L.K.

Midterm 6,8,9,10

Final 10,11,16,17, ~~X~~

8 ☺

Income Statement pg.28

Balance Sheet pg.23

96

Chpt.17 562-570

Profitability Ratio:

1) Profit Margin = $\frac{\text{net income}}{\text{net sales}}$

2) Return on Assets = $\frac{\text{net income}}{\text{total assets}}$

3) Return on Equity = $\frac{\text{net income}}{\text{O.E.}}$

Asset Utilization Ratios:

4) Receivable Turnover = $\frac{\text{sales}}{\text{A/R}}$

5) Average Collection Period = $\frac{\text{A/R}}{\text{average daily Cr. Sales (360 days)}}$

6) Inventory Turnover = $\frac{\text{COGS}}{\text{Inventory}}$

7) Fixed Assets Turnover = $\frac{\text{Sales}}{\text{Fixed Assets}}$

8) Total Assets Turnover = $\frac{\text{Sales}}{\text{Total Assets}}$

Liquidity Ratios:

9) Current Ratio = $\frac{\text{current assets}}{\text{current liabilities}}$

10) Quick Ratio = $\frac{\text{current assets} - \text{inventory}}{\text{current liabilities}}$

Debt Utilization Ratio:

11) debt to total assets = $\frac{\text{total debt}}{\text{total assets}}$

12) Times Interest Earned = $\frac{\text{Income before interest \& taxes}}{\text{Interest}}$

13) Fixed Charge Coverage = $\frac{\text{Income before fixed charges \& taxes}}{\text{Fixed Charges}}$

Foundations of Financial Management

Foundations of Financial Management

Stanley B. Block
Texas Christian University

Geoffrey A. Hirt
DePaul University

Allan Conway
University of Calgary

1988 First Canadian Edition

IRWIN
Homewood, Illinois 60430

To Marj, Janice, and Suzy

Cover photo: Woodfin Camp & Associates,
Craig Aurness, Century City, Calif.

Acquisitions editor: Roderick T. Banister
Project editor: Susan Trentacosti
Production manager: Irene H. Sotiroff
Designer: J. Lo Grasso
Artist: John Foote
Compositor: Carlisle Communications, Ltd.
Typeface: 10½/13 Plantin Roman
Printer: Arcata Graphics/Kingsport

ISBN 0-256-05632-3

Library of Congress Catalog Card No. 87–82520

Printed in the United States of America

1 2 3 4 5 6 7 8 9 0 K 5 4 3 2 1 0 9 8

Preface

This First Canadian Edition of *Foundations of Financial Management* builds on the integrity and experience of four previous U.S. editions while at the same time incorporating substantial new material reflecting the particular environment of Canadian finance.

This edition continues a tradition of presenting the concepts of finance in an enlightening and interesting manner. The careful treatment accorded conceptual material related to valuation, capital structure formation, and risk-return considerations serves to provide the student with a solid background in the theory of finance. The emphasis is on highlighting the key interrelationships and assumptions in financial theory in ways that will allow the student to become financially astute as he or she continues on in his or her career, whether in the field of finance or in some other business specialty.

Many teachers and former students have emphasized the need to present real-world examples to illustrate and support textual material. Care has been taken to integrate actual examples throughout, especially in the sections dealing with long-term financing, working capital management, and external growth through mergers. In addition, much effort was expended in gathering up-to-date data on the size of activity and the contemporary trends developing in various Canadian contexts, such as overall capital markets, the underwriting of new equity issues, mergers and acquisitions, foreign direct investment, the changing financial services industry, and corporate control in Canada.

In terms of structure, the major parts of the book are the Introduction (goals and functions of financial management), Financial Analysis and Planning, Working Capital Management, The Capital Budgeting Process, Long-Term Financing, and Expanding the Perspective of Corporate Finance (mergers and international financial management). A short introductory essay precedes each section and serves as a guide for the material to follow. For example, in the part on capital budgeting, the interrelationship between the time value of money, valuation, the cost of capital, the decision process, and the goals of the firm are laid out for the reader.

The professor who wishes to revise the order of material coverage can easily accomplish that objective. For example, Part Four of the book (time value of money, valuation, etc.) can be presented toward the beginning of the course with working capital (or another topic) moved to a later point. The book covers virtually all topics, but different professors may prefer to cover them in different orders. As is true of most introductory finance texts, it is almost impossible for the instructor to cover every topic so some early decisions must be made.

The textual material is supported by a large number of questions and problems, particularly in the financial analysis and capital budgeting areas. The problems begin at a very basic level and increase in complexity, with optional comprehensive problems at the end of many chapters. The problems were structured to reflect the contemporary corporate environment with risk-return considerations given particular attention.

For their valuable reviews or comments, or for providing me with useful information, I would like to thank Lorne Baxter, Ian Bruce, Ray Carroll, John Churchill, Peter Denhammer, Paul Goodman, Terry Melling, Dave Misener, Don Russell, Doug Short, John Somers, and Peter Walker. To Stanley Block and Geoffrey Hirt I express my gratitude for the work and care they put into the previous U.S. editions of the text and also for the latitude they have allowed me in adapting the book to the Canadian environment and student. I would also like to thank Shelagh Mikulak and Rhonda Evans for their patience in fielding my continual requests for published information. To Christina Larkins and Linda Head go my thanks for their assistance in preparing the manuscript. Finally, I am grateful to all of my students, past and present, whose diligence and vitality make academia a good place to be.

Allan Conway

Contents

PART TWO

Financial Analysis and Planning

PART ONE

Introduction

1 The Goals and Functions of Financial Management

The financial manager's contribution to the success of the firm has become increasingly critical in the 1980s. Some have referred to the era in which we live as the morning after the biggest credit binge in history. In this time of unpredictable economic turns, fluctuating interest rates, inflation and disinflation, painful shortages and gluts, and extremes of optimism and pessimism, the chief financial officer must protect the firm's financial integrity. Indeed, as financial markets become more and more internationalized, the financial officer must bring a global perspective to his or her role. The board of directors and the company's president depend on the financial manager to provide a precious resource—capital—and to ensure that all in the firm manage it in an efficient and profitable fashion. Although there are some financial roles that are specific to the financial manager's position, as you continue on through the book you will realize that much of what is involved in good financial decision making must be understood and implemented by all managers, whether in charge of production, marketing, research, personnel, or another aspect of the firm's operation.

The Field of Finance

The field of finance is closely related to economics and accounting. Therefore, financial managers need to understand the relationships between these fields. Economics provides a structure for decision making in such areas as risk analysis, price theory through supply and demand relationships, comparative return analysis, and so forth. Economics also provides frameworks for understanding the general economic environment in response to which corporate managers must continually adjust the firm's corporate strategy. A financial manager must understand the institutional structure that defines the roles of the Bank of Canada, the chartered banks, the trust companies, the investment dealers, insurance companies, and other organizations whose activities affect the cost and supply of capital. The effective financial manager includes in his or her decision model such economic variables as gross national product, disposable income, inflation, interest rates, and tax policy, among others. These terms will surface throughout the text as they are integrated into the financial process.

Accounting is sometimes referred to as the language of finance because it provides financial data in income statements, balance sheets, and statements of changes in financial position. The effective financial manager knows how to interpret the data in these statements and how to use the information in allocating the firm's resources to create the best possible business organization in the long run. Finance is the link that integrates economic theory with accounting numbers, and all good managers, no matter what their functional specialties, must be able to assess the long-run financial implications of their leadership and decision making.

Many students approaching the field of finance for the first time might wonder what career opportunities exist. For those who develop the right skills, financial positions include banker, corporate treasurer, stockbroker, financial analyst, portfolio manager, investment banker, financial consultant, and personal financial planner. The ambitious finance graduate joining an industrial firm usually aspires to become the chief financial officer who must oversee all of the financial departments within the firm. As you progress through the text you will become familiar with many of these roles in the financing and decision-making processes. A financial manager in the firm may be responsible for decisions ranging from where to locate a new plant to raising funds via a public share issue. Sometimes the task is simply to figure out how to get the highest return on a million dollars of temporarily idle cash between five o'clock one afternoon and eight the next morning. As a result of the importance of the field of finance to business decision making, training in finance has served as a stepping stone to a number of the top corporate positions.

Evolution of Finance as a Field of Study

To appreciate where finance is currently as a field of study, a historical perspective on the shifting emphases over time is essential.

At the turn of the century finance emerged as a field of study separate from economics but still closely linked to it. The major focus of study concentrated upon the instruments and institutions involved in financing the firm. In fact, by then savings and chartered banks, trust companies, and insurance companies were already part of the financial system. The Toronto and Montreal stock exchanges had started up in the 1870s with the Winnipeg, Vancouver, and Alberta exchanges appearing in the early 20th century.

By the 1920s industrialization had developed to the stage that financing corporate growth through stocks and bonds was the chief emphasis. The role of the investment dealer or middleman in a security offering received much attention. No doubt, the great bull market of the 1920s contributed to the emphasis on raising capital. At that time there was no public disclosure of accounting results.

In the 1930s the shock of the Depression ushered in an era of conservatism, and attention shifted to such concerns as preservation of capital, maintenance of liquidity, reorganization of financially troubled corporations, and the bankruptcy process. Company failures, together with questionable treatment of outside investors' interests by insiders, led to the development of securities regulations. A by-product of regulation was the development of published data related to corporate performance. The groundwork was being laid for the sophisticated analysis of corporate information that developed in later decades.

The 1940s and early 1950s seemed to offer little new in the practice of corporate finance. The study methodology had been descriptive or definitional in nature. The emphasis remained on analyzing the firm's financial safety from the point of view of an investor or lender. In the mid-1950s, however, a major shift in emphasis took place. At that time a more analytical, decision-oriented approach began to evolve.

The first area of study to generate the newfound enthusiasm for decision-related analysis was capital budgeting.[1] The financial manager was presented with sophisticated analytical techniques for allocating the firm's scarce resources among competing managers and proposals. Over time this enthusiasm for sophisticated analysis spread to other decision-making issues—such as cash and inventory management, capital structure formulation, and dividend policy. The emphasis had shifted from that of the outsider looking in to that of the corporate manager forced to make important day-to-day decisions affecting the short- and long-term well-being of the firm.

From the late 1960s through today the emphasis of financial management has focused additionally on the relationship between risk and return. The concern has been to maximize the return for a chosen level of risk. This risk-return emphasis was accompanied by corporate implementation of portfolio management strategies, both in an attempt by firms to diversify risk among a number of unrelated industries and as an attempt to divert cash flows away from mature traditional businesses into what looked like more promising new ones. The emergence of holding companies involved in a wide diversity of industries dates to this practice.

High inflation from the 1970s to 1982 created low profitability, large increases in debt, and low stock market values for many companies. Firms were forced to replace plant and equipment (at inflated prices) with borrowed money since they did not have the benefit of large operating cash flows. Some companies borrowed large amounts to buy out other companies on the basis that it was cheaper to buy an existing company than it was to buy an equivalent amount of new productive capacity. By 1981–82, this borrowing binge caught up with many companies as the increased financial risk resulted in record numbers

---

[1]A starting point was Joel Dean, *Capital Budgeting* (New York: Columbia University Press, 1951).

of corporate bankruptcies. By 1987 firms were emphasizing the return aspect of the risk-return trade-off; they did so by focusing on high-profit products while selling off divisions and subsidiaries with marginal or losing profit performances. Such restructuring of assets is resulting in some firms moving away from the unrelated diversification strategy prevalent in the 1960s toward a more narrow strategic focus. This shift toward the return side of the equation has been the partial result of uncertainty arising from increasingly vigorous international competitiveness and rapid changes in the technologies that define product markets and production processes. Accompanying these developments has been a sharpened focus on the financial objectives of the firm. Somewhat critical observations by foreign competitors that Canadian managers are too averse to risk and concentrate too much on short-term financing may be a reflection of this financial emphasis.

Goals of Financial Management

One may suggest that the most important goal for management is "to earn the highest possible profit for the firm." Under this criterion each decision would be evaluated on the basis of its overall contribution to the firm's earnings. While this seems to be a desirable approach, there are some serious drawbacks to selecting profit maximization as the primary goal of the firm.

First, a change in profit may also represent a change in risk. A conservative firm that earned $1.25 per share may become a less desirable investment as its earnings per share increase to $1.50 with an even greater increase in risk.

A second possible drawback to the goal of maximizing profit is that it fails to take into account the timing of benefits. For example, if we could choose between the following two alternatives, we might be indifferent if our emphasis were solely on maximizing earnings.

	Earnings per Share		
	Period One	Period Two	Total
Alternative A	$1.50	$2.00	$3.50
Alternative B	2.00	1.50	3.50

Both investments would provide an additional $3.50 in total earnings per share, but Alternative B is clearly superior because the larger benefits occur earlier. We could reinvest the difference in earnings for Alternative B for an extra period.

Finally, the goal of maximizing profit suffers from the almost impossible task of accurately measuring the key variable, namely, profit. As you will observe throughout the text there are different economic and accounting definitions of profit, each open to its own set of interpretations. Furthermore, new complications related to inflation and international currency translation add to the ambiguity. Constantly improving methods of financial reporting offer some hope although there will always be the need for intelligent interpretation of financial facts.

A Valuation Approach

While there is no question that profits are important, the key issue is how to use them in setting a goal for the firm. The ultimate measure of performance is not what we earned but how the earnings are *valued* by the investor. In making an analysis of the firm, the investor will also consider the risk inherent in the firm's operation, the time pattern over which the firm's earnings increase or decrease, the quality and reliability of reported earnings, and many other factors. The investor is trying to judge the future earning power of the firm, and it is in this context that current and past profitability are important to him or her. The financial manager, in turn, must be sensitive to all of these considerations. He or she must question the impact of each decision on the firm's overall valuation. If a decision maintains or increases the firm's overall value, it is acceptable from a financial viewpoint; otherwise, it should be rejected. This is the one basic principle upon which everything in this text is predicated.

Maximizing Stockholder Wealth

The broad goal of the firm can be brought into focus if we say that the financial manager should attempt to *maximize the wealth of the firm's shareholders* through achieving the highest possible value (that is, stock price) for the firm. This is not a simple task since the financial manager cannot directly control the firm's stock price but can only act in a way that is consistent with the desires of the shareholders in general. Since stock prices are affected by investors' future expectations as well as by the general economic environment, much of what affects stock prices is beyond management's direct control. Even firms with good earnings and favorable financial trends do not always perform well in a declining stock market over the short term.

The concern is not so much with daily fluctuations in stock value as with long-term wealth maximization. This can be a difficult task in light of changing investor expectations. In the 1950s and 1960s the investor emphasis was on maintaining rapid rates of earnings growth. In the 1970s and 1980s investors have become more conservative, putting a premium on lower risk and, at times, high current dividend payments.

Does modern corporate management actually follow the goal of maximizing shareholder wealth as we have defined it? Most of us have heard and read about the fact that in many large corporations stock ownership is diffused and fragmented so that management, with a relatively small ownership position, often controls policy. Under these circumstances management may be more interested in maintaining its own tenure and protecting "private spheres of influence" than in maximizing stockholder wealth. For example, suppose the management of a corporation receives a tender offer to merge the corporation into a second firm. While this offer might be attractive to stockholders, it might be quite unpleasant to present management. Management is often more willing to *satisfice*,[2] while maintaining the status quo, than to maximize.

Although the model of the modern capitalistic society is that company management is free of direct shareholder involvement, the general Canadian situation is strikingly different. As Table 1–1 shows, only 10 of the 100 largest companies in Canada have widely diffused stock

---

[2]This term was popularized by Herbert A. Simon in his seminal study of decision-making processes reported in *Administrative Behavior* (New York: Free Press, 1945). By this term Simon meant that managers have limitations on their abilities to perform and also on their abilities to make correct decisions. In other words, managers were incapable of truly identifying the value-maximizing decision.

Table 1–1
Ownership of largest Canadian industrial corporations*

	Largest 100	Largest 200	Largest 500
Widely held	10	13	40
Canadian controlled	52	107	247
U.S. controlled	27	56	156
U.K. controlled	5	9	25
Japanese controlled	3	8	16
Other controlled	2	7	16

*As determined by dollar sales.

ownership. The corresponding figure is 13 out of the largest 200 and only 40 out of the largest 500. Some 31 percent of our 500 largest companies are subsidiaries of U.S. multinationals. Others, like Northern Telecom, are controlled by larger, widely held Canadian firms. Still others, like Steinberg, are controlled directly by a single family. And still others, like Noranda, are controlled by a holding company that is controlled by another holding company that, in turn, is controlled by one of the two giant Bronfman family trusts. Thus, in general, Canadian managers will very quickly be reminded if they are not acting in the best interests of the controlling group of shareholders. In cases where a corporate parent company is widely held, the top managers in the parent company have discretionary decision-making power, but the decisions of the managers of the controlled Canadian company are monitored very closely. Because so many familiar companies are actually subsidiaries of foreign multinationals, Tables 1–2 and 1–3 were constructed to provide the reader with more information regarding the ownership structure of Canadian industry.

Even in the cases where shares are widely held, there are still reasons that management should act to maximize shareholders' wealth. First, in most cases "enlightened management" is aware that the only way to maintain its position over the long run is to be sensitive to shareholder concerns. Poor stock price performance relative to other companies often leads to undesirable takeovers and proxy fights for control. Second, members of top management often have sufficient stock option incentives to motivate them to achieve market value maximization for their own benefit.

Table 1–2 Largest widely held Canadian industrial corporations

Rank by Sales	*Company*	*Sales (millions)*	*Percent Return on Equity*	*Liabilities/ Equity*	*Percent Canadian*	*Business*
2	Canadian Pacific	$15,040	5.5%	1.1	79.4%	Diversified
4	Bell Canada Enterprises	13,257	16.6	1.3	94.0	Diversified
7	Alcan Aluminum	7,834	6.4	0.6	46.0	Metal manufacture
17	Genstar	4,032	13.3	1.5	60.0	Diversified
23	Nova	3,347	4.6	1.0	97.0	Oil and gas
32	Moore	2,833	17.8	0.1	85.0	Business forms
36	Stelco	2,435	5.5	0.4	97.0	Steel
43	Inco	2,042	5.4	1.0	35.0	Mining
65	George des Epiciers Unis Metro-Richelieu	1,390	negative	2.1	100.0	Retail
89	British Columbia Resources	1,051	negative	4.1	100.0	Mining
128	Federal Industries	719	13.6	1.0	97.0	Transportation
135	Parrish & Heimbecker	684	n.a.	0.3	97.0	—
199	Drug Trading	439	15.2	n.a.	100.0	Drug wholesale

Source: *Canadian Business: Canada's Top 500 Companies*, 1986 Annual.

Table 1–3 Largest controlled Canadian industrial corporations

Rank by Sales	Company	Sales (millions)	Percent Return on Equity	Major Shareholder	Location	Percent Held
1	General Motors of Canada	$18,993	40.5%	General Motors	United States	100.0%
3	Ford Motor Co. of Canada	13,353	19.2	Ford Motor	United States	92.0
5	George Weston	8,880	13.4	Wittington Inv.	Canada	57.8
6	Imperial Oil	8,667	14.9	Exxon	United States	69.6
8	Chrysler Canada	7,041	34.2	Chrysler	United States	100.0
9	Loblaw Companies	6,931	14.4	George Weston	Canada	78.0
10	Shell Canada	6,070	5.9	Shell	Netherlands	72.0
11	Northern Telecom	5,819	22.6	Bell Canada Ent.	Canada	52.0
12	Hudson's Bay	5,272	negative	Woodbridge	Canada	74.0
13	Provigo	4,746	22.8	Unigesco/Sobeys/ Caisse de depot	Canada	49.5
14	TransCanada Pipelines	4,682	16.3	Bell Canada Ent.	Canada	48.0
15	Imasco	4,311	19.7	B.A.T. Industries	United Kingdom	44.1
16	Texaco Canada	4,212	16.1	Texaco	United States	78.0
18	Steinberg	3,845	17.6	Steinberg family	Canada	98.0
19	Sears Canada	3,789	11.9	Sears, Roebuck & Co.	United States	60.5
20	Canada Safeway	3,489	9.2	Safeway Stores	United States	100.0
21	Noranda	3,439	negative	Brascade Resources	Canada	46.0
22	Hiram Walker Resources	3,417	16.0	Interprovincial Pipeline/Olympic & York	Canada	24.9
24	Canada Development	3,257	4.6	Government of Canada	Canada	82.0
25	Total Petroleum	3,250	31.0	Compagnie française des petroles	France	49.9
26	IBM Canada	3,148	25.9	IBM World Trade	United States	100.0

Source: *Canadian Business: Canada's Top 500 companies,* 1986 Annual.

Social Responsibility

Is our goal of stockholder wealth maximization consistent with a concern for social responsibility for the firm? We believe that in most instances the answer is yes. By adopting policies that maximize values in the market, the firm is able to attract capital, provide employment, and offer benefits to its host community. This is the basic strength of the private enterprise system. Only successful business firms have the wherewithal to support the fund drives for fine arts organizations, universities, and so forth that are becoming so prevalent as the 1980s draw to a close.

Nevertheless, certain socially desirable actions, such as installing pollution control equipment, equitable hiring practices, and fair pricing standards, may at times be inconsistent with earning the highest possible profit or achieving maximum valuation in the market. For example, pollution control projects frequently offer a negative return on investment. Does this mean that firms should not exercise social responsibility in regard to pollution control? The answer is no—but certain cost-increasing activities may have to be mandatory rather than voluntary, at least initially, to ensure that the burden falls equally over all business firms.

Functions of Financial Management

Having examined the goals and objectives of financial management, let us turn our attention to the functions it must perform. It is the responsibility of financial management to allocate funds to current and fixed assets, to obtain the best mix of financing alternatives, and to develop an appropriate dividend policy within the context of the firm's objectives. These functions are performed on a day-to-day basis as well as through infrequent approaches to the capital markets to acquire new funds. The daily activities of financial management include credit management, inventory control, and the receipt and disbursement of funds. Less routine functions encompass the sale of stocks and bonds and the establishment of a capital budgeting and dividend plan.

As indicated in Figure 1–1, all of these functions are carried out with the awareness of the need to maintain the proper balance among the profitability and risk components of the firm's situation. The ap-

Figure 1–1
Functions of the financial manager

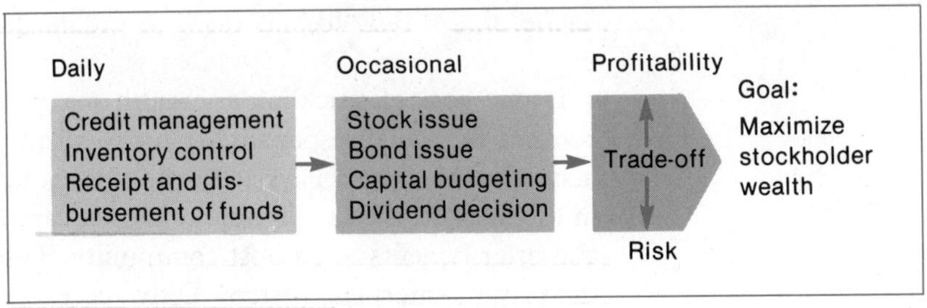

propriate risk-return trade-off must be determined in order to maximize the market value of the firm for its shareholders. The risk-return decision will influence not only the operational side of the business (capital versus labor or product A versus product B) but also the financing mix (stocks versus bonds versus retained earnings).

Forms of Organization

The finance function may be carried out within a number of different forms of organization. Of primary interest are the sole proprietorship, the partnership, and the corporation.

Sole proprietorship This form of organization represents single-person ownership and offers the advantages of simplicity of decision making and low organizational and operating costs. Most small businesses with 1 to 10 employees are sole proprietorships. The major drawback of the sole proprietorship is that there is unlimited liability to the owner. In settlement of the firm's debts he or she can lose not only the capital that has been invested in the business but also personal assets. This drawback can be serious as few lenders are willing to advance funds to a small business without a personal liability commitment from the owner.

The profits or losses of a sole proprietorship are taxed as though they belong to the individual owner. Thus, if a sole proprietorship makes $25,000, the owner will claim the profits in his or her tax return. (In the corporate form of organization the corporation first pays a tax on profits, and then the owners of the corporation pay a tax on any profit distributed.)

Partnership This second form of organization is similar to a sole proprietorship except that there are two or more owners. Multiple ownership makes it possible to raise more capital and to share ownership responsibilities. Most partnerships are formed through an agreement between the participants, known as the *partnership agreement*, which specifies the ownership interest, the methods for distributing profits, and the means for withdrawing from the partnership. For taxing purposes partnership profits or losses are allocated directly to the partners, and there is no double taxation as in the corporate form.

Like the sole proprietorship, the partnership arrangement carries unlimited liability for the owners. While the partnership offers the advantage of *sharing* possible losses, it presents the problem of owners with unequal wealth having to absorb losses. If three people form a partnership with a $10,000 contribution each and the business loses $100,000, one wealthy partner may have to bear a disproportionate share of the losses if the other two partners do not have sufficient personal assets. This form of partnership where all partners assume unlimited liability for the obligations of the business is known as a *general partnership*.

To circumvent this shared unlimited liability feature, a special form of partnership, called a *limited partnership*, can be utilized. Under this arrangement one or more partners are designated general partners and have unlimited liability for the debts of the firm; other partners are designated limited partners and are only liable for their initial contribution. The limited partners are normally prohibited from being active in the management of the firm. You may have heard of limited partnerships in real estate syndications in which a number of limited partners are doctors, lawyers, and chartered accountants with one general partner who is a real estate professional. Not all financial institutions will extend funds to a limited partnership.

Corporation In terms of revenue and profits produced, the corporation is by far the most important type of economic unit. The corporation is unique—it is a legal entity unto itself. Thus, the corporation may sue or be sued, engage in contracts, and acquire property.

A corporation is generally incorporated federally or in a single province with registration in all other provinces in which it carries on business. Although the incorporating procedure varies from province to province, two documents are central to the incorporating procedure, a *company charter* and the *company by-laws*. The charter contains the organization's founding principles and is relatively unalterable. The by-laws contain details of company policies and procedures and can be changed by vote of the board of directors and the shareholders.

Technically, a corporation is owned by stockholders who enjoy the privilege of limited liability, meaning that their liability exposure is generally no greater than their initial investment. However, in the case of small corporations with little in the way of collateral, bankers will generally not lend money to the corporation without a personal guarantee from the owner-manager or a principal shareholder. A corporation also has a continual life and is not dependent on the life span of any one stockholder for maintaining its legal existence.

A key feature of the corporation is the easy divisibility of the ownership interest through the issuance of shares of stock. While it would be nearly impossible to have more than 50 or 100 partners in most businesses, a corporation may have thousands of shareholders. For example, as of the end of 1986 Bell Canada Enterprises, probably the most widely held Canadian company, had 332,400 registered common shareholders. The shareholders' interests are ultimately managed by the corporation's board of directors. The directors, who generally include key management personnel of the firm as well as outside directors not permanently employed by it, serve in a stewardship capacity and may be liable for the mismanagement of the firm or for the misappropriation of funds. According to a study by the Conference Board of Canada, outside directors received, on average, compensation of $7,000 in 1984 for attending an average of six board meetings a year. That amount varied, however, with the size of the firm and with the nature of its industry. Oil and gas companies were the most generous to their outside board members, paying an average of $12,600 per year.[3]

Because the corporation is a separate legal entity, it reports and pays taxes on its *own* income. As previously mentioned, any remaining income paid to the stockholders in the form of dividends will require the payment of a second tax by the stockholders. One of the key disadvantages to the corporate form of organization is this potential

---

[3]These data and other interesting details on Canadian directorship compensation are contained in Prem Benimadhu, *Canadian Directorship Practices: Compensation of Boards of Directors*, Study No. 87 (Ottawa: The Conference Board of Canada, 1985).

double taxation of earnings. The dividend tax credit in Canada's tax system is an attempt to reduce the effect of this double taxation.

Because of the all-pervasive impact of the corporation on our economy and because most growing businesses eventually become corporations, the effects of many decisions in this text are considered from the corporate viewpoint.

Recent Economic Developments

A number of key issues of the late 1970s and 1980s are given special attention in the text. Even though inflation has been significantly reduced from double digits to the 4 percent range during the 1980s, leading economists and financial analysts now accept some degree of inflation as a way of life in Canada and throughout the world. A 4 percent inflation rate is still several times the average rate from 1925 to 1965. The inflation-induced profits of the 1970s and early 1980s are considered somewhat in the past by some, but the intelligent student should not ignore the lessons of inflated phantom profits and undervalued assets of the past two decades. The student should be equally aware of the benefits, drawbacks, and implications of disinflation (a slowing down of price increases). The problems and opportunities related to inflation and disinflation receive particular attention in the later discussion of financial analysis.

A second aspect of contemporary finance is the extreme reliance that financial managers have placed on the use of debt. Debt-to-asset ratios have moved from 48 percent to approximately 60 percent of assets in the last 25 years, and the typical firm's ability to cover its interest expenses has eroded significantly. This is not a short-term, cyclical phenomenon but rather a slow, steady process that has taken place in good times as well as bad. While some firms that were formerly in financial trouble have recovered miraculously (National Sea Products, for instance), other firms in industries such as farm equipment, steel, transportation, construction, and oil are suffering from low profitability, international competition, faltering domestic markets, and high debt. Companies like Massey-Ferguson (farm machinery), Nu-West (residential construction), and Dome Petroleum (oil and gas) encountered hard times not long after having been considered leading Canadian companies in their respective industries. In fact, Dome reported a record loss for Canadian corporations of $2.2 billion for 1986. Dome's multibillion dollar debt, still almost $6 billion after years of restructuring, is a major reason for the company's troubles. Table 1–4 lists 10 of the Canadian companies with high levels of long-term debt outstanding.

Although many of the largest U.S. firms are restructuring their balance sheets by deliberately increasing the use of debt relative to ownership capital (by repurchasing shares of common stock in the open market), many large Canadian companies are involved in attempting to get the amount of debt already on hand down to a manageable level. Mergers and acquisitions of gigantic proportions unheard of in other decades had helped to create much of the debt overload. Firms were often buying or merging with companies in similar and related industries. Rather than just seeking risk reduction through diversification, firms were aquiring greater market share, brand-name products, hidden asset values, or technology—or they were simply looking for size to help them "play the game" in an international arena.

In the oil industry, where opportunities to acquire subsidiaries of foreign multinationals abounded following the implementation of Canada's National Energy Policy, Dome paid over $4 billion to relieve Conoco of Hudson's Bay Oil and Gas while Olympia & York paid over $3 billion to buy Gulf's Canadian subsidiary. In an announced attempt to shield its future prospects from the vagaries of the Canadian economy, Campeau Corporation of Ottawa paid over $4 billion to acquire the New York–based Allied Stores Corporation, an operator of a number of U.S. retailing chains. You should also be aware that some corporations, like Canadian Pacific, have been restructuring their balance sheets by selling off (divesting) unprofitable or unwanted divisions over a period of time.

Table 1–4
Long-term debt, Canadian corporations, December 1986 (millions)

Canadian Pacific	$6,400
Dome Petroleum	5,901
Bell Canada Enterprises	5,640
Canada Development	3,898
Trizec	2,938
Nova	2,739
TransCanada Pipelines	2,613
Noranda	2,251
Genstar	2,310
Alcan Aluminum	1,366

Finally, extreme volatility of interest rates has been a key factor in recent economic environment. In 1969 corporations paid over 8 percent for bank funds. In 1972 the prime rate dropped to 6 percent—then spiraled to almost 11.5 percent in 1974. To the relief of many the prime rate eventually fell to 8.5 percent in 1976. However, an upward movement began with the economic recovery of the late 1970s, and by the early 1980s short-term interest rates surpassed the 20 percent mark before beginning a sharp decline to less than 10 percent by year-end 1986. These rates are portrayed in Figure 1–2 alongside the annual rates of inflation as measured by the consumer price index (CPI). In all years except 1974 and 1975 the prime rate exceeded inflation. Notice that the difference between the prime rate and the inflation rate was very small from about 1972 to 1978, but when inflation began to subside in 1983 the difference was close to 6 percent. This may indicate that lenders do not believe inflation will stay at reasonable levels for good. It would be nice to get back to the 1 percent inflation rate of the early

Figure 1–2
Prime rate versus percent change in the consumer price index (CPI) (average annual rates)*

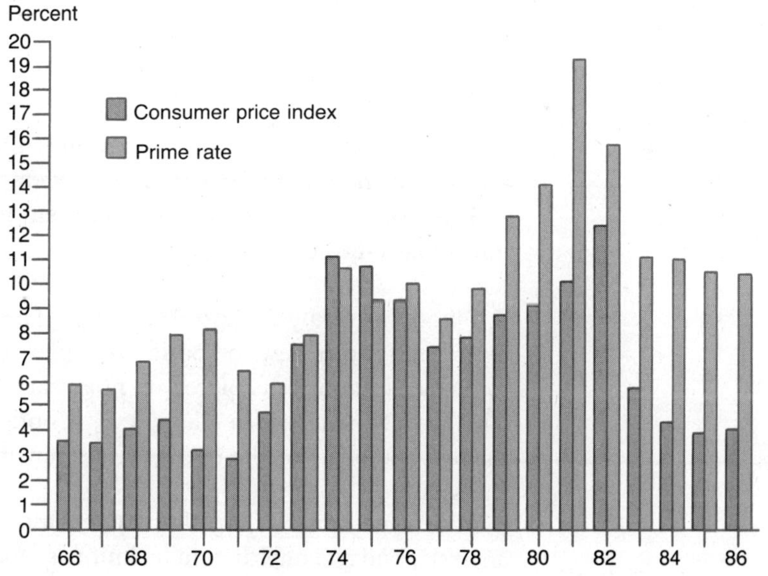

*Prime interest rate is the rate charged by a bank to its best corporate customers.

1960s, but it might be prudent to wait awhile longer before we forget the lessons learned in the management of corporate assets under inflation.

Format of the Text

The material in this text is covered under six major headings. The student progresses from the development of basic analytical skills in accounting and finance to the utilization of decision-making techniques in working capital management, capital budgeting, long-term financing, and other related areas. A total length of 21 chapters should make the text appropriate for one-semester coverage.

The student is given a thorough grounding in financial theory in a highly palatable and comprehensive fashion—with careful attention to definitions, symbols, and formulas. The intent is, above all, that the student develop a thorough understanding of the basic concepts in finance.

Although we prefer to cover the chapters in the order presented, other faculty have moved working capital management so that it follows Part Five. This permits covering the topics of time value of money, valuation, cost of capital, and capital budgeting earlier in the course.

Parts

1. Introduction This section examines the goals and objectives of financial management. The present-day emphasis on decision making and risk management is stressed, with an update of significant events influencing the study of finance.

2. Financial Analysis and Planning The student is first given the opportunity to review the basic principles of accounting as they relate to finance (emphasis is placed on financial statements and funds flow). This review material, in Chapter 2, is optional, and the student may judge whether he or she needs this review before progressing through the section.

Additional material in this part includes a thorough study of ratio analysis, budget construction techniques, and the development of comprehensive pro forma statements. The effect of heavy fixed commitments, in the form of either debt or plant and equipment, is examined in a discussion of leverage.

3. Working Capital Management The techniques for managing the short-term assets of the firm and the associated liabilities are examined. The material is introduced in the context of risk-return analysis. The financial manager must constantly choose between liquid, low-return assets (perhaps marketable securities) and more profitable, less liquid assets (such as inventory). Sources of short-term financing are also considered.

4. The Capital Budgeting Process The decision on capital outlays is among the most significant that a firm will have to make. In terms of study procedure, we attempt to carefully develop "time value of money" calculations, then proceed to the valuation of bonds and stocks, emphasizing present-value techniques. The valuation chapter develops the traditional dividend valuation model and examines bond price sensitivity in response to discount rates and inflation. An appendix presents the supernormal dividend growth model, or what is sometimes called the two-stage dividend model. After careful grounding in valuation practice and theory, we move into an examination of the cost of capital and capital structure. The text then moves to the actual capital budgeting decision, making generous use of previously learned material and employing the concept of marginal analysis. The concluding chapter in this part covers risk-return analysis in capital budgeting with a brief exposure to portfolio theory and a consideration of market value maximization.

5. Long-Term Financing The student is introduced to Canadian financial markets as they relate to corporate financial management. The student considers the sources and uses of funds in the capital markets—with coverage given to warrants and convertibles as well as the more conventional methods of financing. The guiding role of the investment dealer in the distribution of securities is also analyzed. Furthermore, the student is encouraged to think of leasing as a form of debt.

6. Expanding the Perspective of Corporate Finance A chapter on corporate mergers considers external growth strategy and serves as an integrative tool to bring together such topics as profit management, capital budgeting, portfolio considerations, and valuation concepts. A second chapter on international financial management describes the growth of the international financial markets, the rise of multinational business, and the effects on corporate financial management. The issues discussed in these two chapters highlight corporate diversification and risk-reduction attempts prevalent in the 1970s and continuing well into the 1980s.

List of Terms

shareholder wealth maximization	disinflation
sole proprietorship	prime rate
general partnership	limited partnership
inflation	corporation
holding company	restructuring
	diversification

Discussion Questions

1. Some of the early concerns of financial management were related to preservation of capital, maintenance of liquidity, and reorganizations. Do you think these topics are still important in our current economic environment?
2. How has the finance discipline changed since the 1940s and early 1950s? pg. 6
3. What is meant by the goal of maximization of stockholder wealth? Why is profit maximization, by itself, an inappropriate goal? pg. 7-8-9
4. Contrast the liability provisions for a sole proprietorship, a partnership, a limited partnership, and a corporation.
5. Why is the large organization best suited to the corporate form?
6. Why does the financial manager need to be concerned with inflation? With disinflation?
7. What are some ways in which corporations are restructuring their balance sheets and operations?

Selected References

Anderson, Leslie P.; Vergil V. Miller; and Donald L. Thompson. *The Finance Function*. Scranton, Pa.: Intext, 1971.

Anthony, Robert N. "The Trouble with Profit Maximization." *Harvard Business Review* 38 (November–December 1960), pp. 126–34.

Benimadhu, Prem. *Canadian Directorship Practices: Compensation of Boards of Directors*, Study No. 87. Ottawa: The Conference Board of Canada, 1985.

Branch, Ben. "Corporate Objectives and Market Performance." *Financial Management* 2 (Summer 1973), pp. 24–29.

Brennan, Michael J., and Eduardo S. Schwartz. "Regulation and Corporate Investment Policy." *Journal of Finance* 37 (May 1982), pp. 289–300.

Chandler, Alfred D. *The Visible Hand*. Cambridge, Mass.: Belknap, 1977.

"Compensation for Outside Directors." *Harvard Business Review* 57 (November–December 1979), pp. 18–28.

Davis, Keith. "Social Responsibility Is Inevitable." *California Management Review* 19 (Fall 1976), pp. 14–20.

Dean, Joel. *Capital Budgeting*. New York: Columbia University Press, 1951.

Dewing, Arthur S. *The Financial Policy of Corporations*. 5th ed., vol. 1. New York: Ronald, 1953, chap. 1.

Donaldson, Gordon. "Financial Goals: Management vs. Stockholders." *Harvard Business Review* 41 (May–June 1963), pp. 16–29.

Hearth, Douglas, and Janis K. Zaima. "Voluntary Corporate Divestiture and Value." *Financial Management* 13 (Spring 1984), pp. 10–16.

Hill, Lawrence W. "The Growth of the Corporate Finance Function." *Financial Executive* 44 (July 1976), pp. 38–43.

Lewellen, Wilbur G. "Management and Ownership in the Large Firm." *Journal of Finance* 24 (May 1969), pp. 299–322.

Mitchell, Lionel A. *Canadian Business and Management*. Toronto: Metheun, 1987.

Neufeld, E. P. *The Financial System of Canada: Its Growth and Development*. Toronto: MacMillan, 1972.

Seitz, Neil. "Shareholder Goals, Firm Goals and Firm Financing Decisions." *Financial Management* 37 (Autumn 1982), pp. 20–26.

Simon, Herbert A. *Administrative Behavior*. New York: Free Press, 1945.

Solomon, Ezra. *The Theory of Financial Management*. New York: Columbia University Press, 1963, pp. 15–26.

Vance, Jack O. "The Changing Role of the Corporate Financial Executive." *Financial Executive* 31 (March 1963), pp. 27–29.

Weston, J. Fred. "Developments in Finance Theory." *Financial Management* 10 (Tenth Anniversary Issue, 1981), pp. 5–22.

Williamson, Peter J. *Securities Regulation in Canada*. Toronto: University of Toronto Press, 1960.

PART TWO

Financial Analysis and Planning

Introduction

In this day of ever-increasing pressures for more disclosure from provincial securities commissions, and various investor and consumer groups, the presentation and understanding of financial data are critical. Furthermore, increasing complexities in the business environment mean that new methods of reporting the financial condition of the firm are certain to take place. The student must be well positioned to understand the old rules of the game and to appreciate new developments on the horizon.

In Chapter 2, we review some of the basic principles of accounting. The student should have a reasonable understanding of financial statements and related concepts before studying the more analytical material. Students with a strong background in accounting may choose to merely gloss over this material.

We then proceed to a study of company performance through ratio analysis in Chapter 3. The purpose of ratio analysis is to examine financial data on a relative basis. Net profit means very little unless it is compared to some other measure such as sales, total assets, or net worth in an appropriate ratio format. Net income of $100,000 offers little insight, but a ratio of net income to sales of 5 percent may suggest a great deal in comparison to past performance and that of other companies.

An important dimension in financial analysis is a consideration of the impact of inflation and disinflation on the financial fortunes of the firm. The authors present examples showing how changing prices may distort the normally reported income of the firm.

In Chapter 4, we shift the emphasis from "what was" to "what will be" as we go through the process of financial forecasting. To anticipate future financing requirements, the firm must determine what the income statement, balance sheet, and cash budget will look like for the planning period. In the process of financial forecasting, we are forced to make predictions about future sales, inventory levels, receivables, and other accounts, and then to combine our forecasts into a structured set of financial statements. Upon completion of Chapter 4, the student should have a better understanding not only of forecasting but also of all the elements that make up the financial structure of the firm.

As a last topic of consideration in Part Two, we look at management's use of leverage to magnify the results of the firm. By leverage, we mean the utilization of a high percentage of fixed assets or "fixed cost" debt in the management and operation of the firm. As indicated in Chapter 5, if we are able to achieve a high volume of operation, our fixed costs should allow for strong profitability as our revenues go up while much of our costs remains constant. At a low level of operation, perhaps in a recession, the opposite results will take place, and our heavy fixed costs could force us into bankruptcy. We must learn how to handle this two-edged sword in an effective fashion.

2 Review of Accounting

The language of finance flows logically from accounting. In order to ensure that the student is adequately prepared to study important financial concepts, we must lock in the preparatory material from the accounting area. Much of the early frustration suffered by students who have difficulty with finance can be overcome if such concepts as retained earnings, owners' equity, depreciation, and historical/replacement cost accounting are brought into focus.

In this chapter we examine the three basic types of financial statements—the income statement, the balance sheet, and the statement of changes in financial position—with particular attention paid to the interrelationships among these three measurement devices. As special preparation for the financial manager, we briefly examine income tax considerations affecting financial decisions.

Income Statement

The income statement is the major device for measuring the profitability of a firm over a period of time. An example of the income statement is presented in Table 2–1 for the Kramer Corporation.

First, note that the income statement covers a defined period of time, whether it be one month, three months, or a year. The statement is presented in a stair-step or progressive fashion so that we can examine the profit or loss after each type of expense item is deducted.

We start with sales and deduct cost of goods sold to arrive at gross profit. The $500,000 thus represents the difference between what we bought or manufactured our goods for and the sales price. We then subtract selling and administrative expense and depreciation from gross profit to determine our profit (or loss) purely from operations of $230,000.[1] It is possible for a company to enjoy a high gross profit margin (25–50 percent) but a relatively low operating profit because

Table 2–1

KRAMER CORPORATION
Income Statement
For the Year Ended December 31, 1988

1. Sales	$2,000,000
2. Cost of goods sold	1,500,000
3. Gross profits	500,000
4. Selling and administrative expense	220,000
5. Depreciation expense	50,000
6. Operating profit (EBIT)*	230,000
7. Interest expense	20,000
8. Earnings before taxes (EBT)	210,000
9. Taxes	99,500
10. Earnings after taxes (EAT)	110,500
11. Preferred stock dividends	10,500
12. Earnings available to common shareholders	$ 100,000
13. Shares outstanding	100,000
14. Earnings per share	$1.00

*Earnings before interest and taxes.

[1]Depreciation was not treated as part of cost of goods sold in this instance but rather as a separate expense. All or part of depreciation may be treated as part of cost of goods sold, depending on the circumstances.

of heavy expenses incurred in marketing the product and managing the company.

Having obtained operating profit (essentially a measure of how efficient management is in generating revenues and controlling expenses), we now adjust for revenues and expenses not related to operational matters. In this case we pay $20,000 in interest and arrive at earnings before taxes of $210,000. Our tax payments are $99,500, leaving aftertax income of $110,500.

Return to Capital

Before proceeding further, we should note that there are three primary sources of capital—the bondholders, who received $20,000 in interest (item 7); the preferred shareholders, who will receive $10,500 in dividends (item 11); and the common shareholders. After the $10,500 dividend has been paid to the preferred shareholders, there will be $100,000 in earnings available to the common shareholders (item 12). In computing earnings per share, we must interpret this in terms of the number of shares outstanding. As indicated in item 13, there are 100,000 shares outstanding, so the $100,000 of earnings available to the common shareholders may be translated into earnings per share of $1. Needless to say, common shareholders are sensitive to the number of shares outstanding—the more shares, the lower the earnings per share. A corollary to this is that before any new shares are issued, the financial manager must be sure they will eventually generate sufficient earnings to avoid reducing earnings per share.

The $100,000 of profit ($1 earnings per share) may be paid out to the common shareholders in the form of dividends or retained in the company for subsequent reinvestment. The reinvested funds theoretically belong to the common shareholders, who hope they will provide future earnings and dividends. In the case of the Kramer Corporation we assume that $50,000 in dividends will be paid out to the common shareholders, with the balance retained in the corporation for their benefit. A short supplement to the income statement, a statement of retained earnings (see Table 2–2), usually indicates the disposition of earnings.[2]

---

[2]The statement may also indicate any adjustments to previously reported income as well as any restrictions on cash dividends.

Table 2–2

Statement of Retained Earnings
For the Year Ended December 31, 1988

Retained earnings, balance, January 1, 1988	$250,000
Add: Earnings available to common shareholders, 1988	100,000
Deduct: Cash dividends declared in 1988	50,000
Retained earnings, balance, December 31, 1988	300,000

We see that $50,000 has been added to previously accumulated earnings of $250,000.

Price-Earnings Ratio Applied to Earnings per Share

A concept utilized throughout the text is the price-earnings ratio. This refers to the multiplier applied to earnings per share to determine current value. In the case of the Kramer Corporation, earnings per share were $1. If the firm enjoyed a price-earnings ratio of 12, the market value of each share would be $12. The price-earnings ratio (or P/E ratio, as it is commonly called) is influenced by the earnings and the sales growth of the firm, the risk (or volatility in performance), the debt-equity structure of the firm, the dividend payment policy, the quality of management, and a number of other factors. Since companies have various levels of earnings per share, price-earnings ratios allow us to compare the relative market value of many companies based on $1 of earnings per share.

The P/E ratio indicates expectations as to a company's future performance. Firms expected to provide greater than average returns often have P/E ratios higher than the market average P/E ratio. Note that investors' expectations as to future returns do change over time. In turn, this can trigger substantial changes in a company's P/E ratio as indicated in Table 2–3.

Price-earnings ratios, although usually consolidating a great deal of information about a company, can also be confusing at times. When a firm's earnings are dropping rapidly, perhaps even approaching zero, the decline in its stock price may be more gradual. This process can give rise to the appearance of an increasing P/E ratio under adversity. This happens from time to time in cyclical industries, which most of

Table 2–3
Price-earnings ratios for selected companies

		P/E Ratio		
Corporation	*Industry*	*December 31, 1981*	*January 2, 1984*	*January 5, 1987*
Abitibi-Price	Forest products	3.7	26.0	18.6
Bank of Montreal	Banking	3.9	8.3	7.1
Bell Canada	Diversified	7.8	9.1	10.0
Imasco	Tobacco products	7.4	15.1	9.5
John Labatt	Food products	6.6	15.9	8.3
Loblaw Cos.	Grocery chain	6.2	11.2	13.2
PanCanadian	Petroleum	10.3	11.2	13.2
TSE 300	Index	8.6	22.4	17.4

our resource-based industries happen to be. For example, in 1983 Abitibi-Price was trading at multiples in the high 20s because low pulp and newsprint prices kept earnings extremely modest.

Limitations of the Income Statement

The economist defines income as the change in real worth that takes place between the beginning and the end of a specified time period. To the economist an increase in the value of a firm's land as a result of a new airport being built on an adjacent property is an increase in the real worth of the firm. It, therefore, represents income. Similarly, the elimination of a competitor might also increase the firm's real worth and therefore result in income in an economic sense. The accountant does not ordinarily employ such a broad definition of income. Accounting values are established primarily by actual transactions, and income that is gained or lost during a given period is a function of verifiable transactions. While the potential sales price of a company's property may go from $10 million to $20 million as a result of new developments in the area, its stockholders may only perceive a much smaller gain from operations as reported in the accounting statements.

Also, as will be pointed out in Chapter 3, Financial Analysis, there is some flexibility in the reporting of transactions. This means that similar events may result in differing measurements of income at the end of the period. The intent of this section is not to criticize the accounting profession, for it is certainly among the best-organized, best-trained, and best-paid professions, but to alert students to the fact that there is some judgment involved in financial reporting. Therefore, consumers of financial statements must also be prepared to exercise judgment.

Balance Sheet

The balance sheet indicates what the firm owns and how these assets are financed in the form of liabilities or ownership interest. While the income statement purports to show the profitability of the firm, the balance sheet delineates the firm's holdings and obligations. Together these statements are intended to answer two questions: How much did the firm make or lose, and what is a measure of its worth? A balance sheet for the Kramer Corporation is presented in Table 2–4.

Note that the balance sheet is a picture of the firm at a point in time—in this case December 31, 1988. It does not purport to represent the result of transactions for a specific month, quarter, or year but, rather, is a cumulative chronicle of all transactions that have affected the corporation since its inception. In contrast the income statement measures results only over a short, quantifiable period of time. Generally, balance sheet items are stated on an original cost basis rather than at present worth.

Interpretation of Balance Sheet Items

Asset accounts are listed in order of liquidity. The first category of current assets covers items that may be converted to cash within one year (or within the normal operating cycle of the firm). A few items are worthy of mention. *Marketable securities* are temporary investments of excess cash. The value shown in the account is the lower of cost or current market value. *Accounts receivable* include an allowance for bad debts (based on historical evidence) to determine their anticipated collection value. *Inventory* may be in the form of raw material, goods in process, or finished goods, while *prepaid expenses* represent future expense items that have already been paid, such as insurance premiums or rent.

Investments, unlike marketable securities, represent a longer-term commitment of funds (at least one year). They may include stocks,

Table 2–4

KRAMER CORPORATION
Statement of Financial Position (Balance Sheet)
December 31, 1988

Assets

Current assets:		
Cash		$ 40,000
Marketable securities		10,000
Accounts receivable	$ 220,000	
Less: Allowance for bad debts	20,000	200,000
Inventory		180,000
Prepaid expenses		20,000
Total current assets		450,000
Other assets:		
Investments		50,000
Fixed assets:		
Plant and equipment, original cost	1,100,000	
Less: Accumulated depreciation	600,000	
Net plant and equipment		500,000
Total assets		$1,000,000

Liabilities and Owners' Equity

Current liabilities:	
Accounts payable	$ 80,000
Notes payable	100,000
Accrued expenses	30,000
Total current liabilities	210,000
Long-term liabilities:	
Bonds payable, 1995	90,000
Total liabilities	300,000
Owners' equity:	
Preferred stock, 500 shares	50,000
Common stock, 100,000 shares	100,000
Contributed surplus (common stock)	250,000
Retained earnings	300,000
Total owners' equity	700,000
Total liabilities and owners' equity	$1,000,000

bonds, or investments in other corporations. Frequently, the account will contain stock in companies that the firm is acquiring.

Plant and equipment is carried at original cost minus accumulated depreciation. Accumulated depreciation is not to be confused with the depreciation expense item indicated in the income statement in Table 2–1. Accumulated depreciation is the sum of all past and present depreciation charges on currently owned assets, while depreciation expense is the current year's charge. If we subtract accumulated depreciation from the original value, the balance ($500,000) tells us how much of the original cost has not been expensed in the form of depreciation.

Total assets are financed through either liabilities or owners' equity. Liabilities represent financial obligations of the firm and move from current liabilities (due within a year) to longer-term obligations, such as bonds payable in 1995.

Among the short-term obligations, *accounts payable* represent amounts owed on open account to suppliers, while *notes payable* are generally short-term signed obligations to the banker or other creditors. An *accrued expense* is generated when a financial service has been provided or an obligation incurred and payment has not yet taken place. We may owe workers additional wages for services provided or the government taxes on earned income.

In the balance sheet presented in Table 2–4, we see that the $1 million in total assets of the Kramer Corporation was financed by $300,000 in debt and $700,000 in the form of owners' equity. Owners' equity represents the total contribution and ownership interest of preferred and common stockholders.

The *preferred stock* investment position is $50,000, based on 500 shares at $100 par. In the case of *common stock,* 100,000 shares have been issued for $100,000, plus an extra $250,000 in *contributed surplus*[3] for a sum of $350,000. We can assume that the 100,000 shares were originally sold at $3.50 each.

Finally, there is $300,000 in *retained earnings*. This value, previously determined in the statement of retained earnings (Table 2–2), represents the firm's cumulative earnings since inception minus dividends and any other adjustments.

Concept of Net Worth

Owners' equity minus the preferred stock component represents the *net worth,* or *book value,* of the firm. There is some logic to the approach.

---

[3]In most current Canadian circumstances, new common stock is issued on a no par value basis. However, many corporate balance sheets still reflect the historical split between the par value of shares on issue and the premium, termed contributed surplus, paid by investors above that par value.

If you take everything the firm owns and subtract the debt and preferred stock obligation,[4] the remainder belongs to the common stockholder and represents net worth. In the case of the Kramer Corporation, we show:

Total assets	$1,000,000
Total liabilities	300,000
Owners' equity	$ 700,000
Preferred stock obligation	50,000
Net worth assigned to common	$ 650,000
Common shares outstanding	100,000
Net worth, or book value, per share	$6.50

The original cost per share was $3.50; the net worth, or book value, per share is $6.50; and the market value (based on a P/E ratio of 12 and earnings per share of $1) is $12. It is this market value that is of primary concern to the financial manager and the security analyst.

Limitations of the Balance Sheet

Lest we attribute too much significance to the balance sheet, we need to examine some of the underlying concepts supporting its construction. Most of the values on the balance sheet are stated on a historical or original cost basis. This may be particularly troublesome in the case of plant and equipment and inventory, which may now be worth two or three times the original cost or—from a negative viewpoint—may require many times the original cost for replacement.

The accounting profession has been grappling with this problem for decades, and the discussion becomes particularly intense each time inflation rears its ugly head. In January of 1983 the Canadian Institute of Chartered Accountants (CICA) issued a recommendation that large companies disclose inflation-adjusted data. This information was only to be supplementary to the traditional historical cost data. The fact that the inflation-adjusted disclosure is not a requirement has meant that most firms have not adopted the CICA's recommendation.

---

[4]An additional discussion of preferred stock is presented in Chapter 17, Common and Preferred Stock Financing. Preferred stock represents neither a debt claim nor an ownership interest in the firm. It is a hybrid, or intermediate, type of security.

Inflation-adjusted accounting is a relatively new concept in accounting practice, and it will likely undergo modifications over time. Among a number of choices considered, the accounting profession has recommended the use of the *current cost method* (sometimes referred to as replacement cost). This method requires assets to be revalued at their current costs. Until 1984 the U.S. profession had required either the current cost or constant-dollar method for inflation adjustment but, at that time, opted for current cost only. Overall, these adjustments will affect inventory and plant and equipment the most, thus affecting the total asset value of the firm. Those revaluations will also adjust profits for the effects of inflation through changes to depreciation expense and cost of goods sold. During times of rising prices these expenses would be increased, and therefore, profits would be smaller than on a historical-cost basis.

Many financial executives think that the new data will simply confuse most investors, but others see benefits. The most important benefit will be the ability to determine if a company is generating enough cash flow from internal operations to replace worn-out equipment and maintain existing levels of production. Another benefit to investors will come from being able to measure dividends, income, and stock prices in dollars adjusted for inflation. What effect this will have on the market price of common stock and on total stockholder wealth is uncertain. Because the concept of net worth (book value) developed in the previous section is based on historical asset costs (Assets − Liabilities − Preferred stock), net worth may bear little relationship to reality. The use of current cost data to determine book value may or may not be better as an approximation of the stock price. In Table 2–5 we look

Table 2–5
Comparison of market value to book value per share, December 1986

Corporation	*Market Value per Share*	*Book Value per Share*	*Ratio of Market Value to Book Value*
Alcan Aluminum	$38.63	$29.66	1.30
Algoma Steel	11.00	26.67	0.41
Canadian Pacific	11.75	19.25	0.61
CIL	24.75	33.15	0.75
Canron	16.00	14.55	1.10
MacMillan Bloedel	42.38	28.93	1.46
Moore Corporation	28.75	11.01	2.61
National Sea Products	22.88	3.95	5.79
Southam	20.88	7.04	2.97

at large disparities between market value per share and historical book value per share for a number of publicly traded companies at the end of 1986. Besides asset valuation, a number of other factors may explain the wide differences between per share values, such as industry outlook, growth prospects, quality of management, and risk-return expectations.

Cash Flow Statement

In financial reporting the accounting profession requires a third financial statement specifically aimed at supplementing the information provided by the balance sheet and the income statement. The cash flow statement, most commonly called the statement of changes in financial position (SCFP), reports the cash effects of all changes between a beginning and ending balance sheet for a period of time.

The income statement provides information on the measurement of revenues and expenses over a period of time while the balance sheet shows valuations for assets, liabilities, and owners' equity at a point in time. What those two statements do not provide is adequate information on the amount of cash flowing into and out of the business. However, as you will fully realize as you continue through this book, there are many internal and external users of a firm's financial information to whom cash flow information is critical.

In 1974 the CICA defined the content of the funds flow statement to include the financing and investing activities of the enterprise as well as those operating activities that affected cash or working capital. Since 1985 the CICA has required the SCFP to report the changes in cash and cash equivalents (rather than working capital) resulting from the activities of the firm during a given period.

By examining the SCFP analysts can monitor the relative buildup in short-term and long-term assets. Furthermore, they can examine the means of financing used to support any growth in the firm's asset base. They can then make judgments as to the appropriateness of the financing used and its future implications.

Cash flows should be classified under either operating activities, financing activities, or investing activities. The SCFP, or cash flow statement, reports at least the following:

1. Cash provided by operations.
2. Cash flows resulting from extraordinary items.

3. Outlays for acquisitions and proceeds on disposal of assets, by major category, if they are not included in 1 or 2.
4. The issue, assumption, and repayment of debt not included in 1 or 2.
5. The issue, redemption, and acquisition of share capital.
6. The payment of dividends.

Sources and Uses of Cash

If a firm obtains more funds from financing activities than it needs for investing activities, the unused funds increase the company's cash (Sources − Uses = Increase in funds). If the firm invests more funds than it obtains, the company's cash will be reduced correspondingly. Since we know how raising additional equity capital or building a new plant will affect the balance sheet, we can compare the current balance sheet to the previous one and decide what mix of sources and uses caused the change in funding.

In order to illustrate the preceding concepts, we will examine data for the Kramer Corporation for year-end 1987 and 1988. The comparative balance sheet information is provided in Table 2–6.

The question that the cash flow statement is meant to address is: Why did Kramer's cash increase by $10,000 in 1988? In order to explain this increase in cash, we begin by calculating the amount of cash provided by operations.

Cash Provided by Operations

From Table 2–2 we see that Kramer had $100,000 profit available for common stockholders in 1988 and paid $50,000 in common share dividends. This resulted in a net increase in retained earnings of $50,000 for the year.

For the SCFP, however, we must reconstruct more details of the operating cash flow. Table 2–7 summarizes the items that must be taken into account in the Kramer situation. Here the net income figure of $100,000 is adjusted by adding back those items that did not require the use of cash but were deducted in arriving at net income. These include depreciation expense, the increase in accounts payable, and

Table 2–6

KRAMER CORPORATION
Comparative Balance Sheets
For the Years Ending December 31, 1987 and 1988

	Year-End 1987	*Year-End 1988*	*Change*
Assets			
Current assets:			
Cash	$ 30,000	$ 40,000	+$10,000
Marketable securities	10,000	10,000	—
Accounts receivable (net)	170,000	200,000	+ 30,000
Inventory	130,000	180,000	+ 50,000
Prepaid expenses	30,000	20,000	− 10,000
Total current assets	370,000	450,000	—
Investments	50,000	50,000	—
Plant and equipment	1,000,000	1,100,000	—
Less: Accumulated depreciation	550,000	600,000	—
Net plant and equipment	450,000	500,000	+ 50,000
Total assets	$ 870,000	$1,000,000	—
Liabilities and Owners' Equity			
Current liabilities:			
Accounts payable	$ 60,000	$ 80,000	+$20,000
Notes payable	60,000	100,000	+ 40,000
Accrued expenses	40,000	30,000	− 10,000
Total current liabilities	160,000	210,000	—
Long-term liabilities:			
Bonds payable, 1990	60,000	90,000	+ 30,000
Total liabilities	220,000	300,000	—
Owners' equity:			
Preferred stock	50,000	50,000	—
Common stock	100,000	100,000	—
Contributed surplus	250,000	250,000	—
Retained earnings	250,000	300,000	+ 50,000
Total owners' equity	650,000	700,000	—
Total liabilities and owners' equity	$ 870,000	$1,000,000	—

the reduction in prepaid expenses. Items that used cash but were not included in the income calculation are deducted. These include the reduction in accrued expenses, the increase in inventory, and the increase in accounts receivable.

Thus, depreciation expense, never a cash item, must always be added back to income to calculate the cash flow. Increases in accounts receivable represent an operating use of cash while decreases in receiv-

Table 2–7
Kramer Corporation, cash provided by operations for the year ended 1988

Net income (see Tables 2–1 and 2–2)		$100,000
Add: Expense items not requiring use of cash		
Decrease in prepaid expenses	$ 10,000	
Increase in accounts payable	20,000	
Depreciation expense	50,000	80,000
Deduct: Items not providing cash		
Increase in inventory	(50,000)	
Increase in accounts receivable	(30,000)	
Decrease in accrued expenses	(10,000)	(90,000)
Cash provided by operations		$ 90,000

ables provide extra cash. The same holds for changes in inventory. Increases in prepaid expenses or decreases in accrued expenses represent operating uses of cash. Decreases in prepaid expenses or increases in accrued expenses provide cash.

Note that in Table 2–6 the net change in the retained earnings account was $50,000. That reflected net income of $100,000 less dividends paid of $50,000. However, Table 2–7 shows that the net cash provided by Kramer's operations was $90,000.

Other Sources and Uses of Cash

Although changes in a number of the balance sheet accounts, such as accumulated depreciation, have already been taken into account in the operating cash flow calculation above, changes in the plant and equipment, notes payable, bonds payable, and retained earnings accounts must still be included.

The additional investment in plant and equipment represents a use of cash of $100,000. If a fixed asset had been sold, on the other hand, the sale would have been a source of cash.

The increase in the notes payable and in the bonds payable accounts both represent infusions of additional financing and as such are recorded as sources of cash. Reductions in either of those accounts would represent net repayments and as such would be uses of cash.

Finally, the net change in the retained earnings account remains to be explained. While the calculation of the cash flow from operations provides adjustments for all of the operating cash flow effects not reflected in the net income amount, no account has yet been taken of the $50,000 dividend payment. The final cash flow statement would thus look like that in Table 2–8.

Analyzing Cash Flows

In analyzing cash flow statements, we are especially concerned that the uses or buildup in assets are matched against the sources of financing. For example, are increases in long-term assets being supported by profits and long-term borrowing or are they being financed by the riskier route of short-term borrowings? In Tables 2–7 and 2–8 we see that the $100,000 increase in plant and equipment was primarily financed by net income (minus dividends) of $50,000 and a $30,000 increase in the long-term liability, bonds payable.[5] Thus, the situation seems reasonably well in balance. A riskier situation occurs if we attempt to finance virtually all long-term needs with short-term funds. If money becomes "tight" and interest rates go up, continued short-term financing may become either difficult to find or prohibitively

Table 2–8

KRAMER CORPORATION
Statement of Changes in Financial Postition
For the Year Ending December 31, 1988

Sources of cash:		
From operations	$ 90,000	
From borrowings:		
Long-term	30,000	
Short-term	40,000	
Total sources		$160,000
Uses of cash:		
Invested in plant and equipment	100,000	
Dividends	50,000	
Total uses		150,000
Increase in cash		$ 10,000

[5]In a limited sense, depreciation also adds to cash flow, but this topic is deferred until a later section.

expensive. A long-term, short-term imbalance can ultimately lead to insolvency.

The relationship between accounts receivable and accounts payable should also be examined. If we have to finance our customers in the form of receivables, we would like our suppliers to finance us as well. In the present case accounts receivable are increasing 50 percent faster than are payables. In examining the original financial statement in Table 2–6 we observe that the accounts receivable in total ($200,000) greatly exceed accounts payable ($80,000).

The analyst should also examine the relative contribution made by the different sources of financing. In this example the significant contribution to cash flow from operations would indicate that the buildup in receivables and inventory is not excessive. The relatively large investment in plant and equipment deserves further scrutiny.

Depreciation and Cash Flow

One of the most confusing issues for finance students is whether or not depreciation is a source of funds to the corporation. In Table 2–7 we added depreciation to net income in determining the cash flow from operations. The reason we added back depreciation was not because depreciation was a source of new funds but, rather, because we had subtracted this noncash deduction in arriving at net income and have to add it back to determine the actual cash flow effect of operations.

Depreciation represents an attempt to allocate the initial cost of an asset over its useful life. In essence, we attempt to match the annual expense of plant and equipment ownership against the revenues being produced. Nevertheless, the charging of depreciation is purely an accounting entry and does not directly involve the movement of funds. To go from accounting flows to cash flows in Table 2–7 we restored the noncash deduction of $50,000 for depreciation that was subtracted in Table 2–1, the income statement.

Let us examine a very simple case involving depreciation. Assume that we purchase a machine for $500 with a five-year life and that we pay for it in cash. Our depreciation schedule calls for equal depreciation of $100 per year for five years. Assume further that our firm has $1,000 in earnings before depreciation and taxes and that the tax obligation is $450. Note the difference between accounting flows and cash flows for the first two years in Table 2–9.

Table 2–9 Comparison of accounting and cash flows

	Year 1	
	(1) Accounting Flows	(2) Cash Flows
Earnings before depreciation and taxes (EBDT)	$1,000	$1,000
Depreciation	100	100
Earnings before taxes (EBT)	900	900
Taxes	450	450
Earnings after taxes (EAT)	$ 450	450
Purchase of equipment		−500
Depreciation charged without cash outlay		+100
Cash flow		$ 50
	Year 2	
Earnings before depreciation and taxes (EBDT)	$1,000	$1,000
Depreciation	100	100
Earnings before taxes (EBT)	900	900
Taxes	450	450
Earnings after taxes (EAT)	$ 450	450
Depreciation charged without cash outlay		+100
Cash flow		$ 550

Since we took $500 out of cash flow originally (column 2), we do not wish to take it out again. Thus, we add back $100 in depreciation each year to "wash out" the subtraction in the income statement.

Income Tax Considerations

Virtually every financial decision is influenced by federal and provincial income tax considerations. Primary examples are the lease versus purchase decision, the issuance of common stock versus debt decision, and the decision to replace an asset. While the intent of this section is not to review the rules, regulations, and nuances of the Income Tax Act, we will examine, in general, how tax matters influence corporate financial decisions. The primary orientation will be toward the principles governing "corporate" tax decisions, though many of the same principles apply to a sole proprietorship or partnership.

In later chapters there will be references to the specific nature of income tax effects on cash flows under 1987 tax rules. This is especially notable in Chapter 12 where the nature of tax-allowable depreciation is explored in detail and related to the capital budgeting decision. Given the complexity and ever-changing nature of the Canadian tax environment, however, in most cases where tax implications may be important an individual is well-advised to get current tax advice from a tax expert.[6]

Corporate Tax Rate

Corporate tax rates change often both in accordance with government's needs for revenue and also its policy toward industrial encouragement. In this section we will use rates in force as of early 1987, knowing that these will be changed in subsequent budgets by the government of the day.

In 1972 the Tax Act specified a 50 percent corporate tax rate reducing by 1 percent per year until it reached 46 percent. From 1976 to 1987 the federal corporate tax rate has remained at 46 percent. However, the federal government allows a 10 percent tax abatement of all income earned in a province. This abatement is to allow room for the provinces to levy their own taxes on corporations. The guiding principle seems to be that if the provinces then levy their own 10 percent corporate tax, the general corporate tax rate for companies operating in Canada will be 46 percent. The government has included deductions for both small businesses and manufacturing (and processing) businesses as a way to encourage expansion in these types of business.

For small businesses, there is a 21 percent small business deduction on the first $200,000 of active business income of a Canadian-controlled private corporation. Active is interpreted to exclude personal services corporations and specified investment businesses. The basic intent was to reduce the taxes payable, federal and provincial combined, on small businesses to 25 percent from 46 percent. However, as you will see, provisions by the provinces have, in fact, often reduced this to a smaller rate yet. For manufacturing and processing types of industry, there is a 6 percent deduction from the federal rate, aimed at reducing the tax rate to 40 percent for this type of company—19 percent for any portion of income eligible for the small business deduction.

---

[6]The Canadian Minister of Finance, Michael Wilson, has proposed a series of tax reforms to be implemented in mid-1988 which, if approved by Parliament, will result in a number of significant changes in the tax effects of various alternative financial decisions for corporations.

Table 2–10
Provincial tax rates (1986)

	Small Business	Manufacturing and Processing: Small	Manufacturing and Processing: Other	Other
Newfoundland	10.00%	10.00%	16.0%	16.0%
Prince Edward Island	10.00	10.00	15.0	15.0
Nova Scotia	10.00	10.00	15.0	15.0
New Brunswick	5.00	5.00	15.0	15.0
Quebec	3.22	3.22	5.9	5.9
Ontario	10.00	10.00	14.5	15.5
Manitoba	10.00	10.00	17.0	17.0
Saskatchewan	10.00	0.00	17.0	17.0
Alberta	5.00	0.00	5.0	11.0
British Columbia	8.00	8.00	16.0	16.0
Northwest Territories	10.00	10.00	10.0	10.0
Yukon Territory	5.00	2.50	2.5	10.0

Table 2–10 outlines the provincial corporate tax rates. Besides the special treatment accorded small businesses generally, some provinces have instituted a tax holiday for small businesses in their first few years of operation.

Effective Tax Rate Examples

Let us look at several examples of calculating tax payable for a business year ending June 30, 1987. We will assume that the provincial tax rates for 1986 hold for 1987 as well.

1. Nonmanufacturing company—Canadian controlled private corporation—operating in Ontario:

Active business income	$100,000
Federal tax @ 46%	46,000
Less: Provincial abatement @ 10%	10,000
Basic federal tax	36,000
Less: Small business deduction @ 21%	21,000
Federal tax payable	15,000
Add: Provincial tax payable @ 10%	10,000
Total tax payable	25,000

2. Manufacturing company—Canadian controlled private corporation—operating in Saskatchewan:

Active business income	$100,000
Federal tax @ 46%	46,000
Less: Provincial abatement @ 10%	10,000
Basic federal tax	36,000
Less: Manufacturing credit @ 6%	6,000
Less: Small business deduction @ 21%	21,000
Federal tax payable	9,000
Add: Provincial tax payable @ 0%	0
Total tax payable	9,000

3. Manufacturing company—foreign controlled—operating in Prince Edward Island:

Active business income	$100,000
Federal tax @ 46%	46,000
Less: Provincial abatement @ 10%	10,000
Basic federal tax	36,000
Less: Manufacturing credit @ 6%	6,000
Federal tax payable	30,000
Add: Provincial tax payable @ 15%	15,000
Total tax payable	45,000

Depreciation as a Tax Shield

Although depreciation is not a new source of funds, it does provide the important function of shielding part of our income from taxes. Let us examine Corporations A and B with an eye toward depreciation. Corporation A charges off $100,000 in depreciation, while Corporation B charges off none.

	Corporation A	*Corporation B*
Earnings before depreciation and taxes	$400,000	$400,000
Depreciation	100,000	0
Earnings before taxes	300,000	400,000
Taxes (40%)	120,000	160,000
Earnings after taxes	180,000	240,000
Plus: Depreciation charged without cash outlay	100,000	0
Cash flow	$280,000	$240,000
Difference—$40,000		

We compute earnings after taxes and then add back depreciation to get cash flow. The difference between $280,000 and $240,000 indicates that Corporation A enjoys $40,000 more in cash flow. The reason is that depreciation shielded $100,000 from taxation in Corporation A and saved $40,000 in taxes, which eventually showed up in cash flow. Though depreciation is not a new source of funds, it does provide tax shield benefits that can be measured as depreciation times the tax rate, or in this case $100,000 × 0.40 = $40,000. A more comprehensive discussion of depreciation's effect on cash flow is presented in Chapter 12, as part of the long-term capital budgeting decision.[7]

Summary

The financial manager must be thoroughly familiar with the language of accounting in order to administer the financial affairs of the firm.

The income statement provides a measure of the firm's profitability over a specified period of time. Earnings per share represent residual income available to the common shareholder that may be either paid out in the form of dividends or reinvested to generate future profits and dividends. A limitation of the income statement is that it reports income and expenses primarily on a transaction basis and thus may not recognize certain important economic changes as they occur.

The balance sheet is a snapshot of the financial position of the firm at a point in time, with the owners' equity section purporting to represent ownership interest. Because the balance sheet is presented on a historical-cost basis, it may not represent the true value of the firm. Beginning with the 1983 annual reports of large companies, the Canadian Institute of Chartered Accountants (CICA) has recommended inflation-adjusted accounting statements.

The cash flow statement, usually called the statement of changes in financial position, reflects the flows of cash between reporting dates. Through this statement we get a rough picture of operating cash flows and the nature of the firm's investment and financing activities.

Finally, we examine the corporate tax structure and the tax implications of size, location, type of business, and depreciation. The after-tax cost and tax flow implications of these items are important through-

[7]Tax allowable depreciation is referred to as capital cost allowance (CCA). Chapter 12 also outlines the investment tax credit system.

out the text and will be examined in more detail as warranted. Currently proposed tax changes, if implemented, will greatly change the nature of corporate taxation.

List of Terms

income statement	**market-to-book value**
earnings per share	**cash flow statement**
P/E ratio	**historical-cost accounting**
balance sheet	**current-cost accounting**
owners' equity	**constant-dollar accounting**
liquidity	**cash flows**
net worth, or book value	

Discussion Questions

1. Discuss some of the financial variables that have an effect on the price-earnings ratio.
2. What is the difference between book value per share of common stock and market value per share? Why does this disparity occur?
3. Explain how depreciation generates cash flows for the company.
4. What is the difference between accumulated depreciation and depreciation expense? How are they related?
5. How is the income statement related to the balance sheet?
6. Discuss how inflation affects the balance sheet and the income statement. What specific items are most influenced by inflation?
7. What items on the cash flow statement need to be reconciled with the income statement? Why?
8. How can we use a cash flow statement to analyze how a firm's assets were financed?

9. Why is interest expense said to cost the firm approximately half of the actual expense while dividends cost it 100 percent of the outlay?

10. What do inflation-adjusted accounting statements offer to the financial manager and the stockholder?

Problems

1. Ron's Aerobics, Inc., located in downtown Toronto, has the following taxable income for 1986 and 1987.

1986	$ 68,000
1987	142,000

a. Compute the total tax obligation for Ron's Aerobics each year.
b. Compute the average tax rate for each year.

2. Given the following information, prepare, in good form, an income statement for the Nix Corporation. Use the corporate tax rates in Chapter 2 to calculate taxes. Nix is a Vancouver manufacturer.

Selling and administrative expense	$ 90,000
Depreciation expense	50,000
Sales	500,000
Interest expense	20,000
Cost of goods sold	220,000

3. The Singleday Book Company has sold 1,400 finance textbooks to High Tuition University for $35 each. These books cost Singleday $22 each to produce. In addition, Singleday spent $2,000 in selling expense to convince the university to buy its books. Singleday borrowed $15,000 on January 1, 1987, on which it paid 12 percent interest. Both principal and interest were paid on December 31, 1987. Singleday's tax rate is 30 percent. Depreciation expense for the year was $4,000.

Did Singleday make a profit in 1987? Verify with an income statement presented in good form.

4. Classify the following balance sheet items as current or noncurrent.

Inventory
Accounts payable
Preferred stock
Prepaid expenses
Bonds payable
Retained earnings
Marketable securities
Accounts receivable
Plant and equipment
Accrued wages payable

5. Arrange the following income statement items so that they are in the proper order of an income statement.

Depreciation expense
Gross profit
Interest expense
Taxes
Preferred stock dividends
Shares outstanding
Earnings per share
Earnings after taxes
Operating profit
Selling and administrative expense
Sales
Earnings before taxes
Cost of goods sold
Earnings available to common shareholders

6. Identify the following as a source of funds or a use of funds.

Increase in inventory
Decrease in prepaid expenses
Decrease in retained earnings
Increase in cash
Decrease in inventory
Dividend payment
Increase in notes payable
Depreciation expense
Decrease in accounts payable
Increase in investments

7. The Aaron Corporation has an operating profit of $210,000. Interest expense for the year was $15,000, preferred dividends paid were $10,550, and common dividends paid were $37,500. The tax was $69,450. The Aaron Corporation has 25,000 shares of common stock outstanding.

a. Calculate the earnings per share and common dividends per share for the Aaron Corporation.
b. What was the increase in retained earnings for the year?

8. The Elliot Corporation had $450,000 of retained earnings on December 31, 1987. The company paid dividends of $25,000 in 1987 and had retained earnings of $400,000 on December 31, 1986.

How much did Elliot earn during 1987, and what are its earnings per share if 20,000 shares of common stock are outstanding?

9. The Jupiter Corporation has a gross profit of $700,000 and $240,000 in depreciation expense. The Saturn Corporation also has $700,000 in gross profit, with $40,000 in depreciation expense. Selling and administrative expense is $160,000 for each company.

Given that the tax rate is 40 percent, compute the cash flow for both companies. Explain the difference in cash flow between the two firms.

10. Fill in the blank spaces with categories 1 through 7 below.

1. Balance sheet (BS).
2. Income statement (IS).
3. Current assets (CA).
4. Fixed assets (FA).
5. Current liabilities (CL).
6. Long-term liabilities (LL).
7. Owners' equity (OE).

Indicate Whether Item Is on Balance Sheet (BS) or Income Statement (IS)	*If on Balance Sheet, Designate Which Category*	*Item*
1	7	Retained earnings
2		Income tax expense
1	3	Accounts receivable
1	7	Common stock
1	7	Contributed surplus
1	6	Bonds payable, maturity 1999
1	5	Notes payable (six months)
2		Net income
2		Selling and administrative expenses
2 (1)	(3)	Inventories
2		Accrued expenses
1	3	Cash
1	6	Plant and equipment
2		Sales
2		Operating expenses
1	3	Marketable securities
1	5	Accounts payable
2		Interest expense
2		Income tax payable

11. The balance sheet of Neeley Corporation includes the following owners' equity section:

Owners' Equity

Common stock, 100,000 shares outstanding	$ 200,000
Contributed surplus	850,000
Retained earnings	400,000
Total owners' equity	$1,450,000

Assuming there has been only one issue of stock, what was the original selling price of Neeley Company's common stock?

12. Arrange the following items in proper balance sheet presentation.

Accumulated depreciation	$250,000
Retained earnings	73,000
Cash	10,000
Bonds payable	125,000
Accounts receivable	48,000
Plant and equipment—original cost	600,000
Accounts payable	25,000
Allowance for bad debts	3,000
Common stock, 100,000 shares outstanding	100,000
Inventory	50,000
Preferred stock, 1,000 shares outstanding	50,000
Marketable securities	20,000
Investments	8,000
Notes payable	30,000
Contributed surplus (common stock)	80,000

13. Monique's Boutique has assets of $600,000, current liabilities of $150,000, and long-term liabilities of $120,000. There is $75,000 in preferred stock outstanding. Thirty thousand shares of common stock have been issued.

a. Compute book value (net worth) per share.

b. If there is $33,600 in earnings available to common stockholders and Monique's stock has a P/E of 12 times earnings per share, what is the current price of the stock?

c. What is the ratio of market value per share to book value per share?

14. In Problem 13, if the firm sells at two times book value per share, what will the P/E ratio be?

15. Following is the December 31, 1986, balance sheet of Hillcrest Corporation (located in Hamilton):

Current Assets		**Liabilities**	
Cash	$ 10,000	Accounts payable	$ 12,000
Accounts receivable	15,000	Notes payable	20,000
Inventory	25,000	Bonds payable	50,000
Miscellaneous	12,000		
Fixed Assets		**Owners' Equity**	
Plant and equipment	$250,000	Common stock	$ 75,000
Less: Accumulated depreciation	50,000	Paid-in capital	25,000
Net plant and equipment	200,000	Retained earnings	80,000
Total assets	$262,000	Total liabilities and owners' equity	$262,000

Sales for 1987 were $220,000, and cost of goods sold was 60 percent of sales. Depreciation expense was 10 percent of the net plant and equipment at the beginning of the year. Interest expense for the bonds payable was 8 percent, while interest on the notes payable was 10 percent. These interest expenses are based on December 31, 1986, balances. Selling and administrative expenses were $22,000, and the tax rate averaged 18 percent.

During the year 1987 accounts receivable and inventory increased by 10 percent, and accounts payable increased by 25 percent. A new machine was purchased on December 30, 1987, at a cost of $35,000. A cash dividend of $12,800 was paid to common stockholders at the end of 1987. Also, notes payable increased by $6,000, and bonds payable decreased by $10,000.

a. Prepare an income statement for 1987.
b. Prepare a balance sheet as of December 31, 1987.
c. Prepare a statement of changes in financial position similar to Table 2–8.

16. Construct a cash flow statement from the following data for the Madison Corporation.

MADISON CORPORATION

Assets	*Year-End 1986*	*Year-End 1987*	*Change*
Current assets:			
Cash	$ 200,000	$ 220,000	
Marketable securities	70,000	60,000	
Accounts receivable	390,000	430,000	
Inventory	520,000	540,000	
Prepaid expenses	20,000	25,000	
Total current assets	1,200,000	1,275,000	
Plant and equipment:	600,000	790,000	
Less: Accumulated depreciation	160,000	200,000	
Net plant and equipment	440,000	590,000	
Total assets	$1,640,000	$1,865,000	
Liabilities and Owners' Equity			
Current liabilities:			
Accounts payable	$ 265,000	$ 280,000	
Notes payable	200,000	340,000	
Accrued expenses	55,000	65,000	
Total current liabilities	520,000	685,000	
Long-term liabilities:			
Bonds payable, 1994	400,000	360,000	
Total liabilities	920,000	1,045,000	
Owners' equity:			
Preferred stock	100,000	100,000	
Common stock	90,000	100,000	
Contributed surplus	170,000	220,000	
Retained earnings	360,000	400,000	
Total owners' equity	720,000	820,000	
Total liabilities and owners' equity	$1,640,000	$1,865,000	

(*The following questions apply to the Madison Corporation as presented in Problem 16*)

Assume that the Madison Corporation paid out dividends of $15,000 in 1987 and the change in accumulated depreciation is equal to the depreciation expense for the year.

Compute a funds flow statement similar to Table 2–8. (Net income can be defined as change in retained earnings plus dividends paid.)

17. Compute the book value per share for each year for the Madison Corporation. There were 45,000 shares outstanding in 1986, 50,000 in 1987.

18. If the market value of a share of common stock is 1.3 times book value for 1987, what is the firm's P/E ratio for 1987?

19. Has the buildup in fixed assets been financed in a satisfactory manner? Discuss briefly.

Selected References

Arthur Andersen & Co. Study. *Objectives of Financial Statements for Business Enterprises*. Chicago, 1972.

Bierman, Harold, Jr., "Toward a Constant Price-Earnings Ratio." *Financial Analysts Journal* 38 (September–October 1982), pp. 62–65.

CCH Canadian Limited. *Canadian Master Tax Guide*. 40th ed. Toronto, 1985.

Canadian Institute of Chartered Accountants. *CICA Handbook*. Toronto.

________. *Corporate Reporting: Its Future Evolution*. Toronto, 1980.

________. *Financial Reporting in Canada*. 15th ed. Toronto, 1983.

Colley, Geoffrey M. *Tax Principles to Remember*. 1985 ed. Toronto: CICA, 1985.

Helfert, Erich A. *Techniques of Financial Analysis*. 5th ed. Homewood, Ill.: Richard D. Irwin, 1982.

Kroll, Yoman. "On the Differences between Accrual Accounting Figures and Cash Flows: The Case of Working Capital." *Financial Management* 14 (Spring 1985), pp. 75–82.

Matulich, Serge; L. E. Heitger; and T. Var. *Financial Accounting*. 2nd Canadian ed. Toronto: McGraw-Hill Ryerson, 1987.

Norby, William C. "Accounting for Financial Analysis." *Financial Analysts Journal* 38 (July–August 1982), pp. 33–35.

Skinner, Ross M. *Accounting Principles: A Canadian Viewpoint*. Toronto: CICA, 1972.

Welsch, Glenn A.; D. G. Short; and G. R. Chesley. *Fundamentals of Financial Accounting*. 1st Canadian ed. Homewood, Ill.: Richard D. Irwin, 1987.

3 Financial Analysis

In Chapter 2, Review of Accounting, we examined the basic assumptions of accounting and the various components that make up the financial statements of the firm. We now use this fundamental material as a springboard into financial analysis—to evaluate the financial performance of the firm.

The format for the chapter is twofold. In the first part we will use financial ratios to evaluate the relative success of the firm. Various measures such as net income to sales and current assets to current liabilities will be computed for a hypothetical company and examined in light of industry norms and past trends.

In the second part of the chapter we explore further the impact of inflation and disinflation on financial operations over the last decade. Heretofore given scant coverage in financial textbooks, the material is significant for financial managers of the future. The student begins to appreciate the impact of rising prices (or, at times, declining prices) on the various financial ratios. The chapter concludes with a discussion of how other factors—in addition to price changes—may distort the financial statements of the firm. Terms such as *net income to sales, return on investment,* and *inventory turnover* take on much greater meaning when they are evaluated through the eyes of a financial manager who does more than merely pick out the top or bottom line of an income statement. The examples in the chapter are designed from the viewpoint of a financial manager (with only minor attention to accounting theory).

Ratio Analysis

Ratios are used in much of our daily life. We buy cars based on miles per gallon; we evaluate baseball players by earned run averages and batting averages, basketball players by field goal and foul-shooting percentages, and so on. These are all ratios constructed to judge comparative performance. Financial ratios serve a similar purpose, but you must know what is being measured in order to construct a ratio and to understand the significance of the resultant number.

Financial ratios are used to weigh and evaluate the operating performance of the firm. While an absolute value such as earnings of $50,000 or accounts receivable of $100,000 may appear satisfactory, its acceptability can only be measured in relation to other values. For this reason financial managers place heavy emphasis on ratio analysis.

For example, are earnings of $50,000 actually good? If we earned $50,000 on $500,000 of sales (10 percent "profit margin" ratio), that might be quite satisfactory—whereas earnings of $50,000 on $5 million could be disappointing (a meager 1 percent return). After we have computed the appropriate ratio, we must compare our results to those achieved by similar firms in our industry as well as to our own past record of performance. Even then, this "number crunching" process is not fully adequate, and we are forced to supplement our financial findings with an evaluation of company management, physical facilities, and numerous other factors.

For comparative purposes, a number of organizations provide industry data. For example, Dun & Bradstreet compiles data on over 150 different lines of business, while Statistics Canada provides ratios on a number of industry classifications. Quite often the most valuable industry figures come from the various industry associations to which the firms belong—for example, the Canadian Association of Broadcasters. Member firms submit financial information to the association which then publishes it in summary form so that members can analyze their own performances. It is important to remember that we often use ratios of past financial performance to determine our expectations regarding the firm's future success.

Many university and public libraries subscribe to financial services such as The Financial Post Information Service. Financial Post also leases a computer data base as does *The Globe and Mail* under the name of INFO GLOBE. INFO GLOBE, for example, contains annual financial statement data on 1,500 Canadian companies. For the larger of these the data go back to 1974, while three years of quarterly data are available on 350 of the firms. While these data can be used to calculate countless ratios aimed at the measurement of corporate performance, INFO GLOBE also provides software that allows for industry and cross-industry comparisons. The ratios classified in this text represent the most commonly used categories and ratios, but others can also be constructed.

Classification System

We will separate 13 significant ratios into four primary categories.

A. Profitability ratios.
   1. Profit margin.
   2. Return on assets (investment).
   3. Return on equity.

B. Asset utilization ratios.
   4. Receivable turnover.
   5. Average collection period.
   6. Inventory turnover.
   7. Fixed asset turnover.
   8. Total asset turnover.

C. Liquidity ratios.
   9. Current ratio.
   10. Quick ratio.

D. Debt utilization ratios.
   11. Debt to total assets.
   12. Times interest earned.
   13. Fixed charge coverage.

The first grouping, the profitability ratios, allows us to measure the ability of the firm to earn an adequate return on sales, total assets, and invested capital. Many of the problems related to profitability can be explained, in whole or in part, by the firm's ability to effectively employ its resources. Thus, the next category of ratios is asset utilization. Under this heading we measure the speed at which the firm is turning over accounts receivable, inventory, and longer-term assets. In other words, asset utilization ratios measure how many times per year a company sells its inventory or collects its entire accounts receivable. For long-term assets, the utilization ratio tells us how productive the fixed assets are in terms of sales generation.

In Category C, the liquidity ratios, the primary emphasis moves to the firm's ability to pay off short-term obligations as they come due. In Category D, debt utilization ratios, the overall debt position of the firm is evaluated in light of its asset base and earning power.

The users of financial statements will attach different degrees of importance to the four categories of ratios. To the potential investor or security analyst, the critical consideration is profitability, with secondary consideration given to such matters as liquidity and debt utilization. For the banker or trade creditor, the emphasis shifts to the firm's current ability to meet debt obligations. The bondholder, in turn, may be primarily influenced by debt to total assets—while also eyeing the profitability of the firm in terms of its ability to cover debt obligations. Of course, the shrewd analyst looks at all the ratios but with different degrees of attention.

The Analysis

Definitions alone carry little meaning in analyzing or dissecting the financial performance of a company. For this reason we shall apply our four categories of ratios to a hypothetical firm, the Saxton Company, as presented in Table 3–1. The use of ratio analysis is rather like solving a mystery in which each clue leads to a new area of inquiry.

A. Profitability ratios We first look at the profitability ratios. Note that the appropriate ratio is computed for the Saxton Company and is then compared to representative industry data.

Table 3–1
Financial statements for ratio analysis

SAXTON COMPANY
Income Statement
For the Year 1987

Sales (all on credit)	$4,000,000
Cost of goods sold	3,000,000
Gross profit	1,000,000
Selling and administrative expense*	450,000
Operating profit	550,000
Interest expense	50,000
Extraordinary loss	100,000
Net income before taxes	400,000
Taxes (50%)	200,000
Net income	$ 200,000

*Includes $50,000 in lease payments.

Balance Sheet
As of December 31, 1987
Assets

Cash	$ 30,000
Marketable securities	50,000
Accounts receivable	350,000
Inventory	370,000
Total current assets	800,000
Net plant and equipment	800,000
Total assets	$1,600,000

Liabilities and Owners' Equity

Accounts payable	$ 50,000
Notes payable	250,000
Total current liabilities	300,000
Long-term liabilities	300,000
Total liabilities	600,000
Common stock	400,000
Retained earnings	600,000
Total liabilities and owners' equity	$1,600,000

The Saxton Company shows a lower return on the sales dollar (5 percent) than the industry average of 6.5 percent. However, its return on assets (investment) of 12.5 percent exceeds the industry norm of 10 percent. There is only one possible explanation for this occurrence—a more rapid turnover of assets than that generally found within the industry. This is verified in ratio *2b*, in which sales to total assets is 2.5 for the Saxton Company and only 1.5 for the industry. Thus, Saxton earns less on each sales dollar, but it compensates by turning over its assets more rapidly.

Return on total assets as described through the two components of profit margin and asset turnover is part of the Du Pont system of financial analysis.

Return on assets (investment) = Profit margin × Asset turnover

The Du Pont company was a forerunner in stressing that satisfactory return on assets may be achieved through high profit margins or rapid turnover of assets, or a combination of both. We shall also soon observe that under the Du Pont system of analysis, the use of debt may be important. The Du Pont system causes the analyst to examine the sources of a company's profitability. Since the profit margin is an income statement ratio, a high profit margin indicates good cost control, whereas a high asset turnover ratio demonstrates efficient use of the assets on the balance sheet. Different industries have different operating and financial structures. For example, in the heavy capital goods industry the emphasis is on a high profit margin with a low asset turnover—whereas in food retailing the profit margin is low, and the key to satisfactory returns on total assets is a rapid turnover of assets.

A. *Profitability ratios*—

	Saxton Company	*Industry Average*
1. Profit margin = $\frac{\text{Net income}}{\text{Sales}}$	$\frac{\$200{,}000}{\$4{,}000{,}000} = 5\%$	6.5%
2. Return on assets (investment) =		
a. $\frac{\text{Net income}}{\text{Total assets}}$	$\frac{\$200{,}000}{\$1{,}600{,}000} = 12.5\%$	10%
b. $\frac{\text{Net income}}{\text{Sales}} \times \frac{\text{Sales}}{\text{Total assets}}$	5% × 2.5 = 12.5%	6.5% × 1.5 = 10%
3. Return on equity =		
a. $\frac{\text{Net income}}{\text{Owners' equity}}$	$\frac{\$200{,}000}{\$1{,}000{,}000} = 20\%$	15%
b. $\frac{\text{Return on assets (investment)}}{(1 - \text{Debt/Assets})}$	$\frac{0.125}{1 - 0.375} = 20\%$	$\frac{0.10}{1 - 0.33} = 15\%$

Equally important to a firm is its return on equity or ownership capital. For the Saxton Company return on equity is 20 percent versus an industry norm of 15 percent. Thus, the owners of Saxton Company are more amply rewarded than are other shareholders in the industry. This may be the result of one or two factors: a high return on total assets or a generous utilization of debt or a combination thereof. This can be seen through Equation 3*b*, which represents a modified or second version of the Du Pont formula.

$$\text{Return on equity} = \frac{\text{Return on assets (investment)}}{(1 - \text{Debt/Assets})}$$

Note the numerator, return on assets, is taken from Formula 2, which represents the initial version of the Du Pont formula (Return on assets = Net income/Sales × Sales/Total assets). Return on assets is then divided by (1 − Debt/Assets) to account for the amount of debt in the capital structure. In the case of the Saxton Company the modified version of the Du Pont formula shows:

$$\text{Return on equity} = \frac{\text{Return on assets (investment)}}{(1 - \text{Debt/Assets})}$$

$$= \frac{12.5\%}{1 - 0.375} = 20\%$$

Actually, the return on assets of 12.5 percent in the numerator is higher than the industry average of 10 percent, and the ratio of debt to assets in the denominator of 37.5 percent is higher than the industry norm of 33 percent. Both the numerator and denominator contribute to a higher return on equity than the industry average (20 percent versus 15 percent). Note that if the firm had a 50 percent debt-to-assets ratio, return on equity would be up to 25 percent.[1]

$$\text{Return on equity} = \frac{\text{Return on assets (investment)}}{(1 - \text{Debt/Assets})}$$

$$= \frac{12.5\%}{1 - 0.50} = 25\%$$

This does not necessarily mean that debt is a positive influence, only that it can be used to boost return on equity. The ultimate goal for the firm is to achieve maximum valuation for its securities in the marketplace, and this goal may or may not be advanced by using debt to increase return on equity. Because debt represents increased risk, a

[1]The return would be slightly less than 25 percent because of increased financing costs with higher debt.

Figure 3–1
Du Pont analysis

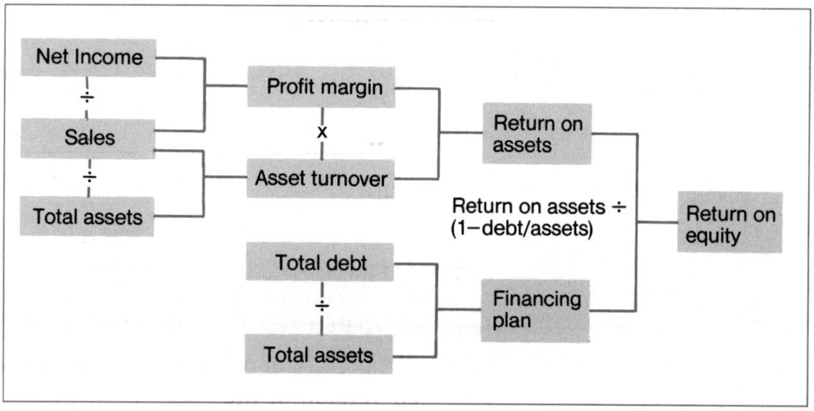

lower valuation of higher earnings is possible.[2] Every situation must be evaluated individually.

The reader may wish to review Figure 3–1, which illustrates the key points in the Du Pont system of analysis.

As an example of the Du Pont analysis, using Table 3–2 let us compare the 1985 data for Imperial Oil and Shell Canada, two diversified oil companies. It is clear that for the year 1985 Imperial's overall profitability far exceeded that of Shell. Looking at the individual elements of the Du Pont formula we see that Imperial's profit margin per dollar of sales was 3.04 times larger than that of Shell. In comparison, the final return on equity figure was 2.21 times larger. Thus, one or both of the asset/turnover or financial leverage relationships have reduced the overall effect of Imperial's superior profit margin.

Looking at asset turnover we see that Shell's was 1.05 times versus a lower .94 times for Imperial. This meant that the return on assets for Imperial was 2.76 times that of Shell versus the 3.04 times that its profit margin exceeded Shell's. Since the overall differential in return on equity was 2.21 times, we can forecast that Shell must have used comparatively more debt in its financing than did Imperial. It turns out that Shell's debt/assets ratio of 56 percent was substantially higher

[2]Further discussion of this point is presented in Chapter 5, Operating and Financial Leverage, and Chapter 10, Valuation and Rates of Return.

Table 3–2
Du Pont analysis of the profitability of Imperial Oil versus Shell Canada

	Profit Margin	×	Asset Turnover	=	Return on Assets	÷	(1 − Debt/Assets)	=	Return on Equity
Imperial	7.3%	×	.94	=	6.9%	÷	(1 − .45)	=	12.6%
Shell	2.4	×	1.05	=	2.5	÷	(1 − .56)	=	5.7

than Imperial's 45 percent. In other words, had Shell's return on assets equaled Imperial's at 6.9 percent, Shell's higher debt/assets ratio would have leveraged its return on equity to 15.7 percent versus Imperial's 12.6 percent return. According to this analysis then, Imperial's profitability was impacted very positively by a high profit margin, while Shell's benefited from a higher asset/turnover and a higher debt ratio.

Finally, as a general statement in computing all the profitability ratios, the analyst must be sensitive to the age of the assets. Plant and equipment purchased 15 years ago may be carried on the books far below its replacement value in an inflationary economy. A 20 percent return on assets purchased in the late 1950s or early 1960s may be inferior to a 15 percent return on newly purchased assets.

B. Asset utilization ratios The second category of ratios relates to asset utilization, and the ratios in this category may well explain why one firm is able to turn over its assets more rapidly than another. Notice that all of these ratios below relate the balance sheet (assets) to the income statement (sales). The Saxton Company's rapid turnover of assets is explained in ratios 4, 5, and 6.

Saxton collects its receivables faster than does the industry. This is shown by receivables turnover of 11.4 times versus 10 times for the industry, and in daily terms by the average collection period of 32 days, which is 4 days faster than that of the industry norm. The average collection period suggests how long, on the average, our customers' accounts stay on our books. The Saxton Company has $350,000 in accounts receivable and $4 million in credit sales, which when divided by 360 days yields average daily credit sales of $11,111. We divide accounts receivable of $350,000 by average daily credit sales of $11,111 to determine how many days credit sales are on the books (32 days).

B. Asset utilization ratios—

	Saxton Company	Industry Average
4. Receivables turnover = $\frac{\text{Sales (credit)}}{\text{Receivables}}$	$\frac{\$4,000,000}{\$350,000} = 11.4$	10 times
5. Average collection period = $\frac{\text{Accounts receivable}}{\text{Average daily credit sales}}$	$\frac{\$350,000}{\$11,111} = 32$	36 days
6. Inventory turnover = $\frac{\text{Cost of goods sold}}{\text{Inventory}}$	$\frac{\$3,000,000}{\$370,000} = 8.1$	7 times
7. Fixed asset turnover = $\frac{\text{Sales}}{\text{Fixed assets}}$	$\frac{\$4,000,000}{\$800,000} = 5$	5.4 times
8. Total asset turnover = $\frac{\text{Sales}}{\text{Total assets}}$	$\frac{\$4,000,000}{\$1,600,000} = 2.5$	1.5 times

In addition, the firm turns over its inventory 8.1 times per year as contrasted with an industry average of 7 times.[3] This tells us that Saxton is able to generate more sales per dollar of inventory than the average company in the industry, and we can assume the firm uses very efficient inventory-ordering and cost-control methods.

The firm maintains a slightly lower ratio of sales to fixed assets (plant and equipment) than does the industry (5 versus 5.4). This is a relatively minor consideration in view of the rapid movement of inventory and accounts receivable. Finally, the rapid turnover of total assets is again indicated (2.5 versus 1.5).

C. Liquidity ratios After considering profitability and asset utilization, the analyst needs to examine the liquidity of the firm. The Saxton Company's liquidity ratios fare quite well in comparison with the industry. Further analysis might call for a cash budget to determine if we can meet each maturing obligation as it comes due.

[3]Credit reporting agencies sometimes show turnover as sales divided by inventory.

C. Liquidity ratios—

	Saxton Company	Industry Average
9. Current ratio = $\frac{\text{Current assets}}{\text{Current liabilities}}$	$\frac{\$800{,}000}{\$300{,}000} = 2.67$	2.1
10. Quick ratio = $\frac{\text{Current assets} - \text{Inventory}}{\text{Current liabilities}}$	$\frac{\$430{,}000}{\$300{,}000} = 1.43$	1.0

D. Debt utilization ratios The last grouping of ratios, debt utilization, allows the analyst to measure the prudence of the debt management policies of the firm.

Debt to total assets of 37.5 percent is slightly above the industry average of 33 percent but well within the prudent range of 50 percent or less. One of the ways to benefit from an inflationary economy is through the utilization of heavy long-term debt, enabling long-standing obligations to be repaid in inflated dollars with the passage of time.

D. Debt utilization ratios—

	Saxton Company	Industry Average
11. Debt to total assets = $\frac{\text{Total debt}}{\text{Total assets}}$	$\frac{\$600{,}000}{\$1{,}600{,}000} = 37.5\%$	33%
12. Times interest earned = $\frac{\text{Income before interest and taxes}}{\text{Interest}}$	$\frac{\$550{,}000}{\$50{,}000} = 11$	7 times
13. Fixed charge coverage = $\frac{\text{Income before fixed charges and taxes}}{\text{Fixed charges}}$	$\frac{\$600{,}000}{\$100{,}000} = 6$	5.5 times

Ratios for times interest earned and fixed charge coverage show that the Saxton Company debt is being well managed compared to the debt management of other firms in the industry. Times interest earned indicates the number of times our income before interest and taxes covers the interest obligation (11). The higher the ratio, the stronger is the interest-paying ability of the firm. The figure for income before interest and taxes in the ratio is the equivalent of the operating profit figure presented in Table 3–1.

Fixed charge coverage measures the firm's ability to meet all fixed obligations rather than interest payments alone, on the assumption that failure to meet any financial obligation will endanger the position of the firm. In the present case the Saxton Company has lease obligations of $50,000 as well as the $50,000 in interest expenses. Thus, the total fixed charge financial obligation is $100,000. We also need to know the income before all fixed charge obligations. In this case we take income before interest and taxes (operating profit) and add back the $50,000 in lease payments.

Income before interest and taxes	$550,000
Lease payments	50,000
Income before fixed charges and taxes	$600,000

The fixed charges are safely covered 6 times, exceeding the industry norm of 5.5 times. The various ratios are summarized in Table 3–3.

Table 3–3
Ratio analysis

	Saxton Company	Industry Average	Conclusion
A. Profitability			
1. Net income to sales	5%	6.5%	Below average
2. Net income to total assets	12.5%	10%	Above average due to high turnover
3. Net income to owners' equity	20%	15%	Good due to ratios 2 and 10
B. Asset utilization			
4. Receivable turnover	11 4	10.0	Good
5. Average collection period	32.0	36.0	Good
6. Inventory turnover	8.1	7.0	Good
7. Fixed asset turnover	5.0	5.4	Below average
8. Total asset turnover	2.5	1.5	Good
C. Liquidity			
9. Current ratio	2.67	2.1	Good
10. Quick ratio	1.43	1.0	Good
D. Debt utilization			
11. Debt to total assets	37.5%	33%	Slightly more debt
12. Times interest earned	11	7	Good
13. Fixed charge coverage	6	5.5	Good

The conclusions reached in comparing the Saxton Company to industry averages are generally valid, though exceptions may exist. For example. a high inventory turnover is considered "good" unless it is achieved by maintaining unusually low inventory levels, which may hurt future profitability.

In summary, the Saxton Company more than compensates for a lower return on the sales dollar by a rapid turnover of assets, principally inventory and receivables, and a wise use of debt. The student should be able to use these 13 measures to evaluate the financial performance of any firm.

Trend Analysis

Over the course of the business cycle, sales and profitability may expand and contract, and ratio analysis for any one year may not present an accurate picture of the firm. Therefore, we look at trend analysis of performance over a number of years. However, without industry comparisons even trend analysis may not present a complete picture. For example, in Figure 3–2 we see that the profit margin for the Saxton Company has improved, while asset turnover has declined. This by itself may look good for the profit margin and bad for asset turnover. However, when compared to industry trends, we see that the firm's profit margin is still below the industry average. On asset turnover Saxton has improved in relation to the industry even though it is in a downward trend. Similar data could be generated for the other ratios.

By analyzing companies in the same industry one company can compare its performance to the industry leader. In the case of the Canadian banking industry the Toronto-Dominion Bank has traditionally been the smallest of the so-called Big Five. Yet it has emerged in recent years as the most consistent performer and the benchmark against which the performance of others is measured. In comparing the Bank of Montreal and the Royal Bank of Canada with Toronto-Dominion we assume that the goal of management is to become the best, not just match the average performance for the industry. Using profit margin and return on equity as selected ratios, Table 3–4 compares these three companies.

If we look at the overall trend in profitability we see a decidedly more profitable picture prior to 1982 than from that year onward. In

Figure 3–2
Trend analysis

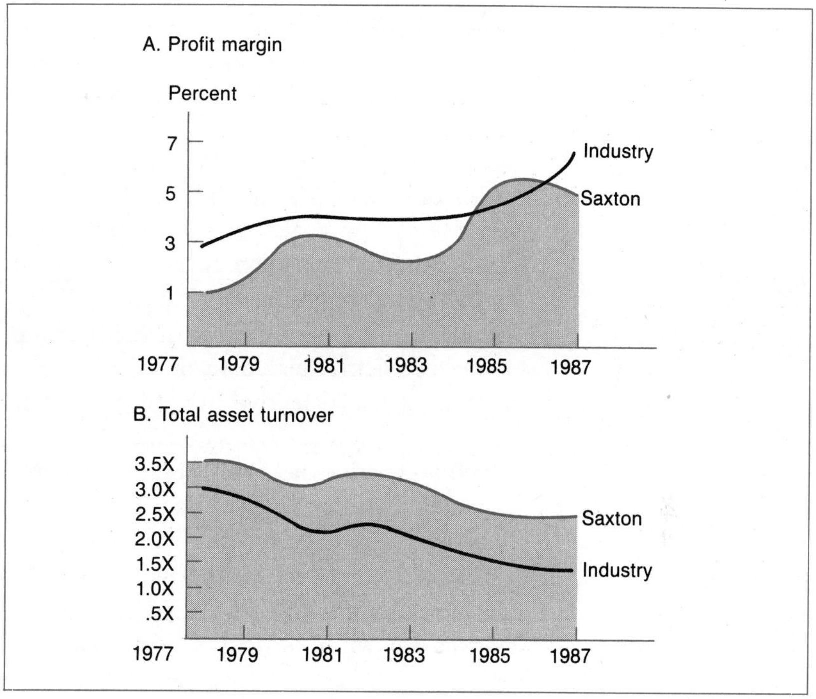

Table 3–4
Trend analysis using an industry leader

	Bank of Montreal		Royal Bank		T–D Bank	
Year	Profit Margin	Return on Equity	Profit Margin	Return on Equity	Profit Margin	Return on Equity
1977	6.1%	*	6.2%	16.1%	8.2%	16.5%
1978	7.5	*	6.9	19.2	7.9	17.6
1979	6.1	18.5%	5.4	17.9	6.6	18.7
1980	4.8	17.2	4.7	17.8	5.8	19.0
1981	4.2	19.9	4.5	20.0	4.9	20.9
1982	2.9	11.4	3.0	12.7	4.9	19.4
1983	4.0	12.6	5.3	16.8	7.2	18.7
1984	3.5	12.1	5.0	13.8	7.4	16.9
1985	4.3	13.1	5.3	13.5	8.4	17.0
1986	4.7	12.1	5.5	13.8	8.4	14.1

*Not enough information to calculate.

fact, the years 1977 to 1980 were expansionary years in the general economy, while 1981 and 1982 were largely beset by recession. The disastrous aftereffect of the merger craze that followed the National Energy Program implementation in late 1981 is very strongly reflected in subsequent results of the Royal and Bank of Montreal. Loan loss provisions related to lending to Third World nations such as Brazil and Mexico have also had a continued dampening effect upon the profitability of Canadian chartered banks despite the strength of domestic operations from 1983 through 1986.

The stronger performance of the Toronto-Dominion Bank, in spite of the problems related to oil merger loans and Third World debt, provides a real incentive to other Canadian chartered banks to strive to improve profitability. In terms of profit margin there is no year in the table where either the Royal or the Bank of Montreal has been able to match that of the T-D Bank. Only once, in 1978, has the Royal Bank been able to better the return on equity of the Toronto-Dominion. It is important to realize that not only did Toronto-Dominion investments realize a higher return per dollar invested but, in addition, the market was willing to pay a higher amount in terms of current share price for each dollar of profitability. In other words the price/earnings multiple of the Toronto-Dominion Bank was higher than those of the other major chartered banks.

Impact of Inflation on Financial Analysis

Prior to, coincident with, or following the computation of financial ratios, we should explore the impact of inflation and other sources of distortion on the financial reporting of the firm. As illustrated in this section, inflation causes phantom sources of profit that may mislead even the most alert analyst. Disinflation also causes certain problems, and we shall eventually consider these as well.

The major problem during inflationary times is that revenue is almost always stated in current dollars, whereas plant and equipment or inventory may have been purchased at lower price levels. Thus, profit may be more a function of increasing prices than of satisfactory performance.

An Illustration

The Stein Corporation shows the accompanying income statement for 1986 (see Table 3–5). At year-end the firm also has 100 units still in inventory at $1 per unit and $200 worth of plant and equipment with a 20-year life.

Assume that in 1987 the number of units sold remains constant at 100. However, inflation causes a 10 percent increase in price, from $2 to $2.20. Total sales will go up to $220 but with no actual increase in physical volume. Further assume the firm uses FIFO inventory pricing, so that inventory first purchased will be written off against current sales. In this case 1986 inventory will be written off against 1987 sales revenue.

The 1987 income statement of the Stein Corporation is shown in Table 3–6.

The company appears to have increased profit by $11 simply as a result of inflation. But not reflected is the increased cost of replacing plant and equipment. Presumably, its replacement cost has increased in an inflationary environment.

As mentioned in Chapter 2, inflation-related information is now recommended for most large companies, although only on a supplemental basis. However, because it is only recommended for Canadian companies,[4] only a small portion of Canadian public companies provide

Table 3–5

STEIN CORPORATION
Net Income for 1986

Sales	$200	(100 units at $2)
Cost of goods sold	100	(100 units at $1)
Gross profit	100	
Selling and administrative expense	20	
Depreciation	10	
Operating profit	70	
Taxes (40%)	28	
Aftertax income	$ 42	

[4]Such information is required in the United States of all companies who must file information with the Securities and Exchange Commission.

Table 3–6

STEIN CORPORATION
Net Income for 1987

Sales	$220	(100 units at 1987 price of $2.20)
Cost of goods sold	100	(100 units at $1.00)
Gross profit	120	
Selling and administrative expense	22	(10% of sales)
Depreciation	10	
Operating profit	88	
Taxes (40%)	35	
Aftertax income	$ 53	

inflation-adjusted information. A study of the reporting procedures adopted by Canadian companies in the first year the CICA recommendation was in effect revealed that only 73 out of 380 firms that met the recommendation requirements filed information on the effects of changing prices.[5] The author concluded that the firms made the choice based upon whether or not the extra costs of compliance exceeded the benefits.

Disinflation Effect

As long as prices continue to rise in an inflationary environment, profits appear to feed on themselves. The main objection is that when price increases moderate (disinflation), there will be a rude awakening for management and unsuspecting stockholders as expensive inventory is charged against softening retail prices. A 15 or 20 percent growth rate in earnings may be little more than an "inflationary illusion." Industries most sensitive to inflation-induced profits are those with cyclical products such as lumber, copper, rubber, and food products and also those in which inventory is a significant percentage of sales and profits.

A leveling off of prices is, of course, not necessarily bad. Even though inflation-induced corporate profits may be going down, investors may be more willing to place their funds in financial assets such as stocks and bonds. The reason for the shift may be a belief that declining

[5] D. B. Thornton, "Current Cost Disclosers and Nondisclosers: Canadian Evidence," *Contemporary Accounting Research* 3, no. 1 (Fall 1986).

inflationary pressures will no longer seriously impair the purchasing power of the dollar. Lessening inflation means that the required return investors demand on financial assets will be going down, and with this lower demanded return, future earnings or interest should receive a higher current valuation.

None of the above happens with a high degree of certainty. To the extent that investors question the permanence of disinflation (leveling off of price increases), they may not act according to the script. That is, lower rates of inflation will not necessarily produce high stock and bond prices unless the price pattern appears sustainable over a reasonable period of time.

Whereas financial assets such as stocks and bonds have the potential (whether realized or not) to do well during disinflation, such is not the case for tangible (real) assets. Precious metals, such as gold and silver, gems, and collectibles, that boomed in the highly inflationary environment of the late 1970s fell off sharply in the 1980s as softening prices caused less perceived need to hold real assets as a hedge against inflation. The shifting back and forth by investors between financial and real assets may take place many times over a business cycle. Financial assets during 1982–87 have performed extremely well. Will they continue to outperform real assets? What are current expectations?

During the years 1983–86 inflation had been about 4 percent, which was substantially less than the previous 10-year average. Some economists think inflation will rapidly increase in the late 1980s because of the large government of Canada deficits and rapid increase in the money supply. Others estimate we may face more disinflation, even to the point of the deflation (actual declining prices) found during the 1930s depression. While most economists are clustered at the middle of these two extremes, there seems to be more uncertainty about the future of inflation now than in the last 20 years. The knowledgeable student will be aware of the ramifications of both inflation and disinflation in financial decision making.

Other Elements of Distortion in Reported Income

The effect of changing prices is but one of a number of problems the analyst must cope with in evaluating a company. Other issues, such as the reporting of revenue, the treatment of nonrecurring items, and the tax write-off policy, cause dilemmas for the financial manager or analyst. The point may be illustrated by considering the income statements for two hypothetical companies in the same industry (see Table 3–7). Both firms had identical operating performances for 1987—but Company A is very conservative in reporting its results, while Company B has attempted to maximize its reported income.

If both companies had reported income of $200,000 in the prior year of 1986, Company B would be thought to be showing substantial growth in 1987 with net income of $650,000, while Company A is reporting a "flat" or no-growth year of $200,000 in 1987. However, we have already established the fact that the companies have equal operating performance.

Explanation of Discrepancies

Let us examine how the inconsistencies in Table 3–7 could take place. Emphasis is given to a number of key elements on the income statement.

Sales Company B reported $200,000 more in sales although actual volume was precisely the same. This may be the result of different concepts of revenue recognition.

Table 3–7

Income Statement
For the Year 1987

	Conservative (A)	*High Reported Income (B)*
Sales	$4,000,000	$4,200,000
Cost of goods sold	3,000,000	2,400,000
Gross profit	1,000,000	1,800,000
Selling and administrative expense	450,000	450,000
Operating profit	550,000	1,350,000
Interest expense	50,000	50,000
Extraordinary loss	100,000	
Net income before taxes	400,000	1,300,000
Taxes (50%)	200,000	650,000
Net income	200,000	650,000
Extraordinary loss (net of tax)		50,000
Net income transferred to retained earnings	$ 200,000	$ 600,000

For example, certain assets may be sold on an installment basis over a long time period. A conservative firm may defer recognition of the revenue until each payment is received, while other firms may attempt to recognize a fully effected sale at the earliest possible date. Similarly, firms that lease assets may attempt to consider a long-term lease as the equivalent of a sale, while more conservative firms such as IBM or Digital Equipment only recognize as revenue each lease payment as it comes due. Although the accounting profession attempts to establish appropriate methods of financial reporting through generally accepted accounting principles, there is variation of reporting among firms.

Cost of goods sold The conservative firm (Company A) may well be using LIFO accounting in an inflationary environment, thus charging the last-purchased, more expensive items against sales, while Company B uses FIFO accounting—charging off less expensive inventory against sales. The $600,000 difference in cost of goods sold may also be explained by varying treatment of research and development costs.

Extraordinary gains/losses Nonrecurring gains or losses may occur from the sale of corporate fixed assets, lawsuits, or similar nonrecurring events. Some analysts argue that such extraordinary events should be included in computing the current income of the firm, while others would leave them off in assessing operating performance. Unfortunately, there is some inconsistency in the manner in which nonrecurring losses are treated in spite of determined attempts by the accounting profession to ensure uniformity of action. The conservative Firm A has written off its $100,000 extraordinary loss against normally reported income, while Firm B carries a subtraction against net income only after the $650,000 amount has been reported. Both had similar losses of $100,000, but Firm B's is shown net of tax implications at $50,000.

Extraordinary gains and losses occur among large companies more often than one might think. For example, Shell Canada incurred extraordinary write-offs of $35 million in 1984 as a result of a corporate restructuring. Canadian Pacific Limited made a net extraordinary charge of $362 million in 1986. This represented the write-down of the value of certain operating assets by $494 million net of gains of $132 million on the divestment of subsidiaries and investments in other companies. In fact, in this age of mergers, tender offers, divestments, and corporate restructurings, understanding the finer points of financial statements becomes more important than ever.

Net Income

Firm A has reported net income of $200,000, while Firm B claims $650,000 before subtraction of extraordinary losses. The $450,000 difference is attributed to different methods of financial reporting, and it should be recognized as such by the analyst. No superior performance has actually taken place. The analyst must remain ever alert in examining each item in the financial statements rather than accepting bottom-line figures.

Summary

The subject of financial analysis was divided into two categories: an examination of ratio analysis and a study of the shortcomings in reported financial data from the viewpoint of a financial manager. Under ratio analysis we developed four categories of ratios: profitability, asset utilization, liquidity, and debt utilization. Each ratio for the firm should be compared to industry measures and analyzed in light of past trends. The use of ratio analysis is rather like the solving of a mystery in which each clue leads to a new area of inquiry.

Financial analysis in the 1980s also calls for an awareness of the impact of inflation and disinflation on the reported income of the firm. Inflation leads to phantom profits which are created as a result of buying goods and reselling them at inflation-induced higher prices. The process is further magnified by the use of FIFO accounting in which older inventory items are costed against current prices. Alternate methods of financial reporting may allow firms with equal performance to report different results.

List of Terms

FIFO
LIFO
replacement cost
inventory profits
Du Pont system of ratio analysis
disinflation
trend analysis
Dun & Bradstreet
profitability ratios
asset utilization ratios
debt utilization ratios

Discussion Questions

1. If we divide users of ratios into short-term lenders, long-term lenders, and stockholders, which ratios would each group be *most* interested in, and for what reasons?

2. Inflation can have significant effects on income statements and balance sheets and, therefore, on the calculation of ratios. Discuss the possible impact of inflation on the following ratios and explain the direction of the impact based on your assumptions.

   a. Return on investment.
   b. Inventory turnover.
   c. Fixed asset turnover.
   d. Debt-to-assets ratio.

3. Explain how the Du Pont system of analysis breaks down return on assets. Also explain how it breaks down return on owners' equity.

4. How would our analysis of profitability ratios be distorted if we used income before taxes? Income before interest and taxes?

5. Is there any validity in rule-of-thumb ratios for all corporations, for example, a current ratio of 2 to 1 or debt to assets of 50 percent?

6. Why is trend analysis helpful in analyzing ratios?

7. What effect will disinflation following a highly inflationary period have on the reported income of the firm?

8. Why might disinflation prove to be favorable to financial assets?

9. Comparisons of income can be very difficult for two companies even though they sell the same products in equal volume. Why?

Problems

1. Watson Data Systems is considering expansion into a new word processing product line. New assets to support expansion will cost $500,000. It is estimated that Watson can generate $1,200,000 in annual sales with a 6 percent profit margin.

   What would net income and return on assets (investment) be for the year?

2. Using the Du Pont method, evaluate the effects of the following relationships for the Lollar Corporation.
   a. Lollar Corporation has a profit margin of 5 percent, and its return on assets (investment) is 13.5 percent. What is its assets turnover?
   b. If the Lollar Corporation has a debt-to-total-assets ratio of 60 percent, what will the firm's return on equity be?
   c. What would happen to return on equity if the debt-to-total-assets ratio decreased to 40 percent? The applicable interest rate is 10 percent and the marginal tax rate is 50 percent.

3. *a.* Trace Manufacturing had an asset turnover of 1.2 times per year. If the return on total assets (investment) was 7.2 percent, what was Trace's profit margin?
   b. The following year, on the same level of assets, Trace's asset turnover declined to 1.0 times and its profit margin was 7.2 percent. How did the return on total assets change from that of the previous year?

4. A firm has sales of $1.2 million, and 10 percent of the sales are for cash. The year-end accounts receivable balance is $360,000. What is the average collection period? (Use a 360-day year.)

5. The balance sheet for the Bryan Corporation is given below. Sales for the year were $3,040,000, with 75 percent of sales on credit.
2,280,000

BRYAN CORPORATION
Balance Sheet 198X

Assets		**Liabilities and Owners' Equity**	
Cash	$ 50,000	Accounts payable	$220,000
Accounts receivable	280,000	Accrued taxes	80,000
Inventory	240,000	Bonds payable (long-term)	118,000
Plant and equipment	380,000	Common stock	250,000
		Retained earnings	282,000
Total assets	$950,000	Total liabilities and owners' equity	$950,000

Compute the following ratios:

a. Current ratio.
b. Quick ratio.
c. Debt to total assets.
d. Asset turnover.
e. Average collection period.

6. The Meredith Corporation's income statement is given below.

   a. What is the times-interest-earned ratio?
   b. What would be the fixed-charge-coverage ratio?

MEREDITH CORPORATION

Sales	$200,000
Cost of goods sold	116,000
Gross profit	84,000
Fixed charges (other than interest)	24,000
Income before interest and taxes	60,000
Interest	12,000
Income before taxes	48,000
Taxes (50%)	24,000
Income after taxes	$ 24,000

7. Using the income statement for the Sports Car Tire Company, compute the following ratios:

   a. The interest coverage.
   b. The fixed charge coverage.

   The total assets for this company equal $40,000. Set up the equation for the Du Pont system of ratio analysis and compute *c*, *d*, and *e*.

   c. Return on investment (assets).
   d. Profit margin.
   e. Total asset turnover.

THE SPORTS CAR TIRE COMPANY

Sales	$20,000
Less: Cost of goods sold	9,000
Gross profit	11,000
Less: Selling and administrative expense	4,000
Less: Lease expense	1,000
Operating profit*	6,000
Less: Interest expense	500
Earnings before taxes	5,500
Less: Taxes (40%)	2,200
Earnings after taxes	$ 3,300

*Equals income before interest and taxes.

8. A firm has net income before taxes of $120,000 and interest expense of $24,000.

a. What is the times-interest-earned ratio?
b. If the firm's lease payments are $40,000, what is the fixed charge coverage?

9. In January 1977 the Status Quo Company was formed. Total assets were $500,000, of which $300,000 consisted of depreciable fixed assets. Status Quo uses straight-line depreciation, and in 1977 it estimated its fixed assets to have useful lives of 10 years. Aftertax income has been $26,000 per year each of the last 10 years. Other assets have not changed since 1977.

a. Compute return on assets at year-end for 1977, 1979, 1982, 1984, and 1986. (Use $26,000 in the numerator for each year.)
b. To what do you attribute the phenomenon shown in part *a*?
c. Now assume that income increased by 10 percent each year. What effect would this have on your above answers? Comment.

10. The Lawton Corporation has the following information on net income and sales. Industry information is also shown.

Year	*Net Income*	*Sales*	*Industry Data on Profit Margin*
1985	$160,000	$2,500,000	6.0%
1986	180,000	3,200,000	4.9
1987	180,000	3,600,000	3.8

As an industry analyst examining the profit margin, are you likely to offer praise or criticism for the firm?

11. The Hobart Corporation shows the following income statement. The firm uses FIFO inventory accounting.

HOBART CORPORATION
Income Statement for 1987

Sales	$100,000	(10,000 units at $10)
Cost of goods sold	50,000	(10,000 units at $5)
Gross profit	50,000	
Selling and administrative expense	5,000	
Depreciation	10,000	
Operating profit.	35,000	
Taxes (40%)	14,000	
Aftertax income.	$ 21,000	

a. Assume in 1988 that the same 10,000 unit volume is maintained but the sales price increases by 10 percent. Because of FIFO inventory policy, old inventory will still be charged off at $5 per unit. Also assume selling and administrative expense will be 5 percent of sales and depreciation will be unchanged. The tax rate is 40 percent. Compute aftertax income for 1988.

b. In part *a*, by what percent did aftertax income increase as a result of a 10 percent increase in the sales price? Explain why this impact took place.

c. Now assume in 1989 the volume remains constant at 10,000 units but the sales price decreases by 15 percent from its 1988 level. Also because of FIFO inventory policy, cost of goods sold reflects the inflationary conditions of the prior year and is $5.50 per unit. Further assume selling and administrative expense will be 5 percent of sales and depreciation will be unchanged. The tax rate is 40 percent. Compute aftertax income.

12. The Diverse Corporation has three subsidiaries:

	Housing	*Shoes*	*Movies*
Sales	$12,000,000	$2,000,000	$6,000,000
Net income (after taxes)	900,000	100,000	500,000
Assets	6,000,000	1,600,000	5,000,000

a. Which division has the lowest return on sales?

b. Which division has the highest return on assets?

c. Compute return on assets for the entire corporation.

d. If the $5 million investment in the movie division is sold off and redeployed in the housing subsidiary at the same rate of return on assets currently achieved in the housing division, what will be the new return on assets for the entire corporation?

13. Construct the current assets section of the balance sheet shown here from the following data:

Yearly sales (credit)	$420,000
Inventory turnover	7 times
Current liabilities	$ 80,000
Current ratio	2
Quick ratio	1.25
Average collection period	36 days

79

Current assets:	$	
Cash		______
Accounts receivable		______
Inventory		______
Total current assets		______

14. The Shannon Corporation has sales of $750,000 and a gross margin of 20 percent. Given the following ratios, fill in the balance sheet below.

Total assets turnover	2.5 times
Cash to total assets	2.0%
Accounts receivable turnover	10.0 times
Inventory turnover	12.0 times
Current ratio	2.0 times
Debt to total assets	45.0%

SHANNON CORPORATION
Balance Sheet, 198X

Assets		**Liabilities and Owners' Equity**	
Cash	______	Current debt	______
Accounts receivable	______	Long-term debt	______
Inventory	______	Total debt	______
Total current assets	______	Net worth	______
Fixed assets	______	Total liabilities and owners' equity	______
Total assets	______		

15. We are given the following information for the Pettit Corporation.

Sales (credit)	$3,000,000
Cash	150,000
Inventory	850,000
Current liabilities	700,000
Asset turnover	1.25 times
Current ratio	2.50 times
Debt-to-assets ratio	40%
Receivables turnover	6 times

Current assets are composed of cash, marketable securities, accounts receivable and inventory. Calculate the following balance sheet items.

a. Accounts receivable.
b. Marketable securities.

c. Fixed assets.
d. Long-term debt.

16. The following data are from U Guessed It Company's financial statements. U Guessed It is a manufacturer of board games for young adults, and it competes with Marker Brothers and Bilton Radley. Sales (all credit) were $20 million for 1988 and cost of goods sold was $16 million.

Sales to total assets	2 times
Total debt to assets	40%
Current ratio	3.0 times
Inventory turnover	4.0 times
Average collection period	18 days
Fixed asset turnover	5.0 times

Fill in the brief balance sheet:

Cash	______	Current debt	______
Accounts receivable	______	Long-term debt	______
Inventory	______	Total debt	______
Total current assets	______	Net worth	______
Fixed assets	______	Total liabilities	
Total assets	______	and equity	______

17. Using the financial statements for the Hobart Corporation, calculate the 13 basic ratios found in the chapter.

HOBART CORPORATION
Balance Sheet
December 31, 1987

Assets

Current assets:	
Cash	$ 50,000
Marketable securities	20,000
Accounts receivable (net)	160,000
Inventory	200,000
Total current assets	430,000
Investments	60,000
Plant and equipment	600,000
Less: Accumulated depreciation	(190,000)
Net plant and equipment	410,000
Total assets	$900,000

Liabilities and Owners' Equity

Current liabilities:	
Accounts payable	$ 90,000
Notes payable	70,000
Accrued taxes	10,000
Total current liabilities	170,000
Long-term liabilities:	
Bonds payable	150,000
Total liabilities	320,000
Owners' equity:	
Preferred stock	100,000
Common stock	80,000
Capital paid in excess of par	190,000
Retained earnings	210,000
Total owners' equity	580,000
Total liabilities and owners' equity	$900,000

HOBART CORPORATION
Income Statement
For the Year Ending December 31, 1987

Sales (on credit)	$1,980,000
Less: Cost of goods sold	1,280,000
Gross profit	700,000
Less: Selling and administrative expenses	475,000*
Operating profit (EBIT)	225,000
Less: Interest expense	25,000
Earnings before taxes (EBT)	200,000
Less: Taxes of 40%	80,000
Earnings after taxes (EAT)	$ 120,000

*Includes $35,000 in lease payments.

18. (*Comprehensive problem*)
Given the financial statements for Jones Corporation and Smith Corporation shown here:

a. To which one would you, as credit manager for a supplier, approve the extension of (short-term) trade credit? Why? Compute all ratios before answering.
b. In which one would you buy stock? Why?

JONES CORPORATION

Current Assets		Liabilities	
Cash	$ 20,000	Accounts payable	$100,000
Accounts receivable	80,000	Bonds payable—10%	80,000
Inventory	50,000		
Long-Term Assets		**Owners' Equity**	
Fixed assets	$500,000	Common stock	$220,000
Less: Accum. dep.	(150,000)		
Net fixed assets	350,000	Retained earnings	100,000
	$500,000		$500,000

Sales (on credit)	$1,250,000
Cost of goods sold	750,000
Gross profit	500,000
Selling and administrative expense	257,000*
Depreciation expense	50,000
Operating profit	193,000
Interest expense	8,000
Earnings before taxes	185,000
Tax expense (50%)	92,500
Net income	$ 92,500

*Includes $7,000 in lease payments.
Jones Corporation has 75,000 shares outstanding.

SMITH CORPORATION

Current Assets		Liabilities	
Cash	$ 35,000	Accounts payable	$ 75,000
Marketable securities	7,500	Bonds payable—10%	210,000
Accounts receivable	70,000		
Inventory	75,000		
Long-Term Assets		**Owners' Equity**	
Fixed assets	$500,000	Common stock	$105,000
Less: Accum. dep.	(250,000)		
Net fixed assets	250,000	Retained earnings	47,500
	$437,500		$437,500

Sales (on credit)	$1,000,000
Cost of goods sold	600,000
Gross profit	400,000
Selling and administrative expense	224,000*
Depreciation expense	50,000
Operating profit	126,000
Interest expense	21,000
Earnings before taxes	105,000
Tax expense	52,500
Net income	$ 52,500

*Includes $7,000 in lease payments.
Smith Corporation has 75,000 shares outstanding.

19. (*Comprehensive problem on trend analysis and industry comparisons.*) Bob Adkins has been approached by his first cousin, Ed Lamar, with a proposal to buy a 15 percent interest in Lamar Swimwear, manufacturers of stylish bathing suits and sunscreen products.

Mr. Lamar is quick to point out the increase in sales that has taken place over the last three years as indicated in the income statement, Exhibit 1. The annual growth rate is 25 percent. A balance sheet for a similar time period is shown in Exhibit 2, and selected industry ratios are presented in Exhibit 3. Note the industry growth rate in sales is only 10–12 percent per year.

There was a steady real growth of 3–4 percent in gross national product during the period under study. The rate of inflation was in the 5–6 percent range.

The stock in the corporation has become available due to the ill health of a current stockholder who is in need of cash. The issue here is not to determine the exact price for the stock but rather whether Lamar Swimwear represents an attractive investment situation. Although Mr. Adkins has a primary interest in the profitability ratios, he will take a close look at all the ratios. He has no fast and firm rules about required return on investment but rather wishes to analyze the overall condition of the firm. The firm does not currently pay a cash dividend, and return to the investor must come from selling the stock in the future. After doing a thorough analysis (including ratios for each year and comparisons to the industry), what comments and recommendations can you offer to Mr. Adkins.

Exhibit 1

LAMAR SWIMWEAR
Income Statement

	198X	*198Y*	*198Z*
Sales (all on credit)	$1,200,000	$1,500,000	$1,875,000
Cost of goods sold	800,000	1,040,000	1,310,000
Gross profit	400,000	460,000	565.000
Selling and administrative expense*	239,900	274,000	304,700
Operating profit (EBIT)	160,100	186,000	260,300
Interest expense	35,000	45,000	85,000
Net income before taxes	125,100	141,000	175,300
Taxes	36,900	49,200	55,600
Net income	$ 88,200	$ 91,800	$ 119,700
Shares	30,000	30,000	38,000
Earnings per share	$2.94	$3.06	$3.15

*Includes $15,000 in lease payments for each year

Exhibit 2

LAMAR SWIMWEAR
Balance Sheet

Assets	*198X*	*198Y*	*198Z*
Cash	$ 30,000	$ 40,000	$ 30,000
Marketable securities	20,000	25,000	30,000
Accounts receivable	170,000	259,000	360,000
Inventory	230,000	261,000	290,000
Total current assets	450,000	585,000	710,000
Net plant and equipment	650,000	765,000	1,390,000
Total assets	$1,100,000	$1,350,000	$2,100,000
Liabilities and Owners' Equity			
Accounts payable	$ 200,000	$ 310,000	$ 505,000
Accrued expenses	20,400	30,000	35,000
Total current liabilities	220,400	340,000	540,000
Long-term liabilities	325,000	363,600	703,900
Total liabilities	545,400	703,600	1,243,900
Common stock	60,000	60,000	76,000
Contributed surplus	190,000	190,000	264,000
Retained earnings	304,600	396,400	516,100
Total owners' equity	554,600	646,400	856,100
Total liabilities and owners' equity	$1,100,000	$1,350,000	$2,100,000

Exhibit 3

Selected industry ratios

	198X	*198Y*	*198Z*
Growth in sales		10.00%	12.00%
Profit margin	7.71%	7.02%	7.90%
Return on assets (investment)	8.09%	8.68%	8.95%
Return on equity	14.31%	15.26%	16.01%
Receivables turnover	9.02 ×	8.86 ×	9.31 ×
Average collection period	39.9 days	40.6 days	38.7 days
Inventory turnover	2.82 ×	3.40 ×	3.41 ×
Fixed asset turnover	1.60 ×	1.64 ×	1.75 ×
Total asset turnover	1.05 ×	1.10 ×	1.12 ×
Current ratio	1.96 ×	2.25 ×	2.40 ×
Quick ratio	1.37 ×	1.41 ×	1.38 ×
Debt to total assets	43.47%	43.11%	44.10%
Times interest earned	6.50 ×	5.99 ×	6.61 ×
Fixed charge coverage	4.70 ×	4.69 ×	4.73 ×
Growth in earnings per share		10.10%	13.30%

Selected References

Altman, Edward I. "Financial Ratios, Discriminant Analysis, and the Prediction of Corporate Bankruptcy." *Journal of Finance* 23 (September 1968), pp. 589–609.

Belkaoui, Ahmed. "Financial Ratios as Predictors of Canadian Takeovers." *Journal of Business Finance and Accounting* 5, no. 1 (January 1978), pp. 93–107.

Benishay, Haskell. "Economic Information in Financial Ratio Analysis." *Accounting and Business Research 2* (Spring 1971), pp. 174–79.

Callard, Charles G., and David C. Kleinman. "Inflation-Adjusted Accounting: Does it Matter?" *Financial Analysts Journal* 41 (May-June 1985), pp. 51–59.

Chen, Kung H., and Thomas A. Shimerda. "An Empirical Analysis of Useful Financial Ratios." *Financial Management* 10 (Spring 1981), pp. 51–60.

Copeland, Ronald M.; Joseph F. Wojdak; and John K. Shank. "The Use of LIFO to Offset Inflation." *Harvard Business Review* 49 (May–June 1971), pp. 91–100.

D'Ambrosio, Charles A. "Truth, Reality and Financial Analysis." *Financial Analysts Journal* 38 (July-August 1982), pp. 24–25.

Davidson, S., and R. L. Weil. "Inflation Accounting." *Financial Analysts Journal* 31 (January–February), pp. 27–31, 70–84.

Friedman, Milton. "Economic Miracles." *Newsweek* 8 (January 21, 1974), p. 80.

Gandolfi, Arthur E. "Inflation, Taxation, and Interest Rates." *Journal of Finance* 37 (June 1982), pp. 797–807.

Garnett, Jeff, and Geoffrey A. Hirt. "Replacement Cost Data: A Study of the Chemical and Drug Industry for Years 1976 through 1978." Study at Illinois State University, January 1980.

Helfert, Erich A. *Techniques of Financial Analysis*. 5th ed. Homewood, Ill.: Richard D. Irwin, 1982, chap. 2.

Jaedicke, Robert K., and Robert T. Sprouse. *Accounting Flows, Income, Funds, and Cash*. Englewood Cliffs, N.J.: Prentice-Hall, 1965, chap. 7.

Lev, Baruch. *Financial Statement Analysis: A New Approach*. Englewood Cliffs, N.J.: Prentice-Hall, 1974, chaps. 2–5.

Modigliani, Franco, and Richard A. Cohn. "Inflation Rational Valuation and the Market." *Financial Analysts Journal* 35 (March–April 1979), pp. 24–44.

Shank, John K. *Price-Level Adjusted Statements and Management Decisions*. New York: Financial Executives Research Foundation, 1975.

Siegel, Joel G. "The 'Quality of Earnings' Concept—A Survey." *Financial Analysts Journal* 38 (March–April 1982), pp. 60–68.

Terborgh, George. "Inflation and Corporate Profits." *Readings in Financial Analysis*. Institute of Chartered Financial Analysts. Homewood, Ill.: Richard D. Irwin, 1973, pp. 153–65.

Thornton, D. B. "Current Cost Disclosers and Nondisclosers: Canadian Evidence." *Contemporary Accounting Research* 3, no. 1 (Fall 1986).

Von Furstenberg, George M., and Burton G. Malkiel. "Financial Analysis in an Inflationary Environment." *Journal of Finance* 32 (May 1977), pp. 575–88.

Wallich, Henry C. "Investment Income during Inflation." *Financial Analysts Journal* 34 (March–April 1978), pp. 34–37.

Waterhouse, J. H. "Managerial Reporting of Non-Historical Cost Accounting Data." Research Paper Series, Canadian CGA Research Foundation, Vancouver, 1984.

Weston, J. Fred. "Financial Analysis: Planning and Control." *Financial Executive* 33 (July 1965), pp. 40–48.

Young, Allen H. "Alternative Estimates of Corporate Depreciation and Profits." *Survey of Current Business* 48 (April and May 1968), pp. 17–28, 16–28.

4 Financial Forecasting

The old notion of the corporate treasurer burning the midnight oil in order to find new avenues of financing before dawn is no longer in vogue. If there is one talent that is essential to the financial manager, it is the ability to plan ahead and to make necessary adjustments before actual events occur. Quite likely we could construct the same set of external events for two corporations (inflation, recession, severe new competition, and so on), and one would survive, while the other would not. The outcome might be a function not only of their risk-taking desires but also of their ability to hedge against risk with careful planning.

While we may assume that no growth or a decline in volume is the primary cause for a shortage of funds, this is not necessarily the case. A rapidly growing firm may witness a significant increase in accounts receivable, inventory, and plant and equipment that cannot be financed in the normal course of business. Assume sales go from $100,000 to $200,000 in one year for a firm that has a 5 percent profit margin on sales. At the same time assume assets represent 50 percent of sales and go from $50,000 to $100,000 as sales double. The $10,000 of profit (5 percent × $200,000) will hardly be adequate to finance the $50,000 asset growth. The remaining $40,000 must come from suppliers, the bank, and perhaps stockholders. The student should recognize that profit alone is generally inadequate to finance significant growth and that a comprehensive financing plan must be developed. All too often the small businessman (and sometimes the big one as well) is mystified by an increase in sales and profits but less cash in the till.

Constructing Pro Forma Statements

The most comprehensive means of financial forecasting is to go through the process of developing a series of pro forma, or projected, financial statements. We will give particular attention to the *pro forma income statement,* the *cash budget,* and the *pro forma balance sheet.* Based on the projected statements, the firm is able to judge its future level of receivables, inventory, payables, and other corporate accounts as well as its anticipated profits and borrowing requirements. The financial officer can then carefully track actual events against the plan and make necessary adjustments. Furthermore, the statements are often required by bankers and other lenders as a guide for the future.

A systems approach is necessary for the development of pro forma statements. We first construct a pro forma income statement based on sales projections and the production plan, then translate this material into a cash budget, and finally assimilate all previously developed material into a pro forma balance sheet. The process of developing pro forma financial statements is depicted in Figure 4–1. We will use a six-month time frame to facilitate the analysis, though the same procedures could be extended to one year or longer.

Pro Forma Income Statement

Assume the Goldman Corporation has been requested by its bank to provide pro forma financial statements for midyear 1988. The pro forma income statement will provide a projection of how much profit the firm anticipates making over the ensuing time period. In developing the pro forma income statement, we will follow four important steps.

Figure 4–1
Development of pro forma statements

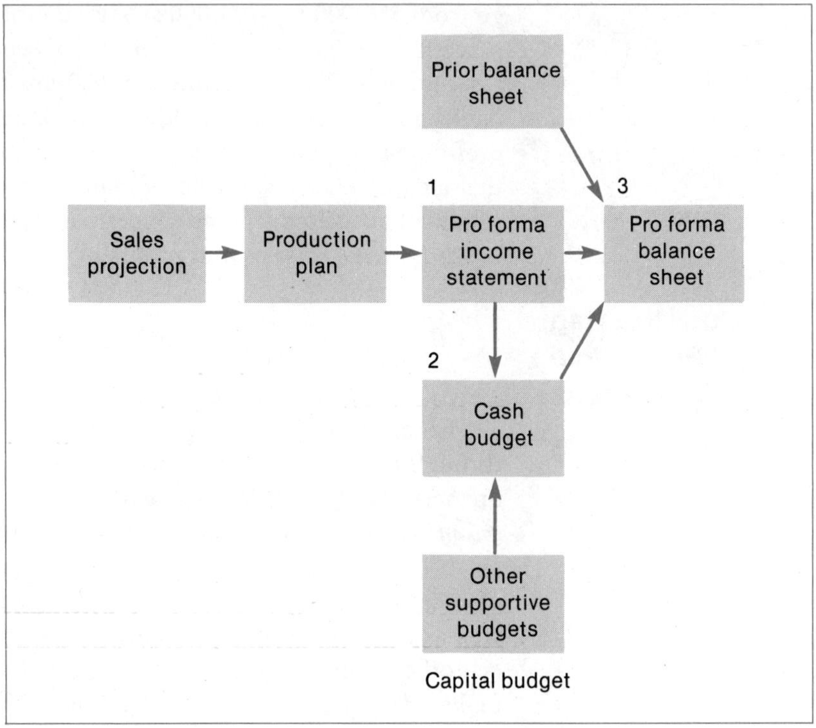

1. Establish a sales projection.
2. Determine a production schedule and the associated use of new material, direct labor, and overhead to arrive at gross profit.
3. Compute other expenses.
4. Determine profit by completing the actual pro forma statement.

Establish a Sales Projection

For purposes of analysis we shall assume the Goldman Corporation has two primary products: wheels and casters. Our sales projection calls for the sale of 1,000 wheels and 2,000 casters at prices of $30 and $35, respectively. As indicated in Table 4–1 we anticipate total sales of $100,000.

Sales projections are best derived from both an external and internal viewpoint. Using the former we analyze our prospective sales in light

Table 4–1
Projected wheel and caster sales (first six months, 1988)

	Wheels	Casters	
Quantity	1,000	2,000	
Sales price	$30	$35	
Sales revenue	$30,000	$70,000	
Total			$100,000

of economic conditions affecting our industry and our company. Statistical techniques such as regression and time series analysis may be employed in the process. Internal analysis calls for the sales department to survey our own salespeople within their territories. Ideally, we would proceed along each of those paths in isolation of the other and then assimilate the results into one meaningful projection.

Determine a Production Schedule and the Gross Profit

Based on anticipated sales we determine the necessary production plan for the six-month period. The number of units produced will depend on the beginning inventory of wheels and casters, our sales projection, and the desired level of ending inventory. Assume that on January 1, 1988, the Goldman Corporation has in stock the items shown in Table 4–2.

We will add the projected quantity of unit sales for the next six months to our desired ending inventory and subtract our stock of beginning inventory (in units) to determine our production requirements.

Units

\+ Projected Sales
\+ Desired ending inventory
− *Beginning* inventory
= Production requirements

Table 4–2
Stock of beginning inventory

	Wheels	Casters	
Quantity	85	180	
Cost	$16	$20	
Total value	$1,360	$3,600	
Total			$4,960

In Table 4–3 we see a required production level of 1,015 wheels and 2,020 casters.

We must now determine the cost to produce these units. In Table 4–2 we saw that the cost of units to stock was $16 for wheels and $20 for casters. However, we shall assume the price of materials, labor, and overhead going into the products is now $18 for wheels and $22 for casters, as indicated in Table 4–4.

The *total* cost to produce the required items for the next six months is shown in Table 4–5.

Cost of goods sold The main consideration in constructing a pro forma income statement is the costs specifically associated with units sold during the time period. Note that in the case of wheels we anticipate sales of 1,000 units, as indicated in Table 4–1, but are producing 1,015, as indicated in Table 4–5, to increase our inventory level by 15 units. For profit measurement purposes we will *not* charge these extra

Table 4–3
Production requirements for six months

	Wheels	Casters
Projected unit sales (Table 4–1)	+1,000	+2,000
Desired ending inventory (assumed to represent 10% of unit sales for the time period)	+100	+200
Beginning inventory (Table 4–2)	−85	−180
Units to be produced	1,015	2,020

Table 4–4
Unit costs

	Wheels	Casters
Materials	$10	$12
Labor	5	6
Overhead	3	4
Total	$18	$22

Table 4–5
Total production costs

	Wheels	Casters	
Units to be produced (Table 4–3)	1,015	2,020	
Cost per unit (Table 4–4)	$18	$22	
Total cost	$18,270	$44,440	$62,710

15 units against current sales.[1] Furthermore, in determining the cost of the 1,000 units sold during the current time period, we will *not* assume that all of the items sold represent inventory manufactured in this period. In the case of the Goldman Corporation we shall assume that it uses FIFO (first-in, first-out) accounting and that it will first allocate the cost of current sales to beginning inventory and then to goods manufactured during the period.

In Table 4–6 we look at the revenue, associated costs of goods sold, and gross profit for both products. For example, 1,000 units of wheels are to be sold at a total revenue of $30,000. Of the 1,000 units, 85 units are from beginning inventory at a $16 cost (see Table 4–2) and the balance of 915 units are from current production at an $18 cost. The total cost of goods sold for wheels is $17,830, yielding a gross profit of $12,170. The pattern is the same for casters, with sales of $70,000, cost of goods sold of $43,640, and gross profit of $26,360. The combined sales for the two products are $100,000, with cost of goods sold of $61,470 and gross profit of $38,530.

At this point we also compute the value of ending inventory for later use in constructing financial statements. As indicated in Table 4–7 the value of ending inventory will be $6,200.

Table 4–6
Allocation of manufacturing cost and determination of gross profits

		Wheels		Casters	Combined
Quantity sold (Table 4–1)		1,000		2,000	3,000
Sales price		$30		$35	
Sales revenue		$30,000		$70,000	$100,000
Cost of goods sold:					
Old inventory (Table 4–2):					
Quantity (units)	85		180		
Cost per unit	$16		$20		
Total		$ 1,360		$ 3,600	
New inventory (the remainder):					
Quantity (units)	915		1,820		
Cost per unit (Table 4–4)	$18		$22		
Total		16,470		40,040	
Total cost of goods sold		17,830		43,640	$ 61,470
Gross profit		$12,170		$26,360	$ 38,530

[1] Later on in the analysis we will show the effect these extra units have on the cash budget and the balance sheet.

Table 4–7
Value of ending inventory

+ Beginning inventory (Table 4–2)	$ 4,960
+ Total production costs (Table 4–5)	62.710
Total inventory available for sales	67,670
− Cost of goods sold (Table 4–6)	61,470
Ending inventory	$ 6,200

Other Expense Items

Having computed total revenue, cost of goods sold, and gross profits, we must now subtract other expense items to arrive at a net profit figure. We deduct general and administrative expenses as well as interest expenses from gross profit to arrive at earnings before taxes, then subtract taxes to determine aftertax income, and finally deduct dividends to ascertain the contribution to retained earnings. For the Goldman Corporation general and administrative expenses are $12,000, interest expense is $1,500, and dividends are $1,500.

Actual Pro Forma Income Statement

Combining the gross profit in Table 4–6 with our assumptions on other expense items we arrive at the pro forma income statement presented in Table 4–8. We anticipate earnings after taxes of $20,024, dividends of $1,500, and an increase in retained earnings of $18,524.

Table 4–8

Pro Forma Income Statement
June 30,1988

Sales revenue	$100,000
Cost of goods sold	61,470
Gross profit	38,530
General and administrative expense	12,000
Operating profit (EBIT)	26,530
Interest expense	1,500
Earnings before taxes (EBT)	25,030
Taxes (20%)	5,006
Earnings after taxes (EAT)	20,024
Common stock dividends	1,500
Increase in retained earnings	$ 18,524

Cash Budget

As previously indicated the generation of sales and profits does not necessarily ensure there will be adequate cash on hand to meet financial obligations as they come due. A profitable sale may generate accounts receivables in the short run but no immediate cash to meet maturing obligations. For this reason we must translate the pro forma income statement into cash flows. In this process we divide the longer-term pro forma income statement into smaller and more precise time frames to order to appreciate the seasonal and monthly patterns of cash inflows and outflows. Some months may represent particularly high or low sales volume or may require dividends, taxes, or capital expenditures.

Cash Receipts

In the case of the Goldman Corporation we break down the pro forma income statement for the first half of 1988 into a series of monthly cash budgets. In Table 4–1 we showed anticipated sales of $100,000 over this time period; we shall now assume these sales can be divided into monthly projections, as indicated in Table 4–9.

A careful analysis of past sales and collection records indicates that 20 percent of sales are collected in the month of sales and 80 percent in the following month. The cash receipt pattern related to monthly sales is shown in Table 4–10. It is assumed that sales for December 1987 were $12,000.

The cash inflows will vary between $11,000 and $23,000, with the high point in receipts coming in May.

We now examine the monthly outflows.

Table 4–9
Monthly sales pattern

January	*February*	*March*	*April*	*May*	*June*
$15,000	$10,000	$15,000	$25,000	$15,000	$20,000

Table 4–10
Monthly cash receipts

	Dec.	Jan.	Feb.	March	April	May	June
Sales	$12,000	$15,000	$10,000	$15,000	$25,000	$15,000	$20,000
Collections (20% of current sales)		3,000	2,000	3,000	5,000	3,000	4,000
Collections (80% of previous month's sales)		9,600	12,000	8,000	12,000	20,000	12,000
Total cash receipts		$12,600	$14,000	$11,000	$17,000	$23,000	$16,000

Cash Payments

The primary considerations for cash payments are monthly costs associated with inventory manufactured during the period (material, labor, and overhead) and disbursements for general and administrative expenses, interest payments, taxes, and dividends. We must also consider cash payments for any new plant and equipment, an item that does not show up on our pro forma income statement.

Costs associated with units manufactured during the period may be taken from the data provided in Table 4–5, Total Production Costs. In Table 4–11 we simply recast these data in terms of materials, labor, and overhead.

We see that the total costs for components in the two products are material, $34,390; labor, $17,195; and overhead, $11,125. We shall assume all of these costs are incurred on an equal monthly basis over the six-month period. Even though the sales volume varies from month to month, we assume we are employing level monthly production to ensure maximum efficiency in the use of various productive resources.

Table 4–11
Component costs of manufactured goods

	Wheels			Casters			
	Units Produced	Cost per Unit	Total Cost	Units Produced	Cost per Unit	Total Cost	Combined Cost
Materials	1,015	$10	$10,150	2,020	$12	$24,240	$34,390
Labor	1,015	5	5,075	2,020	6	12,120	17,195
Overhead	1,015	3	3,045	2,020	4	8,080	11,125
							$62,710

Average monthly costs for materials, labor, and overhead are as shown in Table 4–12.

We shall pay for materials one month after the purchase has been made. Labor and overhead represent direct monthly cash outlays, as is true of interest, taxes, dividends, and assumed purchases of $8,000 in new equipment in February and $10,000 in June. We summarize all of our cash payments in Table 4–13. Past records indicate that $4,500 in materials was purchased in December.

Actual Budget

We are now in a position to bring together our monthly cash receipts and payments into a cash flow statement, illustrated in Table 4–14.

Table 4–12
Average monthly manufacturing costs

	Total Costs	*Time Frame*	*Average Monthly Cost*
Materials	$34,390	6 months	$5,732
Labor	17,195	6 months	2,866
Overhead	11,125	6 months	1,854

Table 4–13
Summary of all monthly cash payments

	Dec.	*Jan.*	*Feb.*	*March*	*April*	*May*	*June*
From Table 4–12:							
Monthly material purchase	$4,500	$ 5,732	$ 5,732	$ 5,732	$ 5,732	$ 5,732	$ 5,732
Payment for material (prior month's purchase)		4,500	5,732	5,732	5,732	5,732	5,732
Monthly labor cost		2,866	2,866	2,866	2,866	2,866	2,866
Monthly overhead		1,854	1,854	1,854	1,854	1,854	1,854
From Table 4–8:							
General and administrative expense ($12,000 over 6 months)		2,000	2,000	2,000	2,000	2,000	2,000
Interest expense							1,500
Taxes (two equal payments)				2,503			2,503
Cash dividend							1,500
Also:							
New equipment purchases			8,000				10,000
Total payments		$11,220	$20,452	$14,955	$12,452	$12,452	$27,953

The difference between monthly receipts and payments is net cash flow for the month.

The primary purpose of the cash budget is to allow the firm to anticipate the need for outside funding at the end of each month. In the present case we shall assume the Goldman Corporation wishes to have a minimum cash balance of $5,000 at all times. If it goes below this amount, the firm will borrow funds from the bank. If it goes above $5,000 and the firm has a loan outstanding, it will use the excess funds to reduce the loan. This pattern of financing is demonstrated in Table 4–15—a fully developed cash budget with borrowing and repayment provisions.

The first line in Table 4–15 shows our net cash flow, which is added to the beginning cash balance to arrive at the cumulative cash balance. The fourth entry is the additional monthly loan or loan repayment, if any, required to maintain a minimum cash balance of $5,000. In order

Table 4–14
Monthly cash flow

	Jan.	Feb.	March	April	May	June
Total receipts (Table 4–10)	$12,600	$14,000	$11,000	$17,000	$23,000	$16,000
Total payments (Table 4–13)	11,220	20,452	14,955	12,452	12,452	27,953
Net cash flow	$ 1,380	($ 6,452)	($ 3,955)	$ 4,548	$10,548	($11,953)

Table 4–15
Cash budget with borrowing and repayment

	Jan.	Feb.	March	April	May	June
1. Net cash flow	$1,380	($6,452)	($3,955)	$4,548	$10,548	($11,953)
2. Beginning cash balance	5,000*	6,380	5,000	5,000	5,000	11,069
3. Cumulative cash balance	6,380	(72)	1,045	9,548	15,548	(884)
4. Monthly loan (or repayment)	—	5,072	3,955	(4,548)	(4,479)	5,884
5. Cumulative loan balance	—	5,072	9,027	4,479	—	5,884
6. Ending cash balance	6,380	5,000	5,000	5,000	11,069	5,000

*We assume that the Goldman Corporation has a beginning cash balance of $5,000 on January 1, 1988, and that it desires a minimum monthly ending cash balance of $5,000.

to keep track of our loan balance, the fifth entry presents cumulative loans outstanding for all months. Finally, we show the cash balance at the end of the month, which becomes the beginning cash balance for the next month.

At the end of January the firm has $6,380 in cash, but by the end of February the cumulative cash position of the firm is negative, necessitating a loan of $5,072 to maintain a $5,000 cash balance. The firm has a loan on the books until May, at which time there is an ending cash balance of $11,069. During the months of April and May the cumulative cash balance is greater than the required minimum cash balance of $5,000, so loan repayments of $4,548 and $4,479 are made to retire the loans completely in May. In June the firm is once again required to borrow $5,884 in order to maintain a $5,000 cash balance.

Pro Forma Balance Sheet

Now that we have developed a pro forma income statement and a cash budget, it is relatively simple to integrate all of these items into a pro forma balance sheet. Because the balance sheet represents cumulative changes in the corporation over time, we first examine the *prior* period's balance sheet and then translate these items through time to represent June 30, 1988. The last balance sheet, dated December 31, 1987, is shown in Table 4–16.

In constructing our pro forma balance sheet for June 30, 1988, some of the accounts from the old balance sheet will remain unchanged, while others will take on new values, as indicated by the pro forma income statement and cash budget. The process is depicted in Figure 4–2.

We present the new pro forma balance sheet as of June 30, 1988, in Table 4–17.

Explanation of pro forma balance sheets Each item in Table 4–17 can be explained on the basis of a prior calculation or assumption.

1. Cash ($5,000)—minimum cash balance as shown in Table 4–15.
2. Marketable securities ($3,200)—remains unchanged from prior period's value in Table 4–16.
3. Accounts receivable ($16,000)—based on June sales of $20,000 in Table 4–10. Twenty percent will be collected that month, while

Table 4–16

Balance Sheet
December 31, 1987

Assets	
Current assets:	
Cash	$ 5,000
Marketable securities	3,200
Accounts	9,600
Inventory	4,960
Total current assets	22,760
Plant and equipment	27,740
Total assets	$50,500
Liabilities and Owners' Equity	
Accounts payable	$ 4,500
Notes payable	0
Long-term debt	15,000
Common stock	10,500
Retained earnings	20,500
Total liabilities and owners' equity	$50,500

Figure 4–2
Development of a pro forma balance sheet

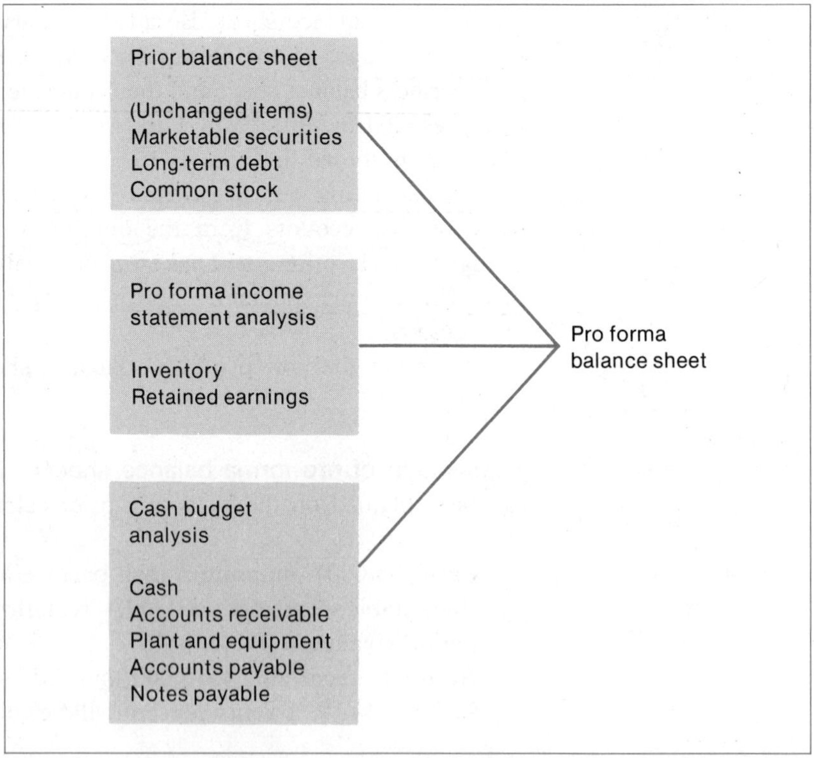

Table 4–17

Pro Forma Balance Sheet
June 30, 1988

Assets	
Current assets:	
1. Cash	$ 5,000
2. Marketable securities	3,200
3. Accounts receivable	16,000
4. Inventory	6,200
Total current assets	30,400
5. Plant and equipment	45,740
Total assets	$76,140
Liabilities and Owners' Equity	
6. Accounts payable	$ 5,732
7. Notes payable	5,884
8. Long-term debt	15,000
9. Common stock	10,500
10. Retained earnings	39,024
Total liabilities and owners' equity	$76,140

80 percent will become accounts receivable at the end of the month.

$20,000 sales
× 80% receivables
$16,000

4. Inventory ($6,200)—ending inventory as shown in Table 4–7.
5. Plant and equipment ($45,740).

Initial value (Table 4–16)	$27,740
Purchases* (Table 4–13)	18,000
Plant and equipment	$45,740

*For simplicity, depreciation is not explicitly considered.

6. Accounts payable ($5,732)—based on June purchases in Table 4–13. They will not be paid until July and thus are accounts payable.
7. Notes payable ($5,884)—the amount we must borrow to maintain our cash balance of $5,000, as shown in Table 4–15.
8. Long-term debt ($15,000)—remains unchanged from prior period's value in Table 4–16.

9. Common stock ($10,500)—remains unchanged from prior period's value in Table 4–16.

10. Retained earnings ($39,024).

Initial value (Table 4–16)	$20,500
Transfer of pro forma income to retained earnings (Table 4–8)	18,524
Retained earnings	$39,024

Analysis of Pro Forma Statement

In comparing the pro forma balance sheet (see Table 4–17) to the prior balance sheet (see Table 4–16), we note that assets are up by $25,640.

Total assets (June 30, 1988)	$76,140
Total assets (Dec. 31, 1987)	50,500
Increase	$25,640

The growth must be financed by accounts payable, notes payable, and profit (as reflected by the increase in retained earnings). Though the company will enjoy a high degree of profitability, it must still look to bank financing of $5,884 to support the increase in assets. This represents the difference between the $25,640 buildup in assets and the $1,232 increase in accounts payable as well as the $18,524 buildup in retained earnings.

Percent-of-Sales Method

An alternative to going through the process of tracing cash and accounting flows to determine financial needs is to assume that accounts on the balance sheet will maintain a given percentage relationship to sales. We then indicate a change in the sales level and ascertain our related financing needs. This is known as the *percent-of-sales method.* For example, for the Howard Corporation, introduced in Table 4–18, we show the following balance sheet accounts in dollars and their percent of sales, based on a sales volume of $200,000.

We observe that cash of $5,000 represents 2.5 percent of sales of $200,000; receivables of $40,000 is 20 percent of sales; and so on. No

Table 4–18

HOWARD CORPORATION
Balance Sheet and Percent-of-Sales Table

Assets		Liabilities and Owners' Equity	
Cash	$ 5,000	Accounts payable	$ 40,000
Accounts receivable	40,000	Accrued expenses	10,000
Inventory	25,000	Notes payable	15,000
Total current assets	70,000	Common stock	10,000
Equipment	50,000	Retained earnings	45,000
Total assets	$120,000	Total liabilities and owners' equity	$120,000

$200,000 Sales
Percent of Sales

Cash	2.5%	Accounts payable	20.0%
Accounts receivable	20.0	Accrued expenses	5.0
Inventory	12.5		25.0%
Total current assets	35.0		
Equipment	25.0		
	60.0%		

percentages are computed for notes payable, common stock, and retained earnings because they are not assumed to maintain a direct relationship with sales volume. Note that each dollar increase in sales will necessitate a 60 cent increase in assets,[2] of which 25 cents will be spontaneously or automatically financed through accounts payable and accrued expenses, leaving 35 cents to be financed by profit or additional outside sources of financing. We will assume the Howard Corporation has an aftertax return of 6 percent on the sales dollar and 50 percent of profits are paid out as dividends.[3]

If sales increase from $200,000 to $300,000, the $100,000 increase in sales will necessitate $35,000 (35 percent) in additional financing. Since we will earn 6 percent on total sales of $300,000, we will show a profit of $18,000. With a 50 percent dividend payout, $9,000 will remain for internal financing. This means that $26,000 out of the

[2]We are assuming equipment increases in proportion to sales. In certain cases there may be excess capacity, and equipment (or plant and equipment) will not increase.

[3]Some may wish to add back depreciation under the percent-of-sales method. Most, however, choose the assumption that funds generated through depreciation (in the sources and uses of funds sense) must be used to replace the fixed assets to which depreciation is applied.

$35,000 must be financed from outside sources. Our formula to determine the need for new funds is:

$$\text{Required new funds (RNF)} = \frac{A}{S}(\Delta S) - \frac{L}{S}(\Delta S) - PS_2(1 - D) \quad (4\text{–}1)$$

where

$\frac{A}{S}$ = Percentage relationship of variable assets to sales [60%]
ΔS = Change in sales [$100,000]
$\frac{L}{S}$ = Percentage relationship of variable liabilities to sales [25%]
P = Profit margin [6%]
S_2 = New sales level [$300,000]
D = Dividend payout ratio

Plugging in the values we show:

60% ($100,000) − 25% ($100,000) − 6% ($300,000) (1 − 0.5) =
$60,000 − $25,000 − $18,000 (0.5) =
$35,000 − $9,000 =
$26,000 required sources of new funds

Presumably the $26,000 can be financed at the bank or through some other appropriate source.

The student will observe that using the percent-of-sales method is a much easier task than tracing through the various cash flows to arrive at the pro forma statements. Nevertheless, the output is much less meaningful, and we do not get a month-to-month breakdown of the data. The percent-of-sales method is a "broad brush" approach, while the development of pro forma statements is more exacting. Of course, whatever methods we use, the results are only as meaningful or reliable as the assumptions about sales and production that went into the numbers.

Sustainable Growth Rate

From the above the question arises: What level of growth can the corporation encounter and still be able to raise the required new funds through additional bank borrowings? The general answer is that highly profitable companies can sustain a high rate of growth, but marginally profitable companies can sustain only low growth. More precisely, if we assume that the debt-to-equity ratio is optimal, the firm's growth in assets can proceed only as quickly as its equity portion expands.

Take the example of the Howard Corporation and assume company management and creditors agree the debt ratio should not increase. This means that a 50 percent growth rate is far in excess of the company's *sustainable growth rate*. Since it has only $9,000 in additional equity being retained from operations, it can add only $2,430 to its notes payable without increasing the debt ratio. This means sales can grow at only one third[4] of the forecast 50 percent amount. In other words, if the equity portion grows by only 16.4 percent, the asset side of the balance sheet can only grow by a maximum of 16.4 percent without increasing the debt ratio. The formula for sustainable growth rate, then, is:

$$\text{Sustainable growth rate (SGR)} = \frac{\text{Net income} \times (1 - D)}{\text{Beginning common equity}} \qquad (4\text{–}2)$$

For the Howard Corporation, the calculation is:

$$\text{SGR} = \frac{\$18{,}000 \times (1 - .5)}{\$55{,}000} = 16.4\%$$

Summary

The process of financial forecasting allows the financial manager to anticipate events before they occur, particularly the need for raising funds externally. An important consideration is that growth itself may call for additional sources of financing because profit is often inadequate to cover the net buildup in receivables, inventory, and other asset accounts.

We develop pro forma financial statements from an overall corporate systems viewpoint. The time perspective is usually six months to a year in the future. In developing a pro forma income statement we begin by making sales projections, then we construct a production plan, and finally we consider all other expenses. From the pro forma income statement we proceed to a cash budget in which the monthly or quarterly cash inflows and outflows related to sales, expenditures,

[4]($9,000 + $2,430)/$35,000.

and capital outlays are portrayed. All of this information can be assimilated into a pro forma balance sheet in which asset, liability, and owners' equity accounts are shown. Any shortage of funds is assumed to be financed through notes payable (bank loans).

We may take a shortcut to financial forecasting through the use of the percent-of-sales method. Under this approach, selected balance sheet accounts are assumed to maintain a constant percentage relationship to sales, and thus for any given sales amount we can ascertain balance sheet values. Once again a shortage of funds is assumed to be financed through notes payable.

List of Terms

pro forma balance sheet
pro forma income statement
cash budget
cost of goods sold
percent-of-sales method
sustainable growth rate

Discussion Questions

1. What are the basic benefits and purposes of developing pro forma statements and a cash budget?
2. Explain how the collections and purchases schedules are related to the borrowing needs of the corporation.
3. With inflation what are the implications of using LIFO and FIFO inventory methods? How do they affect the cost of goods sold?
4. Explain the relationship between inventory turnover and purchase needs.
5. Rapid corporate growth in sales and profits can cause financing problems. Elaborate on this statement.
6. Discuss the advantage and disadvantage of level production schedules in firms whose sales are cyclical.

7. What conditions would help make a percent-of-sales forecast as accurate as pro forma financial statements and cash budgets?

8. Why should management of a profitable company ever worry about growing too rapidly?

Problems

1. Sales for Eastern Sales Company are expected to be 3,000 units for the coming month. The company likes to maintain 15 percent of unit sales for each month in ending inventory. Beginning inventory is 600 units.

   How many units should Eastern Sales produce for the coming month?

2. On December 31 of last year, Wolfson Corporation had in inventory 400 units of its product which cost $21 per unit to produce. During January the company produced 800 units at a cost of $24 per unit.

   Assuming Wolfson Corporation sold 700 units in January, what was its cost of goods sold (assume FIFO inventory method)?

3. At the end of January Dexter Corporation had an inventory of 500 units which cost $15 per unit to produce. During February the company produced 650 units at a cost of $17 per unit.

   If Dexter Corporation sold 900 units in February, what was its cost of goods sold (assume LIFO inventory accounting)?

4. Cox Corporation produces a product with the following costs as of July 1, 1986:

Material	$2 per unit
Labor	4 per unit
Overhead	2 per unit

   Beginning inventory on July 1 was 3,000 units. From July 1 to December 31, 1986, Cox produced 12,000 units. These units had a material cost of $3 per unit. Other costs were the same. Cox uses FIFO inventory accounting.

   Assuming Cox sold 13,000 units during the last six months of the year at $16 each, what will gross profit be? What is the value of ending inventory?

5. Blue Ridge Corporation has forecast credit sales for the fourth quarter of the year:

September (actual)	$50,000
Fourth quarter:	
October	40,000
November	35,000
December	60,000

Experience has shown that 20 percent of sales are collected in the month of sales, 70 percent are collected in the following month, and 10 percent are never collected.

Prepare a schedule of cash receipts for the Blue Ridge Corporation covering the fourth quarter (October through December).

6. The Alberta Corporation has forecast the following sales for the first seven months of the year:

January	$10,000	May	$10,000
February	12,000	June	16,000
March	14,000	July	18,000
April	20,000		

Monthly material purchases are set equal to 30 percent of forecasted sales for the next month. Of the total material costs, 40 percent are paid in the month of purchase and 60 percent in the following month. Labor costs will run $4,000 per month, and fixed overhead is $2,000 per month. Interest payments on the debt will be $3,000 for both March and June. Finally, the Alberta salesmen will receive a 1.5 percent commission on total sales for the first six months of the year, to be paid on June 30.

Prepare a monthly summary of cash payments for the six-month period from January through June. (Note: Compute prior December purchases to help get total material payments for January.)

7. The Boswell Corporation forecasts its sales in units for the next four months as follows:

March	6,000
April	8,000
May	5,500
June	4,000

Boswell maintains an ending inventory for each month in the amount of one and one half times the expected sales in the following month. The ending inventory for February (March's beginning inventory) reflects this policy. Materials cost $5 per unit and are paid in the month after production. Labor cost is $10 per unit and is paid for in the month incurred. Fixed overhead is $12,000 per month. Dividends of $20,000 are to be paid in May. Five thousand units were produced in February.

Complete a production schedule and a summary of cash payments for March, April, and May. Remember that production in any one month is equal to sales plus desired ending inventory minus beginning inventory.

8. The Ace Battery Company has forecast its sales in units as follows:

January	800	May	1,350
February	650	June	1,500
March	600	July	1,200
April	1,100		

Ace always keeps an ending inventory equal to 120 percent of the next month's expected sales. The ending inventory for December (January's beginning inventory) is 960 units, which is consistent with this policy. Materials cost $12 per unit and are paid for in the month after purchase. Labor cost is $5 per unit and is paid in the month the cost is incurred. Overhead costs are $6,000 per month. Interest of $8,000 is scheduled to be paid in March, and employee bonuses of $13,200 will be paid in June.

Prepare a monthly production schedule and a monthly summary of cash payments for the period of January through June. Ace produced 600 units in December.

9. Ed's Waterbeds has made the following sales projections for the next six months. All sales are credit sales.

March	$12,000	June	$14,000
April	16,000	July	17,000
May	10,000	August	18,000

Sales in January and February were $13,500 and $13,000, respectively. Experience has shown that of total sales, 10 percent are uncollectible, 30 percent are collected in the month of sale, 40 percent are collected in the following month, and 20 percent are collected two months after sale.

Prepare a monthly cash receipts schedule for the firm for March through August.

Of the sales expected to be made during the six months from March through August, how much will still be uncollected at the end of August? How much of this is expected to be collected?

10. Warren's Auto Parts has expected sales of $20,000 in September, $25,000 in October, $35,000 in November, and $30,000 in December. Of the company's sales, 20 percent are for cash and 80 percent are on credit. Experience shows that 40 percent of accounts receivable is paid in the month after sale, while the remaining 60 percent is paid two months after. Determine collections for November and December.

Also assume the company's cash payments for November and December are $28,000 and $25,000, respectively. The beginning cash balance in November is $6,000, which is the desired minimum balance.

Prepare a cash budget with borrowing needed or repayments for November and December.

11. Jim Daniels Health Products has eight stores. The firm wishes to expand by two more stores and needs a bank loan to do this. Mr. Hewitt, the banker, will finance construction if the firm can present an acceptable three-month financial plan for January through March. The following are actual and forecasted sales figures:

Actual		*Forecast*		*Additional Information*	
November	$200,000	January	$280,000	April forecast	$330,000
December	220,000	February	320,000		
		March	340,000		

Of the firm's sales 40 percent are for cash, and the remaining 60 percent are on credit. Of credit sales 30 percent are paid in the month after sale, and 70 percent are paid in the second month after sale. Materials cost 30 percent of sales and are purchased and received each month in amounts sufficient to cover the following month's expected sales. Materials are paid for in the month after they are received. Labor expense is 40 percent of sales and is paid in the month of sales. Selling and administrative expense is 5 percent of sales and is also paid in the month of sales. Overhead expense is $28,000 in cash per month. Depreciation expense is $10,000 per month. Taxes of $8,000 will be paid in January, and dividends of $2,000 will be paid in March. Cash at the beginning of January is $80,000, and the desired minimum cash balance is $75,000.

For January, February, and March prepare a schedule of monthly cash receipts, monthly cash payments, and a complete monthly cash budget with borrowing and repayment.

12. Ellis Electronics Company's actual sales and purchases for April and May are shown here along with forecasted sales and purchases for June through September.

	Sales	*Purchases*
April (actual)	$320,000	$130,000
May (actual).	300,000	120,000
June (forecast)	275,000	120,000
July (forecast)	275,000	180,000
August (forecast)	290,000	200,000
September (forecast). . .	330,000	170,000

The company makes 10 percent of its sales for cash and 90 percent on credit. Of the credit sales 20 percent are collected in the month after the sale, and 80 percent are collected two months after. Ellis pays for 40 percent of its purchases in the month after purchase and 60 percent two months after.

Labor expense equals 10 percent of the current month's sales. Overhead expense equals $12,000 per month. Interest payments of $30,000 are due in June and September. A cash dividend of $50,000 is scheduled to be paid in June. Taxes of $25,000 are due in June and September. There is a scheduled capital outlay of $300,000 in September.

Ellis Electronics' ending cash balance in May is $20,000. The minimum desired cash balance is $15,000. Prepare a schedule of monthly cash receipts, monthly cash payments, and a complete monthly cash budget with borrowing and repayments for June through September. The maximum desired cash balance is $50,000. Excess cash (above $50,000) is used to buy marketable securities. Marketable securities are sold before borrowing funds in case of a cash shortfall (less than $15,000).

13. The Meadow Milk Company has plants in five provinces and operates a very large home delivery service. Sales for last year were $100 million, and the balance sheet at year-end is similar in percentage of sales to that of previous years (and this will continue in the future). All assets and current liabilities will vary directly with sales.

Balance Sheet
(in millions)

Assets		Liabilities and Owners' Equity	
Cash	$ 5	Accounts payable	$ 5
Accounts receivable	15	Accrued wages	6
Inventory	30	Accrued taxes	4
Current assets	50	Current liabilities	15
Fixed assets	40	Notes payable	30
		Common stock	25
		Retained earnings	20
Total assets	$90	Total liabilities and owners' equity	$90

Meadow Milk has an aftertax profit margin of 7 percent and a dividend payout ratio of 30 percent.

If sales grow by 10 percent next year, determine how many dollars are needed to finance the expansion. How many dollars will be financed externally and how many internally? (Assume Meadow Milk is already using assets at full capacity and plant must be added.)

14. The Longbranch Western Wear Co. has the following financial statements, which are representative of the company's historical average.

Income Statement

Sales	$200,000
Expenses	158,000
Earnings before interest and taxes	42,000
Interest	2,000
Earnings before taxes	40,000
Taxes	20,000
Earnings after taxes	20,000
Dividends	10,000

Balance Sheet

Assets		Liabilities and Owners' Equity	
Cash	$ 5,000	Accounts payable	$ 5,000
Accounts receivable	10,000	Accrued wages	1,000
Inventory	15,000	Accrued taxes	2,000
Current assets	30,000	Current liabilities	8,000
Fixed assets	70,000	Notes payable	7,000
		Long-term debt	15,000
		Common stock	20,000
		Retained earnings	50,000
Total assets	$100,000	Total liabilities and owners' equity	$100,000

Longbranch is expecting a 20 percent increase in sales next year, and management is concerned about the company's need for external funds. The increase in sales is expected to be carried out without any expansion of fixed assets but rather through more efficient asset utilization in the existing store. Only current liabilities vary directly with sales.

Using a percent-of-sales method, determine whether Longbranch Western Wear has external financing needs. (Hint: A profit margin and payout ratio must be found from the income statement.)

15. Harvard Prep Shops, a clothing chain, had sales of $300 million last year. The business has a steady net profit margin of 15 percent and a dividend payout ratio of 30 percent. The balance sheet for the end of last year is shown.

Balance Sheet
End of Year
(in millions)

Assets		Liabilities and Owners' Equity	
Cash	$ 7	Accounts payable	$ 55
Accounts receivable	28	Accrued expenses	15
Inventory	60	Other payables	20
Plant and equipment	115	Common stock	30
		Retained earnings	90
Total assets	$210	Total liabilities and owners' equity	$210

The firm anticipates there will be a large increase in the demand for tweed sportcoats and deck shoes. An overall sales increase of 25 percent is forecast. All balance sheet accounts are expected to maintain the same percent-of-sales relationships as last year except for common stock and retained earnings. No change in the number of common stock shares is scheduled, and retained earnings will change as dictated by the profits and dividend policy (remember the net profit margin is 15 percent).

a. Will any external financing be required for the firm during the coming year?

b. What would the need for external financing be if the net profit margin increased to 20 percent and the dividend payout ratio was increased to 65 percent?

16. (*Comprehensive problem—external funds*)
The Mansfield Corporation had 1987 sales of $100 million. The balance sheet items that vary directly with sales and the profit margin are as follows:

	Percent
Cash	5%
Accounts receivable	15
Inventory	20
Net fixed assets	40
Accounts payable	15
Accruals	10
Profit margin after taxes	8

The dividend payout rate is 50 percent of earnings, and the balance in retained earnings at the beginning of 1987 was $27 million. Common stock and the company's long-term bonds are constant at $10 million and $5 million, respectively. Notes payable are currently $17 million.

a. How much additional external capital will be required for next year if sales increase 15 percent? (Assume the company is already operating at full capacity.)

b. What will happen to external fund requirements if Mansfield Corporation reduces the payout ratio, grows at a slower rate, or suffers a decline in its profit margin? Discuss each of these separately.

c. Prepare a pro forma balance sheet for 1988 assuming any external funds being acquired will be in the form of notes payable. Disregard the information in part *b* in answering this question (that is, use the original information and part *a* in constructing your pro forma balance sheet).

d. Calculate Mansfield's sustainable growth rate.

17. (*Comprehensive financial forecasting problem—seasonal production*) The difficult part of solving a problem of this nature is to know what to do with the information contained within a story problem. Therefore, this problem will be easier to complete if you rely on Chapter 4 for the format of all required schedules.

The Adams Corporation makes standard-size 2-inch fasteners that it sells for $155 per thousand. Mr. Adams is the majority owner and manages the inventory and finances of the company. He estimates sales for the following months to be:

January	$263,500 (1,700,000 fasteners)
February	186,000 (1,200,000 fasteners)
March	217,000 (1,400,000 fasteners)
April	310,000 (2,000,000 fasteners)
May	387,500 (2,500,000 fasteners)

Last year Adams Corporation's sales were $175,000 in November and $232,500 in December (1,500,000 fasteners).

Mr. Adams is preparing for a meeting with his banker to arrange the financing for the first quarter. Based on his sales forecast and the following information provided by him, your job as his new financial analyst is to prepare a monthly cash budget, a monthly and quarterly pro forma income statement, a pro forma quarterly balance sheet, and all necessary supporting schedules for the first quarter.

Past history shows that the Adams Corporation collects 50 percent of its accounts receivable in the normal 30-day credit period (the month after the sale) and the other 50 percent in 60 days (two months after the sale). It pays for its materials 30 days after receipt. In general, Mr. Adams likes to keep a two-month supply of inventory on hand in anticipation of sales. Inventory at the beginning of December was 2,600,000 units. (This was not equal to his desired two-month supply.)

The major cost of production is the purchase of raw materials in the form of steel rods that are cut, threaded, and finished. Last year raw material costs were $52 per 1,000 fasteners, but Mr. Adams has just been notified that material costs have risen, effective January 1, to $60 per 1,000 fasteners. The Adams Corporation uses FIFO inventory accounting. Labor costs are relatively constant at $20 per thousand fasteners since workers are paid on a piecework basis. Overhead is allocated at $10 per thousand units, and selling and administrative expense is 20 percent of sales. Labor expense and overhead are direct cash outflows paid in the month incurred, while interest and taxes are paid quarterly.

The corporation usually maintains a minimum cash balance of $25,000, and it puts its excess cash into marketable securities. The average tax rate is 40 percent, and Mr. Adams usually pays out 50 percent of net income in dividends to stockholders. Marketable securities are sold before funds are borrowed when a cash shortage is faced. Ignore the interest on any short-term borrowings. Interest on the long-term debt is paid in March, as are taxes and dividends.

As of year-end the Adams Corporation balance sheet was as follows:

ADAMS CORPORATION
Balance Sheet
December 31, 198X

Assets

Current assets:		
Cash	$ 30,000	
Accounts receivable	320,000	
Inventory	237,800	
Total current assets		$ 587,800
Fixed assets:		
Plant and equipment	1,000,000	
Less: Accumulated depreciation	200,000	800,000
Total assets		$1,387,800

Liabilities and Owners' Equity

Accounts payable	$ 93,600	
Notes payable	0	
Long-term debt, 8 percent	400,000	
Common stock	504,200	
Retained earnings	390,000	
Total liabilities and owners' equity		$1,387,800

Selected References

Ansoff, H. Igor. "Planning as a Practical Management Tool." *Financial Executive* 32 (June 1964), pp. 34–37.

Chambers, John C.; Satinder K. Mullick; and Donald D. Smith. "How to Choose the Right Forecasting Technique." *Harvard Business Review* 49 (July–August 1971), pp. 45–74.

Chisholm, R. K., and G. R. Whitaker, Jr. *Forecasting Methods*. Homewood, Ill.: Richard D. Irwin, 1971.

Donaldson, Gordon. "Strategy for Financial Emergencies." *Harvard Business Review* 47 (November–December 1969), pp. 67–79.

Francis, Jack Clark, and Dexter R. Rowell. "A Simultaneous Equation Model of the Firm for Financial Analysis and Planning." *Financial Management* 7 (Spring 1978), pp. 29–44.

Higgins, Robert C. "How Much Growth Can a Firm Afford?" *Financial Management* 6 (Fall 1977), pp. 7–16.

Jaedicke, Robert K., and Robert T. Sprouse. *Accounting Flows: Income, Funds, and Cash*. Englewood Cliffs, N.J.: Prentice-Hall, 1965, chaps. 5 and 6.

Lerner, Eugene M. "Simulating a Cash Budget." *California Management Review* 11 (Winter 1968), pp. 79–86.

Lyneis, James M. "Designing Financial Policies to Deal with Limited Financial Resources." *Financial Management* 4 (Spring 1975), pp. 13–24.

Maier, Steven F.; David W. Robinson; and James H. Vander Weide. "A Short-Term Disbursement Forecasting Model." *Financial Management* 10 (Spring 1981), pp. 9–19.

Parker, George G. C., and Edilberto L. Segura. "How to Get a Better Forecast." *Harvard Business Review* 49 (March–April 1971), pp. 99–109.

Preston, Gerald R. "Considerations in Long-Range Planning." *Financial Executive* (May 1968), pp. 44–49.

Rappaport, Louis H. *SEC Accounting Practice and Procedures*. 3d ed. New York: Ronald, 1972, chap. 21.

Welsch, Glenn A. *Budgeting: Profit Planning and Control*. 2d ed. Englewood Cliffs, N.J.: Prentice-Hall, 1964, chaps. 2 and 11.

Weston, J. Fred. "Forecasting Financial Requirements." *Accounting Review* 33 (July 1958), pp. 427–40.

Wright, Leonard T. *Financial Management: Analytical Techniques*. Columbus, Ohio: Grid, 1974, chap. 4.

5 Operating and Financial Leverage

In the physical sciences as well as in politics the term *leverage* has been popularized to mean the use of special force and effects to produce more than normal results from a given course of action. In business the same concept is applied, with the emphasis on the employment of "fixed-cost" items in anticipation of magnifying returns at high levels of operation. The student should recognize that leverage is a two-edged sword—producing highly favorable results when things go well and quite the opposite under negative conditions.

Leverage in a Business

Assume you are approached with an opportunity to start your own business. You are to manufacture and market industrial parts, such as ball bearings, wheels, and casters. You are faced with two primary decisions.

First, you must determine the amount of fixed-cost plant and equipment you wish to use in the production process. By installing modern, sophisticated equipment, you can virtually eliminate labor in the production of inventory. At high volume you will do quite well, as most of your costs are fixed. At low volume, however, you could face difficulty in making your fixed payments for plant and equipment. If you decide to use expensive labor rather than machinery, you will lessen your opportunity for profit, but at the same time you will lower your exposure to risk (you can lay off part of the work force).

Second, you must determine how you will finance the business. If you rely on debt financing and the business is successful, you will generate substantial profits as an owner, paying only the fixed costs of debt. Of course, if the business starts off poorly, the contractual obligations related to debt could mean bankruptcy. As an alternative you might decide to sell equity rather than borrow, a step that will lower your own profit potential (you must share with others) but minimize your risk exposure.

In both decisions you are making very explicit decisions about the use of leverage. To the extent you go with a heavy commitment to fixed costs in the operation of the firm, you are employing operating leverage. To the extent you utilize debt in the financing of the firm, you are engaging in financial leverage. We shall carefully examine each type of leverage and then show the combined effect of both.

Operating Leverage

Operating leverage reflects the extent to which fixed assets and associated fixed costs are utilized in the business firm. As indicated in Table 5–1, a firm's operating costs may be classified as fixed, variable, or semivariable.

For purposes of analysis, variable and semivariable costs will be combined. In order to evaluate the implications of heavy fixed asset use, we employ the technique of break-even analysis.

Table 5–1
Classification of costs

Fixed	*Variable*	*Semivariable*
Rental	Raw material	Utilities
Depreciation	Factory labor	Repairs and maintenance
Executive salaries	Sales commissions	
Property taxes		

Break-Even Analysis

How much will changes in volume affect cost and profit? At what point does the firm break even? What is the most efficient level of fixed assets to employ in the firm? A break-even chart is presented in Figure 5–1 to answer some of these questions. The number of units produced and sold is shown along the horizontal axis, and revenue and costs are shown along the vertical axis.

Figure 5–1
Break-even chart: Leveraged firm

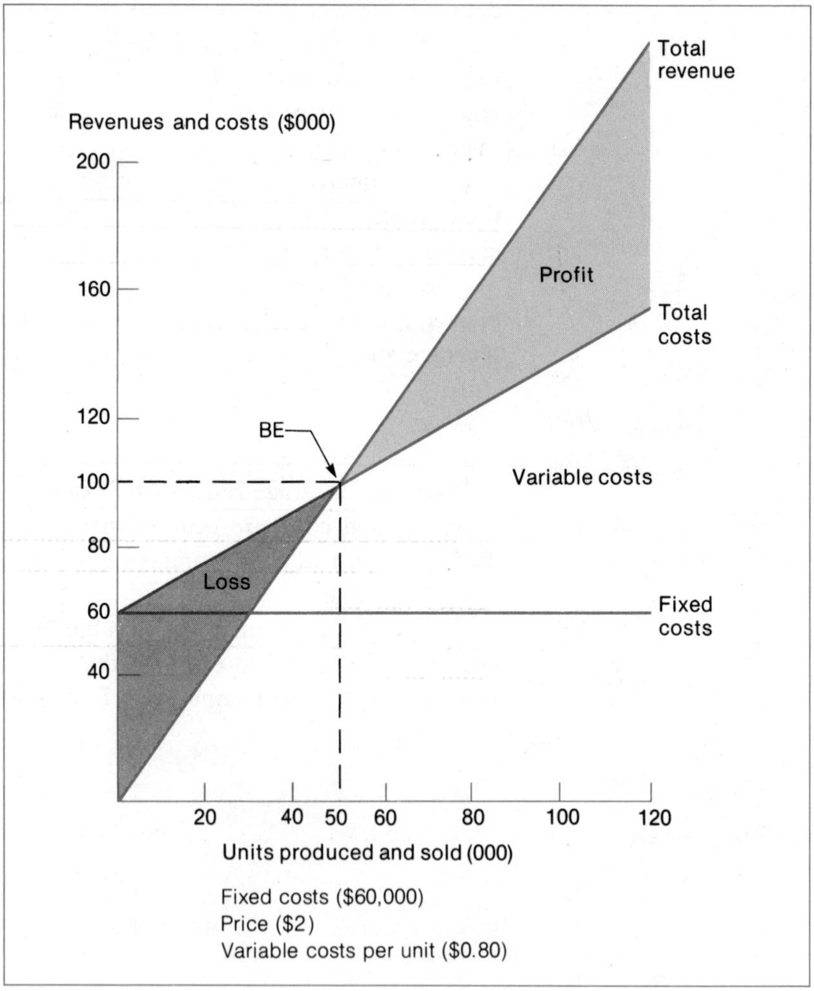

Note, first of all, that our fixed costs[1] are \$60,000, regardless of volume and that our variable costs (at \$0.80 per unit) are added to fixed costs to determine total costs at any point. The total revenue line is determined by multiplying price (\$2) times volume.

Of particular interest is the break-even (BE) point at 50,000 units, where the total costs and total revenue lines intersect. The numbers are as follows:

Units = 50,000

Total Variable Costs (TVC)	*Fixed Costs (FC)*	*Total Costs (TC)*	*Total Revenue (TR)*	*Operating Income (Loss)*
(50,000 × \$0.80) \$40,000	\$60,000	\$100,000	(50,000 × \$2) \$100,000	0

The break-even point for the company may also be determined by use of a simple formula—in which we divide fixed costs by the contribution margin on each unit sold, with the contribution margin defined as price minus variable cost per unit.

$$BE = \frac{\text{Fixed costs}}{\text{Contribution margin}} = \frac{\text{Fixed costs}}{\text{Price} - \text{Variable costs per unit}} = \frac{FC}{P - VC} \quad (5\text{–}1)$$

$$\frac{\$60{,}000}{\$2.00 - \$0.80} = \frac{\$60{,}000}{\$1.20} = 50{,}000 \text{ units}$$

Since we are getting a \$1.20 contribution toward covering fixed costs from each unit sold, minimum sales of 50,000 units will allow us to cover our fixed costs (50,000 units × \$1.20 = \$60,000 fixed costs). Beyond this point we move into a highly profitable range in which each unit of sales brings an increase in operating profit of \$1.20 to the company. As sales increase from 50,000 to 60,000 units, operating profits increase by \$12,000 as indicated in Table 5–2; as sales increase from 60,000 to 80,000 units, profits increase by another \$24,000; and so on. As further indicated in Table 5–2, at low volumes such as 40,000 or 20,000 units our losses are substantial (\$12,000 and \$36,000).

[1]Fixed costs, as used in the operating leverage analysis, include only fixed operating costs and do not include fixed financing charges.

Table 5–2
Volume-cost-profit analysis: Leveraged firm

Units Sold	Total Variable Costs	Fixed Costs	Total Costs	Total Revenue	Operating Income (Loss)
0. . .	0	$60,000	$ 60,000	0	$(60,000)
20,000. . .	$16,000	60,000	76,000	$ 40,000	(36,000)
40,000. . .	32,000	60,000	92,000	80,000	(12,000)
50,000. . .	40,000	60,000	100,000	100,000	0
60,000. . .	48,000	60,000	108,000	120,000	12,000
80,000. . .	64,000	60,000	124,000	160,000	36,000
100,000. . .	80,000	60,000	140,000	200,000	60,000

It is assumed that the firm depicted in Figure 5–1 is operating with a high degree of leverage. The situation is analogous to that of an airline which must carry a certain number of people on board to break even but beyond that point is in a very profitable range.

A More Conservative Approach

Not all firms would choose to operate at the high degree of operating leverage exhibited in Figure 5–1. Fear of falling short of the 50,000-unit break-even level may discourage some companies from heavy utilization of fixed assets. More expensive variable costs may be substituted for automated plant and equipment. Assume that fixed costs for a more conservative firm can be reduced to $12,000—but that variable costs will go from $.80 to $1.60. If the same price assumption of $2 per unit is employed, the break-even level is 30,000 units.

$$BE = \frac{\text{Fixed costs}}{\text{Price} - \text{Variable cost per unit}} = \frac{FC}{P - VC} = \frac{\$12{,}000}{\$2 - \$1.60} = \frac{\$12{,}000}{\$0.40}$$

$$= 30{,}000 \text{ units}$$

With fixed costs reduced from $60,000 to $12,000, the loss potential is small. Furthermore, the break-even level of operations is a comparatively low 30,000 units. Nevertheless, the use of a virtually unleveraged approach has cut into the potential profitability of the more conservative firm, as indicated in Figure 5–2.

Even at high levels of operation, the potential profit is rather small. As indicated in Table 5–3, at a 100,000-unit volume operating income

Figure 5–2
Break-even chart: Conservative firm

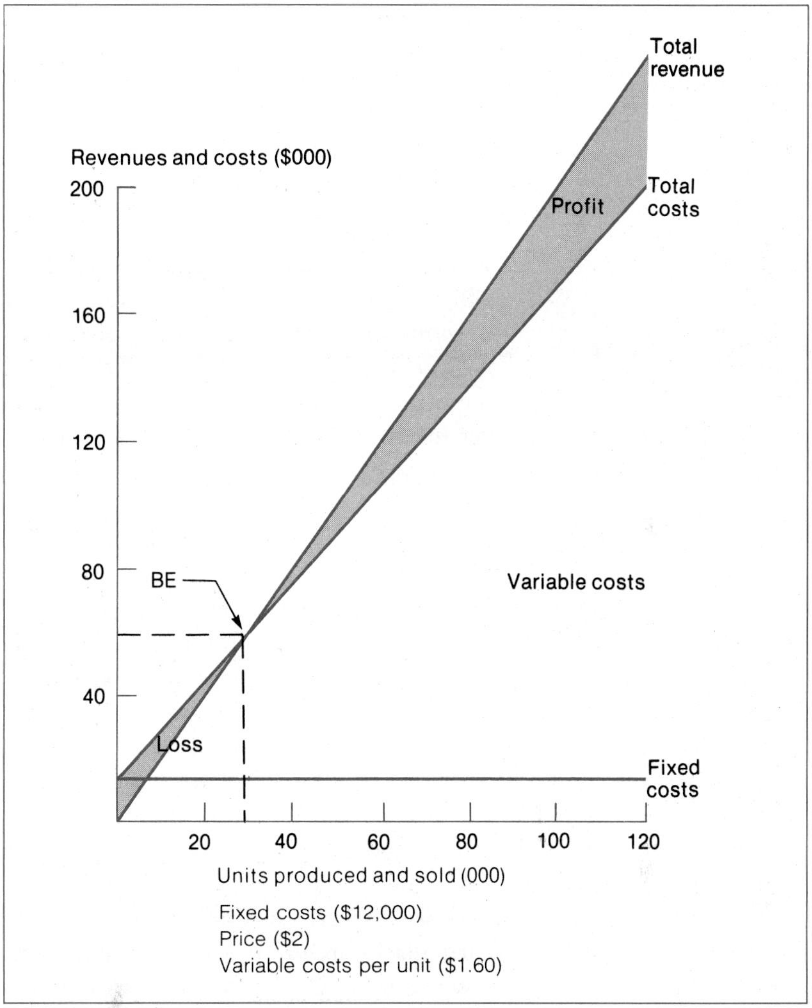

Table 5–3
Volume-cost-profit analysis: Conservative firm

Units Sold	*Total Variable Costs*	*Fixed Costs*	*Total Costs*	*Total Revenue*	*Operating Income (Loss)*
0. . .	0	$12,000	$ 12,000	0	$(12,000)
20,000. . .	$32,000	12,000	44,000	$ 40,000	(4,000)
30,000. . .	48,000	12,000	60,000	60,000	0
40,000. . .	64,000	12,000	76,000	80,000	4,000
60,000. . .	96,000	12,000	108,000	120,000	12,000
80,000. . .	128,000	12,000	140,000	160,000	20,000
100,000. . .	160,000	12,000	172,000	200,000	28,000

is only $28,000—some $32,000 less than that for the "leveraged" firm previously analyzed in Table 5–2.

The Risk Factor

In general, firms in relatively new markets and industries will tend to elect less leveraged positions while firms in more mature industries will choose to employ more operating leverage. For example, if a firm is competing in an emerging industry where the market potential is not yet fully understood and the technology not standardized, locking the firm into fixed costs that require high sales volume based on an as yet unproven technology is highly risky. On the other hand, a firm competing in the pulp and paper industry, where the markets are large but growing slowly and the production processes are highly developed, cannot afford to do anything but invest in high-cost (but very efficient at high volumes) plant and equipment.

Whether management follows the path of high leverage or conservatism also depends on its perceptions about the future. If top management is apprehensive about upcoming economic conditions, a more conservative plan may be undertaken. For a growing business in times of relative prosperity, management might maintain a more aggressive, leveraged position. The firm's competitive position within its industry will also be a factor. Does the firm desire to merely maintain stability or to become a market leader? To a certain extent management should tailor the use of leverage to meet its own risk-taking desires. Those who are risk averse (prefer less risk to more risk) should anticipate a particularly high return before contracting for heavy fixed costs. Others, less averse to risk, may be willing to leverage under more normal conditions. Simply taking risks is not a virtue—bankruptcy courts are filled with risk takers. The important idea, which is stressed throughout the text, is to achieve the best possible return within an acceptable level of risk.

Cash Break-Even Analysis

Our discussion to this point has dealt with break-even analysis in terms of accounting flows rather than cash flows. For example, depreciation has been implicitly included in fixed expenses, but it represents an accounting entry rather than an explicit expenditure of funds. To the extent we were doing break-even analysis on a strictly cash basis, depreciation would be excluded from fixed expenses. In the example of the leveraged firm in Formula 5–1, if we eliminate \$20,000 of "assumed" depreciation from fixed costs, the break-even level is reduced to 33,333 units.

$$\frac{FC}{P - VC} = \frac{(\$60{,}000 - \$20{,}000)}{\$2.00 - \$0.80} = \frac{\$40{,}000}{\$1.20} = 33{,}333 \text{ units}$$

Other adjustments could also be made for noncash items. For example, sales may initially take the form of accounts receivable rather than cash, and the same can be said for the purchase of materials and accounts payable. An actual weekly or monthly cash budget would be necessary to isolate these items.

While cash break-even analysis is helpful in analyzing the short-term outlook of the firm, particularly when it may be in trouble, most break-even analysis is conducted on the basis of accounting flows rather than strictly cash flows. Most of the assumptions throughout the chapter are based on concepts broader than pure cash flows.

Degree of Operating Leverage

Degree of operating leverage (DOL) may be defined as the percentage change in operating income that takes place as a result of a percentage change in units sold.

$$DOL = \frac{\text{Percent change in operating income}}{\text{Percent change in unit volume}} \tag{5–2}$$

Highly leveraged firms, such as those in the auto or construction industry, are likely to enjoy a rather substantial increase in income as volume expands, while more conservative firms will participate to a lesser extent. Degree of operating leverage (DOL) should only be computed over a profitable range of operations. However, the closer DOL is computed to the company break-even point, the higher the number will be due to a large percentage increase in operating income.[2]

[2]While the value of DOL varies at each level of output, the beginning level of volume determines the DOL regardless of the location of the end point.

Let us apply the formula to the leveraged and conservative firms previously discussed. Their income or losses at various levels of operation are summarized in Table 5–4.

We will now consider what happens to operating income as volume moves from 80,000 to 100,000 units.

Leveraged Firm

$$DOL = \frac{\text{Percent change in operating income}}{\text{Percent change in unit volume}} = \frac{\frac{\$24{,}000}{\$36{,}000} \times 100}{\frac{20{,}000}{80{,}000} \times 100}$$

$$= \frac{67\%}{25\%} = 2.7$$

Conservative Firm

$$DOL = \frac{\text{Percent change in operating income}}{\text{Percent change in unit volume}} = \frac{\frac{\$8{,}000}{\$20{,}000} \times 100}{\frac{20{,}000}{80{,}000} \times 100}$$

$$= \frac{40\%}{25\%} = 1.6$$

Table 5–4
Operating income or loss

Units	Leveraged Firm (Table 5–2)	Conservative Firm (Table 5–3)
0	$(60,000)	$(12,000)
20,000	(36,000)	(4,000)
40,000	(12,000)	4,000
60,000	12,000	12,000
80,000	36,000	20,000
100,000	60,000	28,000

We see the DOL is much greater for the leveraged firm, indicating at 80,000 units a 1 percent increase in volume will produce a 2.7 percent change in operating income versus a 1.6 percent increase for the conservative firm.

The formula for degree of operating leverage (DOL) may be algebraically manipulated to read:

$$DOL = \frac{Q(P - VC)}{Q(P - VC) - FC} \qquad (5\text{–}3)$$

where

Q = Quantity at which DOL is computed
P = Price per unit
VC = Variable costs per unit
FC = Fixed costs

Using the newly stated formula for the first firm at $Q = 80{,}000$, with $P = \$2$, $VC = \$0.80$, and $FC = \$60{,}000$:

$$DOL = \frac{\$80{,}000\ (\$2.00 - \$0.80)}{80{,}000\ (\$2.00 - \$0.80) - \$60{,}000}$$

$$= \frac{80{,}000\ (\$1.20)}{80{,}000\ (\$1.20) - 60{,}000} = \frac{96{,}000}{96{,}000 - 60{,}000}$$

$$= 2.7$$

We once again derive an answer of 2.7.[3] The same type of calculation could also be performed for the conservative firm.

---

[3]The formula for DOL may also be rewritten as:

$$DOL = \frac{Q(P - VC)}{Q(P - VC) - FC} = \frac{QP - QVC}{QP - QVC - FC}$$

We can rewrite the second terms as:

QP = S, or Sales (Quantity × Price)
QVC = TVC, or Total variable costs (Quantity × Variable costs per unit)
FC = Total fixed costs (remains the same term)

We then have:

$$DOL = \frac{S - TVC}{S - TVC - FC}, \text{ or } \frac{\$160{,}000 - \$64{,}000}{\$160{,}000 - \$64{,}000 - \$60{,}000} = \frac{\$96{,}000}{\$36{,}000} = 2.7$$

Limitations of Analysis

Throughout our analysis of operating leverage we have assumed that a constant or linear function exists for revenues and costs as volume changes. For example, we have used $2 as the hypothetical sales price at all levels of operation. In the "real world," however, we may face price weakness as we attempt to capture an increasing market, or we may face cost overruns as we move beyond an optimum-size operation. Relationships are not so fixed as we have assumed.

Nevertheless, the basic patterns we have studied are reasonably valid for most firms over an extended operating range (in our example that might be between 20,000 and 100,000 units). It is only at the extreme levels that linear assumptions break down, as indicated in Figure 5–3.

Figure 5–3
Nonlinear break-even analysis

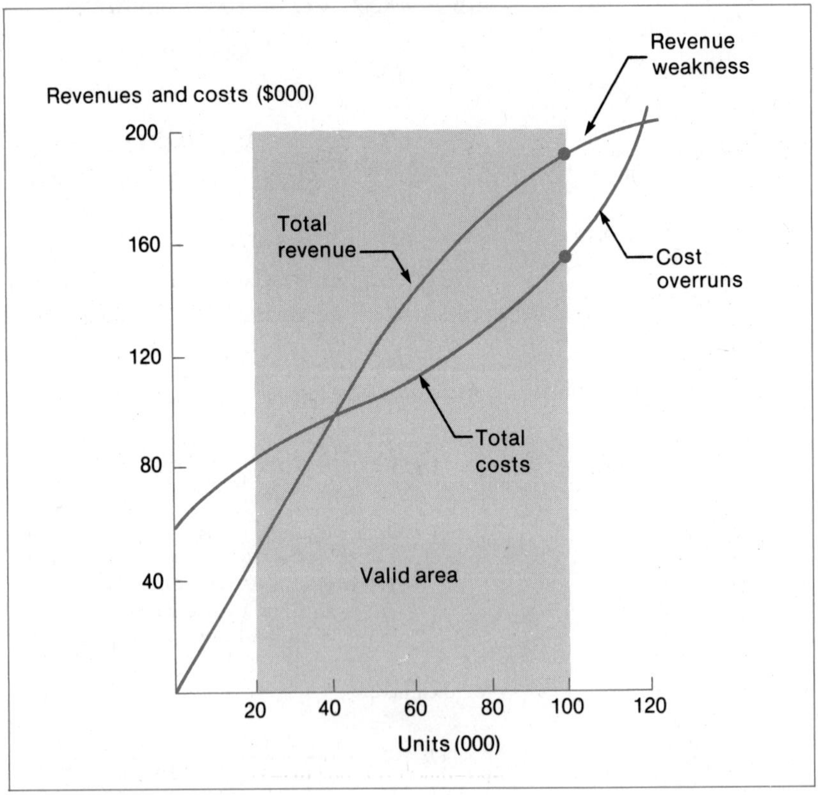

A further word of caution relating to break-even analysis is in order. Although the period of analysis is generally one year, the reality is that a product or venture new to the company will probably not break even within the first few years of operation. This is because it takes time to nurture and realize the market potential. Thus, for such cases one should analyze the break-even possibilities for the situation a few years hence when the market has developed rather than consider just the immediately upcoming year. It is interesting to note that although companies commonly require a new product introduction be profitable by its third year of operation, an important study found it took eight years, on average, for new products to actually turn a profit.[4]

Financial Leverage

Having discussed the effect of fixed costs on the operations of the firm (operating leverage), we now turn to the second form of leverage. Financial leverage reflects the amount of debt used in the capital structure of the firm. Because debt carries a fixed obligation of interest payments, we have the opportunity to greatly magnify our results at various levels of operation. You may have heard of the real estate developer who borrows 100 percent of the costs of his project and will enjoy an infinite return on his zero investment if all goes well.

It is helpful to think of *operating leverage* as primarily affecting the left-hand side of the balance sheet and *financial leverage* as affecting the right-hand side.

Balance Sheet

Assets	*Liabilities and Net Worth*
Operating leverage	Financial leverage

Whereas operating leverage influences the mix of plant and equipment, financial leverage determines how the operation is to be financed.

[4]Ralph Biggadike, "The Risky Business of Diversification," *Harvard Business Review*, May–June 1979, pp. 103–11.

It is entirely possible for two firms to have equal operating capabilities and yet show widely different results because of differing uses of financial leverage.

Impact on Earnings

In studying the impact of financial leverage we shall examine two financial plans for a firm, each employing a significantly different amount of debt in the capital structure. Financing totaling $200,000 is required to carry the assets of the firm.

Total assets—$200,000

	Plan A (Leveraged)	Plan B (Conservative)
Debt (8% interest)	$150,000 ($12,000 interest)	$ 50,000 ($4,000 interest)
Common stock	50,000 (8,000 shares at $6.25)	150,000 (24,000 shares at $6.25)
Total financing.	$200,000	$200,000

Under *leveraged* Plan A we will borrow $150,000 and sell 8,000 shares of stock at $6.25 to raise an additional $50,000, whereas *conservative* Plan B calls for borrowing only $50,000 and acquiring an additional $150,000 in stock with 24,000 shares.

In Table 5–5 we compute earnings per share for the two plans at various levels of "earnings before interest and taxes" (EBIT). These earnings represent the operating income of the firm—before deductions have been made for financial charges or taxes. We assume EBIT levels of 0, $12,000, $36,000, and $60,000.

The impact of the two financing plans is dramatic. Although both plans assume the same operating income, or EBIT, for comparative purposes at each level (say $36,000 in calculation 4) the reported income per share is vastly different ($1.50 versus $0.67). It is also evident that the conservative plan will produce better results at low income levels—but that the leveraged plan will generate much better earnings per share as operating income, or EBIT, goes up. The firm would be indifferent between the two plans at an EBIT level of $16,000 as indicated in Table 5–5.

In Figure 5–4 we graphically demonstrate the effect of the two financing plans on earnings per share.

Table 5–5
Impact of financing plan on earnings per share

	Plan A (Leveraged)	Plan B (Conservative)
1. EBIT (0)		
Earnings before interest and taxes (EBIT)	0	0
– Interest (I)	$(12,000)	$ (4,000)
Earnings before taxes (EBT)	(12,000)	(4,000)
– Taxes (T)*	(6,000)	(2,000)
Earnings after taxes (EAT)	$ (6,000)	$ (2,000)
Shares	8,000	24,000
Earnings per share (EPS)	$(0.75)	$(0.08)
2. EBIT ($12,000)		
Earnings before interest and taxes (EBIT)	$ 12,000	$ 12,000
– Interest (I)	12,000	4,000
Earnings before taxes (EBT)	0	8,000
– Taxes (T)	0	4,000
Earnings after taxes (EAT)	0	$ 4,000
Shares	8,000	24,000
Earnings per share (EPS)	0	$0.17
3. EBIT ($16,000)		
Earnings before interest and taxes (EBIT)	$ 16,000	$ 16,000
– Interest (I)	12,000	4,000
Earnings before taxes (EBT)	4,000	12,000
– Taxes (T)	2,000	6,000
Earnings after taxes (EAT)	$ 2,000	$ 6,000
Shares	8,000	24,000
Earnings per share (EPS)	$0.25	$0.25
4. EBIT ($36,000)		
Earnings before interest and taxes (EBIT)	$ 36,000	$ 36,000
– Interest (I)	12.000	4,000
Earnings before taxes (EBT)	24,000	32,000
– Taxes (T)	12,000	$ 16,000
Earnings after taxes (EAT)	$ 12,000	$ 16,000
Shares	8,000	24,000
Earnings per share (EPS)	$1.50	$0.67
5. EBIT ($60,000)		
Earnings before interest and taxes (EBIT)	$ 60,000	$ 60,000
– Interest (I)	12,000	4,000
Earnings before taxes (EBT)	48,000	56,000
– Taxes (T)	24,000	28,000
Earnings after taxes (EAT)	$ 24,000	$ 28,000
Shares	8,000	24,000
Earnings per share (EPS)	$3,00	$1.17

*The assumption is that large losses can be written off against other income, perhaps in other years, thus providing the firm with a tax savings benefit. The tax rate is 50 percent.

Figure 5–4
Financing plans and earnings per share

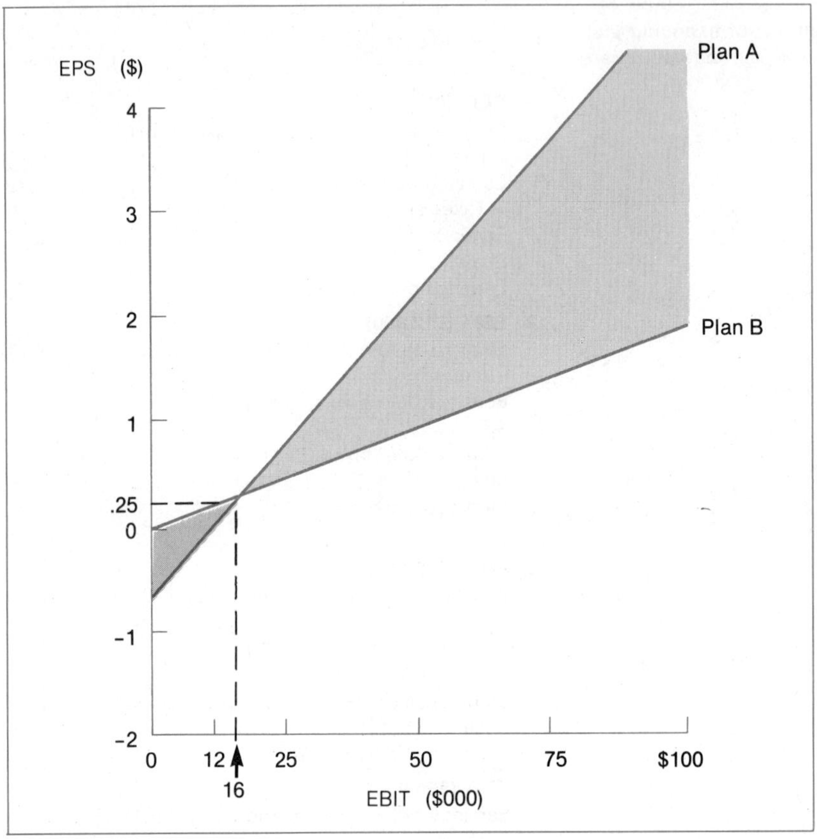

With an EBIT of $16,000 we are earning *8 percent* on total assets of $200,000—precisely the percentage cost of borrowed funds to the firm. The use or nonuse of debt does not influence the answer. Beyond $16,000, Plan A, employing heavy financial leverage, really goes to work, allowing the firm to greatly expand earnings per share as a result of a change in EBIT. For example, at the EBIT level of $36,000, an 18 percent return on assets of $200,000 takes place—and financial leverage is clearly working to our benefit as earnings greatly expand.

Degree of Financial Leverage

As was true of operating leverage, degree of financial leverage measures the effect of a change in one variable on another variable. Degree of financial leverage (DFL) may be defined as the percentage change in earnings (EPS) that takes place as a result of a percentage change in earnings before interest and taxes (EBIT).

$$DFL = \frac{\text{Percent change in } EPS}{\text{Percent change in } EBIT} \tag{5–4}$$

For purposes of computation, the formula for DFL may be conveniently restated as:

$$DFL = \frac{EBIT}{EBIT - I} \tag{5–5}$$

Let's compute the degree of financial leverage for Plan A and Plan B, presented in Table 5–5, at an EBIT level of $36,000. Plan A calls for $12,000 of interest at all levels of financing, and Plan B requires $4,000.

Plan A (leveraged)

$$DFL = \frac{EBIT}{EBIT - I} = \frac{\$36{,}000}{\$36{,}000 - \$12{,}000} = \frac{\$36{,}000}{\$24{,}000} = 1.5$$

Plan B (conservative)

$$DFL = \frac{EBIT}{EBIT - I} = \frac{\$36{,}000}{\$36{,}000 - \$4{,}000} = \frac{\$36{,}000}{\$32{,}000} = 1.1$$

As expected, Plan A has a much higher degree of financial leverage. At an EBIT level of $36,000, a 1 percent increase in earnings will produce a 1.5 percent increase in earnings per share under Plan A but only a 1.1 percent increase under Plan B. DFL may be computed for any level of operation, and it will change from point to point, but Plan A will always exceed Plan B.

Limitations to Use of Financial Leverage

The alert student may quickly observe that if debt is such a good thing, why sell any stock at all? (Perhaps one share to yourself.) With exclusive debt financing at an EBIT level of $36,000, we would have a degree of financial leverage factor (DFL) of 1.8.

$$DFL = \frac{EBIT}{EBIT - I} = \frac{\$36{,}000}{\$36{,}000 - \$16{,}000} = \frac{\$36{,}000}{\$20{,}000} = 1.8$$

(With no stock, we would borrow the full $200,000.)

$$(8\% \times \$200{,}000 = \$16{,}000 \text{ interest})$$

As stressed throughout the text, debt financing and financial leverage offer unique advantages, but only up to a point—beyond that point debt financing may be detrimental to the firm. For example, as we expand the use of debt in our capital structure, lenders will perceive a greater financial risk for the firm. For that reason they may raise the average interest rate to be paid, and they may demand that certain restrictions be placed on the corporation. Furthermore, concerned common stockholders may drive down the price of the stock—forcing us away from the *objective of maximizing the firm's overall value* in the market. The overall impact of financial leverage must be carefully weighed.

This is not to say that financial leverage does not work to the benefit of the firm—it very definitely does if properly used. Further discussion of appropriate debt-equity mixes is covered in Chapter 11, Cost of Capital. For now, we accept the virtues of financial leverage, knowing that all good things must be used in moderation. For firms in industries that offer some degree of stability, are in a positive stage of growth, and are operating in favorable economic conditions, the use of some debt is recommended. In the cases of large utilities like Bell Canada, operating cash flows are forecastable within narrow ranges, thus favoring the use of higher leverage. On the other hand, for companies in industries open to cyclicality or other causes of revenue volatility, use of high levels of leverage may become the cause of significant financial distress as was the case with Dome Petroleum when world oil prices softened in the mid-1980s.

Because firms in a given industry tend to face similar levels of business risk, investors and financial analysts often compare a firm's level of financial leverage to industry averages to estimate whether or not it is excessive. It is therefore incumbent on management to justify clearly any decision to employ a higher amount of leverage than most other firms in its industry. Information on financial leverage for selected Canadian industries is presented in Table 5–6.

Table 5–6
Financial leverage in selected industries (millions, year-end 1984)

Industry	Debt		Equity		
	Short-Term Loans	Long-Term Loans	Preferred	Common*	Long-Term Debt/Equity
Pulp and paper	$ 699	$ 4,958	$ 1,785	$ 7,608	.59
Agriculture	1,328	2,445	1,369	1,953	.74
Oil and gas wells	1,461	12,393	3,747	26,548	.41
Metal mining	929	5,792	1,740	9,890	.50
Bakery products	60	321	195	560	.43
Textile mills	343	547	163	1,559	.32
Clothing	459	120	128	729	.14
Motor vehicles	419	266	149	4,908	.05
Pharmaceuticals	84	32	79	779	.04
Radio and TV	183	1,133	111	1,281	.81
Electric utilities	418	55,095	1,062	14,359	3.57
Wholesale trade	12,667	3,669	3,352	17,755	.17
All nonfinancial	46,162	157,190	32,842	203,849	.67

*Includes retained earnings.
Source: Statistics Canada, *Corporation Financial Statistics*, Fourth Quarter 1986, pp. 61–207.

Combining Operating and Financial Leverage

If both operating and financial leverage allow us to magnify our returns, then we will get maximum leverage through their combined use. We have said that operating leverage affects primarily the asset structure of the firm, while financial leverage affects the debt-equity mix. From an income statement viewpoint, operating leverage determines return from operations, while financial leverage determines how the "fruits of our labor" will be allocated to debt holders and, more importantly, to stockholders in the form of earnings per share. In Table 5–7 we show the combined influence of operating and financial leverage on the income statement. The values in Table 5–7 are drawn from earlier material in the chapter (see Tables 5–2 and 5–5). We assumed in both cases a high degree of operating and financial leverage. The sales volume is 80,000 units.

Table 5–7
Income statement

Sales (total revenue) (80,000 units @ $2)	$160,000	Operating leverage
−Fixed costs	60,000	
−Variable costs ($0.80 per unit)	64,000	
Operating income	$ 36,000	
Earnings before interest and taxes	$ 36,000	Financial leverage
−Interest	12,000	
Earnings before taxes	24,000	
−Taxes	12,000	
Earnings after taxes	$ 12,000	
Shares	8,000	
Earnings per share	$1.50	

The student will observe, first, that operating leverage influences the top half of the income statement—determining operating income. The last item under operating leverage, operating income, then becomes the initial item for determination of financial leverage. "Operating income" and "earnings before interest and taxes" are one and the same, representing the return to the corporation after production, marketing, and so forth—but before interest and taxes are paid. In the second half of the income statement, we then show the extent to which earnings before interest and taxes are translated into earnings per share. A graphical representation of these points is provided in Figure 5–5.

Figure 5–5
Combining operating and financial leverage

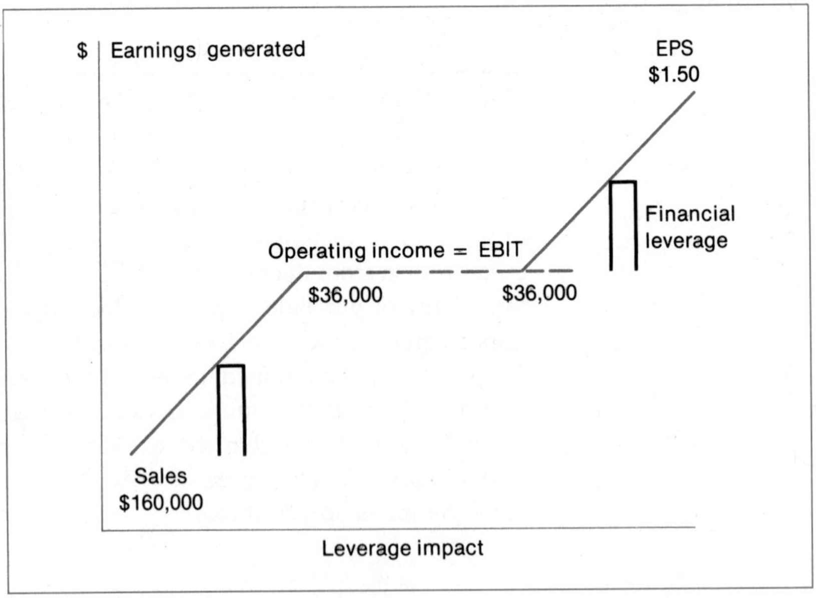

Degree of Combined Leverage

Degree of combined leverage utilizes the entire income statement and shows the impact of a change in sales or volume on bottom-line earnings per share. Degree of operating leverage and degree of financial leverage are, in effect, being combined. Table 5–8 shows what happens to profitability as the firm's sales go from $160,000 (80,000 units) to $200,000 (100,000 units).

The formula for degree of combined leverage is stated as:

$$\text{Degree of combined leverage } (DCL) = \frac{\text{Percent change in } EPS}{\text{Percent change in sales (or volume)}} \quad (5\text{–}6)$$

$$\frac{\text{Percent change in } EPS}{\text{Percent change in sales}} = \frac{\frac{\$1.50}{\$1.50} \times 100}{\frac{\$\ 40{,}000}{\$160{,}000} \times 100} = \frac{100\%}{25\%} = 4$$

Every percentage point change in sales will be reflected in a 4 percent change in earnings per share at this level of operation (quite an impact).

An algebraic statement of the formula is:

$$DCL = \frac{Q\,(P - VC)}{Q(P - VC) - FC - I} \quad (5\text{–}7)$$

From Table 5–8: Q (quantity) = 80,000; P (price per unit) = $2.00; VC (variable costs per unit) = $0.80; FC (fixed costs) = $60,000; I (interest) = $12,000.

Table 5–8
Operating and financial leverage

	(Taken from Table 5–7)		
Sales – $2 per unit (80,000 units)	$160,000	(100,000 → units)	$200,000
– Fixed costs	60,000		60,000
– Variable costs ($0.80 per unit)	64,000		80,000
Operating income = EBIT	36,000		60,000
– Interest	12,000		12,000
Earnings before taxes	24,000		48,000
– Taxes	12,000		24,000
Earnings after taxes	$ 12,000		$ 24,000
Shares	8,000		8,000
Earnings per share	$1.50		$3.00

$$DCL = \frac{80{,}000\ (\$2.00 - \$0.80)}{80{,}000\ (\$2.00 - \$0.80) - \$60{,}000 - \$12{,}000}$$

$$= \frac{80{,}000\ (\$1.20)}{80{,}000\ (\$1.20) - \$72{,}000}$$

$$= \frac{\$96{,}000}{\$96{,}000 - \$72{,}000} = \frac{\$96{,}000}{\$24{,}000} = 4$$

The answer is once again shown to be 4.[5]

A Word of Caution

In a sense we are piling risk upon risk as the two different forms of leverage are combined. Perhaps a firm carrying heavy operating leverage may wish to moderate its position financially, and vice versa. One thing is certain—the decision will have a major impact on the operations of the firm.

Summary

Leverage may be defined as the use of fixed cost items to magnify returns at high levels of operation. Operating leverage primarily affects fixed versus variable cost utilization in the operation of the firm. An

---

[5]The formula for DCL may be rewritten as:

$$DCL = \frac{Q(P - VC)}{Q(P - VC) - FC - I} = \frac{QP - QVC}{QP - QVC - FC - I}$$

We rewrite the second terms as:

QP = S, or Sales (Quantity × Price)
QVC = TVC, or Total variable costs (Quantity × Variable cost per unit)
FC = Total fixed costs (remains the same term)
I = Interest (remains the same term)

We then have:

$$DCL = \frac{S - TVC}{S - TVC - FC - I}$$

$$= \frac{\$160{,}000 - \$64{,}000}{\$160{,}000 - \$64{,}000 - \$60{,}000 - \$12{,}000} = \frac{\$96{,}000}{\$24{,}000} = 4$$

important concept—degree of operating leverage (DOL)—measures the percentage change in operating income as a result of a percentage change in volume. The heavier the utilization of fixed cost assets, the higher DOL is likely to be.

Financial leverage reflects the extent to which debt is used in the capital structure of the firm. Substantial use of debt will place a great burden on the firm at low levels of profitability, but it will help to magnify earnings per share as volume or operating income increases. We combine operating and financial leverage to assess the impact of all types of fixed costs on the firm. There is a multiplier effect when we use the two different types of leverage.

Because leverage is a two-edged sword, management must be sure that the level of risk assumed is in accord with its desires for risk and its perceptions of the future. High operating leverage may be balanced off against lower financial leverage if this is deemed desirable, and vice versa.

List of Terms

break-even analysis
fixed costs
variable costs
contribution margin
nonlinear break-even analysis
leverage (concept in general)
operating leverage
degree of operating leverage (DOL)
financial leverage
degree of financial leverage (DFL)
combined leverage
degree of combined leverage (DCL)

Discussion Questions

1. Discuss the various uses for break-even analysis.
2. What factors would cause a difference in the use of financial leverage for a utility company and an automobile company?

3. Explain how the break-even point and operating leverage are affected by the choice of manufacturing facilities (labor-intensive versus capital-intensive).

4. What role does depreciation play in break-even analysis based on accounting flows? Based on cash flows? Which perspective is longer term in nature?

5. What does risk taking have to do with the use of operating and financial leverage?

6. Discuss the limitations of financial leverage.

7. How does the interest rate on new debt influence the use of financial leverage?

8. Explain how combined leverage brings together operating income and earnings per share.

9. Explain why operating leverage decreases as a company increases sales and shifts away from the break-even point.

10. Why does the starting level of sales determine the degree of operating leverage rather than the ending level of sales?

11. One could say that financial leverage has its most important impact on earnings per share rather than net income after taxes. How would you support this statement?

12. Does being at the EPS indifference point mean that you are always indifferent between two financing plans? Explain.

13. Discuss the concept of operating leverage as you think it would apply to a major, independent television broadcaster.

Problems

1. The Harmon Corporation manufactures baseball bats with Pete Rose's autograph stamped on. Each bat sells for $12 and has a variable cost of $7. There are $20,000 in fixed costs involved in the production process.

   a. Compute the break-even point in units.
   b. Find the sales (in units) needed to earn a profit of $15,000.

2. Draw two break-even graphs—one for a conservative firm using labor-intensive production and another for a capital-intensive firm. Assuming these companies compete within the same industry and have identical sales, explain the impact of changes in sales volume on both firms' profits.

3. The Morgan Tire Company income statement for 1987 is as follows:

MORGAN TIRE COMPANY
Income Statement
For the Year Ended December 31, 1987

Sales (20,000 tires at $60 each)	$1,200,000
Less: Variable costs (20,000 tires at $30)	600,000
Fixed costs	400,000
Earnings before interest and taxes (EBIT)	200,000
Interest expense	50,000
Earnings before taxes (EBT)	150,000
Income tax expense (40%)	60,000
Earnings after taxes (EAT)	$ 90,000

Given this income statement, compute the following:

a. Degree of operating leverage.
b. Degree of financial leverage.
c. Degree of combined leverage.
d. Break-even point in units.

4. The Prima Donna Company provides studios for musicians to give music lessons. The company's income statement for the year 1987 is as follows:

PRIMA DONNA COMPANY
Income Statement
For the Year Ended December 31, 1987

Sales (10,000 lessons at $20 each)	$200,000
Less: Variable costs (10,000 lessons at $5)	50,000
Fixed costs	50,000
Earnings before interest and taxes (EBIT)	100,000
Interest expense	20,000
Earnings before taxes (EBT)	80,000
Income tax expense (40%)	32,000
Earnings after taxes (EAT)	$ 48,000

Given this income statement, compute the following:

a. Degree of operating leverage.
b. Degree of financial leverage.

c. Degree of combined leverage.
d. Break-even point in units (number of music lessons).

5. University Catering sells 50-pound bags of popcorn to university dormitories for $10 a bag. The fixed costs of this operation are $80,000, while the variable costs of the popcorn are $.10 per pound.

a. What is the break-even point in bags?
b. Calculate the profit or loss on 12,000 bags and 25,000 bags.
c. What is the degree of operating leverage at 20,000 bags and 25,000 bags? Why does the degree of operating leverage change as quantity sold increases?
d. If University Catering has an annual interest payment of $10,000, calculate the degree of financial leverage at both 20,000 and 25,000 bags.
e. What is the degree of combined leverage at both sales levels?

6. Sinclair Manufacturing and Boswell Brothers, Inc., are both involved in the production of tile for the homebuilding industry. Their financial information is as follows:

Capital Structure

	Sinclair	*Boswell*
Debt @ 12%	$ 600,000	0
Common stock, $10 per share	400,000	$1,000,000
Total	$1,000,000	$1,000,000
Common shares	40,000	100,000

Operating Plan

	Sinclair	*Boswell*
Sales (50,000 units at $20 each)	$1,000,000	$1,000,000
Less: Variable costs	800,000 ($16 per unit)	500,000 ($10 per unit)
Fixed costs	0	300,000
Earnings before interest and taxes (EBIT)	$ 200,000	$ 200,000

a. If you combine Sinclair's capital structure with Boswell's operating plan, what is the degree of combined leverage? (Round to two places to the right of the decimal point.)
b. If you combine Boswell's capital structure with Sinclair's operating plan, what is the degree of combined leverage?
c. Explain why you got the result you did in part *b*.
d. In part *b*, if sales double, by what percent will EPS increase?

7. Cain Auto Supplies and Able Auto Parts are competitors in the aftermarket for auto supplies. The separate capital structures for Cain and Able are presented below.

Cain		*Able*	
Debt @ 10%	$ 50,000	Debt @ 10%	$100,000
Common stock	100,000	Common stock	50,000
Total	$150,000	Total	$150,000
Common shares	10,000	Common shares	5,000

a. Compute earnings per share if earnings before interest and taxes are $10,000, $15,000, and $50,000 (assume a 30 percent tax rate).

b. Explain the relationship between earnings per share and the level of EBIT.

c. If the cost of debt went up to 12 percent and all other factors remained equal, what would be the break-even level for EBIT?

8. In Problem 7, compute the stock price for Cain if it sells at 12 times earnings per share and EBIT are $40,000.

9. The Norman Automatic Mailer Machine Company is planning to expand production because of the increased volume of mailouts. The increased mailout capacity will cost $2 million. The expansion can be financed either by bonds at an interest rate of 14 percent or by selling 40,000 shares of common stock at $50 per share. The current income statement (before expansion) is as follows:

NORMAN AUTOMATIC MAILER
Income Statement
198X

Sales		$3,500,000
Less: Variable costs	$1,400,000	
Fixed costs	900,000	
Earnings before interest and taxes		1,200,000
Less: Interest expense		400,000
Earnings before taxes		800,000
Less: Taxes @ 40%		320,000
Earnings after taxes		$ 480,000
Shares		100,000
Earnings per share		$4.80

Assume that after expansion, sales are expected to increase by $1.5 million. Variable costs will be 40 percent of sales, and fixed costs will increase by $600,000. The tax rate is 40 percent.

a. Calculate the degree of operating leverage, the degree of financial leverage, and the degree of combined leverage before expansion. (For the degree of operating leverage, use the formula developed in footnote 3; for the degree of combined leverage, use the formula developed in footnote 5. These instructions apply throughout this problem.)
b. Construct the income statement for the two financing plans.
c. Calculate the degree of operating leverage, the degree of financial leverage, and the degree of combined leverage, after expansion, for the two financing plans.
d. Explain which financial plan you favor and the risks involved.

10. Dickinson Company has $12 million in assets. Currently half of these assets are financed with long-term debt at 10 percent and half with common stock having a par value of $8. Ms. Smith, vice president of finance, wishes to analyze two refinancing plans, one with more debt (D) and one with more equity (E). The company earns a return on assets before interest and taxes of 10 percent. The tax rate is 45 percent.

Under Plan D a $3 million long-term bond would be sold at an interest rate of 12 percent, and 375,000 shares of stock would be purchased in the market at $8 per share and retired.

Under Plan E 375,000 shares of stock would be sold at $8 per share, and the $3 million in proceeds would be used to reduce long-term debt.

a. How would each of these plans affect earnings per share? Consider the current plan and the two new plans.
b. Which plan would be most favorable if return on assets fell to 5 percent? Increased to 15 percent? Consider the current plan and the two new plans.
c. If the market price for common stock rose to $12 before the restructuring, which plan would then be most attractive? Continue to assume that $3 million in debt will be used to retire stock in Plan D and $3 million of new equity will be sold to

retire debt in Plan E. Also assume for calculations in part *c* that return on assets is 10 percent.

11. Richards Manufacturing Company has $20 million in assets, 80 percent is financed by debt, and 20 percent is financed by common stock. The interest rate on the debt is 14 percent, and the price of the stock is $20 per share. The firm's president is considering two financing plans for an expansion to $30 million in assets.

Under Plan A the high debt-to-assets ratio will be maintained, but new debt will cost an expensive 18 percent! (The stock will be sold at $20 per share).

Under Plan B only new common stock at $20 per share will be issued. The tax rate is 40 percent.

a. If EBIT is 16 percent on assets, compute earnings per share (EPS) before the expansion and under the two alternatives.
b. What is the degree of financial leverage under each of the three plans?
c. If stock can be sold at $32 per share due to increased expectations about the firm's sales and earnings, what impact would this have on earnings per share for the two expansion alternatives? Compare earnings per share for each.
d. Explain why corporate financial officers are concerned about their stock values.

12. Using annual reports or a financial data base, compare the financial and operating leverage of Bell Canada Enterprises, Imperial Oil, and Canadian Airlines International for the most recent year. Explain the relationship between operating and financial leverage for each company and the resultant combined leverage. What accounts for the differences in leverage among these companies?

13. Mr. Gold is in the widget business. He currently sells 1 million widgets a year at $5 each. His variable cost to produce the widgets is $3 per unit, and he has $1.5 million in fixed costs. His sales-to-assets ratio is five times, and 40 percent of his assets are financed with 8 percent debt, with the balance financed by common stock at $10 per share. The tax rate is 40 percent.

His brother-in-law, Mr. Silverman, says he is doing it all wrong. By reducing his price to $4.50 a widget, he could increase his volume of units sold by 40 percent. Fixed costs would remain constant, and variable costs would remain $3 per unit. His sales-to-assets ratio would be 6.3 times. Furthermore, he could increase his debt-to-assets ratio to 50 percent, with the balance in common stock. It is assumed that the interest rate would go up by 1 percent and that the price of stock would remain constant.

a. Compute earnings per share under the Gold plan.
b. Compute earnings per share under the Silverman plan.
c. Mr. Gold's wife does not think that fixed costs would remain constant under the Silverman plan but that they would go up by 15 percent. If this is the case, should Mr. Gold shift to the Silverman plan, based on earnings per share?

14. Reynolds Calculators Inc. (RCI) is in the process of evaluating the company's break-even position and its operating and financial leverage. RCI has been selling 50,000 calculators per year for the last five years at $10 each. The fixed costs associated with this production are $250,000, and variable costs are $2 per calculator. RCI is currently producing at full capacity and has no debt. Management is expecting sales to increase by 10,000 units per year. To plan for this increase over the next five years, RCI is considering a program that would increase capacity to 100,000 units. The company would borrow $1 million at 12 percent to finance the expansion. They currently have no debt. Fixed costs would immediately rise to $400,000, and variable costs would remain at $2 per unit. The price would stay at $10 per unit.

a. What is the break-even point before expansion and after expansion?
b. What is the degree of operating leverage before expansion? (Use the formula in footnote 3.) What will DOL be one year and five years after expansion?
c. Calculate the degree of financial leverage and the degree of combined leverage before expansion, one year after expansion, and five years after expansion. (For degree of combined leverage, use the formula in footnote 5.) Note that in some calculations degree of financial leverage or degree of combined leverage may be negative.
d. Explain what causes the changes in break-even and leverage measures in calculations in parts *a*, *b*, and *c*.

15. Bertel Bottling Company is considering an expansion of its facilities. Its current income statement is as follows:

Sales	$4,000,000
Less: Variable expense (45% of sales)	1,800,000
Fixed expense	1,600,000
Earnings before interest and taxes (EBIT)	600,000
Interest (6% cost)	120,000
Earnings before taxes (EBT)	480,000
Tax (50%)	240,000
Earnings after taxes (EAT)	$ 240,000
Shares of common stock—200,000	
Earnings per share	$1.20

Bertel Bottling Company is currently financed with 50 percent debt and 50 percent equity (common stock). In order to expand its facilities Mr. Bertel estimates a need for $2 million in additional financing. His investment advisor has laid out three plans for him to consider:

1. Sell $2 million of debt at 9 percent.
2. Sell $2 million of common stock at $20 per share.
3. Sell $1 million of debt at 8 percent and $1 million of common stock at $25 per share.

Variable costs are expected to stay at 45 percent of sales, while fixed expenses will increase to $2.1 million per year. Mr. Bertel is not sure how much this expansion will add to sales, but he estimates that sales will rise by $800,000 per year for the next five years. Occasionally when the weather is cool in early spring and late fall, sales fall about 10 percent, but they usually return to their normal growth pattern the following year.

Mr. Bertel is interested in a thorough analysis of his expansion plans and methods of financing. He would like you to analyze the following:

a. The break-even point for operating expenses before and after expansion (in sales dollars).

b. The degree of operating leverage before and after expansion.

c. The degree of financial leverage before expansion and for all three methods of financing after expansion.

d. In addition, he would like an indifference graph of the three financing methods and your selection of the financing method that best suits his objective of maximizing shareholders' wealth.

16. (*Comprehensive problem for Chapters 2–5*)

BANFF SKI COMPANY
Balance Sheet
December 31,1987

Assets		Liabilities and Owners' Equity	
Cash	$ 40,000	Accounts payable	$1,800,000
Marketable securities	60,000	Accrued expenses	100,000
Accounts receivable	1,000,000	Notes payable (current)	600,000
Inventory	3,000,000	Bonds (10%)	2,000,000
Gross plant and equipment	5,000,000	Common stock (1.5 million shares)	1,500,000
Less: Accumulated depreciation	2,000,000	Retained earnings	1,100,000
Total assets	$7,100,000	Total liabilities and owners' equity	$7,100,000

Income Statement, 1987

Sales (credit)	$6,000,000
Fixed costs*	1,800,000
Variable costs (0.60)	3,600,000
Earnings before interest and taxes	600,000
Less: Interest	200,000
Earnings before taxes	400,000
Less: Taxes @ 40%	160,000
Earnings after taxes	240,000
Dividends	43,200
Increased retained earnings	$ 196,800

*Fixed costs include (*a*) lease expense of $190,000 and (*b*) depreciation of $400,000.

Note: Banff Ski also has $100,000 per year in sinking fund obligations associated with their bond issue. The sinking fund represents an annual repayment of the principal amount of the bond. It is not tax deductible.

Ratios

	Banff Ski (To be filled in)	*Industry*
Profit margin		6.1%
Return on assets		6.5%
Return on equity		8.9%
Receivables turnover		4.9×
Inventory turnover		4.4×
Fixed asset turnover		2.1×
Total asset turnover		1.06×
Current ratio		1.4×
Quick ratio		1.1×
Debt to total assets		27%
Interest coverage		4.2×
Fixed charge coverage		3.0×

a. Analyze Banff Ski Company, using ratio analysis. Compute the ratios above for Banff and compare them to the industry data that are given. Discuss the weak points, strong points, and what you think should be done to improve the company's performance.

b. In your analysis, calculate the overall break-even point in sales and the cash break-even point. Also compute the degree of operating leverage, degree of financial leverage, and degree of combined leverage.

c. Use the information in parts *a* and *b* to discuss the risk associated with this company. Given the risk, decide whether a bank should loan funds to Banff Ski.

Banff Ski Company is trying to plan their funds needed for 1988. The management anticipates an increase in sales of 20 percent, which can be absorbed without increasing fixed assets.

d. What would be Banff's needs for external funds, based on the current balance sheet? Compute RNF (required new funds).

e. What would be the required new funds if the company brings its ratios into line with the industry average during 1988? Specifically examine receivables turnover, inventory turnover, and the profit margin. Use the new values to recompute the factors in RNF (assume liabilities stay the same).

f. Do not calculate, only comment on these questions. How would required new funds change if the company:
(1) Were at full capacity?
(2) Raised the dividend payout ratio?
(3) Suffered a decreased growth in sales?
(4) Faced an accelerated inflation rate?

Selected References

Crowningshield, Gerald R., and George L. Battista. "Cost-Volume-Profit Analysis in Planning and Control." *N.A.A. Bulletin* 45 (July 1963), pp. 3–15.

Ghandhi, J. K. S. "On the Measurement of Leverage." *Journal of Finance* 21 (December 1966), pp. 15–26.

Hobbs, J. B. "Volume-Mix-Price Cost Budget Variance Analysis: A Proper Approach." *Accounting Review* 39 (October 1964), pp. 905–13.

Hugon, J. H. "Break-Even Analysis in Three Dimensions." *Financial Executive* 33 (December 1965), pp. 22–26.

Hunt, Pearson. "A Proposal for Precise Definitions of 'Trading on the Equity' and 'Leverage.' " *Journal of Finance* 16 (September 1961), pp. 377–86.

Jaedicke, Robert K., and Alexander A. Robichek. "Cost-Volume-Profit Analysis under Conditions of Uncertainty." *Accounting Review* 39 (October 1964), pp. 917–26.

Kelvie, W. E., and J. M. Sinclair. "New Technique for Break-Even Charts." *Financial Executive* 36 (June 1968), pp. 31–43.

Krainer, Robert W. "Interest Rates, Leverage, and Investor Rationality." *Journal of Financial and Quantitative Analysis* 12 (March 1977), pp. 1–16.

Lee, Wayne Y., and Henry H. Barker. "Bankruptcy Costs and the Firm's Optimal Debt Capacity: A Positive Theory of Capital Structure." *Southern Economic Journal* 43 (April 1977), pp. 1453–65.

Lev, Baruch. "On the Association between Operating Leverage and Risk." *Journal of Financial and Quantitative Analysis* 9 (September 1974), pp. 627–42.

Levy, Haim, and Robert Brooks. "Financial Break-Even Analysis and the Value of the Firm." *Financial Management* 15, no. 3 (Autumn 1986), pp. 22–26.

Percival, John R. "Operating Leverage and Risk." *Journal of Business Research* 2 (April 1974), pp. 223–27.

Raun, D. L. "The Limitations of Profit Graphs, Break-Even Analysis, and Budgets." *Accounting Review* 39 (October 1964), pp. 927–45.

Rendleman, Richard J., Jr. "The Effects of Default Risk on the Firm's Investment and Financing Decisions." *Financial Management* 7 (Spring 1978), pp. 45–53.

Salit, Sol S. "On the Mathematics of Financial Leverage." *Financial Management* 4 (Spring 1975), pp. 57–66.

Sarig, Oded, and James Scott. "The Puzzle of Financial Leverage Clienteles." *Journal of Finance* 40 (December 1985), pp. 1459–67.

Scott, David F., and Dana J. Johnson. "Financing Policies and Practices in Large Corporations." *Financial Management* 11 (Summer 1982), pp. 51–57.

Scott, David F., and J. D. Martin. "Industry Influence on Financial Structure." *Financial Management* 4 (Spring 1975), pp. 67–73.

PART

THREE

Working Capital Management

Introduction

Working capital policy involves the management of the current assets of the firm and the acquisition of the appropriate financing for those assets. While a firm may be able to sustain a decrease in sales or profitability for some period of time, the need for current assets and the associated financing is now.

Typical working capital decisions involve a determination of the appropriate level of cash, accounts receivable, and inventory that the firm should maintain. On the financing side we must determine whether to carry these assets through credit extension from our supplier, short-term bank loans, or longer-term credit arrangements. The smaller firm usually has a limited number of options.

As we shall see, one of the unfortunate choices of terms in the vernacular of finance and accounting is the phrase "current asset." The normal definition of a current asset is a short-term asset that can be converted to cash within one year or within the normal operating cycle of the firm. Regrettably, as a business begins to grow, some current assets become more "permanent" in nature—perhaps a portion of inventory is not liquidated and a growing volume of receivables, in aggregate, remains on the books. All too often firms think of current assets as being temporary when, in fact, a rather sizable portion require longer-term financing. The lesson about the true nature of current assets is well taught every three or four years, as the Canadian economy finds itself in a credit crunch, and financing cannot be found for "permanent" current assets.

In the initial chapter on working capital, Chapter 6, we examine some of the basic conceptual items related to working capital and the financing decision, with an eye toward the various risk-return alternatives available to the financial manager. We also look at the effects of various production policies on the financing requirements of the firm. In Chapter 7 we look at specific techniques for the management of cash, marketable securities, accounts receivable, and inventory.

Finally, in Chapter 8 we examine the various sources of short-term financing available to the firm. The emphasis is on trade credit, bank financing, and the use of secured loans through the pledging of receivables or inventory as collateral. The relative costs, advantages, and disadvantages of these financing outlets are considered.

6 Working Capital and the Financing Decision

The rapid growth of business firms in the post–World War II period has challenged the ingenuity of financial managers to provide adequate financing. Rapidly expanding sales may cause intense pressure for inventory and receivables buildup—draining the cash resources of the firm. As indicated in Chapter 4, Financial Forecasting, a large sales increase creates an expansion of current assets, especially accounts receivable and inventory. Some of the increased current assets can be financed by the firm's retained earnings, but in most cases internal funds will not provide enough financing, and some external sources of funds must be found. In fact, the faster the growth in sales, the more likely it is that an increasing percentage of financing will be external to the firm. These funds could come from the sale of common stock, preferred stock, long-term bonds, or short-term securities and bank loans or from a combination of short- and long-term sources of funds.

Working capital management involves the financing and management of the current assets of the firm. The financial executive probably devotes more time to working capital management than to any other activity. Current assets, by their very nature, are changing daily, if not hourly, and managerial decisions must be made. "How much inventory is to be carried, and how do we get the funds to pay for it?" Unlike long-term decisions, there can be no deferral of action. While long-term decisions, involving plant and equipment or market strategy, may well determine the eventual success of the firm, short-term decisions on working capital determine whether the firm gets to the long term.

In this chapter we examine the nature of asset growth, the process of matching sales and production, financial aspects of working capital management, and finally, the factors that go into the development of an optimum policy.

The Nature of Asset Growth

Any company that produces and sells a product, whether the product is consumer or industry oriented, will have current assets and fixed assets. If a firm grows, those assets are likely to increase over time. The key to current asset planning is the ability of management to forecast sales accurately and then to match the production schedules with the sales forecast. Whenever actual sales are different from forecasted sales, unexpected buildups or reductions in inventory will occur that will eventually affect receivables and cash flow.

In the simplest case, all of the firm's current assets will be self-liquidating (sold off at the end of a specified time period). For example, assume that at the start of the summer you buy 100 tires to be disposed of by September. It is your intention that all tires will be sold, receivables collected, and bills paid over this time period. In this case, your working capital (current asset) needs are truly short term.

Now let us begin to expand the business. In stage two you add radios, seat covers, and batteries to your operation. Some of your inventory will again be completely liquidated, while other items will form the basic stock for your operation. In order to stay in business you must maintain floor displays and multiple items for selection. Furthermore, not all items will sell. As you eventually grow to more than one store, this "permanent" aggregate stock of current assets will continue to increase. Problems of inadequate financing arrangements are often the result of the businessperson's failure to realize that the firm is carrying not only self-liquidating inventory—but also the anomaly of "permanent" current assets.

The movement from stage one to stage two growth for a typical business is depicted in Figure 6–1. In Panel A the buildup in current assets is temporary—while in Panel B part of the growth in current assets is temporary and part is permanent. (Fixed assets are included in the illustrations, but they are not directly related to the present discussion.)

Controlling Assets—Matching Sales and Production

In most firms fixed assets grow slowly as productive capacity is increased and old equipment is replaced, but current assets fluctuate in the short run, depending on the level of production versus the level

Figure 6–1
The nature of asset growth

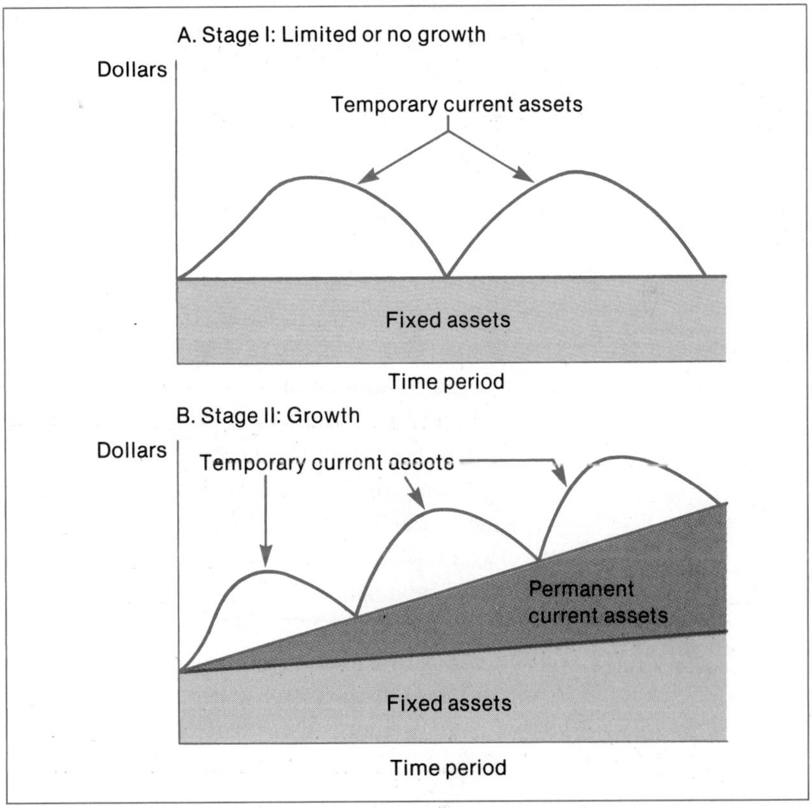

of sales. When the firm produces more than it sells, inventory rises. When sales rise faster than production, inventory declines and receivables rise.

As discussed in the treatment of the cash budgeting process in Chapter 4, some firms employ level production methods to smooth production schedules and use manpower and equipment efficiently at a lower cost. One consequence of level production is that current assets go up and down when sales and production are not equal. Other firms may try to match sales and production as closely as possible in the short run. This allows current assets to increase or decrease with the level of sales and eliminates the large seasonal bulges or sharp reductions in current assets that occur under level production.

Publishing companies are good examples of companies with seasonal sales and an inventory problem. By the nature of the textbook market, heavy sales are made in the third quarter of the year for fall semester sales. The bulk of the sales occurs in July and August and again in December for the second semester. The actual printing and binding of a book has fixed costs that make printing a large number of copies more efficient. Since publishing companies cannot reproduce books on demand, they contract with the printing company to print a fixed number of copies, depending upon expected sales over at least a one-year time period and sometimes based on sales over several years. If the books sell better than expected, the publishing company will order a second or third printing. Orders may have to be placed as much as nine months before the books will actually be needed, and reorders will be placed as much as three or four months ahead of actual sales. If the book declines in popularity, the publisher could get stuck with a large inventory of obsolete books.

Figure 6–2 depicts quarterly sales and earnings per share of a Canadian book publisher, McGraw-Hill Ryerson. This is a good example of a company with seasonal sales. Note that the largest sales and earnings occur in the third quarter of each year. If company management has not planned its inventory correctly, the lost sales or excess inventory could be a serious problem.

Retail firms such as Hudson's Bay and Sears Canada also have seasonal sales patterns. Figure 6–3 shows the quarterly sales and earnings per share of these two companies. These retail companies do not stock a year or more of inventory at one time as do the publishers. They generally sell products made by other firms. Therefore, retail stores

Figure 6–2
Sales and earnings for McGraw-Hill Ryerson

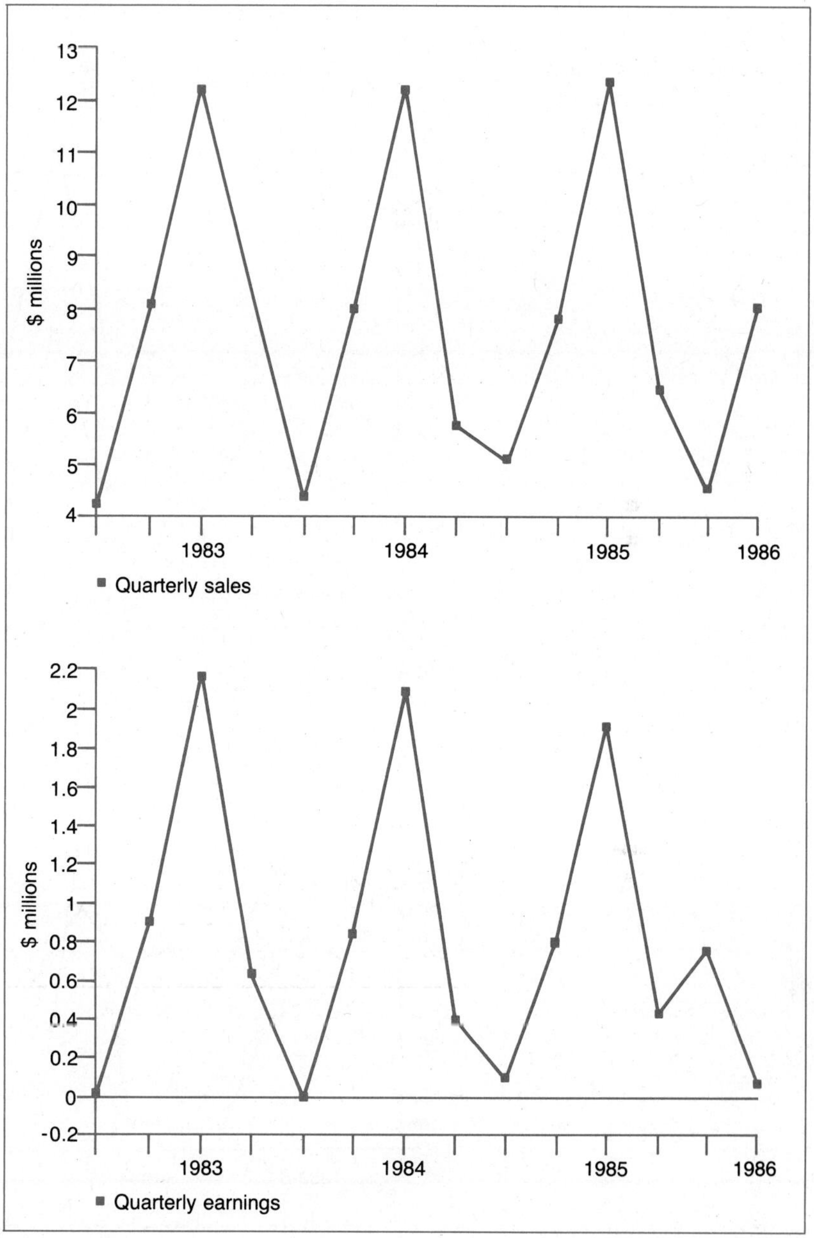

Figure 6–3
Sales and earnings for Hudson's Bay Co. and Sears Canada

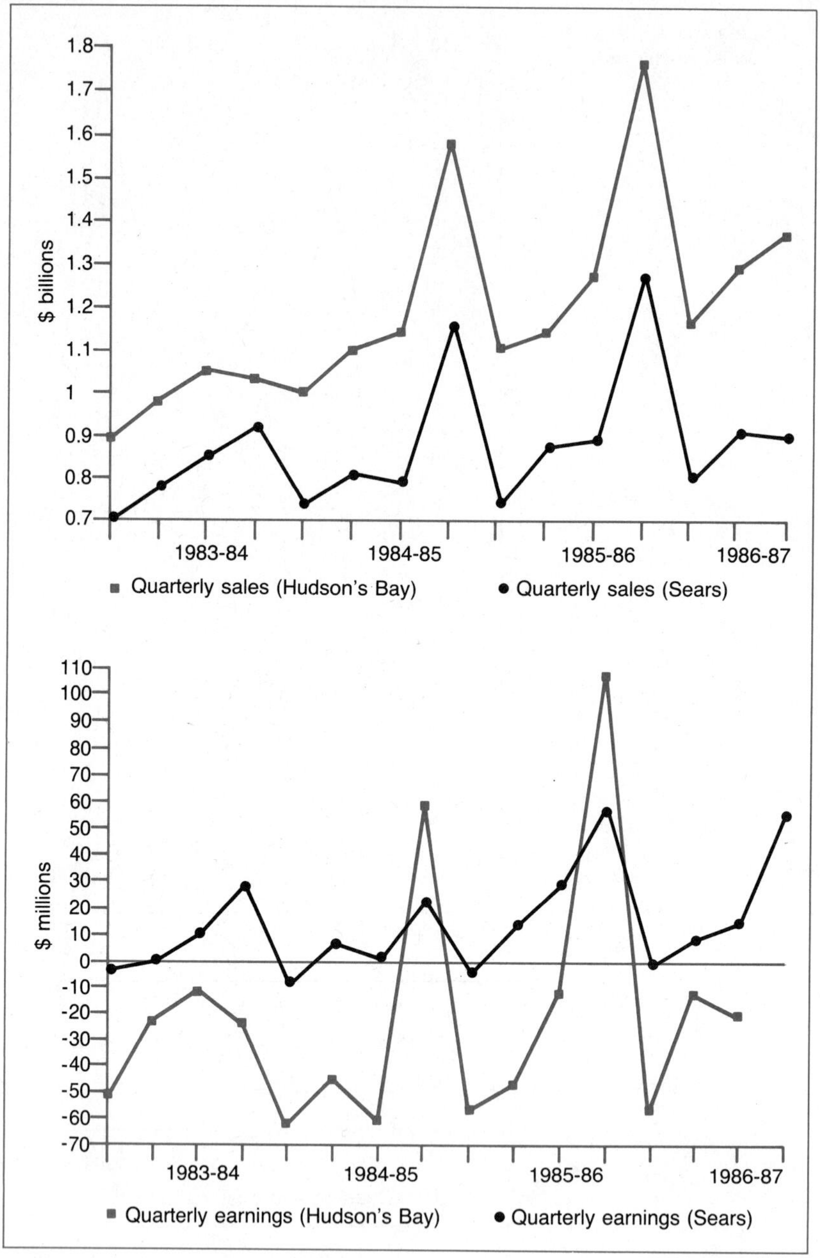

are not involved in deciding level versus seasonal production but, rather, must match sales and inventory. Their suppliers must make the decision to produce on either a level or on a seasonal basis. Since the selling seasons are very much impacted by the weather and holiday periods, the suppliers and retailers cannot avoid inventory risk. The fourth quarter beginning in October and ending in December is the biggest quarter for retailers and usually accounts for 50 percent or more of their annual earnings. Of course, inventory not sold during the Christmas season will probably end up being discounted in January.

Figure 6–3 demonstrates that over several years each peak and trough in quarterly sales was higher for each company. These seasonal peaks and troughs will also be reflected in cash, receivables, and inventory. We see that sales in the fourth quarter are usually 60 to 70 percent higher than those in the first quarter. Note how both companies demonstrate the impact of operating leverage on earnings as discussed in Chapter 5. In fact, Hudson's Bay incurred losses in all but the fourth quarters over the period charted.

As we go through the chapter we shall see that such highly seasonal sales can cause asset management problems. A financial manager must be aware of these to avoid getting caught short of cash or unprepared to borrow if necessary.

Many retail firms have been more successful in matching sales and orders in recent years because of new, computerized inventory control systems linked to on-line point-of-sale terminals. These point-of-sale terminals allow either digital input or use of optical scanners to record the inventory numbers and the amount of each item sold. At the end of the day managers are able to examine sales and inventory levels item by item and, if need be, to adjust orders or production schedules. The predictability of the market will influence the speed with which the manager reacts to this information, while the length and complexity of the ordering or production process will dictate just how fast inventory levels can be changed.

Temporary Assets under Level Production—An Example

In order to get a better understanding of how current assets fluctuate, let us use the example of the Yawakuzi Motorcycle Company, which manufactures in Southern Ontario and sells throughout Canada. Not many Canadians will be buying motorcycles during October through March, but sales will pick up in early spring and summer and will trail off during the fall. Because of the fixed assets and the skilled labor involved in the production process, Yawakuzi decides that level production is the least expensive and the most efficient production method. The marketing department provides a sales forecast for October through September (see Table 6–1).

After reviewing the sales forecast, Yawakuzi decides to produce 800 motorcycles per month, or one year's production of 9,600 divided by 12. A look at Table 6–2 shows how level production and seasonal sales combine to create fluctuating inventory. Assume that October's beginning inventory is one month's production of 800 units. The production cost per unit is $2,000.

The inventory level at cost fluctuates from a high of $9 million in March, the last consecutive month in which production is greater than sales, to a low of $1 million in August, the last month in which sales are greater than production. Table 6–3 combines a sales forecast, a cash receipts schedule, a cash payments schedule, and a brief cash budget in order to examine the buildup in accounts receivable and cash.

In Table 6–3 the *sales forecast* is based on assumptions in Table 6–1. The unit volume of sales is multiplied by a sales price of $3,000 to get sales dollars in millions. Next, *cash receipts* represent 50 percent collected in cash during the month of sale and 50 percent from the prior month's sales. For example, in October this would represent $0.45 million from the current month plus $0.75 million from the prior month's sales.

Table 6–1
Yawakuzi sales forecast (in units)

1st Quarter		*2nd Quarter*		*3rd Quarter*		*4th Quarter*	
October	300	January	0	April	1,000	July	2,000
November	150	February	0	May	2,000	August	1,000
December	50	March	600	June	2,000	September	500

Total sales of 9,600 units at $3,000 each = $28,800,000 in sales.

Table 6–2
Yawakuzi's production schedule and inventory

	Beginning Inventory	+	Production	−	Sales	=	Ending Inventory	Inventory (at cost of $2,000 per unit)
October	800		800		300		1,300	$2,600,000
November	1,300		800		150		1,950	3,900,000
December	1,950		800		50		2,700	5,400,000
January	2,700		800		0		3,500	7,000,000
February	3,500		800		0		4,300	8,600,000
March	4,300		800		600		4,500	9,000,000
April	4,500		800		1,000		4,300	8,600,000
May	4,300		800		2,000		3,100	6,200,000
June	3,100		800		2,000		1,900	3,800,000
July	1,900		800		2,000		700	1,400,000
August	700		800		1,000		500	1,000,000
September	500		800		500		800	1,600,000

Cash payments in Table 6–3 are based on an assumption of level production of 800 units per month at a cost of $2,000 per unit, or $1.6 million, plus payments for overhead, dividends, interest, and taxes.

Finally, the *cash budget* in Table 6–3 represents a comparison of the cash receipts and cash payments schedules to determine cash flow. We further assume that the firm desires a minimum cash balance of $0.25 million. Thus, in October a negative cash flow of $1.1 million brings the cumulative cash balance to a negative $0.85 million, and $1.1 million must be borrowed to provide an ending cash balance of $0.25 million. Similar negative cash flows in subsequent months necessitate expanding the bank loan. For example, in November there is a negative cash flow of $1.325 million. This brings the cumulative cash balance to $ − 1.075 million, requiring additional borrowings of $1.325 million to ensure a minimum cash balance of $0.25 million. The cumulative loan through November (October and November borrowings) now adds up to $2.425 million. Our cumulative bank loan is highest in the month of March.

We now wish to ascertain our total current asset buildup as a result of level production and fluctuating sales for October through September. The analysis is presented in Table 6–4. The cash figures come directly from the last line of Table 6–3. The accounts receivable balance is based on the assumption that accounts receivable represent 50 per-

Impt.

Table 6–3 Sales forecast, cash receipts and payments, and cash budget

	Oct.	Nov.	Dec.	Jan.	Feb.	March	April	May	June	July	Aug.	Sept.
Sales Forecast ($ millions)												
Sales (units)	300	150	50	0	0	600	1,000	2,000	2,000	2,000	1,000	500
Sales (unit price, $3,000)	$0.9	$0.45	$0.15	$ 0	$ 0	$1.8	$3.0	$6.0	$6.0	$6.0	$3.0	$1.5
Cash Receipts Schedule ($ millions)												
50% cash	$0.45	$0.225	$0.075	$ 0	$ 0	$0.9	$1.5	$3.0	$3.0	$3.0	$1.5	$0.75
50% from prior month's sales	0.75*	0.450	0.225	0.075	0	0	0.9	1.5	3.0	3.0	3.0	1.50
Total cash receipts	$1.20	$0.675	$0.300	$0.075	0	$0.9	$2.4	$4.5	$6.0	$6.0	$4.5	$2.25

*Assumes September sales of $1.5 million.

	Oct.	Nov.	Dec.	Jan.	Feb.	March	April	May	June	July	Aug.	Sept.
Cash Payments Schedule ($ millions)												
Constant production of 800 units/month (cost, $2,000 per unit)	$1.6	$1.6	$1.6	$1.6	$1.6	$1.6	$1.6	$1.6	$1.6	$1.6	$1.6	$1.6
Overhead	0.4	0.4	0.4	0.4	0.4	0.4	0.4	0.4	0.4	0.4	0.4	0.4
Dividends and interest	—	—	—	—	—	—	—	—	—	—	1.0	—
Taxes	0.3	—	—	0.3	—	—	0.3	—	—	0.3	—	—
Total cash payments	$2.3	$2.0	$2.0	$2.3	$2.0	$2.0	$2.3	$2.0	$2.0	$2.3	$3.0	$2.0
Cash Budget ($ millions; required minimum balance is $0.25 million)												
Cash flow	$(1.1)	$(1.325)	$(1.7)	$(2.225)	$(2.0)	$(1.1)	$0.1	$2.5	$4.0	$3.7	$1.5	$0.25
Beginning cash	0.25†	0.25	0.25	0.250	0.25	0.25	0.25	0.25	0.25	0.25	1.1	2.60
Cumulative cash balance	$(0.85)	$(1.075)	$(1.45)	$(1.975)	$(1.75)	$(0.85)	$0.35	$2.75	$4.25	$3.95	$2.6	$2.85
Monthly loan or (repayment)	1.1	1.325	1.7	2.225	2.0	1.1	(0.1)	(2.5)	(4.0)	(2.85)	0	0
Cumulative loan	1.1	2.425	4.125	6.350	8.350	9.45	9.35	6.85	2.85	0	0	0
Ending cash balance	0.25	0.25	0.25	0.25	0.25	0.25	0.25	0.25	0.25	1.1	2.6	2.85

†Assumes cash balance of $0.25 million at the beginning of October and that this is the desired minimum cash balance.

Table 6–4
Total current assets, first year ($ millions)

	Cash	Accounts Receivable	Inventory	Total Current Assets
October	$0.25	$0.45	$2.6	$ 3.3
November	0.25	0.225	3.9	4.375
December	0.25	0.075	5.4	5.725
January	0.25	0.000	7.0	7.25
February	0.25	0.000	8.6	8.85
March	0.25	0.90	9.0	10.15
April	0.25	1.50	8.6	10.35
May	0.25	3.00	6.2	9.45
June	0.25	3.00	3.8	7.05
July	1.10	3.00	1.4	5.50
August	2.60	1.50	1.0	5.10
September	2.85	0.75	1.6	5.20

cent of sales in a given month, as the other 50 percent is paid for in cash. Thus, the accounts receivable figure in Table 6–4 represents 50 percent of the sales figure from the second numerical line in Table 6–3. Finally, the inventory figure is taken directly from the last column of Table 6–2, which presented the production schedule and inventory data.

Total current assets start at $3.3 million in October and rise to $10.35 million in the peak month of April. From April through August sales are larger than production and inventory falls to its low of $1.0 million in August, but accounts receivables peak at $3.0 million in the highest sales months of May, June, and July. The cash budget in Table 6–3 explains the cash flows and external funds borrowed to finance asset accumulation. From October to March Yawakuzi borrows more and more money to finance the inventory buildup, but from April to July it eliminates all borrowing as inventory is liquidated and cash balances rise to complete the cycle. In October the cycle starts all over again; but now the firm has accumulated cash which it can use to finance next year's asset accumulation, pay a larger dividend, replace old equipment, or—if growth in sales is anticipated—invest in new equipment to increase productive capacity. Table 6–5 presents the cash budget and total current assets for the second year. Under a simplified no-growth assumption, the monthly cash flow is the same as that of the first year, but beginning cash in October is much higher from the first year's ending cash balance. This lowers the borrowing requirement

Table 6–5 Cash budget and assets for second year with no growth in sales (millions)

	End of First Year	Second Year											
	Sept.	Oct.	Nov.	Dec.	Jan.	Feb.	March	April	May	June	July	Aug.	Sept.
Cash flow	$0.25	$(1.1)	$(1.325)	$(1.7)	$(2.225)	$(2.0)	$(1.1)	$0.1	$2.5	$4.0	$3.7	$1.5	$0.25
Beginning cash	2.60	2.85	1.750	0.425	0.25	0.25	0.25	0.25	0.25	0.25	0.25	3.7	5.2
Cumulative cash balance		1.75	0.425	(1.275)	(1.975)	(1.75)	(0.85)	0.35	2.75	4.25	3.95	5.2	5.45
Monthly loan or (repayment)		—	—	1.525	2.225	2.0	1.1	(0.1)	(2.5)	4.0	(0.25)	—	—
Cumulative loan		—	—	1.525	3.750	5.75	6.85	6.75	4.25	0.25	0	—	—
Ending cash balance	$2.85	$1.75	$0.425	$0.25	$0.25	$0.25	$0.25	$0.25	$0.25	$0.25	$3.70	$5.2	$5.45
						Total Current Assets							
Ending cash balance	$2.85	$1.75	$0.425	$0.250	$0.25	$0.25	$0.25	$0.25	$0.25	$0.25	$3.70	$5.2	$5.45
Accounts receivable	0.75	0.45	0.225	0.075	0	0	0.90	1.50	3.00	3.00	3.00	1.5	0.75
Inventory	1.60	2.60	3.900	5.400	7.00	8.60	9.00	8.60	6.20	3.80	1.40	1.0	1.60
Total current assets	$5.20	$4.80	$4.550	$5.725	$7.25	$8.85	$10.15	$10.35	$9.45	$7.05	$8.10	$7.7	$7.80

Figure 6–4
The nature of asset growth (Yawakuzi)

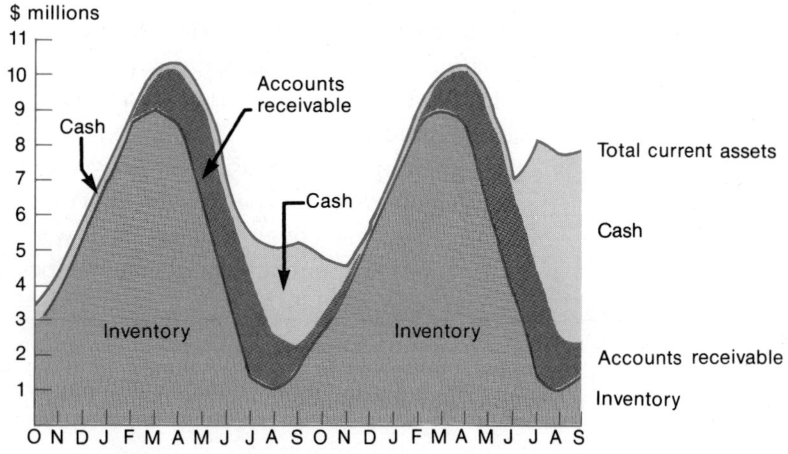

and increases the ending cash balance and total current assets at year-end. Higher current assets are present in spite of the fact accounts receivable and inventory do not change.

Figure 6–4 is a graphic presentation of the current asset cycle. It includes the two years covered in Tables 6–4 and 6–5 assuming level production and no sales growth.

Patterns of Financing

The financial manager's selection of external sources of funds may be one of the firm's most important decisions. The axiom that all current assets should be financed by current liabilities (accounts payable, bank loans, commercial paper, etc.) is subject to challenge when one sees the permanent buildup that can take place in current assets. In the Yawakuzi example the buildup in inventory was substantial, at $9 million. The example had a logical conclusion in that the motorcycles were sold, cash was generated, and current assets became very liquid. What if a much smaller level of sales had occurred? Yawakuzi would be sitting on a large inventory which needed to be financed and would be generating no cash. Theoretically, the firm could be declared technically insolvent (bankrupt) if short-term sources of funds were used but were unable to be renewed when they came due. How would the interest and principal be paid without cash flow from inventory liquidation? The most appropriate financing pattern would be one in which asset buildup and length of financing terms are perfectly matched, as indicated in Figure 6–5.

In the upper part of Figure 6–5 we see that the temporary buildup in current assets is financed by short-term funds. More important, however, permanent current assets, as well as fixed assets, are financed with long-term funds from the sale of stock, the issuance of bonds, or retention of earnings.

Alternative Plans

Only a financial manager with unusual insight and timing could construct a financial plan for working capital that adhered perfectly to the design in Figure 6–5. The difficulty rests in precisely determining what part of current assets is temporary and what part is permanent. Even if dollar amounts could be ascertained, the exact timing of asset liquidation is a difficult matter. To compound the problem, we are never quite sure how much short-term or long-term financing is available at a given point in time. While the precise synchronization of temporary current assets and short-term financing depicted in Figure 6–5 may be the most desirable and logical plan, other alternatives must be considered.

Figure 6–5
Matching long-term and short-term needs

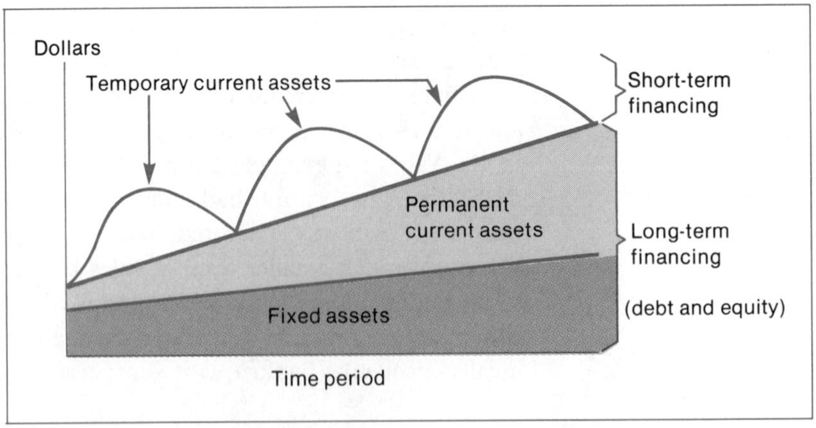

Long-Term Financing

To protect against the danger of not being able to provide adequate short-term financing in tight money periods, the financial manager may rely on long-term funds to cover some short-term needs. As indicated in Figure 6–6, long-term capital is now being used to finance fixed assets, permanent current assets, and part of *temporary current assets.*

By using long-term capital to cover short-term needs, the firm virtually assures itself of having adequate capital at all times. The firm may prefer to borrow a million dollars for 10 years—rather than attempt to borrow a million dollars at the beginning of each year for 10 years and paying it back at the end of each year.

Short-Term Financing (Opposite Approach)

This is not to say that all financial managers utilize long-term financing on a large scale. In order to acquire long-term funds the firm must generally go to the capital markets with a bond or stock offering or must privately place longer-term obligations with insurance companies, wealthy individuals, and so forth. Many small businesses do not have access to such long-term capital and are forced to rely heavily on short-term bank and trade credit. In the capital shortage era of the last decade, even some large businesses were forced to operate with short-term funds.

Figure 6–6
Using long-term financing for part of short-term needs

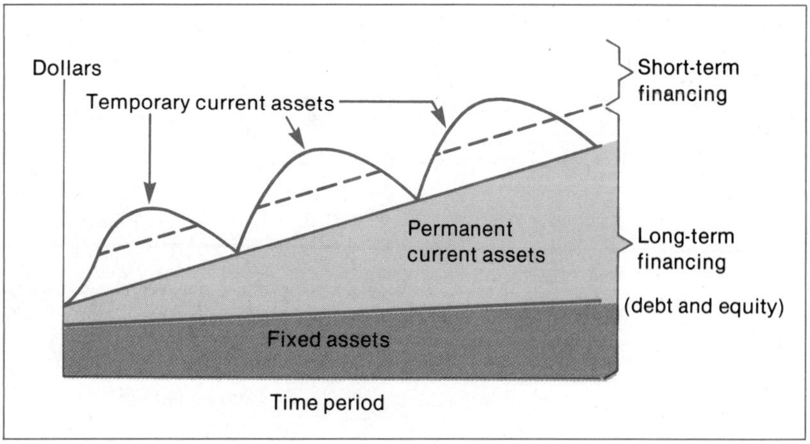

Furthermore, short-term financing does offer some advantages over more extended financial arrangements. As a general rule the interest rate on short-term funds is lower than that on long-term funds. We might surmise then that a firm could develop a working capital financing plan in which short-term funds are used to finance not only temporary current assets but also part of the permanent working capital needs of the firm. As depicted in Figure 6–7, bank and trade credit as well as other sources of short-term financing are now supporting part of the permanent current asset needs of the firm.

The Financing Decision

Some corporations are more flexible than others because they are not locked into a few available sources of funds. Corporations would like many financing alternatives in order to minimize their cost of funds at any point in time. Unfortunately, not many firms are in this enviable position through the duration of a business cycle. During an economic boom period, a shortage of low-cost alternatives exists, and firms often minimize their financing costs by raising funds in advance of forecasted asset needs.

Not only does the financial manager encounter a timing problem, but he also needs to select the right type of financing. Even for companies having many alternative sources of funds, there may be only one or two decisions that will look good in retrospect. At the time the financing decision is made, the financial manager is never sure it is the right one. Should the financing be long-term or short-term, debt or

Figure 6–7
Using short-term financing for part of long-term needs

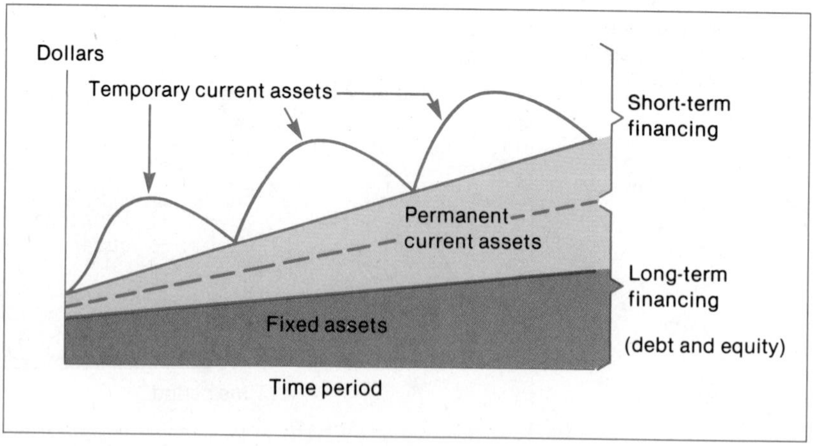

equity, and so on? Figure 6–8 is a decision-tree diagram which shows many of the financing decisions that can be made. At each point a decision is made until a final financing method is reached. In most cases a corporation will use a combination of these financing methods. At all times the financial manager will balance short-term versus long-term considerations against the composition of the firm's assets and the firm's willingness to accept risk. The ratio of long-term financing to short-term financing at any point in time will be greatly influenced by the term structure of interest rates.

Figure 6–8
Decision tree of the financing decision

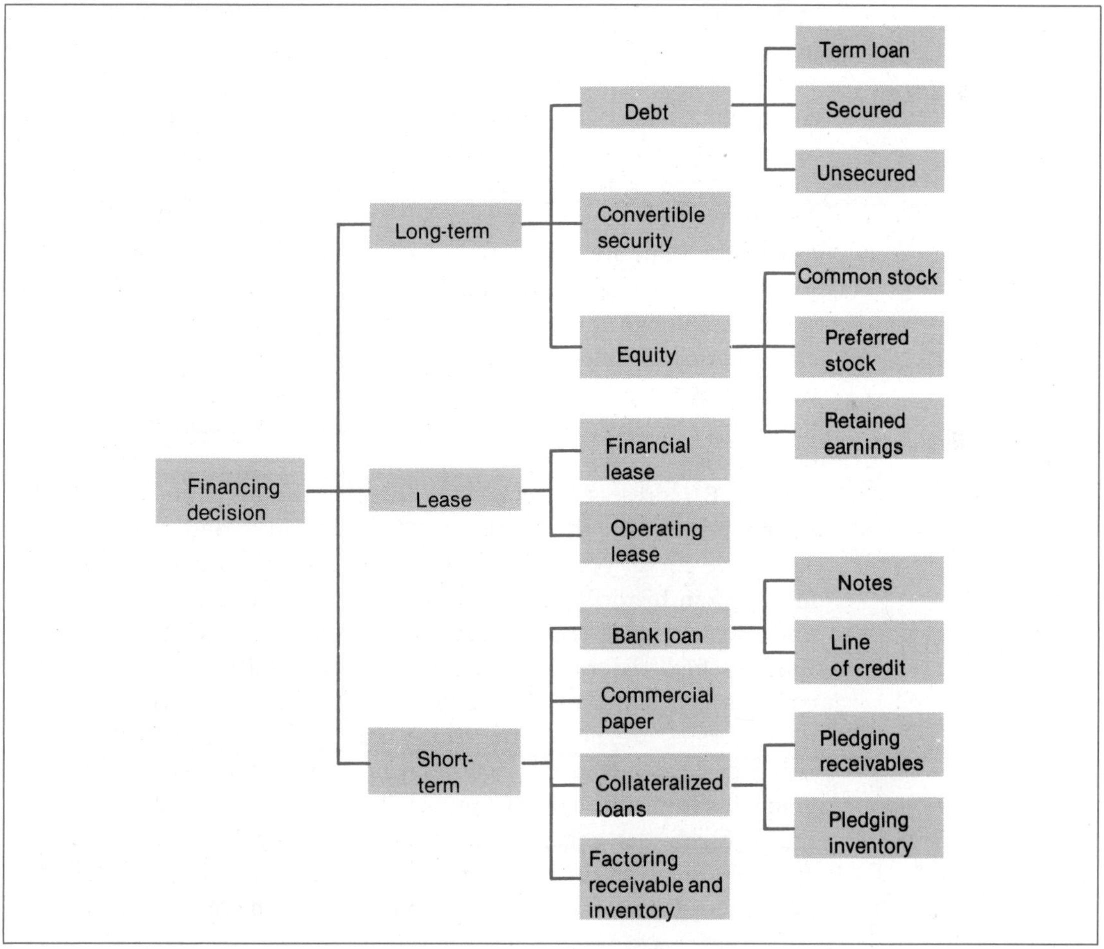

Term Structure of Interest Rates

The term structure of interest rates is often referred to as a yield curve. It shows the interest rate at a specific time for all securities having equal risk but differing maturity dates. Generally, Government of Canada securities are used to construct yield curves because they have many maturities, and each of the securities has an equally low risk of default. Corporate securities will move in the same direction as government securities but will have higher interest rates because of their greater financial risk. Yield curves for both corporations and government securities change daily to reflect current competitive conditions in the money and capital markets, expected inflation, changes in economic conditions, and the strength of the Canadian dollar in international currency markets.

Figure 6–9 depicts four panels of term structures (yield curves) covering 13 years. These four panels present very different pictures of interest-rate cycles over highly unusual economic times.

Panel A shows five yield curves over a period of falling interest rates. The November 1969 curve is called a humped curve because the intermediate rates are higher than both the short- and long-term rates. By March 1970 the curve had shifted to become generally upward sloping, although the slope was rather gradual. The next three curves are progressively more upward sloping, indicating that short-term interest rates tended to decline much more rapidly than did the long-term ones. These upward-sloping yield curves are considered to be the normal case.

Panel B represents interest rate changes in a period of rising rates. If you begin with the January 1978 yield curve and move to each successive curve, you will trace the most dramatic rise in interest rates in Canadian history—caused, in part, by record high inflation rates. You also see that short-term rates on Government of Canada Treasury Bills reached historic highs in the summer of 1981. The July 1981 curve is called downward sloping, or inverted, because short-term interest rates are higher than long-term rates. In fact, through the rising cycle depicted by Panel B you see the term structure going gradually from the normal upward-sloping curve of January 1978 to the relatively flat curves of October 1978, July 1979, and February 1980 and finally to the inverted curves of March and July of 1981. The high interest rates during the latter period were the result of an attempt by the Bank of Canada to break the back of the inflationary spiral (despite a weak economy). By late 1982 the restrictive policy of the bank had reduced inflation to a moderate level but not without a 20-month recession that ended in January 1983. It was that recession that finally caused interest rates to decline as shown in Panel C.

It is important to realize how dramatically interest rates can change in a short period of time. Between June and October of 1982 interest rates on intermediate- and long-term securities dropped by over 3 percentage points. This rapid drop in interest rates during 1982 caused a substantial increase in the prices of long-term bonds, rewarding investors in long-term bonds with annual returns in excess of 40 percent. Many Canadian pension funds did extremely well over that period.

Interest rates are influenced by many variables, but in recent years inflation has had a large effect in boosting interest rates to record levels. As inflation increases lenders charge a premium for the lost purchasing power they will have when the loan is repaid in "cheaper" inflated dollars. Although short-term rates are influenced more by current demands for money than by inflation, long-term rates are greatly affected by the expected rate of inflation over the life of the investment. The downward shift in yield curves between March 1970 and March 1971 can be partly attributed to a decline in the rate of inflation. Conversely, the increasing interest rates over the 1977–81 period were directly related to the spiraling, double-digit inflation and ballooning government deficits.

A business recovery began in January 1983, and Panel D of Figure 6–9 shows the resulting rise in rates from April 1983 to June 1984. As economic growth slowed in late 1984 and as inflation sank to low levels, interest rates dropped to their lowest level in many years, though not to the levels in Panel A. During 1984, 1985, and 1986 inflation was stable at rates of around 4 percent. Panel D shows, as did Panel B, the dramatic changes that can take place in even long-term interest rates. Between June 1984 and August 1986 long-term interest rates in Canada decreased by over 4½ percentage points. Strengthening of the Canadian dollar in terms of the U.S. dollar in foreign exchange markets in early May 1987 led to further reductions in interest rates in Canada as the Bank of Canada moved to moderate the increase in the foreign exchange value of the Canadian dollar. This important relationship between interest rates and the foreign exchange value of the Canadian dollar is covered in Chapter 21, which deals with international finance.

Figure 6–9
A falling term structure

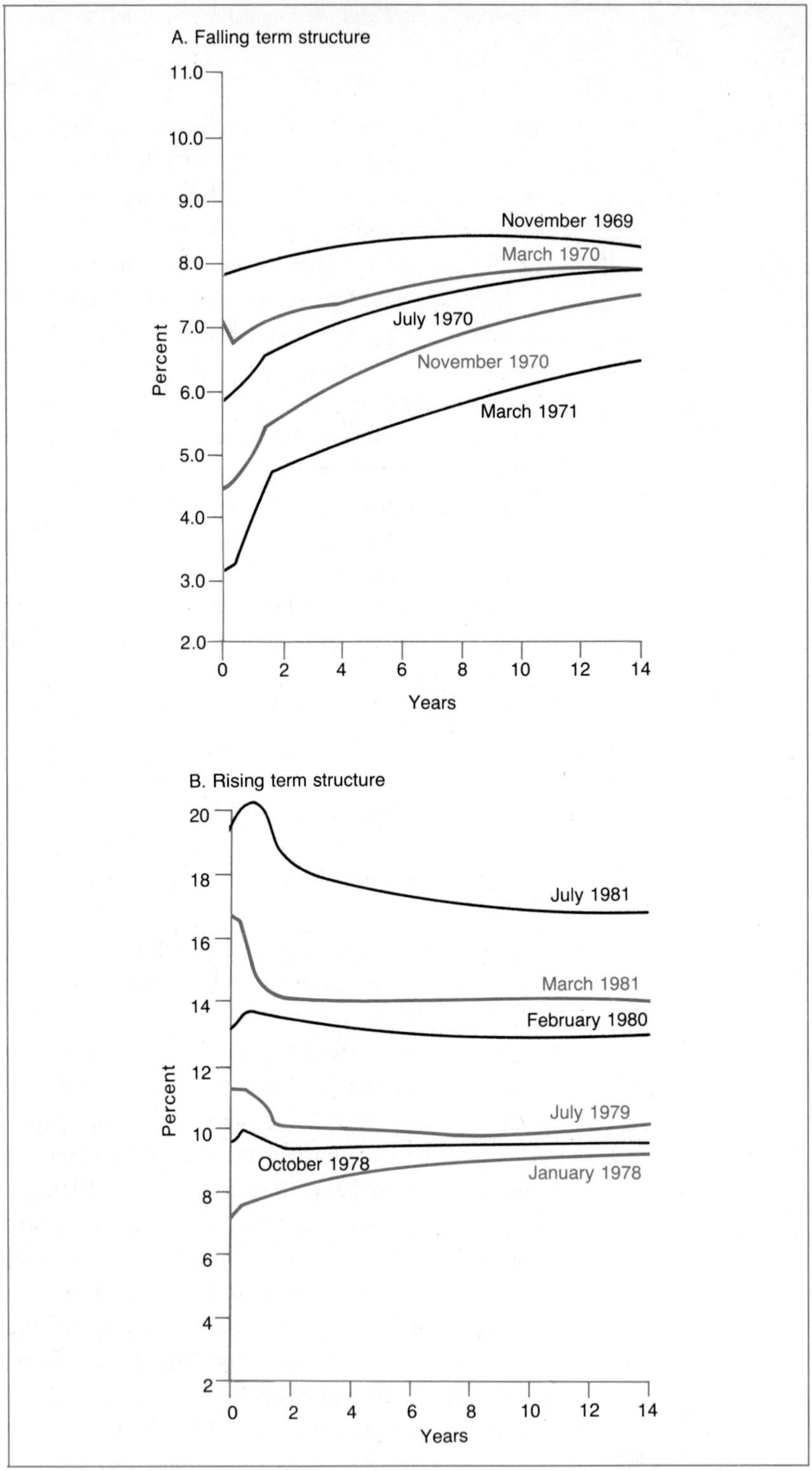

Figure 6–9 *(concluded)*

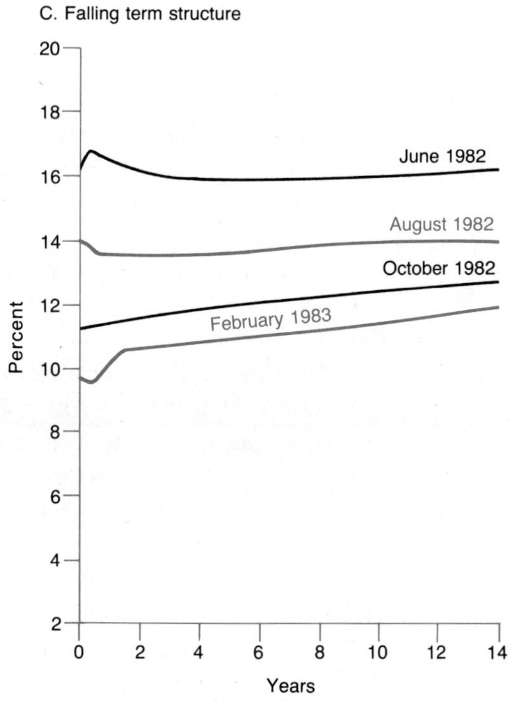

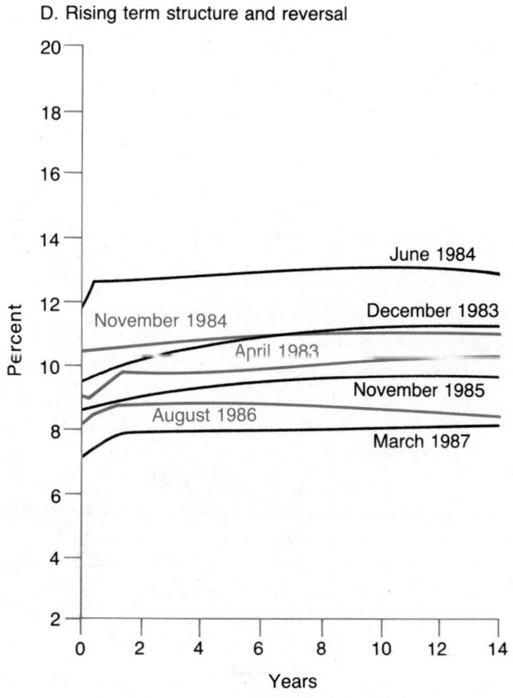

In designing working capital policy, the astute financial manager is interested not only in the term structure of interest rates but also in the relative volatility and the historical level of short-term and long-term rates. Figure 6–10 uses long-term A+ + rated corporate bonds and short-term commercial paper to provide insight into interest rate volatility over a long period of time.

Especially in the period between 1970 and 1983 we see demonstrated the large historical differences in relative volatility between short- and long-term rates. Short-term rates were much more volatile than long-term rates. As a general rule short-term rates have been lower than long-term rates, but there have been a number of exceptions. Note that while short-term rates have fluctuated wildly about long-term rates, since 1965 long-term rates have moved dramatically higher and have consistently stayed well above pre-1965 rates. This is largely due to the fact that in the period from 1965 on, inflation rates have been much higher than they had been previous to that time.

How should a financial manager respond to fluctuating interest rates and changing term structures? When interest rates are high, the fi-

Figure 6–10
Long- and short-term interest rates

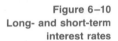

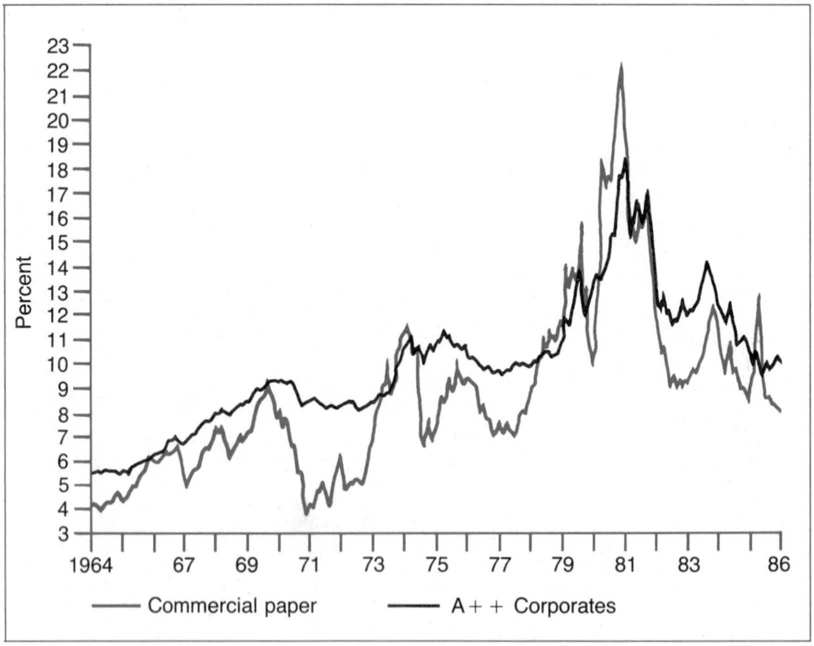

nancial manager generally prefers to borrow short term (if funds are available). As rates decline the financial officer will try to lock in lower rates with long-term borrowing. Some of these long-term funds will be used to reduce short-term debt, and the rest will be available for future expansion. Expansion generally requires additional investment in both fixed assets (plant and equipment) and in working capital.

A Decision Process

Assume we are comparing alternative financing plans for working capital. As indicated in Table 6–6 $500,000 of working capital (current assets) must be financed for the Edwards Corporation. Under Plan A we will finance all our current asset needs with short-term funds, while under Plan B we will finance only a relatively small portion of working capital with short-term money—relying heavily on long-term funds. In either case we will carry $100,000 of fixed assets with long-term financing commitments. As indicated in Part 3 of Table 6–6, under Plan A we will finance total needs of $600,000 with $500,000 of short-term financing and $100,000 of long-term financing, whereas with Plan B we will finance $150,000 short term and $450,000 long term.

Plan A carries the lower cost of financing, with interest of 6 percent on $500,000 of the $600,000 required. We show the impact of both

Table 6–6
Alternative financing plans

EDWARDS CORPORATION

	Plan A	*Plan B*
Part 1. Current assets		
Temporary	$250,000	$250,000
Permanent	250,000	250,000
Total current assets	500,000	500,000
Short-term financing (6%)	500,000	150,000
Long-term financing (10%)	0	350,000
	$500,000	$500,000
Part 2. Fixed assets	$100,000	$100,000
Long-term financing (10%)	$100,000	$100,000
Part 3. Total financing (summary of parts 1 and 2)		
Short-term (6%)	$500,000	$150,000
Long-term (10%)	100,000	450,000
	$600,000	$600,000

Table 6–7
Impact of financing plans on earnings

EDWARDS CORPORATION

Plan A	
Earnings before interest and taxes	$200,000
Interest (short-term): 6% × $500,000	− 30,000
Interest (long-term): 10% × $100,000	− 10,000
Earnings before taxes	160,000
Taxes (50%)	80,000
Earnings after taxes	$ 80,000
Plan B	
Earnings before interest and taxes	$200,000
Interest (short-term): 6% × $150,000	− 9,000
Interest (long-term): 10% × $450,000	− 45,000
Earnings before taxes	146,000
Taxes (50%)	73,000
Earnings after taxes	$ 73,000

plans on bottom-line earnings in Table 6–7.[1] Assuming that the firm generates $200,000 in earnings before interest and taxes, Plan A will provide aftertax earnings of $80,000, while Plan B will generate only $73,000.

Introducing Varying Conditions

Although Plan A, employing cheaper short-term sources of financing, appears to provide $7,000 more in return, this is not always the case. During tight money periods, short-term financing may be difficult to find or may carry exorbitant rates. Furthermore, inadequate financing may mean lost sales or financial embarrassment. For these reasons the firm may wish to evaluate Plans A and B based on differing assumptions about the economy and the money markets.

Expected Value

Past history combined with economic forecasting may indicate an 80 percent probability of normal events and a 20 percent chance of

[1]Common stock is eliminated from the example to simplify the analysis. If it were included, all of the basic patterns would still hold.

extremely tight money. Using Plan A, under normal conditions the Edwards Corporation will enjoy a $7,000 superior return over Plan B (as indicated in Table 6–7). Let us now assume that under disruptive tight money conditions, Plan A would provide a $15,000 lower return than Plan B because of high short-term interest rates. These conditions are summarized inTable 6–8, and an expected value of return is computed. The expected value represents the sum of the expected outcomes under the two conditions.

We see that even when downside risk is considered, Plan A carries a higher expected return of $2,600. For another firm in the same industry that might suffer $50,000 lower returns during tight money conditions, Plan A becomes too dangerous to undertake, as indicated in Table 6–9. Plan A's expected return is now $4,400 less than that of Plan B.

Table 6–8
Expected returns under different economic conditions

EDWARDS CORPORATION

1.	Normal conditions	Expected higher return under Plan A		Probability of normal conditions		Expected outcome
		$7,000	×	.80	=	+ $5,600
2.	Tight money	Expected lower return under Plan A		Probability of tight money		
		($15,000)	×	.20	=	(3,000)
Expected value of return for Plan A versus Plan B					=	+ $2,600

Table 6–9
Expected returns for high-risk firm

1.	Normal conditions	Expected higher return under Plan A		Probability of normal contitions		Expected outcome
		$7,000	×	.80	=	+ $5,600
2.	Tight money	Expected lower return under Plan A		Probability of tight money		
		($50,000)	×	.20	=	(10,000)
Negative expected value of return for Plan A versus Plan B					=	($4,400)

Shifts in Asset Structure

Thus far our attention has been directed to the risk associated with various financing plans. Risk-return analysis must also be carried to the asset side. A firm with heavy risk exposure due to short-term borrowing may compensate in part by carrying highly liquid assets. Conversely, a firm with established long-term debt commitments may choose to carry a heavier component of less liquid, highly profitable assets.

Either through desire or compelling circumstances, business firms have decreased the liquidity of their current asset holdings since the early 1960s. The increased cost of financing current assets resulting from the general rise in interest rates may be the major reason for this decline. For example, in Table 6–10 we see that for Canadian nonfinancial corporations cash and equivalents decreased from 21.36 percent of current assets in 1962 to 14.62 percent in 1981 while inventory increased from 41.84 percent of current assets in 1962 to 47.0 percent in 1981. The ratio of cash and cash equivalents to current liabilities had fallen from 44.55 percent at the end of 1962 to approximately 19.5 percent by 1982, a decline in terms of current liability coverage of over 50 percent. Since 1982 these liquidity percentages have improved although the coverage of current liabilities by cash and equivalents was still 40 percent less in 1986 than it was in 1962. Clearly, Canadian nonfinancial corporations are less liquid today than 25 years ago. In turn, they are far more liquid today than they were during the recession of 1981–82.

The reasons for diminishing liquidity can be traced in part to more sophisticated, profit-oriented financial management as well as better utilization of cash balances via computer. Less liquidity can also be traced to the long-term effect inflation has had on the corporate balance sheet—forcing greater borrowing to carry more expensive assets—and to decreasing profitability during recessions. To demonstrate these effects in terms of current ratio changes, Figure 6–11 graphs the average current ratio over time for Canadian nonfinancial corporations. In the early 1960s, the average current ratio was slightly above 2.0:1. That ratio steadily declined from that time until it reached 1.53:1 as of the end of 1974. After the recession of 1974–75 corporate liquidity increased slightly with the average current ratio remaining between 1.58 and 1.66:1 until the long and severe recession of 1981–82. By the end

Table 6–10 Current asset position ($ billions): Canadian nonfinancial corporations

	Cash and Equivalents		Accounts Receivable		Inventory	
Year	Percent of Current Assets	Percent of Current Liabilities	Percent of Current Assets	Percent of Current Liabilities	Percent of Current Assets	Percent of Current Liabilities
1962	21.36%	44.55%	34.78%	72.45%	41.84%	87.15%
1971	16.49	30.93	40.81	76.55	39.98	74.99
1978	15.78	25.86	39.20	64.07	42.92	70.15
1981	14.62	22.06	38.36	57.88	47.00	70.92
1982	15.11	19.53	39.06	50.45	43.50	56.18
1984	17.99	24.72	39.31	54.01	40.34	55.42
1986	19.09	26.80	39.26	55.12	38.31	53.78

Note: The data for pre-1970 are for all nonfinancial corporations, while those from 1977 on are for nonfinancial corporations having more than $10 million in assets.
Sources: Statistics Canada, *Industrial Corporations, Financial Statistics,* Catalogue #61-003, Quarterly, various.

Figure 6–11
Industrial corporations' current ratio

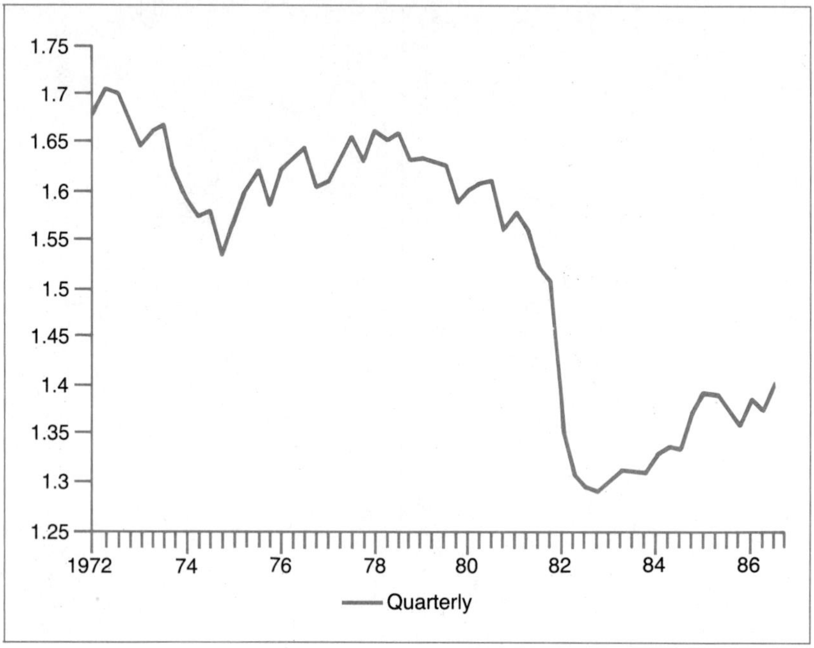

of that recession the average current ratio had fallen to 1.29:1. Even after that recession was over the ratio recovered only modestly to stay at historically low levels between 1.30 and 1.40:1.

Toward an Optimal Policy

As previously indicated the firm should attempt to relate financing patterns to asset liquidity and vice versa. In Table 6–11 a number of different working capital alternatives are presented. Along the top of the table is asset liquidity; along the side, the type of financing arrangement. The combined impact of the two variables is shown in each of the four panels of the table.

Each firm must decide how it wishes to combine asset liquidity and financing needs. The aggressive, risk-oriented firm in Panel 1 of Table 6–11 will borrow short term and maintain relatively low levels of liquidity, hoping to increase profit. It will benefit from low-cost financing and high-return assets, but it will be vulnerable to a credit crunch. The more conservative firm, following the plan in Panel 4,

Table 6–11
Asset liquidity and financing assets

Financing Plan	Low Liquidity	High Liquidity
Short-term	1 High profit High risk	2 Moderate profit Moderate risk
Long-term	3 Moderate profit Moderate risk	4 Low profit Low risk

will utilize established long-term financing and maintain a high degree of liquidity. In Panels 2 and 3 we see more moderate positions in which the firm compensates for short-term financing with highly liquid assets (2) or balances off low liquidity with precommitted, long-term financing (3).

Each financial manager must structure his or her working capital position and the associated risk-return trade-off to meet the company's needs. For firms whose cash flow patterns are predictable, typified by the public utilities sector, a low degree of liquidity can be maintained. Immediate access to capital markets, such as that enjoyed by large, prestigious firms, also allows a greater risk-taking capability. In each case the ultimate concern must be for maximizing the overall valuation of the firm through a judicious consideration of risk-return options.

In the next two chapters we will examine the various methods for managing the individual components of working capital. In Chapter 7 we consider the techniques for managing cash, marketable securities, receivables, and inventory. In Chapter 8 we look at trade and bank credit and also at other sources of short-term funds.

Summary

Working capital management involves the financing and management of the current assets of the firm. A firm's ability to properly manage current assets and the associated liability obligations may determine how well it is able to survive in the short run. To the extent that part of the buildup in current assets is permanent, financial arrangements should carry longer maturities.

The financial manager must also give careful attention to the relationship of the production process to sales. Level production in a seasonal sales environment increases operating efficiency, but it also calls for more careful financial planning. The astute financial manager must also keep an eye on the general cost of borrowing, the term structure of interest rates, and the relative volatility of short- and long-term rates.

The firm has a number of risk-return decisions to consider. Though long-term financing provides a safety margin in availability of funds, its higher cost may reduce the profit potential of the firm. On the asset side, carrying highly liquid current assets assures the bill-paying capability of the firm—but detracts from profit potential. Each firm must tailor the various risk-return trade-offs to meet its own needs. The peculiarities of a firm's industry will have a major impact on the options open to management.

List of Terms

working capital management
self-liquidating assets
"permanent" current assets
temporary current assets
trade credit
level production
point-of-sales terminals
liquidity
term structure of interest rates
expected value
tight money
normal yield curve
inverted yield curve

Discussion Questions

1. Explain how rapidly expanding sales can drain the cash resources of the firm.
2. Discuss the relative volatility of short- and long-term interest rates.
3. What is the significance to working capital management of matching sales and production?
4. How is a cash budget used to help manage current assets?
5. Discuss the impact of inflation on working capital management.

6. "The most appropriate financing pattern would be one in which asset buildup and length of financing terms are perfectly matched." Discuss the difficulty involved in achieving this financing pattern.

7. By using long-term financing to finance part of temporary current assets, a firm may have less risk but lower returns than a firm with a normal financing plan. Explain the significance of this statement.

8. A firm that uses short-term financing methods for a portion of permanent current assets is assuming more risk but expects higher returns than a firm with a normal financing plan. Explain.

9. Since the early 1960s corporate liquidity has been declining. What reasons can you give for this trend?

10. From the data in Table 6–10 and Figure 6–11 what observations about corporate liquidity, besides those mentioned in the text, can you make?

Problems

1. Randolph Equipment Company expects sales next year to be $600,000. Inventory and accounts receivable will have to be increased by $110,000 to accommodate this sales level. The company has a steady profit margin of 10 percent and a 30 percent dividend payout.

   How much external funding will Randolph Equipment Company have to seek? Assume there is no increase in liabilities other than that which will occur with the external funding.

2. Austin Electronics expects sales next year to be $900,000 if the economy is strong, $650,000 of the economy is steady, and $375,000 if the economy is weak. The firm believes there is a 15 percent probability that the economy will be strong, a 60 percent probability of a steady economy, and a 25 percent probability of a weak economy.

   What is the expected level of sales next year?

3. Doris Daycare Centers, Inc., has decided to buy a new computer system with an expected useful life of three years. The cost is $200,000. The company can borrow $200,000 for three years at

12 percent annual interest or for one year at 10 percent annual interest.

How much would Doris Daycare Centers save in interest over the three-year life of the computer system if the one-year loan is utilized and the loan is rolled over (reborrowed) each year at the same 10 percent rate? Compare this to the 12 percent three-year loan. What if interest rates go up to 15 percent in year two and 18 percent in year three? What is the total interest cost now compared to the 12 percent, three-year loan?

4. Assume that Hogan Surgical Instruments Co. has $2 million in assets. If it goes with a low liquidity plan for the assets it can earn a return of 18 percent, but with a high liquidity plan the return will be 14 percent. If the firm goes with a short-term financing plan the financing costs on the $2 million will be 10 percent, and with a long-term financing plan the financing costs on the $2 million will be 12 percent.

a. Compute the anticipated return after financing costs on the most aggressive asset-financing mix (review Table 6–11).
b. Compute the anticipated return after financing costs on the most conservative asset-financing mix.
c. Compute the anticipated return after financing costs on the two moderate approaches to the asset-financing mix.
d. Would you necessarily accept the plan with the highest return after financing costs? Briefly explain.

5. Sherlock Homes, a manufacturer of low-cost mobile housing, has $4.5 million in assets.

Temporary current assets	$1,000,000
Permanent current assets	1,500,000
Fixed assets	2,000,000
Total assets	$4,500,000

Short-term rates are 8 percent. Long-term rates are 13 percent. Earnings before interest and taxes are $960,000. The tax rate is 40 percent.

If long-term financing is perfectly matched (synchronized) with long-term asset needs, and the same is true of short-term financing, what will earnings after taxes be? For an example of perfectly matched plans, see Figure 6–5.

6. In Problem 5 assume the term structure of interest rates becomes inverted, with short-term rates going to 12 percent and long-term rates 4 percentage points lower than short-term rates.

   If all other factors in the problem do not change, what will earnings after taxes be?

7. Plaza Square Inc. has $600,000 in current assets, $250,000 of which are considered permanent current assets. In addition, the firm has $500,000 invested in fixed assets.

   a. Plaza wishes to finance all long-term assets and one half of its permanent current assets with long-term financing costing 10 percent. Short-term financing currently costs 5 percent. Plaza's earnings before interest and taxes are $200,000. Determine Plaza's earnings after taxes under this financing plan. The tax rate is 50 percent.

   b. As an alternative Plaza might wish to finance all long-term assets and permanent current assets plus one half of its temporary current assets with long-term financing. The same interest rates apply as in part *a.* Earnings before interest and taxes will be $200,000. What will be Plaza's earnings after taxes? The tax rate is 50 percent.

   c. What are some of the risks associated with each of these alternative financing strategies?

8. Guardian Inc. is trying to develop an asset financing plan. The firm has $400,000 in temporary current assets and $300,000 in permanent current assets. Guardian also has $500,000 in fixed assets. The tax rate is 40 percent.

   a. Construct two alternative financing plans for Guardian. One of the plans should be conservative, with 75 percent of assets financed by long-term sources, and the other should be aggressive, with only 56.25 percent of assets financed by long-term sources. The current interest rate is 15 percent on long-term funds and 10 percent on short-term financing.

   b. Given that Guardian's earnings before interest and taxes are $200,000, calculate earnings after taxes for each of your alternatives.

   c. What would happen if the short- and long-term rates were reversed?

9. Liz's Health Food Stores has estimated monthly financing requirements for the next six months as follows:

January	$8,000	April	$8,000
February	2,000	May	9,000
March	3,000	June	4,000

Short-term financing will be utilized for the first four months and long-term financing for the last two months. Projected annual interest rates are:

Short Term		*Long Term*	
January	8.07%	May	12%
February	9.0	June	12
March	12.0		
April	15.0		

a. Compute total dollar interest payments for the six months. To convert an annual rate to a monthly rate, divide by 12.

b. If long-term financing at 12 percent had been utilized throughout the six months, would the total dollar interest payments be larger or smaller?

10. Garza Electronics expects to sell 500 units in January, 250 units in February, and 1,000 units in March. December's ending inventory is 700 units. Expected sales for the year are 7,200 units. Garza has decided on a level production schedule of 600 units (7,200 units for the year/12 months = 600 units per month). What is the expected end-of-month inventory for January, February, and March? Show the beginning inventory, production, and sales for each of the three months used to derive the ending inventory.

11. Bombs Away Video Games Corporation has forecasted the following monthly sales:

January	$95,000	July	$ 40,000
February	88,000	August	40,000
March	20,000	September	50,000
April	20,000	October	80,000
May	15,000	November	100,000
June	30,000	December	118,000

Total sales = $696,000

Bombs Away Video Games sells the popular Strafe and Capture video game cartridge. It sells for $5 per unit and costs $2 per unit to produce. A level production policy is followed. Each month's production is equal to annual sales (in units) divided by 12.

Of each month's sales, 30 percent are for cash and 70 percent are on account. All accounts receivable are collected in the month after the sale is made.

a. Construct a monthly production and inventory schedule in units. Beginning inventory in January is 20,000 units. (Note: To do part *a*, you should work in terms of units of production and units of sales.)

b. Prepare a monthly schedule of cash receipts. Sales in the December before the planning year are $100,000. Work part *b* using dollars.

c. Determine a cash payments schedule for January through December. The production costs of $2 per unit are paid for in the month in which they occur. Other cash payments, besides those for production costs, are $40,000 per month.

d. Prepare a monthly cash budget for January through December. The beginning cash balance is $5,000, and that is also the minimum desired.

12. Esquire Products, Inc., expects the following monthly sales:

January	$24,000	May	$ 4,000	September	$25,000
February	15,000	June	2,000	October	30,000
March	8,000	July	18,000	November	38,000
April	10,000	August	22,000	December	20,000

Total sales = $216,000

Cash sales are 40 percent in a given month, with the remainder going into accounts receivable. All receivables are collected in the month following the sale. Esquire sells all of its goods for $2 each and produces them for $1 each. Esquire uses level production, and average monthly production is equal to annual production divided by 12.

a. Generate a monthly production and inventory schedule in units. Beginning inventory in January is 8,000 units. (Note: To do part *a*, you should work in terms of units of production and units of sales.)

b. Determine a cash receipts schedule for January through December. Assume that dollar sales in the prior December were $20,000. Work *b* using dollars.

c. Determine a cash payments schedule for January through December. The production costs ($1 per unit produced) are paid for in the month in which they occur. Other cash payments (besides those for production costs) are $7,000 per month.

d. Construct a cash budget for January through December. The beginning cash balance is $3,000, and that is also the required minimum.

e. Determine total current assets for each month. (Note: Accounts receivable equals sales minus 40 percent of sales for a given month.)

13. Pick a day within the past week and construct a yield curve for that day. Pick a day approximately a year ago and construct a yield curve for that day. How are interest rates different? *The Globe and Mail* should be of help in solving this problem.

Selected References

Archer, Stephen H. "A Model for the Determination of Firm Cash Balances." *Journal of Financial and Quantitative Analysis* 1 (March 1966), pp. 1–11.

Bean, Virginia L., and Reynolds Griffith. "Risk and Return in Working Capital Management." *Mississippi Valley Journal of Business and Economics* 1 (Fall 1966), pp. 28–48.

Bogen, Jules T., ed. *Financial Handbook*. 4th ed. New York: Ronald, 1968, sec. 16.

Brick, John R., and Howard E. Thompson. "Time Series Analysis of Interest Rates: Some Additional Evidence." *Journal of Finance* 33 (March 1978), pp. 93–103.

Budin, Morris, and Van Handel, Robert J. "A Rule-of-Thumb Theory of Cash Holdings by Firm." *Journal of Financial and Quantitative Analysis* 10 (March 1975), pp. 85–108.

Clapin-Pepin, Daniel, and C. Le-Van. "Working Capital Analysis—A Dynamic Model." *CGA Magazine*, March 1985, pp. 9–10.

Cossaboom, Roger A. "Let's Reassess the Profitability-Liquidity Tradeoff." *Financial Executive* 39 (May 1971), pp. 46–51.

Glautier, M. W. E. "Towards a Reformation of the Theory of Working Capital." *Journal of Business Finance* 3 (Spring 1971), pp. 37–42.

Jennings, Joseph A. "A Look at Corporate Liquidity." *Financial Executive* 39 (February 1971), pp. 26–32.

Kahl, Alfred L. "Working Capital Management in Canada: An Exploratory Survey." *Finance* 2, no. 1 (1981), pp. 77–84.

Knight, W. D. "Working Capital Management—Satisfying versus Optimization." *Financial Management* 1 (Spring 1972), pp. 33–40.

Mehta, Dileep R. *Working Capital Management.* Englewood Cliffs, N. J.: Prentice-Hall, 1974.

Smith, Keith V. *Management of Working Capital.* St. Paul, Minn.: West Publishing, 1974.

Stancill, James McN. *The Management of Working Capital.* Scranton, Pa.: Intext, 1971, chaps. 1, 6, and 7.

Van Horne, James C. "A Risk-Return Analysis of a Firm's Working Capital Position." *Engineering Economist* 14 (Winter 1969), pp. 71–89.

Walker, Ernest W. "Towards a Theory of Working Capital." *Engineering Economist* 9 (January–February 1964), pp. 21–35.

Walter, James E. "Determination of Technical Solvency." *Journal of Business* 30 (January 1959), pp. 39–43.

Welter, Paul. "How to Calculate Savings Possible through Reduction of Working Capital." *Financial Executive,* October 1970, pp. 50–58.

7 Current Asset Management

The financial manager must carefully allocate resources among the current assets of the firm—cash, marketable securities, accounts receivable, and inventory. In managing cash and marketable securities, the primary concern should be for safety and liquidity—with secondary attention placed on maximizing profitability. As we move to accounts receivable and inventory, a stiffer profitability test must be met. The investment level should not be a matter of happenstance or historical determination but must meet the same return-on-investment criteria applied to any decision. We may need to choose between a 20 percent increase in inventory and a new plant location or a major research program. We shall examine the decision techniques that are applied to the various forms of current assets.

Cash Management

In the parlance of corporate financial management, the less cash you have, the better off you are. In spite of whatever lifelong teachings you might have learned about the virtues of cash, the corporate manager actively seeks to keep this nonearning asset to a minimum.

The first consideration is to ensure that inflows and outflows of cash are properly synchronized for transaction purposes. Interest-paying marketable securities, held for precautionary purposes, should only be transferred into cash when there is a scheduled need for disbursement. In determining the appropriate cash balance, the firm must carefully assess the payment pattern of customers, the speed at which suppliers and creditors process checks, and the efficiency of the banking system.

Float

Some people are shocked to realize that even the most trusted asset on a corporation's books, "cash," may not portray actual dollars at a given point in time. There are, in fact, two cash balances of importance: the corporation's recorded amount and the amount credited to the corporation by the bank. The difference between the two is labeled *float,* and it exists as a result of the lag between the time when a cheque is written and the eventual clearing of the cheque against a corporate bank account.

Let us examine the use of float. A firm has deposited $1 million in cheques received from customers during the week and has written $900,000 in cheques to suppliers. If the initial balance were $100,000, the corporate books would show $200,000. But what will the bank records show in the way of usable funds? Perhaps $800,000 of the cheques from customers will have cleared their accounts at other banks and been credited to us, while only $400,000 of our cheques may have completed a similar cycle. As indicated in Table 7–1 we have used float to provide us with $300,000 extra in available short-term funds.

Some companies actually operate with a negative cash balance on the corporate books, knowing that float will carry them through at the bank. In the above example the firm may write $1.2 million in cheques

Table 7–1
The use of float to provide funds

	Corporate Books	*Bank Books (usable funds) (amounts actually cleared)*
Initial amount	$ 100,000	$100,000
Deposits	+ 1,000,000	+ 800,000
Cheques	− 900,000	− 400,000
Balance	+$ 200,000	+$500,000
	+$300,000 float	

Table 7–2
Playing the float

	Corporate Books	Bank Books (usable funds) (amounts actually cleared)
Initial amount	$ 100,000	$100,000
Deposits	+ 1,000,000*	+ 800,000*
Cheques	− 1,200,000	− 800,000
Balance	−$ 100,000	+$100,000
	+$200,000 float	

*Assumed to remain the same as in Table 7–1.

on the assumption that only $800,000 will clear by the end of the week, thus leaving it with surplus funds in its bank account. The results, shown in Table 7–2, represent the phenomenon known as "playing the float." A float of $200,000 turns a negative balance on the corporation's books into a positive temporary balance on the bank's books. Obviously, float can also work against you if cheques going out are being processed more quickly than cheques coming in.

Improving Collections

We may expedite the collection and cheque-clearing process through a number of strategies.[1] A popular method is to have customers make payment to a variety of branch offices throughout the country rather than to the corporate headquarters. The local office would then deposit the cheques into a bank account at its local bank branch. In fact, the local office may deposit the cheques directly into an account of the corporate office. The advantage of such a system is that it reduces the time the customer's cheque is in the mail because of the proximity of the branch office.

For those who wish to enjoy the benefits of expeditious cheque clearance at lower costs, a *lockbox system* may replace the role of the local collection offices. Under this plan customers are requested to forward their cheques to a post office box in their geographic region while a local bank picks up the cheques, depositing them in the com-

[1]The chartered banks have cash management advisory groups that can offer valuable consultation on these matters.

pany's account. The company thus retains many of the benefits of regional branch office collections but with reduced corporate overhead.

Extending Disbursements

Perhaps you have heard of the billion-dollar corporation with its headquarters located in the most exclusive office space in downtown New York City but with its primary cheque disbursement center in Fargo, North Dakota. Such a scheme is often put in place by U.S. companies because of the slow cheque-clearing system in that country.[2] In Canada, however, because of the efficiency of the banking system in cheque clearing, such an attempt to extend the float would have no effect. The one opportunity to extend disbursements in Canada involves mailing the cheques from more dispersed locations so that the time in the mail might be extended. For example, a cheque mailed from Vancouver to a Vancouver supplier might spend only one day in the mail, one day in the supplier's processing system, and one day in the cheque-clearing system before the bank transfers the funds out of the mailing firm's bank account. If that same cheque had been mailed from St. John's, Newfoundland, it might have spent another two or three days in the mail, thereby increasing the float.

Cost-Benefit Analysis

An efficiently maintained cash management program can be an expensive operation. The utilization of remote collection and disbursement centers involves additional costs, and banks involved in the process will require that the firm maintain adequate deposit balances or pay sufficient fees to justify their services. Though the use of a lockbox system may reduce total corporate overhead, the costs may still be substantial.

These expenses must be compared to the benefits that may accrue. If a firm has an average daily remittance of $2 million and 1.5 days

[2]See, for example, "Making Millions by Stretching the Float," *Business Week*, November 23, 1974, p. 88.

can be saved in the collection process by establishing a sophisticated collection network, the firm has freed up $3 million for investment elsewhere. Also through stretching the disbursement schedule by one day, perhaps another $2 million will become available for alternate uses. An example of this process is shown in Figure 7–1. If the firm is able to earn 10 percent on the $5 million that is freed up, as much as $500,000 per year may be expended on the administrative costs of cash management before the new costs are equal to the generated revenue.

International Cash Management

Multinational corporations can shift funds around from country to country much as a firm may transfer funds from a local branch bank account in Halifax to the corporation's headquarters account in Mon-

Figure 7–1
Cash management network

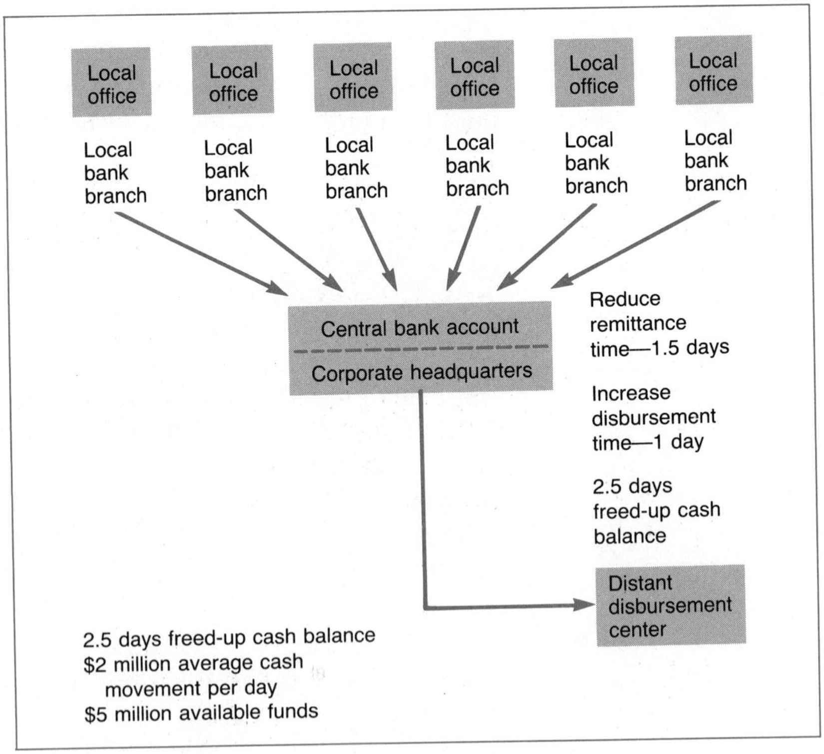

treal. An international electronic funds transfer system called SWIFT has been developed to facilitate this international payments system.

A company may prefer to hold cash balances in one currency rather than another. This may occur either because of future expectations regarding foreign currency rate changes or because of interest rate differentials on short-term investments. In periods when one country's currency has been rising relative to others, financial managers often try to keep as much cash as possible in the country with the "strong" currency. For example, in the early 1980s the U.S. dollar was rising relative to most currencies. At that time there was a tendency to try and keep balances in U.S. bank accounts or in U.S.-dollar-denominated bank accounts in foreign banks. The latter are commonly known as Eurodollar deposits. Because of the growth of the international money markets in size and in scope, they have become an important aspect of cash management. Cash management at the international level employs the same techniques as domestic cash management, using such forecasting devices as the cash budget and daily cash reports, so that excess funds may be collected and invested, until needed, in Eurodollar money market securities or other appropriate investments in securities denominated in strong currencies. A more in-depth coverage of international cash and asset management is presented in Chapter 21.

Marketable Securities

The firm may hold excess funds in anticipation of some major cash outlay such as a dividend payment or partial retirement of debt or as a precaution against an unexpected event. When funds are being held for other than immediate transaction purposes they should be converted from cash into interest-earning marketable securities.[3]

The financial manager has a virtual supermarket of securities from which to choose. Among the factors influencing that choice are yield, maturity, minimum investment required, safety, and marketability. Under normal conditions the longer the maturity period of the security, the higher will be the yield, as displayed in Figure 7–2.[4]

[3]The one possible exception to this principle is found in the practice of holding compensating balances at commercial banks—a topic for discussion in Chapter 8.

[4]Chapter 6 demonstrated some of the different yield-maturity relationships encountered over the last 20 years.

Figure 7–2
An examination of yield and maturity characteristics

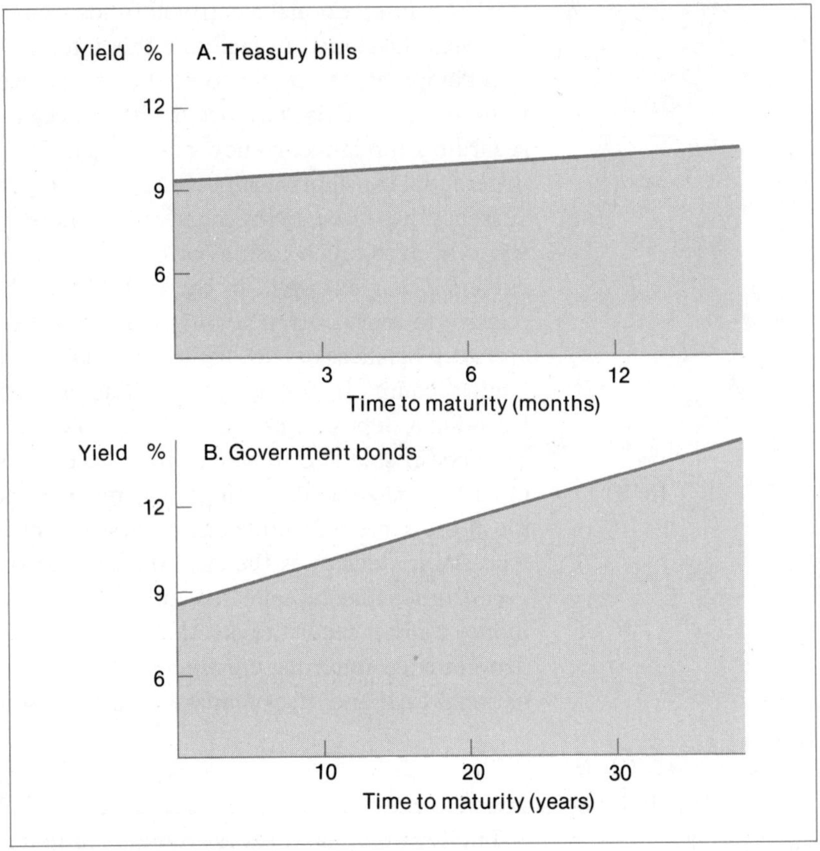

The problem in "stretching out" the maturity of your investment is not that you are legally locked in (you can generally sell your security when you need funds) but that you may have to take a loss to convert the security to cash. A $5,000 government bond issued initially at 9.5 percent, with three years to maturity, may only bring $4,500 if the going interest rate climbs to 11 percent. This risk of price change increases as the maturity date is extended. A complete discussion of "interest rate risk" is included in Chapter 16, Long-Term Debt and Lease Financing.

Various forms of marketable securities and investments, emphasizing the short term, are presented in Table 7–3. The key characteristics of each investment are delineated along with examples of yields for March 31, 1987, when rates were quite low in relation to what they had been

Table 7–3
Types of short-term investments

Investment	Maturity*	Minimum Amount	Safety	Marketability	Yield March 31, 1987
Federal government securities:					
Treasury bills	30 days	$1,000,000	Excellent	Excellent	6.75%
Treasury bills	90 days	1,000,000	Excellent	Excellent	6.92
Nongovernment securities:					
Certificates of deposit (large)	30 days	100,000	Good	Fair	6.00
Certificates of deposit (small)	90 days	1,000	Good	Poor	5.25
Commercial paper	30 days	100,000	Good	Fair	7.08
Bankers' acceptances	90 days	None	Good	Good	7.05
Eurodollar deposits	30 days	1,000,000	Good	Excellent	6.32
LIBOR (London Interbank Offered Rate)	30 days	1,000,000	Good	Excellent	6.40
Savings accounts	Open	None	Excellent	None†	4.75
Bank-swapped deposits	90 days	100,000	Excellent	None	—

*Several of the above securities can be purchased with maturities different than those indicated.
†Though not marketable, these investments are highly liquid because the funds may be withdrawn without penalty.

through much of the early 1980s. For example, 90-day Treasury bills returned slightly over 20 percent during most of the summer of 1981 versus 6.92 percent at March 31, 1987.

Let us examine the characteristics of each security. *Treasury bills* are short-term obligations of the Government of Canada and are a popular place to "park funds" because of a large and active market. Although these securities are originally issued with maturities of 91 days, 182 days, and one year, the investor may buy an outstanding T-bill with as little as one day remaining to maturity (perhaps two prior investors have held it for 45 days each). With the government auctioning 91- and 182-day bills every Thursday and one-year bills every second Thursday, a wide range of choices is always available. Treasury bills are unique in that they trade on a discount basis—meaning that the return received is the difference between the price paid and the maturity value. Although federal government T-bills can be bought at retail in amounts as small as $50,000, the rates quoted are generally for transactions of $1 million or more. The yields on the smaller denominations are substantially less. For example, the rate on a $50,000, 30-day T-bill purchase on March 31, 1987, was 5.25 percent versus

6.75 percent for an amount over $1 million. The fact that the market for Government of Canada T-bills services about $100 billion in securities attests to their popularity as short-term investment vehicles.

Canadian provinces and municipalities, along with their agencies and crown corporations, also issue short-term securities such as Treasury bills. There is a good secondary market for these securities, and they generally provide a slightly higher return than do Government of Canada T-bills.

Commercial paper represents unsecured promissory notes issued to the public by large business corporations. For example, in 1986 the Aluminum Company of Canada decided to raise $300 million via such notes while Imperial Oil targeted $700 million for issue. Finance companies such as the mortgage subsidiaries of the major banks and sales finance companies are very active in the commercial paper market, issuing what is commonly referred to as *finance company paper.* Commercial paper is usually only sold in amounts of $100,000 or more. Maturities range from 30 days to one year with the shorter terms being most popular. Although the market for industrial commercial paper is relatively small it is growing rapidly in Canada.

Bankers' acceptances are short-term securities that generally arise from foreign trade. The acceptance is a draft drawn on a bank for payment when presented to the bank. The difference between a draft and a cheque is that a company does not have to deposit funds at the bank to cover the draft until the bank has accepted the draft for *future* payment of the required amount. This means that the exporter who now holds the bankers' acceptance may have to wait 30, 60, or 90 days to collect the money. Because there is an active market involving some $26 billion in bankers' acceptances they rank closely behind Treasury bills as vehicles for viable short-term investment.

Another popular short-term investment arising from foreign trade is the *Eurocurrency deposit.* The most common Eurocurrency is the U.S. Eurodollar, which is a U.S. dollar held on deposit by foreign banks and in turn loaned out by those banks to anyone seeking dollars. There is a large market for Eurodollar deposits and loans mostly centered in the London international banking market. Because this is a market for large deposits of $1 million or more, only large companies like Bell Canada and Ontario Hydro are active in it.

LIBOR (London Interbank Offered Rate) is the rate offered for dollar deposits in the London market. Thus, companies can lend money (that is, deposit) to banks at that rate. While this is essentially a Eurodollar deposit, the difference is that it is centered only in London rather than in Paris or Frankfurt or some other part of Europe. LIBOR is often used as a base lending rate for companies who may borrow at a floating interest rate of LIBOR plus a small premium. The use of LIBOR is discussed further in Chapter 21, International Financial Management.

Another outlet for investment is the *term deposit*. Depending on the issuing bank or trust company, these deposits may be termed certificates of deposit (CDs), term notes, term deposit receipts, or some other similar name. The investor places his or her funds on deposit at a specified rate over a given time period as evidenced by the certificate received. This is a market for smaller amounts ($1,000 to $100,000) with no secondary market. In these cases the money is invested for specified periods of from one month to seven years.

If the company wants to invest $100,000 or more in a bank deposit, however, it can do so via *bearer deposits* which are transferrable from one investor to another. Although this feature makes bearer deposits somewhat liquid they are still not a very attractive place for temporary excess funds.

The lowest yielding investment may well be a passbook *savings account*. Its relative advantages are that it can accommodate small investments and that it can usually be liquidated with no notice. Thus, although not attractive to the large corporations who have other more lucrative options available, the savings account is still a good short-term investment alternative for small businesses and individuals.

Bank *swapped deposits* have arisen as Canadian companies take advantage of differences in international short-term interest rates. For example, in a typical case the Canadian company would convert Canadian dollars to U.S. dollars and deposit them in a foreign bank. Concurrently, the company would execute a futures contract to sell the U.S. dollars for Canadian dollars when the deposit matures. Thus, the company ends up with a "hedged" U.S. dollar investment.[5] This is attractive if the combination of direct yield and foreign exchange cost or yield generates a higher return than would a straight deposit in Canada.

---

[5]Hedged means that the investor has no foreign exchange risk.

Management of Accounts Receivable

Despite the expansion of credit via bank credit cards and the creation of finance subsidiaries, a substantial portion of the investment in assets by industrial companies continues to be in accounts receivable. According to Statistics Canada, accounts receivable as a percentage of total assets for industrial corporations in Canada has remained between 12 and 15 percent since 1962. In absolute terms they have risen from $7 billion to over $55 billion.[6]

Accounts Receivable as an Investment

As is true of other current assets, accounts receivable should be thought of as an investment. The level of accounts receivable should not be adjudged too high or too low based on historical standards of industry norms, but rather the test should be whether the level of return we are able to earn from this asset equals or exceeds the potential gain from other commitments. For example, if we allow our customers five extra days to clear their accounts, our accounts receivable balance will increase—draining funds from marketable securities and perhaps drawing down the inventory level. We must ask whether we are optimizing our return in light of appropriate risk and liquidity considerations.

An example of a buildup in accounts receivable is presented in Figure 7–3, with supportive financing provided through reducing lower yielding assets and increasing lower cost liabilities.

Credit Policy Administration

In considering the extension of credit there are three primary policy variables to consider in conjunction with our profit objective:

---

[6]The growth in receivables has actually been more dramatic. The 1962 figure represents an estimate for all companies while the later one represents only those corporations with $10 million or more of assets.

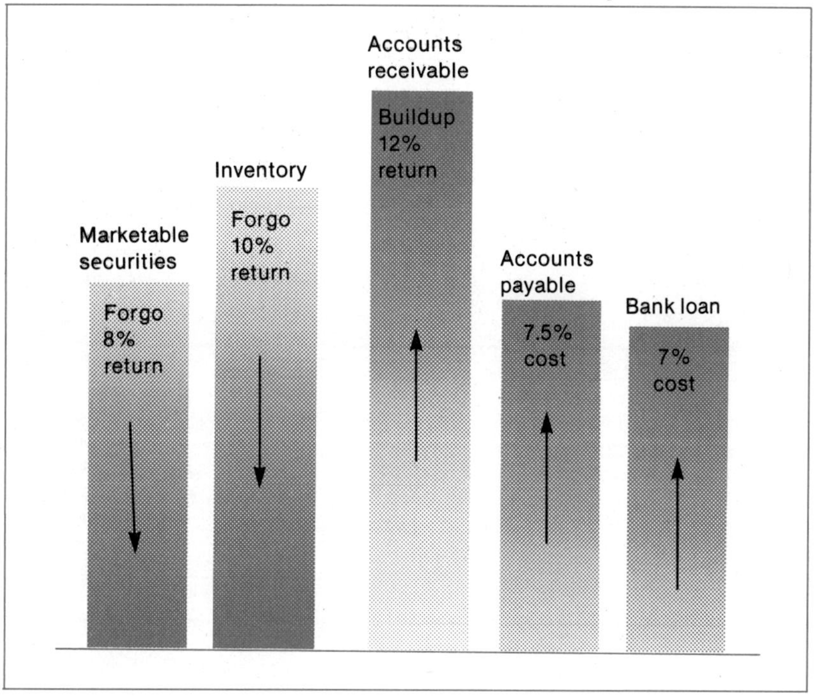

Figure 7–3
Financing growth in accounts receivable

1. Credit standards.
2. Terms of credit.
3. Collection policy.

Credit standards The firm must determine the nature of the credit risk on the basis of prior record of payment, financial stability, current net worth, and other factors. An extensive network of credit information has been developed by credit agencies throughout the country. The most prominent source is Dun & Bradstreet, which publishes a *Reference Book* listing many thousands of business establishments. Information is given on the firm's line of business, net worth, and creditworthiness. An example of the rating system used by Dun & Bradstreet is presented in Table 7–4.

A firm with a BB2 rating has estimated financial strength, based on net worth, of $200,000–$300,000, with an overall composite credit rating of "Good." Besides the *Reference Book*, Dun & Bradstreet can

Table 7–4
Dun & Bradstreet credit rating system

Key to Ratings						
Estimated Financial Strength			Composite Credit Appraisal			
			High	Good	Fair	Limited
5A	Over	$50,000,000	1	2	3	4
4A	$10,000,000 to	50,000,000	1	2	3	4
3A	1,000,000 to	10,000,000	1	2	3	4
2A	750,000 to	1,000,000	1	2	3	4
1A	500,000 to	750,000	1	2	3	4
BA	300,000 to	500,000	1	2	3	4
BB	200,000 to	300,000	1	2	3	4
CB	125,000 to	200,000	1	2	3	4
CC	75,000 to	125,000	1	2	3	4
DC	50,000 to	75,000	1	2	3	4
DD	35,000 to	50,000	1	2	3	4
EE	20,000 to	35,000	1	2	3	4
FF	10,000 to	20,000	1	2	3	4
GG	5,000 to	10,000	1	2	3	4
HH	Up to	5,000	1	2	3	4

also provide extensive individualized credit reports on potential customers.

Certain industries have also developed their own special credit reporting agencies. Even more important are the local credit bureaus that keep close tabs on day-to-day transactions in a given community.

Terms of trade The stated terms of credit extension will have a strong impact on the eventual size of the accounts receivable balance. If a firm averages $5,000 in daily credit sales and allows 30-day terms, the average accounts receivable balance will be $150,000. If customers are carried for 60 days, the firm must maintain $300,000 in receivables, and much additional financing will be required.

In establishing credit terms the firm should also consider the use of a cash discount. Offering the terms 2/10, net 30 enables the customer to deduct 2 percent from the face amount of the bill when paying within the first 10 days, but if the discount is not taken, the customer must remit the full amount within 30 days. As later demonstrated in Chapter 8, Sources of Short-Term Financing, the annualized cost of not taking a cash discount may be substantial.

Collection policy A third area for consideration under credit policy administration is the collection function. A number of quantitative measures may be applied to the credit department of the firm.

a. Average collection period $= \dfrac{\text{Accounts receivable}}{\text{Average daily credit sales}}$

(See ratio 5 in Chapter 3.) An increase in the average collection period may be the result of a predetermined plan to extend credit terms or the consequence of poor credit administration.

b. Ratio of bad debts to credit sales.

An increasing ratio may indicate too many weak accounts or an aggressive market expansion policy.

c. Aging of accounts receivables.

We may wish to determine the amount of time the various accounts have been on our books. If there is a buildup in receivables beyond our normal credit terms, we may wish to take remedial action. Such a buildup is shown in the table presented here.

Age of Receivables, May 31, 1987

Month of Sales	*Age of Account (days)*	*Amounts*
May	0–30	$ 60,000
April	31–60	25,000
March	61–90	5,000
February	91–120	10,000
Total receivables		$100,000

If our normal credit terms are 30 days, we may be doing a poor job of collecting our accounts, with particular attention required on the over-90-day accounts.

An Actual Credit Decision

We now examine a credit decision that brings together the various elements of accounts receivable management. Assume a firm is considering selling to a group of customers that will bring $10,000 in new annual sales, of which 10 percent is forecast to be uncollectible. While this is a very high rate of nonpayment, the critical question is, What is the potential contribution to profitability?

Assume the collection cost on these accounts is 5 percent and the cost of producing and selling the product is 77 percent of the sales dollar. The firm is in a 40 percent tax bracket. The profit on new sales would be as follows:

Additional sales	$10,000
Accounts uncollectible (10% of new sales)	1,000
Annual incremental revenue	9,000
Collection costs (5% of new sales)	500
Production and selling costs (77% of new sales)	7,700
Annual income before taxes	800
Taxes (40%)	320
Annual incremental income after taxes	$ 480

Though the return on sales is only 4.8 percent ($480/$10,000), the return on invested dollars may be considerably higher. Let us assume that the only new investment in this case is a buildup in accounts receivable. (Present working capital and fixed assets are sufficient to support the higher sales level.) Assume analysis of our accounts indicates a turnover ratio of 6 to 1 between sales and accounts receivable. Our new accounts receivable balance will average $1,667.

$$\frac{\text{Sales}}{\text{Turnover}} = \frac{\$10{,}000^{7}}{6} = \$1{,}667$$

Thus, we are committing an average investment of only $1,667 to provide an after-tax return of $480, so that the yield is a very attractive 28.8 percent. If the firm had a minimum required after-tax return of 10 percent, this would clearly be an acceptable investment. We might ask next if we should consider taking on 12 percent or even 15 percent in uncollectible accounts—remaining loyal to our concept of maximizing profit and forsaking any notion about risky accounts being inherently good or bad.

Inventory Management

Inventory can create financing and profit problems for a company. The automobile industry in 1985 and 1986 is a case in point. In the fall of 1985, with bulging inventories of 1985 models, the automobile

[7] We could actually argue that our out-of-pocket commitment to sales is 82 percent times $10,000, or $8,200. This would indicate an even smaller commitment to receivables.

industry instituted a discount financing plan of 7.9 percent interest. While this stimulated sales and cleared 1985 cars out of the dealer showrooms, profits suffered—at General Motors especially. The discount financing was discontinued, but late in 1985 and early in 1986 General Motors found that it had over 80 days of inventory when 60 days is the normal target. Again GM led the industry with 7.9 percent financing.

Inventory is the least liquid of current assets, and it should provide the highest yield to justify investment. While the financial manager may have direct control over the cash management, marketable securities, and accounts receivable, control over inventory policy is generally shared with production management and marketing. Let us examine some key factors influencing inventory management.

Level versus Seasonal Production

A manufacturing firm must determine whether a plan of level or seasonal production should be followed. Level production was discussed in Chapter 6. While level (even) production throughout the year allows for maximum efficiency in the use of manpower and machinery, it may result in unnecessarily high inventory buildups prior to shipment, particularly in a seasonal business. We may have 10,000 bathing suits in stock in November.

If we produce on a seasonal basis the inventory problem is eliminated, but we will then have unused capacity during slack periods. Furthermore, as we shift to maximum operations to meet seasonal needs, we may be forced to pay overtime wages to labor and to sustain other inefficiencies as equipment is overused.

We have a classic problem in financial analysis. Are the cost savings from level production sufficient to justify the extra expenditure in carrying inventory? Let us look at a typical case.

	Production	
	Level	*Seasonal*
Average inventory	$100,000	$70,000
Operating costs—after tax	50,000	60,000

Though we will have to invest $30,000 more in average inventory under level production, we will save $10,000 in operating costs. This represents a 33 percent return on investment. If our required rate of return is 10 percent, this would clearly be an acceptable alternative.[8]

Inventory Policy in Inflation (and Deflation)

The price of copper went from $0.50 to $1.40 a pound and back again in 1973–75 and also showed sharp price volatility in the 1979–82 period. Similar price instability has taken place in wheat, sugar, lumber, and a number of other commodities. Only the most astute inventory manager can hope to prosper in this type of environment. The problem can be partially controlled by taking moderate inventory positions (do not fully commit at one price).

Another way of protecting an inventory position would be by hedging with a futures contract to sell at a stipulated price some months from now.

Rapid price movements in inventory may also have a major impact on the reported income of the firm, a process described in Chapter 3, Financial Analysis. A firm using FIFO (first-in, first-out) accounting may experience large inventory profits when old, less expensive inventory is written off against new high prices in the marketplace. The benefits may be transitory, as the process reverses itself when prices decline.

The Inventory Decision Model

Substantial research has been devoted to the problem of determining optimum inventory size, order quantity, usage rate, and similar considerations. An entire branch in the field of operations research is dedicated to the subject.

In developing an inventory model we must evaluate the two basic costs associated with inventory: the carrying costs and the ordering costs. Through a careful analysis of both of these variables we can determine the optimum order size to place to minimize costs. Carrying

---

[8]The problem may be further evaluated by using the capital budgeting techniques presented in Chapter 12.

costs include interest on funds tied up in inventory, the cost of warehouse space, insurance premiums, and material handling expenses. There is also an implicit cost associated with the dangers of obsolescence and rapid price change. The larger the order we place, the greater the average inventory we will have on hand and the higher the carrying cost.

As a second factor we must consider the cost of ordering and processing inventory into stock. If we maintain a relatively low average inventory in stock, we must order many times, and total ordering cost will be high. The opposite patterns associated with the two costs are portrayed in Figure 7–4.

As the order size increases, carrying costs go up because we have more inventory on hand. With larger orders, of course, we will order less frequently, and overall ordering costs will go down. The approximate trade-off between the two can best be judged by examining the total cost curve. At point *M*, we have appropriately played the advan-

Figure 7–4
Determining the optimum inventory level

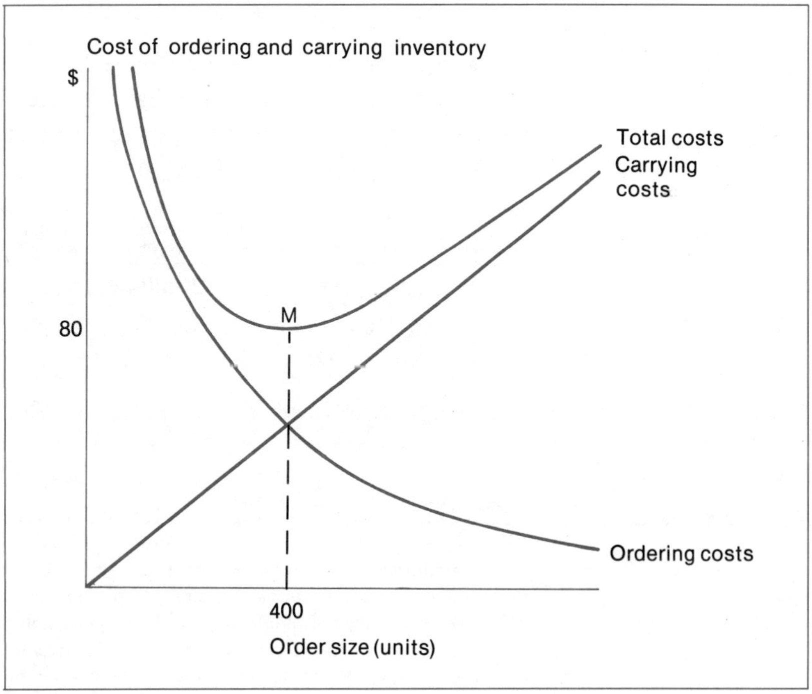

tages and disadvantages of the respective costs against each other. With larger orders, carrying costs will be excessive, while at a reduced order size, constant ordering will put us at an undesirably higher point on the ordering cost curve.

The question becomes, How do we mathematically determine the minimum point (M) on the total cost curve? Under certain fairly reasonable assumptions,[9] we may use the following formula as the first step.

$$EOQ = \sqrt{\frac{2SO}{C}} \tag{7–1}$$

EOQ is the "economic ordering quantity," the amount which it is most advantageous for the firm to order each time. We will determine this value, translate it into average inventory size, and determine the minimum total cost amount (M). The terms in the EOQ formula are defined as follows:

S = Total sales in units
O = Ordering cost for each order
C = Carrying cost per unit in dollars

Let us assume that we anticipate selling 2,000 units, that it will cost us $8 to place each order, and that the price per unit is $1, with a 20 percent carrying cost to maintain the average inventory (the carrying charge per unit is $0.20). Plugging these values into our formula, we show:

$$EOQ = \sqrt{\frac{2SO}{C}} = \sqrt{\frac{2 \times 2{,}000 \times \$8}{\$0.20}} = \sqrt{\frac{\$32{,}000}{\$0.20}} = \sqrt{160{,}000}$$
$$= 400 \text{ units}$$

The optimum order size is 400 units. On the assumption we will use up inventory at a constant rate throughout the year, our average

[9]The assumptions are that inventory usage is at a constant rate, that the amount of time to deliver each order is consistent, and that the delivery date coincides with the point at which we reach a zero level of inventory. It does not consider the problem of stock-outs. A stock-out occurs when a firm is out of a specific inventory item and is unable to sell or deliver the product. Relaxation of these assumptions does not greatly change the calculations.

inventory on hand will be 200 units, as indicated in Figure 7–5. Average inventory equals EOQ/2.

Our total costs with an order size of 400 and an average inventory size of 200 units are computed in Table 7–5.

Point *M* on Figure 7–4 can be equated to a total cost of $80 at an order size of 400 units. At no other order point can we hope to achieve lower costs. The same basic principles of total cost minimization we have applied to inventory can be applied to other assets as well. For example, we may assume that cash has a carrying cost (opportunity cost of lost interest on marketable securities as a result of being in cash) and an ordering cost (transaction costs of shifting in and out of marketable securities) and then work toward determining the optimum level of cash. In each case we are trying to minimize the overall costs and increase the profit and valuation of the firm.

Figure 7–5
Inventory usage pattern

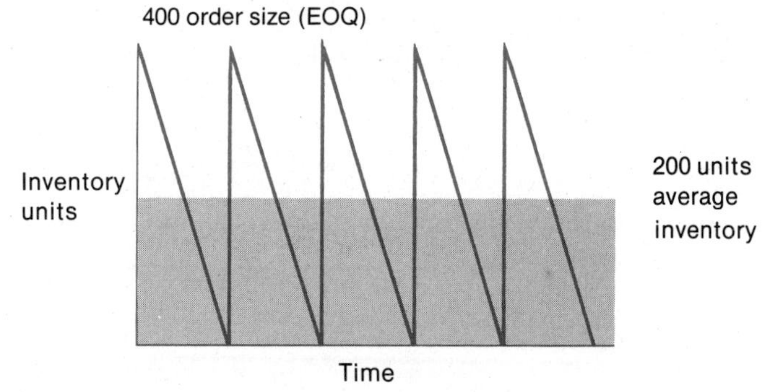

Table 7–5
Total costs for inventory

1. Ordering costs = $\frac{2{,}000 \text{ units}}{400 \text{ order size}}$ = 5 orders

   5 orders at $8 per order = $40

2. Carrying costs = Average inventory in units × Carrying cost per unit

   200 × $0.20 = $40

3.

Order cost	$40
Carrying cost	+40
Total cost	$80

Summary

In cash management our primary goal should be to keep our balances as low as possible consistent with the notion of maintaining adequate funds for transaction purposes. We try to speed the inflow of funds and defer their outflow. Excess short-term funds may be placed in marketable securities—with a wide selection of issues, maturities, and yields from which to choose.

The management of accounts receivable calls for the determination of credit standards and the forms of credit to be offered as well as the development of an effective collection policy.

There is no such thing as bad credit—only unprofitable credit extension. Inventory is the least liquid of the current assets, so it should provide the highest yield. We determine the economic ordering quantity and the optimum average inventory size to minimize the total costs of ordering and carrying inventory.

Other assets may also be subjected to decision models similar to that provided for inventory. In each instance we look at the cost of holding the asset versus the cost of transacting in the asset, and we strive for a minimum value.

List of Terms

float
lockbox system
cost-benefit analysis
Treasury bills
certificates of deposit
commercial paper
Dun & Bradstreet
hedging
futures contract
LIBOR (London Interbank Offered Rate)
economic ordering quantity (EOQ)
carrying costs
trade credit
credit terms
average collection period
aging of accounts receivables
Eurodollars
bankers' acceptances
swapped deposits

Discussion Questions

1. In the management of cash and marketable securities, why should the primary concern be for safety and liquidity rather than profit maximization?
2. Explain briefly how a corporation may use float to its advantage?
3. Why does float exist at all, and what effect does our national banking system have on it?
4. How can a firm operate with a negative cash balance on its corporate books?
5. Explain the similarities and differences between lockbox systems and regional collection offices.
6. Why would a financial manager want to slow down disbursements?
7. Find the going interest rates for the list of marketable securities in Table 7–3. Which security would you choose for a short-term investment? Why?
8. Why are Treasury bills a favorite place for financial managers to invest excess cash?
9. Explain why the bad debt percentage or any other similar credit-control percentage is not the ultimate measure of success in the management of accounts receivable. What is the key consideration?
10. Precisely what does the EOQ formula tell us? What assumption is made about the usage rate for inventory?

Problems

1. Shelia's Society Clothing Manufacturer has collection centers across the country to speed up collections. The company also makes distributions from remote disbursement centers so the firm's cheques take longer in the mail. Average collection time has been reduced by one and one half days and disbursement time increased by one

half day because of these policies. Excess funds are being invested in short-term instruments yielding 11 percent per annum.

a. If the firm has $4 million per day in collections and $3 million per day in disbursements, how many dollars has the cash management system freed up?

b. How much can the firm earn in dollars per year on short-term investments made possible by the freed-up cash?

2. Barney's Antique Shop had annual credit sales of $1,080,000 and an average collection period of 40 days in 1987. Assume a 360-day year.

What was the company's average accounts receivable balance?

3. In Problem 2, if accounts receivable change in 1988 to $140,000 while credit sales are $1,440,000, should we assume the firm has a more or a less lenient credit policy?

4. Western Tires has expected sales of 12,000 tires this year, an ordering cost of $6 per order, and carrying costs of $1.60 per tire.

a. What is the economic ordering quantity?
b. How many orders will be placed during the year?
c. What will the average inventory be?

5. Fisk Corporation is trying to improve its inventory control system and has installed an on-line computer at its retail stores. Fisk anticipates sales of 75,000 units per year, an ordering cost of $8 per order, and carrying costs of $1.20 per unit.

a. What is the economic ordering quantity?
b. How many orders will be placed during the year?
c. What will the average inventory be?
d. What is the total cost of ordering and carrying inventory?

6. (See Problem 5 for basic data.) In the second year, Fisk Corporation finds it can reduce ordering costs to $2 per order but that carrying costs stay the same. Volume remains at 75,000 units.

a. Recompute *a*, *b*, *c*, and *d* in Problem 5 for the second year.
b. Now compare years one and two and explain what happened.

7. Johnson Electronics is considering extending trade credit to some customers previously considered poor risks. Sales would increase by $100,000 if credit is extended to these new customers. Of the new accounts receivable generated, 10 percent will prove to be uncollectible. Additional collection costs will be 3 percent of sales, and production and selling costs will be 79 percent of sales. The firm is in the 40 percent tax bracket.

a. Compute the incremental income after taxes.
b. What will Johnson's incremental return on sales be if these new credit customers are accepted?
c. If the receivable turnover ratio is 6 to 1 and no other asset buildup is needed to serve the new customers, what will Johnson's incremental return on new average investment be?

8. Oscar's chequebook shows a balance of $600. A recent statement from the bank (received last week) shows that all cheques written as of the date of the statement have been paid except numbers 423 and 424, which were for $62 and $40, respectively. Since the statement date, cheques 425, 426, and 427 have been written for $32, $70, and $44, respectively.

There is a 75 percent probability that cheques 423 and 424 have been paid by this time. There is a 40 percent probability that cheques 425, 426, and 427 have been paid.

a. What is the total value of the five cheques outstanding?
b. What is the expected value of payments for the five cheques outstanding?
c. What is the difference between parts *a* and *b*? This represents a type of float.

9. North Pole Snowmobile is considering a switch to level production. Cost efficiencies would occur under level production, and after-tax costs would decline by $30,000, but inventory would increase by $250,000. North Pole Snowmobile would have to finance the extra inventory at a cost of 13.5 percent. Should the company go ahead and switch to level production? How low would interest rates need to fall before level production would be feasible?

10. Anderson Corporation is considering a more liberal credit policy to increase sales but expects that 8 percent of the new accounts will be uncollectible. Collection costs are 5 percent of new sales, production and selling costs are 77 percent, and accounts receivable turnover is five times. Assume income taxes of 40 percent and an increase in sales of $60,000. No other asset buildup will be required to service the new accounts.

a. What is the level of accounts receivable to support this sales expansion?
b. What would be Anderson's incremental after-tax return on investment?
c. Should Anderson liberalize credit if a 15 percent after-tax return on investment is required?

Assume that Anderson also needs to increase its level of inventory to support new sales and that inventory turnover is four times.

d. What would be the total incremental investment in accounts receivable and inventory to support a $60,000 increase in sales?
e. Given the income determined in part *b* and the investment determined in part *d,* should Anderson extend more liberal credit terms?

11. Fashion Furniture is evaluating the extension of credit to a new group of customers. Although these customers will provide $180,000 in additional credit sales, 12 percent are likely to be uncollectible. The company will also incur $14,000 in additional collection expense. Production and marketing costs represent 70 percent of sales. The firm is in a 40 percent tax bracket and has a receivables turnover of five times. No other asset buildup will be required to service the new customers.

a. Should Fashion Furniture extend credit to these customers, assuming it has a 10 percent desired return?
b. Should credit be extended if 15 percent of the new sales prove uncollectible?
c. Should credit be extended if the receivables turnover drops to 1.5 and 12 percent of the accounts are uncollectible?

12. Reconsider Problem 11. Assume the average collection period is 120 days. All other factors are the same (including 12 percent uncollectibles). Should credit be extended?

(Problems 13–16 are a series and should be taken in order.)

13. Dome Metals has credit sales of $144,000 yearly with credit terms of net 30 days, which is also the average collection period. Dome does not offer a discount for early payment, so its customers take the full 30 days to pay.

What is the average receivables balance? Receivables turnover?

14. If Dome offered a 2 percent discount for payment in 10 days and every customer took advantage of the new terms, what would the new average receivables balance be? Use the full sales of $144,000 for your calculation of receivables.

15. If Dome reduces its bank loans, which cost 10 percent, by the cash generated from reduced receivables, what will be the net gain or loss to the firm (don't forget the 2 percent discount)? Should it offer the discount?

16. Assume the new trade terms of 2/10, net 30 will increase sales by 15 percent because the discount makes Dome price competitive. If Dome earns 20 percent on sales before discounts, should it offer the discount? (Consider the same variables as you did for Problems 13 through 15.)

17. (*Comprehensive problem on receivables and inventory policy*)
Logan Distributing Company of Ottawa sells fans and heaters to retail outlets throughout the East. Joe Logan, the president of the company, is thinking about changing the firm's credit policy to attract customers away from competitors. The present policy calls for a 1/10, net 30 cash discount. The new policy would call for a 3/10, net 50 cash discount. Currently, 30 percent of Logan customers are taking the discount, and it is anticipated that this number would go up to 50 percent with the new discount policy. It is further anticipated that annual sales would increase from a level of $400,000 to $600,000 as a result of the change in the cash discount policy.

The increased sales would also affect the inventory level carried by Logan. The average inventory carried by Logan is based on a determination of an EOQ. Assume sales of fans and heaters increase from 15,000 to 22,500 units. The ordering cost for each order is $200, and the carrying cost per unit is $1.50 (these values will not change with the discount). The average inventory is based on EOQ/2. Each unit in inventory has an average cost of $12.

Cost of goods sold is equal to 65 percent of net sales, general and administrative expenses are 15 percent of net sales, and interest payments of 14 percent will only be necessary for the increase in the accounts receivable and inventory balances. Taxes will be 40 percent of before-tax income.

a. Compute the accounts receivable balance before and after the change in the cash discount policy. Use the net sales (total sales minus cash discounts) to determine the average daily sales.

b. Determine EOQ before and after the change in the cash discount policy. Translate this into average inventory (in units and dollars) before and after the change in the cash discount policy.

c. Complete the income statement.

	Before Policy Change	*After Policy Change*
Net sales (sales − cash discount)		
Cost of goods sold		
Gross profit		
General and administrative expenses		
Operating profit		
Interest on increase in accounts receivable and inventory (14 percent).		
Income before taxes		
Taxes		
Income after taxes		

d. Should the new cash discount policy be utilized? Briefly comment.

Selected References

Annett, William. "A Swap in Time Saves—How to Trade Interest Rates." *CGA*, April 1986, pp. 74–75.

Batlin, C. A., and Susan Hinko. "Lockbox Management and Value Maximization." *Financial Management* 10 (Winter 1981), pp. 39–44.

Baumol, William J. "The Transactions Demand for Cash: An Inventory Theoretic Approach." *Quarterly Journal of Economics* 65 (November 1952), pp. 545–56.

Beman, Lewis. "A Big Payoff from Inventory Controls." *Fortune* 104 (July 27, 1981), pp. 76–80.

Block, Stanley B. "Accounts Receivable as an Investment." *Credit and Financial Management* 76 (May 1974), pp. 32–35, 40.

Budin, Morris, and Robert J. Van Handel. "Rule-of-Thumb Theory of Cash Holdings by Firm." *Journal of Financial and Quantitative Analysis* 10 (March 1975), pp. 85–108.

Emery, Gary W. "Some Empirical Evidence on the Properties of Daily Cash Flow." *Financial Management* 10 (Spring 1981), pp. 21–28.

Hofer, C. F. "Analysis of Fixed Costs in Inventory." *Management Accounting* (September 1970), pp. 15–17.

Irwin, Tom R. "Cash Flow Management . . . A State of Mind." *Cost & Management* 58, no. 1 (January–February 1984), pp. 42–45.

Kim, Yong H.; Joseph C. Atkins; and Walter Dolde. "Evaluating Investments in Accounts Receivable: A Maximizing Framework." *Journal of Finance* 33 (May 1978), pp. 403–12.

Magee, John F. "Guides to Inventory Policy, 1–3." *Harvard Business Review* 34 (January–February 1956), pp. 49–60; 34 (March–April 1956), pp. 103–16; and 34 (May–June 1956), pp. 57–70.

Miller, Merton H., and Daniel Orr. "The Demand for Money by Firms: Extension of Analytic Results." *Journal of Finance* 23 (December 1968), pp. 735–59.

_______. "A Model of the Demand for Money by Firms." *Quarterly Journal of Economics* 80 (August 1966), pp. 413–35.

Miller, Tom W., and Bernell K. Stone. "Daily Cash Modeling and Seasonal Resolution: Alternative Models and Techniques for Using the Distribution Approach." *Journal of Financial and Quantitative Analysis* 20 (September 1985), pp. 335–51.

Patterson, Harlan R. "New Life in the Management of Corporate Receivables." *Credit and Financial Management* 72 (February 1970), pp. 15–18.

Rodriguez, Rita M., and Eugene E. Carter. *International Financial Management.* 2nd ed. Englewood Cliffs, N.J.: Prentice-Hall, 1979.

Schiff, Michael. "Credit and Inventory Management." *Financial Executive* 40 (November 1972), pp. 28–33.

Smith, Keith V. *Management of Working Capital.* St. Paul, Minn.: West Publishing, 1974, sec. 4.

Walford, J. Stewart. "The Canadian Money Market—The Secret Is Out." *Canadian Banker* 93, no. 1 (February 1986), pp. 26–30.

8 Sources of Short-Term Financing

In Chapter 8 we examine the cost and availability of the various outlets for short-term funds with primary attention to trade credit from suppliers, bank loans, corporate promissory notes, foreign borrowing, and loans against receivables and inventory. It is sometimes said the only way to be sure a bank loan will be approved is to convince the banker you don't really need the money. The learning objective of this chapter will be quite the opposite—namely, to demonstrate how required funds can be made available on a short-term basis from the various suppliers of credit.

Figure 8–1 shows the overall profile of various sources and forms of debt in financing nonfinancial Canadian corporations. As of the end of 1984 this group of companies owed a total of $616 billion to creditors. Among the larger Canadian companies short-term financing comprised 37 percent of the overall total debt. In this chapter we will deal with the sources that provide that short-term financing. Chapter 16 will

Figure 8–1
Structure of the debt of nonfinancial private (sector) corporations in Canada

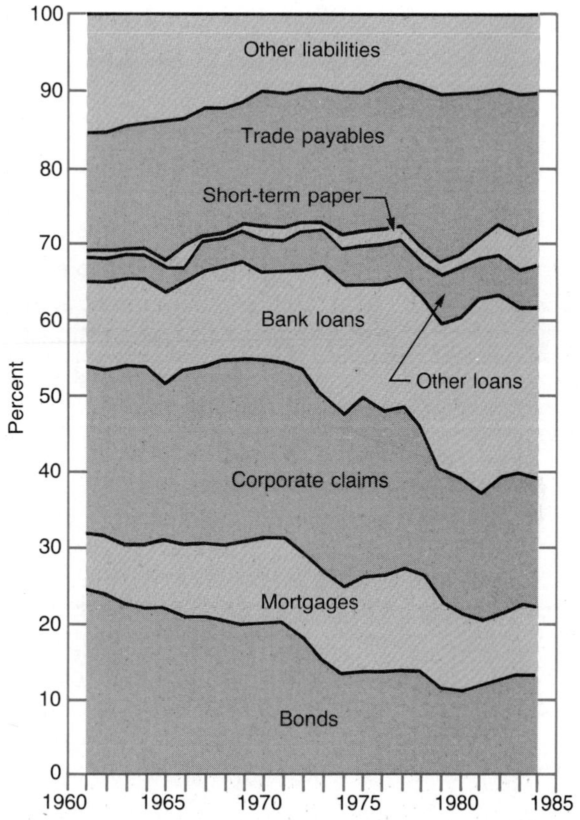

Source: *National Balance Sheet Accounts,* CAI/BS13/214, Statistics Canada.

explore, in depth, the longer-term sources of that debt while Chapter 21 will examine the international sources.

Trade Credit

The largest provider of short-term credit is usually at the firm's doorstep—the manufacturer or seller of goods and services. Approximately 45 percent of short-term financing is in the form of accounts payable or trade credit. Trade payables are a spontaneous source of funds, growing as the business expands on a seasonal or long-term basis and contracting in a like fashion.

Payment Period

Trade credit is extended for 30 to 60 days although that varies by industry. For example, many suppliers of foodstuffs, like ice cream, to small retailers give only 10 days to pay. Many firms attempt to "stretch the payment period" in order to provide additional short-term financing. This is an acceptable form of financing as long as it is not carried to an abusive extent. Going from a 30- to a 35-day average payment period may be tolerated within the trade, while stretching payments to 65 days might alienate suppliers and cause a diminishing credit rating with Dun & Bradstreet and local credit bureaus. A major variable in determining the payment period is the possible existence of a cash discount.

Cash Discount Policy

A cash discount allows for a reduction in price if payment is made within a specified time period. A 2/10, net 30 cash discount means we can deduct 2 percent if we remit our funds 10 days after billing, but failing this, we must pay the full amount by the 30th day.

On a \$100 billing we could pay \$98 up to the 10th day or \$100 at the end of 30 days. If we fail to take the cash discount we will get to use \$98 for 20 more days for a \$2 fee. The interest rate on the use of that money is then a whopping 37.23 percent. Note that we first consider the interest cost and then convert this to an annual basis. The standard formula for approximating this interest cost is:

$$\begin{aligned}\text{Cost of failing to take a cash discount} &= \frac{\text{Discount percent}}{100\text{ percent} - \text{Discount percent}} \\ &\quad \times \frac{365}{\text{Final due date} - \text{Discount period}} \qquad (8\text{–}1) \\ &= \frac{2\%}{100\% - 2\%} \times \frac{365}{30 - 10} \\ &= 2.04\% \times 18.25 = 37.23\%\end{aligned}$$

This formula fails to account for the cumulative effect of being able to earn interest on the interest in each succeeding 20-day period after the first period. Therefore, the real rate of interest is more like 43 percent.[1]

Cash discount terms may vary. For example, on a 2/10, net 90 basis, it would cost us only 9.3 percent not to take the discount and to pay the full amount after 90 days.

$$\frac{2\%}{100\% - 2\%} \times \frac{365}{90 - 10} = 2.04\% \times 4.56 = 9.30\%$$

In each case we must ask ourselves whether bypassing the discount and using the money for a longer period of time is the cheapest means of financing. In the first example, with an approximated cost of 37.23 percent, it probably is not. We would be better off borrowing $98 for 20 days at some lesser rate. For example, at 10 percent interest we would pay 54 cents[2] in interest as opposed to $2 under the cash discount policy. With the 2/10, net 90 arrangement, the cost of missing the discount is only 9.3 percent, and we may choose to let our suppliers carry us for an extra 80 days.

Net Credit Position

In Chapter 2, Review of Accounting, we defined accounts receivable as a use of funds and accounts payable as a source. The firm should closely watch the relationship between the two to determine its net credit position. If a firm has average daily sales of $5,000 and collects in 30 days, the accounts receivable balance will be $150,000. If this is associated with average daily purchases of $4,000 and a 25-day average payment period, the average accounts payable balance is $100,000—indicating $50,000 more in credit extended than received. Changing this situation to an average payment period of 40 days increases the accounts payable to $160,000 ($4,000 × 40). Accounts payable would then exceed accounts receivable by $10,000, thus leaving funds for other needs. Larger firms tend to be net providers of trade credit

---

[1]The methods and rationale for such compounding are covered in Chapter 9.

[2] $\frac{20}{365} \times 10\% \times \$98 = \$.54$

(relatively high receivables), with smaller firms in the user position (relatively high payables). Of course, anyone who has dealt with the large retail chains knows how carefully they manage their payables, using them as an important source of funds.

Bank Credit

Banks may provide funds to finance seasonal needs, product line expansions, long-term growth, and so on. The preferred type of loan from the point of view of most bankers is a self-liquidating loan the use of which generates cash flows that will form a built-in or automatic repayment scheme. Although financing by Canadian banks has traditionally been more for short-term than long-term needs, that situation has changed dramatically in recent years. As of mid-1985 over 60 percent of the almost $50 billion owed by mid-size and large-size Canadian nonfinancial corporations to banks were classed as long-term debt. In addition, through the process of renewing old loans many of the 90- or 180-day agreements take on the characteristics of longer-term financing.

Major changes are taking place in banking today that are centered on the concept of "full-service banking." The modern banker's function is much broader than merely accepting deposits, making loans, and processing cheques. At present a banking institution may be providing investment services, a credit card operation, real estate lending, data processing services, and helpful advice in cash management or international trade. This wide array of services has become possible over time because of periodic changes in the Bank Act—current contemplation of changes in restrictions on bank ownership may further expand the types of operations with which a bank may become involved.

Unlike the U.S. situation, where banking has traditionally been a state-by-state industry, banking in Canada has been carried on on a national basis. In the 1970s the concept of regional banks to service the needs of Western Canadians was embedded in the operations of the Northland Bank, the Canadian Commercial Bank, and the Bank of British Columbia. Downturns in the oil industry and in western real estate values put these banks into insolvent positions so that the first two have gone out of existence while the third has been taken over by the subsidiary of a large foreign bank. Ongoing deregulation of the financial industries in Canada seems destined to create greater competition among financial institutions such as commercial banks, trust companies, caisses populaire, insurance companies, and securities dealers.

We will look at a number of terms generally associated with banking (and other types of lending activity) and consider the significance of each. Attention is directed to the prime interest rate, compensating balances, the term loan arrangement, and methods of computing interest.

Prime Rate - what bank of Canada charges banks

This is the rate the bank charges its most creditworthy customers, and it is scaled up proportionally to reflect the various credit classes. At certain slack loan periods in the economy, banks may actually charge top customers less than the published prime rate; however, such activities are difficult to track. The average customer can expect to pay 1 or 2 percent above prime, while in tight money periods a builder in a speculative construction project may pay 5 or more percentage points over prime.

Figure 8–2 presents the annual average prime rate from 1968 until early 1987 for Canada compared with the United States. While the period before 1968 does not show up, it should be pointed out that interest rates in the 1950s and early 1960s were relatively stable. Beginning in 1965 and continuing into the present the prime rate became highly volatile, moving as much as 10 percentage points in the 12-month period leading up to August 1981 when it hit a high point of 22.75 percent. In fact, from Figure 8–2 we see the prime rate in the early 1980s above 20 percent for several months before sharply declining. With lower inflation from 1982 to 1985 interest rates followed the same pattern, and the prime ended 1986 at 9¾ percent falling further to 9¼ percent in the first two months of 1987.

Compensating Balances

In providing loans and other services, banks have sometimes in the past required that business customers maintain a minimum average account balance, herein referred to as a compensating balance. The required amount is usually computed as a percentage of customer loans

Figure 8–2
Prime interest rate movements

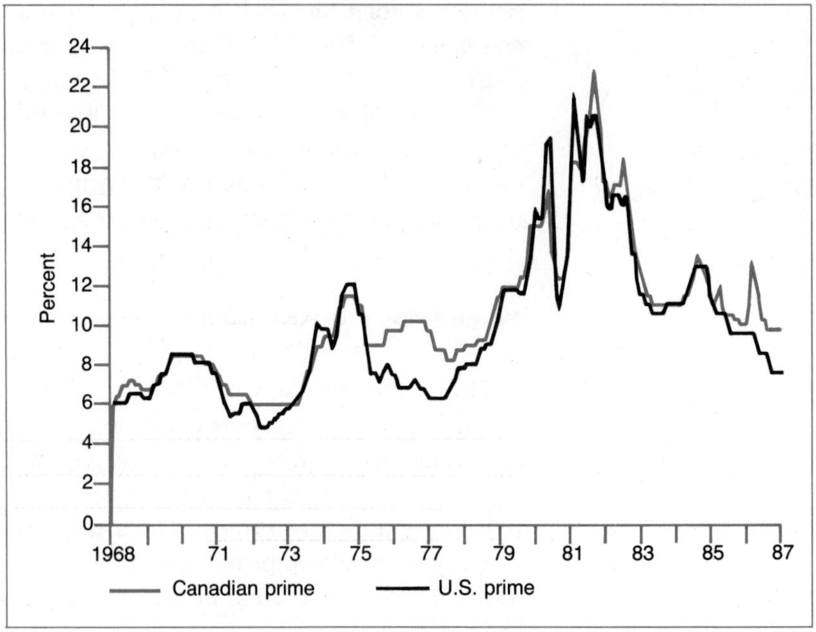

outstanding or as a percentage of bank commitments toward future loans to a given account. A common ratio used to be 20 percent against outstanding loans though market conditions tended to influence the percentages.

Some view the compensating balance requirement as an unusual arrangement. Where else would you walk into a business establishment, buy a shipment of goods, and then be told that you could not take 20 percent of the purchase home with you? If you borrowed $100,000, paying 8 percent interest on the full amount with a 20 percent compensating balance requirement, you would be paying $8,000 for the use of $80,000 in funds, or an effective rate of 10 percent.

The amount that must be borrowed to end up with the desired sum of money is simply figured by taking the needed funds and dividing by $(1 - c)$, where c is the compensating balance expressed as a decimal. For example, if you need $100,000 in funds you must borrow $125,000 to ensure that the intended amount will be available. This would be calculated as follows:

$$\text{Amount to be borrowed} = \frac{\text{Amount needed}}{(1 - c)}$$

$$= \frac{\$100{,}000}{(1 - 0.2)}$$

$$= \$125{,}000$$

A check on this calculation could be done to see if we actually end up with the use of $100,000:

$125,000	Loan
−25,000	20% compensating balance requirement
$100,000	Available funds

Under the Bank Act borrowers must agree to the compensating balance requirement, and Canadian banks must disclose the full cost of the loan, which is increased by the need for a compensating balance. In fact, however, banks seem to be making most of their loans these days without the requirement for the compensating balance, preferring instead to charge interest rates consistent with their cost of funds. The emphasis has turned to doing more intensive analysis of the profitability of each loan.

Maturity Provisions

As previously indicated, bank loans have been traditionally short term in nature (though perhaps renewable). In the last decade there has been a movement to the use of the term loan in which credit is extended for a period of one to seven years. The loan is usually repaid in monthly or quarterly installments over its life rather than in one single payment. Only superior credit applicants, as measured by working capital strength, potential profitability, and competitive position, can qualify for term loan financing.

Bankers are hesitant to fix a single interest rate to a term loan. The more common practice is to allow the interest rate to change with market conditions. Thus, the interest rate on a term loan may be tied to the prime rate and will change (float) with it. A good customer may have its rate set at prime plus 1 percent, for example. More will be said on term loans in Chapter 16 when we discuss longer-term financing.

Cost of Commercial Bank Financing

The effective interest rate on a loan is based on the loan amount, the dollar interest paid, the length of the loan, and the method of repayment. It is easy enough to observe that $60 interest on a $1,000 loan for one year would carry a 6 percent interest rate; but what if the same loan were for 120 days? To come to an approximate answer to that question we use the formula:

$$\begin{aligned}\text{Effective rate} &= \frac{\text{Interest}}{\text{Principal}} \times \frac{\text{Days in the year}}{\text{Days loan is outstanding}} \\ &= \frac{\$60}{\$1{,}000} \times \frac{365}{120} \qquad (8\text{–}2)\\ &= 6\% \times 3 = 18.25\%\end{aligned}$$

Since we have use of the funds for only 120 days, the effective rate is approximately 18.25 percent. If we took into account the accumulation of interest on the interest in the second and third 120-day periods, we would come to an annual interest rate of slightly over 19 percent. To highlight the effect of time, if you borrowed $20 for only 10 days and paid back $21, the effective interest rate would be over 180 percent—a gross violation of our sense of what is ethical.

$$\frac{\$1}{\$20} \times \frac{365}{10} = 5\% \times 36.5 = 182.5\%$$

Not only is the time dimension of a loan important but also the way in which interest is charged. We have assumed that interest would be paid when the loan comes due. If the bank deducts the interest in advance (discounts the loan), the effective rate of interest increases. For example, a $1,000 one-year loan with $60 of interest deducted in advance represents the payment of interest on only $940, or an effective rate of 6.38 percent.

$$\begin{aligned}\text{Effective rate on discounted loan} &= \frac{\text{Interest}}{\text{Principal} - \text{Interest}} \\ &\times \frac{\text{Days in the year}}{\text{Days loan is outstanding}} \qquad (8\text{–}3)\\ &= \frac{\$60}{\$1{,}000 - \$60} \times \frac{365}{365} = \frac{\$60}{\$940} = 6.38\%\end{aligned}$$

Interest Costs with Compensating Balances

When a loan is made with compensating balances the effective interest rate is the stated interest rate divided by $(1 - c)$, where c is the compensating balance expressed as a decimal. Assume that 6 percent is the stated annual rate and that a 20 percent compensating balance is required.

$$\text{Effective rate with compensating balances} = \frac{\text{Interest rate}}{(1 - c)} \quad (8\text{–}4)$$

$$= \frac{6\%}{(1 - 0.2)}$$

$$= 7.5\%$$

If dollar amounts are used and the stated rate is unknown, Formula 8–5 can be used. The assumption is that we are paying $60 interest on a $1,000 loan but are only able to use $800 of the funds. The loan is for a year.

$$\begin{array}{l}\text{Effective}\\ \text{rate with}\\ \text{compensating}\\ \text{balances}\end{array} = \frac{\text{Interest}}{\text{Principal} - \begin{array}{c}\text{Compensating}\\ \text{balance in dollars}\end{array}} \times \frac{\text{Days in the year (365)}}{\text{Days loan is outstanding}} \quad (8\text{–}5)$$

$$= \frac{\$60}{\$1{,}000 - \$200} \times \frac{365}{365} = \frac{\$60}{\$800} = 7.5\%$$

Of course, it may arise that the firm has ongoing cash needs greater than the compensating balance required. In theory the compensating balance is supposed to be above and beyond those needs. However, in some cases the compensating balance requirement does not require the firm to have more cash on hand than it otherwise would. In such cases the firm would not use Formula 8–4 or 8–5 to adjust the effective rate of the loan.

Rate on Installment Loans

The most confusing borrowing arrangement to the average bank customer or consumer is the installment loan. An installment loan calls for a series of equal payments over the life of the loan. Though federal legislation prohibits a misrepresentation of interest rates on loans to customers, it would be possible for a loan officer or an overanxious salesperson to quote a rate on an installment loan that is approximately half the true rate.

Assume you borrow $1,000 on a 12-month installment basis, with regular monthly payments to apply to interest and principal, and the interest requirement is $60. Though it might be suggested that the rate on the loan is 6 percent ($60/$1,000), this is clearly not the case. It is true you will pay a total of $60 in interest, but you do not have the use of $1,000 for one year. Rather, you are paying back the $1,000 on a monthly basis, with an average outstanding loan balance for the year of a little more than $500. The effective rate of interest is 11.08 percent. Formula 8–6 can be used for approximating the effective rate of interest on an installment loan.

$$\text{Rate on installment loan} = \frac{2 \times \text{Annual number of payments} \times \text{Interest}}{(\text{Total number of payments} + 1) \times \text{Principal}} \qquad (8\text{–}6)$$

$$= \frac{2 \times 12 \times \$60}{13 \times \$1{,}000} = \frac{\$1{,}440}{\$13{,}000} = 11.08\%$$

The Credit Crunch Phenomenon

In 1969–70, 1973–74, and 1979–81 the economy went through a period of extreme credit shortage in the banking sector and other financial markets. This suggests that we seem to find ourselves in the midst of a tight money situation once in every four to five years. The anatomy of such a credit crunch has been as follows. The Bank of Canada tightens the growth in the money supply in its battle against inflation, causing a decrease in funds available for lending and an increase in interest rates. To compound the difficulty, business requirements for funds may be increasing to carry inflation-laden inventory and receivables. The increase in general interest rates causes a third problem—the withdrawal of savings deposits from our financial institutions, all in search of higher returns. The net result is that there simply are not enough lendable funds to go around. Recent policy changes by the Bank of Canada reverting away from trying to control the growth of the money supply directly will mean that future credit shortages, if they develop, will arise in an at least slightly different fashion.

Recent history has taught us that the way *not* to deal with credit shortages is to impose artificial limits on interest rates in the form of restrictive usury laws or extreme governmental pressure. In 1969–70 the prime rate went to 8.5 percent in a tight money period—a level not high enough to bring the forces of demand and supply together, and little credit was available. In 1974 the prime rose to 11.5 percent, a rate truly reflecting market conditions, and funds were available. The same was true in 1980 and 1981 as the prime went to 20 percent and higher, but funds were available for borrowers.

Between 1978 and 1982 the Bank of Canada had put increasing emphasis on "attempting" to control the rate of growth in the money supply at a steady pace and allowing interest rates to move freely. This helps to explain part of the volatility in interest rates in the last few years up to the mid-80s. Current Bank of Canada policy is seemingly aimed at influencing the level of the Canadian dollar on international exchange markets by managing interest rates. As such it is highly dependent on economic circumstances in the U.S. economy.[3]

Financing through Commercial Paper

ex: Visa

For large, prestigious firms commercial paper may provide an outlet for raising funds. Commercial paper represents a short-term, unsecured promissory note issued to the public in minimum units of $25,000. Rather than paying interest, commercial paper is sold at a discount from the maturity value, the depth of the discount determining the rate of return. As Figure 8–3 indicates (see page 234), the amount of commercial paper outstanding has increased dramatically, rising from $2 billion in 1970 to over $13 billion in 1985. This large increase in the commercial paper market reflects the eagerness of qualified companies to borrow at the lowest possible rate available. The larger market that has emerged in the last five years has improved the ability of corporations to raise short-term funds.

Commercial paper falls into two categories. First, there are finance companies, such as Avco Financial Services of Canada, Canadian Tire Acceptance Corporation, and Household Finance Corporation, that

[3]See Chapter 21 for a better understanding of why this is so.

issue paper primarily to institutional investors such as pension funds, insurance companies, and money market mutual funds. Paper sold by financial firms such as Canadian Tire Acceptance is referred to as *finance paper,* and since it is usually sold directly to the lender by the finance company, it is also referred to as *direct paper.* Sales finance, consumer loan, and other financial institutions use the commercial paper market to fund their ordinary course of business. The second type of commercial paper is sold by industrial or utility firms, like Stelco or Bell Canada Enterprises, that use an intermediate dealer network to distribute their paper. This is referred to as *dealer paper.* Nonfinancial corporations account for just under $4 billion in commercial paper debt, often issuing it to fund seasonal fluctuations in inventory or accounts receivable.

Advantages of Commercial Paper

The growing popularity of commercial paper can be attributed largely to its relative cheapness compared to short-term bank debt. For example, commercial paper may be issued at below the prime interest rate. As indicated in the last column of Table 8–1, this rate differential is generally between .5 and 2 percent except during times of extremely tight money. Differentials of over 2 percent during the tight money of 1981 partially account for the surge in commercial paper activity at that time. At the same point in time the differential in the U.S. market had reached 5 percent, causing an even greater expansion in the issuance of commercial paper in that market.

A second advantage of commercial paper is that no compensating balance requirements are associated with its issuance, though the firm is generally required to maintain commercial bank lines of approved credit equal to the amount of the paper outstanding (a procedure somewhat less costly than compensating balances). Finally, a number of firms enjoy the prestige associated with being able to float their commercial paper in what is considered a "snobbish market" for funds.

Limitations on the Issuance of Commercial Paper

Historically, commercial paper activity has sometimes led to problems. In 1965 the default of the Atlantic Acceptance Corporation was a reminder to the lenders of the risks involved. In the huge U.S.

Table 8–1
Comparison of commercial paper rate to bank prime rate

Year	Bankers' Acceptances	Commercial Paper (90-day)	Bank Prime	Prime minus Commercial Paper
	Average Interest Rate at December 31			
1968	6.50%	6.65%	6.75%	.10%
1969	8.90	9.17	8.50	(.67)
1970	6.10	5.58	7.50	1.92
1971	4.15	4.32	6.00	1.68
1972	4.80	5.15	6.50	1.35
1973	9.30	10.25	9.50	(.75)
1974	9.78	10.25	11.00	.75
1975	9.23	9.32	9.75	.43
1976	8.25	8.05	9.75	1.70
1977	7.15	7.23	8.25	1.02
1978	10.23	10.78	11.50	.72
1979	13.85	14.20	15.00	.80
1980	18.45	17.75	18.25	.50
1981	14.93	15.65	17.25	1.65
1982	10.20	10.25	12.50	2.25
1983	9.57	9.85	11.00	1.15
1984	10.10	10.00	11.25	1.25
1985	9.45	9.40	10.00	1.60
1986	8.16	8.40	9.75	1.35

commercial paper market, Penn Central Railroad went bankrupt in 1970 with $85 million in "bad" commercial paper floating around. This caused many lenders in the market to panic and refuse to roll over (renew) existing paper as it came due. The market shrank by 15 percent from May to December of that year, and the unnerving situation almost caused Chrysler Financial Corporation to be towed away.

The lesson to be learned is that although the funds provided through the issuance of commercial paper are cheaper than bank loans, they are also less predictable. Along with the higher rate on a bank loan, a firm may also be buying a degree of loyalty and commitment that is unavailable in the commercial paper market. Therefore, lines of credit at a commercial bank are important in protecting the firm against adverse turns of events in the money markets.

Bankers' Acceptances

Figure 8–3 displays the prominent role played by bankers' acceptances in short-term debt financing in recent years. This instrument accounted for almost $18 billion of borrowings at the end of 1985 versus

Figure 8–3
Corporate short-term paper

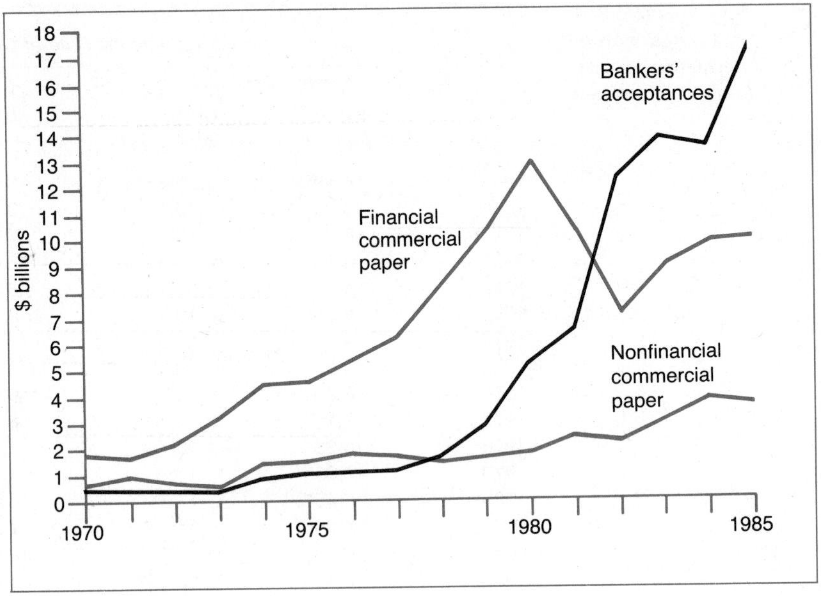

$1 billion 10 years earlier. The main use of bankers' acceptances has been to finance inventories of finished goods in transit to the buyers. As you can well imagine, companies engaged in foreign trade find this form of financing especially helpful given the long lead times involved.

As an example, consider a case where a Canadian company is importing machinery from a German manufacturer, agreeing to pay in 180 days. The Canadian company would arrange a letter of credit with a Canadian bank. Under the letter of credit the bank agrees to accept a draft drawn by the German company on the Canadian importer. Hence, the term bankers' acceptance is used to signify the accepted draft once it has been sent by the exporter to the importer's bank. By accepting the draft, the bank has substituted its creditworthiness for that of the customer. If the bank is one of our major banks, the draft becomes a highly marketable money market instrument. This means that the German manufacturer does not have to hold the draft until the due date, but rather, it can sell it in the money market at a discount from its face value. The discount allows the buyer of the bankers' acceptance to realize a return for holding the acceptance until the 180-day payment period is up.

Foreign Borrowing

NO

An increasing source of funds for Canadian firms has been the large Eurocurrency market. Loans from foreign banks denominated in U.S. dollars (the most common currency) are called Eurodollar loans. Such loans are usually short term to intermediate term in maturity. Many multinational corporations are finding cheaper ways of borrowing in foreign markets. A new approach in the 1980s has been for financial managers to borrow *foreign currencies* either directly or through foreign subsidiaries at very favorable interest rates. The companies *convert* the borrowed francs or marks to dollars, which are then sent to Canada to be used by the parent company. There is, however, foreign exchange exposure risk associated with these loans. This topic is given greater coverage in Chapter 21.

Unsecured Bank Loans

Almost any firm would prefer to borrow on an unsecured basis. Short-term, unsecured loans may be extended by a bank to a borrower under a line of credit, a revolving-credit agreement, or on a transaction basis.

Line of credit Credit lines are usually established on a year-to-year basis between a bank and its customer. The line of credit is an agreement whereby the bank sets out the maximum amount it will allow the firm to owe it at any one time. The amount of the line depends on an assessment of the firm's creditworthiness. The line of credit is usually evidenced by a letter from the bank. However, the letter does not legally bind the bank to extend credit to the customer on demand. If the creditworthiness of the customer were to change or if the bank were to become tight for funds, the bank might refuse to lend money under the line of credit agreement. In practice, however, a bank would be very reluctant not to honour its commitments under lines of credit.

The arrangement for lines of credit is an important role of the financial manager. For example, as of late 1986 Northern Telecom had committed operating lines of credit of $125 million available from three Canadian chartered banks as well as an $80 million line renewable monthly for 18 months from the Chemical Bank of New York. In addition, Northern had revolving credit agreements with Canadian banks for another $155 million.

Revolving credit agreements The basic differences between the revolving credit agreement and the line of credit are that the revolving credits are usually for periods longer than one year, and they usually involve a fee calculated as a fraction of the unused portion of the credit. Technically, because they are for periods longer than one year, revolving credits are generally classed as intermediate rather than short-term financing.

Transaction loans Sometimes a borrower needs a loan to fund one particular project. In such cases a line of credit or a revolving credit agreement do not make sense. The bank might finance a company to finish work on a piece of machinery which is to be delivered on contract to a large customer. When the machine is delivered and paid for, the firm would repay its debt to the bank.

Use of Collateral in Short-Term Financing

Despite the fact that firms prefer to borrow on an unsecured (no-collateral) basis, if the borrower's credit rating is too low or its need for funds too great, the lending institution will require that certain assets be pledged. A secured credit arrangement generally helps the borrower obtain funds that would otherwise be unavailable.

In any loan the lender's primary concern, however, is whether the borrower's capacity to generate cash flow is sufficient to liquidate the loan as it comes due. Few lenders would make a loan strictly on the basis of collateral. Collateral is merely a stopgap device to protect the lender when all else fails. The bank or finance company is in business to collect interest, not to repossess and resell assets. Though a number of different types of assets may be pledged, our attention will be directed to accounts receivable and inventory.

Accounts Receivable Financing

Accounts receivable financing may include *pledging* accounts receivable as collateral for a loan or an outright *sale* (factoring) of receivables. Receivables financing is popular because it permits borrowing to be tied directly to the level of asset expansion at any given time. As the level of accounts receivable goes up we are able to borrow more.

A drawback is that this is a relatively expensive method of acquiring funds, so it must be carefully compared to other forms of credit. Accounts receivable represent valuable short-term assets, and they should be committed only where the appropriate circumstances exist. An ill-advised accounts receivable financing plan may exclude the firm from a less expensive bank term loan. Let us investigate more closely the characteristics and the costs associated with the pledging and selling of receivables.

Pledging Accounts Receivable

The lending institution will generally stipulate which of the accounts receivable are of sufficient quality to serve as collateral for a loan. For example, banks will generally not accept accounts receivable that are more than 90 days old. The firm may borrow up to 60–65 percent of the value of the acceptable collateral from a bank. The loan percentage will depend on the financial strength of the borrowing firm and on the credit risk of its accounts. The lender will have full recourse against the borrower in the event any of the accounts go bad. The interest rate in a receivables borrowing arrangement is generally 1 to 3 percent in excess of the prime rate.

The interest is computed against the loan balance outstanding, a figure that may change quite frequently, as indicated in Table 8–2. In the illustration interest is assumed to be 12 percent annually, or approximately 1 percent per month. In month 1, the firm can borrow $6,000 against $10,000 in acceptable receivables and must pay $60 in interest. Similar values are developed for succeeding months.

Table 8–2
Receivable loan balance

	Month 1	*Month 2*	*Month 3*	*Month 4*
Total accounts receivable	$11,000	$15,100	$19,400	16,300
Acceptable receivables (to bank)	10,000	14,000	18,000	15,000
Loan balance (60%)	6,000	8,400	10,800	9,000
Interest—1% per month	60	84	108	90

Factoring Receivables

Factoring companies deal only with companies that produce physical product rather than service companies. In Canada there are only a handful of factoring companies active in any one of the major cities such as Accord Business Credit Inc. in Toronto and Boston Factors in Montreal. Smaller manufacturers in the apparel, consumer electronics, furniture, and automotive aftermarket industries are the prime users of factoring services. Factoring companies may provide accounts receivable management alone or combined with receivables-based financing.

The factoring company may be used as a direct substitute for the firm's accounts receivable department. The client firm sells its product and sends a copy of the invoice to the factor which then takes over collection responsibility. The invoiced customers still pay the client firm, but the factor keeps track of payments, sends follow-up notices to late payers, and so forth. As part of the service the factor usually provides a credit guarantee. This guarantee provides that if a factor cannot collect a legitimate accounts receivable within a specified period, often 180 days, the factor will pay the client firm for the receivable and take possession of it itself. Rates for this management service, including the credit guarantee, are 1 to 2 percent per month. Thus, although the factor's service is not cheap, the client firm may save on bad debt expenses as well as administrative costs related to managing collections.

Factoring companies will also provide financing based on receivables as collateral. For a rate of prime plus 1½–3 percent the factor might actually advance a higher proportion of the value of receivables, sometimes as much as 80 to 90 percent.

Consider, as an illustration, a case where a factor administers all of a client's receivables and advances 80 percent of their value as an operating loan. If $100,000 a month is processed at a 2 percent commission and a 12 percent annual borrowing rate is charged on the loan, the total effective cost of the borrowing is often calculated as approximately 42 percent on an *annual* basis.

2.50%	Commission (2%/80% advanced)
1.00%	Interest for one month (12% annual/12)
3.50%	Total fee monthly
3.50%	Monthly × 12 = 42% annual rate

The important part of the factoring analysis, however, is to determine what portion of the cost relates to the administration and credit guarantee service and to determine if that is reasonable. If the equivalent cost of a secured loan from the bank was also 12 percent, then the company would have to determine if the commission costs of 2 percent per month or $24,000 per year are justified by administrative and credit loss savings. For example, if the firm estimated that factoring would save $10,000 in credit checking and clerical costs as well as avoid a ½ percent bad debt experience, the estimated savings would be $22,000 per year versus a cost of $24,000.

$10,000	Administrative cost savings
12,000	Bad debt savings ($100,000 × .005 × 12)
$22,000	

If, on the other hand, the firm estimated that the factor would insure receivables upon which it expected a bad debt experience of 1 percent or more, choosing to factor its receivables would be a sound financial decision.

Asset-Backed Public Offerings

A new wrinkle in accounts receivable financing has surfaced in the United States. It is the sale of receivables by large firms in public offerings. While factoring has long been one way of selling receivables, public offerings of securities backed by receivables as collateral gained respectability when General Motors Acceptance Corporation made a public offering of $500 million of asset-backed securities in December of 1985.

These asset-backed securities are nothing more than the sale of receivables. In former years companies that sold receivables were viewed as short of cash, financially shaky, or in some sort of financial trouble. While this negative perception has yet to be overcome, new issues of receivables-backed securities by companies such as Sperry Corporation, Marine Midland Bank, and General Motors may succeed in changing this perception. Sperry's securities are backed by computer leases, and so far the others are backed by automobile loans. If these new offerings are successful, more firms such as Ford, Chrysler, and other large companies may follow suit in Canada as well.

The public sale of receivables involves other problems in addition to the image one. Computer systems need to be upgraded to service securities and handle the paperwork. In order for GMAC to offer such a large public issue, they had to change their whole data-processing system to keep track of the loans for the investors in the securities. Additionally, regulatory roadblocks stand in the way of banks (which have the potential to be the largest segment of this new market). Not all loans are repaid, and risk to the purchaser of receivables-backed securities exists. Even though current loss rates on loans were about one half of 1 percent in late 1985, bad debts can be as much as 5 to 10 percent in tight money markets. What may develop is either self-insured guaranteed payment by the selling company or outside insurance firms guaranteeing the repayment of the offering in total. While this short-term market is still relatively small by money market standards, it could provide an important avenue for corporate liquidity and short-term financing in the future.

Inventory Financing

We may also borrow against inventory to acquire funds. The extent to which inventory financing may be employed is based on the marketability of the pledged goods, their associated price stability, and the perishability of the product. Another significant factor is the degree of physical control that can be exercised over the product by the lender. We can relate some of these factors to the stages of inventory production and the nature of lender control.

Stages of Production

Raw materials and finished goods are likely to provide the best collateral, while goods in process may only qualify for a small percentage loan. For a firm holding such widely traded raw materials as lumber, metals, grain, cotton, and wool, a loan of 70–80 percent is possible. The lender may only have to place a few quick phone calls to dispose of the goods at market value if the borrower fails to repay the loan. For standardized finished goods, such as tires, canned goods, and building products, the same principle would apply. On the other hand, goods in process, representing altered but unfinished raw materials, may qualify for a loan of only one fourth their value or less.

Nature of Lender Control

The methods for controlling pledged inventory go from the simple to the complex, providing ever-greater assurances to the lender but progressively higher administrative costs.

Blanket inventory liens The simplest method is for the lender to have a general claim against the inventory of the borrower. Specific items are not identified or tagged, and there is no physical control.

Trust receipts A trust receipt is an instrument acknowledging that the borrower holds the inventory and proceeds from sales in trust for the lender. Each item is carefully marked and specified by serial number. When sold, the proceeds are transferred to the lender, and the trust receipt is cancelled. Also known as *floor planning,* this financing device is very popular among auto and industrial equipment dealers and in the television and home appliance industries. Although it provides tighter control than does the blanket inventory lien, it still does not give the lender direct control over inventory—only a better and more legally enforceable system of tracing the goods.

Warehousing Under this arrangement goods are physically identified, segregated, and stored under the direction of an independent warehousing company. The firm issues a warehouse receipt to the lender, and goods can be moved only with the lender's approval.

The goods may be stored on the premises of the warehousing firm, an arrangement known as *public warehousing,* or on the borrower's premises—under a *field warehousing* agreement. When field warehousing is utilized it is still an independent warehousing company that exercises control over inventory.

Appraisal of Inventory Control Devices

While the more structured methods of inventory financing appear somewhat restrictive, they are well accepted in certain industries. For example, field warehousing is popular in grain storage and food canning. Well-maintained control measures do involve substantial administrative expenses, and they raise the overall costs of borrowing. The costs of inventory financing may run 15 percent or higher. As is true of accounts receivable financing, the extension of funds is well synchronized with the need.

Summary

A firm in search of short-term financing must be aware of all the institutional arrangements that are available. The easiest access is to trade credit provided by suppliers as a natural outgrowth of the buying and reselling of goods. Larger firms tend to be net providers of trade credit, while smaller firms are net users.

Bank financing has traditionally been in the form of short-term, self-liquidating loans. Banks are still an important source of this type of financing even as they have greatly increased their activity in longer-term lending. A financially strong customer will be offered the prime, or lowest rate, with the rates to other accounts scaled up appropriately. The use of compensating balances traditionally tended to increase the effective yield to the bank. More commonly today, however, compensating balances serve as a device to compensate the bank for the many services it provides to a commercial account.

An alternative to bank credit for the large, prestigious firm is the use of commercial paper. Though generally issued at a rate below prime it is an impersonal means of financing that may "dry up" during difficult financing periods.

Firms are also turning to foreign sources of funds, either through the Eurocurrency market or through borrowing foreign currency directly.

A firm may borrow on an unsecured basis by arranging a bank line of credit, a revolving credit, or a transaction loan. By using a secured form of financing the firm ties its borrowing requirements directly to its asset buildup. It may pledge its accounts receivable as collateral or sell them outright, as well as borrow against inventory. Though secured-asset financing devices may be expensive, they may well fit the credit needs of the firm, particularly those of a small firm that cannot qualify for premium bank financing or the commercial paper market.

List of Terms

trade credit	receivables factoring
self-liquidating loan	pledging receivables
prime rate	blanket inventory liens
compensating balances	trust receipt
commercial paper	transaction loan
bankers' acceptance	public warehousing
line of credit	field warehousing
revolving credit	discounted loan

Discussion Questions

1. Under what circumstances would it be advisable to borrow money to take a cash discount?
2. Discuss the relative use of credit between large and small firms. Which group is generally in the net creditor position and why?
3. What is the prime interest rate? How does the average bank customer fare in regard to the prime interest rate? Are companies ever allowed by banks to borrow at less than prime?
4. What advantages do compensating balances have for banks? Are the advantages to banks necessarily disadvantages to corporations?
5. A borrower is often confronted with a stated interest rate and an effective interest rate. What is the difference, and which one should the financial manager recognize as the true cost of borrowing?
6. Commercial paper may show up on corporate balance sheets as either a current asset or a current liability. Explain this statement.
7. What are the advantages of commercial paper in comparison wih bank borrowing at the prime rate? What are the disadvantages?
8. What is the major advantage of a bankers' acceptance?

9. Discuss the major types of collateralized short-term loans.

10. What is an asset-backed public offering?

Problems

1. Compute the cost of not taking the following cash discounts:

   a. 2/10, net 50.
   b. 2/15, net 40.
   c. 3/10, net 45.
   d. 3/10, net 180.

2. Your bank will lend you $2,000 for 45 days at a cost of $25 interest. What is your effective rate of interest?

3. Dr. Johnson is going to borrow $3,000 for one year at 12 percent interest. What is the effective rate of interest if the loan is discounted?

4. Beasley Furniture Company is borrowing $300,000 for one year at 11 percent from First Canadian National Bank. The bank requires a 20 percent compensating balance. What is the effective rate of interest? What would the effective rate be if the company were required to make 12 equal monthly payments of $27,750 each to retire the loan? In Formula 8–6 use the funds the firm can effectively utilize (amount borrowed − compensating balance).

5. Randall Corporation plans to borrow $200,000 for one year at 12 percent from the Bank of Winnipeg. There is a 20 percent compensating balance requirement. Randall Corporation keeps minimum transaction balances of $10,000 in the normal course of business. This idle cash counts toward meeting the compensating balance requirement.

   What is the effective rate of interest?

6. The treasurer for the Moncton Gold Sox baseball team is seeking a $20,000 loan for 180 days from the Atlantic National Bank. The stated interest rate is 14 percent, and there is a 10 percent compensating balance requirement. The treasurer always keeps a minimum of $1,500 in the baseball team's chequing account. These

funds count toward meeting any compensating balance requirements.

What is the effective rate of interest on this loan?

7. Spicer Corporation plans to borrow $100,000. Western Bank will lend the money at $\frac{1}{2}$ percent over the prime rate of $11\frac{1}{2}$ percent (12 percent total) and requires a compensating balance of 20 percent. Principal in this case refers to funds the firm can effectively use in the business.

What is the effective rate of interest?

What would the effective rate be if Spicer were required to make four quarterly payments to retire the loan?

8. Your company plans to borrow $5 million for 12 months, and your banker gives you a stated rate of 14 percent interest. You would like to know the effective rate of interest for the following types of loans. (Each of the following parts stands alone.)

a. Simple 14 percent interest with a 10 percent compensating balance.
b. Discounted interest.
c. An installment loan (12 payments).
d. Discounted interest with a 5 percent compensating balance.

9. If you borrow $4000 at $500 interest for one year, what is your effective interest cost for the following payment plans?

a. Annual payment.
b. Semiannual payments.
c. Quarterly payments.
d. Monthly payments.

10. Lewis and Clark Camping Supplies Inc. is borrowing $45,000 from the Imperial Bank. The total interest is $12,000. The loan will be paid by making equal monthly payments for the next three years.

What is the effective rate of interest on this installment loan?

11. Mr. Hugh Warner is a very cautious business man. His supplier offers trade credit terms of 3/10, net 80. Mr. Warner never takes the discount offered, but he pays his suppliers in 70 days rather than the 80 days allowed so he is sure the payments are never late.

What is Mr. Warner's cost of ignoring the cash discount?

12. The Reynolds Corporation buys from its suppliers on terms of 2/10, net 40. Reynolds has not been utilizing the discount offered and has been taking 55 days to pay its bills. The suppliers seem to accept this payment pattern, and Reynold's credit rating has not been adversely affected.

Mr. Duke, Reynolds Corporation vice president, has suggested that the company begin to take the discount offered. Duke proposes that the company borrow from its bank at a stated rate of 14 percent. The bank requires a 20 percent compensating balance on these loans. Current account balances would not be available to meet any of this compensating balance requirement.

Do you agree with Mr. Duke's proposal?

13. In Problem 12, if the compensating balance requirement were 10 percent instead of 20 percent, would you change your answer? Do the appropriate calculation.

14. Burt's Department Store needs $300,000 to take a cash discount of 3/10, net 70. A bank will loan the money for 60 days at an interest cost of $8,100.

a. What is the effective rate on the bank loan?
b. How much would it cost (in percentage terms) if Burt did not take the trade discount but paid the bill in 70 days instead of 10 days?
c. Should Burt borrow the money to take the discount?
d. If the bank requires a 20 percent compensating balance, how much must Burt borrow to end up with the $300,000?
e. What would be the effective interest rate in part *d* if the interest charge for 60 days were $10,125? Should Burt borrow with the 20 percent compensating balance? (He has no funds to count against the compensating balance requirement.)

15. Ajax Box Company is negotiating with two banks for a $100,000 loan.

Eastern Bank requires a 20 percent compensating balance, discounts the loan, and wants to be paid back in four quarterly payments. Central Bank requires a 10 percent compensating balance, does not discount the loan, but wants to be paid back in 12 monthly installments. The stated rate for both banks is 8 percent. Compensating balances will be subtracted from the $100,000 in determining the available funds in part *a*.

a. Which loan should Ajax accept?
b. Recompute the effective cost of interest, assuming that Ajax ordinarily maintains at each bank $20,000 in deposits which will serve as compensating balances.
c. How much did the compensating balances inflate your interest costs? Does your choice of banks change if the assumption in part *b* is correct?

16. Ewing Oil Supplies sells to the 12 accounts listed below.

Account	*Receivables Balance Outstanding*	*Average Age of the Account over the Last Year*
A.	$ 50,000	35 days
B.	80,000	25
C	120,000	47
D.	10,000	15
E.	250,000	35
F.	60,000	51
G	40,000	18
H.	180,000	60
I	15,000	43
J	25,000	33
K.	200,000	41
L.	60,000	28

J&R Financial Corporation will lend 90 percent against account balances that have averaged 30 days or less, 80 percent for account balances between 30 and 40 days, and 70 percent for account balances between 40 and 45 days. Customers that take over 45 days to pay their bills are not considered as acceptable accounts for a loan.

The current prime rate is 12 percent, and J&R Financial Corporation charges 3 percent over prime to Ewing Oil Supplies as its annual loan rate.

a. Determine the maximum loan for which Ewing Oil Supplies could qualify.
b. Determine how much one month's interest expense would be on the loan balance determined in part *a*.

17. The Montreal Garment Co. is considering whether to continue financing its receivables with the First National Bank or to switch to the Better Factoring Co. Ltd. Montreal Garment has found that, on average, its customers (mostly small to medium-sized retailers) take 60 days to pay for merchandise. Historically, the bad debt losses ranged between 1 and 2 percent of sales. The bank has been advancing 65 percent of all receivables outstanding less than 75 days (about 80 percent of total receivables) and charging a rate of prime (currently 10 percent) plus 2 percent. Given the competitive nature of the industry, Montreal Garment has found itself habitually short of cash.

Better Factoring has offered to finance 85 percent of all receivables outstanding for less than 75 days at prime plus 1 percent if it can also manage Montreal's receivables for a fee of 2½ percent of the gross value of receivables invoices per month, including credit insurance. Since this offer would provide about $132,000 of much needed additional working capital at 1 percent less than the bank's rate, Montreal Garment's treasurer, Jean Higgins, was very anxious to sign a deal with Better Factoring before they revoked their offer. Jean estimated that the factoring service would save her company another $25,000 annually in collection costs.

What recommendation would you make to Ms. Higgins?

Selected References

Abraham, Alfred B. "Factoring—The New Frontier for Commercial Banks." *Journal of Commercial Bank Lending* 53 (April 1971), pp. 32–43.

Anstie, R. "The Historical Development of Pledge Lending in Canada." *The Canadian Banker,* Summer 1967, pp. 81–90.

Baxter, Nevins D., and Harold T. Shapiro. "Compensating Balance Requirements: The Results of a Survey." *Journal of Finance* 19 (September 1964), pp. 483–96.

Begert, Brian, and D. R. Capozza. "Reviving Fixed-Rate Loans through Financial Futures." *Canadian Banker* 91, no. 2 (April 1984), pp. 12–17.

Block, Stanley B. "Financial and Management Strategy for Bank Holding Companies." *Bank Administration* 48 (August 1972), pp. 14–16.

Crane, Dwight B., and William L. White. "Who Benefits from a Floating Prime Rate?" *Harvard Business Review* 50 (January–February 1972), pp. 121–29.

Denonn, Lester E. "The Security Agreement." *Journal of Commercial Bank Lending* 50 (February 1968), pp. 32–40.

Hawkins, Gregory D. "An Analysis of Revolving Credit Agreements." *Journal of Financial Economics* 59 (March 1982), pp. 59–81.

Hirt, Geoffrey A., and Stanley B. Block. *Fundamentals of Investment Management*. 2nd ed. Homewood, Ill.: Richard D. Irwin, 1986.

James, Christopher. "An Analysis of Bank Loan Rate Indexation." *Journal of Finance* 37 (June 1982), pp. 809–25.

Kolb, Robert W., and Raymond Chiang. "Improving Performance Using Interest-Rate Futures." *Financial Management* 10 (Autumn 1981), pp. 72–79.

Lev, Baruch. *Financial Statement Analysis: A New Approach*. Englewood Cliffs, N.J.: Prentice-Hall, 1974, chap. 11.

Monroe, Ann. "Sales of Receivables by Big Firms Gain Respect in Public Offerings." *The Wall Street Journal*, December 2, 1985, p. 41.

Nadler, Paul S. "Compensating Balances and the Prime at Twilight." *Harvard Business Review* 50 (January–February1972), pp. 112–20.

Quarles, J. Carson. "The Floating Lien." *Journal of Commercial Bank Lending* 53 (November 1970), pp. 51–58.

Robichek, Alexander A., and Stewart C. Myers. *Optimal Financing Decisions*. Englewood Cliffs, N.J.: Prentice-Hall, 1965, chap. 5.

Rose, Peter S. "Loan Pricing in a Volatile Economy." *Canadian Banker* 92, no. 5 (October 1985), pp. 44–49.

Sarpkaya, S. *The Money Market in Canada*. 2nd ed. Toronto: Butterworth, 1980.

Schwartz, Robert A. "An Economic Model of Trade Credit." *Journal of Financial and Quantitative Analysis* 9 (September 1974), pp. 643–58.

Seiden, Martin H. "The Quality of Trade Credit." Occasional Paper No. 87. New York: National Bureau of Economic Research, 1964.

Selden, Richard T. *Trends and Cycles in the Commercial Paper Market*. New York: National Bureau of Economic Research, 1963.

Selected issues of *Bank of Canada Review*.

Smith, Keith V. *Management of Working Capital*. St. Paul, Minn.: West Publishing, 1974.

PART FOUR

The Capital Budgeting Process

Introduction

A capital budgeting decision is one that involves the allocation of funds to projects that will have a life of at least one year and usually much longer. Examples might include the development of a major new product, a plant site location, or equipment replacement. Because we may be locked into our decision for 10–20 years and large sums of money are usually involved, the capital budgeting decision must be approached with great care. Basic capital budgeting decisions determine whether there is under- or overcapacity in a given firm or within an industry. The problem has been complicated by the introduction of nonprofitable, but at times necessary, government regulations for pollution control and safety provisions.

The capital budgeting decision is of interest not only to students of finance but also to those who desire careers in accounting, marketing, production management, and a number of other areas. Whether the marketing manager gets a new product approved for production and distribution may be a function of how well he or she provides data into the capital budgeting process and understands the analysis.

Because the capital budgeting process is long term in nature, we must develop a methodology for translating future inflows and outflows to the present. Thus, our first step will be to consider the time value of money in Chapter 9. Our understanding of compound sum, present value, annuities, and yields allows us to move back and forth between the future and the present. The student may be particularly interested in the extensive summary and review material at the end of the chapter.

We then move to the topic of valuation of sources of financing in Chapter 10. By understanding what measures investors use to determine required rates of return and current values for bonds, preferred stock, and common stock, we are also considering what the corporation must pay for these funds. The chapter on valuation thus naturally extends into the next chapter on cost of capital (financing) to the firm. As described in Chapter 11 the cost of capital represents the weighted cost of the various sources of financing to the firm and is generally a minimum standard for accepting an investment. The capital asset pricing model, an analytical approach to relating individual asset returns to market returns, is considered briefly in Chapter 11 and is also covered in Appendix 11A.

In Chapter 12 we bring together the concepts of time value of money and cost of capital to develop actual investment decisions. Though a number of methods of evaluating capital investments are discussed, such as the payback method and the internal rate of return method, the primary emphasis is on the net present value method. Here we discount future flows from an investment at the cost of capital to see whether they equal or exceed the required investment. If the answer is positive, we know we have earned the cost of financing the project. Because these investment decisions depend upon the aftertax cash flow-generating capability of a project, the tax impact is carefully considered.

In Chapter 13 we study risk in the capital budgeting decision process. Most managers and investors are risk averse—that is, all things being equal, they would prefer a certain predictable outcome of 10 percent, rather than a 50–50 chance of going broke or doubling their money (this is an extreme case). To reflect these preferences we incorporate a penalty for large risk in our decision-making process. A more risky investment may have to provide a higher return than a less risky investment. Since the objective of financial management is to maximize the market value of the firm and the wealth of its shareholders, we must determine the appropriate mix of profitability and risk to achieve this objective. As part of the analytical procedures introduced in the chapter, simulation techniques to approximate future outcomes are considered.

9 The Time Value of Money

In 1624 the Indians sold Manhattan Island at the ridiculously low figure of $24. But wait, was it really ridiculous? If the Indians had merely taken the $24 and reinvested it at 6 percent annual interest up to 1987, they would have had $37 billion, an amount sufficient to repurchase most of New York City. If the Indians had been slightly more astute and had invested the $24 at 7.5 percent compounded annually, they would now have close to $6,000,000,000,000 (6 trillion)—and tribal chiefs would now rival oil sheikhs as the richest people in the world. Another popular example is that $1 received 1,987 years ago, invested at 6 percent, could now be used to purchase all the wealth in the world.

While not all examples are this dramatic, the time value of money figures in many day-to-day decisions. Understanding the effective rate on a business loan, the mortgage payment in a real estate transaction, or the true return on an investment is dependent on understanding the time value of money. As long as an investor is able to garner a positive return on idle dollars, distinctions must be made between money received today and money received in the future. The investor/lender essentially demands that a financial "rent" be paid on his or her funds as current dollars are set aside today in anticipation of higher returns in the future.

Relationship to the Capital Outlay Decision

The decision to purchase new plant and equipment or to introduce a new product in the market requires using capital allocating or capital budgeting techniques. Essentially, we must determine whether future benefits are sufficiently large to justify current outlays. It is important that we develop the mathematical tools of the time value of money as the first step toward making capital allocating decisions. Let us now examine the basic terminology of "time value of money."

Compound Sum—Single Amount

In determining the compound sum we measure the future value of an amount that is allowed to grow at a given interest rate over a period of time. Assume an investor has $1,000 and wishes to know its worth after four years if it grows at 10 percent per year. At the end of the first year he will have $1,000 × 1.10, or $1,100. By the end of year two, the $1,100 will have grown to $1,210 ($1,100 × 1.10). The four-year pattern is indicated below.

1st year	$1,000	×	1.10	=	$1,100
2nd year	$1,100	×	1.10	=	$1,210
3rd year	$1,210	×	1.10	=	$1,331
4th year	$1,331	×	1.10	=	$1,464

After the fourth year the investor has accumulated $1,464. Because compounding problems often cover a long period of time, a more generalized formula is necessary to describe the compounding procedure. We shall let:

S = Compound sum
P = Principal or present value

i = Interest rate
n = Number of periods

The simple formula is:

$$S = P(1 + i)^n$$

In the present case, P = \$1000, i = 10 percent, n = 4, so we have:

$$S = \$1000(1.10)^4, \text{ or } \$1,000 \times 1.464 = \$1,464$$

The term $(1.10)^4$ is found to equal 1.464 by multiplying 1.10 four times itself (the fourth power) or by using logarithms. An even quicker process is using an interest rate table, such as Table 9–1, for the compound sum of a dollar. With n = 4 and i = 10 percent, the value is also found to be 1.464.

The table tells us the amount that \$1 would grow to if it were invested for any number of periods at a given interest rate. We multiply this factor times any other amount to determine the compound sum. An expanded version of Table 9–1 is presented at the back of the text in Appendix A.

In determining the compound sum, we will shorten our formula from $S = P(1 + i)^n$ to:

$$S = P \times IF_s \qquad (9\text{–}1)$$

where IF_s equals the interest factor found in the table.

If \$10,000 were invested for 10 years at 8 percent, the compound sum, based on Table 9–1, would be:

$$S = P \times IF_s\ (n = 10, i = 8\%)$$
$$S = \$10,000 \times 2.159 = \$21,590$$

Table 9–1
Compound sum of \$1 (IF_s)

Periods	*1%*	*2%*	*3%*	*4%*	*6%*	*8%*	*10%*
1	1.010	1.020	1.030	1.040	1.060	1.080	1.100
2	1.020	1.040	1.061	1.082	1.124	1.166	1.210
3	1.030	1.061	1.093	1.125	1.191	1.260	1.331
4	1.041	1.082	1.126	1.170	1.262	1.360	1.464
5	1.051	1.104	1.159	1.217	1.338	1.469	1.611
10	1.105	1.219	1.344	1.480	1.791	2.159	2.594
20	1.220	1.486	1.806	2.191	3.207	4.661	6.727

Present Value— Single Amount

In recent years the sports pages have been filled with stories of athletes who receive multimillion dollar contracts for signing with sports organizations. Perhaps you have wondered how the Oilers or Blue Jays can afford to pay such fantastic sums. The answer may lie in the concept of present value—a sum payable in the future is worth less today than the stated amount.

The present value is the exact opposite of the compound sum. For example, earlier we determined that the compound sum of $1,000 for four periods at 10 percent was $1,464. We could reverse the process to state that $1,464 received four years into the future, with a 10 percent interest or discount rate, is worth only $1,000 today—its present value. The relationship is depicted in Figure 9–1.

The formula for present value is derived from the original formula for the compound sum.

$$S = P(1 + i)^n \text{ Compound sum}$$

$$P = S\left[\frac{1}{(1 + i)^n}\right] \text{ Present value}$$

Figure 9–1
Relationship of present value and compound sum

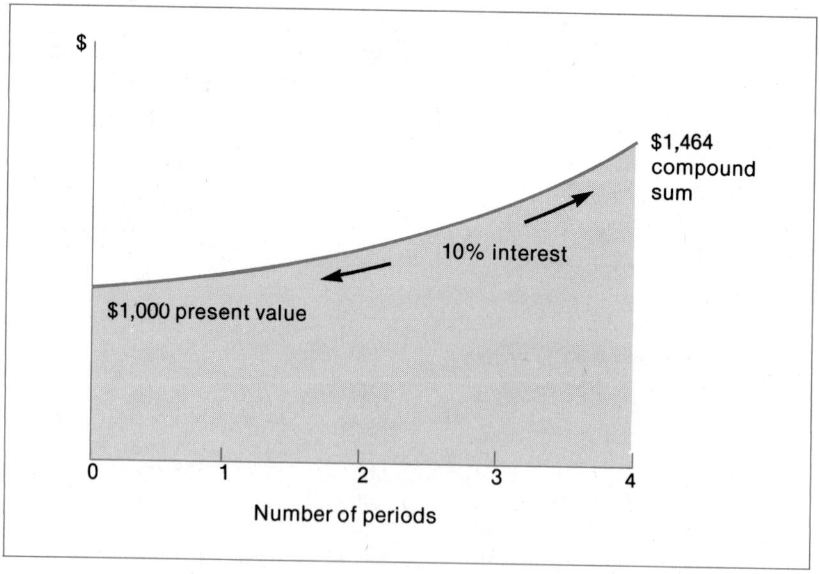

Table 9–2
Present value of $1 ($IF_{pv}$)

Periods	1%	2%	3%	4%	6%	8%	10%
1	0.990	0.980	0.971	0.962	0.943	0.926	0.909
2	0.980	0.961	0.943	0.925	0.890	0.857	0.826
3	0.971	0.942	0.915	0.889	0.840	0.794	0.751
4	0.961	0.924	0.888	0.855	0.792	0.735	0.683
5	0.951	0.906	0.863	0.822	0.747	0.681	0.621
10	0.905	0.820	0.744	0.676	0.558	0.463	0.386
20	0.820	0.673	0.554	0.456	0.312	0.215	0.149

An expanded table is presented in Appendix B.

The present value can be determined by solving for a mathematical solution to the above formula or by using Table 9–2, the present value of a dollar. In the latter instance we restate the formula for present value as:

$$P = S \times IF_{pv} \tag{9–2}$$

Once again IF_{pv} represents the interest factor found in appropriate Table 9–2.

Let's demonstrate that the present value of $1,464, based on our assumptions, is $1,000 today.

$$P = S \times IF_{pv}\ (n = 4,\ i = 10\%)\ [\text{Table 9–2}]$$
$$P = \$1{,}464 \times 0.683 = \$1{,}000$$

Compound Sum—Annuity

Our calculations up to now have dealt with single amounts rather than annuity values, which may be defined as a series of consecutive payments or receipts of equal amount. The annuity values are generally assumed to occur at the end of each period. If we invest $1,000 at the end of each year for four years and our funds grow at 10 percent, what is the compound sum of this annuity? One solution method is to find the compound sum for each payment and then total to find the compound sum of an annuity (see Figure 9–2). Figure 9–2 illustrates that the compound sum for the annuity is $4,641. Although this is a four-period annuity, the first $1,000 comes at the *end* of the first period and has but three periods to run; the second $1,000 at the end of the second

Figure 9–2
Compounding process for annuity

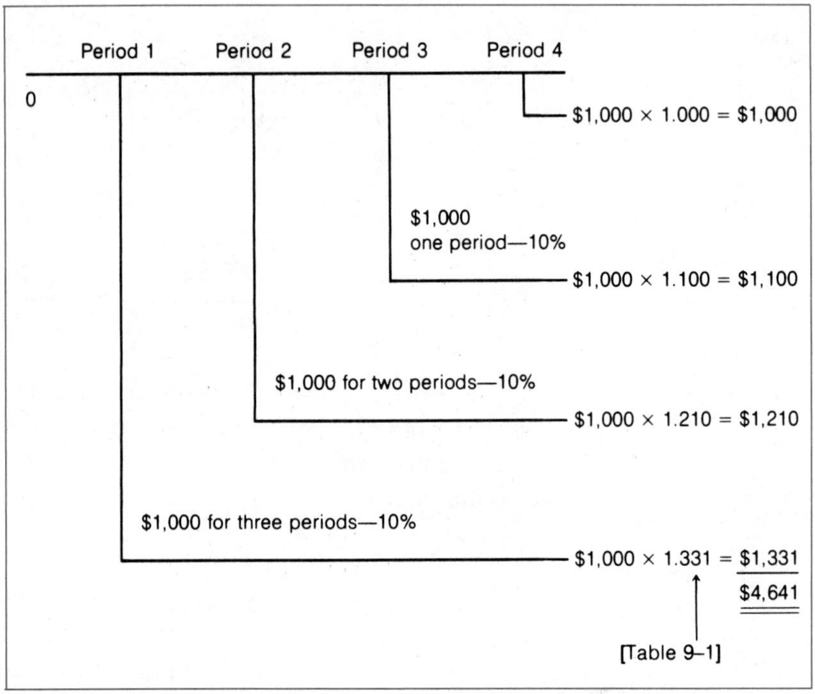

period, with two periods remaining—and so on down to the last $1,000 at the end of the fourth period. The final payment (period 4) is not compounded at all.

Because the process of compounding the individual values is quite tedious, special tables are also available for annuity computations. We shall refer to Table 9–3, the compound sum of an annuity of $1. Let us define R as the annuity value and use Formula 9–3 for the compound sum of an annuity.[1] Note that in the IF term the first subscript, $_s$, indicates compound sum and the second subscript, $_a$, indicates that we are dealing with an annuity.

$$S = R \times IF_{sa}\ (n = 4, i = 10\%) \qquad (9\text{–}3)$$
$$S = \$1{,}000 \times 4.641 = \$4{,}641$$

[1] $S = R(1 + i)^{n-1} + R(1 + i)^{n-2} + \ldots R(1 + i)^1 + R(1 + i)^0$

$$= R\left[\frac{(1 + i)^n - 1}{i}\right] = R \times IF_{sa}$$

Table 9–3
Compound sum of an annuity of \$1 (IF_{sa})

Periods	1%	2%	3%	4%	6%	8%	10%
1. . .	1.000	1.000	1.000	1.000	1.000	1.000	1.000
2. . .	2.010	2.020	2.030	2.040	2.060	2.080	2.100
3. . .	3.030	3.060	3.091	3.122	3.184	3.246	3.310
4. . .	4.060	4.122	4.184	4.246	4.375	4.506	4.641
5. . .	5.101	5.204	5.309	5.416	5.637	5.867	6.105
10. . .	10.462	10.950	11.464	12.006	13.181	14.487	15.937
20. . .	22.019	24.297	26.870	29.778	36.786	45.762	57.275
30. . .	34.785	40.588	45.575	56.085	79.058	113.280	164.490

An expanded table is presented in Appendix C.

If a wealthy relative offered to set aside \$2,500 a year for you for the next 20 years, how much would you have to your credit after 20 years if the funds grew at 8 percent?

$$S = R \times IF_{sa}\ (n = 20,\ i = 8\%)$$
$$S = \$2{,}500 \times 45.762 = \$114{,}405$$

A rather tidy sum considering that a total of only \$50,000 has been invested over the 20 years.

Present Value—Annuity

To find the present value of an annuity, the process is reversed. In theory each individual payment is discounted back to the present, and then all of the discounted payments are added up, yielding the present value of the annuity. Table 9–4 allows us to eliminate extensive calculations and to find our answer directly. In Formula 9–4 the term A refers to the present value of the annuity.[2] Once again, assume that $R = \$1{,}000$, $n = 4$, and $i = 10$ percent—only now we want to know the present value of the annuity. Note that in the IF term the first

---

[2] $$A = R\left[\frac{1}{(1+i)}\right]^1 + R\left[\frac{1}{(1+i)}\right]^2 + \ldots R\left[\frac{1}{(1+i)}\right]^n = R\left[\frac{1 - \frac{1}{(1+i)^n}}{i}\right]$$
$$= R \times IF_{pva}$$

Table 9–4
Present value of an annuity of \$1 (IF_{pva})

Periods	1%	2%	3%	4%	6%	8%	10%
1 . . .	0.990	0.980	0.971	0.962	0.943	0.926	0.909
2 . . .	1.970	1.942	1.913	1.886	1.833	1.783	1.736
3 . . .	2.941	2.884	2.829	2.775	2.673	2.577	2.487
4 . . .	3.902	3.808	3.717	3.630	3.465	3.312	3.170
5 . . .	4.853	4.713	4.580	4.452	4.212	3.993	3.791
8 . . .	7.652	7.325	7.020	6.733	6.210	5.747	5.335
10 . . .	9.471	8.983	8.530	8.111	7.360	6.710	6.145
20 . . .	18.046	16.351	14.877	13.590	11.470	9.818	8.514
30 . . .	25.808	22.396	19.600	17.292	13.765	11.258	9.427

An expanded table is presented in Appendix D.

subscript, $_{pv}$, represents present value and that the second subscript, $_a$, indicates an annuity.

$$A = R \times IF_{pva}\ (n = 4,\ i = 10\%) \tag{9–4}$$
$$A = \$1{,}000 \times 3.170 = \$3{,}170$$

Determining the Annuity Value

In our prior discussion of annuities we assumed that the unknown value was the compound sum or the present value—with specific information available on the annuity value (R), the interest rate, and the number of periods or years. In certain cases our emphasis may shift to solving for one of these other values (on the assumption that compound sum or present value is given). For now, we will concentrate on determining an unknown annuity value.

Annuity Equaling a Compound Sum

Assuming we wish to accumulate \$4,641 after four years at a 10 percent interest rate, how much must be set aside at the end of each of the four periods? We take the previously developed statement for the compound sum of an annuity and solve for R.

$$S = R \times IF_{sa}$$

$$R = \frac{S}{IF_{sa}} \tag{9–5}$$

S is given as \$4,641, and IF_{sa} (interest factor) may be determined from Table 9–3 (compound sum of an annuity). Whenever you are working with an annuity problem relating to compound sum, you employ Table 9–3, regardless of the variable that is unknown. For $n = 4$ and $i = 10$ percent, IF_{sa} is 4.641. Thus R equals \$1,000.

$$R = \frac{S}{IF_{sa}} = \frac{\$4{,}641}{4.641} = \$1{,}000$$

The solution is the exact reverse of that previously presented under the discussion of the compound sum of an annuity. As a second example assume that the director of the Women's Tennis Association must set aside an equal amount for each of the next 10 years in order to accumulate \$100,000 in retirement funds and that the return on deposited funds is 6 percent. Solve for the annual contribution, R.

$$R = \frac{S}{IF_{sa}} \ (n = 10, i = 6\%)$$

$$R = \frac{\$100{,}000}{13.181} = \$7{,}587$$

Annuity Equaling a Present Value

In this instance we assume you know the present value and you wish to determine what size annuity can be equated to that amount. Suppose your wealthy uncle presents you with \$10,000 now to help you get through the next four years of college. If you are able to earn 6 percent on deposited funds, how much can you withdraw at the end of each year for four years? We need to know the value of an annuity equal to a given present value. We take the previously developed statement for the present value of an annuity and reverse it to solve for R.

$$A = R \times IF_{pva}$$

$$R = \frac{A}{IF_{pva}} \qquad (9\text{–}6)$$

The appropriate table is Table 9–4 (present value of an annuity). We determine an answer of \$2,886.

$$R = \frac{A}{IF_{pva}} \quad (n = 4,\ i = 6\%)$$

$$R = \frac{\$10{,}000}{3.465} = \$2{,}886$$

The flow of funds would follow the pattern in Table 9–5. Annual interest is based on the beginning balance for each year.

The same process can be used to indicate necessary repayments on a loan. Suppose a homeowner signs a $40,000 mortgage to be repaid over 20 years at 8 percent interest. How much must he or she pay annually to eventually liquidate the loan? In other words, what annuity paid over 20 years is the equivalent of a $40,000 present value with an 8 percent interest rate?

$$R = \frac{A}{IF_{pva}} \quad (n = 20,\ i = 8\%)$$

$$R = \frac{\$40{,}000}{9.818} = \$4{,}074$$ [3]

Part of the payments to the mortgage company will go toward the payment of interest, with the remainder applied to debt reduction, as indicated in Table 9–6.

If this same process is followed over 20 years, the balance will be reduced to zero. The student might note that the homeowner will pay over $41,000 of *interest* during the term of the loan, as indicated below.

Total payments ($4,074 for 20 years)	$81,480
Repayment of principal	−40,000
Payments applied to interest	$41,480

Table 9–5
Relationship of present value to annuity

Year	Beginning Balance	Annual Interest (6 percent)	Annual Withdrawal	Ending Balance
1	$10,000.00	$600.00	$2,886.00	$7,714.00
2	7,714.00	462.84	2,886.00	5,290.84
3	5,290.84	317.45	2,886.00	2,722.29
4	2,722.29	163.71	2,886.00	0

[3] The actual mortgage could be further refined into monthly payments of approximately $340.

Table 9–6
Payoff table for loan (amortization table)

Period	Beginning Balance	Annual Payment	Annual Interest (8 percent)	Repayment on Principal	Ending Balance
1 . . .	$40,000	$4,074	$3,200	$ 874	$39,126
2 . . .	39,126	4,074	3,130	944	38,182
3 . . .	38,182	4,074	3,055	1,019	37,163

Determining the Yield on an Investment

In our discussion thus far we have considered the following time value of money problems.

	Formula		Table	Appendix
Compound sum—single amount	(9–1)	$S = P \times IF_s$	9–1	A
Present value—single amount	(9–2)	$P = S \times IF_{pv}$	9–2	B
Compound sum—annuity	(9–3)	$S = R \times IF_{sa}$	9–3	C
Present value—annuity	(9–4)	$A = R \times IF_{pva}$	9–4	D
Annuity equaling a compound sum	(9–5)	$R = \dfrac{S}{IF_{sa}}$	9–3	C
Annuity equaling a present value	(9–6)	$R = \dfrac{A}{IF_{pva}}$	9–4	D

In each case we knew three out of the four variables and solved for the fourth. We will follow the same procedure once again, but now the unknown variable will be *i*, the interest rate, or yield on the investment.

Yield—Present Value of a Single Amount

An investment producing $1,464 after four years has a present value of $1,000. What is the interest rate, or yield, on the investment?

We take the basic formula for the present value of a single amount and rearrange the terms.

$$P = S \times IF_{pv}$$

$$IF_{pv} = \frac{P}{S} = \frac{\$1,000}{\$1,464} = 0.683 \qquad (9\text{–}7)$$

The determination of IF_{pv} does not give us the final answer—but in effect, it scales down the problem so that we may ascertain the answer from Table 9–2, the present value of $1. A portion of Table 9–2 is presented below.

Periods	*1%*	*2%*	*3%*	*4%*	*5%*	*6%*	*8%*	*10%*
2	0.980	0.961	0.943	0.925	0.907	0.890	0.857	0.826
3	0.971	0.942	0.815	0.889	0.864	0.840	0.794	0.751
4	0.961	0.924	0.888	0.855	0.823	0.792	0.735	0.683

Read down the left-hand column of the table until you have located the number of periods in question (in this case $n = 4$), and read across the table for $n = 4$ until you have located the computed value of IF_{pv}. We see that for $n = 4$ and IF_{pv} equal to 0.683, the interest rate, or yield, is 10 percent. This is the rate that will equate $1,464 received in four years to $1,000 today.

If an IF_{pv} value does not fall under a given interest rate, an approximation is possible. For example, with $n = 3$ and $IF_{pv} = 0.861$, 5 percent may be suggested as an approximate answer.

Interpolation may also be used to find a more precise answer. In the above example, we write out the two IF_{pv} values that the designated IF_{pv} (0.861) falls between and take the difference between the two.

IF_{pv} at 5%	0.864
IF_{pv} at 6%	0.840
	0.024

We then find the difference between the IF_{pv} value at the lowest interest rate and the designated IF_{pv} value.

IF_{pv} at 5%	0.864
IF_{pv} designated	0.861
	0.003

We next express this value (0.003) as a fraction of the preceding value (0.024) and multiply by the difference between the two interest rates (6 percent minus 5 percent). The value is added to the lower interest rate (5 percent) to get a more exact answer of 5.125 percent rather than the estimated 5 percent.

$$
\begin{aligned}
5\% + \frac{0.003}{0.024}(1\%) &= \\
5\% + 0.125\,(1\%) &= \\
5\% + 0.125\% &= 5.125\%
\end{aligned}
$$

Yield—Present Value of an Annuity

We may also find the yield related to any other problem. Let's look at the present value of an annuity. Take the basic formula for the present value of an annuity and rearrange the terms.

$$A = R \times IF_{pva}$$

$$IF_{pva} = \frac{A}{R} \quad (9\text{–}8)$$

The appropriate table is Table 9–4 (the present value of an annuity of $1). Assuming that a $10,000 investment will produce $1,490 a year for the next 10 years, what is the yield on the investment?

$$IF_{pva} = \frac{A}{R} = \frac{\$10{,}000}{\$1{,}490} = 6.710$$

If the student will flip back to Table 9–4 and read across the columns for $n = 10$ periods, he will see that the yield is 8 percent.

The same type of approximated or interpolated yield that applied to a single amount can also be applied to an annuity when necessary.

Special Considerations in Time Value Analysis

We have assumed that interest was compounded or discounted on an annual basis. This assumption will now be relaxed. Contractual arrangements, such as an installment purchase agreement or a corporate bond contract, may call for semiannual, quarterly, or monthly compounding periods. The adjustment to the normal formula is quite simple. To determine n, multiply the number of years by the number of compounding periods during the year. The factor for i is then determined by dividing the quoted annual interest rate by the number of compounding periods.

Case 1—Find the compound sum of a $1,000 investment after five years at 8 percent annual interest, compounded semiannually.

$$n = 5 \times 2 = 10 \qquad i = 8 \text{ percent} \div 2 = 4 \text{ percent}$$

Since the problem calls for the compound sum of a single amount, the formula is $S = P \times IF_s$. Using Table 9–1 for $n = 10$ and $i = 4$ percent, the answer is $1,480.

$$S = P \times IF_s$$
$$S = \$1{,}000 \times 1.480 = \$1{,}480$$

Case 2—Find the present value of 20 quarterly payments of $2,000 each to be received over the next five years. The stated interest rate is 8 percent per annum. The problem calls for the present value of an annuity.

$$A = R \times IF_{pva}\ (n = 20,\ i = 2\%)\ [\text{Table 9–4}]$$
$$A = \$2{,}000 \times 16.351 = \$32{,}702$$

Patterns of Payment

Time value of money problems may evolve around a number of different payment or receipt patterns. Not every situation will involve a single amount or an annuity. For example, a contract may call for the payment of a different amount each year over a three-year period. To determine present value, each payment is discounted (see Table 9–2) to the present and then summed.

(Assume 8% discount rate)

1. 1,000 × 0.926 =	$ 926
2. 2,000 × 0.857 =	1,714
3. 3,000 × 0.794 =	2,382
	$5,022

A more involved problem might include a combination of single amounts and an annuity. If the annuity will be paid at some time in the future, it is referred to as a deferred annuity and requires special treatment. Assume the same problem as above, but with an annuity of $1,000 that will be paid at the end of each year from the fourth through the eighth year. With a discount rate of 8 percent, what is the present value of the cash flows?

1.	$1,000	Present value = $5,022
2.	2,000	
3.	3,000	
4.	1,000	Five-year annuity
5.	1,000	
6.	1,000	
7.	1,000	
8.	1,000	

We know that the present value of the first three payments is $5,022, but what about the annuity? Let's diagram the five annuity payments.

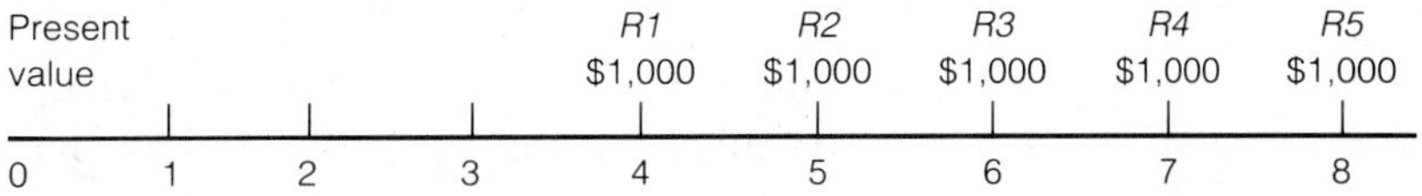

The information source is Table 9–4, the present value of an annuity of $1. For $n = 5$, $i = 8$ percent, the discount factor is 3.993—leaving a "present value" of the annuity of $3,993. However, tabular values only discount to the beginning of the first stated period of an annuity—in this case the beginning of the fourth year, as diagramed below.

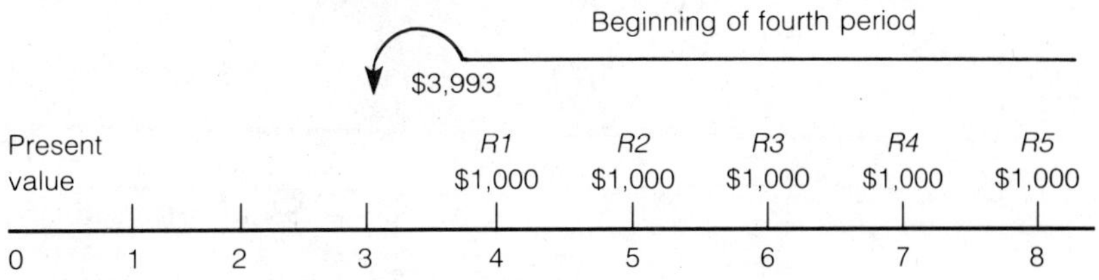

Each number represents the end of the period; that is, 4 represents the end of the fourth period.

The \$3,993 must finally be discounted back to the present. Since this single amount falls at the beginning of the fourth period—in effect, the equivalent of the end of the third period—we discount back for three periods at the stated 8 percent interest rate. Using Table 9–2, we have:

$$P = S \times IF_{pv}\ (n = 3, i = 8\%)$$
$$P = \$3{,}993 \times 0.794 = \$3{,}170 \text{ (actual present value)}$$

The last step in the discounting process is shown below.

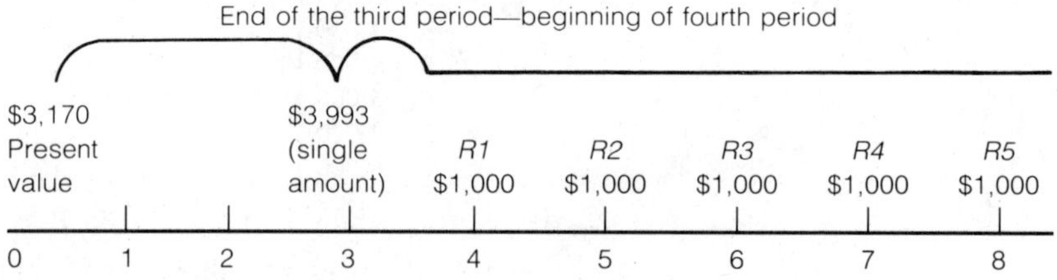

A *second method* for finding the present value of a deferred annuity is to:

1. Find the present value factor of an annuity for the total time period. In this case, where $n = 8$, $i = 8\%$, the IF_{pva} is 5.747.

2. Find the present value factor of an annuity for the total time period (8) minus the deferred annuity period (5).

$$8 - 5 = 3$$
$$n = 3, i = 8\%$$

The IF_{pva} value is 2.577.

3. Subtract the value in step 2 from the value in step 1, and multiply by R.

$$\begin{array}{r} 5.747 \\ -2.577 \\ \hline 3.170 \end{array}$$

$3.170 \times \$1{,}000 = \$3{,}170$ (present value of the annuity)

The figure \$3,170 is precisely the same answer for the present value of the annuity as that reached by the first method. The present value of the five-year annuity may now be added to the present value of the inflows over the first three years to arrive at the total value.

$5,022	First three period flows
+3,170	Five-year annuity
$8,192	Total present value

Special Review of the Chapter

In working a time value of money problem, the student should determine, first, whether the problem deals with compound sum or present value and, second, whether a single sum or an annuity is involved. The major calculations in Chapter 9 are summarized below.

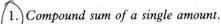

1. *Compound sum of a single amount.*
   Formula: $S = P \times IF_s$
   Table: 9–1 or Appendix A.
   When to use: In determining the future value of a single amount.
   Sample problem: A invests $1,000 for four years at 10 percent interest. What is the value at the end of the fourth year?

2. *Present value of a single amount.*
   Formula: $P = S \times IF_{pv}$
   Table: 9–2 or Appendix B.
   When to use: In determining the present value of an amount to be received in the future.
   Sample problem: A will receive $1,000 after four years at a discount rate of 10 percent. How much is this worth today?

3. *Compound sum of an annuity.*
   Formula: $S = R \times IF_{sa}$
   Table: 9–3 or Appendix C.
   When to use: In determining the future value of a series of consecutive, equal payments (an annuity).
   Sample problem: A will receive $1,000 at the end of each period for four periods. What is the accumulated value (future worth) at the end of the fourth period if money grows at 10 percent?

4. *Present value of an annuity.*
   Formula: $A = R \times IF_{pva}$
   Table: 9–4 or Appendix D.

When to use: In determining the present worth of an annuity.
Sample problem: A will receive $1,000 at the end of each period for four years. At a discount rate of 10 percent, what is the current worth?

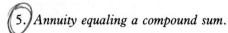

5. *Annuity equaling a compound sum.*

Formula: $R = \frac{S}{IF_{sa}}$

Table: 9–3 or Appendix C.
When to use: In determining the size of an annuity that will equal a future value.
Sample problem: A needs $1,000 after four periods. With an interest rate of 10 percent, how much must be set aside at the end of each period to accumulate this amount?

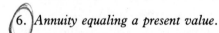

6. *Annuity equaling a present value.*

Formula: $R = \frac{A}{IF_{pva}}$

Table: 9–4 or Appendix D.
When to use: In determining the size of an annuity equal to a given present value.
Sample problems:

a. What four-year annuity is the equivalent of $1,000 today with an interest rate of 10 percent?

b. A deposits $1,000 today and wishes to withdraw funds equally over four years. How much can he withdraw at the end of each year if funds earn 10 percent?

c. A borrows $1,000 for four years at 10 percent interest. How much must be repaid at the end of each year?

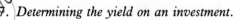

7. *Determining the yield on an investment.*

Formulas	Tables	
a. $IF_{pv} = \frac{P}{S}$	9–2, Appendix B	Yield—present value of a single amount
b. $IF_{pva} = \frac{A}{R}$	9–4, Appendix D	Yield—present value of an annuity

When to use: In determining the interest rate (i) that will equate an investment with future benefits.
Sample problem: A invests $1,000 now, and the funds are expected to increase to $1,360 after four periods.
What is the yield on the investment:

$$\text{Use } IF_{pv} = \frac{P}{S}$$

8. *Less than annual compounding periods.*

Semiannual	Multiply $n \times 2$	Divide i by 2	(then use normal formula)
Quarterly	Multiply $n \times 4$	Divide i by 4	
Monthly	Multiply $n \times 12$	Divide i by 12	

When to use: If the compounding period is more (or perhaps less) frequent than once a year.
Sample problem: A invests $1,000 compounded semiannually at 8 percent per annum over four years. Determine the future sum.

9. *Patterns of payment—deferred annuity.*

Formulas	*Tables*	
$A = R \times IF_{pva}$	9–4, Appendix D	*Method 1*
$P = S \times IF_{pv}$	9–2, Appendix B	

When to use: If an annuity begins in the future.
Sample problem: A will receive $1,000 per period, starting at the end of the fourth period and running through the end of the eighth period. With a discount rate of 8 percent, determine the present value.

The student is encouraged to work the many problems found at the end of the chapter.

List of Terms

compound sum	**compound sum of annuity**
present value	**semiannual compounding**
interest factor (*IF*)	**annuity**
discount rate	**yield**

Discussion Questions

1. How is the compound sum (Appendix A) related to the present value of a single sum (Appendix B)?
2. How is the present value of a single sum (Appendix B) related to the present value of an annuity (Appendix D)?
3. Why does money have a time value?
4. Does inflation have anything to do with making a dollar today worth more than a dollar tomorrow?
5. Adjust the annual formula for a compound sum of a single amount at 12 percent for 10 years to a semiannual compounding formula. What are the interest factors (IF_s) for the two assumptions? Why are they different?
6. If, as an investor, you had a choice of daily, monthly, or quarterly compounding, which would you choose? Why?
7. What is a deferred annuity?
8. List five different financial applications of the time value of money.

Problems

1. What is the present value of:

   a. $8,000 in 10 years at 6 percent?
   b. $16,000 in 5 years at 12 percent?
   c. $25,000 in 15 years at 8 percent?
   d. $1,000 in 40 periods at 20 percent?

2. If you invest $12,000 today, how much will you have:

   a. In 6 years at 7 percent?
   b. In 15 years at 12 percent?
   c. In 25 years at 10 percent?
   d. In 25 years at 10 percent (compounded semiannually)?

3. How much would you have to invest today to receive:

   a. $12,000 in 6 years at 12 percent?
   b. $8,000 in 5 years at 20 percent?
   c. $20,000 in 10 years at 6 percent?
   d. $15,000 in 15 years at 8 percent?
   e. $10,000 in 20 years at 25 percent?
   f. $5,000 each year for 10 years at 8 percent?
   g. $30,000 each year for 20 years at 6 percent?
   h. $40,000 each year for 40 years at 5 percent?

4. Mr. Elite invests $80,000 in an old, classic Rolls-Royce. He expects it to increase in value 12 percent per year for the next five years. How much will his car be worth after five years?

5. Mr. Sampson will receive $6,500 a year for the next 14 years from his trust. If an 8 percent interest rate is applied, what is the current value of the future payments?

6. Ms. Graham has been depositing $1,500 in her savings account every December starting in 1979. Her account earns 5 percent, compounded annually. How much will she have in December of 1988? (Assume that a deposit is made in 1988.)

7. At a growth rate (interest rate) of 8 percent annually, how long will it take for a sum to double? to triple? Select the year that is closest to the correct answer.

8. If you owe $4,000 payable at the end of five years, what amount should your creditor accept in payment immediately if he or she could earn 7 percent on his or her money?

9. Mr. Flint retired as president of the Color Tile Company but is currently on a consulting contract for $45,000 per year for the next 10 years.
   a. If Mr. Flint's opportunity cost (potential return) is 10 percent, what is the present value of his consulting contract?
   b. Assuming that Mr. Flint will not retire for two more years and will not start to receive his 10 payments until the end of the third year, what would be the value of his deferred annuity?

10. Your grandfather has offered you a choice of one of the three following alternatives: $5,000 now; $1,000 a year for eight years; or $12,000 at the end of eight years. Assuming you could earn 11 percent annually, which alternative should you choose? If you could earn 12 percent annually, would you still choose the same alternative?

11. You need $30,750 at the end of eight years, and your only investment outlet is a 12 percent long-term certificate of deposit (compounded annually). With the certificate of deposit, you make an initial investment at the beginning of the first year.

   a. What single payment could be made at the beginning of the first year to achieve this objective?
   b. What amount could you pay at the end of each year annually for eight years to achieve this same objective?

12. On January 1, 1985, Mr. Strong bought 100 shares of stock for $13 per share. On December 31, 1987, he sold the stock for $20.50 per share.

   What is his annual rate of return? Interpolate to find the exact answer.

13. Dr. Emily Smart bought 1,000 shares of Quality Steel Products stock for $5 per share on January 1, 1982. Using interpolation, find her exact annual rate of return if she sells the stock:

   a. On December 31, 1983, for $6 per share.
   b. On December 31, 1986, for $7.85 per share.
   c. On December 31, 1989, for $11 per share.

14. Dr. John Foresight has just invested $2,790 for his son (age one). This money will be used for his son's education 17 years from now. He calculates he will need $30,000 for his son's education by the time the boy goes to school.

What rate of return will Mr. Foresight need in order to achieve this goal?

15. Donald Johnson has just given an insurance company $20,000. In return, he will receive an annuity of $1,800 for 20 years.

At what rate of return must the insurance company invest this $20,000 in order to make the annual payments? Interpolate.

16. Brian Hirt started a paper route on January 1, 1981. Every three months, he deposits $250 in his bank account, which earns 8 percent annually but is compounded quarterly. On December 31, 1985, he used the entire balance in his bank account to invest in a certificate of deposit at 12 percent annually.

How much will he have on December 31, 1988?

17. Mary Mills has retired after 35 years with the Electric Company. Her total pension funds have an accumulated value of $300,000, and her life expectancy is 18 more years. Her pension fund manager assumes she can earn an 8 percent return on her assets.

What will her yearly annuity be for the next 18 years?

18. Dr. T. Account, an accounting professor, invests $50,000 in a dude ranch that is expected to increase in value by 9 percent per year for the next five years. He will take the proceeds and provide himself with a 10-year annuity.

With a 9 percent interest rate, how much will this annuity be?

19. You wish to retire in 20 years, at which time you want to have accumulated enough money to receive an annuity of $12,000 for 25 years after retirement. During the period before retirement you can earn 8 percent annually, while after retirement you can earn 10 percent on your money.

What are your annual contributions to the retirement fund to allow you to receive the $12,000 annuity?

20. If you borrow $9,725 and are required to repay the loan in five equal annual installments of $2,500, what is the interest rate associated with the loan?

21. If your uncle borrows $50,000 from the bank at 10 percent interest over the eight-year life of the loan, what equal annual payments must be made to discharge the loan, plus pay the bank its required rate of interest (round to the nearest dollar)? How much of his first payment will be applied to interest? To principal? How much of his second payment will be applied to each?

22. Darla Lewis has purchased an annuity to begin payment at the end of 1989 (that is the date of the first payment). Assume it is now the end of 1986. The annuity is for $12,000 per year and is designed to last eight years.

    If the discount rate for this problem is 11 percent, what is the most she should have paid for this annuity?

23. Jim Thomas borrows $70,000 at 12 percent interest toward the purchase of a home. His mortgage is for 30 years.

    a. How much will his annual payments be? (Although home payments are usually on a monthly basis, we shall do our analysis on an annual basis for ease of computation. We get a reasonably accurate answer.)

    b. How much interest will he pay over the life of the loan?

    c. How much should he be willing to pay to get out of a 12 percent mortgage and into a 10 percent mortgage with 30 years remaining on the mortgage? Assume that current interest rates are 10 percent.

24. Your younger sister, Susie, will start college in five years. She has just informed your parents that she wants to go to Collegiate U., which will cost $8,000 per year for four years (assumed to come at the end of each year). Anticipating Susie's ambitions, your parents started investing $1,000 per year five years ago and will continue to do so for five more years.

    How much *more* will your parents have to invest each year for the next five years to have the necessary funds for Susie's education? Use 10 percent as the appropriate interest rate throughout this problem (for discounting or compounding).

25. Susie (from Problem 24) is now 18 years old (five years have passed), and she wants to get married instead of going to school. Your parents have accumulated the necessary funds for her education.

Instead of her schooling, your parents are paying $2,433 for her current wedding and plan to take a year-end vacation costing $4,000 per year each year for the next three years.

How much will your parents have at the end of three years to help you with graduate school, which you will start then? You plan to work on a master's and perhaps a Ph.D. If graduate school costs $5,450 per year, approximately how long will you be able to stay in school based on these funds? Use 10 percent as the appropriate interest rate throughout this problem.

26. You are chairperson of the investment retirement fund for the local Actors Guild. You are asked to set up a fund of semiannual payments to be compounded semiannually to accumulate a sum of $50,000 after 10 years at an 8 percent annual rate (20 payments). The first payment into the fund is to take place six months from today, and the last payment is to take place at the end of the 10th year.

a. Determine how much the semiannual payment should be. (Round all values to whole numbers.)

On the day after the sixth payment is made (the beginning of the fourth year), the interest rate goes up to a 10 percent annual rate, and you can earn a 10 percent annual rate on the funds that have accumulated as well as on all future payments into the fund. Interest is to be compounded semiannually on all funds.

b. Determine how much the revised semiannual payments should be after this rate change (there are 14 remaining payments and compounding dates). The next payment will be in the middle of the fourth year. (Round all values to whole numbers.)

Selected References

Bierman, Harold, Jr.; Charles P. Bonini; and Warren H. Hausman. *Quantitative Analysis for Business Decisions*. 7th ed. Homewood, Ill.: Richard D. Irwin, 1986.

_______; and Seymour Smidt. *The Capital Budgeting Decision*. 5th ed. New York: Macmillan, 1980.

Boness, A. James. *Capital Budgeting*. New York: Praeger Publishers, 1972.

Cissell, Robert, and Helen Cissell. *Mathematics of Finance*. 4th ed. Boston: Houghton Mifflin, 1972.

Draper, Jean E., and Jane S. Klingman. *Mathematical Analysis*. New York: Harper & Row, 1967.

Howell, James E., and Daniel Teichroew. *Mathematical Analysis for Business Decisions*. Rev. ed. Homewood, Ill.: Richard D. Irwin, 1971.

Jean, William H. *Capital Budgeting: The Economic Evaluation of Investment Projects*. Scranton, Pa.: International Textbook, 1969.

Johnson, R. W. *Capital Budgeting*. Belmont, Calif.: Wadsworth, 1970.

Osteryoung, Jerome. *Capital Budgeting: Long-Term Asset Selection*. Columbus, Ohio: Grid, 1974, chap. 3.

Peterson, David E. *A Quantitative Framework for Financial Management*. Homewood, Ill.: Richard D. Irwin, 1969.

Solomon, Ezra. "The Arithmetic of Capital-Budgeting Decisions." *Journal of Business* 29 (April 1956), pp. 124–29.

10 Valuation and Rates of Return

In Chapter 9 we considered the basic principles of the time value of money. In this chapter we will use many of those concepts to determine how financial assets (bonds, preferred stock, and common stock) are valued and how investors establish the rates of return they demand. In the next chapter we will use material from this chapter to determine the overall cost of financing to the firm. Once we know how much bondholders and stockholders demand in the way of rates of return, we then observe what the corporation is required to pay them in order to attract their funds. The cost of corporate financing (capital) is subsequently used in analyzing whether a project is acceptable for investment or not. These relationships are depicted in Figure 10–1.

Valuation Concepts

The valuation of a financial asset is based on determining the present value of future cash flows. Thus, we need to know the value of future cash flows and the discount rate to be applied to the future cash flows to determine the current value.

Figure 10–1
The relationship between time value of money, required return, cost of financing, and investment decisions

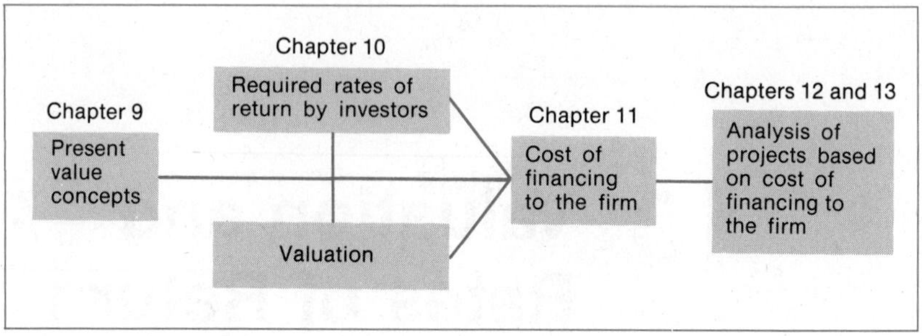

The market-determined required rate of return, which is the discount rate, depends on the market's perceived level of risk associated with the individual security. Also important is the idea that required rates of return are competitively determined among the many companies seeking financial capital. For example, IBM, due to its low financial risk, relatively high return, and strong market position in computers, is likely to raise debt capital at a significantly lower cost than can Dome Petroleum or Algoma Steel, two financially troubled firms. This implies that investors are willing to accept a lower return for a lower risk, and vice versa. In the way described above, the market allocates capital to companies based on estimates of risk, efficiency, and expected returns—which are based to a large degree on past performance. The reward to the manager for efficient use of capital in the past is a lower required return for investors than that of competing companies that did not manage their financial resources as well.

Throughout the balance of this chapter concepts of valuation to corporate bonds, preferred stock, and common stock will be applied. Although we describe the basic characteristics of each form of security as part of the valuation discussion, extended discussion of each security is deferred until later chapters.

Valuation of Bonds

As previously stated, the value of a financial asset is based on the concept of determining the present value of future cash flows. Let's start our exploration of this process by applying it to bond valuation. A bond provides an annuity stream of interest payments and a $1,000 principal payment at maturity.[1] Investors discount these future cash flows to determine the current price of the bond. The discount factor used is called the yield to maturity (Y). The value of Y is determined in the bond markets and represents the required rate of return demanded by investors on a bond of a given risk and maturity. More will be said about the concept of yield to maturity in the next section.

The price of a bond is thus equal to the present value of regular interest payments discounted by the yield to maturity added to the present value of the principal (also discounted by the yield to maturity). This relationship can be expressed mathematically as follows.

$$P_b = \sum_{t=1}^{n} \frac{I_t}{(1 + Y)^t} + \frac{P_n}{(1 + Y)^n} \qquad (10\text{–}1)$$

where

P_b = Price of the bond
I_t = Interest payments
P_n = Principal payment at maturity
t = Number corresponding to a period; running from 1 to n
n = Total number of periods
Y = Yield to maturity (or required rate of return)

The first term in the equation says to take the sum of the present values of the interest payments (I_t); the second term directs you to take the present value of the principal payment at maturity (P_n). The discount rate used throughout the analysis is the yield to maturity (Y). The answer derived is referred to as P_b (the price of the bond). The analysis is carried out for n periods.

Let's consider an example where I_t (interest payments) equals \$100; P_n (principal payment at maturity) equals \$1,000; Y (yield to maturity) is 10 percent; and n (total number of periods) equals 20. This means that P_b (the price of the bond) would equal:

$$P_b = \sum_{t=1}^{20} \frac{\$100}{(1 + .10)^t} + \frac{\$1{,}000}{(1 + .10)^{20}}$$

[1]Most corporate bonds have a \$1,000 par value. If the par value is higher or lower, then that value would be used.

Although the price of the bond could be determined with logarithms, it is much simpler to use present value tables. We take the present value of the interest payments and then add this value to the present value of the principal payment at maturity.

Present value of interest payments In this case we determine the present value of a $100 annuity for 20 years.[2] The discount rate is 10 percent. Using Appendix D, the present value of an annuity, we find the following:

$$A = R \times IF_{pva}\ (n = 20,\ i = 10\%)$$
$$A = \$100 \times 8.514 = \$851.40$$

Present value of principal payment (par value) at maturity This single value of $1,000 will be received after 20 years. Note the term *principal payment at maturity* is used interchangeably with *par value* or *face value* of the bond. We discount $1,000 back to the present at 10 percent. Using Appendix B, the present value of a single amount, we find the following:

$$P = S \times IF_{pv}\ (n = 20,\ i = 10\%)$$
$$P = \$1{,}000 \times .149 = \$149$$

The current price of the bond, based on the present value of interest payments and the present value of the principal payment at maturity, is $1,000.40.

Present value of interest payments	$ 851.40
Present value of principal payment at maturity	149.00
Total present value, or price, of the bond	$1,000.40

The price of the bond in this case is essentially the same as its par, or stated, value to be received at maturity of $1,000.[3] This is because the annual interest rate is 10 percent (the annual interest payment of $100 divided by $1,000), and the yield to maturity, or discount rate, is also 10 percent. When the interest rate on the bond and the yield

[2]For now we are using *annual* interest payments for simplicity. Later in the discussion, we will shift to semiannual payments and more appropriately determine the value of a bond.

[3]The slight difference is due to the rounding procedures in the tables.

to maturity are equal, the bond will trade at par value. Later we shall examine the mathematical effects of varying the yield to maturity above or below the interest rate on the bond. But first, let's more fully examine the concept of yield to maturity.

Concept of Yield to Maturity

In the previous example the yield to maturity used as the discount rate was 10 percent. The yield to maturity, or discount rate, is the rate of return required by bondholders. The bondholder, or any investor for that matter, will allow *three* factors to influence his or her required rate of return.

1. The required real rate of return—This is the rate of return the investor demands for giving up current use of the funds on a noninflation-adjusted basis. It is the financial "rent" the investor charges for using his or her funds for one year, five years, or any given time period. Historically, the real rate of return demanded by investors has been about 2 to 3 percent. Throughout the 1980s the real rate of return has been much higher; that is, 5 to 7 percent.

2. Inflation premium—In addition to the real rate of return discussed above, the investor requires a premium to compensate for the eroding effect of inflation on the value of the dollar. It would hardly satisfy an investor to have a 3 percent total rate of return in a 5 percent inflationary economy. Under such circumstances the lender (investor) would be paying the borrower 2 percent (in purchasing power) for use of the funds. This would represent an irrational course of action. No one wishes to *pay* another party to use his or her funds. The inflation premium added to the real rate of return ensures that this will not happen. The size of the inflation premium will be based on the investor's expectations about future inflation. In the mid-1980s the inflation premium has been of the magnitude of 3 to 4 percent. In the late 1970s it was in excess of 10 percent.

If one combines the real rate of return (1) and the inflation premium (2), the *risk-free rate of return* is determined. This is the rate that compensates the investor for the current use of his or her funds and for the loss in purchasing power due to inflation, but not for taking risks.

As an example, if the real rate of return were 3 percent and the inflation premium were 4 percent, we would say the risk-free rate of return was 7 percent.[4]

3. Risk premium—We must now add the risk premium to the risk-free rate of return. This is a premium associated with the special risks of a given investment. Of primary interest to us are two types of risks: *business risk* and *financial risk*. Business risk relates to the possible inability of the firm to hold its competitive position and maintain stability and growth in its earnings. Financial risk relates to the possible inability of the firm to meet its debt obligations as they come due. In addition to the two forms of risk mentioned above, the risk premium will be greater or less for different types of investments. For example, because bonds possess a contractual obligation for the firm to pay interest and repay principal to bondholders, they are considered less risky than common stock where no such obligation exists.[5]

The risk premium of an investment may range from as low as zero on a very short-term Canadian government-backed security to 10 to 15 percent on a gold mining expedition. Typical risk premiums range from 2 to 6 percent. We shall assume that in the investment we are examining the risk premium is 3 percent. If we add this risk premium to the two components of the risk-free rate of return developed in 1 and 2, we arrive at an overall required rate of return of 10 percent.

+ Real rate of return	3%
+ Inflation premium	4%
= Risk-free rate	7%
+ Risk premium	3
= Required rate of return	10%

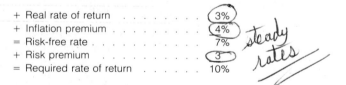

In this instance we assume we are evaluating the required return on a bond issued by a firm. If the security had been the common stock of the same firm, the risk premium might have been 5 to 6 percent, thus making the required rate of return 12 to 13 percent.

[4]Actually, a slightly more accurate representation would be: Risk-free rate = (1 + real rate of return) (1 + inflation premium) − 1. We would show: (1.03) (1.04) − 1 = 1.0712 − 1 = .0712 = 7.12 percent.

[5]On the other hand, common stock carries the potential for unlimited return when the corporation is very profitable.

As we conclude this section, then, please recall that the required rate of return on a bond is effectively identical to the required yield to maturity.

Changing the Yield to Maturity and the Impact on Bond Valuation

In the earlier bond value calculation the interest rate was 10 percent ($100 annual interest on a $1,000 par value bond) while the yield to maturity was also 10 percent. Under those circumstances, the price of the bond was equal to its par value. Let us now assume that conditions in the market cause the yield to maturity to change.

Increase in inflation premium For example, assume the inflation premium goes up from 4 to 6 percent while all else remains constant. The required rate of return would now become 12 percent.

+ Real rate of return	3%
+ Inflation premium	6
= Risk-free rate	9%
+ Risk premium	3
= Required rate of return	12%

This increase in the required rate of return, or yield to maturity, on the bond will cause its price to change.[6] A bond that pays only 10 percent interest when the required rate of return (yield to maturity) is 12 percent will have its price fall below its former value of approximately $1,000. The new price of the bond, as computed below, is $850.90.

Present value of interest payments—We take the present value of a $100 annuity for 20 years. The discount rate is 12 percent. Using Appendix D:

$$A = R \times IF_{pva}\ (n = 20, i = 12\%)$$
$$A = \$100 \times 7.469 = \$746.90$$

[6]Of course, the required rate of return on all other financial assets will also go up proportionally.

Present value of principal payment at maturity—We take the present value of $1,000 after 20 years. The discount rate is 12 percent. Using Appendix B:

$$P = S \times IF_{pv}\ (n = 20,\ i = 12\%)$$
$$P = \$1,000 \times .104 = \$104$$

Total present value—

Present value of interest payments	$746.90
Present value of principal payment at maturity	104.00
Total present value, or price, of the bond	$850.90

In this example increasing inflation causes the required rate of return (yield to maturity) to go up. This, in turn, causes the bond price to fall by approximately $150. A similar effect will take place if the business risk increases or the demanded level for the *real* rate of return becomes higher.

Decrease in inflation premium Of course, the opposite effect will occur if the required rate of return goes down because of lower inflation, less risk, or some other factor. Let's consider what happens if the inflation premium declines, causing the required rate of return (yield to maturity) to go down to 8 percent.

The 20-year bond with the 10 percent interest rate would now sell for $1,196.80.

Present value of interest payments—

$$A = R \times IF_{pva}\ (n = 20,\ i = 8\%) \quad \text{[Appendix D]}$$
$$A = \$100 \times 9.818 = \$981.80$$

Present value of principal payment at maturity—

$$P = S \times IF_{pv}\ (n = 20,\ i = 8\%) \quad \text{[Appendix B]}$$
$$P = \$1,000 \times .215 = \$215$$

Total present value—

Present value of interest payments	$ 981.80
Present value of principal payment at maturity	215.00
Total present value, or price, of the bond	$1,196.80

The price of the bond has now risen $196.80 above par value. This is certainly in line with the expected result because the bond is paying 10 percent interest when the required yield in the market is only 8 percent. The 2 percent differential on a $1,000 par value bond represents $20 per year. The investor will receive this differential for the next 20 years. The present value of $20 for the next 20 years at the current market rate of interest of 8 percent is approximately $196.80. This explains why the bond is trading at $196.80 over its stated, or par, value.

The further the yield to maturity on a bond falls away from the stated interest rate on the bond, the greater the price change effect will be. This is illustrated in Table 10–1 for the 10 percent interest rate, 20-year bonds discussed in this chapter.

We see clearly that different yields to maturity have a significant impact on the price of a bond.[7]

Time to Maturity

The impact of a change in yield to maturity on valuation is also affected by the remaining time to maturity. The effect of a bond paying 2 percent more or less than the going rate of interest is much greater for a 20-year bond than it is for a 1-year bond. In the latter case the investor will only be gaining or giving up $20 for one year. That is certainly not the same as having this differential for an extended period of time. Let's once again return to the 10 percent interest rate bond and show the impact of a 2 percent decrease or increase in yield to maturity for varying *times* to maturity. The values are shown in Table 10–2 and graphed in Figure 10–2. The upper part of Figure 10–2 shows how the amount (premium) above par value is reduced as the

---

[7]The reader may observe that the impact of a decrease or increase in interest rates is not equal. For example, a 2 percent decrease in interest rates will produce a $196.80 gain in the bond price, and an increase of 2 percent causes a $149.10 loss. While price movements are not symmetrical around the price of the bond when the time dimension is the maturity date of the bond, they are symmetrical around the duration of the bond. The duration represents the weighted average time period to recapture the interest and principal on the bond. While these concepts go beyond that appropriate for an introductory finance text, the interested reader may wish to consult Geoffrey A. Hirt and Stanley B. Block, *Fundamentals of Investment Management*, 2nd ed. (Homewood, Ill.: Richard D. Irwin, 1986), or Frank K. Reilly, *Investments*, 2nd ed. (Hinsdale, Ill.: Dryden Press, 1985).

Table 10–1
Bond price table

(10 Percent Interest Payment, 20 Years to Maturity)

Yield to Maturity	Bond Price
2%	$2,308.10
4	1,825.00
6	1,459.00
7	1,317.40
8	1,196.80
9	1,090.90
10	1,000.00*
11	920.30
12	850.90
13	789.50
14	735.30
16	643.90
20	513.00
25	407.40

*This value was computed earlier as $1,000.40 due to rounding. The correct value is $1,000.00.

Table 10–2
Impact of time to maturity on bond prices

Time Period in Years (of 10 percent bond)	Bond Price with 8 Percent Yield to Maturity	Bond Price with 12 Percent Yield to Maturity
0	$1,000.00	$1,000.00
1	1,018.60	982.30
5	1,080.30	927.50
10	1,134.00	887.00
15	1,170.90	864.11
20	1,196.80	850.90
25	1,213.50	843.30
30	1,224.80	838.50

number of years to maturity becomes smaller and smaller. Figure 10–2 should be read from left to right. The lower part of the figure shows how the amount (discount) below par value is reduced with progressively fewer years to maturity. Clearly, the longer the maturity, the greater the impact of changes in yield.

Determining Yield to Maturity from the Bond Price

Up until now we have used yield to maturity as well as other factors, such as the interest rate on the bond and number of years to maturity,

Figure 10–2
Relationship between time to maturity and bond price*

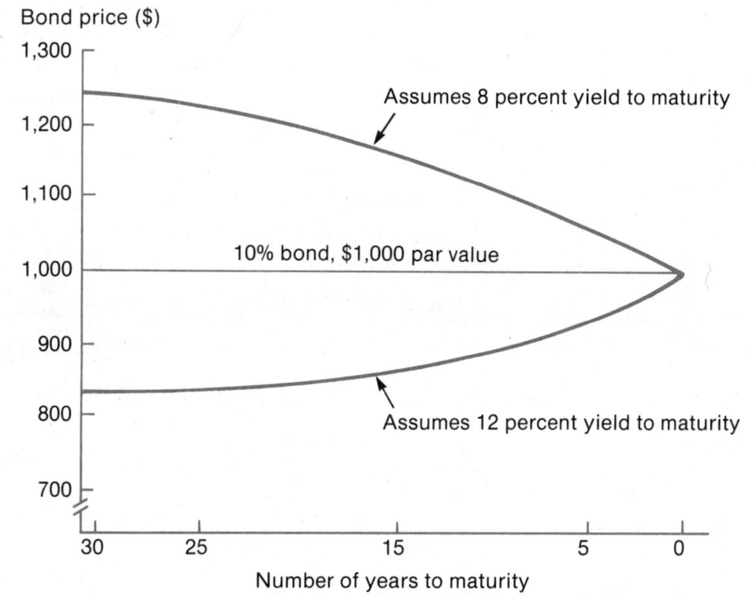

*The relationship in the graph is not symmetrical in nature.

to determine the price of the bond. We shall now assume we know the price of the bond, the interest rate on the bond, and the years to maturity, and we wish to determine the yield to maturity. Once we have computed this value, we have determined the rate of return investors are demanding in the marketplace to provide for inflation, risk, and other factors.

Let's once again present Formula 10–1.

$$P_b = \sum_{t=1}^{n} \frac{I_t}{(1 + Y)^t} + \frac{P_n}{(1 + Y)^n}$$

We now try to determine the value Y, the yield to maturity, that will equate the interest payments (I_t) and the principal payment (P_n) to the price of the bond (P_b). This is similar to the calculations to determine yield in the prior chapter.

Assume a 15-year bond pays $110 per year (11 percent) in interest and $1,000 after 15 years in principal repayment. The current price of the bond is $932.21. We wish to determine the yield to maturity, or discount rate, that equates future flows with the current price.

In this trial-and-error process, the first step is to choose an initial percentage in the tables to try as the discount rate. Since the bond is trading below the par value of $1,000, we know the yield to maturity (discount rate) must be above the quoted interest rate of 11 percent. Let's begin the trial-and-error process.

A 13 percent discount rate As a first approximation, we might try 13 percent and compute the present value of the bond as follows:

Present value of interest payments—

$$A = R \times IF_{pva}\ (n = 15,\ i = 13\%) \qquad \text{[Appendix D]}$$
$$A = \$110 \times 6.462 = \$710.82$$

Present value of principal payment at maturity—

$$P = S \times IF_{pv}\ (n = 15,\ i = 13\%) \qquad \text{[Appendix B]}$$
$$P = \$1{,}000 \times .160 = \$160$$

Total present value—

Present value of interest payments	$710.82
Present value of principal payment at maturity	160.00
Total present value, or price, of the bond	$870.82

The answer of $870.82 is below the current bond price of $932.21. This indicates we have used too high a discount rate in creating too low a value.

A 12 percent discount rate As a next step in the trial-and-error process, we will try 12 percent.

Present value of interest payments—

$$A = R \times IF_{pva}\ (n = 15,\ i = 12\%) \qquad \text{[Appendix D]}$$
$$A = \$110 \times 6.811 = \$749.21$$

Present value of principal payment at maturity—

$$P = S \times IF_{pv}\ (n = 15,\ i = 12\%) \qquad \text{[Appendix B]}$$
$$P = \$1{,}000 \times .183 = \$183$$

Total present value—

Present value of interest payments	$749.21
Present value of principal payment at maturity	183.00
Total present value, or price, of the bond	$932.21

The answer matches precisely the price of $932.21 for the bond being evaluated. That indicates that the correct yield to maturity for the bond is 12 percent. Of course, if the computed value were slightly different from the price of the bond, we could use interpolation to arrive at the correct answer. An example of interpolating to derive yield to maturity is presented in Appendix 10A.

Formula for bond yield Because it is a tedious process to determine the bond yield to maturity through trial and error, an approximate answer can also be found by using Formula 10–2.

$$\text{Approximate yield to maturity } (Y') = \frac{\text{Annual interest payment} + \dfrac{\text{Principal payment} - \text{Price of the bond}}{\text{Number of years to maturity}}}{\dfrac{\text{Price of the bond} + \text{Principal payment}}{2}} \qquad (10\text{–}2)$$

Plugging in the values from the just completed analysis of yield to maturity, we show:

$$= \frac{\$110 + \dfrac{\$1{,}000 - \$932.21}{15}}{\dfrac{\$932.21 + \$1{,}000}{2}}$$

$$= \frac{\$110 + \dfrac{\$67.79}{15}}{\dfrac{\$932.21 + \$1{,}000}{2}}$$

$$= \frac{\$110 + \$4.52}{\$966.11}$$

$$= \frac{\$114.52}{\$966.11} = 11.84\%$$

The answer of 11.84 percent is a reasonably good approximation of the exact yield to maturity of 12 percent.[8] We use the prime (′) symbol after Y to indicate the answer based on Formula 10–2 is only an approximation.

Note the numerator of Formula 10–2 represents the average annual income over the life of the bond and the denominator represents the average investment. That is, in the numerator we take the annual interest payment of $110 and add that to the average annual change in the bond value over 15 years which is computed as $4.52. This provides average annual income of $114.52. In the denominator we average the original price of $932.21 with the final value of $1,000 that we will receive at maturity to get the average investment over the 15-year holding period.

It should be pointed out that in computing yield to maturity on a bond, financially oriented hand-held calculators and software programs for microcomputers can be extremely helpful. There are also useful bond tables in libraries. Nevertheless, it is important that students also understand the mechanics that go into the calculations.

As we have discussed throughout, the yield to maturity is the required rate of return demanded by bondholders. More importantly for our purposes here, it also indicates the current cost to the corporation to issue bonds. In the prior example the corporation had issued bonds at 11 percent, but market conditions changed and the current price of the bond fell to $932.21. At this current price the ongoing yield to maturity increased to 12 percent (11.84 percent, using the approximation method). If the corporate treasurer were to issue new bonds today, he would have to respond to the current market-demanded rate of 12 percent rather than the initial yield of 11 percent. Only by understanding how investors value bonds in the marketplace can the corporate financial officer properly assess the cost of that source of financing to the corporation.

Semiannual Interest and Bond Prices

Up until now in our bond analysis we have been considering examples where interest was paid annually. In actuality, most bonds pay interest

---

[8]The greater the premium or discount and the longer the period to maturity, the less accurate the approximation.

semiannually. Thus, a 10 percent interest rate bond may actually pay \$50 twice a year instead of \$100 annually. To make the conversion from an annual to semiannual analysis, we follow three steps.

1. Divide the annual interest rate by two.
2. Multiply the number of years by two.
3. Divide the annual yield to maturity by two.

Assume a 10 percent, \$1,000 par value bond has a maturity of 20 years. The annual yield to maturity is 12 percent. In following the three steps above, we would show:

1. 10%/2 = 5% semiannual interest rate; therefore, 5% × \$1,000 = \$50 semiannual interest.
2. 20 × 2 = 40 periods to maturity.
3. 12%/2 = 6% yield to maturity, expressed on a semiannual basis.

In computing the price of the bond issued, on a semiannual analysis, we show:

Present value of interest payments—We take the present value of a \$50 annuity for 40 periods. The semiannual discount rate is 6 percent. Using Appendix D:

$$A = R \times IF_{pva}\ (n = 40, i = 6\%)$$
$$A = \$50 \times 15.046 = \$752.30$$

Present value of principal payment at maturity—We take the present value of \$1,000 after 40 periods, using a 6 percent discount rate. Note that once we go to a semiannual analysis with the interest payments, we consistently follow the same approach in discounting back the principal payment; otherwise, we would be using semiannual and annual calculations on the same bond. Using Appendix B:

$$P = S \times IF_{pv}\ (n = 40, i = 6\%)$$
$$P = \$1{,}000 \times .097 = \$97$$

Total present value—

Present value of interest payments	\$752.30
Present value of principal payment at maturity	97.00
Total present value, or price, of the bond	\$849.30

The answer of \$849.30 is slightly below that which we found previously for the same bond, assuming an annual interest rate (\$850.90). In terms of accuracy the semiannual analysis is a more acceptable method. It is the method used in most bond tables, for example. As is true in many finance texts, the annual interest rate approach is given first for ease of presentation, and then the semiannual basis is given. In the problems at the back of the chapter, you will be asked to do problems on both an annual and semiannual interest payment basis.

Valuation and Preferred Stock

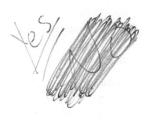

Preferred stock usually represents a perpetuity. In other words, it has no maturity date. It is valued in the market without any principal payment since it has no ending life. If preferred stock had a maturity date, the analysis would be similar to that of the preceding bond example. Preferred stock has a fixed dividend payment carrying a higher order of precedence than common stock dividends, but not the binding contractual obligation of interest on debt. Preferred stock, being a hybrid security, has neither the ownership privilege of common stock nor the legally enforceable provisions of debt. To value a perpetuity such as preferred stock, we first consider the formula:

$$P_p = \frac{D_p}{(1 + K_p)^1} + \frac{D_p}{(1 + K_p)^2} + \frac{D_p}{(1 + K_p)^3} + \dots + \frac{D_p}{(1 + K_p)^\infty} \quad (10\text{–}3)$$

where

P_p = Price of preferred stock
D_p = Annual dividend for preferred stock It is a constant value
K_p = Required rate of return, or discount rate, applied to preferred stock dividends

Note the formula calls for taking the present value of an infinite stream of constant dividend payments at a discount rate equal to K_p. Because we are dealing with an infinite stream of payments, Formula 10–3 can be reduced to a much more usable form as indicated in Formula 10–4.

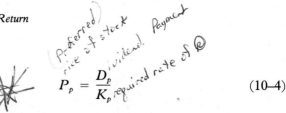

$$P_p = \frac{D_p}{K_p} \tag{10–4}$$

According to Formula 10–4 all we have to do to find the price of preferred stock (P_p) is to divide the constant annual dividend payment (D_p) by the required rate of return that preferred stockholders are demanding (K_p). For example, if the annual dividend were \$10 and the stockholder required a 10 percent rate of return, the price of preferred stock would be \$100.

$$P_p = \frac{D_p}{K_p} = \frac{\$10}{.10} = \$100$$

As was true in our bond valuation analysis, if the rate of return required by security holders changes, the value of the financial asset (in this case, preferred stock) will change. You may also recall that the longer the life of an investment, the greater the impact of a change in required rate of return. It is one thing to be locked into a low-paying security for one year when the rate goes up; it is quite another to be locked in for 10 or 20 years. With preferred stock, you have a *perpetual* security, so the impact is at a maximum. Assume in the prior example that because of higher inflation or increased business risk, K_p (the required rate of return) increases to 12 percent. The new value for the preferred stock shares then becomes:

$$P_p = \frac{D_p}{K_p} = \frac{\$10}{.12} = \$83.33$$

Of course, if the required rate of return were reduced to 8 percent, the opposite effect would take place. The preferred stock price would be recomputed as:

$$P_p = \frac{D_p}{K_p} = \frac{\$10}{.08} = \$125$$

It is not surprising that preferred stock is now trading well above its original price of \$100. It is still offering a \$10 dividend (10 percent of original offering price of \$100) while the market is demanding only an 8 percent yield. In order to match the \$10 dividend with the 8 percent rate of return, the market price will advance to \$125.

Determining the Required Rate of Return (Yield) from the Market Price

depends on market

In our analysis of preferred stock, we have used the value of the annual dividend (D_p) and the required rate of return (K_p) to solve for the price of preferred stock (P_p). We could change our analysis to solve for the required rate of return (K_p) as the unknown, given that we knew the annual dividend (D_p) and the preferred stock price (P_p). We take Formula 10–4 and rewrite it as Formula 10–5, where the unknown is the required rate of return (K_p).

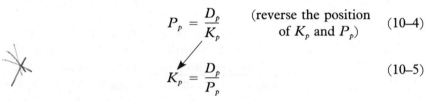

$$P_p = \frac{D_p}{K_p} \quad \text{(reverse the position of } K_p \text{ and } P_p\text{)} \qquad (10\text{–}4)$$

$$K_p = \frac{D_p}{P_p} \qquad (10\text{–}5)$$

Using Formula 10–5, if the annual preferred dividend (D_p) is \$10 and the price of preferred stock (P_p) is \$100, the required rate of return (yield) would be 10 percent.

$$K_p = \frac{D_p}{P_p} = \frac{\$10}{\$100} = 10\%$$

If the price goes up to \$130, the yield will be only 7.69 percent.

$$K_p = \frac{\$10}{\$130} = 7.69\%$$

We see that the rise in market price causes quite a decline in the yield.

Valuation of Common Stock

The value of a share of common stock to the shareholder is the *present value* of an expected stream of *future dividends*. Although in the short run stockholders may be influenced by a change in earnings or other variables, the ultimate value of any holding rests with the distribution of earnings in the form of dividend payments. Though the stockholder may benefit from the retention and reinvestment of earnings by the corporation, at some point the earnings must be translated into cash flow for the stockholder. A stock valuation model based on future expected dividends can be stated as:

$$P_0 = \frac{D_1}{(1 + K_e)^1} + \frac{D_2}{(1 + K_e)^2} + \frac{D_3}{(1 + K_e)^3} + \ldots + \frac{D_\infty}{(1 + K_e)^\infty} \quad (10\text{–}6)$$

where

P_0 = Price of the stock today
D = Dividend for each year
K_e = Required rate of return for common stock (discount rate)

This formula, with modification, is generally applied to three different circumstances:

1. No growth in dividends.
2. Constant growth in dividends.
3. Variable growth in dividends.

No Growth in Dividends

Under the no-growth circumstance, common stock is very similar to preferred stock. The common stock pays a constant dividend each year. For that reason we merely translate the terms in Formula 10–5, which applies to preferred stock, to apply to common stock. This is shown as new Formula 10–7.

$$P_0 = \frac{D_0}{K_e} \quad (10\text{–}7)$$

where

P_0 = Price of common stock today
D_0 = Current annual common stock dividend (a constant value)
K_e = Required rate of return for common stock

Assume D_0 = \$1.86 and K_e = 12 percent; the price of the stock would be \$15.50

$$P_0 = \frac{\$1.86}{.12} = \$15.50$$

A no-growth policy for common stock dividends does not hold much appeal for investors and so is seen infrequently in the real world.

Constant Growth in Dividends

A firm that increases dividends at a constant rate is a more likely circumstance. Perhaps a firm decides to increase its dividends by 5 or 7 percent per year. Under such a circumstance, Formula 10–6 converts to Formula 10–8.

$$P_0 = \frac{D_0(1+g)^1}{(1+K_e)^1} + \frac{D_0(1+g)^2}{(1+K_e)^2} + \frac{D_0(1+g)^3}{(1+K_e)^3} + \ldots + \frac{D_0(1+g)^\infty}{(1+K_e)^\infty} \quad (10\text{–}8)$$

where

P_0 = Price of common stock today
$D_0(1+g)^1$ = Dividend in year 1, D_1
$D_0(1+g)^2$ = Dividend in year 2, D_2, and so on
g = Constant growth rate in dividends
K_e = Required rate of return for common stock (discount rate)

In other words, the current price of the stock is the present value of the future stream of dividends growing at a constant rate. If we can anticipate the growth pattern of future dividends and determine the discount rate, we can ascertain the price of the stock.

For example, assume the following information:

D_0 = Latest 12-month dividend (assume \$1.87)
D_1 = First year, \$2.00 (growth rate, 7%)
D_2 = Second year, \$2.14 (growth rate, 7%)
D_3 = Third year, \$2.29 (growth rate, 7%)
etc., etc.
K_e = Required rate of return (discount rate), 12%

then

$$P_0 = \frac{\$2.00}{(1.12)^1} + \frac{\$2.14}{(1.12)^2} + \frac{\$2.29}{(1.12)^3} + \ldots + \frac{\text{Infinite dividend}}{(1.12)^\infty}$$

To find the price of the stock we take the present value of each year's dividend. This is no small task when the formula calls for us to take the present value of an *infinite* stream of growing dividends. Fortunately, Formula 10–8 can be compressed into a much more usable form if two circumstances are satisfied.

1. The dividend growth rate (g) must be constant.
2. The discount rate (K_e) must exceed the growth rate (g).

These assumptions are usually made to reduce the complications in the analytical process. They then allow us to reduce or rewrite Formula 10–8 as Formula 10–9. Formula 10–9 is the basic equation for finding the value of common stock and is referred to as the dividend valuation model.

$$P_0 = \frac{D_1}{K_e - g} \qquad (10\text{–}9)$$

This is an extremely easy formula to use in which:[9]

P_0 = Price of the stock today
D_1 = Dividend at the end of the first year (or period)
K_e = Required rate of return (discount rate)
g = Constant growth rate in dividends

---

[9]In order to derive this relationship we multiply both sides of Equation 10–8 by $(1 + K_e)/(1 + g)$ and subtract Equation 10–8 from the product. The result is

$$\frac{P_0(1 + K_e)}{(1 + g)} - P_0 = D_0 - \frac{D_0(1 + g)^\infty}{(1 + K_e)^\infty}$$

Because K_e is larger than g, the last term on the right-hand side goes to zero because of the infinite exponent. That leaves us with

$$P_0\left[\frac{1 + K_e}{1 + g} - 1\right] = D_0$$

$$P_0\left[\frac{(1 + K_e) - (1 + g)}{1 + g}\right] = D_0$$

$$P_0(K_e - g) = D_0(1 + g)$$

$$P_0 = \frac{D_1}{K_e - g}$$

Based on the current example:

D_1 = \$2.00
K_e = .12
g = .07

and P_0 is computed as:

$$P_0 = \frac{D_1}{K_e - g} = \frac{\$2.00}{.12 - .07} = \frac{\$2.00}{.05} = \$40$$

Thus, given that the stock has a \$2 dividend at the end of the first period, a discount rate of 12 percent, and a constant growth rate of 7 percent, the current price of the stock is \$40.

Let's take a closer look at Formula 10–9 and the factors that influence valuation. For example, what is the anticipated effect on valuation if K_e (the required rate of return, or discount rate) increases as a result of inflation or increased risk? Intuitively, we would expect the stock price to decline if investors demand a higher return and the dividend and growth rate remain the same. This is precisely what happens.

If D_1 remains at \$2 and the growth rate (g) is 7 percent, but K_e increases from 12 percent to 14 percent, using Formula 10–9, the price of the common stock will now be \$28.57. This is considerably lower than its earlier value of \$40.

$$P_0 = \frac{D_1}{K_e - g} = \frac{\$2.00}{.14 - .07} = \frac{\$2.00}{.07} = \$28.57$$

Similarly, if the growth rate (g) increases while D_1 and K_e remain constant, the stock price can be expected to increase. Assume D_1 = \$2, K_e is set at its earlier level of 12 percent, and g increases from 7 percent to 9 percent. Using Formula 10–9 once again, the new price of the stock would be \$66.67.

$$P_0 = \frac{D_1}{K_e - g} = \frac{\$2.00}{.12 - .09} = \frac{\$2.00}{.03} = \$66.67$$

We should not be surprised to see that an increasing growth rate has enhanced the value of the stock.

Stock valuation based on future stock value The discussion of stock valuation to this point has related to the concept of the present value of future dividends. This is a valid concept, but suppose we wish to approach the issue from a slightly different viewpoint. Assume we are going to buy a stock and hold it for three years and then sell it. We wish to know the present value of our investment. This is somewhat like the bond valuation analysis. We will receive a dividend for three years (D_1, D_2, D_3) and then a price (payment) for the stock at the end of three years (P_3). What is the present value of the benefits? What we do is add the present value of three years of dividends and the present value of the stock price after three years. Assuming a constant-growth dividend analysis, the stock price after three years is simply the present value of all future dividends after the third year (from the fourth year on). Thus, the current price of the stock in this case is nothing other than the present value of the first three dividends, plus the present value of all future dividends (which is equivalent to the stock price after the third year). Saying the price of the stock is the present value of all future dividends is also the equivalent of saying it is the present value of a dividend stream for a number of years plus the present value of the price of the stock after that time period. The appropriate formula is still $P_0 = D_1/(K_e - g)$, which we have been using throughout this part of the chapter.

Determining the Required Rate of Return from the Market Price

In our analysis of common stock we have used the first year's dividend (D_1), the required rate of return (K_e), and the growth rate (g) to solve for the stock price (P_0) based on Formula 10–9.

$$P_0 = \frac{D_1}{K_e - g} \text{ (Previously presented Formula 10–9)}$$

We could change the analysis to solve for the required rate of return (K_e) as the unknown, given that we know the first year's dividend (D_1), the stock price (P_0), and the growth rate (g). We take the formula above and algebraically change it to provide Formula 10–10.

$$P_0 = \frac{D_1}{K_e - g} \qquad (10\text{–}9)$$

$$K_e = \frac{D_1}{P_0} + g \qquad (10\text{–}10)$$

This formula allows us to compute the required return (K_e) from the investment. Returning to the basic data from the common stock example:

K_e = Required rate of return (to be solved)
D_1 = Dividend at the end of the first year \$2.00
P_0 = Price of the stock today \$40
g = Constant growth rate .07

$$K_e = \frac{\$2.00}{\$40} + 7\% = 5\% + 7\% = 12\%$$

In this instance we would say the stockholder demands a 12 percent return on his common stock investment. Of particular interest are the individual parts of the formula for K_e that we have been discussing. Let's write out Formula 10–10 again.

$$K_e = \frac{\text{First year's dividend}}{\text{Common stock price}} \left(\frac{D_1}{P_0}\right) + \text{Growth } (g)$$

The first term represents the dividend yield the stockholder will receive, and the second term represents the anticipated growth in dividends, earnings, and stock price. While we have been describing the growth rate primarily in terms of dividends, it is assumed the earnings and stock price will also grow at that same rate over the long term if all else holds constant. You should also observe that the formula above represents a total return concept. The stockholder is receiving a current dividend plus anticipated growth in the future. If the dividend yield is low, the growth rate must be high to provide the necessary return. Conversely, if the growth rate is low, a high dividend yield will be expected.

The Price–Earnings Ratio Concept and Valuation

- multiplier

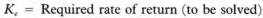

In Chapter 2 we introduced the concept of the price–earnings ratio. The price–earnings ratio represents a multiplier applied to current earnings to determine the value of a share of stock in the market. It is considered a pragmatic, everyday approach to valuation. If a stock has earnings per share of \$3 and a price–earnings (P/E) ratio of 12 times, it will carry a market value of \$36. Another company with the same earnings but a P/E ratio of 15 times will enjoy a market price of $45.

The price–earnings ratio is influenced by the earnings and sales growth of the firm, the risk (or volatility in performance), the debt-equity structure of the firm, the dividend policy, the quality of management, and a number of other factors. Firms that have bright expectations for the future tend to trade at high P/E ratios while the opposite is true of low P/E firms.

For example, the average P/E for all Toronto Stock Exchange firms was 21 in mid-1987, although Dylex traded at a P/E of 43 because of the bright prospects for specialty retailing. At the same time, the Royal Bank of Canada traded at a relatively low P/E of 9.5 because of the large exposure of Canadian banks to potential loan losses related to large loans made to energy companies and to Third World governments.

Price–earnings ratios can be looked up in many financial newspapers. Quotations from the *Financial Times of Canada* are presented in Table 10–3. Note that the third column after the company name shows the annual dividend and the fourth column shows the dividend yield. The last column shows the P/E ratio. For Abitibi-Price it was 23.2, indicating that the current price of $34½ represented 23.2 times annual earnings.[10] The remaining columns show the closing price for the week, the change in price over the week, weekly sales volume, the high and low prices over the past year, and latest reported earnings.

The P/E ratio represents an easily understood, pragmatic approach to valuation that is widely used by stockbrokers and individual investors. The dividend valuation approach (based on the present value of dividends) we have been using throughout the chapter is more theoretically sound and likely to be used by sophisticated financial analysts. Actually, to some extent, the two concepts can be brought together. A stock that has a high required rate of return (K_e) because of its risky nature will generally have a low P/E ratio. Similarly, a stock with a high expected growth rate (g) will normally have a high P/E ratio. In the first example, both methods provide a low valuation, while in the latter case, both methods provide a high valuation.

[10]The price–earnings ratio is not shown for some companies because they do not have positive earnings on which to base the calculation, or because it is the preferred stock of the company which is shown, in which case the P/E ratio is not relevant because preferred stock does not have earnings per share as such.

Table 10–3
Stock quotations

Close	Change on week	Sales 100s		12 mo. Hi	Lo	Divi-dend	% Yield	Latest fiscal year earnings	Latest interim earnings	P E ratio
			A							
16	-¼	527	AGF Pf f	19⅛	10	.36	2.3	Nov86.75	Feb3m.27	18.8
6	-⅛	100	AHA Auto Tch	10	5½	.00	.0	Dec86.43	Mar3m.12	15.4
10½	-⅜	491	AMCA Int'l	16¾	9	.00	.0	Dec86 2.76D	Mar3m.37D	
24⅛	¼	79	AMCA Pf 8.84	25⅝	22⅜	2.21	9.2			
23½	⅛	102	Amca Pf 9.5%	27¼	19	2.38	10.1			
24⅜	⅛	37	AMCA 9.25%	25½	22⅜	2.31	9.5			
5	-⅛	60	ARC Intl	5¾	4.25	.00	.0		Jan9m.11	
0.16	-.01	363	Abaterra En	.30	.10	.00	.0	Apr86.19D	Jan9m.14D	
2.05	-.35	543	Abermin Corp	3.45	1.12	.00	.0	Dec86.06D		
0.90	.05	89	Abermin Wt	1.80	.40	.00	.0			
34½	¾	484	Abitibi-Prce	43	21	.60	1.7	Dec86 1.50	Mar3m.29	23.2
10⅜	⅜	276	Abitibi Wts	15½	3.50	.00	.0			
3.00	-.30	569	Acadia Mnl	4.30	1.25	.00	.0			
0.82	.07	169	Access ATM	3.15	.47	.00	.0	Sep86 1.06D	Dec3m.41D	
4.85	-.15	57	Accgrph Cl A	8⅛	2.25	.00	.0	Aug86.17D	Feb6m.05D	
18¼	-¼	1	Acklands	21	15⅞	.60	3.3	Nov86.59	May6m.34	35.1
0.37	-.02	63	Adanac Mng	.75	.16	.00	.0			
4.45	.05	99	Agassiz Res	4.65	3.15	.00	.0	Jun85.29	Mar9m.07	24.9
30¼	-1½	815	Agnico Eagle	45	21⅝	.20U	.9	Dec86.37	Mar3m.07	54.1
6½		20	Agra Inds Wt	6½	6½	.00	.0			
15¾	¾	40	Agra Ind ClA	17	12	.20	1.3	Jul86.59	Apr9m.49	21.9
15¾	¾	56	Agra Cl-B f	17	12	.24	1.5	Jul86.59	Apr9m.49	21.9
14½	-⅜	116	Ahed Corp	20½	2.50	.00	.0	Nov83.01	Feb3m.02D	
0.30		44	Albany O&G	.41	.13	.00	.0	Dec83.01	Sep9m.00D	
20¼	-⅜	3012	Alta Energy	22¼	9¾	.30	1.5	Dec86.72	Mar3m.34	22.3
29⅛	-1	345	Alta 11.25Pf	35½	27	2.81	9.7			
29¾		174	Alta En Pf 2	30⅜	21⅝	1.94	6.5			
14½	⅛	241	Alta Nat Gas	16	11¾	.68	4.7	Dec86.89	Mar3m.23	17.7
39¾	-⅞	9082	Alcan Alum	43¼	25.41	.60U	2.0	Dec86 1.45	Mar3m.39	18.3
25¾		99	Alexis 7.4%	26⅜	25⅛	1.85	7.2			
10⅛	-⅝	152	Algo Grp A	11	7¾	.25	2.5	Dec86.71	Mar3m.20	14.3
2.85	-.45	125	Algo Wt A	3.90	1.10	.00	.0			
22½		39	Algoma Cnt R	24	19	.40	1.8	Dec86.70	Mar3m.08D	35.2
16	-¼	114	Algoma Steel	18¾	10	.00	.0	Dec86 4.65D	Mar3m.07	
18	¼	52	Algoma 8% Pf	19⅜	12¾	2.00	11.1			
18½	½	74	Algoma P2.00	19	13½	2.00	10.8			
1.50	.12	453	Altex Res	1.70	.45	.00	.0	Dec86.06	Mar3m.01	
25	⅛	210	Alum $2 Pfd	27¼	24½	2.00	8.0			
26¼	¼	88	Alm 2.3125Pf	27¼	25¾	2.31	8.8			
26⅛	⅛	73	Alum 2.1875U	27⅜	25½	2.19U	8.4			
24⅝	½	84	Alum Cda PfC	25⅝	23¾	1.89	7.7			
24½	¼	84	Alum Cda PfD	26	23¾	1.88U	7.7			
26	⅜	10	Almn Co $2.0	26¼	25¼	2.00	7.7			
25⅜	⅜	68	Almn Co PfdE	26¾	25	2.16	8.5			
21	-2	6760	Amer Bar Res	28⅝	6.93	.00	.0	Dec86.35	Mar3m.12	53.2
6⅜	-⅞	1630	Amer Bar Wt	9½	1.10	.00	0			
2.85	-.45	899	Amcn Bar GWt	4.25	1.60	.00	0			
19	-3½	140	Amcn Bar IR	25	9¼	.00	0			
1.48	.03	163	Amer Eagle	1.85	1.00	.00	.0	Dec86.10D	Mar3m.04D	
47¾	-¼	3	Amer Exprss	49	38	.76U	2.1	Dec86 2.78	Mar3m.28	13.2
0.38		177	Amer Leduc	.45	.23	.00	.0	Aug86.02	Feb6m.02	
3.40	-.40	452	Amir Mines	4.50	3.30	.00	.0			
19	-1½	8	Andres ClB	25⅜	17¼	.52	2.7	Mar87 1.10		17.3
19½	-½	29	Andres ClA f	25¾	17	.60	3.1	Mar87 1.10		17.7
0.38		242	Anglo Cdn Mn	.90	.18	.00	.0			
37½	½	3	AngloCn$3.15	40¼	37	3.15	8.4			
0.88		1612	Anthes Ind	.99	.50	.00	.0	Oct86.12	Jan3m.03	6.8
16¼	-⅛	3	Arbor Cap A	18½	14½	.07	.4	Oct86.47	Jan3m.20	28.5
16¼	¼	34	Arbor Cp B f	17	14⅞	.07	.4	Oct86.47	Jan3m.20	28.5
39⅞	-2⅛	1	Argus $2.5Pf	49	31⅛	2.50	6.3			
31⅜	⅛	14	Argus $2.7Pf	33	29	2.70	8.6			
0.70	-.04	145	Argyyl A f	.88	.45	.00	0	Dec86 1.41D	Mar3m.01D	
0.03	-.01	50	Argyll En Rt	.04	.03	.00	.0			
12⅝	-½	3007	Asamera	15⅜	7⅛	.20	1.6	Dec86.48D	Mar3m.08	
3.45	-.15	429	Asamera Wts	4.50	.80	.00	.0			
28	½	153	Asamera 8% C	29¼	20⅜	2.00	7.1			
12⅝	-¾	1144	Asamera 7%	15⅝	9½	1.05	8.3			
6¼		14	Asbestos	8¼	2.40	.00	.0	Dec86 5.37D		
0.59	.04	920	Ascot Invest	.73	.15	.00	.0	Dec85.17D		
3.45	.20	65	Assoc Porcup	5½	1.35	.00	.0	Jun86.01D	Dec6m.00	
10		4	Astrl Bel Af	15½	10	.15	1.5	Feb86.42	Nov9m.23	28.6
10½	¼	13	Astrl Bel Bf	15⅛	10¼	.15	1.4	Feb86.42	Nov9m.23	30.0
11⅜		4722	Atco Cl I f	12¼	7½	.20	1.8	Mar87.91		12.5
11⅛	-¼	46	Atco Cl II	12	7½	.20	1.8	Mar87.91		12.2
1.95		1	At Coast Cop	2.30	1.20	.00	.0	Dec86.00	Mar3m.01	
11	-1	63	Atl Shop A	13⅞	10	.12	1.1	Mar87 1.56		7.1
27¼	¼	4	Atl Shop Pfd	28⅛	27	2.31	8.5			
1.55	-.10	1382	Atlants Intl	1.80	.45	.00	.0	Dec86.36D	Mar3m.01	

Reprinted permission of *Financial Times of Canada,* June 29, 1987, p. 29.

Variable Growth in Dividends

In the discussion of common stock valuation we have considered procedures for firms that had no growth in dividends and for firms that had a constant growth. Most of the discussion and literature in finance assumes a constant growth dividend model. However, there is also a third case, and that is one of variable growth in dividends. The most common variable growth model is one in which the firm experiences supernormal (very rapid) growth for a number of years and then levels off to more normal, constant growth. The supernormal growth pattern is often experienced by firms in emerging industries, such as in the early days of electronics or microcomputers.

In evaluating a firm with an initial pattern of supernormal growth, we first take the present value of dividends during the exceptional growth period. We then determine the price of the stock at the end of the supernormal growth period by taking the present value of the normal, constant dividends that follow the supernormal growth period. We discount this price to the present and add it to the present value of the supernormal dividends. This gives us the current price of the stock. A numerical example of a supernormal growth rate evaluation model is presented in Appendix 10B at the end of this chapter.

Finally, in the discussion of common stock valuation models readers may ask about the valuation of companies that currently pay no dividends. Since virtually all our discussion has been based on values associated with dividends, how can this "no dividend" circumstance be handled? One approach is to assume that even for the firm that pays no current dividends, at some point in the future, stockholders will be rewarded with cash dividends. We then take the present value of their deferred dividends.

A second approach to valuing a firm that pays no cash dividend is to take the present value of earnings per share for a number of periods and add that to the present value of a future anticipated stock price. The discount rate applied to future earnings is generally higher than the discount rate applied to future dividends.

Summary and Review of Formulas

The primary emphasis in this chapter is on valuation of financial assets: bonds, preferred stock, and common stock. Regardless of the security being analyzed, valuation is normally based on the concept of determining the present value of future cash flows. Thus, we draw on many of the time-value-of-money techniques developed in Chapter 9. Inherent in the valuation process is a determination of the rate of return demanded by investors. When we have computed this value, we have also identified what it will cost the corporation to raise new capital. Let's specifically review the valuation techniques associated with bonds, preferred stock, and common stock.

Bonds

The price, or current value, of a bond is equal to the present value of interest payments (I_t) over the life of the bond plus the present value of the principal payment (P_n) at maturity. The discount rate used in the analytical process is the yield to maturity (Y). The yield to maturity (required rate of return) is determined in the marketplace by such factors as the *real* rate of return, an inflation premium, and a risk premium.

The equation for bond valuation was presented as Formula 10–1.

$$P_b = \sum_{t=1}^{n} \frac{I_t}{(1 + Y)^t} + \frac{P_n}{(1 + Y)^n} \qquad [10\text{–}1]$$

The actual terms in the equation are solved by the use of present value tables. We say the present value of interest payments is:

* $A = R \times IF_{pva}\ (n = \_\_\_\_,\ i = \_\_\_\_)$ [Appendix D]

while the present value of the principal payment at maturity is:

* $P = S \times IF_{pv}\ (n = \_\_\_\_,\ i = \_\_\_\_)$ [Appendix B]

Adding these two values together gives us the price of the bond. We may use annual or semiannual analysis.

The value of the bond will be strongly influenced by the relationship of the yield to maturity in the market to the interest rate on the bond and also the length of time to maturity.

If we know the price of the bond, the size of the interest payments, and the maturity of the bond, we can solve for the yield to maturity through a trial-and-error approach (discussed in the chapter and ex-

*formula on pg 293

panded in Appendix 10A), by an approximation approach as presented in Formula 10–2, or by using financially oriented calculators or computer software.

Preferred Stock

In determining the value of preferred stock, we are taking the present value of an infinite stream of level dividend payments. This would be a tedious process if it were not for the fact that the mathematical calculations can be compressed into a simple formula. The appropriate equation is Formula 10–4.

$$P_p = \frac{D_p}{K_p} \qquad [10\text{–}4]$$

According to Formula 10–4, to find the preferred stock price (P_p) we take the constant annual dividend payment (D_p) and divide this value by the rate of return that preferred stockholders are demanding (K_p).

If, on the other hand, we know the price of the preferred stock and the constant annual dividend payment, we can solve for the required rate of return on preferred stock as:

$$K_p = \frac{D_p}{P_p} \qquad [10\text{–}5]$$

Common Stock

The value of common stock is also based on the concept of the present value of an expected stream of future dividends. Unlike preferred stock, the dividends are not necessarily level. The firm and shareholders may experience:

1. No growth in dividends.
2. Constant growth in dividends.
3. Variable or supernormal growth in dividends.

It is the second circumstance that receives most of the attention in the financial literature. If a firm has constant growth (g) in dividends

(D) and the required rate of return (K_e) exceeds the growth rate, Formula 10–9 can be utilized.

$$P_0 = \frac{D_1}{K_e - g} \qquad [10\text{–}9]$$

In using Formula 10–9 all we need to know is the value of the dividend at the end of the first year, the required rate of return, and the discount rate. Most of our valuation calculations with common stock utilize Formula 10–9.

If we need to know the required rate of return (K_e) for common stock, Formula 10–10 can be employed.

$$K_e = \frac{D_1}{P_0} + g \qquad [10\text{–}10]$$

The first term represents the dividend yield on the stock and the second term, the growth rate. Together they provide the total return demanded by the investor.

List of Terms

yield to maturity
real rate of return
inflation premium
risk premium
perpetuity
dividend valuation model
dividend yield
price-earnings ratio (P/E)
supernormal growth
discount rate
required rate of return

Discussion Questions

1. How is valuation of financial assets by investors related to the cost of financing (cost of capital) for the firm?

2. How is valuation of any financial asset related to future cash flows?

3. Why might investors demand a lower rate of return for an investment in IBM as compared to Dome Petroleum?

4. What are the three factors that influence the rate of return demanded by investors?

5. If inflationary expectations increase, what is likely to happen to yield to maturity on bonds in the marketplace? What is also likely to happen to the price of bonds?

6. Why is the remaining time to maturity an important factor in evaluating the impact of a change in yield to maturity on bond prices?

7. What are the three adjustments that have to be made in going from annual to semiannual bond analysis?

8. Why is a change in required yield for preferred stock likely to have a greater impact on price than a change in required yield for bonds?

9. What type of dividend pattern for common stock is similar to the dividend payment for preferred stock?

10. What two conditions must be met to go from Formula 10–8 to Formula 10–9 in using the dividend valuation model?

$$P_0 = \frac{D_1}{K_e - g} \qquad \text{[Formula 10–9]}$$

11. What are the two components that make up the required rate of return on common stock?

12. What are some factors that might influence a firm's price-earnings ratio?

13. How does a firm's price-earnings ratio relate to K_e? to g?

14. How is the supernormal growth pattern likely to vary from the more normal, constant growth pattern?

15. What approaches can be taken in valuing a firm's stock when there is no cash dividend payment?

Problems

(For the first nine bond problems, assume interest payments are on an annual basis)

1. The Lone Star Company has $1,000 par value bonds outstanding at 9 percent interest. The bonds will mature in 20 years. Compute the current price of the bonds if the present yield to maturity is:

a. 6 percent.
b. 8 percent.
c. 12 percent.

2. The Hartford Telephone Company has a $1,000 par value bond outstanding that pays 11 percent annual interest. The current yield to maturity on such bonds in the market is 14 percent. Compute the price of the bond based on these maturity dates:

a. 30 years.
b. 15 years.
c. 1 year.

3. For Problem 2 graph the relationship in a manner similar to the bottom half of Figure 10–2 in the chapter. Also explain why the pattern of price change takes place.

4. The Perry Refrigerator Company issued bonds in 1983 at $1,000 per bond. The bonds had a 25-year life when issued, and the annual interest payment was then 12 percent. This return was in line with required returns by bondholders at that point in time as described below:

Real rate of return	3%
Inflation premium	6
Risk premium	3
Total return	12%

Assume that in 1988 the inflation premium is only 4 percent and is appropriately reflected in the required return (or yield to maturity) of the bonds. The bonds have 20 years remaining until maturity.

Compute the new price of the bond.

5. Ron Rhodes calls his broker to inquire about purchasing a bond of Golden Years Recreation Corporation. His broker quotes him a price of $1,170. Ron is concerned that the bond might be overpriced based on the factors involved. The $1,000 par value bond pays 13 percent annual interest, and it has 18 years remaining until maturity. The current yield to maturity on similar bonds is 11 percent.

   Do you think the bond is overpriced? Do the necessary calculations.

6. Lawrence Alexander III specializes in buying deep discount bonds. These represent bonds that are trading at well below par value. He has his eye on a bond issued by the Fulton Steamship Company. The $1,000 par value bond pays 5 percent annual interest and has 15 years remaining to maturity. The current yield to maturity on similar bonds is 12 percent.

   a. What is the current price of the bond?
   b. By what percent will the price of the bond increase between now and maturity?
   c. What is the annual compound rate of growth in the value of the bond? (An approximate answer is acceptable.)

7. Bonds issued by the Lawton Corporation have a par value of $1,000, which, of course, is also the amount of principal to be paid at maturity. The bonds are currently selling for $870. They have 10 years remaining to maturity. The annual interest payment is 10 percent ($100).

   Compute the approximate yield to maturity using Formula 10–2.

8. Bonds issued by the Norton Corporation have a par value of $1,000, are selling for $1,075, and have 15 years remaining to maturity. The annual interest payment is 12.5 percent ($125).

   Compute the approximate yield to maturity using Formula 10–2.

NO

9. *Optional*—for Problem 8, use the techniques in Appendix 10A to combine a trial-and-error approach with interpolation to find a more exact answer.

(For the next two problems, assume interest payments are on a semiannual basis)

10. Ami Brian is considering a bond investment in Wilmette Music Company. The $1,000 par value bonds have a quoted annual interest rate of 12 percent, and interest is paid semiannually. The yield to maturity on the bonds is 10 percent annual interest. There are 15 years to maturity.

Compute the price of the bonds based on semiannual analysis.

11. You are called in as a financial analyst to appraise the bonds of Granny's Karate and Judo Schools, a national chain of self-defense programs. The $1,000 par value bonds have a quoted annual interest rate of 9 percent, which is paid semiannually. The yield to maturity on the bonds is 12 percent annual interest. There are 20 years to maturity.

a. Compute the price of the bonds based on semiannual analysis.
b. With 20 years remaining to maturity, if yield to maturity goes down to 8 percent, what will be the new price of the bonds?

12. The preferred stock of the Hilton Chocolate Company pays an annual dividend of $6. It has a required return of 8 percent.

Compute the price of the preferred stock.

13. The Shipley Software Corporation has preferred stock outstanding that pays an annual dividend of $12. It has a price of $108.

What is the required rate of return (yield) on the preferred stock?

14. X-Tech Company issued preferred stock many years ago. It carries a fixed dividend of $5 per share. With the passage of time, yields have soared from the original 5 percent to 12 percent (yield is the same as required rate of return).

a. What was the original issue price?
b. What is the current value of this preferred stock?
c. If the yield on preferred shares declines in general, how will the price of the preferred stock be affected?

(*All of the following problems pertain to the common stock section of the chapter*)

15. Stagnant Iron and Steel currently pays a $4.20 annual cash dividend (D_0). They plan to maintain the dividend at this level for the foreseeable future as no future growth is anticipated.

If the required rate of return by common stockholders (K_e) is 12 percent, what is the price of the common stock?

16. Allied Coal will pay a common stock dividend of $3.40 at the end of the year (D_1). The required return on common stock (K_e) is 14 percent. The firm has a constant growth rate (g) of 8 percent.
Compute the current price of the stock (P_0).

17. Matson Chemical Company will pay a dividend of $2.50 per share in the next 12 months (D_1). The required rate of return (K_e) is 12 percent, and the constant growth rate is 5 percent.

a. Compute P_0.

(In the remaining questions in this problem all variables remain the same except the one specifically changed. Each question is independent of the others.)

b. Assume K_e, the required rate of return, goes up to 14 percent, what will be the new value of P_0?
c. Assume the growth rate (g) goes up to 8 percent, what will be the new value of P_0?
d. Assume D_1 is $3, what will be the new value of P_0?

18. The Fleming Corporation paid a dividend of $4 last year. Over the next 12 months, the dividend is expected to grow at 8 percent, which is the constant growth rate for the firm (g). The new dividend after 12 months will represent D_1. The required rate of return (K_e) is 13 percent.
Compute the price of the stock (P_0).

19. Rick's Department Stores has had the following pattern of earnings per share over the last five years.

Year	Earnings per Share
1983	$4.00
1984	4.20
1985	4.41
1986	4.63
1987	4.86

The earnings per share have grown at a constant rate (on a rounded basis) and are expected to do so in the future. Dividends represent 40 percent of earnings.

Project earnings and dividends for the next year (1988).

If the required rate of return (K_e) is 13 percent, what is the anticipated stock price at the beginning of 1989?

20. A firm pays a \$4 dividend at the end of year one (D_1), has a stock price of \$50 (P_0), and a constant growth rate (g) of 5 percent.

Compute the required rate of return (K_e).

21. A firm pays a \$2.20 dividend at the end of year one (D_1), has a stock price of \$80 (P_0), and a constant growth rate (g) of 13 percent.

a. Compute the required rate of return (K_e).

Indicate whether each of the following changes would make the required rate of return (K_e) go up or down. (Each question is separate from the others. No actual numbers are necessary.)

b. The stock price increases.
c. The dividend payment increases.
d. The expected growth rate increases.

22. Hunter Petroleum Corporation paid a \$2 dividend last year. The dividend is expected to grow at a constant rate of 5 percent over the next three years. The required rate of return is 12 percent (this will also serve as the discount rate in this problem). Round all values to three places to the right of the decimal point where appropriate.

a. Compute the anticipated value of the dividends for the next three years. That is, compute D_1, D_2, and D_3; for example, D_1 is \$2.10 (\$2.00 × 1.05).
b. Discount each of these dividends back to the present at a discount rate of 12 percent and then sum them.
c. Compute the price of the stock at the end of the third year (P_3).

$$P_3 = \frac{D_4}{K_e - g}$$

(D_4 is equal to D_3 times 1.05)

d. After you have computed P_3, discount it back to the present at a discount rate of 12 percent for three years.
e. Add together the answers in part *b* and part *d* to get P_0, the current value of the stock. This answer represents the present

value of the first three periods of dividends plus the present value of the price of the stock after three periods (which, in turn, represents the value of all future dividends).

f. Use Formula 10–9 to show that it will provide approximately the same answer as part *e*.

$$P_0 = \frac{D_1}{K_e - g} \qquad [10\text{–}9]$$

For Formula 10–9, use $D_1 = \$2.10$, $K_e = 12$ percent, and $g = 5$ percent. (The slight difference between the answers to part *e* and part *f* is due to rounding.)

Selected References

Barnes, Amir, and Dennis E. Logue. "The Evaluation Forecasts of a Security Analyst." *Financial Management* 2 (Summer 1975), pp. 38–45.

Friend, Irwin, and Marshall Blume. "The Demand for Risky Assets." *American Economic Review* 75 (December 1975), pp. 900–22.

Gooding, Arthur E. "Quantification of Investors' Perceptions of Common Stocks: Risk and Return Dimensions." *Journal of Finance* 30 (December 1975), pp. 1301–16.

Hirt, Geoffrey A., and Stanley B. Block. *Fundamentals of Investment Management*. 2nd ed. Homewood, Ill.: Richard D. Irwin, 1986.

McEnally, Richard W. "A Note on the Return of High Risk Common Stock." *Journal of Finance* 29 (March 1974), pp. 199–202.

Nelson, Charles R. "Inflation and Rates of Return on Common Stocks." *Journal of Financc* 31 (May 1976), pp. 471–83.

Norgaard, Richard L. "An Examination of the Yields of Corporate Bonds and Stocks." *Journal of Finance 29* (September 1974), pp. 1275–86.

Olsen, I. J. "Valuation of a Closely Held Corporation." *Journal of Accounting* 128 (August 1969), pp. 35–47.

Reilly, Frank K. *Investments*. 2nd ed. Hinsdale, Ill.: Dryden Press, 1985.

Vandell, Robert F., and Jerry L. Stevens. "Personal Taxes and Equity Security Pricing." *Financing Management* 11 (Spring 1984), pp. 31–40.

Appendix 10A: The Bond Yield to Maturity Using Interpolation

We will use a numerical example to demonstrate this process. Assume a 20-year bond pays $118 per year (11.8 percent) in interest and $1,000 after 20 years in principal repayment. The current price of the bond is $1,085. We wish to determine the yield to maturity or discount rate that equates the future flows with the current price.

Since the bond is trading above par value at $1,085, we can assume the yield to maturity must be below the quoted interest rate of 12 percent (the yield to maturity would be the full 12 percent at a bond price of $1,000). As a first approximation, we will try 10 percent. Annual analysis is used.

Present value of interest payments—

$$A = R \times IF_{pva}\ (n = 20,\ i = 10\%) \qquad \text{[Appendix D]}$$
$$A = \$118 \times 8.514 = \$1{,}004.65$$

Present value of principal payment at maturity—

$$P = S \times IF_{pv}\ (n = 20,\ i = 10\%) \qquad \text{[Appendix B]}$$
$$P = \$1{,}000 \times .149 = \$149$$

Total present value—

Present value of interest payments	$1,004.65
Present value of principal payment at maturity	149.00
Total present value or price of the bond	$1,153.65

The discount rate of 10 percent gives us too high a present value in comparison to the current bond price of $1,085. Let's try a higher discount rate to get a lower rate. We will use 11 percent.

Present value of interest payments—

$$A = R \times IF_{pva}\ (n = 20,\ i = 11\%) \qquad \text{[Appendix D]}$$
$$A = \$118 \times 7.963 = \$939.63$$

Present value of principal payment at maturity—

$$P = S \times IF_{pv}\ (n = 20,\ i = 11\%) \qquad \text{[Appendix B]}$$
$$P = \$1{,}000 \times .124 = \$124.00$$

Total present value—

Present value of interest payments	$ 939.63
Present value of principal payment at maturity	124.00
Total present value or price of the bond	$1,063.63

The discount rate of 11 percent gives us a value slightly lower than the bond price of $1,085. The rate for the bond must fall between 10 and 11 percent. Using linear interpolation, the answer is 10.76 percent.

$1,153.65	*PV* @ 10%	$1,153.65	*PV* @ 10%
1,063.63	*PV* @ 11%	1,085.00	bond price
$ 90.02		$ 68.65	

$$10\% + \frac{\$68.65}{\$90.02}(1\%) = 10\% + .76(1\%) = 10.76\%$$

Problem

10A–1. Bonds issued by the Peabody Corporation have a par value of $1,000, are selling for $890, and have 18 years to maturity. The annual interest payment is 8 percent.

Find yield to maturity by combining the trial-and-error approach with interpolation, as shown in this appendix. (Use an assumption of annual interest payments.)

Appendix 10B: Valuation of a Supernormal Growth Firm

The equation for the valuation of a supernormal growth firm is:

$$P_0 = \sum_{t=1}^{n} \frac{D_t}{(1 + K_e)^t} + P_n \left(\frac{1}{1 + K_e}\right)^n \qquad (10B–1)$$

(Supernormal growth period) (After supernormal growth period)

Actually, the formula is not difficult to use. The first term calls for determining the present value of the dividends during the supernormal growth period. The second term calls for computing the present value of the future stock price as determined at the end of the supernormal growth period. If we add the two together we arrive at the current stock price. We are adding together the two benefits the stockholder will receive: a future stream of dividends during the supernormal growth period and the future stock price.

Let's assume the firm paid a dividend over the last 12 months of \$1.67; this represents the current dividend rate. Dividends are expected to grow by 20 percent per year over the supernormal growth period (n) of three years. They will then grow at a normal constant growth rate (g) of 5 percent. The required rate of return (discount rate) as represented by K_e is 9 percent. We first find the present value of the dividends during the supernormal growth period.

(1) Present value of supernormal dividends—

D_0 = \$1.67. We allow the value to grow at 20 percent per year over the three years of supernormal growth.

$D_1 = D_0\,(1 + .20) = \$1.67\,(1.20) = \$2.00$

$D_2 = D_1\,(1 + .20) = \$2.00\,(1.20) = \$2.40$

$D_3 = D_2\,(1 + .20) = \$2.40\,(1.20) = \$2.88$

We then discount these values back at 9 percent to find the present value of dividends during the supernormal growth period.

	Supernormal Dividends	Discount Rate $K_e = 9\%$	Present Value of Dividends during the Supernormal Period
D_1	\$2.00	.917	\$1.83
D_2	2.40	.842	2.02
D_3	2.88	.772	2.22
			\$6.07

The present value of the supernormal dividends is \$6.07. We now turn to the future stock price.

(2) Present value of future stock price—We first find the future stock price at the end of the supernormal growth period. This is found by taking the present value of the dividends that will be growing at a normal, constant rate after the supernormal period. This will begin *after* the third (and last) period of supernormal growth.

Since after the supernormal growth period the firm is growing at a normal, constant rate (g = 5 percent) and K_e (the discount rate) of 9 percent exceeds the new, constant growth rate of 5 percent, we have fulfilled the two conditions for using the constant dividend growth model after three years. That is, we can apply Formula 10–9 (without subscripts for now).

$$P = \frac{D}{K_e - g}$$

In this case, however, D is really the dividend at the end of the fourth period because this phase of the analysis starts at the beginning of the fourth period and D is as of the *end* of the first period of analysis in the formula. Also, the price we are solving for now is the price at the beginning of the fourth period which, of course, is the same concept as the price at the end of the third period (P_3).

We thus say:

$$P_3 = \frac{D_4}{K_e - g} \quad \text{(10–B2)}$$

D_4 is equal to the previously determined value for D_3 of \$2.88 moved forward one period at the constant growth rate of 5 percent.

$$D_4 = \$2.88\ (1.05) = \$3.02$$

Also:

$$K_e = .09 \text{ discount rate (required rate of return)}$$
$$g = .05 \text{ constant growth rate}$$
$$P_3 = \frac{D_4}{K_e - g} = \frac{\$3.02}{.09 - .05} = \frac{\$3.02}{.04} = \$75.50$$

This is the value of the stock at the end of the third period. We discount this value back to the present.

Stock Price after Three Years	*Discount Rate* K_e = 9%*	*Present Value of Future Price*
\$75.50	.772	\$58.29

*Note: *n* is equal to 3.

The present value of the future stock price (P_3) of \$75.50 is \$58.29.

By adding together the answers in part (1) and part (2) of this appendix, we arrive at the total present value, or price, of the supernormal growth stock.

(1) Present value of dividends during the normal growth period	\$ 6.07
(2) Present value of the future stock price	58.29
Total present value, or price	\$64.36

The process we have just completed is presented in Figure 10B–1. The student who wishes to develop skills in growth analysis should work Problem 10B–1.

Figure 10B–1
Stock valuation under supernormal growth analysis

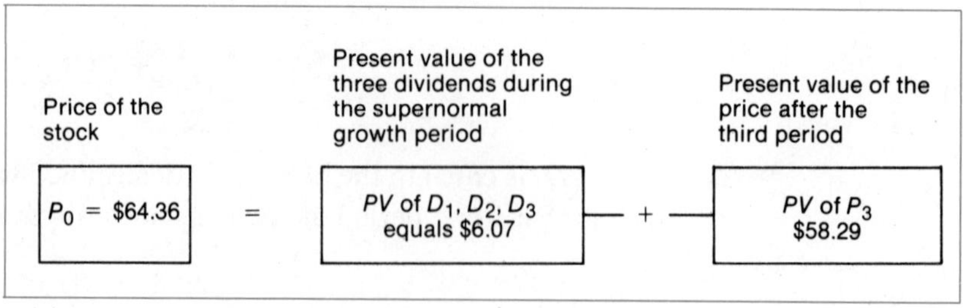

Problem

10B–1. The McMillan Corporation paid a dividend of \$2.40 over the last 12 months. The dividend is expected to grow at a rate of 25 percent over the next three years (supernormal growth). It will then grow at a normal, constant rate of 6 percent for the foreseeable future. The required rate of return is 14 percent (this will also serve as the discount rate).

a. Compute the anticipated value of the dividends for the next three years (D_1, D_2, and D_3).

b. Discount each of these dividends back to the present at a discount rate of 14 percent and then sum them.

c. Compute the price of the stock at the end of the third year (P_3).

$$P_3 = \frac{D_4}{K_e - g} \qquad \text{[Review Appendix 10B–1 for the definition of } D_4\text{]}$$

d. After you have computed P_3, discount it back to the present at a discount rate of 14 percent for three years.

e. Add together the answers in part *b* and part *d* to get the current value of the stock. (This answer represents the present value of the first three periods of dividends plus the present value of the price of the stock after three periods.)

11 Cost of Capital

Throughout the previous two chapters a number of references were made to discounting future cash flows in solving for the present value. The vexing problem at this point is: How do you determine the appropriate discount rate in a given situation? To demonstrate the importance of the answer to this question, it might be helpful to explore a rather simple, but not uncommon, type of problem. Suppose a young doctor is rendered incapable of practicing medicine due to an auto accident in the last year of her residency. In a subsequent legal action the court determines that the best approximation of her future earning potential before the accident was $100,000 a year for the next 30 years. How much, then, will the court award the young woman as a single payment to compensate her for the lost earning power? To assign a settlement value, the court must still determine the appropriate rate to use to discount those future earnings estimates. As well might be the case, suppose further that her lawyer argues for a 5 percent discount rate while the insurance company lawyers argue for a 12 percent rate.

What present value will the court assign to these inflows? If it accepts the arguments of the doctor's lawyer, the settlement value becomes \$1,537,300. If, on the other hand, it accepts the arguments made by the insurance company's lawyers, the assigned value becomes \$805,500. The choice between these two discount rates represents a \$730,000 difference in the amount awarded to the injured doctor. As you see, the difference is not trivial.

In the corporate finance setting the more likely circumstance is where an investment, if made today, promises a set of inflows in the future. To decide whether the expected future inflows justify the current investment we need to know the appropriate discount rate. The purpose of this chapter is to set down the methods and procedures for making that determination.

If we invest money today to receive benefits in the future, how much must we earn on it? If you said we must be certain we are earning at least as much as it costs us to acquire the funds for investment, you were right. That amount, in essence, is the minimum acceptable return. Thus, if the firm's cost of funds is 12 percent, then all normal projects must be tested to make sure they earn at least 12 percent.[1] By using this as the discount rate we can decide whether we can reasonably expect to earn the financial cost of doing business.

The Overall Concept

How does the firm determine the cost of its funds or, more properly stated, the *cost of capital?* Suppose a plant superintendent wishes to borrow funds at 6 percent (after-tax cost) to purchase a conveyor system, while the division manager suggests common shares be sold at an effective cost of 15 percent to finance the development of a new digital component for one of the company's products. As you see, judging each investment against the specific means of financing used to fund it runs the risk of making investment selection decisions arbitrary and inconsistent. For example, picture financing the conveyor system having an 8 percent return with 6 percent debt while also evaluating the digital component project having a 14 percent return

[1]The term *normal* is used because the method under discussion would not be appropriate for considering a new venture in a high-risk area, for example.

against the 15 percent cost of the common stock. If projects and financing are matched in this way, the project with the lower return would be accepted and the project with the higher return would be rejected. In reality, if stock and debt are sold in equal proportions, the average cost of financing would be 10.5 percent (one half debt at 6 percent and one half stock at 15 percent). With a 10.5 percent average cost of financing, we would now reject the 8 percent conveyor system and accept the 14 percent component project. This would be a rational and consistent decision. Though an investment financed by low-cost debt might appear acceptable at first glance, the use of debt might increase the overall risk of the firm (as discussed in Chapter 5), eventually making all forms of financing more expensive. Therefore, the general conclusion has been that each project must be measured against the overall cost of funds to the firm.

The determination of cost of capital can best be understood by examining the capital structure of a hypothetical firm, the Baker Corporation, in Table 11–1. Note that the after-tax costs of the individual sources of financing are determined, weights are then assigned to each, and finally, a weighted average cost is determined. It is important to realize that the relevant costs are those related to new funds which might be raised in future financings rather than the costs of funds raised to fund investments in the past. In the remainder of the chapter each of these procedural steps is examined.

K opportunity cost

Each element in the capital structure has an explicit or opportunity cost associated with it, herein referred to by the symbol *K*. This cost is directly related to the valuation concepts developed in the previous chapter. It is important to realize that the cost of a security is a function of how the security is valued. Once we decide on the proper method for valuing a particular security, the mathematics involved are relatively

Table 11–1
Cost of capital—Baker Corporation

		Cost (after-tax)	Weights	Weighted Cost
Debt	K_d	6.34%	30%	1.90%
Preferred stock	K_p	10.94	10	1.09
Common equity (retained earnings)	K_e	12.00	60	7.20
Weighted average cost of capital	K_a			10.19%

simple. Since debt is probably the most straightforward element of the capital structure, we will begin our analysis by exploring how its cost might be calculated by a firm's financial analyst.

Cost of Debt

The cost of debt is measured by the interest rate, or yield, that would have to be paid to bondholders to persuade them to buy our bonds. A simple case might involve our being able to sell $1,000 bonds, paying $100 in annual interest for $1,000. Our cost of debt would thus be 10 percent. Of course, the computation becomes a little more difficult if our $1,000 bonds sell for an amount more or less than $1,000. If this is the case, we could use the yield-to-maturity formula discussed in Chapter 10.

For example, assume the firm is preparing to issue new debt. To determine the likely cost of the new debt in the marketplace, the firm will compute the yield on its currently outstanding debt. This is not the rate at which the old debt was issued but, rather, the rate that investors are demanding today for holding the firm's debt. It may be that the debt issue is paying $112 per year in interest, has a 20-year life, and is currently selling for $950. Of course, we are interested in the current yield to maturity on the debt. To find it we could use the trial-and-error process described in the previous chapter. That is, we could experiment with discount rates until we found the rate that equates the present value of interest payments of $112 for 20 years plus the present value of a $1,000 payment at maturity with a current market value of $950. A simpler process would be to calculate the approximate yield to maturity using Formula 10–2 from the prior chapter. That formula is reproduced below and relabeled Formula 11–1 to fit the numbering system in this chapter.

$$\text{Approximate yield to maturity } (Y') = \frac{\text{Annual interest payment} + \dfrac{\text{Principal payment} - \text{Price of the bond}}{\text{Number of years to maturity}}}{\dfrac{\text{Price of the bond} + \text{Principal payment}}{2}} \qquad (11\text{–}1)$$

For the bond under discussion, the approximate yield to maturity (Y_{me}) would be:

$$= \frac{\$112 + \dfrac{\$1{,}000 - \$950}{20}}{\dfrac{\$950 + \$1{,}000}{2}}$$

$$= \frac{\$112 + \dfrac{\$50}{20}}{\dfrac{\$1{,}950}{2}}$$

$$= \frac{\$112 + \$2.50}{\$975}$$

$$= \frac{\$114.50}{\$975} = 11.74\%$$

In many cases you will not have to compute the yield to maturity. It will be available from other sources, like the financial pages of various daily and weekly newspapers or from one of the larger investment dealers who deal in bond trading. The type of information available on a sample of outstanding bonds is presented in Table 11–2. If the firm involved is Interprovincial Pipeline, for example, the financial manager could observe that debt maturing in 2004 would have a yield to maturity of 11.25 percent. This is true in spite of the fact that the debt was originally issued at 13.40 percent.

Once the bond yield is determined through the formula or the tables (or is given to you), you must adjust the yield for tax considerations. In other words, yield to maturity indicates how much the corporation has to pay on a *before-tax* basis. The interest payment on debt, however, is a tax-deductible expense. Since interest is tax deductible, the true cost of the bond is less than the interest paid because the government is picking up part of the cost by allowing the firm to pay less taxes. The after-tax cost of debt is actually the yield to maturity times one minus the tax rate.[2] This is presented as Formula 11–2.

---

[2]The yield may also be thought of as representing the interest cost to the firm after consideration of all selling and distribution costs, though no explicit representation is given to these costs in relationship to debt. These costs are usually quite small, and they are often bypassed entirely in some types of loans. For those who wish to explicitly include this factor in Formula 11–1, we would have:

$$K_d = [\text{Yield}/(1 - \text{Distribution costs})]\ (1 - T)$$

Table 11–2 Sample bond information

Issue	Interest Payable	Maturity	Price	Yield	Rating
Algoma Steel	7.375%	October 1, 1987	$ 95.85	10.00%	B+
. . . .	8.750	March 31, 1991	94.00	10.25	B+
. . . .	10.375	June 1, 1993	99.30	10.50	B+
C-I-L	12.375	December 15, 1993	110.70	10.37	A+
. . . .	14.500	April 15, 1996	116.15	11.75	A+
. . . .	10.625	July 15, 1996	103.05	10.15	A+
Interprovincial. . . .	9.875	December 1, 1990	100.85	9.65	A+
. . . .	8.625	May 1, 1993	94.20	9.75	A+
. . . .	11.375	February 1, 1996	105.05	10.55	A+
. . . .	10.125	May 1, 1996	99.85	10.15	A+
. . . .	10.875	July 15, 1996	104.00	10.25	A+
. . . .	13.400	April 1, 2004	116.50	11.25	A+
Maritime Tel	10.375	June 15, 1999	98.40	10.60	A+
. . . .	10.950	December 15, 2005	102.05	10.70	A+

Sources: Canadian Bond Rating Service; *Canadian Bond Prices;* FP Information Services.

$$K_d(\text{Cost of debt}) = Y(\text{Yield})\,(1 - T) \qquad (11\text{–}2)$$

The term *yield* in the formula is interchangeable with yield to maturity or approximate yield to maturity. In using the approximate-yield-to-maturity formula earlier in this section, we determined that the *current* required yield on existing debt is 11.74 percent. We shall assume that new debt can be issued at the same going market rate[3] and that the firm is in a 46 percent tax bracket. Applying the tax adjustment factor, the after-tax cost of debt would be 6.34 percent.

$$\begin{aligned} K_d(\text{Cost of debt}) &= Y(\text{Yield})\,(1 - T) \\ &= 11.74\%(1 - .46) \\ &= 11.74\%(.54) \\ &= 6.34\% \end{aligned}$$

Please refer back to Table 11–1 and observe in column 1 that the after-tax cost of debt for Baker Corporation is the 6.34 percent that we have just computed.

[3]The rate will probably be slightly higher to reflect the fact that bonds trading at a discount from par ($950 in this case) generally pay a lower yield to maturity than par value bonds because of possible tax advantages and higher leverage potential.

Cost of Preferred Stock

The cost of preferred stock is similar to the cost of debt in that a constant annual payment is made, but dissimilar in that there is no maturity date on which a principal payment must be made. Thus, the determination of the yield on preferred stock is simpler than determining the yield on debt. All you have to do is divide the annual dividend by the current price (this process was discussed in Chapter 10). This represents the rate of return to preferred stockholders as well as the annual cost to the corporation for the preferred stock issue.

To determine the cost of a new issue of preferred shares we have to make one slight alteration to this process by dividing the dividend payment by the *net* price or proceeds received by the firm. Since a new share of preferred stock has a selling cost (flotation cost), the proceeds to the firm are equal to the selling price in the market minus the flotation cost. The cost of preferred stock is presented as Formula 11–3.[4]

$$K_p(\text{cost of preferred}) = \frac{D_p}{P_p - F} \qquad (11\text{–}3)$$

where

K_p = Cost of preferred stock
D_p = Annual dividend on preferred stock
P_p = Price of preferred stock
F = Flotation, or selling, cost

In the case of the Baker Corporation the annual dividend is \$10.50, the preferred stock price is \$100, and the flotation, or selling, cost is estimated at \$4. The effective cost of preferred shares becomes:

$$K_p = \frac{D_p}{P_p - F} = \frac{\$10.50}{\$100 - 4} = \frac{\$10.50}{\$96} = 10.94\%$$

Because a preferred stock dividend is not a tax-deductible expense, there is no downward tax adjustment. If you now refer back to Table

[4]Note that in Chapter 10, K_p was presented with no adjustment for flotation charges. Some may wish to formally add an additional subscript to K_p to indicate we are now talking about the cost of *new* preferred. The adjusted symbol would be K_{pn}.

11–1 you will observe in column 1 that 10.94 percent is the cost of preferred stock in the Baker Corporation example.

Cost of Common Equity

Determining the cost of common stock in the capital structure is a much more involved task than was the case for debt or preferred shares. The out-of-pocket cost is the cash dividend, but one cannot merely assume that the percentage cost of common stock is simply the current year's dividend divided by the market price.

$$\frac{\text{Current dividend}}{\text{Market price}}$$

If such an approach were followed, the common stock costs for selected Canadian corporations in December 1986 would have been 2.1 percent for Abitibi-Price, 1.6 percent for CAE Industries, 2.7 percent for Jannock Corporation, and 1.9 percent for Guardian Capital. It is obvious that if new common stock were thought to be so cheap, those firms would have no need to issue other securities and could profitably finance projects that earned only 3 or 4 percent. The question still remaining, then, is: How do we determine the correct effective cost of common stock to the firm?

Valuation Approach

The cost of common stock is a function of the pricing and performance demands of current and future stockholders. An appropriate approach is to develop a model for valuing common stock that is dependent on the required return demanded from it

In Chapter 10 the constant dividend growth model yielded the following relationship between stock price and demanded return:

$$P_0 = \frac{D_1}{K_e - g}$$

in which

P_0 = Price of the stock today
D_1 = Dividend at the end of the first year (or period)

K_e = Required rate of return
g = Constant growth rate in dividends

We then found we could rearrange the terms in the formula to solve for K_e instead of P_0. This was presented in Formula 10–10 in the prior chapter. We present the formula once again here as Formula 11–4.

$$K_e = \frac{D_1}{P_0} + g \qquad (11\text{–}4)$$

The required rate of return (K_e) is equal to the dividend at the end of the first year (D_1), divided by the price of the stock today (P_0), plus a constant growth rate (g). Although the growth rate applies directly to dividends, it must also apply to earnings over the long term. The formula's assumption that there is a constant relationship between earnings per share and dividends per share (that is, a constant payout ratio) assures the ability to sustain the growth in dividend payments.

In the Baker Corporation example, the expected dividend for this year is \$2, the current stock price is \$40, the dividends have been and are expected to continue to grow at a rate of 7 percent. Given that information we would calculate K_e to be equal to 12 percent.

$$K_e = \frac{D_1}{P_0} + g = \frac{\$2}{\$40} + 7\% = 5\% + 7\% = 12\%$$

This result assumes that stockholders expect to receive a 5 percent return on their investment by way of dividends and a 7 percent return by way of an increase in the price of their shares. Thus, they are investing in this stock on the basis that they demand and expect to receive a 12 percent return on their investment.

Alternate Calculation of the Required Return on Common Stock

An alternate model for calculating the required return on common stock is represented by the capital asset pricing model (CAPM). The attributes of this model are covered in Appendix 11A, so we will consider it only briefly at this point. Some proclaim the capital asset pricing model as an important advance in our attempts to value common stock valuation, while others suggest it is not a valid description of how the real world operates.

Under the capital asset pricing model, the required return for common stock (or other investments) can be described by the following formula.

$$K_j = R_f + \beta(K_m - R_f) \qquad (11\text{–}5)$$

where

K_j = Required return on common stock
R_f = Risk-free rate of return; often taken as equivalent to the current rate on short-term, Government of Canada Treasury Bills.
β = Beta coefficient. The beta measures the historical volatility of an individual stock's return relative to a stock market index. A beta greater than 1 indicates greater volatility (as measured by price movements) than the market, while the reverse would be true for a beta less than 1.
K_m = Return in the market as measured by an appropriate index

In the Baker Corporation example, the following values might apply:

$$R_f = 9\%$$
$$K_m = 11\%$$
$$\beta = 1.5$$

K_j, based on Formula 11–5, would then equal:

$$K_j = 9\% + 1.5(11\% - 9\%) = 9\% + 1.5(2\%)$$
$$= 9\% + 3\% = 12\%$$

In this case we have structured the data so that K_j (the required return under the capital asset pricing model) would equal K_e (the required return under the dividend valuation model). In both cases the computations lead to a 12 percent estimate as the cost of common equity. In real life circumstances it will rarely turn out that the two models give exactly the same estimate.

For now, we shall use the dividend valuation model exclusively; that is, we shall use $K_e = D_1/P_0 + g$ in preference to $K_j = R_f + \beta\ (K_m - R_f)$. Those who wish to study the capital asset pricing model further are referred to Appendix 11A.

Cost of Retained Earnings

Up to this point we have discussed the cost (required return) of common stock in a general sense. We have not really specified who is supplying the funds. One obvious supplier of common stock equity capital is the purchaser of new shares of common stock. This is not the only source, however. Retained earnings constitute what is referred to as an internal as opposed to external funding source. Statistics Canada reported that as of the beginning of 1985,[5] Canadian nonfinancial corporations' balance sheets showed $112 billion of their historical financing came from retained earnings and $90 billion from common share issues. Thus, for the universe of firms as a whole, retained earnings form the most important source of ownership or equity capital investment funds.

Accumulated retained earnings represent the past and present earnings of the firm minus previously distributed dividends. Retained earnings, by law, belong to the current stockholders. They can either be paid out to the current stockholders in the form of dividends or reinvested in the firm. Thus, as current earnings are retained in the firm for reinvestment, they represent a source of equity capital supplied by the current shareholders. Just because the firm did not have to go to the market to raise new funds does not mean, however, that these internally generated funds are free. In other words, there is an opportunity cost involved—the funds could be paid out as dividends to the current stockholders who could then redeploy them by buying other stocks, bonds, real estate, and so forth. The expected rate of return on these alternative investments becomes the opportunity cost of not having paid out the earnings in dividends. It seems reasonable to assume stockholders could earn a return equivalent to that provided by their present investment in the firm (on an equal risk basis).[6] This represents $D_1/P_0 + g$. Given that in the securities markets there are literally thousands of investments from which to choose, it is not implausible to assume the stockholder can take dividend payments and reinvest them to provide a comparable yield.

[5]This represented the most recent published data as of July 1987. Preferred shares accounted for $33 billion of funding.

[6]Chapter 14, in dealing with the concept of efficient markets, provides more insight into why this assumption is reasonable.

Computing the cost of retained earnings takes us back to where we began our discussion of the cost of common stock. The cost of retained earnings is equivalent to the rate of return on the firm's common stock. This is the opportunity cost. Thus, we say the cost of common equity in the form of retained earnings is equal to the required rate of return on the firm's stock.[7]

$$K_e\text{(Cost of common equity in the form of retained earnings)} = \frac{D_1}{P_0} + g \qquad (11\text{–}6)$$

Thus, K_e not only represents the required return on common stock as previously defined, but it also represents the cost of equity in the form of retained earnings. Therefore, the cost of retained earnings for the Baker Corporation becomes 12 percent.

$$K_e = \frac{\$2}{\$40} + 7\% = 5\% + 7\% = 12\%$$

Please refer back to Table 11–1 and observe in column 1 that 12 percent is the value we used for the cost of retained earnings.

Cost of New Common Stock

Let's now consider the other source of equity capital, new common stock. If we are issuing *new* common stock, we must earn a slightly higher return than K_e, which represents the required rate of return of

[7]One could make the seemingly logical suggestion that this is not a perfectly equivalent relationship. For example, if stockholders receive a distribution of retained earnings in the form of dividends, they may have to pay taxes on the dividends before they can reinvest them in equivalent yield investments. Additionally, the stockholder may incur brokerage costs in the process. For these reasons, one might suggest the opportunity cost of retained earnings is less than the rate of return on the firm's common stock. The current majority view, however, is that the appropriate cost for retained earnings is equal to the rate of return on the firm's common stock. The strongest argument for this equality position is that for a publicly traded company, a firm always has the option of buying back some of its shares in the market. Given that this is so, it is assured a return of K_e. Thus, the firm should never make an alternative investment that has an expected equity return of less than K_e. Nevertheless, some students may wish to look into the minority view as well. In the event a tax adjustment is made, the cost of retained earnings can be represented as $K_r = K_e\,(1 - t_r)$ where K_r is the cost of retained earnings, K_e is the required return on common stock, and t_r is the average stockholder marginal tax rate on dividend income.

present stockholders. The higher return is needed to cover the distribution costs of the new securities. If the required return for present stockholders were 12 percent and shares were quoted to the public at \$40, a new distribution of securities would need to earn slightly more than 12 percent to compensate for sales commissions and other expenses. The corporation will not receive the full \$40 because of these. The formula for K_e is restated as K_n (the cost of new common stock) to reflect this requirement.

$$\text{Common stock} \quad K_e = \frac{D_1}{P_0} + g$$

$$\text{New common stock } K_n = \frac{D_1}{P_0 - F} + g \qquad (11\text{–}7)$$

The only new term is F (flotation, or selling, costs).

Assume

$$D_1 = \$2$$
$$P_0 = \$40$$
$$F = \$4$$
$$g = 7\%$$

then

$$K_n = \frac{\$2}{\$40 - \$4} + 7\%$$
$$= \frac{\$2}{\$36} + 7\%$$
$$= 5.6\% + 7\% = 12.6\%$$

The cost of new common stock to the Baker Corporation is 12.6 percent. This value will be used more extensively later in the chapter. New common stock was not included in the original assumed capital structure for the Baker Corporation presented in Table 11–1.

Overview of Common Stock Costs

For those of you who are suffering from an overexposure to *K*s in the computation of cost of common stock, let us reiterate the two common stock formulas you will be using in the rest of the chapter and in solving the problems at the end of the chapter.

$$K_e\text{(Cost of common equity in the form of retained earnings)} = \frac{D_1}{P_0} + g$$

$$K_n\text{(Cost of new common stock)} = \frac{D_1}{P_0 - F} + g$$

The primary emphasis will be on K_e for now, but later in the chapter we will also use K_n when we discuss the marginal cost of capital.

Optimal Capital Structure—Weighting Costs

Having established the techniques for computing the cost of the various elements in the capital structure, we must now discuss methods of assigning weights to these costs. We will attempt to weight capital components in accordance with our desire to achieve a minimum overall cost of capital. For purposes of this discussion, Table 11–1 (Cost of Capital for the Baker Corporation) is reproduced here.

		Cost (after-tax)	*Weights*	*Weighted Cost*
Debt	K_d	6.34%	30%	1.90%
Preferred stock	K_p	10.94	10	1.09
Common equity (retained earnings)	K_e	12.00	60	7.20
Weighted average cost of capital	K_a			10.19%

How does the firm decide on the appropriate weights for debt, preferred stock, and common stock financing? In other words, why not use all debt for future financing since the above chart indicates it is substantially cheaper than the alternatives? The answer is that the use of debt beyond a reasonable point will probably greatly increase the firm's financial risk and thereby drive up the costs of all sources of financing.

One way for us to explore this critical point is to have you assume you are going to start your own company and are considering three different capital structures. For ease of presentation, only debt and equity (common stock) are being considered. As it happens the costs of the components in the capital structure change each time you vary the proposed debt-equity mix (weights).

	Cost (after-tax)	Weights	Weighted Cost
Financial Plan A:			
Debt	6.5%	20%	1.3%
Equity	12.0	80	9.6
			10.9%
Financial Plan B:			
Debt	7.0%	40%	2.8%
Equity	12.5	60	7.5
			10.3%
Financial Plan C:			
Debt	9.0%	60%	5.4%
Equity	15.0	40	6.0
			11.4%

We see that the firm is able to reduce the cost of capital by including more debt financing as we consider Plan B versus Plan A. Beyond a point, however, the continued use of debt becomes unattractive causing increases in the costs of the various sources of financing that more than offset the benefit of substituting cheaper debt for more expensive equity. In our example that point seems to occur somewhere around the debt/equity mix represented by Plan B. Traditional financial theory maintains there is a U-shaped cost-of-capital curve relative to debt-equity mixes for the firm, as illustrated in Figure 11–1.[8] In this illustration, the optimum capital structure occurs at a 40 percent debt-to-equity ratio.

Most firms are able to use 30–50 percent debt in their capital structure without exceeding norms acceptable to creditors and investors. Distinctions should be made, however, between firms that carry high or low business risks. As discussed in Chapter 5, Operating and Financial Leverage, a growth firm in a reasonably stable industry can afford to absorb more debt than its counterparts in cyclical industries. Examples of debt use by companies in various industries are presented in Table 11–3.

In determining the appropriate capital mix the firm generally begins with its present capital structure and ascertains whether that structure

[8]A dissenting viewpoint was expressed by Professors Modigliani and Miller in which they maintained that the cost of capital is constant over all debt-equity mixes (in other words, the increased cost effect of higher leverage exactly offsets any potential net cost advantage of substituting debt for equity). Their assumption of perfect markets and their neglect of tax considerations were strongly challenged. They later modified their position to include tax and bankruptcy considerations as well as the possibility of an optimal debt-equity mix.

Figure 11–1
Cost of capital curve

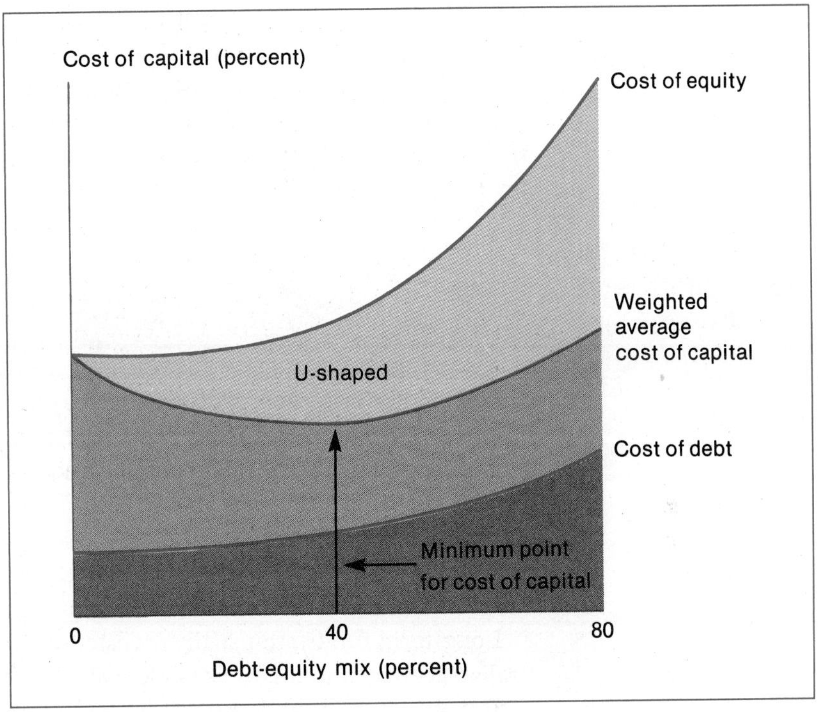

Table 11–3
Debt as a percentage of total assets

Selected Companies with Industry Designation	Percent
Seagram (spirits and wines)	45%
Canadian Pacific (conglomerate)	69
Bank of Montreal (commercial bank)	95
Nova Corp. (oil, gas, petrochemicals)	76
Dofasco (steel)	47
Noranda (mining)	59
GSW (appliances)	50
Gandalf Technologies (microelectronics)	31
Inter-City Gas (gas distribution)	88
Abitibi-Price (forest products)	50
Baton Broadcasting (communications)	22
Campeau (real estate development)	91

Source: Annual reports.

is optimal.[9] If not, subsequent financing should carry the firm toward a financing mix that is deemed more desirable. It is important for the reader to note that only the costs of new or incremental financing should be considered. The historical costs of financing to the firm are not relevant except to the extent they provide clues as to what future financing costs are likely to be.

Capital Acquisition and Investment Decision Making

So far, the various costs of financial capital and the optimum capital structure have been discussed. Financial capital, as you know, consists of bonds, preferred stock, and common equity. These forms of financial capital appear on the corporate balance sheet under liabilities and equity. The money raised by selling these securities, along with the earnings retained in the firm, is invested in the real capital of the firm, the long-term productive assets of plant and equipment.

Long-term funds are usually invested in long-term assets, with several asset-financing mixes possible over the business cycle. Obviously, a firm wants to provide all of the necessary financing at the lowest possible cost. This generally leads the financial manager to attempt to sell common stock when prices are relatively high to minimize the cost of equity.[10] The financial manager also wants to sell debt at low interest rates. Since there is short-term and long-term debt, he needs to know how interest rates move over the business cycle and when to use short-term versus long-term debt.

Thus, the task is for the firm to find a balance between debt and equity that achieves its minimum cost of capital. Although we discussed minimizing the overall cost of capital K_a at a single debt-to-equity ratio, firms seem, in reality, to operate within a relevant range of debt to equity before they become penalized with a higher overall cost because of increased risk.

Figure 11–2 shows a theoretical cost-of-capital curve at three different points in time. As we move from time period t to time period

---

[9]Market value rather than book value should be used—though in practice book value is commonly used.

[10]In Chapter 14 we will discuss the rationality of such "market timing" in more detail.

$t + 2$, falling interest rates and rising stock prices cause a downward shift in K_a. This graph is meant to illuminate two basic points: (1) the firm wants to keep its debt-to-equity ratio between *x* and *y* at all times; and (2) the firm would rather finance its long-term needs at $K_{a^{t+2}}$ than at K_{a^t}. Corporations do have some leeway in the money and capital markets such that it is not uncommon for the debt-to-equity ratio to fluctuate between *x* and *y* over a business cycle. Note, however, that the firm already at point *y* has lost the flexibility of increasing its debt-to-equity ratio without incurring the penalty of higher capital costs.

Cost of Capital in the Capital Budgeting Decision

It is always the current cost of capital for each source of funds that is important when making a capital budgeting decision. Historical costs for past funding may have very little to do with current costs against

Figure 11–2
Cost of capital over time

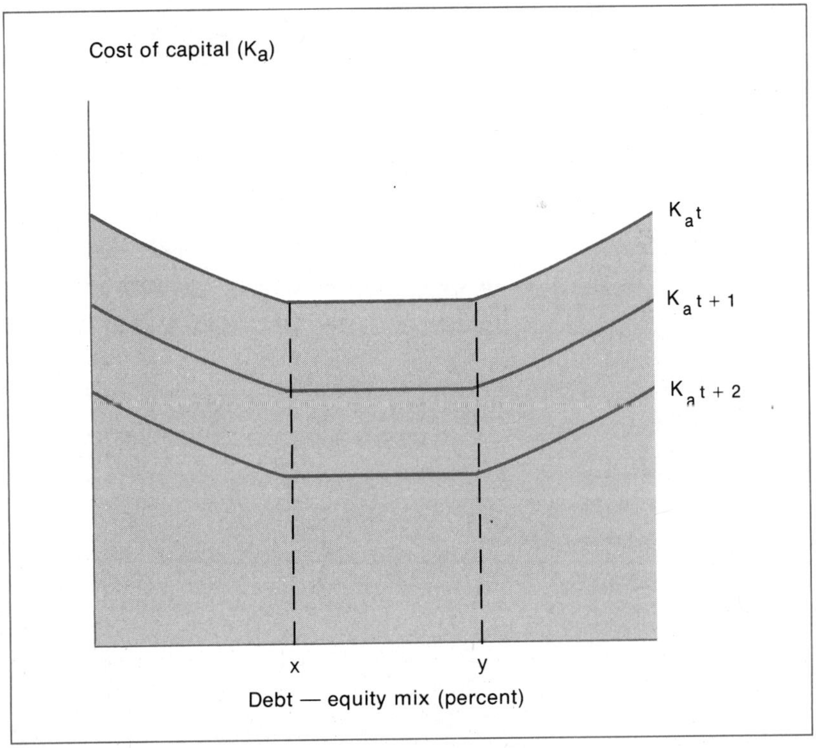

which future potential returns must be measured. When raising new financial capital, a company will tap the various sources of financing over a reasonable period of time. Regardless of the particular source of funds the company is using for the purchase of an asset, the required rate of return or discount rate will be the weighted average cost of capital. As long as the company earns its cost of capital, the common stock value of the firm will be maintained since stockholder expectations are being met. For example, assume the Baker Corporation was considering making an investment in eight projects with the returns and costs shown in Table 11–4. These projects could be viewed graphically and merged with the weighted average cost of capital in order to make a capital budgeting decision, as indicated in Figure 11–3.

Notice that the Baker Corporation is contemplating a total of $95 million in projects. Given that the weighted average cost of capital is 10.19 percent, however, it should choose only projects A through E, or $50 million in new assets. Selecting assets F, G, and H would probably reduce the market value of the common stock because these projects do not provide a return equal to the overall costs of raising funds.

The Marginal Cost of Capital

Nothing guarantees the Baker Corporation that its component cost of capital will stay constant for as much money as its wants to raise even if a given capital structure is maintained. If a large amount of financing is desired, the market may demand a higher cost of capital for each extra increment of funds desired. The point is analogous to the fact that you may be able to go to your relatives and best friends

Table 11–4
Investment projects available to the Baker Corporation

Projects	*Expected Returns*	*Cost ($ millions)*
A	16.00%	$10
B	14.00	5
C	13.50	4
D	11.80	20
E	10.40	11
F	9.50	20
G	8.60	15
H	7.00	10
		$95

Figure 11–3
Cost of capital and investment projects for the Baker Corporation

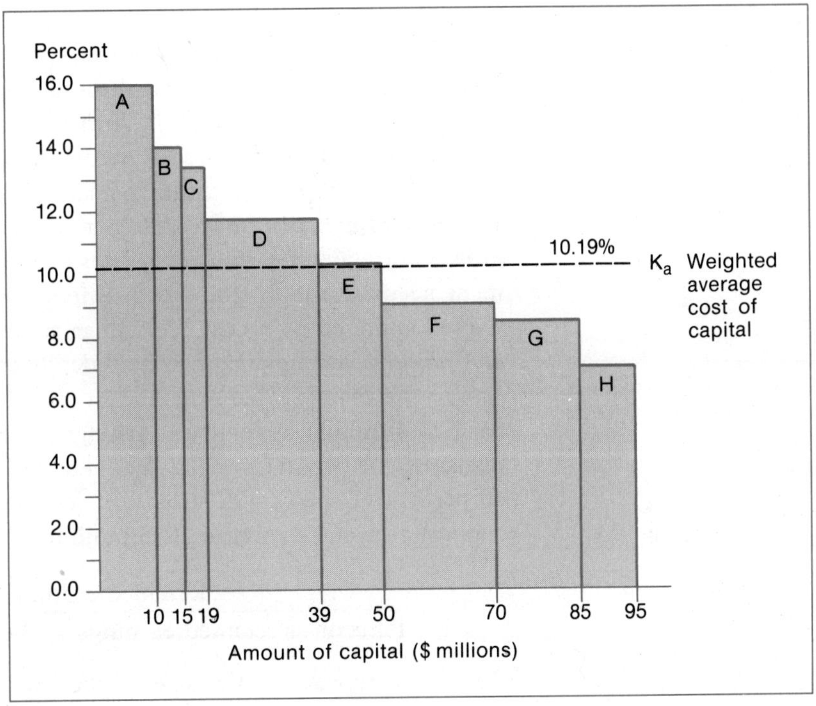

and raise funds for an investment at 10 percent. After you have exhausted the lending or investing power of those closest to you, you will have to look to other sources, and the marginal cost of your capital will probably go up.

As a background for this discussion, the cost of capital table for the Baker Corporation is reproduced again.

		Cost (after-tax)	Weights	Weighted Cost
Debt	K_d	6.34%	30%	1.90%
Preferred stock	K_p	10.94	10	1.09
Common equity (retained earnings)	K_e	12.00	60	7.20
Weighted average cost of capital	K_a			10.19%

We need to review the nature of the firm's capital structure in order to explain the concept of marginal cost of capital as it applies to the firm. Note that 60 percent of the firm's capital is in the form of common equity. This equity (ownership) capital is represented by retained earnings. Management has learned through experience that 60 percent is the amount of equity capital the firm must maintain to keep a balance, acceptable to security holders, between fixed income securities and equity ownership. The astute reader has already realized, however, that depending upon how quickly the firm's capital needs expand, the growth in retained earnings may not be enough to support the investment needs of the firm and to maintain a balanced capital structure. Capital supplied by retained earnings is limited to the amount of past and present earnings that can be redeployed into the investment projects of the firm.[11] Take a point in time when the Baker Corporation has \$23.4 million of retained earnings available for investment. Since management has determined that retained earnings should represent 60 percent of the capital structure, retained earnings are adequate to support a capital structure of \$39 million. More formally, we say that:

$$X = \frac{\text{Retained earnings}}{\text{Percent of retained earnings in the capital structure}} \qquad (11\text{–}8)$$

(Where X represents the size of the capital structure that retained earnings will support.)

$$X = \frac{\$23.4 \text{ million}}{.60}$$
$$= \$39 \text{ million}$$

Once \$39 million of capital is in place, retained earnings will no longer be adequate to keep the equity portion of the capital structure above 60 percent. Lenders and investors will become concerned if common equity (ownership) capital falls below 60 percent. Because of

---

[11]This basic concept, known as sustainable growth rate, is an important one for the student or practitioner of finance to grasp. Too often managers have assumed that as long as their firms were profitable, they could continue to grow as quickly as possible. Rude awakenings sometimes followed when banks refused to advance any more loans to the cash-strapped firms. The basic formula for determining the internally sustainable growth rate of the firm is:

$$\text{Sustainable growth rate} = \frac{\text{Earnings}(1 - \text{Dividend payout ratio})}{\text{Beginning equity}}$$

In other words, assuming that the firm's debt ratio is optimal, the rest of the balance sheet can grow no faster than the equity portion.

this, *new* common stock will be needed to supplement retained earnings to provide the 60 percent common equity component for the firm. That is, after $39 million in capital is passed, additional common equity capital will be in the form of new common stock rather than retained earnings.

In the upper portion of Table 11–5 we see the original cost of capital that we have been discussing throughout the chapter. This applies up to a total capital amount of $39 million. After $39 million the concept of marginal cost of capital becomes important. The cost of capital goes up as shown on the lower portion of the table.

K_{mc}, in the lower portion of the table, represents the *marginal* cost of capital, which becomes 10.55 percent after $39 million. The cost of capital increases for capital above $39 million because the invested common equity is now in the form of new common stock rather than retained earnings. The after-tax (A/T) cost of the latter is slightly more than the former because of flotation costs (F). The equation for the cost of new common stock was shown earlier in the chapter as Formula 11–7. In this circumstance it is calculated:

$$K_n = \frac{D_1}{P_0 - F} + g = \frac{\$2}{\$40 - \$4} + 7\%$$

$$= \frac{\$2}{\$36} + 7\% = 5.6\% + 7\% = 12.6\%$$

Table 11–5
Cost of capital for different amounts of financing

		After-Tax Cost	Weights	Weighted Cost
First $39 million:				
Debt.	K_d	6.34%	.30	1.90%
Preferred.	K_p	10.94	.10	1.09
Common equity*.	K_e	12.00	.60	7.20
				K_a = 10.19%
Next $11 million:				
Debt.	K_d	6.34%	.30	1.90
Preferred.	K_p	10.94	.10	1.09
Common equity†	K_n	12.60	.60	7.56
				K_{mc} = 10.55%

*Retained earnings.
†New common equity.

The flotation cost (F) of $4 makes the cost of new common stock 12.60 percent. This is higher than the 12 percent cost of retained earnings we have been using and therefore causes the increase in the marginal cost of capital.

To carry the example a bit further, let us assume the cost of debt of 6.34 percent applies only to the first $15 million of debt the firm raises. After that, the after-tax cost of debt will rise to 7.9 percent because of the need to tap more expensive sources. Since debt represents 30 percent of the capital structure for the Baker Corporation, the cheaper form of debt will be available to support the capital structure up to $50 million. We derive the $50 million by using Formula 11–9.

$$Z = \frac{\text{Amount of lower cost debt}}{\text{Percent of debt in the capital structure}} \qquad (11\text{–}9)$$

(Where Z represents the size of the capital structure in which lower cost debt can be utilized)

$$Z = \frac{\$15 \text{ million}}{.30}$$
$$= \$50 \text{ million}$$

After the first $50 million of capital is raised, lower-cost debt will no longer be available to make up 30 percent of the capital structure. After $50 million in total financing, the after-tax cost of debt will go up to the previously specified 7.9 percent. The marginal cost of capital for over $50 million in financing is shown in Table 11–6.

This increase in the cost of debt causes another rise in the marginal cost of capital (K_{mc}) to 11.02 percent after $50 million of financing. You should observe that the capital structure with over $50 million of financing reflects both the increase in the cost of debt and the continued

Table 11–6
Cost of capital for increasing amounts of financing

		Cost (after-tax)	Weights	Weighted Cost
Over $50 million:				
Debt (higher cost)	K_d	7.90%	.30	2.37%
Preferred stock	K_p	10.94	.10	1.09
Common equity				
(new common stock)	K_n	12.60	.60	7.56
			K_{mc} =	11.02%

exclusive use of new common stock to represent additional common equity capital.

We could carry on this process by next considering at what point an increase in the cost of preferred stock would be demanded by investors, or at what points the costs of debt or new common stock will increase as more and more capital is required. For now, however, it is important that you merely understand the basic process and can think it through when the details of an actual situation are at hand.

To summarize, then, we have calculated that the Baker Corporation has a basic weighted average cost of capital of 10.19 percent. This chapter was devoted to demonstrating the development of that value. Table 11–1 presented it originally. We found, however, that as the firm's investment plans required it to substantially expand its capital structure, the weighted average cost of capital increased. This process demonstrated the concept of marginal cost of capital. The first increase, or break point, occurred at $39 million. At that point the marginal cost of capital went up to 10.55 percent as a result of having to raise new common stock (in other words we passed the firm's sustainable growth rate). The second increase in the cost of capital occurred when the total required capital structure passed $50 million. Past there, the marginal cost of capital increased to 11.02 percent as a result of the need to utilize more expensive sources of debt. These marginal changes are summarized below.

Amount of Financing	*Marginal Cost of Capital*
0–$39 million	10.19%
$39–50 million	10.55
Over $50 million	11.02

Remember that this discussion of marginal cost of capital is highly dependent upon the investment opportunities available to the firm and, in turn, has a great effect upon them. Figure 11–3 shows the estimated returns from investment for projects A through H. Figure 11–4 reproduces the returns originally shown in Figure 11–3 and, in addition, includes the concept of marginal cost of capital. Observe that the marginal cost of capital (dotted lines) increases even as the marginal returns (straight lines) decrease.

In the earlier Figure 11–3 presentation, the Baker Corporation seemed justified in choosing projects A through E representing capital expen-

Figure 11–4
Marginal cost of capital and Baker Corporation investment alternatives

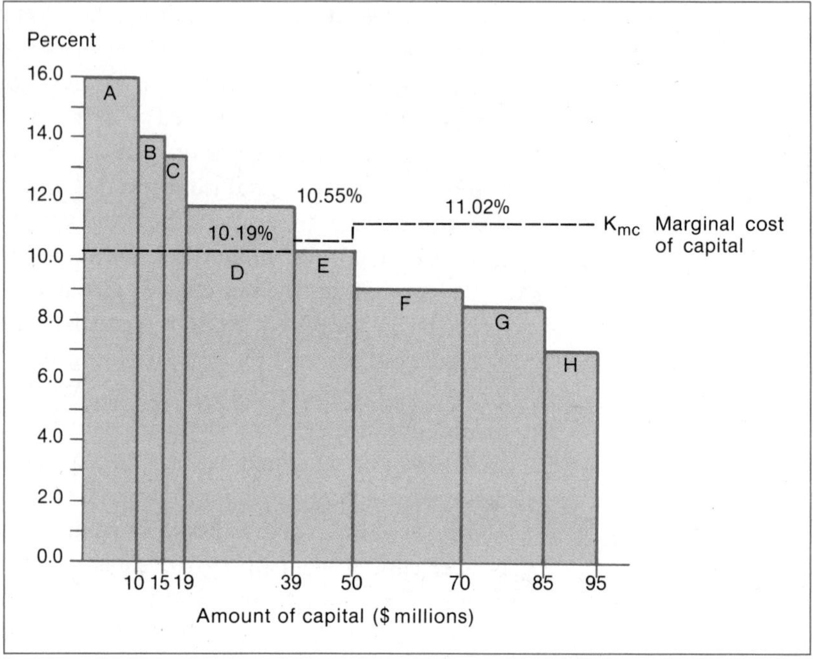

ditures of $50 million. Figure 11–4 represents a more sophisticated consideration of the investment alternatives and, as such, tells a slightly different story. Because of the increasing marginal cost of capital, the returns exceed the cost of capital for only the first $39 million of projects. This means that only projects A through D will be deemed acceptable.

Despite the importance of the marginal cost of capital, for purposes of most of our discussion of capital budgeting decisions in the next chapter we will assume we are operating on the initial flat part of the marginal cost of capital curve in Figure 11–4. This will mean that most of our decisions will be made based on the initial weighted average cost of capital. Such an approach is generally acceptable, but it is up to the astute financial analyst to realize when this will not be the case. If there seem to be very real financing consequences involved with taking on marginal projects, he or she must take them into account.

Summary

The cost of capital is a critical component in the valuation of a firm and its prospects. It is determined by computing the costs of various sources of financing and weighting them in proportion to their expected representation in future financings. The cost of each component in the capital structure is closely associated with the valuation of that source. For debt and preferred stock the cost is directly related to the current yield, with the cost of debt reduced downward to reflect the tax deductibility of interest costs.

For common stock the cost of retained earnings (K_e) is the current dividend yield on the security plus the anticipated future rate of growth in dividends. Minor adjustments must be made to the formula to determine the cost of new common stock issues. A summary of the Baker Corporation's capital costs, as developed throughout the chapter, is presented in Table 11–7.

The weights for each of the elements in the capital structure should be chosen with a view to minimizing the overall cost of capital. While debt is usually the "cheapest" form of financing, excessive use of debt may increase the financial risk of the firm and drive up the costs of all sources of financing. The wise financial manager attempts to ascertain which level of debt will result in the lowest overall cost of capital. That level of debt defines the optimum capital structure. Once the optimum capital structure has been established, the weighted average cost of capital is used as the discount rate in converting future cash flows to

Table 11–7
Cost of components in the capital structure

1	Cost of debt	$K_d = \text{Yield}(1 - T) = 6.34\%$	Yield = 11.74% T = Corporate tax rate, 46%
2	Cost of preferred stock	$K_p = \dfrac{D_p}{P_p - F} = 10.94\%$	D_p = Preferred dividend, $10.50 P_p = Price of preferred stock, $100 F = Flotation costs, $4
3	Cost of common equity (retained earnings)	$K_e = \dfrac{D_1}{P_0} + g = 12\%$	D_1 = First year common dividend, $2 P_0 = Price of common stock, $40 g = Growth rate, 7%
4	Cost of new common stock . . .	$K_n = \dfrac{D_1}{P_0 - F} + g = 12.60\%$	Same as above, with F = Flotation costs, $4

their present value. The major decision rule, then, is to determine if an investment proposal will earn at least the cost of the firm's financing. Investments that earn more than that cost increase the value of the firm (or "create value").

The marginal cost of capital is important in considering what happens to a firm's cost of capital as it tries to finance large requirements for funds. First, the company will use up its access to retained earnings with the cost of financing rising as higher-cost new common stock is substituted for retained earnings. Common stock will be needed in order to maintain the optimum capital structure (that is, the appropriate debt-to-equity ratio). Needs for larger amounts of financial capital can also cause the costs of the individual means of financing to rise by raising the interest rates the firm must pay or by depressing the price of the stock because more is offered for sale than the market wants to absorb at the old price.

List of Terms

financial capital
optimum capital structure
common equity
cost of capital
weighted average cost of capital
marginal cost of capital
dividend valuation model
flotation costs
capital asset pricing model (CAPM)

Discussion Questions

1. Why do we use the overall cost of capital for investment decisions even when an investment will be funded by only one source of capital (for example, debt)?
2. How does the cost of a source of capital relate to the valuation concepts presented in Chapter 10?
3. In computing the cost of capital, do we use the historical costs of existing debt and equity or the current costs as determined in the market? Why?

4. Why would the cost of debt be less than the cost of preferred stock if both securities were priced to yield 10 percent in the market?

5. What are the two sources of equity (ownership) capital for the firm?

6. Explain what we mean when we say retained earnings has an opportunity cost associated with it?

7. Why is the cost of retained earnings the equivalent of the firm's own required rate of return on common stock (K_e)?

8. Why is the cost of new common stock (K_n) higher than the cost of retained earnings (K_e)?

9. How are the component weights determined in arriving at the lowest weighted average cost of capital?

10. Modigliani and Miller previously maintained that the cost of capital is constant for all debt-equity mixes. The traditional approach maintains that the cost curve is U-shaped. Explain the difference in the logic between the two approaches.

11. Identify other variables (ratios) besides the debt-to-equity ratio that you think will influence a company's cost of capital. You may wish to refer to Chapter 3 for possibilities.

12. It is generally maintained that if the company cannot earn a rate of return greater than its cost of capital it should not make investments. Explain the logic behind such a statement. Might there ever be an occasion when this statement is false.

13. What effect would inflation have on a company's cost of capital? (Hint: Think about how inflation influences interest rates, stock prices, corporate profits, and growth.)

14. Explain the concept of marginal cost of capital?

Problems

1. Orbit Enterprises can issue debt yielding 12 percent. The company is in a 40 percent tax bracket. What is its after-tax cost of debt?

2. Calculate the after-tax cost of debt under each of the following conditions.

	Yield	Corporate Tax Rate
a.	8.0%	16%
b.	14.0	46
c.	11.5	24

3. Calculate the after-tax cost of debt on a bond issue yielding 12 percent. The issuing company pays tax at a rate of 42 percent and will incur distribution costs of 1 percent on this bond issue. (See text footnote 2.)

4. Oxford Clothiers has a $1,000 par value bond outstanding with 20 years to maturity. The bond issue carries an annual interest payment of $95 and is currently selling for $920 per bond. Oxford Clothiers is in a 35 percent tax bracket. The firm wishes to know what the after-tax cost of a new bond issue is likely to be. The risk and maturity date on the new issue are judged to be similar to those on the old one.

   a. Compute the yield to maturity expected on the new issue.
   b. What, then, will the after-tax cost of debt be?

5. Interprovincial Pipelines is planning to issue debt that will mature in the year 2004. In many respects the issue is similar to currently outstanding debt of the corporation. Using Table 11–2 in the chapter, identify:

   a. The yield to maturity on similar (in terms of maturity) outstanding debt for the firm.
   b. Assume that because the new debt will be issued at par, the required yield to maturity will be .15 percent lower than the value observed in part *a*. Add this factor to the observation from *a* to arive at your estimate of what rate Interprovincial will have to offer on the new debt. Why might the new issue at par be acceptable at a slightly lower yield than the old debt selling at a premium?
   c. If the firm is in a 46 percent tax bracket, what is the after-tax cost of debt?

6. Schuss, Inc., can sell preferred stock for $60 with an estimated flotation cost of $3. The preferred stock is anticipated to pay $7 per share in dividends.

   a. Compute the cost of a preferred stock for Schuss, Inc.
   b. Do we need to make a tax adjustment for the issuing firm?

7. The Holtz Corporation sold a new issue of preferred stock for $100 per share 10 years ago. The stock provided a 9 percent yield at the time of issue. The preferred stock is now selling for $85.

   a. What is the current cost of preferred stock to the Holtz Corporation? (Disregard flotation costs.)
   b. If a 5 percent flotation (selling) cost is presently involved in issuing new preferred stock, what is the current cost to Holtz of a preferred stock issue? [Hint: Divide the answer in part *a* by (1 − flotation percentage).]

8. Ellington Electronics wants you to calculate its cost of common stock. During the next 12 months, the company expects to pay dividends (D_1) of $1.50 per share while the current price of its common stock is $30 per share. The expected growth rate is 8 percent for earnings per share and for dividends per share.

   a. Compute the cost of retained earnings (K_e). Use Formula 11–6.
   b. If a $2 per share flotation cost is involved, compute the cost of new common stock (K_n). Use Formula 11–7.

9. Compute K_e and K_n under the following circumstances:

   a. D_1 = $4.60, P_0 = $60, g = 6%, F = $4.00.
   b. D_1 = $0.25, P_0 = $20, g = 10%, F = $1.50.
   c. E_1 (earnings at the end of period one) = $6, payout ratio equals 30 percent, P_0 = $25, g = 4.5%, F = $2.
   d. D_0 (dividend at the beginning of the first period) = $3, growth rate for dividends and earnings per share (g) = 7%, P_0 = $42, F = $3.

10. Sam's Fine Garments sells jackets and sport coats in suburban shopping malls throughout the country. Business has been good as indicated by the six-year growth in earnings per share. The earnings have grown from $1.00 to $1.87.

a. Use Appendix A at the back of the text to determine the compound annual rate of growth in earnings.

b. Based on the growth rate determined in part *a*, project earnings for next year (E_1). Round to two decimal places.

c. Assume the dividend payout ratio has historically been, and is expected to continue to be, 40 percent. Compute D_1.

d. The current price of the stock is $15. Using the growth rate (g) from part *a* and D_1 from part *c*, compute K_e.

e. If the flotation cost is $1.75, compute the cost of new common stock (K_n).

11. The Tyler Oil Company's capital structure is as follows:

Debt	.35%
Preferred stock	.15
Common equity	.50

The after-tax cost of debt is 7 percent; the cost of preferred stock is 10 percent; and the cost of common equity (in the form of retained earnings) is 13 percent.

Calculate Tyler Oil Company's weighted average cost of capital in a manner similar to that used for Table 11–1.

12. As an alternative to the capital structure shown in Problem 11 for the Tyler Oil Company, an outside consultant has suggested the following.

Debt	.60%
Preferred stock	5
Common equity	.35

Under this new, more debt-oriented arrangement, the after-tax cost of debt would become 8.8 percent; the cost of preferred stock, 10.5 percent; and the cost of common equity (in the form of retained earnings), 15.5 percent.

Recalculate Tyler Oil Company's weighted average cost of capital if it decides to aim toward restructuring its financing mix as suggested.

Which financing plan is better? Why?

13. Given the following information, calculate the weighted average cost of capital for Genex Corporation. Line up the calculations in the order shown in Table 11–1.

Percent of capital structure:	
Debt	35%
Preferred stock	10
Common equity	55

Additional information:	
Bond coupon rate	13%
Bond yield	11%
Dividend, common expected	\$3.00
Dividend, preferred	\$10.00
Price, common	\$50.00
Price, preferred	\$98.00
Flotation cost, preferred	\$5.50
Growth rate, historical	8%
Corporate tax rate	30%

14. Brunswick Atlantic Corporation is trying to calculate its cost of capital for use in a capital budgeting decision. Mr. Krone, the vice president of finance, has given you the following information and has asked you to compute the weighted average cost of capital. The company currently has outstanding a bond with a 9 percent coupon rate and a convertible bond with a 6½ percent coupon rate. Brunswick Atlantic's investment dealer has informed Mr. Krone that bonds of equal risk and credit rating are currently selling to yield 13 percent. The common stock has a price of \$30 per share and an expected dividend (D_1) of \$1 per share. Brunswick Atlantic's historical growth rate of dividends and earnings per share has been 15 percent, but security analysts on Bay Street expect this growth to slow to 12 percent in future years. The preferred stock is selling at \$50 per share and carries a dividend of \$5 per share. The corporate tax rate is 40 percent. The flotation costs are 4 percent of the selling price for preferred stock. The optimum capital structure for Brunswick Atlantic seems to consist of about 30 percent debt, 10 percent preferred stock, and 60 percent common equity. Retained earnings are expected to be sufficient to support foreseeable investment plans.

Compute the cost of capital for the individual components in the capital structure and then calculate the weighted average cost of capital (similar to Table 11–1).

15. Western Electric Utility Company faces increasing needs for capital. Fortunately, it has an A+ credit rating. The corporate tax rate is 46 percent. Western's treasurer is trying to determine the corporation's current weighted average cost of capital in order to assess the profitability of proposed capital projects. Historically, the corporation's earnings and dividends per share have increased at about a 5 percent annual rate. Western common stock is selling at $50 per share, and the company intends to pay a $4 per share dividend. The company's $100 preferred stock has been yielding 9 percent in the current market. Flotation costs for the company have been estimated by its investment advisor to be $2 per share for preferred stock. The company's optimum capital structure is estimated as 40 percent debt, 15 percent preferred stock, and 45 percent common equity in the form of retained earnings. Refer to the table below on bond issues to gain some insight into probable bond yields payable by Western.

Data on Bond Issues

Issue	*Rating*	*Price*	*Yield to Maturity*
Utilities:			
Maritime Tel & Tel 10⅜s 1999	A+	$1,027.50	9.98%
Bell Canada 9⅖s 2002	A++	991.30	9.51
Consumers' Gas 10.45s 1999	A	1,023.80	10.10
Industrials:			
Bank of N.S. 9½s 1997	A+	992.50	9.61%
Genstar 10¾s 1999	B++	1,017.50	10.49
Woolworth 10s 2003	A	981.30	10.24

Compute the following from the preceding information.

a. Cost of debt.
b. Cost of preferred stock.
c. Cost of common equity in the form of retained earnings.
d. Weighted average cost of capital.

16. The Nolan Corporation finds that it is necessary to determine its marginal cost of capital. Nolan's current capital structure calls for 45 percent debt, 15 percent preferred stock, and 40 percent common equity. Initially, common equity will be in the form of retained earnings (K_e) and then new common stock (K_n). The costs of the various sources of financing are as follows: debt, 5.6 percent; preferred stock, 9 percent; retained earnings, 12 percent; and new common stock, 13.2 percent.

a. What is the initial weighted average cost of capital? (Include debt, preferred stock, and common equity in the form of retained earnings, K_e.)
b. If the firm has $12 million in retained earnings, past what amount of total capital will the firm not be able to sustain further growth by reinvesting retained earnings?
c. What will the marginal cost of capital be immediately after that point? (The exception is that equity will remain at 40 percent of the capital structure, but additional amounts will all be in the form of new common stock, K_n.)
d. The 5.6 percent cost of debt referred to above applies only to the first $18 million of debt. After that the cost of debt will be 7.2 percent. Past what amount of total capital will there be a change in the cost of debt?
e. What will the marginal cost of capital be immediately after that point?

17. Hailey Mills, an apparel manufacturer, is in the process of expanding its productive capacity to introduce a new line of products. Current plans call for a possible expenditure of $100 million on four projects of equal size ($25 million) but with different returns. Project A will increase the firm's processed yarn capacity and has an expected return of 15 percent after taxes. Project B will increase the capacity for woven fabrics and carries a return of 13.5 percent. Project C, a venture into synthetic fibers, is expected to earn 11.2 percent, and Project D, an investment to move the firm into the dye and textile chemical business, is expected to show a 10.5 percent return.

The firm's capital structure consists of 40 percent debt and 60 percent common equity, and this will continue in the future. There is no preferred stock.

Hailey Mills has $15 million in retained earnings above what is required to keep a 40/60 debt-equity ratio. Once a capital structure in which equity represents only 60 percent of total financing is reached, all additional equity financing must come in the form of new common stock.

Common stock is selling for $30 per share, and underwriting costs are estimated at $3 if new shares are issued. Dividends for the next year are estimated at $1.50 per share, and per share earnings and dividends have grown consistently at 9 percent per year.

The yield on comparative bonds has been hovering around 11 percent. The investment dealer feels that the first $20 million of bonds could be sold to yield 11 percent, while additional debt might require a 2 percent premium and be marketed to yield 13 percent. The corporate tax rate is 45 percent.

a. Based on the two sources of financing, what is the initial weighted average cost of capital?

b. Past what total amount of capital will retained earnings be unavailable to support further investment?

c. What will be the marginal cost of capital immediately after that point?

d. Past what total capital size will there be a change in the cost of debt?

e. What will be the marginal cost of capital immediately past that point?

f. Based on the information about potential returns on investments in the first paragraph and information on marginal cost of capital (in parts *a*, *c*, and *e*), how large a capital investment budget should the firm plan on?

g. Graph the answer determined in part *f*.

18. (*Comprehensive problem*)
Logan Manufacturing is a very large company with common stock listed on the Toronto and Montreal Stock Exchanges and bonds traded over-the-counter. As of the current balance sheet, it has three bond issues outstanding:

$100 million of 8¾ percent series 2000
$50 million of 6 percent series 1990
$150 million of 4 percent series 1989

The vice president of finance is planning to sell $150 million of bonds next year to replace the debt due to expire in 1989. At present, market yields on similar A++ bonds are 10.8 percent.

Logan also has $100 million of 4.5 percent noncallable preferred stock outstanding, but it has no intentions of selling any new preferred stock at any time in the future. The preferred stock originally sold for $100 per share and is currently trading at $47 per share.

The company has had very volatile earnings, but its dividends per share have had a very stable growth rate of 5 percent, and management intends to continue to increase dividends gradually. The expected dividend in the upcoming year is $2.80 per share, while the common stock is selling for $45 per share. The company's investment advisor has quoted Logan the following flotation costs: $2 per share for preferred stock and $1.90 per share for common stock.

On the advice of its investment advisor, Logan has kept its debt at 50 percent of assets and its equity at 50 percent. Logan sees no need to sell either common or preferred stock in the foreseeable future as it generates enough internal funds for its investment needs (when these funds are combined with the additional debt financing they make possible). Logan's corporate tax rate is 46 percent.

Compute the cost of capital for the following:

a. Bond (debt) (K_d).
b. Preferred stock (K_p).
c. Common equity in the form of retained earnings (K_e).
d. New common stock (K_n).
e. Weighted average cost of capital.

Selected References

Alberts, W. W., and S. H. Archer. "Some Evidence on the Effect of Company Size on the Cost of Equity Capital." *Journal of Financial and Quantitative Analysis* 8 (March 1973), pp. 229–42.

Archer, Stephen H., and Leroy G. Faerber. "Firm Size and the Cost of Equity Capital." *Journal of Finance* 21 (March 1966), pp. 69–84.

Arditti, F. D. "The Weighted Average Cost of Capital: Some Questions on Its Definition, Interpretation, and Use." *Journal of Finance* 28 (September 1973), pp. 1001–8.

Beranek, William. "The Cost of Capital, Capital Budgeting, and the Maximization of Shareholder Wealth." *Journal of Financial and Quantitative Analysis* 10 (March 1975), pp. 1–21.

Bierman, Harold, Jr., and Jerome E. Hass. "Capital Budgeting under Uncertainty: A Reformulation." *Journal of Finance* 28 (March 1973), pp. 119–20.

Brennan, Michael J. "A New Look at the Weighted Average Cost of Capital." *Journal of Business Finance* 5, no. 1 (1973), pp. 24–30.

Brigham, Eugene F., and Keith V. Smith. "The Cost of Capital to the Small Firm." *Engineering Economist* 13 (Fall 1967), pp. 1–26.

Conine, Thomas E., Jr., and Maury Tamarkin. "Divisional Cost of Capital Estimation: Adjusting for Leverage." *Financial Management* 14 (Spring 1985), pp. 154–58.

Elton, Edwin J., and Martin J. Gruber. "The Cost of Retained Earnings—Implications of Share Repurchase." *Industrial Management Review* 9 (Spring 1968), pp. 87–104.

Fowler, D. J.; C. H. Rorke; and V. M. Jog. "Thin Trading and Beta Estimation Problems on the Toronto Stock Exchange." *Journal of Business Administration* 12 (Fall 1980), pp. 77–90.

Fuller, Russell J., and Halbert S. Kerr. "Estimating the Divisional Cost of Capital: An Analysis of the Pure-Play Technique." *Journal of Finance* 36 (December 1981), pp. 997–1009.

Gordon, Myron J., and Paul J. Halpern. "Cost of Capital for a Division of a Firm." *Journal of Finance* 29 (September 1974), pp. 153–63.

Lewellen, Wilbur G. *The Cost of Capital*. Belmont, Calif.: Wadsworth, 1969.

Lintner, John. "The Cost of Capital and Optimal Financing of Corporate Growth." *Journal of Finance* 18 (May 1963), pp. 292–310.

Long, Susan W. "Risk-Premium Curve vs. Capital Market Line: Differences Explained." *Financial Management* 7 (Spring 1978), pp. 60–64.

Modigliani, F., and M. Miller. "The Cost of Capital, Corporation Finance, and the Theory of Investment." *American Economic Review* 48 (June 1958), pp. 261–96.

Morin, R. A. "Market Line Theory and the Canadian Equity Market." *Journal of Business Administration* 12 (Fall 1980), pp. 57–76.

Nantell, Timothy J., and C. Robert Carlson. "The Cost of Capital as a Weighted Average." *Journal of Finance* 30 (December 1975), pp. 343–55.

Ofer, Aharon R. "Investors' Expectations of Earnings Growth, Their Accuracy, and Effects on the Structure of Realized Rates of Return." *Journal of Finance* 30 (May 1975), pp. 509–23.

Roll, Richard. "A Critique of the Asset Pricing Theory's Test. Part 1., On the Past and Potential Testability of the Theory." *Journal of Financial Economics* 4 (March 1977), pp. 129–76.

———. "Ambiguity when Performance Is Measured by the Securities Market Line." *Journal of Finance* 33 (September 1978), pp. 1051–70.

Sharpe, William F. "Capital Asset Prices: A Theory of Market Equilibrium under Conditions of Risk." *Journal of Finance* 19 (September 1964), pp. 1425–42.

Solomon, Ezra. "Measuring a Company's Cost of Capital." *Journal of Business* 28 (October 1955), pp. 240–52.

Appendix 11A: Cost of Capital and the Capital Asset Pricing Model (Optional)

The Capital Asset Pricing Model

The capital asset pricing model (CAPM) relates the risk-return tradeoffs of individual assets to market returns. Common stock returns over time have generally been used to test this model since stock prices are widely available and efficiently priced, as are market indexes of stock performance. In theory the CAPM encompasses all assets, but in practice it is difficult to measure returns on all types of assets or to find an all-encompassing market index. For our purposes we will use common stock returns to explain the model, and occasionally we will generalize to other assets.

The basic form of the CAPM is a linear relationship between returns on individual stocks and the market over time. By using least squares regression analysis, the return on an individual stock, K_j, is expressed in Formula 11A–1.

$$K_j = \alpha + \beta K_m + e \quad (11A\text{–}1)$$

where

K_j = Return on individual common stock of a company
α = Alpha, the intercept on the y-axis
β = Beta, the coefficient
K_m = Return on the market (usually an index of stock returns is used)
e = Error term of the regression equation

As indicated in Table 11A–1 and Figure 11A–1, this equation uses historical data to generate the beta coefficient (β), a measurement of the return performance of a given stock versus the return performance of the market. Assume we want to calculate a beta for Parts Associates, Inc. (PAI), and that we have the performance data for that company and the market shown in Table 11A–1. The relationship between PAI and the market appears graphically in Figure 11A–1.

The alpha term in Figure 11A–1 of 2.8 percent is the y-intercept of the linear regression. It is the expected return on PAI stock if returns on the market are zero. However, if the returns on the market are expected to approximate the historical rate of 12.4 percent, the expected return on PAI would be $K_j = 2.8 + 0.9(12.4) = 14.0$ percent. This maintains the historical relationship. If the returns on the market are expected to rise to 18 percent next year, expected return on PAI would be $K_j = 2.8 + 0.9\ (18.0) = 19$ percent.

Notice that we are talking in terms of expectations. The CAPM is an exceptional (ex ante) model, and there is no guarantee that historical data will reoccur. One area of empirical testing involves the stability

Table 11A–1
Performance of PAI and the market

	Rate of Return on Stock	
Year	PAI	Market
1	12.0 %	10.0 %
2	16.0	18.0
3	20.0	16.0
4	16.0	10.0
5	6.0	8.0
Mean return	14.0 %	12.4 %
Standard deviation	4.73%	3.87%

Figure 11A–1
Linear regression of returns between PAI and the market

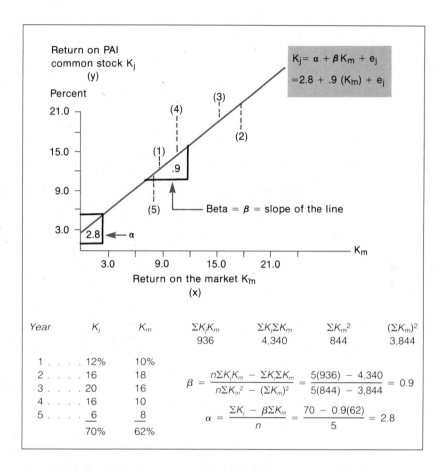

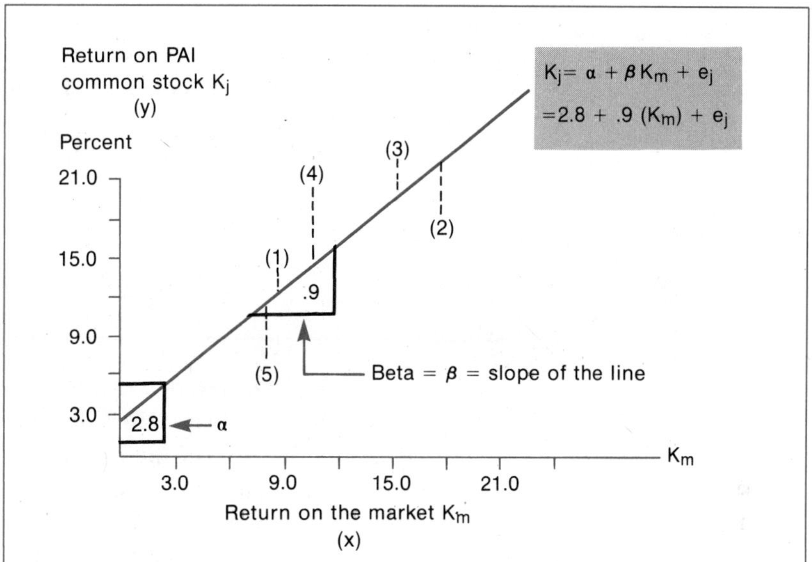

Year	K_j	K_m
1	12%	10%
2	16	18
3	20	16
4	16	10
5	6	8
	70%	62%

$\Sigma K_j K_m$	$\Sigma K_j \Sigma K_m$	ΣK_m^2	$(\Sigma K_m)^2$
936	4,340	844	3,844

$$\beta = \frac{n\Sigma K_j K_m - \Sigma K_j \Sigma K_m}{n\Sigma K_m^2 - (\Sigma K_m)^2} = \frac{5(936) - 4{,}340}{5(844) - 3{,}844} = 0.9$$

$$\alpha = \frac{\Sigma K_j - \beta \Sigma K_m}{n} = \frac{70 - 0.9(62)}{5} = 2.8$$

and predictability of the beta coefficient based on historical data. Research has indicated that betas are more useful in a portfolio context (for groupings of stocks) because the betas of individual stocks are less stable from period to period than portfolio betas. In addition, there seems to be a tendency for individual betas to approach 1.0 over time.

The Security Market Line

The capital asset pricing model evolved from Formula 11A–1 into a risk premium model where the basic assumption is that in order for investors to take more risk they must be compensated by larger expected returns. Investors should also not accept returns that are less then they can get from a riskless asset. For CAPM purposes it is assumed that short-term government of Canada Treasury bills may be considered a riskless asset.[1] When viewed in this context, an investor must achieve an extra return above that obtainable from a Treasury bill in order to induce the assumption of more risk. This brings us to the more common and theoretically useful model:

$$K_j = R_f + \beta(K_m - R_f) \qquad (11A\text{–}2)$$

where

R_f = Risk-free rate of return
β = Beta coefficient from Formula 11A–1
K_m = Return on the market index
$K_m - R_f$ = Premium or excess return of the market versus the risk-free rate (since the market is riskier than R_f, the assumption is that the expected K_m will be greater than R_f)
$\beta(K_m - R_f)$ = Expected return above the risk-free rate for the stock of Company j, given the level of risk.

The model centers on beta, the coefficient of the premium demanded by an investor to invest in an individual stock. For each individual security, beta measures the sensitivity (volatility) of the security's return to the market. By definition, the market has a beta of 1.0, so that if an individual company's beta is 1.0, it can expect to have returns as volatile as the market and total returns equal to the market. A company with a beta of 2.0 would be twice as volatile as the market and would be expected to generate more returns, whereas a company with a beta of 0.5 would be half as volatile as the market. For example, assuming that the risk-free rate is 9.0 percent and that the expected return in the market is 11 percent, the following returns would occur with betas of 2.0, 1.0, and 0.5.

[1]A number of studies have also indicated that longer-term government securities may form a base to use in calculating R_f.

$$K_2 = 9.0\% + 2.0\,(11.0\% - 9.0\%) = 13\%$$
$$K_1 = 9.0\% + 1.0\,(11.0\% - 9.0\%) = 11\%$$
$$K_{.5} = 9.0\% + 0.5\,(11.0\% - 9.0\%) = 10\%$$

Basically beta measures the riskiness of an investment relative to the market. In order to outperform the market, one would have to assume more risk by selecting assets with betas greater than 1.0. Another way of looking at the risk-return trade-off would be that if less risk than the market is desired, an investor would choose assets with a beta of less than 1.0. Beta is a good measure of a stock's risk when the stock is combined into a portfolio, and therefore it has some bearing on the assets a company acquires for its portfolio of real capital.

In Figure 11A–1 individual stock returns were compared to market returns, and the beta from Formula 11A–1 was shown. From Formula 11A–2, the risk premium model, a generalized risk-return graph called the security market line (SML) can be constructed that identifies the risk-return trade-off of any common stock (asset) relative to the company's beta. This is shown in Figure 11A–2.

The required return for all securities can be expressed as the risk-free rate plus a premium for risk. Thus, we see that a stock with a beta of 1.0 would have a risk premium of 2 percent added to the risk-free rate of 9 percent to provide a required return of 11 percent. Since a beta of 1.0 implies risk equal to the market, the return is also at the overall market rate. If the beta is 2.0, twice the market risk premium

Figure 11A–2
The security market line (SML)

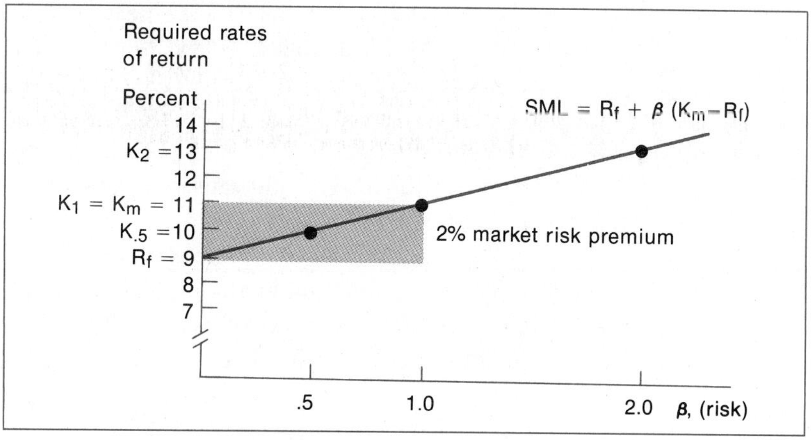

of 2 percent must be earned, and we add 4 percent to the risk-free rate of 9 percent to determine the required return of 13 percent. For a beta of 0.5, the required return is 10 percent.

Cost of Capital Considerations

When calculating the cost of capital for common stock, remember that K_e is equal to the expected total return from the dividend yield and capital gains.

$$K_e = \frac{D_1}{P_0} + g$$

K_e is the return required by investors based on expectations of future dividends and growth. The SML provides the same information but in a market-related risk-return model. As required returns rise, prices must fall to adjust to the new equilibrium return level, and as required returns fall, prices rise. Stock markets are generally efficient, and when stock prices are in equilibrium, the K_e derived from the dividend model will be equal to K_j derived from the SML.

The SML helps us to identify several circumstances that can cause the cost of capital to change. Figure 11–2 in Chapter 11 examined required rates of returns over time with changing interest rates and stock prices. Figure 11A–3 does basically the same thing, only through the SML format.

When interest rates increase from the initial period (R_{f1} versus R_{f0}), the security market line in the next period is parallel to SML_0, but higher. What this means is that required rates of return have risen for every level of risk as investors desire to maintain their risk premium over the risk-free rate. The market rate will not always change by a percentage equal to that of the change in the risk-free rate. A steeper slope for the SML could cause a greater change in the required market returns.

One very important variable influencing interest rates is the rate of inflation. As inflation increases, lenders try to maintain their real dollar purchasing power, so they increase the required interest rates to offset inflation. The risk-free rate can be thought of as:

$$R_f = RR + IP$$

Figure 11A–3
The security market line and changing interest rates

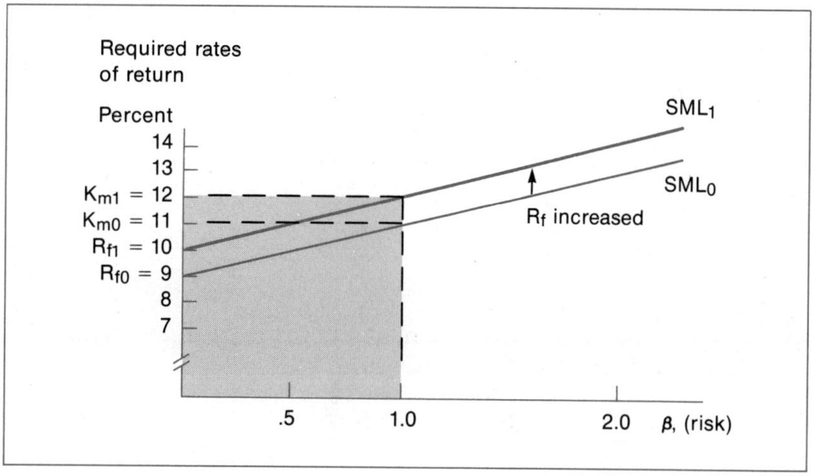

where

RR is the real rate of return on a riskless government security when inflation is zero.

IP is an inflation premium that compensates lenders (investors) for loss of purchasing power.

An upward shift in the SML indicates that the prices of all assets will shift downward as interest rates move up. In Chapter 10, Valuation and Rates of Return, this was demonstrated in the discussion which showed that when market interest rates went up, bond prices adjusted downward to make up for the lower coupon rate (interest payment) on the old bonds.

Another factor affecting the cost of capital is a change in risk preferences by investors. As investors become more pessimistic about the economy, they require larger premiums for assuming risk. This desire for more returns per unit of risk causes the SML to increase its slope, as indicated in Figure 11A–4. This change in risk premiums causes $(K_{m0} - R_f)$ to increase from 11 percent minus 9 percent, a 2 percent risk premium, to $(K_{m1} - R_f)$, a 4 percent risk premium (13 percent minus 9 percent). Any asset riskier than the market would have a larger increase in the required return. In many instances rising interest rates and pessimistic investors go hand in hand, so the SML may change its slope and intercept at the same time. This combined effect would

Figure 11A–4
The security market line and changing investor expectations

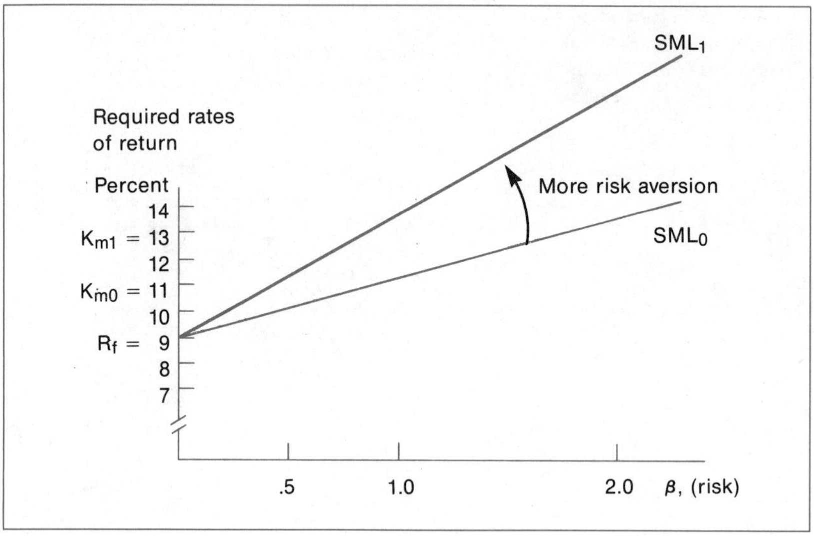

cause severe drops in the prices of risky assets and much larger required rates of return for such assets.

The capital asset pricing model and the security market line have been presented to further your understanding of market-related events that impact the firm's cost of capital, such as market returns and risk, changing interest rates, and changing risk preferences.

While the capital asset pricing model has received criticism because of the difficulties of dealing with the betas of individual securities and because of the problems involved in consistently constructing the appropriate slope of the SML to represent reality, it provides some interesting insights into risk-return measurement.

List of Terms

capital asset pricing model	**risk-free rate of interest**
security market line	**market risk premium**

Discussion Questions

11A–1. How does the capital asset pricing model help explain changing costs of capital?

11A–2. Why does K_e approximate K_j, or why does $D_1/(P_0 - g)$ approximate $R_f + \beta (K_m - R_f)$?

11A–3. How does the SML react to changes in the rate of interest, changes in the rate of inflation, and changing investor expectations?

Problems

11A–1. Assume that $R_f = 6$ percent and $K_m = 10$ percent. Compute K_j for the following betas, using Formula 11A–2.

a. 0.7
b. 1.4
c. 2.0

11A–2. In the preceding problem, an increase in interest rates increases R_f to 7.5 percent, and other factors increase K_m to 11 percent. Compute K_j for the three betas of 0.7, 1.4, and 2.0.

12 The Capital Budgeting Decision

Capital investment decisions are among the most significant a firm's management will have to make. A decision to build a new plant or expand into a foreign market may influence the performance of the firm over the next decade or more. In making these long-term commitments of a firm's resources, the management is settling the firm into a strategic direction that can often only be changed by incurring huge writedowns. A wrong decision on a large capital outlay can lead to great financial stress and even bankruptcy for a firm. Dome's $4 billion purchase of Hudson's Bay Oil and Gas, based on what turned out to be an incorrect estimate of the direction of future world oil prices, effectively crippled the firm's ability to compete and looks like it will ultimately lead to either the bankruptcy of Dome or its purchase by another company. Managers in Canada's important but cyclical pulp and paper industry are constantly faced with decisions regarding large capital investments to modernize or expand their operations. Historically, new plants in that industry have often been constructed and become operative just as the demand for forest products declined, exposing the firms to declining revenues despite the increased costs created by the new investments.

The capital budgeting decision involves the planning of expenditures for a project with a life of at least one year and usually a considerably longer period. In general, the capital expenditure decision requires extensive planning to ensure that engineering and marketing information is available, product design is completed, necessary patents are acquired, production costs are fully understood, and the capital markets are tapped for the necessary funds. Throughout this chapter we will use the techniques developed in our discussion of the time value of money to equate future cash flows to present ones. The firm's cost of capital will be used as the basic discount rate.

A major problem in analyzing capital budgeting decisions is that as the time horizon moves further into the future, decision makers become more and more uncertain about annual costs and inflows. Estimates of such items as economic conditions, customer requirements, technological change, and the development of foreign competition become more and more speculative. In Canada's resource-based industries, the need to contemplate multibillion dollar decisions with 20- and 30-year return horizons makes capital budgeting decisions particularly difficult. A good example of the difficulty in forecasting future competitive conditions can be observed in the development of the hand calculator industry in the mid-1970s. A number of firms had tooled up in the early 1970s in the hope of being first to break through the $100 price range for pocket calculators. These firms assumed that penetration of the $100 barrier would bring a large market share and high profitability. However, technological advancement, price cutting, and the appearance of Texas Instruments in the consumer market drove prices down by 60–90 percent and made the $100 pocket calculator a museum piece. Rapid Data Systems, the first entry into the under-$100 market, went into bankruptcy. Of course, not all new developments are quite so perilous, and a number of techniques, which will be treated in the next chapter, have been devised to cope with the impact of uncertainty on decision making.

In this chapter capital budgeting will be studied under the following major topical headings: administrative considerations, accounting flows versus cash flows, methods of ranking investment proposals, selection strategy, combining cash flow analysis and selection strategy, and the replacement decision. A large part of this chapter, as well, is devoted to exploring the impact of Canadian tax law and development incentives on depreciation and capital budgeting decisions.

Administrative Considerations

A good capital budgeting program requires that a number of steps be taken in the decision-making process.

1. Search and discovery of investment opportunities.
2. Collection of data.
3. Evaluation of alternatives and decision making.
4. Plan implementation.
5. Ongoing reevaluation and adjustment.

The search for new opportunities is the least emphasized, though perhaps the most important, of the five steps. Although it is outside the scope of this book to suggest procedures for developing an organization that is conducive to innovation and creative thinking, the marginal return of such an organization is likely to be high (and a high marginal return is the essence of capital budgeting).[1]

The collection of data should go beyond engineering data and market surveys. It must attempt to identify possible important events and capture the relative likelihood of their occurrence. The probabilities of increases or slumps in product demand may be evaluated from statistical analysis, while other outcomes may have to be estimated subjectively. The likely competitive reaction of other industry participants to any new investment by our firm is an important element to be considered in this analysis.

After all data have been collected and evaluated, the final decision must be made. Generally, determinations involving relatively small amounts will be made at the department or division level, while major expenditures can only be approved by top management.[2] Once a plan

[1] See, for example, H. Allan Conway and N. A. McGuinness, "Idea Generation in Technology-Based Firms," *Journal of Product Innovation Management* 4 (1986), pp. 276–91, for an investigation of the factors that influence the new product search process.

[2] The reader must realize that because of the complexity and uncertainty surrounding many of these capital budgeting decisions, the actual process of managerial review and

Figure 12–1
Capital budgeting procedures

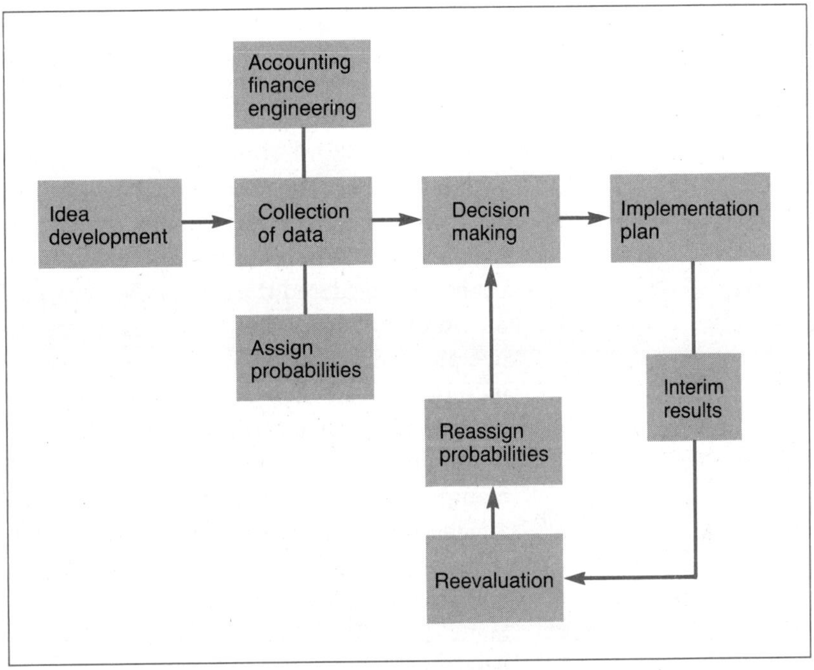

is developed and implemented a constant monitoring of the results of a given decision may indicate that a whole new set of probabilities must be developed based on actual experience. This may cause an initial decision to then be reevaluated and perhaps reversed. The preceding process is outlined in Figure 12–1.

The Notion of Incremental Cash Flows

From an analytical standpoint the task in capital budgeting is to identify the amount and timing of all *incremental* cash flows related to a possible investment and to use the discounting techniques explored

evaluation may be as important as the financial forecasts explicit in the financial analysis. Although this book will concentrate on the use of financial techniques, we refer you to Joseph L. Bower, *Managing the Resource Allocation Process* (Boston: Division of Research, Harvard Business School, 1970), for an excellent treatment of capital budgeting in the overall corporate decision-making context.

in Chapter 9 to equate those incremental cash flows to present values. By the term *incremental cash flows* we mean those cash inflows and outflows that will occur if we decide to make a given capital investment but will not occur if we decide not to make the investment. For example, if we were considering the replacement of an older machine with a new one, the cost of the new machine would be an incremental cash outflow, while any money we received on the sale of the old machine would be a capital inflow (or the net incremental investment could be considered the cost of the new machine minus the resale value of the old). If the same operator at the same wage were required to operate either machine, the machine operator's wages would not be an incremental cash flow and, therefore, would be ignored in the analysis. If, on the other hand, the new machine required a more skilled operator at a higher wage, the difference in operators' wages would be an incremental cash outflow. The identification of the incremental cash flows attached to a particular capital budgeting decision is a critical task and requires careful thought and judgment on the part of the capital budgeting analyst. Much of the rest of this chapter is devoted to considering methods of identifying the timing and amounts of incremental cash flows.

Accounting Flows versus Cash Flows

In capital budgeting decisions the emphasis is on cash flow rather than reported income. In accounting the concentration is on assigning the costs of an asset to those periods during which the asset provides economic benefit to the firm. In order to analyze a capital investment proposal, we will often have to be able to translate accounting profit figures into actual cash flows.

One of the important differences between accounting profits and the timing of cash flows relates to depreciation. Because depreciation does not represent an actual expenditure of current funds, it is added back to profit to determine the amount of cash flow generated in the current period.[3]

[3] As explained in Chapter 2, depreciation is not a new source of funds (except in tax savings) but represents a noncash expense.

Table 12–1 tries to capture the effect of adding back depreciation to the accounting profit to arrive at the actual cash flow. In that table the Alston Corporation has $50,000 of new equipment to be depreciated on a straight-line basis over 10 years ($5,000 per year). The firm has $20,000 in earnings before depreciation and taxes and is in a 50 percent tax bracket. The firm shows $7,500 in earnings after taxes. To arrive at the cash flow figure of $12,500 we add the noncash deduction of $5,000 in depreciation to the accounting profit number. An even more dramatic illustration of the difference between accounting and cash flow is provided by the situation shown in Table 12–2. That table demonstrates what would happen if the depreciation expense for Alston had been $20,000 rather than $5,000. Net earnings before and after taxes would have been zero, but the company ends the year with $20,000 more in the bank than it had at the beginning.

To the capital budgeting specialist the concentration on cash flow rather than accounting figures seems obvious. It is sometimes harder for practicing managers to consider cash flows, therefore ignoring the

Table 12–1
Cash flow for Alston Corporation

Earnings before depreciation and taxes (cash flow)	$20,000
Depreciation (noncash expense)	5,000
Earnings before taxes	15,000
Taxes (cash outflow)	7,500
Earnings after taxes	7,500
Depreciation	+5,000
Cash flow	$12,500

Alternative method of cash flow calculation

Cash inflow (EBDT)	$20,000
Cash outflow (taxes)	−7,500
Cash flow	$12,500

Table 12–2
Revised cash flow for Alston Corporation

Earnings before depreciation and taxes	$20,000
Depreciation	20,000
Earnings before taxes	0
Taxes	0
Earnings after taxes	0
Depreciation	+20,000
Cash flow	$20,000

effects that will be reported in the historical cost accounting statements. Assume, for example, you are the president of a widely held firm listed on the Toronto Stock Exchange and must select between two investment alternatives. Over the next year it is estimated that Proposal A will provide zero in after-tax earnings and $100,000 in cash flow, while Proposal B, calling for no depreciation, will provide $50,000 in both after-tax earnings and cash flow. As president of a publicly traded firm you well realize that security analysts are constantly penciling in their projections of your earnings for the next quarter, and you fear your stock may drop dramatically if earnings are lower than they project, even if by a small amount. Although a capital budgeting analysis indicates that Proposal A is a superior investment, you may be more sensitive to reported after-tax earnings than to cash flow and, therefore, select Proposal B. This type of understandable sensitivity among managers leads to periodic criticism of them for being overly concerned with the short-term impact of a decision rather than its longer-term economic benefits.

The student must be sensitive to the concessions to short-term pressures that are sometimes made by top executives. Interestingly, some observers have held that modern financial decision-making tools reinforce this tendency.[4] Nevertheless, in the material that follows, the emphasis is on the use of proper evaluation techniques aimed at identifying the best economic choice and, therefore, at providing long-term wealth maximization.

Methods of Ranking Investment Proposals

Three widely used methods for evaluating capital expenditures will be considered, along with the shortcomings and advantages of each.

1. Payback method.
2. Internal rate of return.
3. Net present value.

[4] See, for example, Robert Hayes and William Abernathy, "Managing Our Way to Economic Decline," *Harvard Business Review,* July–August 1980, pp. 67–77, for a widely read and quoted criticism of the tendency of users of modern financial decision-making techniques to become very short-term oriented.

The first method is widely used in practice in spite of the fact that it has some serious theoretical shortcomings. Approaches 2 and 3 are more comprehensive, and one or the other should be applied to most situations.

Payback Method

The payback method simply computes the time required to recoup the initial investment. To examine how it works consider a situation where we are called upon to select between Investment A and Investment B, the after-tax cash flows for which are shown in Table 12–3.

It would take two years to receive net cash inflows of $10,000, the amount of the initial investment, under Investment A. Thus, we say the payback period for Investment A is 2 years, while for Investment B it is 3.8 years. In the latter case we would recover $6,000 in the first three years, $4,000 short of the full $10,000 investment. Since the fourth year has a total inflow of $5,000, we assume we would be 80 percent of the way through the fourth year ($4,000/$5,000) before we had recovered the additional $4,000 needed to make up the original $10,000. Thus, the payback period for Investment B is computed as 3.8 years.

In using the payback method to select Investment A, two important considerations are ignored. First of all, there is no consideration of the amount of cash flow generated after the initial investment is recaptured. The $2,000 in Year 3 for Investment A is ignored, as is the $5,000 in Year 5 for Investment B. Even if the $5,000 inflow in Year 5 were $50,000, it would have no impact on the decision. Second, the method fails to consider the time value of money. If we had two possible $10,000

Table 12–3
Investment alternatives

	Net Cash Inflows (of a $10,000 investment)	
Year	Investment A	Investment B
1	$5,000	$1,500
2	5,000	2,000
3	2,000	2,500
4		5,000
5		5,000

investments with the following inflow patterns, the payback method would rank them equally.

Year	Early Returns	Late Returns
1	$9,000	$1,000
2	1,000	9,000
3	1,000	1,000

Although both investments have a payback period of two years, the first alternative is clearly superior because the $9,000 comes in the first year rather than the second.

The payback method does have some features that help to explain its use by corporate management. It is easy to understand, and it places a heavy emphasis on liquidity. A proposed project must recoup the initial investment quickly, or it will not qualify (most corporations use a maximum time horizon of three to five years). A rapid payback may be particularly important to firms in industries characterized by rapid technological developments or other sources of uncertainty. Given that some decisions may only be justifiable on the basis of cash flow estimates far in the future (and therefore relatively more uncertain), managers often opt for the decisions with the more predictable cash flow estimates.

Nevertheless, the payback method, concentrating as it does on only the initial years of investment, fails to definitively discern the optimum or most economic solution to a capital budgeting problem. The analyst is therefore required to consider the more comprehensive capital budgeting methods.

Internal Rate of Return

The internal rate of return (IRR) calls for determining the yield on an investment, that is, calculating the interest rate that equates the cash outflows (cost) of an investment with the subsequent cash inflows. The simplest case would be an investment of $100 which provides $120 after one year, or a 20 percent internal rate of return. For more complicated situations we use Appendix B (present value of a single amount) and Appendix D (present value of an annuity) and the techniques described in Chapter 9, The Time Value of Money. For example, a

$1,000 investment returning an annuity of $244 per year for five years provides an internal rate of return of 7 percent, as indicated by the following calculation and use of Appendix D.

1. First divide the investment (present value) by the annuity.

$$\frac{\text{(Investment)}}{\text{(Annuity)}} = \frac{\$1{,}000}{\$244} = 4.1\ (IF_{pva})$$

2. Then proceed to Appendix D (present value of an annuity). The factor of 4.1 for five years indicates a yield of 7 percent.

Whenever an annuity is being evaluated, annuity interest factors (IF_{pva}) can be used to find the final IRR solution. If an uneven cash inflow is involved, we are not so lucky. We need to use a trial-and-error method. The first questions are: Where do we start? What interest rate should we pick for our first trial? Assume we are once again called upon to evaluate the two investment alternatives in Table 12–3, only this time using the internal rate of return to rank the two projects. Because neither proposal represents a precise annuity stream, we must use the trial-and-error approach to determine an answer. We begin with Investment A, a new drill press that qualifies for a 20 percent capital cost allowance (CCA) rate for income tax allowable depreciation. Capital cost allowance will be discussed in detail later in the chapter where the calculation of the tax allowable depreciation for this machine is calculated in Table 12–9. The relevant tax rate is 40 percent. Note that the net cash flow increment is calculated by adding back depreciation to the before-tax cash savings while subtracting any additional taxes incurred because of increased earnings.

Net Operating Cash Flows
(on a $10,000 net capital outlay)

Investment A

Year	*(1) Increased Revenue*	*(2) Increase in CCA*	*(3) Increased Taxable Income*	*(4) Increased Taxes (@40%)*	*(5) Increased Cash Flow (1) − (4) + (2)*
1. . .	$6,000	$1,000	$5,000	$2,000	$5,000
2. . .	4,133	1,800	2,333	933	5,000
3. . .	(27)	1,440	(1,467)	(587)	2,000

1. In order to find a beginning value to start our first trial, average the inflows as if we were really getting an annuity.

$$\begin{array}{r} \$5{,}000 \\ 5{,}000 \\ \underline{2{,}000} \\ \$12{,}000/3 = \$4{,}000 \end{array}$$

2. Then divide the investment by the "assumed" annuity value in Step 1.

$$\frac{\text{(Investment)}}{\text{(Annuity)}} = \frac{\$10{,}000}{\$4{,}000} = 2.5\ (IF_{pva})$$

3. Proceed to Appendix D to arrive at a *first approximation* of the internal rate of return, using:

$$IF_{pva}\ \text{factor} = 2.5$$
$$n\text{(period)} = 3$$

The factor falls between 9 and 10 percent. This is only a first approximation—our actual answer will be closer to 10 percent or higher because our method of average cash flows theoretically moved receipts from the first two years into the last year. This averaging understates the actual internal rate of return. The same method would overstate the IRR for Investment B because it would move cash from the last two years into the first three years. Since we know that cash flows in the early years are worth more and increase our return, we can usually gauge whether our first approximation is overstated or understated.

4. Next, enter into a trial-and-error process to arrive at an answer. Because these cash flows are uneven rather than an annuity, we need to use Appendix B. We will begin with 10 percent and then try 12 percent.

Year	*10 Percent*
1	\$5,000 × 0.909 = \$ 4,545
2	5,000 × 0.826 = 4,130
3	2,000 × 0.751 = 1,502
	\$10,177

At 10 percent, the present value of the inflows exceeds \$10,000—we therefore use a higher discount rate.

Year	*12 Percent*
1	\$5,000 × 0.893 = \$4,465
2	5,000 × 0.797 = 3,985
3	2,000 × 0.712 = 1,424
	\$9,874

At 12 percent, the present value of the inflows is less than \$10,000—thus, the discount rate is too high.

The answer must fall between 10 percent and 12 percent, indicating an approximate answer of 11 percent.

If we want to be more accurate, the results can be *interpolated*. Because the internal rate of return is determined when the present value of the inflows (PV_I) equals the present value of the outflows (PV_O), we need to find a discount rate that equates the PV_I to the cost of $10,000 ($PV_O$). The total difference in present values between 10 percent and 12 percent is $303.

$10,177	PV_I @10%	$10,177	PV_I @10%
9,874	PV_I @12%	10,000	(cost)
$ 303		$ 177	

The solution at 10 percent is $177 away from $10,000. Actually the solution is ($177/$303) percent of the way between 10 and 12 percent. Since there is a 2 percent difference between the two rates used to evaluate the cash inflows, we need to multiply the fraction by 2 percent and then add our answer to 10 percent for the final answer of:

$$10\% + (\$177/\$303)\ (2\%) = 11.17\%\ \text{IRR}$$

For Investment B the same process will yield an answer of 14.33 percent (you may wish to confirm this).

Investment B

Year	Increased Revenue	+	Increased CCA	−	Increased Taxes (@40%)	=	Increased Cash Flow
1	$ 167		$1,000		$(333)		$1,500
2	(867)		1,800		(1,067)		2,000
3	807		1,440		(253)		2,500
4	5,645		1,152		1,797		5,000
5	6,182		922		2,105		5,000

The use of the internal rate of return calls for the prudent selection of Investment B in preference to Investment A, the exact opposite of the conclusion reached under the payback method.

	Investment A	Investment B	Selection
Payback method.	2 years	3.8 years	Quickest payback: Investment A
Internal rate of return . . .	11.17%	14.33%	Highest yield: Investment B

The final selection of any project under the internal-rate-of-return method will also depend upon the yield exceeding some minimum cost standard, usually based on the cost of capital to the firm.

Under Canada's tax system depreciation for tax purposes on many capital items is calculated on a declining-balance method. If this applies to the investment in question, the calculation of internal rate of return becomes more complicated because the value of the depreciation shield may continue at ever diminishing amounts well past the economic life of the asset. For simplicity we have ignored the value of tax savings past Year 3 for Investment A and Year 5 for Investment B. Since there are leftover tax savings in these examples, however, the true internal rates of return are higher than those calculated. The handling of declining-balance depreciation tax shields in capital budgeting decision making is discussed later in this chapter.

Net Present Value

The final method of investment selection is to determine the net present value of an investment. This is done by discounting the inflows over the life of the investment to determine whether they equal or exceed the required investment. The basic discount rate is usually the cost of capital to the firm. If we once again evaluate Investments A and B—using an assumed cost of capital or a discount rate of 10 percent—we arrive at the following figures for net present value:

$10,000 Investment, 10-Percent Discount Rate

Year	Investment A		Year	Investment B	
1	$5,000 × 0.909 =	$ 4,545	1	$1,500 × 0.909 =	$ 1,364
2	5,000 × 0.826 =	4,130	2	2,000 × 0.826 =	1,652
3	2,000 × 0.751 =	1,502	3	2,500 × 0.751 =	1,878
		$10,177	4	5,000 × 0.683 =	3,415
			5	5,000 × 0.621 =	3,105
					$11,414
Present value of inflows		$10,177	Present value of inflows		$11,414
Present value of outflows . . .		10,000	Present value of outflows . . .		10,000
Net present value		$ 177	Net present value		$ 1,414

While both proposals appear to be acceptable, Investment B has a considerably higher net present value than Investment A.[5] Under most circumstances the net present value and internal rate of return methods give theoretically correct answers, and the subsequent discussion will be restricted to these two approaches. A summary of the various conclusions reached under the three methods is presented in Table 12–4.

Selection Strategy

In both the internal rate of return and net present value methods the profitability must equal or exceed the cost of capital for the project to be potentially acceptable. However, other distinctions are necessary—namely, whether the projects are *mutually exclusive or not*. If investments are mutually exclusive the selection of one alternative will preclude the selection of any other alternative. Assume we are going to build a specialized assembly plant in Central Canada, and four cities are under consideration, only one of which will be picked. In this situation we select the alternative with the highest acceptable yield or the highest net present value and disregard all others. Even if certain locations provide a marginal return in excess of the cost of capital, they

Table 12–4
Capital budgeting results

	Investment A	*Investment B*	*Selection*
Payback method	2 years	3.8 years	Quickest payout: Investment A
Internal rate of return . . .	11.17%	14.33%	Highest yield: Investment B
Net present value	$177	$1.414	Highest net present value: Investment B

[5] A further possible calculation under the net present value method is the profitability index.

$$\text{Profitability index} = \frac{\text{Present value of the inflows}}{\text{Present value of the outflows}}$$

For Investment A the profitability index is 1.0177 ($10,177/$10,000), and for Investment B it is 1.1414 ($11,414/$10,000). The profitability index is used to place returns from different size investments onto a common measuring standard.

may be rejected. In the table below, the possible alternatives are presented.

Mutually exclusive alternatives	*IRR*	*Net Present Value (thousands)*
Oakville	15%	$300
Sarnia	12	200
Ottawa	11	100
Cost of capital	**10**	—
Windsor	9	(100)

Among the mutually exclusive alternatives, only Oakville would be selected. Of course, if the alternatives were not mutually exclusive (for example, much-needed multiple retail outlets), we would accept all of the alternatives that provided a return in excess of our cost of capital. Only Windsor would then be rejected.

Applying this logic to Investments A and B in the prior discussion and assuming a cost of capital of 10 percent, only Investment B would be accepted if the alternatives were mutually exclusive, while both would clearly qualify if they were not mutually exclusive.

	Investment A	*Investment B*	*Accepted if Mutually Exclusive*	*Accepted if Not Mutually Exclusive*
Internal rate of return	11.17%	14.33%	B	A, B
Net present value	$177	$1,414	B	A, B

The discussion to this point has assumed that the internal rate of return and net present value methods will call for the same decision. Although this is generally true, there are exceptions. Two rules may be stated:

1. Both methods will accept or reject the same investments based on minimum return or cost of capital criteria. If an investment has a positive net present value, it will also have a yield in excess of the cost of capital.
2. In certain limited cases, however, the two methods may give different answers in selecting the best investment from a range of acceptable alternatives.

Reinvestment Assumption

It is only under this second set of events that a preference for one method over the other must be established. A prime characteristic of the internal rate of return is the assumption that all inflows can be reinvested at the same yield as that generated by the investment being analyzed. For example, in the case of the aforementioned Investment A yielding 11.17 percent, the assumption is made that the dollar amounts coming in each year can, in fact, be reinvested at that rate. For Investment B, with a 14.33 percent internal rate of return, the new funds are assumed to be reinvested at this high rate. The relationships are presented in Table 12–5.

For investments with a very high IRR it may be unrealistic to assume that reinvestment can take place at an equally high rate. The net present value method, depicted in Table 12–6, makes the more conservative assumption that each inflow can be reinvested at the cost of capital or discount rate.

The reinvestment assumption under the net present value method allows for a measure of consistency. Inflows from each project are

Table 12–5
The reinvestment assumption—internal rate of return ($10,000 investment)

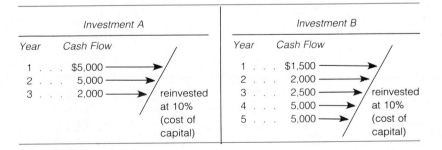

Investment A (11.17% IRR)			*Investment B (14.33% IRR)*		
Year	*Cash Flow*		*Year*	*Cash Flow*	
1 . . .	$5,000 →		1 . . .	$1,500 →	
2 . . .	5,000 →		2 . . .	2,000 →	
3 . . .	2,000 →	reinvested at 11.17%	3 . . .	2,500 →	reinvested at 14.33%
			4 . . .	5,000 →	
			5 . . .	5,000 →	

Table 12–6
The reinvestment assumption—net present value ($10,000 investment)

Investment A			*Investment B*		
Year	*Cash Flow*		*Year*	*Cash Flow*	
1 . . .	$5,000 →		1 . . .	$1,500 →	
2 . . .	5,000 →		2 . . .	2,000 →	
3 . . .	2,000 →	reinvested at 10% (cost of capital)	3 . . .	2,500 →	reinvested at 10% (cost of capital)
			4 . . .	5,000 →	
			5 . . .	5,000 →	

assumed to have the same investment opportunity yielding a return equal to the firm's cost of capital.

Capital Rationing

At times management may place a dollar constraint on the amount of funds that can be invested in a given period. The executive planning committee may emerge from a lengthy capital budgeting session to announce that only $5 million may be spent on new capital projects this year. Although $5 million may represent a large sum, it is still an artificially determined constraint and not the product of marginal analysis in which all projects with positive net present values are accepted.

Perhaps a management team may adopt a posture of capital rationing because it fears the risks attached to rapid growth strategies or because it is hesitant to use external sources of financing. However, in a purely theoretical sense, capital rationing hinders a firm from maximizing value. With capital rationing as indicated in Table 12–7, acceptable projects must be ranked, and only those with the highest positive net present value are accepted. Under capital rationing only Projects A through C, calling for $5 million in investment, will be accepted. Although Projects D and E have returns exceeding the cost of funds, as evidenced by a positive net present value, they will not be accepted under capital rationing.

Why, then, would experienced managers impose a capital constraint? Besides the periodic reluctance to go to external sources for funding, many times the reason probably derives from one of two other sources.

In some cases the concern is with how many new projects the current management team can oversee at one time. In other words, the con-

Table 12–7
Capital rationing

	Project	Investment	Total Investment	Net Present Value
Capital rationing solution	A	$2,000,000		$400,000
	B	2,000,000		380,000
→	C	1,000,000	$5,000,000	150,000
	D	1,000,000		100,000
Best solution →	E	800,000	6,800,000	40,000
	F	800,000		(30,000)

straint being imposed is actually one related to available management talent even though it is presented as a restriction on the amount of capital available. Thus, although the projects might look good under the assumption that their implementation will be supervised by experienced company managers, they are less attractive if additional new managers must be employed. Another case relates to industries where the experience with forecasting future demand has been so unsuccessful that management deliberately funds new projects in relation to cash near at hand. This has often been the situation with Canada's forest products industry, which accounts for 1 in 10 jobs in the country. This latter form of capital rationing is really a qualitative way of dealing with high levels of uncertainty.

Net Present Value Profile

An interesting way to summarize the characteristics of an investment is through the use of the net present value profile. The profile allows us to graphically portray the net present value of a project at different discount rates. Let's apply the profile to the investments we have been discussing. The projects are summarized again below.

After-Tax Cash Inflows
(of a $10,000 investment)

Year	*Investment A*	*Investment B*
1	$5,000	$1,500
2	5,000	2,000
3	2,000	2,500
4		5,000
5		5,000

To apply the net present value profile you need to know *three* characteristics about an investment:

1. *The net present value at a zero discount rate.* Actually, that is easy to determine. With no discount rate, the present values and future values are the same. For Investment A the net present value would be $2,000 ($5,000 + $5,000 + $2,000 − $10,000). For Investment B the answer is $6,000 ($1,500 + $2,000 + $2,500 + $5,000 + $5,000 − $10,000).

2. *The net present value as determined by a normal discount rate* (such as the cost of capital). For these two investments we used a discount rate of 10 percent. As summarized in Table 12–4, the net present values for the two investments at that discount rate were $177 for Investment A and $1,414 for Investment B.
3. *The internal rate of return for the investments.* Once again referring to Table 12–4 we see the internal rate of return is 11.17 percent for Investment A and 14.33 percent for Investment B. The reader should also realize that the internal rate of return is the discount rate that allows the project to have a net present value of zero. This characteristic will become more important when we present our graphic display.

We summarize the information about discount rates and net present values for each investment here and, graphically, in Figure 12–2.

Investment A

Discount Rate	*Net Present Value*
0	$2,000
10%	177
11.17%(IRR)	0

Investment B

Discount Rate	*Net Present Value*
0	$6,000
10%	1,414
14.33%(IRR)	0

Note that in Figure 12–2 we have graphed the three points for each investment. For example, for Investment A we showed a $2,000 net present value at a zero discount rate, a $177 net present value at a 10 percent discount rate, and a zero net present value at an 11.17 percent discount rate. We then connected the points. The same procedure was applied to Investment B. The reader can also visually approximate what the net present value for the investment projects would be at other discount rates (such as 5 percent).

In the above example the net present value of Investment B was superior to Investment A at every point. This is not always the case

Figure 12–2
Net present value profile

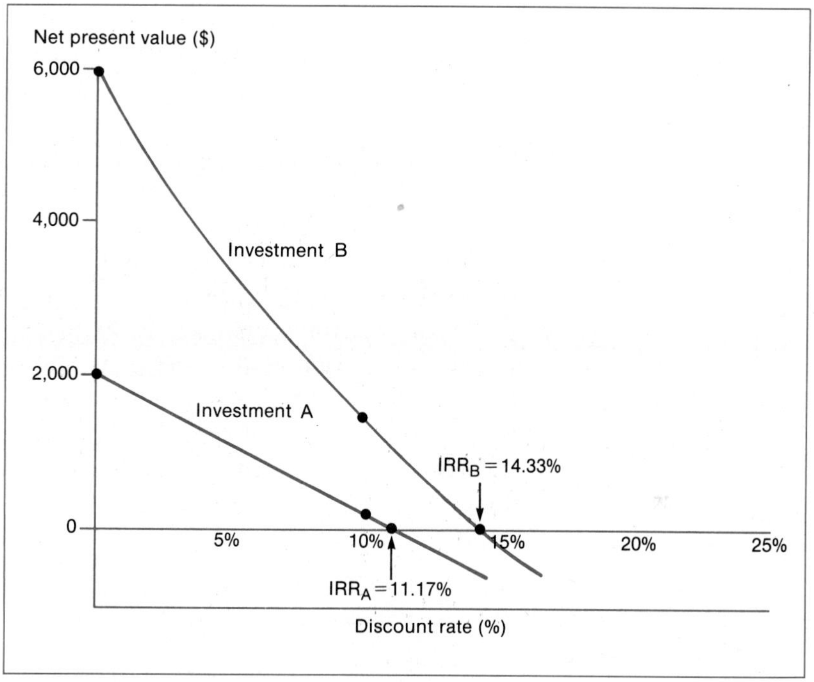

in comparing projects. To illustrate, let's introduce a new project, Investment C, and then compare it with Investment B.

Characteristics of Investment C

Investment C
($10,000 investment)

Year	*After-Tax Cash Inflows*
1	$9,000
2	3,000
3	1,200

1. The net present value at a zero discount rate for this project is $3,200 ($9,000 + 3,000 + 1,200 − 10,000).
2. The net present value at a 10 percent discount rate is $1,560.
3. The internal rate of return is 22.51 percent.

You could compute these values for yourself, but that is really not necessary at this point.

Comparing Investment B to Investment C in Figure 12–3, we observe that at low discount rates, Investment B has a higher net present value than Investment C. However, at high discount rates, Investment C has a higher net present value than Investment B. The actual crossover point is at approximately 8.7 percent. That is to say, if you had to choose between Investment B and Investment C, your answer would be dependent on the discount rate. At low rates (below 8.7 percent) you would opt for Investment B. At higher rates (above 8.7 percent) you would select Investment C. Since the cost of capital is presumed to be 10 percent, you would probably prefer Investment C (remember, though, that the cost of capital can change).

Why does Investment B do well compared to Investment C at low discount rates and relatively poorly compared to Investment C at high

Figure 12–3
Net present value profile with crossover

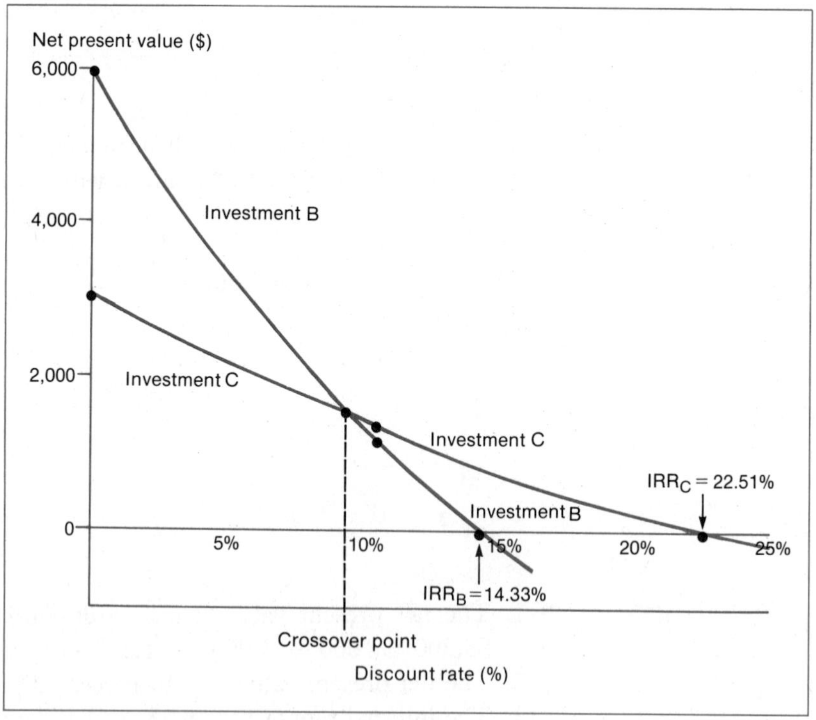

discount rates? This difference is related to the timing of inflows. Let's examine the inflows.

	Cash Inflows (of a $10,000 investment)	
Year	Investment B	Investment C
1	$1,500	$9,000
2	2,000	3,000
3	2,500	1,200
4	5,000	
5	5,000	

Investment B has heavy late inflows ($5,000 in both the fourth and fifth years), and these are more strongly penalized by high discount rates. Investment C has extremely high early inflows that are less affected by high discount rates than are later flows.

As previously mentioned in the chapter, if the investments are not mutually exclusive and capital is not being rationed, we would probably accept both Investment B and Investment C at discount rates below 14.33 percent. Below that discount rate they both have positive net present values. On the other hand, if we can select only one, the decision may well turn on the choice of a discount rate. Observe in Figure 12–3 that at a discount rate of 5 percent, we would select Investment B, at 10 percent we would select Investment C, and so on. The net present value profile helps us make such decisions.

Capital Cost Allowance

In order to analyze the anticipated cash flow patterns under any investment proposal we will have to know how to take into account the effects of tax-allowable depreciation on our cash flow estimates. Although financial accounting entries for depreciation have no cash flow effects, tax-allowable depreciation expenses do. The Income Tax Act of Canada lays out a system of allocating depreciation that reduces the tax payable for profitable firms and therefore is important in estimating the cash flow effects of proposed project investments.

Depreciation was originally authorized under the Income War Tax Act of 1917, which made it tax deductible on any straight-line basis acceptable to the minister. During World War II, accelerated depreciation was introduced to encourage expansion of wartime production capacity. Virtually every federal budget in recent years has included measures implementing new government policy directions through amendments to the system of capital cost allowances.

For tax-deductible depreciation purposes, assets are divided into a number of classes, each of which is assigned a depreciation rate. All the assets of a given class form what is called an asset pool. Unfortunately for those of us trying to calculate the tax shield resulting from depreciation expense, most of the asset classes call for declining-balance depreciation methods as a result of the new income tax act implemented in 1949. A sampling of depreciation classes (subject to the declining-balance rule), their accompanying depreciation rates, and some of the items that might be assigned to a particular class are included in Table 12–8.

The amount of depreciation allowable under the tax act is called *Capital Cost Allowance (CCA)*. Of the CCA classes, some of the larger amounts involving capital investment projects often fall under Class 3 (buildings) and Class 8 (machinery). Table 12–9 calculates the CCA for the assets (drill presses, Class 8) involved in Investments A and B considered earlier in this chapter.

Note that any increases in a pool are eligible for only half the normal CCA in the year of addition. Under the *half-rate rule,* introduced in November 1981, only half the normal CCA for most assets is allowed as a tax-deductible expense in the year of acquisition. This rule does

Table 12–8
Declining-balance tax depreciation classes

Class	*Rate*	*Assets*
Class 3	5%	Buildings, windmills, telegraph poles
Class 5	10	Pulp and paper mills
Class 7	15	Boats, ships
Class 8	20	Most machinery, radio communications equipment
Class 9	25	Aircraft
Class 10	30	Automobile equipment, computer hardware
Class 11	35	Billboards
Class 12	100	Dishes, motion picture films, computer software
Class 16	40	Taxicabs, autos for short-term rental
Class 30	40	Unmanned telecommunications spacecraft
Class 33	15	Timber resource property

Table 12–9
Capital cost allowance for Investment A or B

Year 1:	
Net original cost	$10,000
Less: Capital cost allowance ½($10,000 × .20)	1,000
Undepreciated capital cost*	$ 9,000
Year 2:	
Less: Capital cost allowance ($9,000 × .20)	1,800
Undepreciated capital cost	$ 7,200
Year 3:	
Less: Capital cost allowance ($7,200 × .20)	1,440
Undepreciated capital cost	$ 5,760
Year 4:	
Less: Capital cost allowance ($5,760 × .20)	1,152
Undepreciated capital cost	$ 4,608
Year *n*:	
Undepreciated capital cost (for year $n - 1$)	
Less: Capital cost allowance (UCC in year $n - 1 \times .20$)	
Equals: Undepreciated capital cost (for year *n*)	

*UCC for short.

not apply to most Class 12 assets, normally written off 100 percent in the first year. Property in Classes 14 and 15 (see Table 12–11) is also exempt from the half-rate rule because of the depletion nature of those allowances.

Once an asset has been assigned to a given CCA pool, depreciation is calculated on the undepreciated capital cost (UCC) of the pool of assets rather than on a single individual asset. What we have calculated above is the maximum CCA a firm can deduct for a given year. Of course, there may be circumstances where a firm would want to claim less than the maximum allowable CCA. For example, if the firm were in a loss situation and expected to be for many years hence, it might decide that taking the maximum CCA allowable might only reduce the tax shield available in the future while there is no income to shield from tax presently.[6]

[6] Up until 1982 a firm could carry losses forward for five years or back one to apply them against taxable income. For losses incurred in 1983 or later, the carryover rule is forward seven or back three years. Thus, the consideration to delay or not to delay CCA expenses is not a straightforward one although the later rule makes delay a less likely choice.

Addition and Disposal of Assets

When an asset is purchased its purchase price is added to the pool. When an asset is sold, on the other hand, the lower of the sale price or its original cost is deducted. If an asset is sold for more than its original cost, the difference is treated as a capital gain for tax purposes.

Assume Firm XYZ chose to buy the drill press (Press A) under Investment A in Year 1 and then also bought the press (Press B) under Investment B in Year 2. Assume also these are the only assets in Class 8. The undepreciated capital cost balance for Class 8 assets at the end of Year 3 would then be $12,960 (from Table 12–9 we see it would include $5,760 from A and $7,200 from B).

Suppose that in Year 4 XYZ sells both of the drill presses in Class 8 after which no assets remain in that pool. The liquidation of the pool could give rise to a number of different tax effects depending upon the amounts for which the assets were sold. (See Table 12–10.)

Under Outcome 1 the pool has a leftover balance of $2,960 as the resale value of the assets declined more quickly than allowed for under the CCA schedule. That leftover balance is termed a *terminal loss* and is tax deductible in Year 4. Under Outcome 2 the amount realized on the sale of the assets is exactly equal to the previous UCC, and the pool balance is zero, leaving no need for further adjustment. In Outcome 3 the sale price exceeds the UCC. More depreciation was deducted than the difference between the purchase and resale prices. The $2,040 is added to revenue in Year 4 and termed *depreciation recapture*. Outcome 4 generates both a capital gain of $2,000 on the resale of A and depreciation recapture of $4,240 to eliminate the negative balance that would still be left in the pool after accounting for the capital gain.

Table 12–10
Liquidation of asset pool

	Outcome 1	*Outcome 2*	*Outcome 3*	*Outcome 4*
Year 3:				
UCC	$12,960	$12,960	$12,960	$12,960
Year 4:				
Sale price—A	5,000	7,000	7,500	12,000
Sale price—B	5,000	5,960	7,500	7,200
Balance in pool	$ 2,960	$ 0	$(2,040)	$(4,240)

Table 12–11
Straight-line CCA classes

Class 13	Certain leasehold improvements (to be depreciated over the life of the lease)
Class 14	Certain patents, franchises, or licenses for a limited period (to be depreciated over the life of the asset)
Class 15	Woods assets (depreciated depending on the amount cut in the year)
Class 20	Class 3 or 6 buildings included in a development project approved under the Area Development Incentives Act (20 percent CCA rate)
Class 24	Water pollution control equipment
Class 27	Air pollution equipment
Class 29	Certain machinery and equipment
Class 34	Certain electrical generating equipment

Straight-Line CCA Classes

Some classes of capital items are not subject to rules of declining balance but, rather, may be depreciated for tax purposes on a straight-line basis. Table 12–11 lists some examples of classes subject to straight-line CCA.[7]

Investment Tax Credit

The current investment tax credit (ITC) was originally a temporary measure that provided a 5 percent tax credit with respect to qualified buildings or equipment acquired between June 23, 1975, and June 30, 1976. Since that time various governments have added qualified scientific research expenditures, qualified transportation equipment, and certified property to the list of assets that qualify for the investment tax credit. Besides being used to encourage expansion of the types of businesses favored by government policymakers, the investment tax credit has been used to encourage investment in certain geographical regions. Investment tax credits available in the mid-1980s included:

[7] Classes 24, 27, 29, and 34 are subject to a 50 percent CCA rate. The net effect of the half-rate rule is to make the effective depreciation schedule for these classes 25 percent, 50 percent, and 25 percent over the three-year period it will take to fully depreciate the asset. One of the tax changes being considered by Finance Minister Michael Wilson for introduction in mid-1988 would lengthen the time it takes to write off asset purchases in these accelerated depreciation classes.

Qualified property for use in:	
Gaspe/Atlantic Provinces	20%
Other designated regions in Canada	10
Elsewhere in Canada	7
Qualified scientific research expenditures:	
By CCPC* eligible for small business deduction	35
In Gaspe/Atlantic Provinces	30
In other designated areas of Canada	20
Elsewhere in Canada	20
Qualified transportation equipment	7
Certified property for use in manufacturing, processing in selected incentive areas	50
Qualified construction equipment	7
Certain approved projects on Cape Breton Island	50

*Canadian-controlled private corporation.

Unlike the CCA tax shield, investment tax credits represent direct dollar givebacks irrespective of whether or not the firm is taxable. In the case of a new $100,000 machine (Class 8) bought by a profitable firm, the first-year cash flow effect generated by tax savings would be the tax shield or

$$\tfrac{1}{2}\,(20\% \times \$100{,}000 \times \text{tax rate})$$

For a firm whose tax rate is 46 percent that becomes $4,600. On the other hand, if that machine were bought to be used for scientific research purposes in Southern Ontario, it would qualify for a 20 percent investment tax credit which would result in a $20,000 tax reduction no matter what the tax rate. Remember, though, the receipt of an investment tax credit reduces the amount available for capital cost allowance. In the second case the $20,000 tax credit would mean that a net amount of only $80,000 would be added to the CCA pool instead of the machine's total cost of $100,000. This would reduce the first-year tax shield from CCA to $3,680. Along with the $20,000 tax credit that makes the maximum possible tax-related cash flow effect $23,680 versus $4,600 for equipment not qualifying for the ITC.

Combining Cash Flow Analysis and Selection Strategy

To explore how the system affects the project cash flow, consider a situation where a firm is deciding whether to add two new vehicles to its fleet of delivery vans. By referring to Table 12–8 above we see that these vehicles would be placed in the CCA Class 10 asset pool which carries a 30 percent CCA rate. Consider also that since the Class 10 pool had a balance of $52,000 coming into the current year, these vans would be purchased for $30,000, and no other assets will be added to the pool in the current year. The sale of an old pickup for $500 is the only other transaction expected to cause an adjustment to the balance in the asset pool. The undepreciated capital cost of the pool would thus become $81,500 ($52,000 + $30,000 − $500) if the vans were purchased.

Beginning UCC	$52,000
Additions to the pool	30,000
Dispositions from the pool	500
Undepreciated capital cost	$81,500

In the current year the maximum allowable CCA in respect to automobile equipment would be

[Beginning UCC + ½(Additions − Dispositions)] × CCA rate

If the vans are purchased, the balance in the Class 10 asset pool will increase by $30,000. Table 12–12 demonstrates the change in the de-

Table 12–12
Tax allowed depreciation expense for vans

Year	Beginning UCC Effect	CCA Calculation	Change in CCA Available
1988	$30,000	½($30,000 × .30)	$4,500
1989	25,500	$25,500 × .30	7,650
1990	17,850	17,850 × .30	5,355
1991	12,495	12,495 × .30	3,749
1992	8,746	8,746 × .30	2,624
.	.	.	.
.	.	.	.

preciation tax shield available in the first few years that will result if the vans are purchased.

In other words, after Year 1 we have created a steadily declining balance in perpetuity. For the investment decision analysis, we need to calculate the present value of the CCA tax shield. Given how the CCA system operates, we must provide the present value of a perpetual CCA tax shield. The general formula to account for the tax shield effect can be developed[8] then as

$$\frac{CdT_c}{r + d}$$

where

C = Capital cost of an acquired asset
d = CCA rate for the asset class
T_c = Corporate tax rate
r = Discount rate

In adjusting this formula for the half-rate rule, we obtain

$$\frac{CdT_c}{r + d} \times \frac{1 + .5r}{1 + r}$$

One further complication to the present value calculation must be included to make it complete. In the normal course of events we would expect at some time in the future to resell those two vans. Additionally, we would expect to have other values still in the Class 10 CCA pool. Therefore, we would realize a cash inflow on the sale of the vans but lose the CCA tax shield associated with that value in future years. This causes a need to adjust the CCA tax shield formula as follows to take into account the estimated timing and amount of the salvage value:

---

[8] The development is exactly the same as for the dividend growth model derived in Chapter 10. The major conceptual difference is only that g (growth rate) is negative. Thus, we have

$$PV = \frac{C_1}{1 + r} + \frac{C_1(1 - d)}{(1 + r)^2} + \frac{C_2(1 - d)^2}{(1 + r)^3} + \ldots$$
$$= \frac{C_1}{r - (-d)}$$

$$PV \text{ of CCA tax shield} = \left[\frac{CdT_c}{r+d} - \left(\frac{SdT_c}{r+d} \times \frac{1}{(1+r)^n}\right)\right] \times \frac{1+.5r}{1+r} \qquad (12\text{–}1)$$

where

$S =$ Salvage value
$n =$ Number of years in the future we intend to sell off the assets.

Since $C_1 = CdT_c$, we get

$$PV = \frac{CdT_c}{r+d}$$

Therefore, if in the case of the proposed van purchases we expected to sell them after four years usage at an estimated value of $2,000 each, and if the company's estimated cost of capital was 12 percent, the present value of the depreciation tax shield from the vans would be:

$$PV = \left[\frac{\$30{,}000 \times .30 \times .46}{.12 + .30} - \left(\frac{\$4{,}000 \times .30 \times .46}{.12 + .30} \times \frac{1}{(1+.12)^4}\right)\right] \times \frac{1+.5(.12)}{1+.12}$$

$$= [\$9{,}857 - (\$1{,}314 \times .636)]\,[.9464]$$
$$= \$8{,}537$$

What remains to be done to decide whether or not to buy the vans? That decision will rest on whether the estimated increase in future cash flows resulting from the purchase and use of the vans in the business more than offsets their initial cost. This means we will next have to estimate the incremental cash flow effects (in addition to the depreciation effect). Say, for example, we estimate the new vans will allow the business to generate $33,000 per year in extra sales and those extra sales will also require $16,000 per year in extra operating costs. The present value of the incremental operating cash flows would be as shown in Table 12–13.

To determine the advisability of buying the vans we must now compare the present value of the incremental cash flows against the capital outlay. (See Table 12–14.)

Thus, on the basis of this financial analysis the investment in the vans will clearly create value. It may be, however, that there are other effects of this decision that have not been quantified or are very difficult

Table 12–13
Present value of incremental cash flows

Year	Cash Flow	(1 − t)	×	PV Factor (12%)	=	Present Value
1	$17,000	(.54)	×	0.893	=	$ 8,198
2	17,000	(.54)	×	0.797	=	7,316
3	17,000	(.54)	×	0.712	=	6,536
4	17,000	(.54)	×	0.636	=	5,838
Present value of operating increases						$27,888
Present value of salvage ($4000 × .636)						2,544
Present value of depreciation tax shield						8,537
Present value of incremental cash flows						$38,969

Table 12–14
Net present value van purchase decision

Present value of incremental cash flows	$38,969
− Initial investment	30,000
Net present value	$ 8,969

to quantify. For example, the addition of the two vans may implicitly reduce the amount of time a supervisor spends on his or her present duties. Management should then factor in any additional overall company effects against the favorable result of the information already included.

IRR and Capital Cost Allowance

In our drill press examples earlier in the chapter we omitted the tax savings on CCA charged in the years after the drill presses were no longer to be used. We also omitted any consideration of salvage value on the resale of those presses. We will now calculate the effect of the inclusion of those items on the internal rate of return.

Recall for Investment A the net capital outlay for the press was $10,000, and the new press was expected to result in annual pretax cash savings of $3,667, $4,600, and $337, respectively, over three years. Taking into account the tax rate of 40 percent and the maximum CCA available in each of the three years the press would be in operation, we calculated an internal rate of return of 11.17 percent.

If we estimated that the press would be sold at the end of Year 3 for $1,000 with other assets still left in the Class 8 pool, there would then be an additional inflow of $1,000 cash for Year 3 of our analysis plus some ongoing tax-shield effects in later years, shown as follows:

Net Operating Cash Flows
on Investment A

Year		Increased Cash Flow
1	. . . .	$3,667
2	. . . .	4,600
3	. . . .	1,337
1–∞	. . . .	Tax savings on CCA

Using trial and error as the basis of finding the appropriate discount rate and Formula 12–1 for the calculation of the present value of the CCA tax shield, we would find that the internal rate of return on the investment comes out to be 12.47 percent. Thus, the inclusion of salvage value and the ongoing CCA tax benefit has a major impact on this investment decision.

The Replacement Decision

Our discussion of capital budgeting thus far has centered on projects being considered as net additions to the present plant and equipment. Many capital budgeting decisions are made, however, because of the availability of new machinery to replace older models. Such decisions are referred to as replacement decisions. For example, plant engineers are constantly faced with the need to determine if a new machine incorporating the latest in technology can do a job more efficiently than the one currently used.

These replacement decisions bring additional considerations to the capital budgeting problem. For example, the sale of the old machine must be included in the analysis. This sale will produce a cash inflow that partially offsets the purchase price of the new machine. In Canada, unlike in the United States, the sale of the old machinery will generally not have any tax consequences that will require special handling. In the unlikely case it is sold for more than its original purchase price, there will, however, need to be an allowance made for capital gains tax payable.

The replacement decision can be analyzed by using a total analysis of both the old and the new machine or by using an incremental analysis. We will use the incremental approach which emphasizes the changes in cash flow between using the old and the new machine.

Consider the situation in which the Dalton Corporation purchased a computer two years ago for $100,000. The asset is included under CCA Class 10 (30 percent rate). It can currently be sold in the market for $40,000. A new replacement computer would cost $150,000 and would also become a Class 10 asset. A 10 percent investment tax credit would be available on the new computer.

The estimated cost savings and other benefits attributable to installing the new computer are between $20,000 and $45,000 per year for each of the next five years. This would show up as a net increase in earnings before depreciation and taxes. The estimate is that at the end of that period, either of the old or the new computers would be replaced. At that time it is estimated the new computer under consideration could be sold for only $30,000 while the old computer would have no salvage value. The firm is in a 46 percent tax bracket and has a 12 percent cost of capital.

As the first step we have to determine the net additional cost of the new computer. The purchase price of $150,000 is partially offset by the investment tax credit and by the cash inflow from the sale of the old computer (see Table 12–15).

The effect of the lost tax shield attached to the old computer need not be taken into account here as there will be tax calculations related to the sale. That is in spite of the fact the depreciation taken thus far on the computer would have been less than the difference between its purchase price and the realization on its sale. Instead, it is handled by the fact that we will consider the net change in the Class 10 UCC balance rather than the salvage value and new purchase effects separately.

The basic capital budgeting question in this circumstance becomes, then: *Are the anticipated incremental gains from the replacement of the old computer by the new large enough to justify the net cost of $95,000?*

The answer to that question will depend on a cash flow analysis of (1) the incremental increase in depreciation and the related tax shield benefits and (2) the operating benefits.

Table 12–15
Net price of the new computer

Price of the new computer	$150,000
− Investment tax credit (10%)	15,000
Net price of new computer	$135,000
− Cash inflow from sale of old computer	40,000
Net cost of new computer	$ 95,000

Incremental Depreciation

As mentioned earlier, the net increase in undepreciated capital cost would be $95,000 if the replacement decision were taken. That means the present value of the depreciation tax shield can be calculated by using formula 12–1.

$$PV = \left[\frac{\$95{,}000 \times .30 \times .46}{.12 + .30} - \left(\frac{\$30{,}000 \times .30 \times .46}{.12 + .30} \times \frac{1}{(1 + .12)^5}\right)\right] \times \frac{1 + .5(.12)}{1 + .12}$$

$$= (\$31{,}214 - (\$9{,}857 \times .567))\,(.9464)$$

$$= \$24{,}251$$

Cost Savings

The second type of benefit that requires consideration relates to the cost savings that can be realized by installing the new computer. As previously stated, these are estimated at between $20,000 and $45,000 per year over the next five years. The after-tax benefits are summarized in Table 12–16. In Table 12–16 the cost savings were multiplied by one minus the tax rate to calculate the value of the savings on an after-tax basis.

We are now in a position to compare the present value of incremental cash flows to the net cost of buying a new computer and to thus determine the financial attractiveness of such a decision.

Table 12–16
Analysis of incremental cost savings benefits

(1) Year	(2) Cost Savings	(3) (1 − Tax Rate)	(4) After-Tax Savings	(5) PV Factor (12%)	(6) Present Value
1 . . .	$20,000	0.54	$10,800	0.893	$ 9,644
2 . . .	38,000	0.54	20,520	0.797	16,354
3 . . .	40,000	0.54	21,600	0.712	15,379
4 . . .	45,000	0.54	24,300	0.636	15,455
5 . . .	45,000	0.54	24,300	0.567	13,778
Present value of cost savings benefits . . .					$ 70,610
Present value of salvage ($30,000 × .567) . . .					17,010
Present value of tax shield benefits . . .					24,251
Present value of incremental benefits . . .					$111,871

Present value of incremental benefits	$111,871
Net cost of new computer	95,000
Net present value	$ 16,871

According to the estimates used in this investment analysis, the net present value is positive. Thus, the purchase of the new computer can be recommended on the basis of the financial analysis. There may be other costs attached to this decision that have not yet been quantified but which are worth at least $16,871 to the company. If so, the fact the financial analysis thus far revealed a positive net present value should not dissuade management from closely analyzing whether there will be other costs (or benefits) that have not been included in this analysis.

Summary

The capital budgeting decision involves the planning of expenditures for a project with a life of at least one year and usually a considerably longer one. Although top management is often anxious about the impact of decisions on short-term reported income, the planning of capital expenditures dictates adopting a longer time horizon. Three primary methods are used to analyze capital investment proposals: payback, internal rate of return, and net present value. The first method, although widely used, has some serious theoretical flaws. The latter two, because they take into account the timing and overall amount of cash flows, are more complete methods for assessing capital budgeting decisions. Under certain circumstances the net present value method is superior over the internal rate of return.

Although capital budgeting techniques are economically rational by design, the combination of future uncertainty and information complexity means that decision inputs are highly dependent on managerial judgment. Projects with large initial investments, with long time horizons, and facing a high degree of future uncertainty are particularly difficult to justify using capital budgeting or any other analytical technique. In Chapter 13 we will examine how differing levels of risk can be factored into the capital budgeting decision-making process.

Investment alternatives may be classified as either mutually exclusive or not mutually exclusive. If they are mutually exclusive the selection of one alternative will preclude the selection of all other alternatives, and projects with a positive net present value may be eliminated. The same may also be true under capital rationing, a method under which management determines the maximum amount that can be invested in any one time period.

Tax considerations are also a major factor in capital budgeting decisions. In this chapter we have considered the effects of tax-allowable depreciation (capital cost allowance) and investment tax credits (ITC) in relation to the analysis. At this time in Canada the tax system is being used to attempt to encourage investment in some of the less-affluent regions of the country and also to attempt to channel investments toward research and development.

List of Terms

planning horizon	**cash flow**
payback	**capital cost allowance**
internal rate of return	**undepreciated capital cost**
net present value	**investment tax credit**
mutually exclusive	**reinvestment assumption**
capital rationing	**net present value profile**
terminal loss	**depreciation recapture**

Discussion Questions

1. What are the important administrative considerations in the capital budgeting process?
2. Why does capital budgeting rely for analysis on cash flows rather than net income effects?
3. What are the weaknesses of the payback method? Why do so many managers use it?
4. What is normally used as the discount rate under the net present value method? Why?

5. What does the term *mutually exclusive investments* mean?

6. If a corporation has projects that will earn more than the cost of capital, should it ration capital?

7. What is the net present value profile? What three points (characteristics) should be determined to create the profile?

8. What else, besides the forecast IRR and NPV, might top management consider in making capital budgeting decisions?

9. Generally speaking, what effect does the capital cost allowance system have on the timing of depreciation tax shield benefits?

10. What is the investment tax credit? How does it affect the capital budgeting decision?

Problems

1. Assume a corporation has annual earnings before depreciation and taxes of $60,000 and depreciation of $30,000, and it is in the 46 percent tax bracket. Compute its yearly cash flow.

2. Assume a $50,000 investment and the following after-tax cash flows for two alternatives.

Year	Investment A	Investment B
1	$10,000	$20,000
2	11,000	25,000
3	13,000	15,000
4	16,000	
5	24,000	

Which alternative would you select under the payback method?

3. Now assume that in Problem 2 you used the net present value method with a 10 percent discount rate. Would your answer change? Make the relevant calculations and explain the logic behind your answer.

4. You buy a new piece of equipment for $19,254, and you receive a net after-tax cash inflow of $3,000 per year for 10 years. What is the internal rate of return?

5. Bevan's Department Store is contemplating the purchase of a new machine at a cost of $13,566. The machine will provide $3,000 per year in after-tax cash flow for six years. Bevan has a cost of capital of 11 percent.

   Using the internal-rate-of-return method, evaluate this project and indicate whether it should be undertaken. Interpolate to find the exact answer (for this interpolation, refer to techniques in Chapter 9 if necessary).

6. DeBarry Corporation makes an investment of $50,000 which yields the following after-tax cash flows:

Year	Cash Flow
1	$10,000
2	10,000
3	16,000
4	18,000
5	20,000

   a. What is the net present value at a 9 percent discount rate?

   b. What is the internal rate of return? Use the interpolation procedure from this chapter.

   c. In this problem would you make the same decision under both parts *a* and *b?*

7. The Green Goddess Salad Oil Company is considering the purchase of a new machine that would increase the speed of bottling and save money. The net cost of this machine is $45,000. The annual after-tax net cash flows are projected as follows. The salvage value is included in the Year 5 cash flow projection and is equal to the amount of the asset not already depreciated at that time.

Year	Cash Flow
1	$15,000
2	20,000
3	25,000
4	10,000
5	5,000

   a. If the cost of capital is 10 percent, what is the net present value of selecting the new machine?

   b. What is the internal rate of return?

   c. Should the project be accepted? Why?

8. You are asked to evaluate the following two projects for the Boring Corporation. Using the net present value method, combined with the profitability index approach described in footnote 2 of this chapter, which project would you select? Use a discount rate of 10 percent.

Project X (Videotapes of the Weather Report) ($10,000 investment)		Project Y (Slow-Motion Replays of Commercials) ($30,000 investment)	
Year	After-Tax Cash Flow	Year	After-Tax Cash Flow
1	$5,000	1	$15,000
2	3,000	2	8,000
3	4,000	3	9,000
4	3,600	4	11,000

9. The Suboptimal Glass Company uses a process of capital rationing in its decision making. The firm's cost of capital is 13 percent. It will only invest $60,000 this year. It has determined the internal rate of return for each of the following projects.

Project	Project Size	Internal Rate of Return
A	$10,000	15.0%
B	30,000	14.0
C	25,000	16.5
D	10,000	17.0
E	10,000	23.0
F	20,000	11.0
G	15,000	16.0

a. Pick out the projects the firm should accept.

b. If Projects D and E were mutually exclusive, how would that affect your overall answer? That is, what projects would you accept in expending the $60,000?

10. Keller Construction Company is considering two new investments. Project E calls for the purchase of earth-moving equipment. Project H represents the investment in a hydraulic lift. Keller wishes to use a net present value profile in comparing the projects. The expected salvage value is included in the cash flows and is equal to the incremental undepreciated capital cost attributable to the equipment at the end of the projects. The investment and cash flow patterns are as follows:

Project E ($20,000 investment)	
Year	After-Tax Cash Flow
1	$ 5,000
2	6,000
3	7,000
4	10,000

Project H ($20,000 investment)	
Year	After-Tax Cash Flow
1	$16,000
2	5,000
3	4,000

a. Determine the net present value of the projects based on a zero discount rate.
b. Determine the net present value of the projects based on a 9 percent discount rate.
c. Graph a net present value profile for the two investments similar to Figure 12–3.
d. If the two projects are not mutually exclusive, what would your acceptance or rejection decision be if the cost of capital (discount rate) were 10 percent? (Use the net present value profile for your decision; no actual numbers are necessary.)
e. If the two projects are mutually exclusive (the selection of one precludes the selection of the other), what would be your decision if the cost of capital were (1) 6 percent, (2) 13 percent, (3) 18 percent? Once again, use the net present value profile for your answer.

11. Luft Watch Company is considering an investment of $15,000, which produces the following after-tax inflows.

Year	Cash Flow
1	$8,000
2	7,000
3	4,000

You are going to use the net present value profile to approximate the value for the internal rate of return. Please follow these steps.

a. Determine the net present value of the project based on a zero discount rate.
b. Determine the net present value of the project based on a 10 percent discount rate.
c. Determine the net present value of the project based on a 20 percent discount rate (it will be negative).

d. Draw a net present value profile for the investment and observe the discount rate at which the net present value is zero. This is an approximation of the internal rate of return on the project.
e. Actually compute the internal rate of return based on the interpolation procedure presented in this chapter. Compare your answers in parts *d* and *e*.

12. The Stevens Company will invest $50,000 in a project. Extra working capital accounts for $10,000 of the $50,000. The firm's discount rate (cost of capital) is 9 percent. The investment is projected to provide the following after-tax inflows not including the expected recovery of the working capital investment at the end of the project.

1	$10,000
2	10,000
3	16,000
4	18,000
5	10,000

The internal rate of return is 12.8 percent.

a. If the reinvestment assumption of the net present value method is used, what will be the total value of the inflows after five years? (Assume the inflows come at the end of each year.)
b. If the reinvestment assumption of the internal rate of return method is used, what will be the total value of the inflows after five years?
c. Generally, is one reinvestment assumption likely to be better than another?

13. XYZ Corporation has decided to sell one of its office buildings for $5 million. This building is part of the Class 3 (5 percent) CCA pool, and XYZ had it built five years ago at a cost of $4.5 million. XYZ's tax rate is 40 percent. XYZ uses 12 percent as its cost of capital.

a. If the Class 3 UCC at the start of the year in question was $12 million (and this was the only disposal), what would the tax consequences of the sale of the building be?
b. If the Class 3 UCC at the start of the year of the sale was $4 million, what would the tax effect of the sale be?
c. If the UCC at the start of the year was $6 million and this was the last building in the pool, what would be the tax treatment?

14. A $95,000 investment is to be depreciated for tax purposes using the maximum capital cost allowance available.

a. If the investment represents a fleet of automobiles for a telephone utility, what will be the allowable depreciation rate?
b. How much will the addition of the automobiles increase the allowable dollar depreciation in Year 1? in Year 2?
c. If the investment had been for machinery, what difference would that have made in the depreciation rate allowed?
d. What difference will it make when the cars are scrapped for next to nothing after five years (the company's autos tend to accumulate very high mileage, and the company has therefore adopted the practice of giving them away to interested employees when their usefulness to the company ceases)?

15. The Brunswick Corporation will purchase a $40,000 piece of production machinery with an estimated useful life of five years. The new machine is expected to allow an increase in sales of $65,000 per year, while increased incremental costs will amount to $35,000 per year. The firm is in a 46 percent income tax bracket. Complete the following table to determine the first-year cash flow effect of the investment.

Increased sales	________
Increased costs	________
Earnings before depreciation and taxes	________
Depreciation	________
Earnings before taxes	________
Taxes	________
Earnings after taxes	________
Depreciation	________
Net cash flow	________

16. Acme Auto Parts Ltd. has gained approval for a special developmental project on Cape Breton Island. It intends to invest $1.5 million in a new plant and another $800,000 in new equipment.

a. Assuming the tax rules governing investment tax credits and CCA remain the same as represented in this chapter, compute the investment tax credit available to Acme.
b. What will be the original capital cost base for depreciation purposes?
c. Compute the present value of the investment tax credit and capital cost allowance combined (Acme uses 10 percent as its discount rate).

17. (*Basic investment decision*)
The Bryant Car Rental Corporation is contemplating expanding its short-term rental fleet by 25 automobiles at a cost of $275,000. It expects to keep the autos for only two years and to sell them at the end of that period for 60 percent, on average, of what they cost. The plan is to generate $8,500 of incremental revenue per additional auto in each year of operation. The controller estimates that other costs will amount to 10 cents per kilometre on an average of 40,000 kilometres per car per year. She also estimates the new business will require an investment of $5,000 in additional working capital. The firm is in a 40 percent tax bracket and uses 13 percent as a cost of capital.

Should Bryant purchase the automobiles? Do all the necessary calculations to substantiate your recommendation.

18. (*Basic investment decision*)
MicroElectronics Ltd. is considering the investment of $60,000 in a new machine that will allow it to do research on developing a new microchip for use in hearing aids. The machine will be assigned to CCA Class 8. The firm is considered a Canadian-controlled private corporation eligible for the small business tax deduction.

If the machine is purchased, MicroElectronics expects to be able to develop an entirely new product for the hearing aid market ready for sale about two years after the machine is purchased. This new product is anticipated to provide revenues of $116,000 per year for the seven years after introduction and to have associated expenses of $88,000 per year for the first five of those years and $101,000 for the last two. Other development costs associated with the new product in the initial two years are estimated at $15,000 per year. The firm's controller estimates its cost of capital at 14 percent and that $.10 in additional working capital is required for every $1 in extra sales.

Should MicroElectronics purchase the new machine? Do all relevant calculations to support your recommendation.

19. (*Replacement decision*)
Nelson Technology purchased a radio communication system three years ago for $258,000. It has a potential buyer for the system who is willing to pay $78,000. A new system will cost $320,000 and is eligible for a 10 percent investment tax credit.

It is estimated the new system would provide the following stream of cost savings over the next five years:

Year	*Cost Savings*
1.	$95,000
2.	86,000
3.	72,000
4.	60,000
5.	58,000

The tax rate is 46 percent, and the estimated cost of capital is 11 percent.

a. What is the net cost of the new system?
b. What will be the incremental effect on the depreciation tax shield?
c. Compute the after-tax benefits of the cost savings.
d. Determine the present value of the incremental tax shield and cost savings benefits.

Should the new system be purchased?

20. (*Comprehensive problem*)
Upon graduating from college, Steven MacLean joined the financial analysis section of a large Canadian industrial concern, Ontario Corporation. Shortly thereafter Steven was assigned to help out in the financial analysis of a proposed acquisition by Ontario of a firm in a business quite unlike any of Ontario's traditional businesses. After a month of searching, Steven had assembled the following additional information:

a.

TARGET FIRM
Balance Sheet at 12/31/87
(000s)

Cash	$ 150	Current liabilities	$ 150
Accounts receivable . . .	400		
Inventory	600	Long-term debt	750
Net fixed assets	2,100	Equity	2,350
Total	$3,250		$3,250

b. Target Firm's sales for 1987 had been $3.5 million, and because it was operating at full capacity it looked as if all classes of assets would increase at a pace directly proportional to any increase in sales.

c. The interest rate on Target's long-term debt was 12.5 percent with annual interest payments being made at the end of each year.

d. Steven recommended the long-term debt be maintained after the acquisition.

e. Target had 2 million shares outstanding at the end of 1987 which had traded recently at prices around $1.50 per share.

f. The following estimates of sales and earnings before interest and taxes were the most reliable Steven had come across:

Year	*Annual Sales (millions)*	*Annual EBIT*
1	$3.7	$650,000
2	4.0	700,000
3	4.1	720,000
4	4.2	720,000
5	4.0	690,000
6–10	4.3	700,000

In arriving at EBIT, depreciation expenses of $140,000 per year had been deducted.

g. Expenditures on fixed assets would be necessary to allow for growth and to replace worn-out equipment. Steven estimated that $200,000 per year would be required in Years 1–5 with $80,000 per year thereafter.

h. The income tax rate for both firms was expected to remain at 46 percent.

i. Ontario Corporation used 13 percent as its cost of equity and had a weighted average cost of capital of 11 percent.

Compute the price Steven should recommend that Ontario Corporation offer to pay for each of Target Firm's shares.

Selected References

Abdelsamad, Moustafa. *A Guide to Capital Expenditure Analysis*. New York: American Management Association, 1973.

Bacon, Peter W. "The Evaluation of Mutually Exclusive Investments." *Financial Management* 6 (Summer 1977), pp. 55–58.

Bernhard, Richard H. "Mathematical Programming Models for Capital Budgeting—A Survey, Generalization, and Critique." *Journal of Financial and Quantitative Analysis* 4 (June 1969), pp. 111–58.

Bierman, Harold, Jr., and Seymour Smidt. *The Capital Budgeting Decision*. 4th ed. New York: Macmillan, 1975.

Bower, Joseph L. *Managing the Resource Allocation Process*. Boston: Division of Research, Harvard Business School, 1970.

Brick, Ivan, and Daniel G. Weaver. "A Comparison of Capital Budgeting Techniques in Identifying Profitable Investments." *Financial Management* 13 (Winter 1984), pp. 29–39.

Donaldson, Gordon. "Strategic Hurdle Rates for Capital Investment." *Harvard Business Review* 50 (March–April 1972), pp. 50–58.

Dorfman, Robert. "The Meaning of Internal Rates of Return." *Journal of Finance* 36 (December 1981), pp. 1010–21.

Durand, David. "Comprehensiveness in Capital Budgeting." *Financial Management* 10 (Winter 1981), pp. 7–13.

Hyndman, R. M. "The Efficacy of Recent Corporate Tax Reductions for Manufacturing." *Canadian Tax Journal* XXII (January–February 1974), pp. 84–97.

Johnson, Robert W. *Capital Budgeting*. Belmont, Calif.: Wadsworth, 1970.

Kim, Suk H., and Edward Farragher. "Current Capital Budgeting Practices." *Management Accounting* (June 1981), pp. 26–30.

Klommer, Thomas. "Empirical Evidence of the Adoption of Sophisticated Capital Budgeting Techniques." *Journal of Business* 45 (July 1972), pp. 387–97.

MacDonald, W. A., and G. E. Cronkwright, eds. *Income Taxation in Canada*. Scarborough, Ontario: Prentice-Hall Canada, 1987.

Mao, James C. T. "The Internal Rate of Return as a Ranking Criterion." *Engineering Economist* 11 (Winter 1966), pp. 1–13.

Matukonis, Michael. "Appropriate Application of the Investment Tax Credit in Capital Budgeting Decisions." Manuscript, State University of New York College at Oneonta, 1985.

Murdick, Robert G., and Donald D. Deming. *The Management of Corporate Expenditures*. New York: McGraw-Hill, 1968.

Murphy, George J. "The Influence of Taxation on Canadian Corporate Depreciation Practices." *Canadian Tax Journal* XX (May–June 1972), pp. 233–39.

Oakford, Robert V. *Capital Budgeting*. New York: Ronald, 1970.

Petty, J. William; David F. Scott, Jr.; and Monroe M. Bird. "The Capital Expenditure Decision-Making Process of Large Corporations." *Engineering Economist* 20 (Spring 1975), pp. 159–72.

Rappaport, Alfred, and Robert A. Taggart, Jr. "The Evaluation of Capital Expenditure Proposals under Inflation." *Financial Management* 11 (Spring 1982), pp. 5–13.

Sarnat, M., and H. Levy. "The Relationship of Rules of Thumb to the Internal Rate of Return: A Restatement and Generalization." *Journal of Finance* 24 (June 1969), pp. 479–89.

Van Horne, James C. "A Note on Biases in Capital Budgeting Introduced by Inflation." *Journal of Financial and Quantitative Analysis* 6 (January 1971), pp. 653–58.

Weaver, James B. "Organizing and Maintaining a Capital Expenditure Program." *Engineering Economist* 20 (Fall 1974), pp. 1–36.

Welch, Robert. "The Effect on Capital Budgeting Decisions of Recent Changes in the CCA Calculation." *Cost and Management*, May–June 1982, pp. 52–53.

13 Risk and Capital Budgeting

No one area is more essential to financial decision making than the evaluation and management of risk. The price of a firm's stock is, to a large degree, influenced by the amount of risk that investors perceive to be inherent in the firm's operations. We are constantly trying to achieve the appropriate mix between profitability and risk to satisfy those with a stake in the affairs of the firm in order to achieve the goal of wealth maximization for shareholders.

The difficulty is not in finding viable investment alternatives but in determining where we want to be on the risk-return scale. Would we prefer a 25 percent potential return on a new product in oil-sensitive Western Europe or a safe 8 percent return on an extension of our current product line in our home territory? The question can only be answered in terms of profitability, the risk position of the firm, and management and stockholder disposition toward risk. In this chapter we examine additional definitions of risk, its measurement, its incorporation into the *capital budgeting* process, and the basic tenets of portfolio theory.

Definition of Risk in Capital Budgeting

Risk may be defined in terms of the variability of possible outcomes from a given investment. If funds are invested in a 30-day Government of Canada Treasury bill, the outcome is certain and there is no variability—hence no risk. On the other hand, if we invest the same funds in a gold-mining expedition in the deepest wilds of Africa, the variability of possible outcomes is great and we say the project is replete with risk.

The student should observe that risk is measured not only in terms of losses but also in terms of uncertainty.[1] We say that gold mining carries a high degree of risk not just because you may lose your money but because there is a wide range of possible outcomes. Observe in Figure 13–1 examples of three investments with different risk characteristics. Note that in each case the distributions are centered on the same expected value ($20,000) but that the variability (risk) increases as we move from Investment A to Investment C. Because you may *gain* or *lose* the most in Investment C, it is clearly the riskiest of the three.

The Concept of Risk Averse

A basic assumption in financial theory is that most investors and managers are risk averse—that is, for a given situation they would prefer relative certainty to uncertainty. In Figure 13–1, therefore, they would prefer Investment A over Investments B and C, despite the fact that all three investments have the same expected value of $20,000. You are probably risk averse too. Assume you have saved $1,000 for your last year in college and are challenged to flip a coin, double or nothing. Heads, you end up with $2,000—tails, you are broke. Given that you are not enrolled at the University of Nevada at Las Vegas or that you are not an inveterate gambler, you will probably stay with your certain $1,000.

---

[1]We use the term *uncertainty* in its normal sense, rather than in the more formalized sense in which it is sometimes used in decision theory to indicate that insufficient evidence is available to estimate a probability distribution.

Figure 13–1
Variability and risk

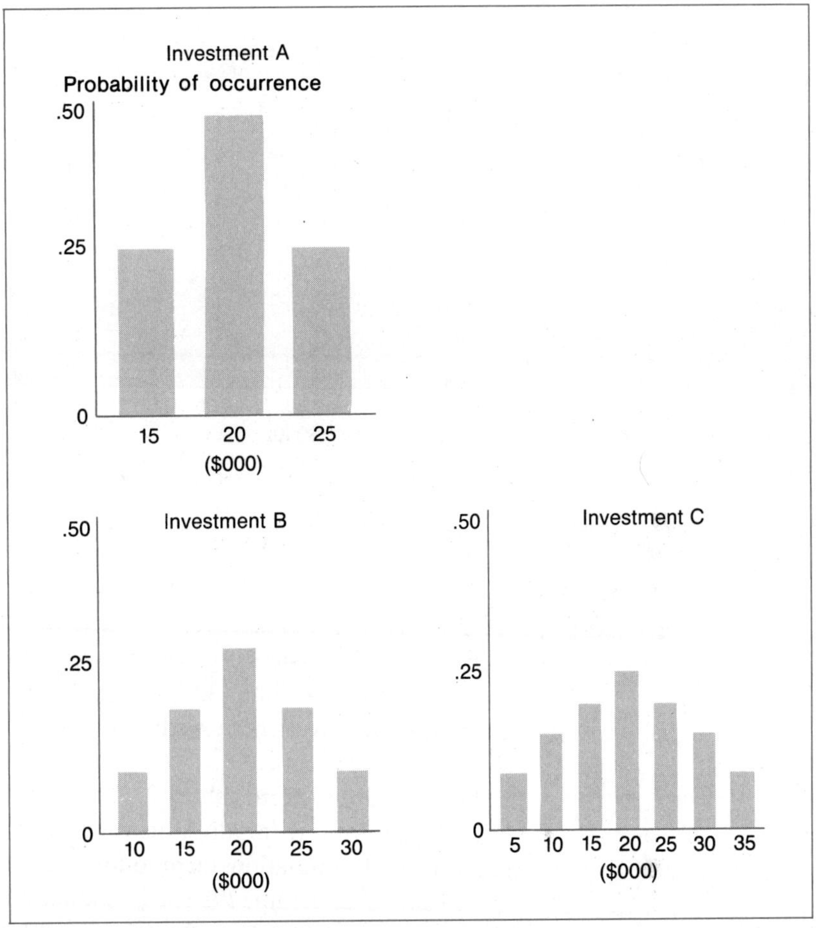

This is not to say that investors or businessmen are unwilling to take risks—but rather that they will require a higher expected value or return for risky investments. In Figure 13–2 we compare a low-risk proposal with an expected value of $20,000 to a high-risk proposal with an expected value of $30,000. The higher expected return may well compensate investors for absorbing greater risk.

Throughout the chapter we will develop methods for incorporating a higher demanded return for risky investments. For Evel Knievel, back in the 1970s, it was $7 million to jump over the Snake River Canyon—for a corporation, it may be a bonus return of 5 percent over the cost of capital.

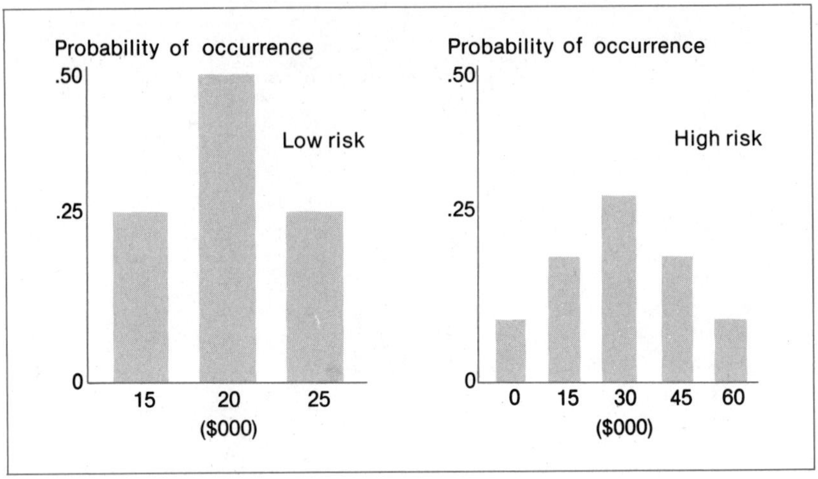

Figure 13–2
Risk-return trade-off

Actual Measurement of Risk

A number of basic statistical devices may be employed to measure the extent of risk inherent in any given situation. Assume we are examining an investment with the probability of possible outcomes shown in Table 13–1.

The probabilities in Table 13–1 may be based on past experience, industry ratios and trends, interviews with company executives, and sophisticated simulation techniques. The probability values may be quite easy to determine for the introduction of a mechanical stamping process in which the manufacturer has 10 years of past data, but difficult to assess for a new product in a foreign market. In one study that compared the present value of actual results with that of forecasted results for capital projects, new products were found, on average, to realize only 10 percent of the forecasted returns. Sales expansion proj-

Table 13–1
Probability distribution of outcomes

Outcome	*Probability of Outcome*	*Assumptions*
$300	.2	Pessimistic
600	.6	Moderately successful
900	.2	Optimistic

ects realized an average of 60 percent while cost reduction projects realized, on average, 110 percent of their forecasted returns.[2] Because of the difficulty of estimating future results it is, therefore, important to analyze carefully the range and probability of possible outcomes.

With the data before us, we compute two important statistical measures—the expected value and the standard deviation. The expected value is a weighted average of the outcomes times their probabilities.

$$\bar{D} \text{ (expected value)} = \Sigma DP \qquad (13\text{–}1)$$

D		P		DP
300	×	.2	=	\$ 60
600	×	.6	=	360
900	×	.2	=	180
				\$600 = ΣDP

The expected value is \$600. We then compute the standard deviation—the measure of dispersion or variability around the expected value. The formula for the standard deviation is quite simple:

$$\sigma \text{ (standard deviation)} = \sqrt{\Sigma(D - \bar{D})^2 P} \qquad (13\text{–}2)$$

The following steps should be followed:

Step 1: Subtract the Expected Value ($\bar{D}$) from Each Outcome (D)	Step 2: Square ($D - \bar{D}$)	Step 3: Multiply by P and Sum	Step 4: Determine the Square Root
D − $\bar{D}$ = $(D - \bar{D})$	$(D - \bar{D})^2$	P $(D - \bar{D})^2P$	
300 − 600 = −300	90,000	× .20 = 18,000	
600 − 600 = 0	0	× .60 = 0	
900 − 600 = +300	90,000	× .20 = 18,000	
		36,000	$\sqrt{36{,}000}$ = \$190

The standard deviation of \$190 gives us a rough average measure of how far each of the three outcomes falls away from the expected value. Generally, the larger the standard deviation (or spread of outcomes), the greater is the risk, as indicated in Figure 13–3.

[2]Reported in Joseph L. Bower, *Managing the Resource Allocation Process* (Homewood, Ill.: Richard D. Irwin, 1972), pp. 9–10.

Figure 13–3
Probability distribution with differing degrees of risk

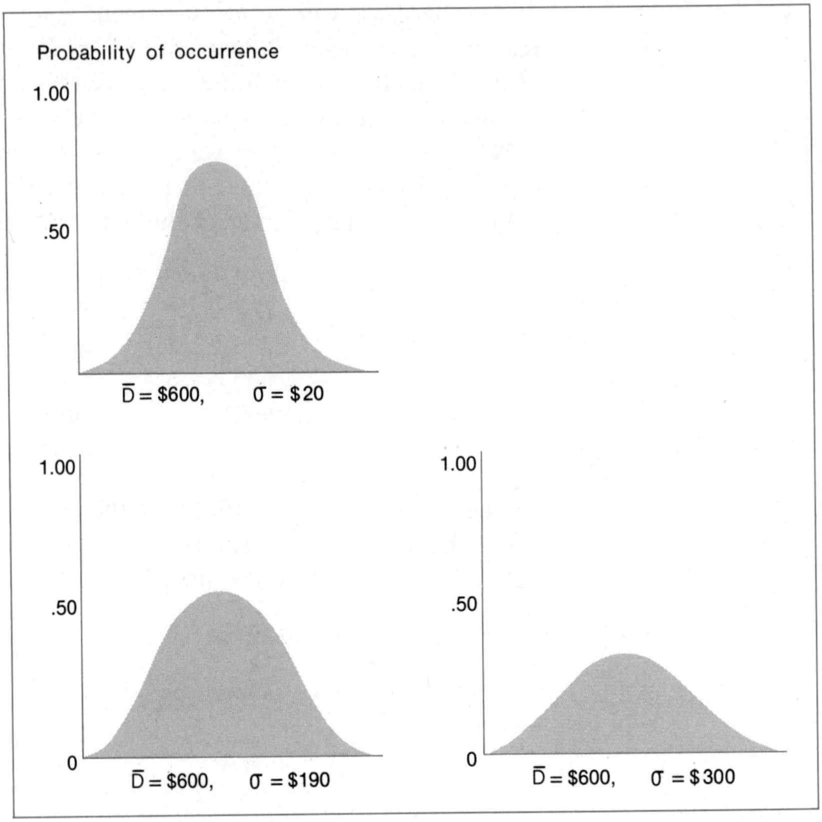

The student will note that in Figure 13–3 we compare the standard deviation of three investments with the same expected value of $600. If the expected values of the investments were quite different (such as $600 versus $6,000), a direct comparison of the standard deviations for each distribution would not be very helpful in measuring risk. In Figure 13–4 we show such an occurrence.

Note that the investment in Panel A of Figure 13–4 appears to have a high standard deviation—but not when related to the expected value of the distribution. A standard deviation of $600 on an investment with an expected value of $6,000 may indicate less risk than a standard deviation of $190 on an investment with an expected value of only $600.

We can eliminate the size difficulty by developing a third measure, the coefficient of variation (V). This rather imposing term calls for

Figure 13–4

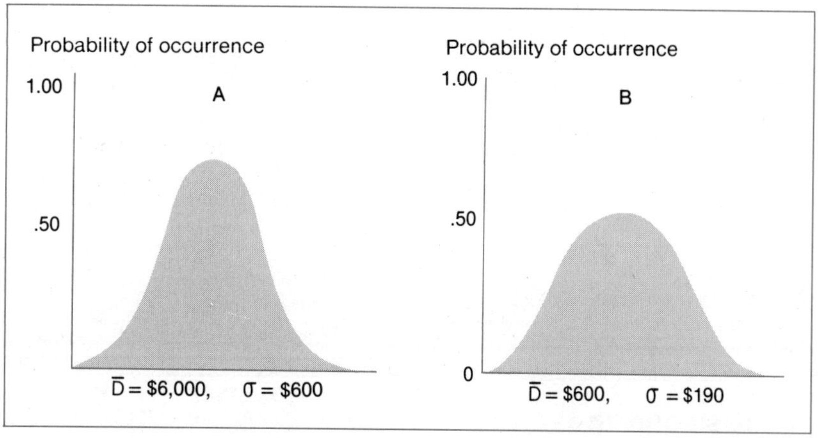

nothing more difficult than dividing the standard deviation of an investment by the expected value. Generally, the larger the coefficient of variation, the greater is the risk.

$$\text{Coefficient of variation } (V) = \frac{\sigma}{\bar{D}} \qquad (13\text{–}3)$$

For the investments in Panels A and B of Figure 13–4, we show:

$$\begin{array}{cc} A & B \\ \dfrac{600}{6{,}000} = .10 & \dfrac{190}{600} = .317 \end{array}$$

We have correctly identified the second investment as carrying the greater risk.

Another risk measure, the beta (β), is widely used with portfolios of common stock. Beta measures the volatility of returns on an individual stock relative to a stock market index of returns such as the Toronto Stock Exchange 300 stock index.[3] A common stock with a beta of 1.0 is said to be of equal risk with the market. Stocks with betas greater than 1.0 are riskier than the market, while stocks with betas of less than 1.0 are less risky than the market. Table 13–2 presents a sample of betas for several well-known companies from 1981 to 1986.

[3]Other market measures may also be utilized.

Table 13–2
Betas for a five-year period (1981–1986)

Company Name	Beta
Alcan Aluminum	0.74
Bell Canada Enterprises	0.66
Campbell Red Lake Mines	0.72
Campbell Resources	1.39
Carling O'Keefe	1.18
Dome Mines	1.49
INCO	1.23
MacMillan Bloedel	1.10
Northern Telecom	1.55
Westcoast Transmission	0.41

Risk and the Capital Budgeting Process

How can risk analysis be used effectively in the capital budgeting process? In Chapter 12, The Capital Budgeting Decision, we made no explicit distinction between risky and nonrisky events.[4] We showed the amount of the investment and the annual returns—making no comment about the riskiness or likelihood of achieving these returns. We know that enlightened investors and managers need further information. A $1,400 investment that produces "certain" returns of $600 a year for three years is not the same as a $1,400 investment that produces returns with an expected value of $600 for three years—but a high coefficient of variation. Investors, being risk averse by nature, will apply a stiffer test to the second investment. How can this new criterion be applied to the capital budgeting process?

Risk-Adjusted Discount Rate

A favored approach to adjusting for risk is to use different discount rates for proposals with different risk levels. A project that carries a normal amount of risk and does not change the overall risk composure of the firm should be discounted at the cost of capital. Investments carrying

[4]Our assumption was that the risk factor could be considered as constant for various investments.

greater than normal risk will be discounted at a higher rate; and so on. In Figure 13–5 we show a possible risk/discount rate trade-off scheme. Risk is assumed to be measured by the coefficient of variation (V).

The normal risk for the firm is represented by a coefficient of variation of 0.30. An investment with this risk would be discounted at the firm's normal cost of capital of 10 percent. As the firm selects riskier projects with, for example, a V of 0.90, a risk premium of 5 percent is added for an increase in V of 0.60. If the company selects a project with a coefficient of variation of 1.20, it will now add another 5 percent risk premium for this additional V of 0.30. Notice that the same risk premium of 5 percent was added for a smaller increase in risk. This is an example of being increasingly risk averse at higher levels of risk and potential return.

Figure 13–5
Relationship of risk to discount rate

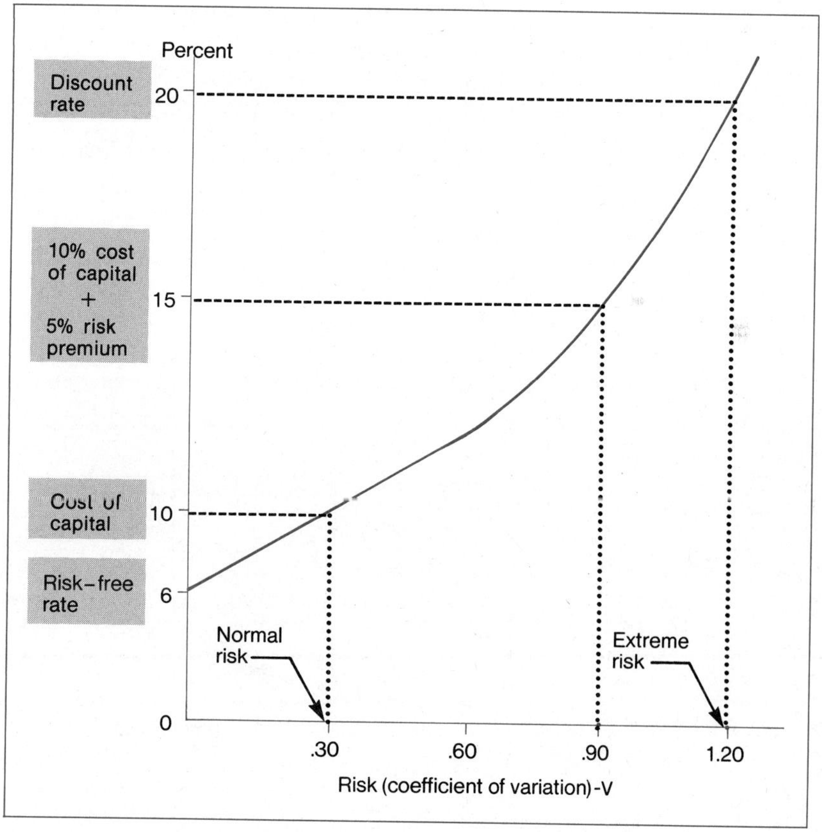

Increasing Risk over Time

It seems our ability to forecast accurately diminishes as we forecast farther out in time. As the time horizon becomes longer, more uncertainty enters the forecast. In 1985, Esso Resources was planning a $13 billion investment in a steam-injection oil sands plant at Cold Lake, Alberta, while Shell Canada had plans for a similar plant at Peace River. The rapid decline in world oil prices in early 1986 (from about U.S. $26 per barrel to less than $10), due to Saudi Arabia's policy of flooding the market with cheap oil, led Esso and Shell to postpone these huge capital investments. According to their managements, these projects cannot be reconsidered until the long-term outlook is for stable oil prices even though the world price of oil has recovered to over U.S. $20 per barrel by mid-1987. These unexpected events create a higher standard deviation in cash flow estimates and increase the risk associated with long-lived projects. Figure 13–6 depicts the relationship between risk and time.

Even though a forecast of cash flows shows a constant expected value, Figure 13–6 shows that the range of outcomes and probabilities increase as we move from Year 2 to Year 10. The standard deviations

Figure 13–6
Risk over time

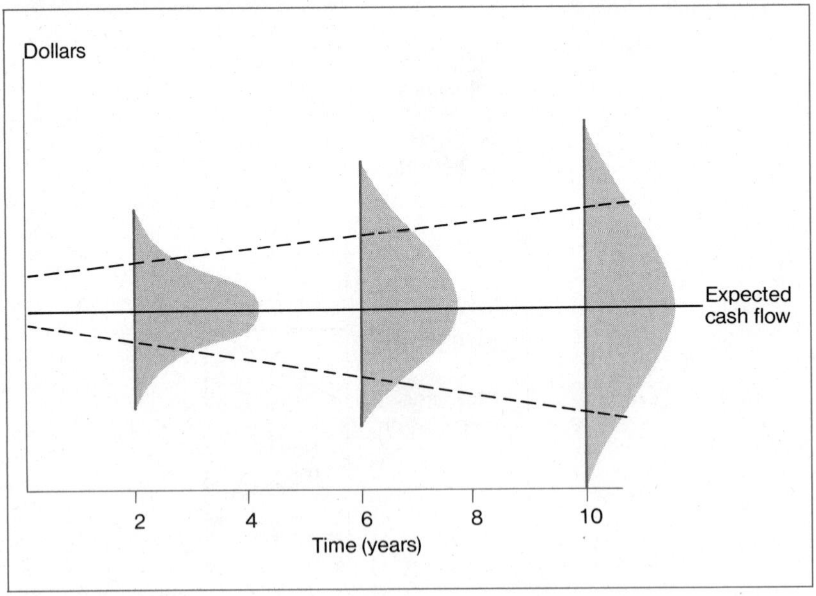

increase for each forecast of cash flow. If cash flows were forecast as easily for each period, all distributions would look like the first one for Year 2. Using progressively higher discount rates to compensate for risk tends to penalize late flows more than early flows, and this is consistent with the notion that risk is greater for longer-term cash flows than for near-term cash flows.

Qualitative Measures

Rather than relate the discount rate—or required return—to the coefficient of variation or possibly the beta, management may wish to set up risk classes based on qualitative considerations. Examples are presented in Table 13–3. Once again we are equating the discount rate to the perceived risk.[5]

Example—risk-adjusted discount rate In Chapter 12 we compared two $10,000 investment alternatives and indicated that each had a positive net present value (at a 10 percent cost of capital). The analysis is reproduced in Table 13–4.

Table 13–3
Risk categories and associated discount rates

	Discount Rate
Low or no risk (repair to old machinery)	6%
Moderate risk (new equipment)	8
Normal risk (addition to normal product line)	10
Risky (new product in related market)	12
High risk (completely new market)	16
Highest risk (new product in foreign market)	20

[5]Throughout all of this note the difficulty implied for managers trying to gain approval for "new" ideas with long development time horizons. Taking into account Canada's relatively inferior position with respect to most new technologies, its relatively high manufacturing costs, its need to depend upon selling into foreign markets, and the purported risk averseness of the Canadian people, you have the definition of a very serious impediment to investment for the long-term development of the Canadian industrial economy.

Table 13–4
Capital budgeting analysis

Year	Investment A (10% discount rate)		Year	Investment B (10% discount rate)	
1 . . .	$5,000 × 0.909 =	$ 4,545	1 . . .	$1,500 × 0.909 =	$ 1,364
2 . . .	5,000 × 0.826 =	4,130	2 . . .	2,000 × 0.826 =	1,652
3 . . .	2,000 × 0.751 =	1,502	3 . . .	2,500 × 0.751 =	1,878
		$10,177	4 . . .	5,000 × 0.683 =	3,415
			5 . . .	5,000 × 0.621 =	3,105
					$11,414
Present value of inflows . . .		$10,177	Present value of inflows . . .		$11,414
Investment		10,000	Investment		10,000
Net present value		$ 177	Net present value		$ 1,414

Though both proposals are acceptable, if they were mutually exclusive only Investment B would be undertaken. But what if we add a risk dimension to the problem? Assume that Investment A calls for an addition to the normal product line and is assigned a discount rate of 10 percent. Further assume that Investment B represents a new product in a foreign market and must carry a 20 percent discount to adjust for the large risk component. As indicated in Table 13–5 our answers are reversed, and Investment A is now the only acceptable one of the two alternatives.

Other methods besides the risk-adjusted discount rate are also used to evaluate risk in the capital budgeting process. The spectrum runs from a seat-of-the-pants "executive preference" approach to sophisticated computer-based statistical analysis. All methods, however, include a common approach—that is, they must give recognition to the riskiness of a given investment proposal and make an appropriate adjustment for risk.[6]

[6]As an example, each value might be penalized for lack of certainty (adjusted for risk), and then a risk-free discount rate might be applied to the resultant values. This is termed the *certainty equivalent approach*. In practice, the expected value for a given year is multiplied by a percentage figure indicating the degree of certainty and then translated back to the present at a risk-free discount rate (less than the cost of capital). Items with a high degree of certainty are multiplied by 100 percent, less certain items by 75 percent, and so on down the scale.

Table 13–5
Capital budgeting decision adjusted for risk

Year	Investment A (10% discount rate)		Year	Investment B (20% discount rate)	
1 . . .	$5,000 × 0.909 =	$ 4,545	1 . . .	$1,500 × 0.833 =	$ 1,250
2 . . .	5,000 × 0.826 =	4,130	2 . . .	2,000 × 0.694 =	1,388
3 . . .	2,000 × 0.751 =	1,502	3 . . .	2,500 × 0.579 =	1,448
		$10,177	4 . . .	5,000 × 0.482 =	2,410
			5 . . .	5,000 × 0.402 =	2,010
					$ 8,506
Present value of inflows . . .		$10,177	Present value of inflows. . .		$ 8,506
Investment		10,000	Investment		10,000
Net present value		$ 177	Net present value		$(1,494)

Simulation Models

Computers make it possible to simulate various economic and financial outcomes, using a large number of variables. Thus, simulation is one way of dealing with the uncertainty involved in forecasting the outcomes of capital budgeting projects or other types of decisions. A Monte Carlo simulation model uses random variables for inputs. By programming the computer to randomly select inputs from probability distributions, the outcomes generated by a simulation are distributed about a mean so that instead of generating one return or net present value, a range of outcomes with standard deviations is provided. A simulation model relies on repetition of the same random process as many as several hundred times. Since the inputs are representative of what one might encounter in the real world, many possible combinations of returns are generated.

One of the benefits of simulation is its ability to test various possible combinations of events. This sensitivity testing allows the planner to ask "what if" questions, such as: What will happen to the returns on this project if oil prices go up? Go down? What effect will a 5 percent increase in interest rates have on the net present value of this project? The analyst can use the simulation process to test out possible changes in economic policy, sales levels, inflation or any other variable included in the modeling process. Some simulation models are driven by sales forecasts with assumptions to derive income statements and balance sheets. Others generate probability acceptance curves for capital budgeting decisions by informing the analyst about the probabilities of having a positive net present value.

For example, each distribution in Figure 13–7 will have a value picked randomly and used for one simulation. The simulation will be run many times, each time selecting a new random variable to generate the final probability distribution for the net present value (at the bottom). For that probability distribution, the expected values are on the horizontal axis, and the probability of occurrence is on the vertical axis. The outcomes also indicate something about the riskiness of the project, which is indicated by the overall dispersion.

Figure 13–7
Simulation flow chart

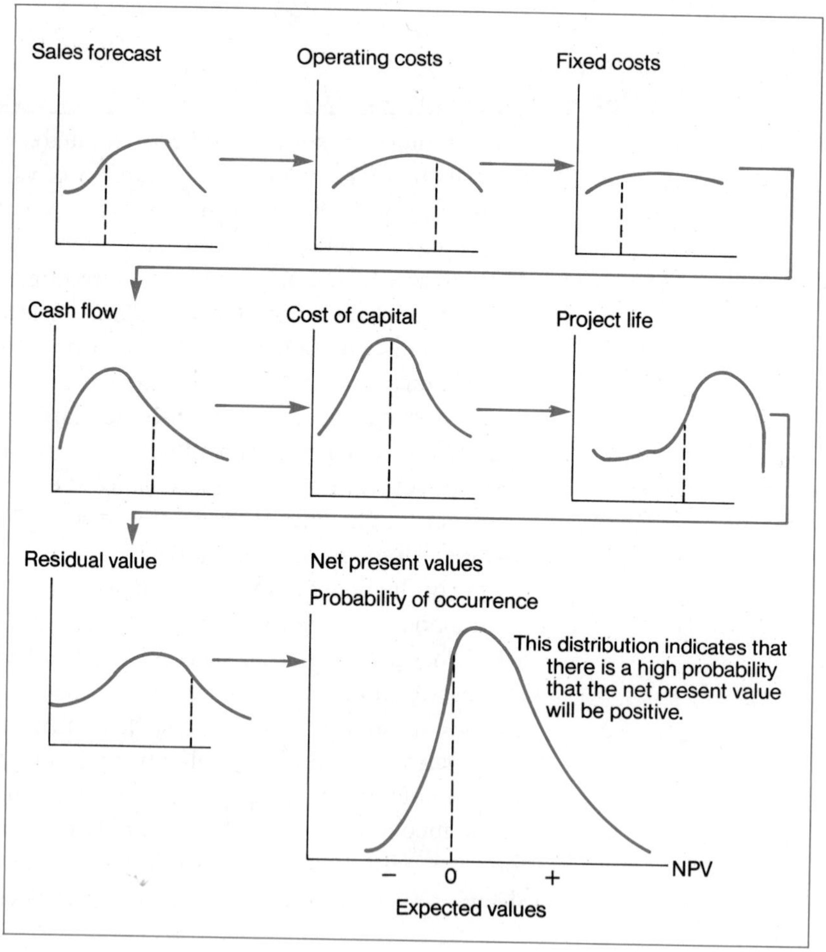

Decision Trees

Decision trees help lay out the sequence of decisions that can be made and present a tabular or graphical comparison resembling the branches of a tree, which highlight the differences between investment choices. In Figure 13–8 we examine a semiconductor firm considering two choices: (A) expanding the production of semiconductors for sale to end users of these tiny chips or (B) entering the highly competitive home computer market by using the firm's technology. The cost of both projects is the same $60 million, but the net present value (NPV) and risk are different.

If the firm expands its semiconductor capacity (Project A), it is assured of some demand so that a high likelihood of a positive rate of return exists. The market demand for these products is volatile over time, but long-run growth seems to be a reasonable expectation as the emphasis on technology increases. If the firm expands into the home computer market (Project B), it faces stiff competition from many existing firms. It stands to lose more money if expected sales are low

Figure 13–8
Decision trees

	(1) Expected Sales	(2) Probability	(3) Present Value of Cash Flow from Sales ($ millions)	(4) Initial Cost ($ millions)	(5) NPV (3) − (4) ($ millions)	(6) Expected NPV (2) × (5) ($ millions)
Start → A: Expand semiconductor capacity	High	.50	$100	$60	$40	$20.00
	Moderate	.25	75	60	15	3.75
	Low	.25	40	60	(20)	(5.00)
					Expected NPV =	$18.75
Start → B: Enter home computer market	High	.20	$200	$60	$140	$28.00
	Moderate	.50	75	60	15	7.50
	Low	.30	25	60	(35)	(10.50)
					Expected NPV =	$25.00

than it would under option A, but it will make more if sales are high. Even though project B has a higher expected NPV than project A, its extra risk does not make for an easy choice. Clearly, more analysis would have to be done before management made the final decision between these two projects. Nevertheless, the decision tree has identified some critical areas where managerial judgment must be exercised.

The Portfolio Effect

Up to this point we have been primarily concerned with the risk inherent in an *individual* investment proposal. While this approach is quite useful, we also need to consider the impact of a given investment on the overall risk of the firm—the "portfolio effect."[7] For example, we might undertake an investment in the building products industry that appears to carry a high degree of risk—but if our primary business is the manufacture of electronic components for industrial use, we may actually diminish the overall risk exposure of the firm. Why? Because electronic component sales expand when the economy does well and falter in a recession. The building products industry reacts in the opposite fashion—performing poorly in boom periods and generally reacting well in recessionary periods. By investing in the building products industry, an electronic components manufacturer could actually smooth out the cyclical fluctuations inherent in its business and reduce overall risk exposure, as indicated in Figure 13–9.

The risk reduction phenomenon is demonstrated by a less dispersed probability distribution. We say the standard deviation for the entire company (the portfolio of investments) has been reduced.

Portfolio Risk

Whether a given investment will change the overall risk of the firm depends on its relationships to other investments. If one airline purchases another, there is very little risk reduction. Highly correlated

[7]Here the portfolio of investments refers to plant, equipment, new products, and so forth, rather than stocks and bonds.

Figure 13–9
Portfolio considerations in evaluating risk

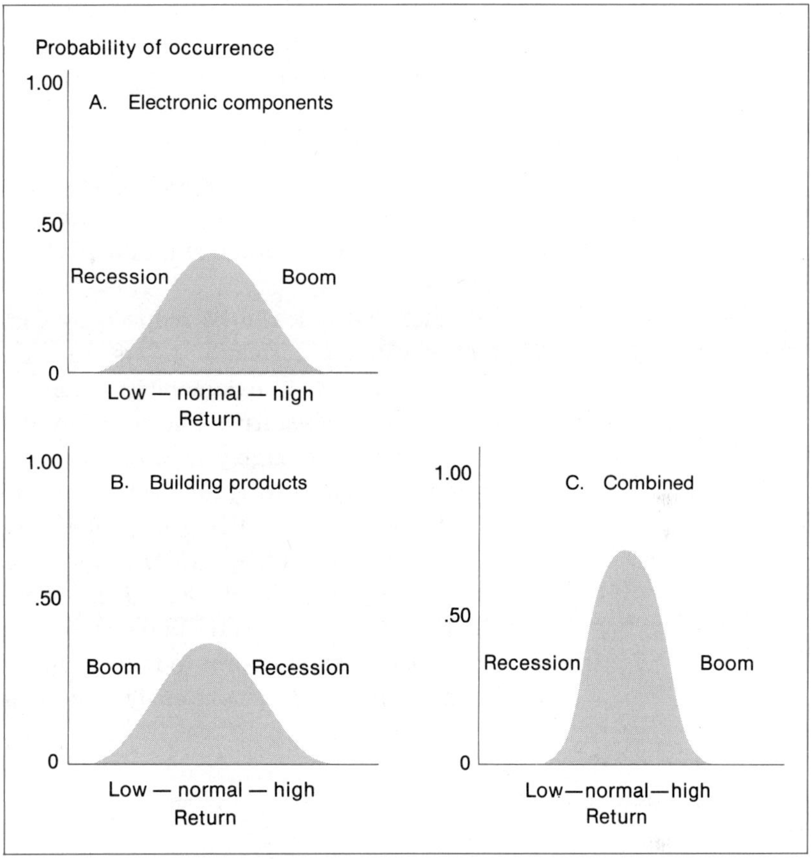

investments, that is, projects which move in the same direction in good times as well as bad, do little or nothing to diversify away risk. Projects moving in opposite directions (for example, building products and electronic components) are referred to as being negatively correlated and provide a high degree of risk reduction.

Finally, projects that are totally uncorrelated provide some overall reduction in portfolio risk—though not as much as negatively correlated investments. For example, if a beer manufacturer purchases a textile firm, the projects are neither positively nor negatively correlated, but the purchase will reduce the overall risk of the firm simply through the "law of large numbers." If you have enough unrelated projects going on at one time, good and bad events will probably even out.

The extent of correlation among projects is represented by a new term called the *coefficient of correlation*—a measure that may take on values anywhere from -1 to $+1$.[8] Examples are presented in Table 13–6.

In the real world very few investment combinations take on values as extreme as -1 or $+1$, or for that matter exactly 0. The more likely case is a point somewhere in between, such as $-.2$ negative correlation or $+.3$ positive correlation, as indicated along the continuum in Figure 13–10.

The fact that risk can be reduced by combining risky assets with low or negatively correlated assets can be seen by the example of Conglomerate, Inc. Conglomerate has fairly average returns and standard deviations of returns. The company is considering the purchase of two separate but large companies with sales and assets equal to its own. Management is struggling with the decision since both companies have a 14 percent rate of return, which is 2 percent higher than that of Conglomerate, and they have the same standard deviation of returns as that of Conglomerate, at 2.82 percent. This information is presented in the first three columns of Table 13–7.

Since management desires to reduce risk (σ) and to increase returns at the same time, it decides to analyze the results of each combination.[9]

Table 13–6
Measures of correlation

Coefficient of Correlation	*Condition*	*Example*	*Impact on Risk*
−1	Negative correlation	Electronic components, building products	Large risk reduction
0	No correlation	Beer, textile	Some risk reduction
+1	Positive correlation	Two airlines	No risk reduction

[8]Coefficient of correlation is not to be confused with coefficient of variation—a term used earlier in the chapter.

[9]In Chapter 20 you will evaluate a merger situation in which there is no increase in earnings, only a reduction in the standard deviation. Because the lower risk may mean a higher price-earnings ratio, this could, of course, be beneficial.

Figure 13–10
Levels of risk reduction as measured by the coefficient of correlation

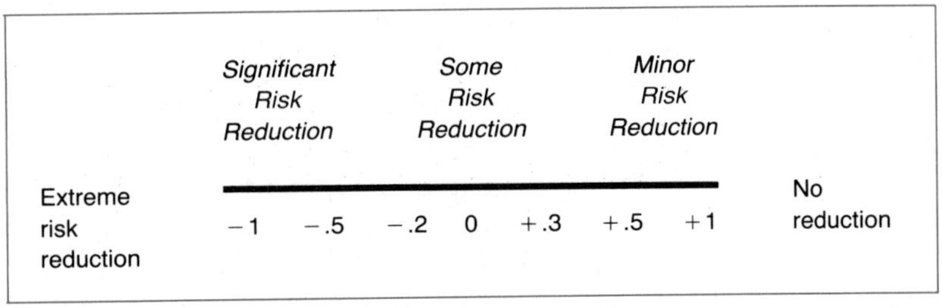

Table 13–7
Rates of return for Conglomerate, Inc., and two merger candidates

Year	(1) Conglomerate, Inc.	(2) Positive Correlation, Inc. +1.0	(3) Negative Correlation, Inc. −.9	(1) + (2) Conglomerate, Inc. + Positive Correlation, Inc.	(1) + (3) Conglomerate, Inc. + Negative Correlation, Inc.
1	14%	16%	10%	15%	12%
2	10	12	16	11	13
3	8	10	18	9	13
4	12	14	14	13	13
5	16	18	12	17	14
Mean return	12%	14%	14%	13%	13%
Standard deviation of returns (σ)	2.82%	2.82%	2.82%	2.82%	.63%
Correlation coefficients with Conglomerate, Inc.				+1.0	−.9

These are shown in the last two columns in Table 13–7. A combination with Positive Correlation, Inc., increases the mean return to 13 percent but maintains the exact same standard deviation of returns (no risk reduction). Why? Because the coefficient of correlation is + 1.0 and no diversification benefits are achieved. A combination with Negative Correlation, Inc., also increases the mean return to 13 percent, but it reduces the standard deviation of returns to 0.63 percent, a significant reduction in risk. This occurs because of the offsetting relationship of returns between the two companies, as evidenced by the coefficient of correlation of −.9. When one company has high returns, the other has low returns, and vice versa.

Evaluation of Combinations

The firm should evaluate all possible combinations of projects, determining which will provide the best trade-off between risk and return. In Figure 13–11 we see a number of alternatives that might be available to a given firm. Each point represents a combination of different possible investments. For example, point *F* might represent a semiconductor manufacturer combining three different types of semiconductors, plus two calculators, and two products in totally unrelated fields. In choosing between the various points or combinations, management should have two primary objectives:

1. Achieve the highest possible return at a given risk level.
2. Allow the lowest possible risk at a given return level.

All the best opportunities will fall along the leftmost sector of the diagram (line *C–F–G*). Each point on the line satisfies the two objectives of the firm. Any point to the right is less desirable.

After we have developed our best risk-return line, known in the financial literature as the "efficient frontier," we must determine where on the line our firm should be. There is no universally correct answer.

Figure 13–11
Risk-return trade-offs

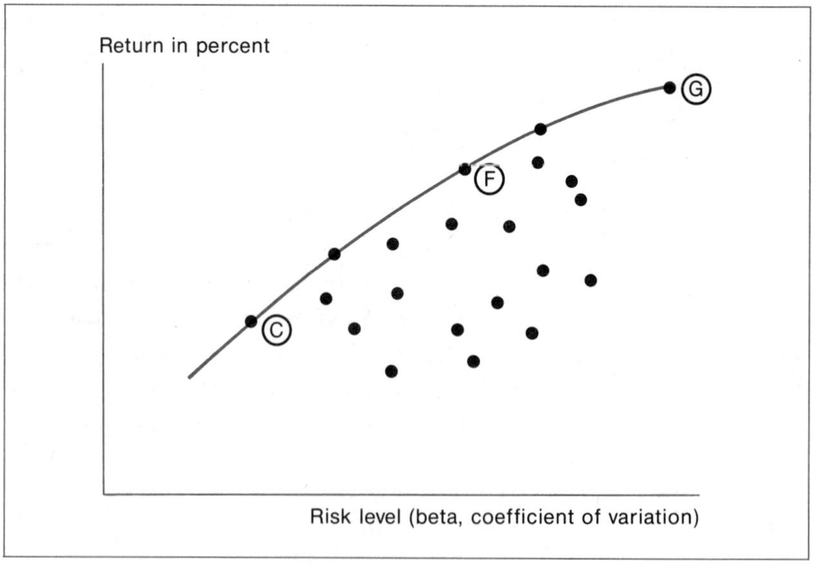

To the extent we are willing to take large risks for superior returns, we will opt for some point on the upper portion of the line—such as *G*. A more conservative selection might be *C or F*.

The Share Price Effect

The firm must be sensitive to the wishes and demands of shareholders. To the extent that unnecessary or undesirable risks are taken, a higher discount rate and lower valuation will probably be assigned to our stock in the market. Higher profits, resulting from risky ventures, could have a result opposite from that intended. In raising the coefficient of variation, or beta, we could be lowering the overall valuation of the firm.

The aversion of investors to unpredictability (and the associated risk) is confirmed by observing the relative valuation given to cyclical stocks versus highly predictable growth stocks in the market. Metals, autos, and housing stocks generally trade at an earnings multiplier well below that for industries with level, predictable performance such as drugs, soft drinks, and even alcohol or cigarettes. Each company must carefully analyze its own situation to determine the appropriate trade-off between risk and return. The changing desires and objectives of investors tend to make the task somewhat more difficult.

Summary

Risk may be defined as the variability of the potential outcomes from an investment. The less predictable the outcomes, the greater is the risk. Both management and investors tend to be risk averse—that is, all things being equal, they would prefer to take less risk rather than greater risk.

The most commonly employed method to adjust for risk in the capital budgeting process is to alter the discount rate based on the perceived risk level. High-risk projects will carry a risk premium, producing a discount rate well in excess of the average cost of capital.

In assessing the risk components in a given project, management may rely on simulation techniques to generate probabilities of possible outcomes and decision trees to help isolate the key variables to be evaluated.

Management must consider not only the risk inherent in a given project but also the impact of a new project on the overall risk of the firm (the portfolio effect). Negatively correlated projects have the most favorable effect on smoothing out business cycle fluctuations. The firm may wish to consider all combinations and variations of possible projects and to select only those that provide a total risk-return trade-off consistent with its goals.

List of Terms

risk	**portfolio effect**
risk averse	**coefficient of correlation**
expected value	**efficient frontier**
standard deviation	**beta**
coefficient of variation	**simulation**
risk-adjusted discount rate	**decision tree**

Discussion Questions

1. If corporate managers are risk averse, does this mean they will not take risks? Explain.
2. Discuss the concept of risk and how it might be measured.
3. When is the coefficient of variation a better measure of risk than the standard deviation?
4. Explain how the concept of risk can be incorporated into the capital budgeting process.
5. If risk is to be analyzed in a qualitative way, place the following investment decisions in order from the lowest risk to the highest risk.

   a. New equipment.
   b. Completely new market.
   c. Repair old machinery.
   d. New product in a foreign market.
   e. New product in a related market.
   f. Addition to a product line.

6. Assume a company whose performance is highly correlated with the general economy is evaluating six projects, of which two are positively correlated with the economy, two are negatively correlated, and two are not correlated with it at all. Which two projects would you select to minimize the company's overall risk?

7. Assume a firm has several hundred possible investments and wants to analyze the risk-return trade-off for portfolios of 20 projects. How should it proceed with the evaluation?

8. Explain the effect of the risk-return trade-off on the market value of common stock.

9. What is the purpose of using simulation analysis?

10. Why might an analyst set up a decision tree in attempting to make a decision?

Problems

1. Pabst Dental Supplies is evaluating the introduction of a new product. The possible levels of unit sales and the probabilities of their occurrence are given.

Possible Market Reaction	*Sales in Units*	*Probabilities*
Low response	20	.10
Moderate response	40	.20
High response	65	.40
Very high response	80	.30

a. What is the expected value of unit sales for the new product?
b. What is the standard deviation of unit sales?

2. Possible outcomes for three investment alternatives and their probabilities of occurrence are given below.

	Alternative 1		*Alternative 2*		*Alternative 3*	
	Outcomes	*Probability*	*Outcomes*	*Probability*	*Outcomes*	*Probability*
Failure	50	.2	90	.3	80	.4
Acceptable	80	.4	160	.5	200	.5
Successful	120	.4	200	.2	400	.1

Rank the three alternatives in terms of risk (compute the coefficient of variation).

3. Five investment alternatives have the following returns and standard deviations of returns.

Alternative	Returns: Expected Value	Standard Deviation
A	$ 1,000	$200
B	3,000	300
C	3,000	400
D	5,000	700
E	10,000	900

a. Using the coefficient of variation, rank the five alternatives from lowest risk to highest risk.
b. If you were to choose between alternatives B and C only, would you need to use the coefficient of variation? Why?

4. Mary Beth Clothes is considering opening one more suburban outlet. An after-tax cash flow of $100 per week is expected from two stores that are being evaluated. Both stores have positive net present values.

Which store site would you select based on the distribution of these cash flows? Use the coefficient of variation as your measure of risk.

Site A		Site B	
Probability	Cash Flows	Probability	Cash Flows
.2	50	.1	20
.3	100	.2	50
.3	110	.4	100
.2	135	.2	150
		.1	180

5. Western Dynamite Co. is evaluating two different methods of blowing up old buildings for commercial purposes over the next five years. Method one (implosion) is relatively low in risk for this business and will carry a 10 percent discount rate. Method two (explosion) is more dangerous and will call for a discount rate of

15 percent. Either investment will require an initial capital outlay of $100,000. The inflows from projected business over the next five years are given below. Which method should be selected, using net present value analysis?

Years	Method 1	Method 2
1	$25,000	$28,000
2	30,000	32,000
3	38,000	39,000
4	31,000	33,000
5	19,000	25,000

6. Canadian Metal, Mining, and Petroleum is examining two projects for investment. The first project is an oil-well drilling project in the Beaufort Sea at a cost of $500 million, and the second project is the expansion of an aluminum smelter in Mapletree, Quebec, at a cost of $500 million. The oil wells are expected to produce a deferred cash flow of $100 million per year in Years 5 through 10 and $200 million per year in Years 11 through 20. The aluminum smelter is expected to generate cash flows of $80 million yearly in Years 2 through 25. The cost of capital is 12 percent.

a. Which investment should be made?

b. If the oil-well project justifies an extra 4 percent premium over the normal cost of capital because of its riskiness, how does the investment decision change?

7. Larry's Athletic Lounge is planning an expansion program to increase the sophistication of the exercise equipment. Larry is considering some new equipment priced at $20,000 with an estimated life of five years. Larry is not sure how many members the new equipment will attract, but he estimates that his increased yearly cash flows for the next five years will have the following probability distribution. Larry's cost of capital is 14 percent.

P (probability)	Cash Flow
.2	$2,400
.4	4,800
.3	6,000
.1	7,200

a. What is the expected cash flow?
b. What is the expected net present value and internal rate of return?
c. Should Larry buy the new equipment?

8. Mr. John Backster, a retired executive, desires to invest a portion of his assets in rental property. He has narrowed his choices down to two apartment complexes, Windy Acres and Hillcrest Apartments. After conferring with the present owners, Mr. Backster has developed the following estimates of the cash flows for these properties.

Windy Acres		Hillcrest Apartments	
Probability	Yearly After-Tax Cash Flow	Probability	Yearly After-Tax Cash Flow
.1 . . .	$10,000	.2 . . .	$15,000
.2 . . .	15,000	.3 . . .	25,000
.4 . . .	30,000	.4 . . .	35,000
.2 . . .	45,000	.1 . . .	45,000
.1 . . .	50,000		

a. Find the expected cash flow from each apartment complex.
b. What is the coefficient of variation for each apartment complex?
c. Which apartment complex has more risk?

9. Mr. Backster, in making his decision, feels he is likely to hold the complex of his choice for about 10 years, and he will use this time period for decision-making purposes. Either apartment complex can be acquired for $100,000. Mr. Backster uses a risk-adjusted discount rate when considering investments with a coefficient of variation (V) greater than .35. He estimates his cost of capital to be 12 percent. For projects with a V between .35 and .40, he adds 2 percent to the cost of capital, and for those with a V between .4 and .5, he adds 4 percent. Mr. Backster would not consider an investment with a V of more than .5.

a. Compute the risk-adjusted net present values for Windy Acres and Hillcrest Apartments. (Use cash flow figures from the previous problem.)
b. Which investment should Mr. Backster accept if the two investments are mutually exclusive? If the investments are not

mutually exclusive and no capital rationing takes place, how would your decision be affected?

10. Wardrobe Clothing Manufacturers is preparing a strategy for the fall season. One strategy is to go to a highly imaginative new, four-gold-button sport coat with special emblems on the front pocket. The all-wool product will be available for males and females alike. A second option would be to produce a traditional blue blazer line. The market research department has determined that the new, four-gold-button coat and the traditional blue blazer line offer the following probabilities of outcomes and related cash flows.

	New Coat		Blazer	
Expected Sales	Probability	Present Value of Cash Flows from Sales	Probability	Present Value of Cash Flows from Sales
Fantastic	.4	$240,000	.2	$120,000
Moderate	.2	180,000	.6	75,000
Dismal	.4	0	.2	65,000

The initial cost to get into the new coat line is $100,000 in designs, equipment, and inventory. The blazer line would carry an initial cost of $60,000.

a. Diagram a complete decision tree of possible outcomes similar to Figure 13–8. Take the analysis all the way through the process of computing expected NPV (last column for each investment).

b. Given the analysis in part *a*, would you automatically make the investment indicated?

11. The Canada Pipeline Company projects the following pattern of inflows from an investment. The inflows are spread over time to reflect delayed benefits. Each year is independent of the others.

Year 1		Year 5		Year 10	
Cash Inflow	Probability	Cash Inflow	Probability	Cash Inflow	Probability
65	.20	50	.25	40	.30
80	.60	80	.50	80	.40
95	.20	110	.25	120	.30

The expected value for all three years is \$80.

a. Compute the standard deviation for each of the three years.
b. Diagram the expected values and standard deviations for each of the three years in a manner similar to Figure 13–6.
c. Assuming a 6 percent and a 12 percent discount rate, complete the table below for present value factors.

Year	IF_{pv} 6 Percent	IF_{pv} 12 Percent	Difference
1	.943	.893	.050
5	—	—	—
10	—	—	—

d. Is the increasing risk over time, as diagrammed in part *b*, consistent with the larger differences in IF_{pv}s over time as computed in part *c*?
e. Assume the initial investment is \$135. What is the net present value of the investment at a 12 percent discount rate? Should the investment be accepted?

12. When returns from a project can be assumed to be normally distributed, such as those shown in Figure 13–6 (represented by a symmetrical, bell-shaped curve), the areas under the curve can be determined from statistical tables based on standard deviations. For example, 68.26 percent of the distribution will fall within one standard deviation of the expected value ($\bar{D} \pm 1\sigma$). Similarly, 95.44 percent will fall within two standard deviations ($\bar{D} \pm 2\sigma$), and so on. An abbreviated table of areas under the normal curve is shown here.

Number of σ's from Expected Value	+ or −	+ and −
0.5	0.1915	0.3830
1.0	0.3413	0.6826
1.5	0.4332	0.8664
1.96	0.4750	0.9500
2.0	0.4772	0.9544

Assume Project A has an expected value of \$20,000 and a standard deviation (σ) of \$4,000.

a. What is the probability that the outcome will be between \$16,000 and \$24,000?
b. What is the probability that the outcome will be between \$14,000 and \$26,000?
c. What is the probability that the outcome will be at least \$12,000?
d. What is the probability that the outcome will be less than \$27,840?
e. What is the probability that the outcome will be less than \$16,000 or greater than \$26,000?

13. Chilton Airlines is seeking to diversify its business and lower its risk. Currently, it is examining three companies—an auto parts company, an airline food service company, and an oil company. Each of these companies can be bought at the same multiple of earnings. The following represents information about the companies.

Company	Correlation with Chilton Airlines	Sales ($ millions)	Average Earnings ($ millions)	Standard Deviation in Earnings ($ millions)
Chilton Airlines	+ 1.0	$80	$15	$ 5
Auto Parts Company	+ .2	80	15	$ 7.5
Airline Food Service Company	+ .8	80	15	$ 5
Oil Company	− .6	80	15	$10

a. Discuss what would happen to Chilton Airlines' portfolio risk return if it bought the auto parts company? The airline food service company? The oil company?
b. If you were going to buy one company, which would you choose? Why?
c. If you were going to buy two companies, which would you choose? Why?

14. *(Comprehensive problem)*
Tobacco Company of Canada is a very stable billion dollar company with sales growth of about 5 percent per year in good or bad economic conditions. Because of this stability (correlation coefficient with the economy of + .3 and a standard deviation of sales

of about 5 percent from the mean), Mr. Weed, the vice president of finance, thinks the company can absorb some small risky company which could add quite a bit of return without increasing the company's risk very much. He is currently trying to decide which of two companies he will buy. Tobacco Company's cost of capital is 10 percent.

Computer Whiz Company (cost $75 million)		*Atlantic Micro-Technology (cost $75 million)*	
Probability	*After-Tax Cash Flows for 10 Years (in $ millions)*	*Probability*	*After-Tax Cash Flows for 10 years (in $ millions)*
.3	$ 6	.2	$(1)
.3	10	.2	3
.2	16	.2	10
.2	25	.3	25
		.1	31

a. What is the expected cash flow from both companies?
b. Which company has the lower coefficient of variation?
c. Compute the net present value of each company.
d. Which company would you pick, based on net present values?
e. Would you change your mind if you added the risk dimensions into the problem? Explain.
f. What if Computer Whiz had a correlation coefficient with the economy of +.5 and AMT had one of −.1? Which of the companies would give you the best portfolio effects for risk reduction? Which would give you the highest potential returns?
g. What might be the effect of the acquisitions on the market value of Tobacco Company's stock?

15. Virgil Trucking Company is considering the purchase of 50 new diesel trucks that are 15 percent more fuel efficient than the ones the firm is now using. Mr. George R. Kell, the president, has found that the company uses an average of 30 million litres of diesel fuel per year at a price of $.40 per litre.

Mr. Kell assumes that the price of diesel fuel is an external market force he cannot control and that any increased costs of fuel will be passed on to the shipper through higher rates. If this is true, then fuel efficiency would save more money as the price of diesel fuel rose. Mr. Kell has come up with two possible forecasts as shown below—each of which he feels has about a 50 percent chance of coming true. Under assumption number one, diesel prices will stay relatively low; under assumption number two, diesel prices will rise considerably.

Fifty new trucks will cost Virgil Trucking $4.0 million. They qualify for a 30 percent CCA pool. No investment tax credit will be available. The firm has a tax rate of 40 percent and a cost of capital of 16 percent.

a. First compute the yearly expected costs of diesel fuel for both assumption one (relatively low prices) and assumption two (high prices) from the forecasts below:

Forecast for assumption one:

Probability (same for each year)	*Price of Diesel Fuel per Litre*		
	Year 1	*Year 2*	*Year 3*
.1	$.30	$.333	$.37
.2	.333	.38	.40
.3	.40	.43	.50
.2	.45	.50	.55
.2	.50	.55	.60

Forecast for assumption two:

Probability (same for each year)	*Price of Diesel Fuel per Litre*		
	Year 1	*Year 2*	*Year 3*
.1	$.42	$.47	$.50
.3	.43	.57	.67
.4	.55	.67	.75
.2	.60	.75	.85

b. What will be the dollar savings in diesel expenses each year for assumption one and for assumption two?

c. Find the cash flow after taxes for both forecasts.

d. Compute the net present value of the truck purchases for each fuel forecast assumption and the combined net present value (that is, weight the NPVs by .5).

e. If you were Mr. Kell, would you go ahead with this capital investment?

f. How sensitive to fuel prices is this capital investment?

Selected References

Arditti, Fred D. "Risk and the Required Return on Equity." *Journal of Finance* 22 (March 1967), pp. 14–36.

Blume, M. E. "On the Assessment of Risk." *Journal of Finance* 26 (March 1971), pp. 95–117.

Breen, William J., and Eugene M. Lerner. "Corporate Financial Strategies and Market Measures of Risk and Return." *Journal of Finance* 28 (May 1973), pp. 339–51.

Chen, Son-Nan, and William T. Moore. "Investment Decisions under Uncertainty: Application of Estimation Risk in the Hiller Approach." *Journal of Financial and Quantitative Analysis* 17 (September 1982), pp. 425–37.

Fabozzi, Frank J. "The Use of Operations Research Techniques for Capital Budgeting Decisions: A Sample Survey." *Journal of Operations Research Society* 29 (1978), pp. 39–42.

Green, Richard C., and Sanjay Stivastava. "Risk Aversion and Arbitrage." *Journal of Finance* 40 (March 1985), pp. 257–68.

Hayes, Robert H. "Incorporating Risk Aversion into Risk Analysis." *Engineering Economist* 20 (Winter 1975), pp. 99–121.

Hertz, David B. "Investment Policies that Pay Off." *Harvard Business Review* 46 (January–February 1968), pp. 96–108.

________. "Risk Analysis in Capital Investment." *Harvard Business Review* 22 (January–February 1964), pp. 95–106.

Hillier, Frederick S. "A Basic Model for Capital Budgeting of Risky Interrelated Projects." *Engineering Economist* 17 (Fall 1971): pp. 1–30.

Lessard, Donald R., and Richard S. Bower. "Risk-Screening in Capital Budgeting." *Journal of Finance* 28 (May 1973), pp. 331–38.

Levy, Haim, and Marshall Sarnat. "The Portfolio Analysis of Multiperiod Capital Investment under Conditions of Risk." *Engineering Economist* 16 (Fall 1970), pp. 1–19.

Lewellen, Wilber G., and Michael E. Long. "Simulation versus Single-Value Estimates in Capital Expenditure Analysis." *Decision Sciences* 3 (1972), pp. 19–33.

Magee, J. F. "How to Use Decision Trees in Capital Investment." *Harvard Business Review* 42 (September–October 1964), pp. 79–96.

Markowitz, Harry. "Portfolio Selection." *Journal of Finance* 7 (March 1952), pp. 77–91.

Osteryoung, Jerome S.; Elton Scott; and Gordon S. Roberts. "Selecting Capital Projects with the Coefficient of Variation." *Financial Management* 6 (Summer 1977), pp. 65–70.

Richardson, L. K. "Do High Risks Lead to High Returns?" *Financial Analysts Journal* 26 (March–April 1970), pp. 88–99.

Salazar, Rudolfo C., and Subrata K. Sen. "A Simulation Model of Capital Budgeting under Uncertainty." *Management Science* 15 (December 1968), pp. 161–79.

Sharpe, William F. *Portfolio Theory and Capital Markets.* New York: McGraw-Hill, 1970.

Stapleton, R. C. "Portfolio Analysis, Stock Valuation, and Capital Budgeting Decision Rules for Risky Projects." *Journal of Finance* 26 (March 1971), pp. 95–117.

Van Horne, James C. "Capital Budgeting Decisions Using Combinations of Risky Investments." *Management Science* 13 (October 1966), pp. 84–92.

PART

FIVE

Long-Term Financing

Introduction

The methods of long-term financing available to the firm are diverse and constantly changing. At times there appears to be a battleground in which the federal and provincial governments, large corporations, and small businesses are fighting one another for available funds. There has been much concern over the reluctance of investors to channel capital into new venture investments in Canada. There has also been concern over competition due to the funds requirements of the federal government as it scrambles to compensate for its huge budget deficits. Whether a shortage of investment capital for business as a whole exists is a debatable point. It is certain, however, that the average business of small to medium size has historically faced, and continues to face, difficulty in attracting equity investors and long-term lenders.

In Chapter 14 we take a close look at Canada's securities markets with an eye toward the emerging international market system and the radical changes taking place in regulations controlling industry competition. Chapter 15 examines the actual process of selling securities to the public through an investment dealer. The investment dealer is responsible for the analysis, pricing, and distribution of stocks or bonds and serves as the middleman between the corporation and the public. As part of our discussion of investment underwriting, we consider the advantages and disadvantages of going public—that is, of selling stock to the general public in the over-the-counter market or through an organized exchange—rather than maintaining ownership in private hands. The reasons for the cyclical nature of the new issues market and the buoyancy of it in the mid-1980s are explored in detail. Also, we consider the underwriting activity and comparative financial strength of Canadian investment dealers as they prepare for competition with larger foreign-based investment firms after deregulation.

In Chapters 16 and 17 we study the advantages, disadvantages, and limitations of long-term debt, preferred stock, and common stock. Under long-term debt financing we also consider the lease alternative to borrowing funds for the outright purchase of an asset. In Chapter 17 the importance of preferred shares and subordinated voting common shares in Canadian corporate financing are examined. The controversy surrounding the attempted takeover of Canadian Tire by its franchised dealers, through an offer of what amounts to a staggering premium for the voting common while making no offer for the nonvoting, is explored in detail.

In Chapter 18 we examine the corporation's decision as to whether it should pay out earnings in the form of dividends or retain them to fund future projects. The chapter considers dividend policy in relation to its impact on shareholder expectations and market value maximization.

Corporate securities that may be converted into common stock or that have special provisions for the purchase of common stock are considered in Chapter 19. The investment features of convertibles and warrants are evaluated along with their potential use in corporate finance.

14 Capital Markets in Canada

Security markets are generally separated into short-term and long-term markets. The short-term markets are composed of government bills and bonds with maturities up to three years and of other fixed-income securities with maturities of one year or less. These short-term markets are referred to as money markets. The securities most commonly traded in these markets, such as Treasury bills, commercial paper, and negotiable certificates of deposit, were previously discussed under working capital and cash management and will not be covered again.

The long-term markets are called capital markets and consist of securities having maturities greater than one year. The most common corporate securities in this category are bonds, common stock, preferred stock, and convertible securities. These securities are found on the firm's balance sheet under the designation long-term liabilities and equities. Taken together with the retained earnings, these long-term securities comprise the firm's capital structure.

In the following chapters of this part we will be looking at how the capital markets are organized and integrated into the corporate and economic system of Canada. We will also study how corporate securities are sold by investment dealers and examine the rights, contractual obligations, and unique features of each type of security.

Competition for Funds in the Capital Markets

In order to put corporate securities into perspective, it is necessary to look at other securities that are available in the capital markets. The federal government, provincial governments, and local municipalities all compete with one another for a limited supply of financial capital, with the capital markets serving as a way of allocating the available capital among competing possible users. Therefore, the ultimate investor chooses among many kinds of securities, both corporate and noncorporate. The investor will generally do this so as to maximize his return for any given level of risk.

Figure 14–1 depicts the composition of long-term funds raised in the Canadian capital markets from 1965 through 1986.[1] Strikingly, it shows that, over that time period, corporate securities issues comprised only 37 percent of the total, while government securities made up the rest.[2] It also shows that both the corporate and noncorporate markets are large and have grown substantially over the past 20 years. The total amount of new securities issues with maturities of more than one year had risen from $2 billion in 1965 to about $4.5 billion in 1970. Over the next 15 years that amount had expanded by almost 800 percent so that, in 1985, it stood at just under $40 billion. The fact that the total funds raised in Canadian capital markets had not exceeded $10 billion in a single year before 1975 makes the $30 billion plus activity in each year since 1983 all the more significant historically.

---

[1]Note that even larger amounts of money were being raised in the short-term money markets, as shown in Figure 8–3, Chapter 8.

[2]As a point of comparison it is interesting to note that in the larger U.S. capital market, corporate capital constituted 40 percent, indicating that despite the absolute size of the corporate sector in that economy, its capital market activity is still much smaller that that of the federal, state, and local governments. The total funds raised in the U.S. capital markets in 1984 were $422 billion or over 10 times the amount raised in Canadian capital markets.

Figure 14–1
Composition of funds (net) raised in Canadian capital markets by corporations and governments

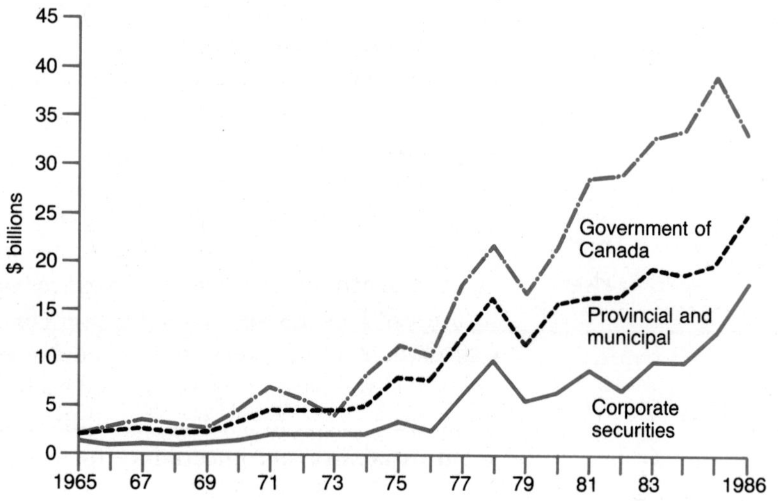

Source: *Bank of Canada Review,* Series F6, selected issues.

Government Securities

Government of Canada securities In accordance with government fiscal policy, the Bank of Canada manages the federal government's debt in order to balance budgetary inflows and outflows. When deficits are incurred, the government can sell short-term or long-term securities to finance the shortfall.

Figure 14–1 depicts only the long-term element of that financing. Over the total 22-year period for which Figure 14–1 presents information, long-term Government of Canada financing averaged 35 percent of the total for all long-term funds raised in Canadian capital markets. Since 1981, however, large fiscal deficits have meant that long-term Government of Canada financing has accounted for over 40 percent of the total. Because of the size of the deficits, the government has had to go to the bond markets at least once a month in recent years for the purpose of either rolling over maturing debt or for financing revenue shortfalls. It remains to be seen if the Government of Canada can find an effective policy for reducing the deficit and thereby government borrowing.

Besides the mounting deficits, the government's demand for long-term capital is also dependent upon the relationship between long-term and short-term interest rates. The discussion of the term structure of interest rates in Chapter 6 demonstrates the volatile nature of short-term rates. During 1981 and 1982 the skyrocketing of short-term interest rates had the effect of shifting the government's dependence away from short-term funding toward long-term sources. With the later return to lower short-term interest rates in 1983, the federal government returned to a more normal balance between short- and long-term securities. This has shortened the average maturity on Government of Canada debt from 7 years in 1979 to 5½ years in 1985. With over 40 percent of the debt being refinanced each year,[3] continued refundings in addition to net new needs for additional financing causes concerns about instability and uncertainty for both the money and the capital markets.

Provincial and municipal government bonds The fact that the provinces issued between $6.5 billion and $10 billion of new securities over and above refundings each year since 1980 makes them important borrowers in the bond market. Historically, the provinces had borrowed mainly long term to fund capital projects, but recent budget deficits have led them to become active in the short-term market as well. Because certain provinces (for example, Quebec) and certain provincial crown corporations borrow actively in foreign as well as in domestic markets, usually about one quarter to one third of provincial financings are done outside of Canadian markets. In 1986 foreign provincial financings were an exceptionally high 53 percent of total provincial long-term borrowing.

Municipal bonds comprise a small portion of the bond market. In 1986 they amounted to only $430 million above refundings. Because most municipal debentures are relatively illiquid, they tend to be purchased mainly by institutions.

During the 1965 to 1986 time period provincial and municipal bonds together accounted for some 31 percent of the total funds raised in

---

[3]As of December 31, 1985, Government of Canada marketable debt stood at $149.8 billion with $59.4 billion of that in Treasury bills and $19.7 billion in bonds with less than three years to maturity.

Canadian capital markets. Historically, then, provincial bonds have been a large component of the long-term securities market in Canada. Only in recent years has the federal government become a more important player in this market.

Corporate Securities

Corporate bonds Over the time period represented in Figure 14–1 corporate securities comprised 34 percent of the value of net new long-term financing in Canadian markets. Of corporate securities bond financings were 24 percent of the total. Although the corporate bond has been an important element of Canadian markets historically, the overall balance between raising new capital via stock or bond issues has been very volatile. Until the late 1970s bond financings dominated stock issues. This was understandable in light of the historically low price-earnings ratios in the early and mid-1970s, which made management unenthusiastic about issuing stock. In the 1982 to 1985 period, by way of contrast, domestic bond issues were an almost negligible source of new corporate financing. In fact, 72 percent of the value of bonds placed by Canadian firms between 1980 and 1986 was issued in foreign markets. Much of the rest was issued domestically via private placement.

Preferred stock Figure 14–2 provides comparative data on the use of various capital market financing alternatives by Canadian firms. It shows that preferred stock is a surprisingly important source of corporate financing in Canada. While comprising only 6 percent of long-term financing in the United States over the period 1970 to 1985,[4] it accounted for almost 36 percent in Canada.

This difference in importance of preferred share funding in Canada versus the United States is somewhat a result of differences in the tax treatment of corporate dividends coupled with the prevalence of holding company controlling ownership of Canadian companies. In both countries interest payments are tax deductible to a corporation while dividends are not. In the United States dividends received are taxed

[4]*Federal Reserve Bulletins.*

Figure 14–2
Corporate financings in Canadian capital markets

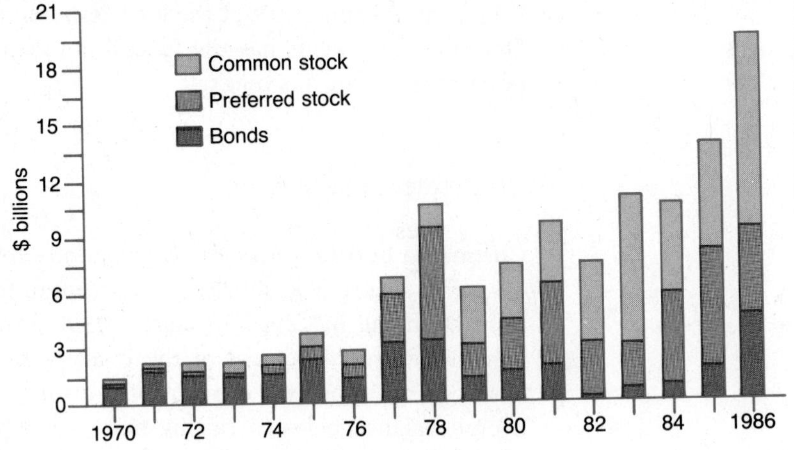

Source: *Bank of Canada Review*, Series F10, selected issues.

at the full personal rate. Regulated public utilities, who can pass the tax disadvantage of preferred shares versus debt on to the customer, are the major issuers of preferred shares in the United States. In Canada dividend income is generally not taxable when paid from one Canadian corporation to another. There is a dividend tax credit accorded to individual investors.[5] The tax advantage of debt over preferred share financing is thus erased in certain circumstances and reduced in most others.

Common stock Somewhat surprisingly in the mind of the average Canadian, the sale of common stock during the period 1970–1986 averaged only 40 percent of total corporate long-term financing. When the total long-term funding activity in Canadian capital markets is considered, common stock accounted for only about 14 percent of all long-term financings over that period. The small percentage of new common stock issued and the periodic variance of that percentage illustrate that common stock has not been reliable as a regular source of new long-term financing for corporations.

---

[5]See Chapter 18 for a description of the dividend tax credit.

Equity Financing in General

The year-to-year variance in common stock versus debt issuance, as shown by Figure 14–2, is striking. Note that in 1979 common stock issues accounted for only $1.1 billion or about one ninth of the corporate funds raised in the Canadian capital market. In 1983 common stock issues amounted to $7.5 billion or well over two thirds of the total.

Although one must be careful in assigning simple explanations to such variations, there do seem to be some partial explanations available. Basically, it is safe to say that the general "bumpiness" of financing issues will lead a given firm to issue a large amount of debt at one point in time. This will often, then, be followed by a large amount of equity as the next financing in order to keep the debt-to-equity ratio in the appropriate range. This does not explain, however, general trends by the whole population of firms toward debt or equity. In 1980 and 1981, for example, heavy acquisition activity, largely spurred on by the National Energy Program and by low stock market values, was financed largely by debt. Much of that debt was in the form of bank financing. In 1981 nonfinancial corporations' bank indebtedness increased by a net amount of almost $16.5 billion.

The interesting question is why so much debt was used in the financings. We will touch on this issue again later in Chapter 20, but basically, part of the reason lies in the very rationale for making the acquisitions in the first place. Generally, low stock market values made managers reluctant to sell shares in their own firms even though they made them anxious to buy those of other firms. Conversely, in 1983 through 1987, when the stock market was assigning much higher valuations than in 1981, corporate managements undertook to rebuild their corporate balance sheets by issuing equity to achieve more normal debt/equity ratios. In 1983, for example, Canadian nonfinancial private corporations' net issues of stock were over $6 billion while their bank indebtedness decreased by $7.6 billion.

Such an explanation of debt versus equity issuance means that managers attempt to time their issues of common stock. Empirical studies in the United States and in Great Britain have shown that stock issues tend to be more popular after prices have risen than after they have fallen.[6] At least two observations on this behaviour should be of interest to all serious students and/or practitioners of financial management. First, an increased market value for a firm's shares increases its capacity to incur debt. Yet firms substitute equity for debt on their balance sheets at that time. Second, managers seem to believe equity is expensive when stock markets are low by historic standards (and vice versa). This implies they have some notion of the stock market generally underpricing and overpricing equity rather than as placing a rational value on it at all points in time.

Figure 14–3 is a graphic representation of debt-to-equity ratios among Canadian nonfinancial private corporations. It shows that over the 25-year period ending in 1984, the debt-to-book-equity ratio has been generally rising, so that by 1984 it was about 1:4:1 versus about 1:1 in the early 1960s. On the other hand, that ratio has not increased since the mid-1970s. When some value for equity based on current

Figure 14–3
Debt-to-equity ratios for nonfinancial private corporations

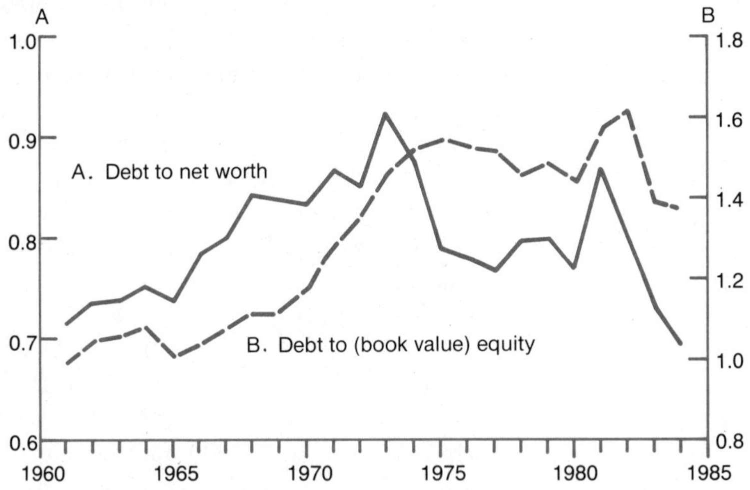

Source: *National Balance Sheet Accounts,* chart 19, p. xxix.

[6]R. A. Taggart, "A Model of Corporate Financing Decisions," *Journal of Finance* 32 (December 1977), pp. 1467–84; and P. Marsh, "The Choice between Equity and Debt: An Empirical Study," *Journal of Finance* 37 (March 1982), pp. 121–44.

value accounting is used, the debt-to-equity ratio seems to be trending down from a peak reached in 1973.[7]

Internal versus External Sources of Funds

Thus far the discussion has centered on corporations raising long-term financing externally using bonds, preferred stock, and common stock. However, funds generated and retained from on-going operations have historically been an even more important source of funds to the corporation. These internally generated funds are generally designated as retained earnings and accounting expense amounts for depreciation and other noncash items. In the previous discussion of cost of capital in Chapter 11, the cost of retained earnings was considered, while Chapter 12 demonstrated how the capital budgeting decision is significantly impacted by the noncash nature of depreciation charges.

Table 14–1 summarizes the flow of funds for nonfinancial private corporations in Canada during 1986 as a way to give the reader some insight into where corporate funds get absorbed and from where they are generated.

Table 14–1
Canadian nonfinancial private corporations: Funds flow, 1986 (in billions)

Expenditures		*Sources of Funds*	
Capital investment	$47,662	Operations:	
Inventories	2,205	Retained earnings	$11,759
Accounts receivable	223	Depreciation	29,222
Other financial assets	18,145	Trade payables	(389)
	68,235	Loans	(1,736)
Discrepancy	3,885	Commercial paper	7,955
	$72,090	Mortgages	749
		Bonds	4,547
		Associated corp.	5,699
		Stock issues	13,337
		Other liabilities	947
			$72,090

Source: Statistics Canada, *Financial Flow Accounts*, 1986, quarter 4, table 2–2.

[7]See Chapter 11 for a discussion of debt capacity.

From Table 14–1 we see that cash from operations accounted for 56.9 percent of the funds generated. Figure 14–4 shows the ratio of internally generated versus externally generated corporate funds over the period 1965–1986. Although corporations had relied primarily on internally generated funds prior to the mid-1960s, Figure 14–4 shows a roughly equal weighting of internal and external funding over the whole period since 1965. Because the inflationary spiral that began in the mid-60s made equipment depreciation amounts inadequate for the investment required to replace it, one would have suspected a more dramatic shift toward external financing sources.

The ability to reinvest internally generated funds[8] insulates managerial decision making to some extent from the scrutiny of objective outside analysts. It is not uncommon for firms that have limited investment opportunities in traditional businesses to look elsewhere to invest internally generated funds rather than pay them out to shareholders. Although it is probably true that managers would make less

Figure 14–4
Internal versus external generation of corporate funding requirements

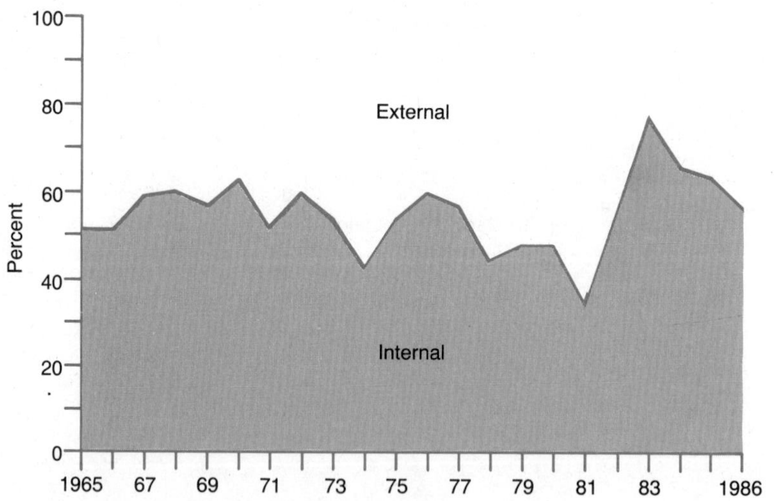

Source: Statistics Canada, *Financial Flow Accounts*, various issues.

[8]Remember, earnings could be paid out to shareholders as dividends requiring firms to raise and justify to external investors the funds for new investments.

investment decisions if they had to approach external sources for each investment, it is not clear that this would result in better investment decisions by managers. For one thing, such a system would be awkward and costly. Second, it would require managers to make public every detail of their planned competitive strategy which might deprive their companies of the benefits of a unique industrial initiative. The current system whereby managers are held accountable for the outcomes of their decisions after the fact and only on an aggregated basis is probably necessary for good management practice although it may also allow mediocre practices to go undetected for some time. In the end investors cannot monitor the actions of management in "real time." Therefore, since investors must trust in management's ability to choose the best options, it is extremely important to ensure that the best possible individuals occupy managerial positions.

The Supply of Capital Funds

In a three-sector economy consisting of business, government, and households, the major supplier of funds for investment is the household sector. Corporations and the federal government have traditionally been net demanders of funds. Figure 14–5 diagrams the flow of funds through our basic three-sector economy.

As households receive wages and transfer payments from the government and wages and dividends from corporations, they generally save some portion of their income. These savings are usually funneled to financial intermediaries that in turn make investments in the capital markets with the funds received from the household sector. This is known as indirect investment. The types of financial institutions that channel funds into the capital markets are specialized and diverse. Funds may flow into the chartered banks, trust companies, mortgage companies, and credit unions. Households may also purchase mutual fund shares, invest in life insurance, or participate in some form of private pension plan or profit sharing. All of these financial institutions act as intermediaries; they help make the flow of funds from one sector of the economy to another very efficient and competitive. Without intermediaries, the cost of funds would be higher, and the efficient allocation of funds to the best users at the lowest cost would not take place.

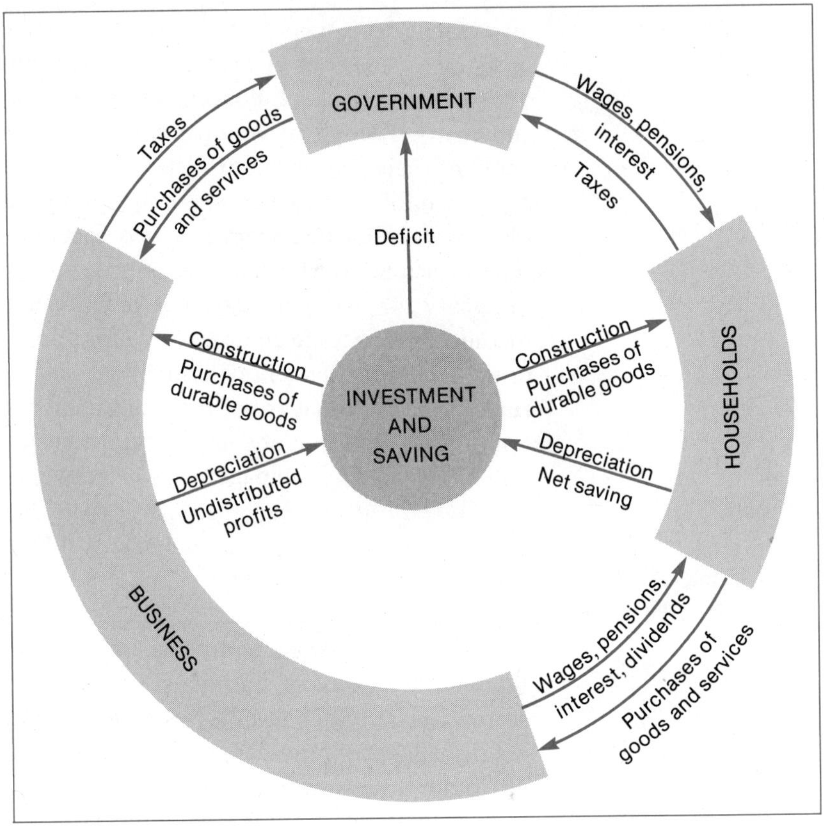

Figure 14–5
Flow of funds through the economy

The Role of the Security Markets

Security markets exist to facilitate the allocation of capital among households, corporations, and governmental units, with financial institutions acting as intermediaries. Just as financial institutions specialize in their services and investments, so are the capital markets divided into many functional subsets, with each specific market serving a certain type of security. For example, the common stocks of some of the largest corporations are traded on the Toronto Stock Exchange, whereas government securities are traded by government security dealers in the over-the-counter markets.

After a security is sold initially as an original offering, it will then trade in its appropriate market among all kinds of investors. This trading activity is known as secondary trading since funds flow among investors rather than into the corporation from an investor. Secondary trading is vitally important as it provides liquidity for investors and keeps prices competitive among alternative security investments.

Security markets provide liquidity in two ways. First, they enable corporations to raise funds by selling new issues of securities rapidly and at competitive prices. Second, they allow the investor who purchases securities to sell them with relative ease and speed and thereby to turn a paper asset into cash at will. Ask yourself the question, "Would I buy securities if there were no place to sell them?" You would probably think twice before committing funds to an illiquid investment. It follows, then, that without markets, corporations and governmental units would not be able to raise the large amounts of capital necessary for economic growth. Therefore, the presence and efficient management of security markets in Canada is vitally important to individuals, corporations, and governments alike.

The Organization of the Security Markets

The competitive structure and organization of the security markets have changed considerably since the early 1970s. In this section we present the current organization of the markets, provide an update of significant events of the last few years, and make a small conjecture about the nature of the security markets well into the 1980s. The most common division of security markets is between organized exchanges and over-the-counter markets. Each will be examined separately.

The Organized Exchanges

An organized stock exchange is a marketplace where buyers and sellers of securities come together for the purpose of trading securities. Prices on an exchange are established competitively according to conditions of supply and demand. Canadian exchanges facilitate the trading of common and preferred shares, rights and warrants, listed options, financial instrument futures, and some commodities.

Organized exchanges are either regional or national in scope. Each exchange has a central location where all buyers and sellers meet in an auction market to transact purchases and sales. Buyers and sellers are not actually present on the floor of the exchange but are represented by brokers who act as their agents. These brokers are registered members of the exchange by virtue of having purchased one or more seats on the particular exchange.

Each exchange has its own governing body whose job it is to do the administration and policy setting for the stock exchange. Each governing body is made up of permanent officers of the exchange, members of the brokerage community, and individuals representing the community outside of the brokerage industry.

In Canada there are five stock exchanges located in Montreal, Toronto, Winnipeg, Calgary, and Vancouver. Member firms are allowed to own more than one seat and on the Toronto (TSE), Alberta (ASE), and Vancouver (VSE) exchanges are entitled to one vote per seat to a maximum of three votes. The Montreal Exchange (ME) has no such maximum. Table 14–2 shows the comparative volumes of these exchanges.

From Table 14–2 we see that the Toronto Stock Exchange is by far the most important, accounting for some 75 percent of the dollar volume of trading in listed stocks. Over 4.9 billion shares were traded on the TSE in 1986. At the other end of the share trading spectrum is the Winnipeg exchange whose importance is really as a commodities exchange. Share volume at Vancouver is 70 percent of that at Toronto,

Table 14–2
Percentage of listed stock trading in Canada by exchange

	Toronto	Montreal	Vancouver	Alberta	Winnipeg
By share volume:					
1965	55.0%	25.2%	17.7%	2.0%	0.1%
1975	42.3	12.2	44.1	1.3	0.1
1980	47.9	7.1	41.0	3.9	0.1
1985	47.2	9.2	40.2	3.2	0.1
1986	49.7	11.1	35.4	3.7	0.1
By dollar volume:					
1965	67.1	26.2	6.4	0.2	0.1
1975	70.4	23.8	5.4	0.3	0.1
1980	77.1	10.1	11.5	1.2	0.1
1985	76.4	16.4	4.8	0.5	0.1
1986	75.3	18.9	5.3	0.6	0.1

while share trading value is only 7 percent of Toronto's indicating the relative low price of VSE-listed stocks. This is largely due to the fact that Vancouver is mostly active with trade in speculative junior mining and oil issues. The Montreal Exchange declined in importance after the election in 1976 of a separatist government but has gained volume in more recent years. The small Alberta Stock Exchange in Calgary deals mainly in provincially based companies.

Listing requirements The listing requirements differ from exchange to exchange. For example, the Montreal Exchange requires a minimum net income for an industrial company listing of $100,000 in the year previous to listing, while the TSE requires a minimum pre-tax cash flow of $200,000 and Alberta, a profit of $25,000. Many Canadian stocks are listed on more than one Canadian exchange in addition to being listed on exchanges in other countries. The most prevalent outside country for listing is the United States where 110 Canadian stocks were listed as of the end of 1985.

Since most of the largest Canadian companies are traded on the TSE, it is not surprising that its listing requirements are more stringent than the others. Although each case is decided on its own merits, the minimum requirements for a company to be listed as an "industrial" on the Toronto Stock Exchange for the first time are as follows:[9]

1. In the fiscal year immediately preceding the application, some pre-tax profitability and a minimum pre-tax cash flow of $200,000; average pre-tax cash flow of at least $150,000 for the two years preceding application, although consideration is given based on evidence of future profitability; working capital minimum of $350,000 with minimum net tangible assets of $1 million.
2. A minimum of 200,000 shares publicly held with at least 200 shareholders owning a board lot or more of shares; however, there can be as few as 100,000 public shares if the product of the number of publicly held shares multiplied by the number of public shareholders owning a board lot or more is equal to or greater than 40 million.
3. A minimum of $350,000 market value of issued shares owned by the public.

[9]The TSE also had less stringent requirements for listing in the mining and oil and gas categories.

Corporations desiring to be listed on exchanges have made the decision that public availability of the stock on an exchange will benefit their shareholders. The benefits will occur either by providing liquidity to owners or by allowing the company a more viable means for raising external capital for growth and expansion. The company must pay a nonrecurring listing fee determined by the number of shares to be listed. An annual sustaining fee is also paid in order to keep the listing in good standing.

The exchanges have the authority to withdraw a listed security's trading or listing privileges either temporarily or permanently. Such actions would be taken to protect the interests of the investors or at the request of the company in respect of its own securities.

The Over-the-Counter Markets

Corporations trading in the over-the-counter market (OTC) are referred to as unlisted. There is no central location for the OTC market, but instead a network of brokers and dealers is linked together by computer display terminals, telephones, and teletypes. While the organized exchanges trade by auction, the OTC market is a way of carrying out trading by negotiation.

Many dealers and brokers make markets in the same security and thus create prices on the active stocks. With the advent of a centralized computer to keep track of all trades and prices, potential traders have up-to-the-minute price information on all competing traders.

According to the Investment Dealers Association, the overall OTC market in North America involves over 50,000 stocks and 14,000 bonds. Although the shares of a few conservative industrial companies trade over the counter, the average price of securities traded is lower, making the dollar volume traded much less than that of the organized exchanges. Since 1969 Quebec brokers have been required to report statistics on unlisted trading in Quebec to the Quebec Securities Commission. Since 1970 the Investment Dealers Asssociation and the Ontario Securities Commission have operated a reporting system for designated unlisted industrial stocks. In the early 1980s there were about 1,000 securities in this group, of which about 200 would trade in a given week.

In contrast to the Canadian situation where very few stocks trading over the counter could obtain listing on the TSE, in the United States there are many large companies trading over the counter. Such well-known companies as Apple Computer, MCI Communications, and Intel are included in that group. The National Association of Securities Dealers in the United States estimates that at least 600 of the over-the-counter stocks would meet the very stringent listing requirements of the New York Stock Exchange (NYSE).

Historically, trading in bonds and debentures in Canada has occurred in the OTC market. In a given year the value of trading in bond and money market securities on the OTC markets can be 10 times or more greater than the value of trading on Canada's five stock exchanges.

Recent Developments in Trading

In recent years the nature of doing business in the stock market has changed and will probably continue to evolve. By early 1986 more than half of the trades on the TSE were occurring via the Computer Assisted Trading System (CATS). With the use of this system orders are executed directly without the use of floor traders. In 1986 a system called Canadian Over-the-Counter Automated Trading System (COATS) was introduced by the Ontario Securities Commission for trading unlisted stocks.

Up until April 1, 1983, the exchanges had fixed the commissions to be charged by brokers. Since that time rates have been set competitively as they have been in the United States since 1975.[10] Such a move has provided an entry availability for discount brokers who simply execute trades while offering no analytic information to customers. By late 1986 two of the major chartered banks had gotten into the discount brokerage business partially as a way to retain the cash balances investors would otherwise keep on deposit with investment dealers. If this discount competition intensifies, it will lead the traditional investment brokers to start unbundling their charges so that information is paid for separately from trading commissions. After three years of operation, however, the penetration of discount brokers in Canada was still minimal—5 percent of trades versus 20 percent in the United States. Although the deregulation of rates definitely decreased brokerage costs

[10]With the growing internationalization of markets and interlisting of stocks, sophisticated investors had the ability to negotiate cheaper trades in New York and elsewhere. The Canadian move was a reaction to this reality.

for large, institutional investors, it seemed to have led to increased charges for the individual investor.

In comparison to the New York markets, the secondary markets in Canada are thin, with few buyers and sellers. This condition makes it difficult to carry out large transactions without a significant price effect. While the Canadian equities market has consisted almost entirely of exchange-listed stocks, New York has a large over-the-counter market as well as a "third" market that takes place among the dealers outside of the exchanges. Even in exchange trading on the NYSE, dealers play a much larger role acting as specialists who make markets in given stocks. All of this has historically meant a seller would have to give up his stock at a lower price, on the TSE versus the NYSE, in order to make it marketable. The extremely liquid markets in the United States thus tended to attract business away from Canadian markets. In order to reduce this relatively higher price of liquidity, the Toronto Stock Exchange has been urging a larger role for dealers acting as principals rather than brokers in stock trading.

It is probably safe to say that over the next decade securities markets will become more competitive as computer systems are employed to do more and more of the trading and as innovations are found to make the secondary markets more liquid.

Market Efficiency

We have mentioned competitive and efficient markets all through this chapter, but so far we have not given criteria to judge whether the Canadian securities markets are indeed competitive and efficient markets.

Criteria of Efficiency

There are several concepts of market efficiency, and there are many degrees of efficiency, depending on which market we are talking about. Markets in general are efficient when: (1) prices adjust rapidly to new information; (2) there is a continuous market in which each successive trade is made at a price close to the previous price (the faster the price responds to new information and the smaller the differences in price changes, the more efficient the market); and (3) the market can absorb large dollar amounts of securities without destabilizing the price.

A key variable affecting efficiency is the certainty of the income stream. The more certain the expected income, the less volatile price movements will be. Fixed-income securities, with known maturities, have reasonably efficient markets. The most efficient market is that for Government of Canada securities, with the short-term Treasury bill market being exemplary. Corporate bond markets are somewhat efficient but less so than government bond markets. A question still widely debated and researched by academics is whether markets for common stock are truly efficient.

The Efficient Market Hypothesis

If stock markets are efficient, it is very difficult for investors to select portfolios of common stocks that can outperform the stock market in general. That is because all relevant and available information would already be reflected in the stock prices. In the terminology of capital budgeting, then, purchases and sales of stocks in an efficient market are zero-NPV transactions.

This concept of market efficiency is called the efficient market hypothesis, and it has been stated in three forms which have been designated the weak, semistrong, and strong forms. The weak form simply states that prices reflect all of the information contained in the past price history. This implies that past price information is unrelated to future prices so that attempting to extrapolate trends will generate no additional gains to investors. This noncorrelation of future price movements with past price movements has been referred to as a "random walk" and has received much empirical validation. The second level of efficiency is the semistrong form. It states that prices reflect all "public" information. Most of the research in this area focuses on changes in public information, such as announcements of company earnings forecasts, and on the measurement of how rapidly prices converge to a new equilibrium after the release of new information.[11] This research has concluded that this information was rapidly reflected in the stock price. A third level of efficiency, the strong form, states

[11]See, for example, G. Mandelker, "Risk and Return: The Case of Merging Firms," *Journal of Financial Economics* 1 (December 1974), pp. 303–35; and G. Charest, "Returns to Dividend Splitting Stocks on the Toronto Stock Exchange," *Journal of Business Administration* 12 (Fall 1980), pp. 1–18.

that all information, both "private" and "public," is immediately reflected in stock prices. Under this form of market efficiency, efficient markets should prevent insiders and large institutions from being able to make profits in excess of the market in general. A number of analyses of the portfolio performance of mutual fund managers has shown that this group of investors does no better than the market as a whole.

Much research in recent years has been focused on the measurement of market efficiency. As communications systems advance information will get disseminated more quickly and accurately. Furthermore, securities laws are forcing fuller disclosure of inside corporate data. The research has shown that our capital markets generally function well. Disclosure of more and better information, therefore, should be digested and reflected in stock prices, allowing for even better valuations.

Securities Regulation—A Changing Environment

Much of our discussion of the role of the organized exchanges above centered on the self-regulatory role of the exchanges with regard to their members and clients. Besides the stock exchanges, the Investment Dealers' Association is an important player in the self-regulation of securities markets. Stock exchanges impose listing requirements, demand regular financial statements, demand notice of material changes in corporate affairs, establish trading rules to protect the public, and enact special rules to govern takeover bids exercised through the exchanges. One interesting TSE regulation is that no financial institution outside of the securities industry can own more than 10 percent of a member firm. As you will see later in this section, that rule had to change before June 1987. The Investment Dealers' Association establishes minimal capital limits for member firms, maintains a fund to reimburse clients in case of a member firm's failure, monitors the ethics of clients' conduct, and sets up courses of instruction for securities industry employees.

Despite the conscientious attempts at self-regulation by the industry, governments still have little confidence in the adequacy of self-regulation. As mentioned in Chapter 1, the policing of fraudulent or unfair practices has been a major concern of these regulatory bodies since the 1930s.

Because regulation of the securities industry is a provincial responsibility, each of the provinces has its own securities commission. However, most provinces adopt the regulations of the Ontario Securities Commission as the majority of major companies are listed and trade on the Toronto Stock Exchange. The general exception to that uniformity of provincial approach is Quebec. Although the need to generally improve the policing of market-related activities is an ongoing priority, as of 1987 the world of regulation relating to ownership policy was undergoing a massive reorientation.

The Four Pillars of Finance

In order to understand the current changing regulatory situation in the securities industry, we must review the philosophies that underlay the historical regulation of the whole financial sector in Canada. Because of concerns over conflict of interest, the basic structural foundation has been one called the four pillars of finance. There were to be banks, trust companies, insurance companies, and securities dealers. Thus, the reasoning went, a bank would not be caught in the bind of having to decide whether to lend money from a trust account to a corporate client. Another hallmark of the financial sector has been restrictions on nonresident ownership. This was ostensibly to safeguard investors and depositors as regulators would have more control over Canadian residents. In addition, various rules have been aimed at preventing self-dealing. Thus, regulations prevent nonfinancial firms from owning financial firms. In banking restrictions have been aimed at preventing one individual or group from buying control for the same reason.

Over the past 20 years, however, there has been significant erosion of the separation of function among these four sectors. Trust companies provide chequing and other facilities competitive with banks. Securities firms pay interest on clients' account balances. Since changes to the 1967 and 1980 Bank Acts, banks have moved into mortgage lending, personal lending, leasing and factoring services, and discount brokerage. However, banks are still prohibited from trust activities and underwriting securities in Canada. They already have subsidiaries that do offshore underwriting.

Table 14–3 shows the capital bases of each of the groups within the Canadian financial industry. As can be readily seen, the investment

Table 14–3 Shareholders' equity of the four pillars of finance (in millions)

	July 1986	Five-Year Growth Rate
Charted banks	$20,028	21%
Trust companies	3,172	12
Life insurers	12,998	11
Investment dealers	577	11

dealers have miniscule capital bases when compared to the others, especially the banks. This small capital base is a current concern to industry firms as proposed changes in regulation promise to alter the competitive environment dramatically.

Although there had traditionally been a policy of separating the real and financial sectors in Canada, conglomerates with financial subsidiaries started to appear. Peter and Edward Bronfman's Trilon Corporation controlled Royal Trust, London Life, Triathlon Leasing, Eurobrokers Investment Corp., and Trilon Bancorp. Paul Desmarais' Power Financial Corp. controlled Investors Syndicate, Great West Life Assurance, and Montreal Trust, while Imasco, the tobacco products giant, took over Canada Trust, the sixth largest financial institution in the country.

Current Directions in Regulation

Only the fear of foreign ownership seemed to have survived the test of time and corporate ingenuity. Historically, increasing activity by foreign investment dealers had led the Ontario government in 1971 to enact legislation limiting nonresident ownership of securities firms to 25 percent in total and to 10 percent for any single nonresident. After years of study in the 1980s Ontario task forces recommended upholding the twin policy goals of maintaining the four pillars concept and of keeping the industry Canadian. In an attempt to open the industry up to more competition, however, they did recommend raising the limits on foreign ownership to 30 percent and also allowing other financial institutions to participate on the same basis as nonresidents. This restriction on other financial institutions related to Ontario's fear of undue corporate concentration, especially because of the size of the Canadian chartered banks.

Although the foregoing represented the preferred position of the Ontario government, Canada's federal government had other objectives. It wanted to allow the banks to control 100 percent of securities firms so that the country's investment industry would have the financial muscle to compete with the investment Goliaths of the United States and Japan. In addition, Ottawa was looking at banks and financial service, already a major component of Canada's export activity, to become major factors in future export growth. Canada's banks were well positioned to become major players in the U.S. banking industry as it went from a local, state system to a national system. No bank in the United States had ever managed thousands of branches continentwide as had the large Canadian banks. Thus, as the large U.S. investment houses welcomed the idea of open access to Canada's securities industry, the Canadian banks were anxious to see deregulation of the U.S. banking sector.

In negotiations Ottawa's objectives of ensuring competition seemed to win out over Ontario's concerns related to Canadian ownership and investor protection. In late 1986 Ontario had agreed to make the legislative changes to allow foreign interests to own up to 100 percent of investment dealers by 1988. They also agreed to amend the Securities Act to allow the same for banks and trust companies. At the same time Quebec allowed the Bank of Nova Scotia to set up a 100 percent owned securities subsidiary putting pressure on Ottawa and Ontario to catch up. The Bank of Nova Scotia was able to do this under an obscure clause in the Bank Act that allowed banks to take control of an off-limits company for two years before divesting. As this book goes to print the expectation is that banks, insurance companies, and trust companies will be able to enter the Ontario securities industry by July of 1987, with wholly owned foreign interests able to compete by mid-1988. Companies owning interests in the nonfinancial sector are to be constrained from entry or buying controlling ownership of financial institutions. However, for those commercially linked companies already owning financial firms, a grandfather clause will restrict them to no greater than 65 percent ownership.

Summary

In this chapter we presented the concept of a capital market in which corporations compete for funds not only among themselves but with governmental units of all kinds. Corporations only account for about

35 percent of all funds raised in the capital market. Up until the late 1970s bond financings dominated equity issues, but during the 1980s the opposite was true. We also depicted a three-sector economy consisting of households, corporations, and governmental units and showed how funds flow through the capital markets from suppliers of funds to the ultimate users. This process is highly dependent upon the efficiency of the financial institutions that act as intermediaries in channeling the funds to the most productive users.

Security markets are divided into organized exchanges and over-the-counter markets. Brokers act as agents for stock exchange transactions, and dealers make markets over the counter at their own risk as owners of the securities they trade. The Toronto Stock Exchange is the largest of the organized exchanges. We explored some of its major characteristics, such as its relative size, the liquidity it provides corporations and investors, and its requirements for listing securities. Although the OTC market for stock is not significant in Canada, corporate bond trades and trades in municipal, provincial, and federal government securities are transacted over the counter.

Throughout this chapter we have tried to present the concept of efficient markets doing an important job in allocating financial capital. We find the existing markets struggling to provide liquidity for both the corporation and the investor while they adjust efficiently to new information. Because of the laws governing the markets, much information is available for investors, and this in itself creates more competitive prices. Moreover, there are few cases of fraud and manipulation. In the future we expect even more efficient markets with expanded roles for the investment dealers aimed at increasing liquidity for secondary trading.

Historically, regulations in the securities industry have been aimed at maintaining Canadian ownership and avoiding conflicts of interest. The latter meant prohibiting securities firm ownership by other financial and nonfinancial firms. Currently proposed changes in regulation promise to increase industry competitiveness by allowing ownership by foreign interests and by other financial institutions. Given the relatively small equity position of Canadian investment dealers, this will cause investment firms to seriously consider raising new capital or selling out to larger financial institutions. Regulators continue to propose that companies with nonfinancial interests still be constrained from controlling securities or any Canadian financial firm.

List of Terms

money markets
capital markets
Treasury bills
internal corporate funds
external corporate funds
financial intermediaries
three-sector economy
secondary trading
Toronto Stock Exchange
Montreal Exchange
over-the-counter markets
brokers
dealers
third market
market efficiency
Securities Commission
Bank Act
Investment Dealers Association
four pillars of finance

Discussion Questions

1. Name the major competitors for funds in the capital markets.
2. How does the economy influence the amount of funds raised by the federal government in the long-term markets?
3. Discuss the average maturity of the federal government's marketable interest-bearing public debt and the implications for the money and capital markets if the present trend continues.
4. What has been the percentage composition of long-term financing by corporations from 1970 through 1986?
5. Comment on the use of external versus internal sources of funds by corporations in the 1970s and 1980s. What has caused this shifting pattern?
6. Explain the role of financial intermediaries in the flow of funds through the economy.
7. Discuss the importance of security markets for both the corporation and the stockholder or bondholder.
8. What is the difference between organized exchanges and over-the-counter markets?

9. Why does the Toronto Stock Exchange have listing requirements? What are the major requirements? How do they compare with the listing requirements of the other exchanges?

10. How would you define efficient securities markets?

11. The efficient market hypothesis is interpreted in a weak form, a semistrong form, and a strong form. How can we differentiate its various forms?

12. Why do we have the "four pillars of finance" concept in Canada?

13. What are the implications of the changing regulations governing the Canadian securities industry?

Selected References

Canadian Securities Institute. Canadian Securities Course. Toronto, 1983.

Dann, Larry Y.; David Myers; and Robert J. Raab. "Trading Rules, Large Blocks, and the Speed of Price Adjustment." *Journal of Financial Economics* 4 (January 1977), pp. 3–22.

Hunter, W. T. *Canadian Financial Markets.* Peterborough: Broadview Press, 1986.

Jensen, Michael C. "Some Anomalous Evidence Regarding Market Efficiency." *Journal of Financial Economics* 5 (June–September 1978).

Malkiel, Burton. *A Random Walk down Wall Street.* 4th ed. New York: W. W. Norton, 1985.

Neufeld, E. P. *The Financial System of Canada.* Toronto: MacMillan, 1972.

Oppenheimer, Henry, and Gary Schlarbaum. "Investing with Ben Graham: An Ex Ante Test of the Efficient Markets Hypothesis." *Journal of Financial and Quantitative Analysis* 16 (September 1981), pp. 341–60.

Pattison, J. C. *Financial Markets and Foreign Ownership.* Toronto: Ontario Economic Council, 1978.

Peters, J. P. *Economics of the Canadian Corporate Bond Market.* Montreal: McGill-Queen's University.

Ross, A. *The Money Traders: Inside Canada's Stock Markets.* Toronto: Collins, 1984.

Selected Issues of *Bank of Canada Review.*

Shaw, D. "The Cost of Going Public in Canada." *Financial Executive* (July 1969) pp. 21–22.

Shaw, D., and Ross Archibald. *The Management of Change in the Canadian Securities Industry.* Toronto: The Toronto Stock Exchange, 1977.

Shearer, R. A.; J. F. Chant; and D. E. Bond. *The Economics of the Canadian Financial System.* 2nd ed. Toronto: Prentice-Hall Canada, 1984.

Van Horne, James C. *Financial Markets Rates and Flows.* Englewood Cliffs, N.J.: Prentice-Hall, 1978.

Ziegel, J. S.; L. Waverman; and P. W. Conklin, eds. *Canadian Financial Institutions: Changing the Regulatory Environment.* Toronto: Ontario Economic Council, 1986.

15 Investment Underwriting: Public and Private Placement

In Chapter 15 we will examine the role of the investment dealer, the advantages and disadvantages of selling securities to the public, and the private placement of securities with insurance companies, pension funds, and other lenders. We will also examine the characteristics of the extremely active new issues market in 1985 and 1986 and who the major players have been in investment underwriting in Canada.

The Role of Investment Underwriting

The investment dealer is the great link between the corporation in need of funds and the investor. As a middleman the investment dealer is responsible for designing and packaging a security offering and selling the securities to the public. This so-called corporate finance fraternity within the investment dealer community has long been thought of as an elite group—with appropriate memberships in the country club, the yacht club, and other such venerable institutions. The roller coaster performances of the securities markets in the late 1960s, 70s, and 80s have altered the picture somewhat. Competition has become the new way of doing business in which even the fittest must merge to survive, while others are forced to drop out of the game. The scheduled entrance as new players in the Canadian securities markets of the Canadian chartered banks and of large foreign investment banking firms, following deregulation, promises to test the skills of even the fittest.

Enumeration of Functions

As a middleman in the distribution of securities, the investment dealer plays a number of key roles.

Underwriter By the mid-1980s the investment dealer had become a risk taker in most cases. This occurred because of the relative growth of so-called bought deals which have become common in Canada since 1983. In a bought deal the investment dealer contracts to buy securities from the corporation and resell them to other securities dealers and the public. By giving a "firm commitment" to purchase the securities from the corporation, the dealer is said to underwrite any risks that might be associated with a new issue. While the risk may be fairly low in handling a bond offering for Bell Canada Enterprises or for Northern Telecom in a stable market, such may not be the case in selling the shares of a less-known firm in a very volatile market environment. In 1985 almost two thirds of the corporate underwritings were bought deals.

Though the public offerings of most large, well-established firms usually require the investment dealers to assume the risk of distribution, issues for relatively unknown corporations are still handled on a "best-efforts" or commission basis. Because this distribution practice had been the industry standard until 1983, it is often referred to as a traditional underwriting. A new issue by a small Alberta company, Plastifab Ltd., in September 1986 provides an example of a hybrid deal. Dominion Securities Ltd. undertook to purchase about one third of the $5 million issue and sell the remaining two thirds on a best-efforts basis.[1] Because only one half of the issue sold, the underwriter fared much better than if it had underwritten the whole deal.

Market maker During distribution and in later time periods the investment dealer may make a market in a given security—that is, engage in the buying and selling of the security to ensure a liquid market. It may also provide research on the firm to encourage active investor interest.

Advisor The investment dealer may advise clients on a continuing basis about the types of securities to be sold, the number of shares or units for distribution, and the timing of the sale. A company considering a stock issuance to the public may be persuaded, in counsel with an investment dealer, to borrow the funds from an insurance company or, if stock is to be sold, to wait for two more quarters of earnings before going to the market. The investment dealer also provides important advisory services in the area of mergers and acquisitions, leveraged buyouts, and corporate restructuring.

Agency functions The investment dealer may act as an agent for a corporation that wishes to place its securities privately with an insurance company, a pension fund, or a wealthy individual. In this instance the investment dealer will shop around among potential investors and negotiate the best possible deal for the corporation. It may also serve as an agent in merger and acquisition transactions. Because of the many critical roles the investment dealer plays, it may be requested to have a representative sit on the board of directors of the client company.

The Distribution Process

The actual distribution process requires the active participation of a number of parties. The principal or managing investment dealer will usually call upon other investment houses to share the burden of risk and to aid in the distribution. To this end they will form an under-

[1]The fact the issue was an early qualifier for the Alberta Stock Savings Plan was a complication in the minds of investors and probably accounted for the partial underwriting and also the partial distribution.

writing syndicate composed of as a few as 2 or as many as 100 investment houses. In Figure 15–1 we see a typical case in which a hypothetical firm, the Maxwell Corporation, wishes to issue 250,000 additional shares of stock with Wood Gundy as the managing underwriter and an underwriting syndicate of 15 firms.

The banking syndicate will purchase shares from the Maxwell Corporation and distribute them through the channels of distribution. Syndicate members will act as wholesalers in distributing the shares to brokers and dealers who will eventually sell the shares to the public. Large investment houses are usually vertically integrated, acting as underwriter-dealer-broker and capturing more fees and commissions.

The Spread

The spread represents the total compensation available to those who participate in the distribution process. In a 1986 new issue 2 million shares of West Fraser Timber Company stock were offered at a public or retail price of $20.50 each. The underwriters paid a price of $19.3725

Figure 15–1
Distribution process in investment banking

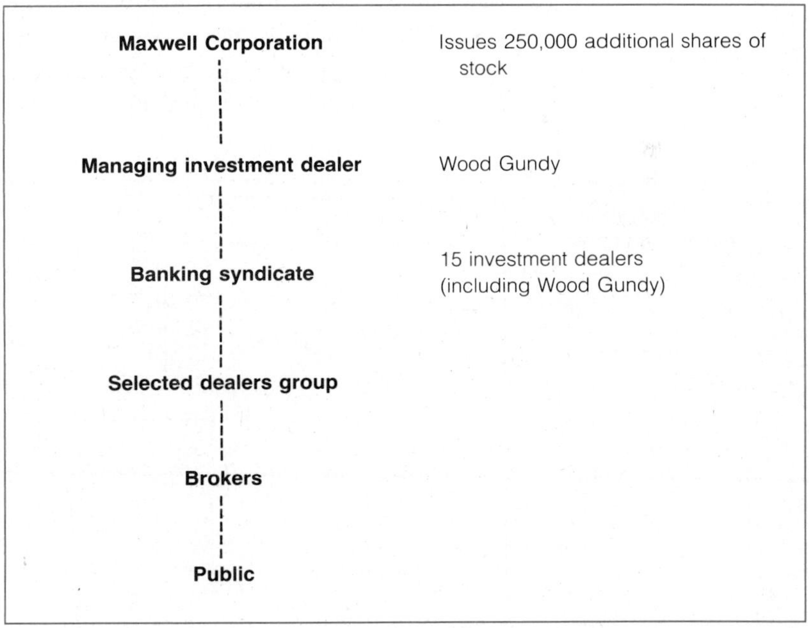

per share to West Fraser. The $1.1275 differential between the public price and the proceeds to the issuing company is known as the total spread. In a typical case such a spread of $1.1275 might be divided up among the participants in a manner like that depicted in Figure 15–2.

The farther down the dealer is in the distribution process, then, the higher the price it must pay for shares. The managing underwriter pays $19.3725 while dealers in the selling group syndicate pay $20.00. This also means that a dealer, by reselling as far down the distribution chain as it can, stands to make a higher profit. If, for example, the managing underwriter resells a volume of shares to a member of the selling group syndicate, it will earn .6225 per share; for each share the managing underwriter resells directly to the public it will make $1.1275.

The total spread of $1.1275 in the sample case represents 5.5 percent of the offering price. In general, the larger the dollar value of an issue, the smaller will be the spread as a percentage of the offering price. Certain company expenses like printing and legal costs are largely fixed, again increasing the flotation cost percentages for smaller versus larger issues. For the West Fraser Timber Company issue, the company's direct issue expenses were estimated at $275,000 or about two thirds of 1 percent of the total issue proceeds. Thus, the total flotation costs for the issue were just over 6 percent of the total proceeds. For a larger stock issue this percentage might be more in the 4 percent range, while for a $5 million issue, a percentage cost of 8 percent or more might

Figure 15–2
Allocation of underwriting spread

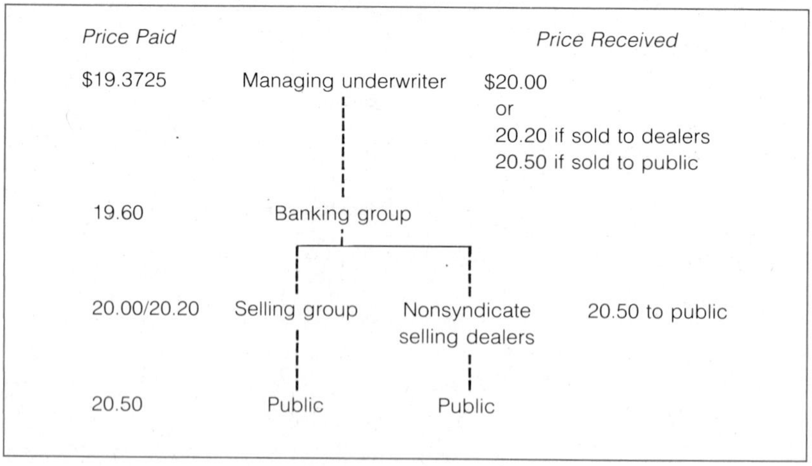

be reasonably expected. When the spread plus out-of-pocket costs are considered, therefore, the total cost of a new issue is substantial. In the planned $5 million Plastifab issue discussed earlier, the expected flotation costs were 8.8 percent of the expected proceeds.

Before leaving the subject of flotation costs, it is important to realize that for the purposes of Figure 15–2, we assumed the shares were sold at their offering price of $20.50. It is possible, however, that an issue may not be salable at the offering price and will have to be sold for a lesser amount. Such may come about because of adverse market conditions arising before the distribution is completed or simply because the issue was mispriced relative to the prices of other competing securities. In situations where the issue is sold to the public for less than the offering price, the actual realized commissions of the underwriting group will be less than the amounts originally planned for.

Pricing the Security

Because the syndicate members purchase the stock for redistribution in the marketing channels, they must be careful about the pricing of the stock. When a stock is sold to the public for the first time (that is, the firm is going public), the managing investment dealer will do an in-depth analysis of the company to determine its value. The study will include an analysis of the firm's industry, financial characteristics, and anticipated earnings and dividend-paying capability. Based on appropriate valuation techniques, a tentative price will be assigned and compared to that commanded by the common shares of similar firms in a given industry. If the industry's average price-earnings ratio is 10, for example, the issue price should probably not be set very far above this norm. Besides the fundamental valuation and the industry comparison the anticipated public demand for the new issue will be a major factor in pricing.

Rather than new issues, however, the majority of common stock flotations handled by investment dealers are additional issues of stocks or bonds for companies already trading publicly. In such cases the price will generally be set at a level slightly below the current market price for the company's common stock. This process, known as underpricing, helps create a receptive market for the securities thereby reducing somewhat the pricing risk borne by the underwriting syndicate.

At times an investment dealer will handle large blocks of securities for existing stockholders. Because the number of shares may be too large to trade in normal channels, the investment dealer will manage the issue and price the stock below current prices to the public. Such a process is known as a secondary offering, in contrast to a primary offering in which corporate securities are sold directly by the corporation.

Dilution

The actual or perceived dilutive effect on shares currently outstanding is a problem facing companies when they issue additional securities. In the case of the Maxwell Corporation the 250,000 new shares may represent a 10 percent increment to shares currently in existence. Earnings of $5 million on 2.5 million shares prior to the offering would indicate earnings per share of $2. With 250,000 new shares to be issued, earnings per share will temporarily slip to $1.82.

Of course, the proceeds from the sale of new shares may well be expected to provide the increased earnings necessary to bring earnings back to or to surpass $2 per share. While financial theory dictates that a new equity issue should not be undertaken if it diminishes the overall wealth of current stockholders, there may be a time lag in the recovery of earnings per share as a result of the increased shares outstanding, especially if the proceeds are invested in a relatively new business development. For this reason there may be a temporary weakness in a stock when an issue of additional shares is proposed. In most cases this is overcome with the passage of time as the wisdom of management's financial decision making is demonstrated.

Market Stabilization

Another problem may set in when the actual public distribution begins—namely, unanticipated weakness in the stock or bond market. Since the sales group has made a firm commitment to purchase stock at a given price for redistribution, it is essential that the price of the stock remain relatively strong. If, in the hypothetical Maxwell Company situation, syndicate members were committed to purchasing the stock at $20 or better, they could be in trouble if the sales price fell to $19 or $18. The managing underwriter is generally responsible for stabilizing the offering during the distribution period and may accomplish this by repurchasing securities as the market price moves below the initial public offering price.

The period of stabilization usually lasts two or three days after the initial offering, but it may extend up to 30 days for difficult-to-distribute securities. In a very poor market environment stabilization may be virtually impossible to achieve. When Xerox Canada Inc. of Toronto went public in 1984 only half the issue sold. The second half of the deal could only be sold by adding half a warrant and selling the securities to financial institutions for $16, down from the original $19 price. Thus, the investment dealers, led by Wood Gundy, took an enormous $4.6 million loss because rising interest rates caused deteriorating stock prices. The fact that such a loss occurred on the issue of such a high-quality stock indicates the risks involved in the underwriting process.

Aftermarket

The investment dealer is also interested in how well the underwritten security behaves after the distribution period—for its ultimate reputation rests on bringing strong securities to the market. This is particularly true for initial public offerings.

Research has indicated that initial public offerings often do well in the immediate aftermarket. For example, one of these studies examined approximately 500 firms and determined that there were excess returns of 10.9 percent, on average, one week after issue (the term *excess return* refers to movement in the price of the stock above and beyond the market). There were also positive excess returns of 11.6 percent for a full month after issue but a negative market-adjusted performance of -3.0 percent one full year after issue.[2] Because the managing underwriter may underprice the issue initially to ensure a successful offering, there is quite often a jump in value after the issue first goes public. The efficiency of the market eventually takes hold so that sustained long-term performance is very much dependent on the quality of the issue and the market conditions at play.

[2]Frank K. Reilly, "New Issues Revisited," *Financial Management* 6 (Winter 1977), pp. 28–42.

Changes in the Investment Industry

During the time period that up and down market conditions have challenged the brokerage industry, the corporate finance function of the investment dealers has been rapidly expanding. The growth in corporate finance revenue has not been predominantly in the underwriting area but rather in other functions performed. Major increases have taken place in corporate finance and merger/acquisition advisory services. The fact that in 1985 securities firms averaged a 20 percent return on investment versus 5 percent for all industries has made the Canadian investment industry an attractive target for potential new entrants.

Additionally, investment underwriting is becoming much more internationally oriented causing many firms to become global in nature. For example, Dominion Securities Ltd. generated about 20 percent of its business overseas in 1986. As another indication of internationalization, 60 percent of the largest share offering ever undertaken by a Canadian company, $517 million issued by Gulf Canada in 1987, was distributed outside of Canada.

The investment underwriting industry has become much more competitive on the basis of performance. Furthermore, there has been a reaffirmation of the value of vertical integration. Firms that were at one time primarily specializing in underwriting and corporate client services have moved into more broadly based brokerage distribution services.

Increasing foreign competition poses a particular threat for the Canadian securities industry. The traditionally small capital bases of Canadian dealers put them at a distinct disadvantage with bought deals[3] and global, 24-hour securities trading[4] becoming common. The response of the industry has been a spate of mergers and the going public of many Canadian securities firms. By late 1986 11 Canadian investment houses had gone public or had announced plans to do so. This certainly denotes a marked changed in the investment industry environment as

[3]In a bought deal the investment dealer must commit to the newly issued shares for its own account before reselling them without any recourse to defining market conditions under which it could back away from the deal.

[4]This requires significant expenditures on securities trading hardware and software.

it was only in 1983 that the first of Canada's securities firms to go public did so. Within days of one another in September 1986 details were announced of a $100 million public offering by Canada's largest brokerage house, Dominion Securities Ltd., and of a merger by Nesbitt Thompson Bongard Inc. with F. H. Deacon Hodgson Inc. to increase the merged firm's capital to $125 million. Changes in Ontario Securities Commission legislation were expected to permit up to 20 foreign full-service investment dealers to operate in the Ontario markets.

Table 15–1 lists the 10 largest investment dealers, ranked by total capital, and financial performance information to the extent available as of the end of 1986.

As foreign investment banks and Canadian chartered banks readied themselves to expand their operations in the Canadian securities industry, the prices for stock exchange seats skyrocketed. In mid-1986 a seat on the TSE sold for only $37,000. The T-D Bank paid $191,000 to buy a seat in March 1987, while Prudential-Bache Securities (of New York) paid $301,000 in mid-April. On April 29, 1987, Daiwa Securities, the world's second largest securities firm,[5] bought a TSE

Table 15–1
Ten largest investment dealers

Company	Total Capital (in thousands)	Revenue (in thousands)	Shareholders' Capital (in thousands)	1986 Earnings (in thousands)	Return on Average Total Capital
1. Dominion Securities Inc.	$274,971	$305,426	$214,971	$95,508	47.9%
2. Wood Gundy Inc.	168,331	n.a.	n.a.	49,807	35.0%
3. Gordon Capital Corp.	155,100	n.a.	n.a.	n.a.	n.a.
4. Nesbitt Thomson Deacon, Inc.	118,936	187,798*	102,896	17,037*	n.a.
5. McLeod Young Weir Ltd.	108,149	n.a.	n.a.	n.a.	n.a.
6. Burns Fry Ltd.	107,558	198,861	75,297	54,115	58.0%
7. Richardson Greenshields	67,531	n.a.	n.a.	n.a.	n.a.
8. Loewen, Ondaatje, McCutcheon	59,412	62,000	59,412	15,465	38.7%
9. Merrill Lynch Canada	56,293	174,527	52,293	11,453	21.5%
10. Levesque, Beaubien	55,223	123,462	17,175	22,044	54.9%

*Nine-month figures.
Source: *The Financial Post 500*, Summer 1987.

[5]The largest at that time was Komura Securities, also of Japan.

seat for $361,000. Similar increases in price and demand occurred on the Montreal and Vancouver exchanges. This sudden expansion in industry competition made for record salaries and demand for newly graduating MBAs (Masters in Business Administration). For example, in the spring of 1987 Daiwa Securities' Toronto office expanded from 1 to 20 employees—mostly new MBA graduates—with plans to expand to 40 or 50.

Besides the increased competition nationally and internationally among traditional securities firms, the incursions by other financial sector firms into the securities business and the advent of financial services conglomerates, first in the United States, then in Canada, will have an effect on how the industry develops. The major Canadian banks are interested in participating directly in investment banking activity while the Royal Bank and the Toronto Dominion Bank have already entered the brokerage end of the industry. The high profitability reported by some of Canada's securities dealers (for example, Dominion Securities Pitfield's returns of 75 percent on equity in 1985) have naturally attracted the attention of other financial institutions.

In the United States nonbrokerage firms moved into the brokerage area through acquisitions in the early 1980s. Since the acquired brokerage houses were also engaged in investment banking activities, acquiring firms obtained investment banking capabilities as well. The merger of Prudential Insurance Company with Bache Halsey Stuart Shields was the first of these types of mergers. In retrospect as of year-end 1986, Prudential and Sears, who acquired Dean Witter Reynolds, are both having problems generating significant profits from their brokerage and investment banking acquisitions. Only American Express, which acquired the retail broker Shearson Loeb Rhoades and then the investment banker Lehman Brothers, is having some success with the merged firms. There have been no significant combinations with nonbrokerage companies since these acquisitions. However, these acquisitions spurred traditional securities firms such as Merrill Lynch, Salomon Brothers, and others to accelerate their expansion plans and more than triple their staffs over the last 10 years.

Thus far in Canada none of the largest investment dealers has become part of a financial conglomerate. The readying of industry competitors for the day when a major player could be a subsidiary of a chartered bank or of American Express, and so on, has led to the consolidation of financial resources among fewer and fewer investment dealers.

Underwriting Activity in Canada

Table 15–2 presents the comparative information on the leading underwriters of securities issued by Canadian corporations and governments.

The data show that Wood Gundy, the most active Canadian underwriter, participated in 38 percent of all new corporate issues, while Dominion Securities, the second most active, participated in 30 percent. Of the $14.2 billion raised domestically, some 16 percent was issued via private placement. While 30 percent of Canadian corporate issues were placed internationally, only 24 percent of the underwritings of the top five Canadian dealers were placed internationally. This was because 9 of the largest 10 underwriters for Canadian corporate issues internationally were non-Canadian investment bankers. Given that the foreign securities firms already had these strong relationships with many of Canada's largest corporations, they were a potentially potent force in the Canadian domestic market as deregulation allowed them wider access from 1988 on.

Bought deals outpaced traditional underwritings in 1985 by a two-to-one margin. As one would expect a very high percentage of international issues were on a bought basis whereas private domestic placements tended to be on a commission basis.

Table 15–2 does not show that each firm tended to have its own specialty. Dominion Securities was the leader in domestic public issues while Burns Fry was the most active in private placements. In the international arena Union Bank led the way with Wood Gundy being the only Canadian dealer among the 10 most active.

As activity in Canadian markets becomes more and more open to international competition and as more and more activity becomes centered on the large markets of New York, London, and Tokyo, the needs for size and efficiency strike many Canadian securities firms as being paramount.

Size Criteria for Going Public

Although there are no prescribed, or official, size criteria for approaching the public markets, the well-informed corporate financial

Table 15–2 Leading Canadian underwriters, 1985

	Total Underwritings		Corporate Underwritings									
			Total		Debt		Equity		Bought		Private*	
Dealer	Amount (in millions)	Number	Amount (in millions)	Number	Amount (in millions)	Number	Amount (in millions)	Number	Dollars	Number	Dollars	Number
Wood Gundy	$5,205	275	$ 2,994	152	$1,268	78	$1,726	74	58%	63%	16%	17%
Dominion Securities	4,578	195	2,899	120	703	45	2,196	75	64	60	7	13
McLeod Young Weir	3,387	144	2,076	95	786	33	1,290	62	36	46	25	17
Burns Fry	2,263	72	1,963	85	956	36	1,007	29	56	36	32	40
Nesbitt Thomson	N/A	N/A	1,059	43	222	11	837	32	69	58	4	12
Market totals	—	—	$20,400	402	—	—	—	—	64%	63%	16%	—

*As percent of domestic underwritings only.
Source: *Financial Post* estimates, as reported May 3, 1986.

officer of a private company should have some feel for what his or her options are. Can a company with $10 million in sales even consider a public offering?

In the United States the most prestigious investment houses tend to concentrate on underwriting large companies. Because of the absolute difference in size of American versus Canadian investment firms, it is not surprising that even the largest of Canadian firms are often involved in relatively small securities issues. The Plastifab issue discussed earlier is a good example. The underwriter, Dominion Securities, was the largest player in the Canadian corporate domestic issues market. Yet the Plastifab issue was for only $5 million. In fact, Plastifab's sales had been only $9.9 million and profits $580 thousand for the previous fiscal year. From Table 15–2, we can quickly calculate that Dominion Securities' average underwriting was for $24 million. This indicates the firm was probably involved in a number of small issues as well as large ones.

Public versus Private Financing

Our discussion to this point has assumed the firm was distributing stocks or bonds in the public markets (through the organized exchanges or over the counter, as explained in Chapter 14). However, many companies, by choice or circumstance, prefer to remain private in nature—restricting their financial activities to direct negotiations with bankers, insurance companies, and so forth. Let us evaluate the advantages and the disadvantages of public versus private financing and then explore the avenues open to a privately financed firm.

Advantages of Being Public

First of all the corporation may tap the security markets for a greater amount of funds by selling securities directly to the public. With 4 million individual stockholders in the country, combined with hundreds of institutional investors, the greatest pool of funds is channeled toward publicly traded securities. Furthermore, the attendant prestige of a public security may be helpful in bank negotiations, executive recruitment, and the marketing of products.

Stockholders of a heretofore private corporation may also sell part of their holdings if the corporation decides to go public. A million-share offering may contain 500,000 authorized but unissued corporate shares (a primary offering) and 500,000 existing stockholder shares (a secondary offering). The stockholder is able to achieve a higher degree of liquidity and to diversify his or her portfolio. A publicly traded stock with an established price may also be helpful for estate-planning purposes.

Finally, going public allows the firm to play the merger game, using marketable securities for the purchase of other firms. The high visibility of a public offering may even make the firm a potential recipient of attractive offers for its own securities.

Disadvantages of Being Public

The company must make all information available to the public through securities commissions filings. Not only is this tedious, time consuming, and expensive, but important corporate information on profit margins and product lines must be divulged. For Canadian firms that are also listed on the New York Stock Exchange, the filings required by the U.S. Securities and Exchange Commission are even more extensive than those required by Canadian regulators. Because of the need to provide information, a company president must adapt himself to being a public relations representative to all interested members of the securities industry.

Another disadvantage of being public is the tremendous pressure for short-term performance placed on the firm by security analysts and large institutional investors. Quarter-to-quarter earnings reports can become more important to top management than providing a long-run stewardship plan for the company. A capital budgeting decision calling for the selection of Alternative A—carrying a million dollars higher net present value than Alternative B—may be discarded in favor of the latter because Alternative B adds two cents more to next quarter's earnings per share.

In a number of cases the blessings of having a publicly quoted security may become quite the opposite. Although a security may have had an enthusiastic reception in a strong "new issues" market such as that of 1961–62, 1967–68, or 1985–87, a dramatic erosion in value may later take place, causing embarrassment and anxiety for stockholders and employers.

A final disadvantage is the high cost of going public. For example, for issues of under a million dollars the underwriting spread plus the out-of-pocket cost may run well over 10 percent.

Public Offerings

A Classic Example of Instant Wealth—EDS Goes Public

The U.S. market has provided us with some spectacular stories of entrepreneurs becoming wealthy by going public. A case in point was Electronic Data Systems (EDS) and H. Ross Perot. In September 1968 Perot took EDS public, and within one month he found himself worth $300 million. The original EDS offering was at 118 times current earnings (the norm is 10 to 15 times earnings). After one month in the hot new issues market of 1967–68, the stock was trading at over 200 times earnings. By 1970 EDS had a quoted market value of $1.5 billion. All of this was accomplished by a firm with a few hundred employees.

Although Canadian history does not provide spectacular stories of wealth like EDS, going public has been important for many Canadian entrepreneurs. In the West Fraser Timber situation discussed earlier in the chapter, about 18 percent of the company's equity was sold to the public for approximately $40 million. The intent was to reduce the company's long-term debt of $92 million thereby positioning the firm to expand via acquisition when the right opportunity came along. Thus, the members of the founding Ketcham family were able to have more equity capital injected into the firm without relinquishing control. A year after the new issue the company's stock was selling for $27.25 or 33 percent more than the issue price. Since that return[6] was substantially higher than the average return on the TSE over that period, an investor who bought and held shares originally would have been pleased. On the other hand, the holders of the 82 percent not issued to the public fared well also.

[6]The dividend was very small.

When New Issues Get Hot

During 1986 the Montreal Exchange attracted 177 new company listings, more than double the 1985 total. The Toronto Stock Exchange listed 165 new companies in 1986, up from 73 the previous year. The reason for the upsurge in new issues activity? An ongoing, four-year-old bull market in equities, resulting in earnings multiples of about 15 times earnings made going public very attractive for young companies.[7] Part of the freneticness of the current pace may be a fear that this attractive "window of opportunity" for new market issues may close at any time.

When the prices for existing stocks are historically high there are few obvious bargains to be had. Investors seem to then look to the new issues market to provide the potential for an exciting price appreciation. The data in Table 15–3 summarize the investment performance of public companies listed for the first time over a two-month period in 1985. The table shows a number of very highly positive results along with a couple of negatives. Over the ensuing year four of the issues performed better than the TSE composite index while three performed worse.

Table 15–3
New listings on the TSE, July and August 1985

Company	*Public Offering Price*	*Recent Price*	*Percent Change from Offering*
Lonvest Corp.	$20.00	$25.13	+ 25%
First Mercantile Currency	10.00	7.28	− 15
Fund Inc. Q.A.		1.10(w)	
Calgary Centre Holdings Pr.	25.00	26.38	+ 6
Dicon Systems	4.25	8.50	+100
Access ATM Network Inc.	8.25	2.35	− 72
Tuckahoe Financial	3.50	4.60	+ 50
Corp. Cl. A		.65(w)	
X-Cal Resources Ltd.	.75	.81	+ 8
TSE composite percent change			+ 7%

Source: *Financial Times of Canada,* September 1986.

[7]By the spring of 1987 they had risen to an average of 20 times earnings.

Private Placement

Private placement refers to the selling of securities directly to insurance companies, pension funds, and wealthy individuals rather than through the security markets. The financing device may be employed by a growing firm that wishes to avoid or defer an initial public stock offering or by a publicly traded company that wishes to incorporate private funds into its financing package. The relative importance of private versus public placement is indicated in Table 15–4. That table shows that over the 1983 to 1986 period $5.5 billion of new equities were raised privately through the facilities of the TSE. That amount represented 15 percent of all equity raised.

The advantages of private placement are worthy of note. First of all, there is no lengthy, expensive registration process with the securities commissions. Second, the firm has considerably greater flexibility in negotiating with one or a handful of insurance companies, pension funds, or bankers than is possible in a public offering. Because there is no securities registration or underwriting, the initial costs of a private placement may be considerably lower than those of a public issue. However, on an interest-bearing security, the interest rate is usually higher to compensate the investor for holding a less liquid obligation.

Going Private and Leveraged Buyouts

Throughout the years there were always some firms going from being public to being private. In the 1970s a number of firms gave up their

Table 15–4
New equity financing, Toronto Stock Exchange, 1983–1986 (millions)

	1986	*1985*	*1984*	*1983*	*Percentage Summary*
Public offerings	$ 9,999	$8,003	$6,139	$5,731	80%
Private placements	2,328	803	874	1,515	15
Rights offerings	727	123	127	771	5
Total	$13,054	$8,929	$7,141	$8,117	100%

public listings to go private, but these were usually small firms. Management figured they could save several hundred thousand dollars a year in annual report expenses, legal and auditing fees, and security analysts' meetings—a significant amount for a small company.

In the 1980s, however, a number of very large U.S. corporations have been going private and not just to save several hundred thousand dollars. The answer seems to be in management's desire to manage for the long-term without the short-term performance demands the stock market places upon corporations. Private firms do not have to please analysts with short-term performance. Although large Canadian firms have not followed suit in going private yet, there are indeed many chief executives who wish from time to time to be subject to less intense demands relating to current reported profits.

There are basically two ways to accomplish going private. First, a publicly owned company can be purchased by a private company. Second, the company can repurchase all publicly traded shares from the stockholders. Both methods have been in vogue and can be accomplished through the use of a leveraged buyout. In a leveraged buyout either the management or some other investor group borrows the needed cash to repurchase all the shares of the company. After the repurchase the company exists with a lot of debt and heavy interest expense. What worries many analysts is that the borrowing is done at banks rather than through the securities markets. They claim this may cause a misdirection of capital into nonproductive activities (leveraged buyouts) instead of capital formation for new ventures and products. An additional fallout when a large firm goes private is that common stock outstanding tends to disappear leaving fewer investment choices for investors.

Usually management of the private company must sell off assets to reduce the debt load, and a corporate restructuring occurs where divisions and products are sold and assets redeployed into new higher return areas. Over the long run these strategies could be rewarding and these companies could again become publicly owned, but that has not been the typical occurrence to date. Table 15–5 lists nine U.S. firms going private in 1985 with prices in excess of one half billion dollars and a total value of over $14 billion.

In Canada leveraged buyouts have sometimes become a method for repatriating ownership of what were formerly Canadian divisions of foreign multinationals. For example, a group of Canadian managers successfully negotiated the purchase of B. F. Goodrich's Canadian

Table 15–5
Large U.S. firms going private in 1985

	Value (in millions)
Beatrice Corp.	$ 6,200
Storer Communications, Inc.	2,510
Levi Strauss & Co.	1,450
Northwest Industries, Inc.	1,000
Uniroyal, Inc.	836
Denny's, Inc.	734
SCOA Industries	637
Scovill, Inc.	523
Parsons Corp.	518
Total value	$14,408

Source: *The Wall Street Journal,* August 12, 1985, p. 13.

industrial products division and run it as a private corporation under the name Epton Industries. In another case a group of Canadian investors bought American Can Inc.'s Canadian subsidiary. That group followed up its acquisition with a $55 million issue of subordinate voting shares presumably to ease the debt load caused by the buyout. This availability of these Canadian subsidiaries to be bought stems from a number of global corporate strategic conditions. As the multinational corporations switch to global product production strategies, smaller Canadian operations established to serve only the Canadian market may no longer make sense in the overall corporate plan. In other cases the traditional businesses around which the Canadian subsidiaries were founded may have become deemphasized by corporate decision makers as newer, more exciting market developments are pursued.

Summary

The role of the investment dealer is critical to the distribution of securities in the Canadian economy. The investment dealer serves as an underwriter or risk taker by purchasing the securities from the issuing corporation and redistributing them to the public. The dealer may continue to maintain a market in the distributed securities long after they have been sold to the public. The dealer can also help a company sell a new issue on a "best-efforts" basis. Investment dealers also serve as advisors to corporations and have become more important to corporations in the 1980s in providing advice on mergers, acquisitions, leveraged buyouts, and hostile takeover attempts.

The advantages of selling securities in the public markets must be weighed against the disadvantages. While going public may give the corporation and major stockholders greater access to funds as well as additional prestige, these advantages may quickly disappear in a down market. Furthermore, the corporation must open its books to the public and orient itself to the supposed short-term emphasis of investors.

Investment dealers have become larger and consolidated into fewer firms in just the last few years. The industry may become dominated by the large dealers who are able to take down large blocks of securities and compete in a more international market. Despite their exceptional historical profitability, Canadian investment dealers face the future with serious concerns about impending competition from the mammoth foreign investment bankers, entry into the industry by Canadian chartered banks, and the effects of 24-hour worldwide trading centered in the New York, London, and Tokyo markets.

Private placement—or the direct distribution of securities to large insurance companies, pension funds, and wealthy individuals—may bypass the rigors of securities commission registration and allow more flexibility in terms. A number of U.S. corporations actually changed their structure from public to private during the bear market of 1973–74. This trend has become evident again in 1984 and 1985 with many large companies going private through leveraged buyouts. While much of the debt used in leveraged buyouts comes from the banking industry, only the public markets can meet the vast capital needs of Canadian corporations. Leveraged buyouts provide a mechanism for former subsidiaries of foreign multinationals to become controlled by Canadian investors who were often the subsidiary managers.

List of Terms

investment dealer
underwriting
market maker
underwriting syndicate
managing underwriter
underwriting spread
dilution of earnings
market stabilization
public placement
private placement
going private
bull market
bear market
secondary offering
bought deal
leveraged buyout

Discussion Questions

1. In what way is an investment dealer a risk taker?
2. What is the purpose of market stabilization activities during the distribution process?
3. Discuss how an underwriting syndicate decreases risk for each underwriter and at the same time facilitates the distribution process.
4. Discuss the reason for the differences between underwriting spreads for stocks and bonds.
5. Explain how the price-earnings ratio is related to the pricing of a new security issue and the dilution effect.
6. Explain why the new issues market periodically becomes extremely popular. What are the dangers of a "hot" new issues market?
7. Comment on the market performance of companies going public, both immediately after the offering has been made and some time later. Relate this to research that has been done in this area.
8. Discuss key changes that have been going on in the investment dealer-brokerage community in terms of vertical integration. Also who are some of the new participants in the industry?
9. Discuss the benefits accruing to a company traded in the public securities markets.
10. What are some reasons why a corporation may prefer to remain privately held?
11. If a company wished to raise capital by way of a private placement, where would it look for funds?
12. How does a leveraged buyout work? What does the debt structure of the firm normally look like after a leveraged buyout? What might be done to reduce the debt?
13. What effect does a leveraged buyout have on the future strategic choices open to the company's management?

Problems

1. The Hamilton Corporation currently has 4 million shares of stock outstanding and will report earnings of $6 million in the current year. The company is considering the issuance of 1 million additional shares that will net $30 per share to the corporation.

   a. What is the immediate dilution potential for this new stock issue?

   b. Assume the Hamilton Corporation can earn 10.5 percent on the proceeds of the stock issue in time to include it in the current year's results. Should the new issue be undertaken based on earnings per share?

2. Walton and Company is the managing investment dealer for a major new underwriting. The price of the stock to the investment dealer is $18 per share. Other syndicate members may buy the stock for $18.25. The price to the selected dealers group is $18.80, with a price to brokers of $19.20. Finally, the price to the public is $19.50.

   a. If Walton and Company sells its shares to the dealer group, what will the percentage return be?

   b. If Walton and Company performs the dealer's function also and sells to brokers, what will the percentage return be?

   c. If Walton and Company fully integrates its operation and sells directly to the public, what will its percentage return be?

3. Becker Brothers is the managing underwriter for a 1 million share issue by Jay's Hamburger Heaven. Becker Brothers is "handling" 10 percent of the issue. Their price is $25, and the price to the public is $26.40.

   Becker also provides the market stabilization function. During the issuance the market for the stock turned soft, and Becker was forced to purchase 40,000 shares in the open market at an average price of $25.75. They later sold the shares at an average value of $23.

   Compute Becker Brothers *overall* gain or loss from managing this issue.

4. Winston Sporting Goods is considering a public offering of common stock. Its investment dealer has informed the company that

the retail price will be $18 per share for 600,000 shares. The company will receive $16.50 per share and will incur $150,000 in registration, accounting, and printing fees.

a. What is the spread on this issue in percentage terms? What are the total expenses of the issue as a percentage of total value (at retail)?

b. If the firm wanted to net $18 million from this issue, how many shares must be sold?

5. Ashley Homebuilding is about to go public. The investment firm of Blake Webber and Company is attempting to price the issue. The homebuilding industry generally trades at a 25 percent discount below the P/E ratio on the TSE 300 Stock Index. Assume that index currently has a P/E ratio of 12. Ashley can be compared to the homebuilding industry as follows:

	Ashley	*Homebuilding Industry*
Growth rate in earnings per share	12%	10%
Consistency of performance	Increased earnings 4 out of 5 years	Increased earnings 3 out of 5 years
Debt to total assets	55%	40%
Turnover of product	Slightly below average	Average
Quality of management	High	Average

Assume in assessing the initial P/E ratio the investment advisor will first determine the appropriate industry P/E based on the TSE 300 Index. Then a half point will be added to the P/E ratio for each consideration in which Ashley is superior to the industry norm, and a half point will be deducted for an inferior comparison. On this basis, what should the initial P/E be for Ashley Homebuilding?

6. The Landry Corporation needs to raise $1 million of debt via a 25-year issue. If it places the bonds privately, the interest rate will be 11 percent. Thirty thousand dollars in out-of-pocket costs will be incurred. For a public issue the interest rate will be 10 percent, and the underwriting spread will be 4 percent. There will be $100,000 in out-of-pocket costs.

The plan is for interest on the debt to be paid semiannually and for the debt to be outstanding for the full 25-year period at the end of which time it will be repaid. Which plan offers the higher net present value? For each plan compare the net amount of funds initially available (inflow) to the present value of future payments to determine net present value. Use a discount rate of approximately the after-tax cost of debt. The corporate tax rate is 48 percent.

7. Midland Corporation has a net income of $15 million and 6 million shares outstanding. Its common stock is currently selling for $40 per share. Midland plans to sell common stock in order to set up a major new production facility costing $21,660,000. The production facility will not produce any profit in Year 1. Thereafter, it is expected to earn a 15 percent return on the investment. Stanley Morgan and Co., an investment firm, plans to sell the issue to the public for $38 per share with a spread of 5 percent.

   a. How many shares of stock must be sold to net $21,660,000? (Note: Ignore out-of-pocket costs in this problem.)
   b. Why is the investment dealer selling the stock at less than its current market price?
   c. What are the current earnings per share (EPS) and the price-earnings ratio before the issue (based on a stock price of $40)? What will be the price per share immediately after the sale of stock if the P/E stays constant?
   d. Compute the EPS and the price (P/E stays constant) after the new production facility begins to produce a profit. Assume for the sake of this computation that the earning power of its other assets remains constant and that no dividends are being paid.
   e. Are the shareholders better off because of the sale of stock and the resultant investment? What other financing strategy could the company have tried in order to increase earnings per share? What would you recommend?

8. The Presley Corporation is about to go public. It currently has after-tax earnings of $7.5 million, and 2.5 million shares are owned by the present stockholders (the Presley family). The new public issue will represent 600,000 new shares and will be offered to the public at $20 per share, with a 5 percent spread on the offering price. There will also be $200,000 in out-of-pocket costs to the corporation.

a. Compute the net proceeds to the Presley Corporation.
b. Compute the earnings per share immediately before the stock issue.
c. Compute the earnings per share immediately after the stock issue.
d. Determine what rate of return must be earned on the net proceeds to the corporation so there will not be a dilution in earnings per share during the year of going public.
e. Determine what rate of return must be earned on the proceeds to the corporation so there will be a 5 percent increase in earnings per share, over what it would have been with no new issue, during the year of going public.

9. I. B. Michaels has a chance to participate in a new public offering by Hi-Tech Microcomputers. His broker informs him that there is a very strong demand for the 500,000 shares to be issued. His broker's firm is assigned 15,000 shares in the distribution and will allow Michaels, a relatively good customer, 1.5 percent of their 15,000 share allocation.

The initial offering price is $30 per share. There is a strong aftermarket, and the stock goes to $33 one week after issue. One full month after issue Mr. Michaels is quite pleased to observe his shares are selling for $34.75. He is content to place his shares in a lockbox and eventually use their anticipated increased value to help send his son to college many years in the future. However, one year after the distribution, he looks up the shares in *The Globe and Mail* and finds they are trading at $28.75.

a. Compute the total dollar profit or loss on Mr. Michael's shares one week, one month, and one year after the purchase. In each case compute the profit or loss against the initial purchase price.
b. Also compute this percentage gain or loss from the initial $30 price and compare this to the results that might be expected in an investment of this nature based on prior research. Assume the overall stock market was basically static during the period of observation.
c. Why might a new public issue be expected to have a strong aftermarket?

10. *(Comprehensive problem—impact of new public offering)*
The Bailey Corporation, a manufacturer of medical supplies and

equipment, is planning to sell its shares to the general public for the first time. The firm's investment banker, Robert Merrill and Company, is working with Bailey Corporation in determining a number of items. Information on the Bailey Corporation follows:

BAILEY CORPORATION
Income Statement
For the Year 198X

Sales (all on credit)	$42,680,000
Cost of goods sold	32,240,000
Gross profit	10,440,000
Selling and administrative expenses	4,558,000
Operating profit	5,882,000
Interest expense	600,000
Net income before taxes	5,282,000
Taxes	2,120,000
Net income	$ 3,162,000

BAILEY CORPORATION
Balance Sheet
As of December 31, 198X

Assets

Current assets:	
Cash	$ 250,000
Marketable securities	130,000
Accounts receivable	6,000,000
Inventory	8,300,000
Total current assets	14,680,000
Net plant and equipment	13,970,000
Total assets	$28,650,000

Liabilities and Owners' Equity

Current liabilities:	
Accounts payable	$ 3,800,000
Notes payable	3,550,000
Total current liabilities	7,350,000
Long-term liabilities	5,620,000
Total liabilities	12,970,000
Owners' equity:	
Common stock (1,800,000 shares)	8,100,000
Retained earnings	7,580,000
Total owners' equity	15,680,000
Total liabilities and owners' equity	$28,650,000

a. Assume that 800,000 new corporate shares will be issued to the general public. What will earnings per share be immediately after the public offering? (Round to two places to the right of the decimal point). Based on a price-earnings ratio of 12, what will be the initial price of the stock? Use earnings per share after the distribution in the calculation.

b. Assuming an underwriting spread of 5 percent and out-of-pocket costs of $300,000, what will be the net proceeds to the corporation?

c. What return must the corporation earn on the net proceeds to have earnings per share equal those from before the offering? How does this compare with the current return on the total assets on the balance sheet?

d. Now assume that of the initial 800,000 share distribution, 400,000 belong to current stockholders and 400,000 are new shares, with the latter to be added to the 1.8 million shares currently outstanding. What will earnings per share be immediately after the public offering? What will be the initial market price of the stock? Assume a price-earnings ratio of 12 and use earnings per share after the distribution in the calculation.

e. Assuming an underwriter spread of 5 percent and out-of-pocket costs of $300,000, what will net proceeds to the corporation be?

f. What return must the corporation now earn on the net proceeds to have earnings per share equal those from before the offering? How does this compare with current return on the total assets on the balance sheet?

Selected References

Block, Stanley B., and Marjorie T. Stanley. "The Price Movement Pattern and Financial Characteristics of Companies Approaching the Unseasoned Securities Market in the Late 1970s." *Financial Management* 9 (Winter 1980), pp. 30–36.

Canadian Securities Institute. *Canadian Securities Course*. Toronto, 1983.

Cohan, Avery B. *Private Placements and Public Offerings: Market Shares since 1935*. Chapel Hill: School of Business Administration, University of North Carolina, 1961.

Friend, Irwin, et al. *Investment Banking and the New Issues Market*. Cleveland: World, 1967.

Hess, Alan C., and Peter A. Frost, "Tests for Price Effects of New Issues of Seasoned Securities." *Journal of Finance* 37 (March 1982), pp. 11–25.

Ibbotsen, Roger G. "Price Performance of Common Stock New Issues." *Journal of Financial Economics* 2 (September 1975), pp. 253–72.

Johnson, Keith B.; T. Gregory Morton; and M. Chapman Findlay III. "An Empirical Analysis of the Flotation Cost of Corporate Securities, 1971–1972." *Journal of Finance* 30 (September 1975), pp. 1129–33.

Logue, Dennis E. "On the Pricing of Unseasoned New Issues, 1965–1969." *Journal of Financial and Quantitative Analysis* 8 (January 1973), pp. 91–103.

McDonald, J. G., and A. K. Fisher. "New Issue Stock Price Behavior." *Journal of Finance* 27 (March 1972), pp. 97–102.

Nair, Richard S. "Investment Banking: Judge Medina in Retrospect." *Financial Analysts Journal* 16 (July–August 1960), pp. 35–40.

Reilly, Frank K. "New Issues Revisited." *Financial Management* 6 (Winter 1977), pp. 28–42.

Shaw, David. "The Cost of Going Public in Canada." *Financial Executive*, July 1969, pp. 21–22.

"The Scorecard on New Issues." *Underwriters Performance Record*. Wayne, N. J.

16 Long-Term Debt and Lease Financing

The Shakespearean quote of "Neither a borrower nor a lender be" hardly applies to corporate financial management. The virtues and drawbacks of debt usage were considered in Chapter 5, Operating and Financial Leverage, and in Chapter 11, Cost of Capital. One can only surmise that today's financial managers, many of whom were educated in the 1950s and 1960s, remember the advantages a bit better than the disadvantages. Debt usage has been at unprecedented levels in the late 1970s and 1980s.

In Chapter 16 we will consider the importance of debt in the Canadian economy, the nature of long-term debt instruments, the mechanics of bond yields and pricing, and the decision to call back or refund an existing bond issue. Finally, lease financing will be considered as a special case of long-term debt financing. We give particular attention to accounting rule changes that affect leasing.

The Expanding Role of Debt

The debt of Canadian nonfinancial private corporations has increased more than tenfold since 1961. This growth has been the result of rapid business expansion, the impact of inflationary pressures, and at times, a relatively weak stock market.

Rapid expansion of the economy has placed pressures on corporations to raise even larger amounts of borrowed capital. Because of this continuously expanded level of borrowing, benchmarks to judge capital adequacy have had to be reconsidered by those evaluating the quality of corporate bond issues. In effect, the borrowing quality of the average corporation has deteriorated significantly since the 1960s. Figure 16–1 attempts to capture the effects of this extra borrowing on the safety margin of pre-tax, pre-interest earnings (operating and nonoperating) over interest charges. From about six times interest earned in the early 1970s, the average interest coverage ratio has steadily declined for Canadian industrial corporations so that it hovered between two and three times interest earned in the mid-1980s. The slippage to 1.91 in 1982, the result of high interest rates and recession-induced operating

Figure 16–1
Interest coverage—Canadian industrial corporations, 1972–1985

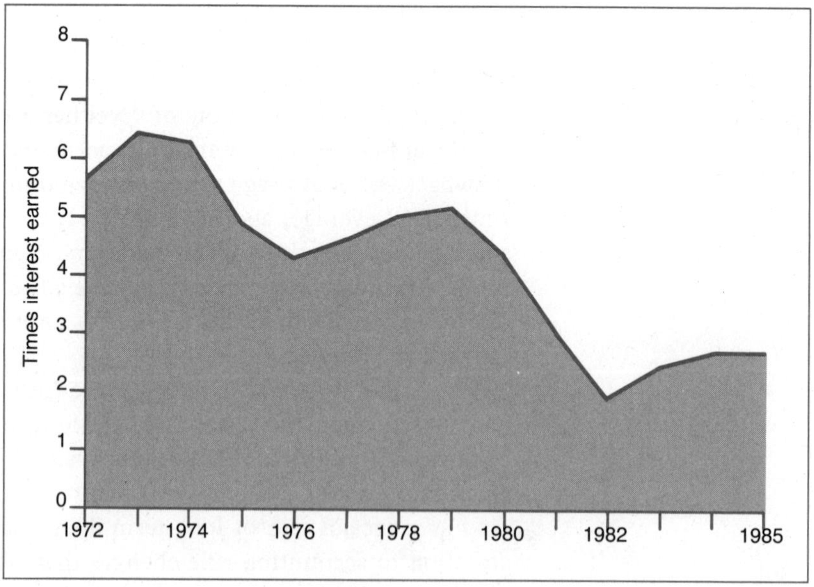

profit declines, shows the danger involved in carrying high debt loads. If only pre-tax, pre-interest "operating" earnings are considered for 1982, the interest coverage ratio becomes a meager 1.45 times. The exclusion of "other income" in the ratio calculation results in similar effects in the other years displayed.

With the decline in the interest-paying capability of corporate borrowers, a number of large corporations have actually defaulted on their obligations, and a number of smaller firms have been liquidated. In the event such unwelcome situations occur, it is the "debt contract" that dictates a leader's potential influence over the corporation's affairs and a given lender's relative bargaining position. Thus, the terms and conditions included in the debt contract are very important in determining the quality of the debtholder's security.

The Debt Contract

The corporate bond represents the basic long-term debt instrument for most large corporations. The bond agreement specifies such basic items as the par value, the coupon rate, and the maturity date.

Par value (face value) The initial value of the bond. Most corporate bonds are traded in $1,000 units.

Coupon rate The actual interest rate on the bond, usually payable in semiannual installments. To the extent that interest rates in the market go above or below the coupon rate after the bond has been issued, the market price on the bond will change from the par value. A bond paying a 10 percent coupon rate on par value will certainly trade at a discount from par value in a market in which 12 percent interest is commonplace.

Maturity date The final date on which repayment of the bond principal is due.

The bond agreement is supplemented by a much longer document termed a *bond indenture*. The indenture, often containing over 100 pages of complicated legal wording, covers every minute detail surrounding the bond issue—including collateral pledged, methods of repayment, restrictions on the corporation, and procedures for initiating claims against the corporation. An independent trustee (for example, Royal Trust or Montreal Trust) is appointed by the corporation to administer the bond indenture provisions under the guidelines of the trust acts of the individual provinces. Let us examine two key items in any bond agreement: the security provisions and the methods of repayment.

Security Provisions

A secured claim is one in which specific assets are pledged to bondholders in the event of default. Only infrequently are pledged assets actually sold off and the proceeds distributed to bondholders. Typically, the defaulting corporation is reorganized, and existing claims are partially satisfied by issuing new securities to the participating parties. Of course, the stronger and better secured the initial claim, the higher the quality of the new security to be received in exchange. When a defaulting corporation is reorganized for failure to meet obligations, existing management may be terminated and, in extreme cases, held legally responsible for any imprudent actions.

A number of terms are used to denote collateralized or secured debt. Under a mortgage agreement, real property (plant and equipment) is pledged as security for the loan. A mortgage may be senior or junior in nature, with the former requiring satisfaction of claims before payment is given to the latter. Bondholders may also attach an after-acquired property clause, requiring that any new property be placed under the original mortgage.

The student should realize that not all secured debt will carry every protective factor, but rather its provisions result from careful negotiations through which some safeguards are included, others rejected. Generally, the greater the protection offered a given class of bondholders, the lower is the interest rate on the bond. Bondholders are willing to assume some degree of risk to receive a higher yield.

Unsecured Debt

A number of corporations issue debt that is not secured by a specific claim to assets. The term *debenture* refers to a long-term, unsecured corporate bond. Among the major participants in debenture offerings are such prestigious firms as Bell Canada Enterprises and Imperial Oil. Because of the legal problems associated with "specific" asset claims in a secured bond offering, the trend is decidedly to unsecured debt—allowing the bondholder a general claim against the corporation rather than a specific lien against an asset.

Even unsecured debt may be divided between high-ranking and subordinated debt. A *subordinated debenture* is an unsecured bond in which payment to the holder will take place only after designated senior debenture holders are satisfied. The hierarchy of creditor obligations for secured as well as unsecured debt is presented in Figure 16–2 along with consideration of the position of shareholders. For a further discussion of payment of claims and the hierarchy of obligations, see Appendix 16A, "Financial Alternatives for Distressed Firms," which also covers bankruptcy considerations.

Figure 16–2
Priority of claims

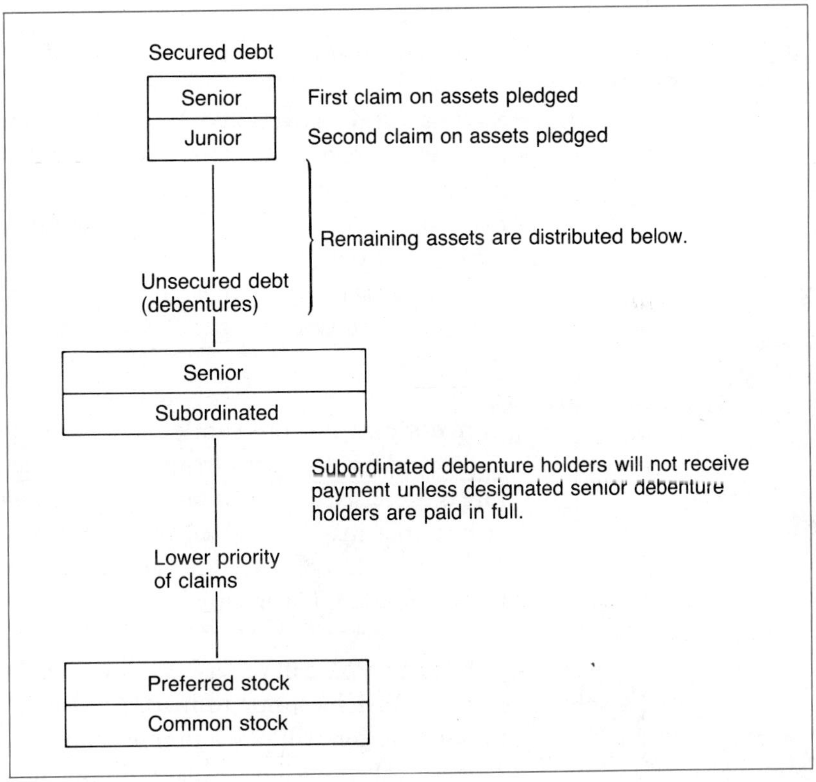

Methods of Repayment

The method of repayment for bond issues may not always call for one lump-sum disbursement at the maturity date. Historically, some Canadian and British government bond issues were perpetual in nature. In the case of one unusual U.S. issue, West Shore Railroad, 4 percent bonds are not scheduled to mature until 2361 (almost 400 years in the future). Nevertheless, most bonds have some orderly or preplanned system of repayment. In addition to the simplest arrangement—a single-sum payment at maturity—bonds may be retired by serial payments, through sinking-fund provisions, through conversion, or through a call feature.

Serial payments Bonds may be paid off in installments, or serial payments, over the life of the issue. Each bond has its own predetermined date of maturity and receives interest only to that point. Although the total issue may span 20 years, 15 or 20 different maturity dates may be assigned specific dollar amounts.

Sinking-fund provision A less structured but considerably more popular method of debt retirement is through the use of a sinking fund. Under this arrangement semiannual or annual contributions are made by the corporation into a fund administered by the trustee for purposes of debt retirement. The trustee takes the proceeds and goes into the market to purchase bonds from willing sellers. If no willing sellers are available a lottery system will be used among outstanding bondholders.

Conversion A more subtle method of reducing debt outstanding is to provide for debt conversion into common stock. Although this feature is exercised at the option of the bondholder, a number of incentives or penalties may be utilized to encourage conversion. The mechanics of convertible bond trading are discussed at length in Chapter 19, Convertibles and Warrants.

Call feature A call provision allows the corporation to call in or force in the debt issue prior to maturity. In the event it exercises the call the corporation will pay a premium over par value of 5 to 10 percent. Modern call provisions usually do not take effect until the bond has been outstanding at least 5 to 10 years so as to allow an original investor to reap some reward if he/she timed the purchase to buy the bonds before a general decrease in interest rates. Generally, the call premium declines over time, usually by ½ to 1 percent per year after the call period begins. A corporation may decide to call in outstanding debt issues when interest rates on new securities are considerably lower than those on previously issued debt. (The purpose would be to get the high-cost, old debt off the books.)

Now that the key features of the bond indenture have been discussed we will discuss an actual bond situation. Table 16–1 presents the information from *The Corporate Bond Record* on Genstar Corporation bonds. We see that Genstar had seven outstanding public bond issues at the time, issued between June 1, 1975, and October 15, 1981, and ranging between 7 percent and 17½ percent interest payable on the face amounts. One of the issues, the 11¾ percent bond sold on June 1, 1975, consisted of an original offering of $30 million. As of December 31, 1984, bonds from that issue worth $14,871,000 were still outstanding. A check of the sinking-fund requirement reveals that retirement of $1.5 million per year was required from 1976 to 1994. In other words, the company was required to retire the bond evenly over each year of its 20-year life. The fact that almost half of the bonds were outstanding at the end of 1984 indicates that Genstar did not exercise its option to retire bonds earlier than specified in the bond indenture. Note that the premium for redemption in the first year was 11.25 percent decreasing by 0.65 percent per year. Thus, a bond called in June of 1988 would require a retirement premium of 3.45 percent. This means that Genstar would pay $1,034.50 for every $1,000 bond redeemed.

– when a bond is cashed, you are paid whatever t. interest rate is

Bond Prices, Yields, and Ratings

The financial manager must be sensitive to interest rate changes and price movements in the bond market. The treasurer's interpretation of market conditions will influence the timing of new issues, the coupon rate offered, the maturity date, and the necessity for a call provision. Lest the student of finance think that bonds maintain stable, long-term price patterns, he or she need merely examine bond pricing during the period 1977–82. When the market interest rate on outstanding 30-

Table 16–1
Details on corporate debt

GENSTAR CORPORATION

10% S.F. Debentures, due June 1, 1989

Issued:	US$50,000,000	(1979)	Payable: Euro. U.S.
O/S:	US$38,991,000		Interest: June 1

25% of issue purchased before maturity

Redemption: Not redeemable prior to June 1, 1983. Thereafter redeemable at 102.50 to May 31, 1984; premium decreasing by 0.50 of 1% per annum to May 31, 1988; thereafter at par.

Purchase and Sinking Fund: Purchase Fund—The Purchase agent will endeavour to purchase at prices not in excess of 98.50, US$2,000,000 of debentures during each of the years ending June 1, 1980 and 1981; and US$1,000,000 during each of the years ending June 1, 1982 and 1983.

Sinking fund—Sufficient to retire US$2,500,000 per annum on June 1 in each of the years 1984 to 1988, inclusive.
Trustee: Montreal Trust Co.
Lead Underwriter: Société Générale de Banque S.A.

17.5% Debentures, due Oct. 15, 1989

Issued:	US$75,000,000	(1981)	Payable: Euro. U.S.
O/S:	US$74,975,000		Interest: Oct 15

Redemption: Not redeemable prior to Oct. 15, 1986; therafter redeemable at 102.0 to Oct. 14, 1987; at 101.0 to Oct. 14, 1988; therafter at par. The company may redeem all but not part of the debentures at par if withholding taxes imposed.

Trustee: Montreal Trust Co.

Lead Underwriter: Société Général de Banque S.A.

14.75% S.F. Debentures, due Apr. 15, 1991

Issued:	US$50,000,000	(1981)	Payable: Euro. U.S.
O/S:	US$43,700,000		Interest: Apr. 15

21% of issue purchased before maturity

Redemption: Redeemable at 101.50 to Apr. 14, 1986; premium decreasing by 0.25 of 1% per annum to 100.5 on Apr. 14, 1990; thereafter at par.

Purchase and Sinking Fund: Purchase Fund—The purchase agent will endeavor to purchase in each 12-month period ending Apr. 15, 1987 to 1990, inclusive, not less than US$3,750,000.

Sinking Fund—Sufficient to retire US$2,100,000 on Apr. 15 in each of the years 1982 to 1986, inclusive.

Trustee: Montreal Trust Co.

Lead Underwriter: Société Générale de Banque S.A.

7% Debentures, due Apr. 30, 1991

Issued:	S.Fr.$100,000,000	(1981)	Payable: Euro. S.Fr.
O/S:	S.Fr.$100,000,000		Interest: Apr. 30

Table 16–1 (*concluded*)

Redemption: Not redeemable prior to Apr. 20, 1987. Thereafter redeemable at 101 to Apr. 29, 1988; at 100.50 to Apr. 29, 1989; thereafter at par. If the company is required to make additional payments to interest, it may redeem all but not part of the debentures at 102.00 in the 12 months ending Apr. 30, 1982; at 101.50 in 1983; at 101.00 in 1984; at 100.50 in 1985; thereafter at par.

Purchase Fund: The company will undertake to purchase S.Fr. 5,000,000 within 60 days prior to Apr. 30 in each of the years 1987 through to 1990, inclusive.

Trustee: Montreal Trust Co.

Lead Underwriter: Credit Suisse

11.75% S.F. Debentures, due June 1, 1995

Issued:	$30,000,000	(1975)	Payable: Cdn.
O/S:	$14,871,000		Interest: June 1; Dec. 1

95% of issue purchased before maturity

Redemption: Redeemable at 111.25 to Mar. 31, 1976; premium decreasing by 0.65 of 1% per annum to 100.2 on Mar. 31, 1993; thereafter at par.

Sinking Fund: Sufficient to retire on June 1 in each of the years 1976 to 1994, inclusive, $1,500,000.

Trustee: Montreal Trust Co.

Lead Underwriter: Dominion Securities Pitfield

11.25% S.F. Debentures, due Mar. 15, 1996

Issued:	$50,000,000	(1976)	Payable: Cdn.
O/S:	$34,490,000		Interest: Mar. 15; Sept 15

70% of issue purchased before maturity

Redemption: Redeemable at 111.25 on or before Mar. 14, 1977; premium decreasing by 0.60 of 1% per annum to 105.85 on Mar. 14, 1986; thereafter premium decreasing by 0.65 of 1% per annum to 100.65 on Mar. 14, 1994; thereafter at par.

Purchase and Sinking Fund: Purchase Fund—The company shall purchase in each 12-month period ending Mar. 14, 1977 to 1981, inclusive, at least $2,500,000.
Sinking Fund—Sufficient to retire on Mar. 15 in each of the years 1982 to 1995, inclusive, $2,500,000.

Trustee: Montreal Trust Co.

Lead Underwriter: Wood Gundy

10.75% Debentures, due June 15, 1999

Issued:	$50,000,000	(1979)	Payable: Cdn.
O/S:	$46,000,000		Interest: June 15; Dec. 15

Private placement.

Source: *The Corporate Bond Record 1986* (Toronto: The Financial Post Information Service), pp. 102–103.

year, AAA corporate bonds went from 9.5 percent to 18.3 percent, the average price of such existing bonds dropped about 48 percent. Imagine the disillusionment of a conservative investor during that period as she watched her $1,000, 9.5 percent, top-quality bond decline to be quoted at $525.[1] Though most bonds are virtually certain to be redeemed at their face value at maturity ($1,000 in this case), this is small consolation to the bondholder who has many decades to wait while his or her capital is tied up making below market returns.

As indicated above the price of a bond is intimately tied to current interest rates. A bond paying 9.5 percent ($95 a year) will fare quite poorly when the going market rate is 18.3 percent ($183 a year). In order to maintain a market in the older issue, the price is adjusted downward to reflect current market demands. The longer the life of the issue, the greater the influence of interest rate changes on the price of the bond.[2] The same process will work in reverse if interest rates go down. The value of a 30-year, $1,000 bond initially issued to yield 18.3 percent would rise to $1,800 if interest rates declined to 9.5 percent (assuming the bond is not callable). An illustration of interest rate effects on bond prices is presented in Table 16–2 for a bond paying 12 percent interest. It is very important to observe that years to maturity as well as market interest rates have a strong influence on bond prices.

Over the past four decades long-term interest rates have shown a definite upward trend, as shown in Figure 16–3. Until the mid-1980s

Table 16–2
Interest rates and bond prices (the bond pays 12 percent interest)

Years to Maturity	Rate in the Market (percent)				
	8%	10%	12%	14%	16%
1	$1,038.16	$1,018.54	$1,000	$981.48	$963.98
15	1,345.52	1,153.32	1,000	875.54	774.48
25	1,429.92	1,182.92	1,000	862.06	754.98

Note: This table is based on semiannual interest payments, with annualized interest rates.

[1]Bond prices are generally quoted as a percentage of original par value. In this case the quote would read 52½.

[2]This is known as Malkiel's second theory of bonds. In fact, it is only completely true when the coupon rate of the bond is equal to or greater than the original discount rate.

Figure 16–3
Long-term yields on debt

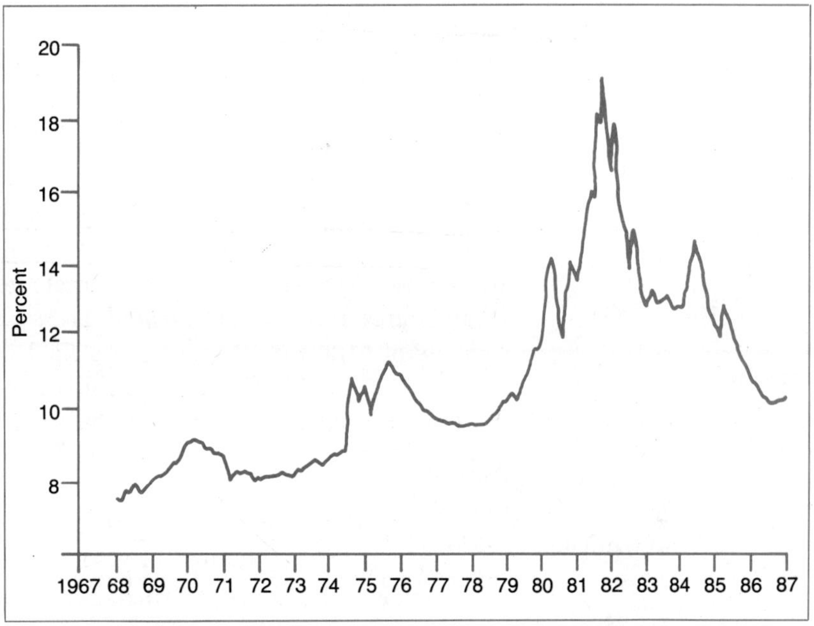

rate declines had seldom lasted more than a year which fact necessitated rapid action by participants who wished to catch the market while rates were still low. There has been, however, a substantial decline in long-term interest rates in the mid-1980s (albeit from rates that were extremely high in a historical comparison).

Bond Yields

Bond yields are quoted on three different bases: coupon rate, current yield, and yield to maturity. We will apply each to a $1,000 par value bond paying $100 per year interest for 10 years. The bond is currently selling in the market for $900.

Coupon rate (nominal yield) Stated interest payment divided by the par value.

$$\frac{\$100}{\$1{,}000} = 10\%$$

Current yield Stated interest payment divided by the current price of the bond.

$$\frac{\$100}{\$900} = 11.11\%$$

Yield to maturity The interest rate that will equate future interest payments and the payment at maturity to the current market price. This represents the concept of the internal rate of return. In the present case an interest rate of approximately 11.58 percent will equate interest payments of \$100 for 10 years and a final payment of \$1,000 to the current price of \$900. A simple formula may be used to approximate yield to maturity.[3] This formula was initially presented in Chapter 10.

$$\text{Approximate yield to maturity } (Y') = \frac{\text{Annual interest payment} + \dfrac{\text{Principal payment (par)} - \text{Price of the bond}}{\text{Number of years to maturity}}}{\dfrac{\text{Price of the bond} + \text{Principal payment (par)}}{2}} \quad (16\text{–}1)$$

$$= \frac{\$100 + \dfrac{\$1{,}000 - \$900}{10}}{\dfrac{\$900 + \$1{,}000}{2}}$$

$$= \frac{\$100 + \dfrac{\$100}{10}}{\dfrac{\$1{,}900}{2}}$$

$$= \frac{\$100 + \$10}{\$950} = \frac{\$110}{\$950} = 11.58\%$$

Extensive bond tables indicating yields to maturity are also available. When financial analysts speak of bond yields, the general assumption is that they are speaking of yields to maturity. This is deemed to be the most significant measure of return.

[3] The greater the discount or premium and the longer the period to maturity, the less accurate is the approximation.

Bond Ratings

Rating services provide an objective assessment of the investment quality of securities. Issuing corporations and investors alike pay close attention to the bond ratings assigned by bond rating services. In Canada, Dominion Bond Rating Services and Canadian Bond Rating Service provide independent bond ratings. In the United States, Moody's Investor Service and Standard & Poor's Corporation perform a similar service.

The higher the rating assigned a given issue, the lower will be the interest payments required to satisfy potential investors. This is because the higher rating indicates a lower amount of risk. A major industrial corporation may be able to issue a 30-year bond with an 11 percent yield to maturity because it is rated A++ by the Canadian Bond Rating Service while a smaller, regional firm may only qualify for a B+ rating and be forced to pay 13½ to 14 percent. (See Table 16–3.)

As an example of a rating system, Canadian Bond Rating Service provides seven categories of ranking:

A++ A+ A B++ B+ B C

The first two categories represent high quality (for example, Bell Canada); the next three, medium to good quality; rating B signifies poor quality, while rating C signifies speculative. High and low mod-

Table 16–3
Long-term corporate bond ratings and yield averages

Rating	*Average Yield* *April 1, 1987*	*Average Yield* *July 1, 1982*
Utility:		
A++	9.31%	17.29%
A+	10.10	17.35
A	10.17	17.51
B++	10.43	18.05
Industrial:		
A++	9.63	17.06
A+	10.05	17.41
A	10.25	17.90
B++	10.42	19.18
B+	11.10	25.42

Source: Canadian Bond Rating Service.

ifiers are also added to each of the ranges to make the rating even more precise.

Bonds receive ratings based on the corporation's ability to make interest payments, its consistency of performance, its size, its debt-equity ratio, its working capital position, and a number of other factors. Rating services are extremely interested in the quality of the corporation's management although it seems the judgment of that is often a function of the consistency and adequacy of the firm's financial ratios. The yield spread between higher- and lower-rated bonds varies with economic conditions. If investors are pessimistic about the economic outlook, they may accept as much as 3 percent less to hold high-quality securities while in normal times the spread may be only 1 percent.

Examining Actual Bond Offerings

Information on three actual bond offerings is shown in Table 16–4 to illustrate the various terms we have used.

Recall that the true return on a bond issue is measured by yield to maturity (the last column of Table 16–4). Looking at the Abitibi-Price bonds we note that they are unsecured, as indicated by the term *debentures*. Furthermore, they have a sinking-fund requirement for the retirement of debt. The bonds carry an A (high) rating which puts them on the border between good and very good quality. The bonds carry a market price of $982.50 because the interest rate at time of

Table 16–4
Outstanding bond issues (May 1987)

		Rating	*Price*	*Yield to Maturity*
Abitibi-Price 11s	Sinking fund debentures due March 1995	A (High)	$ 982.50	11.34%
Dofasco 10⅜s	Debentures due March 1996	A++	971.30	10.88
Dominion Textile 14s	Sinking fund debentures due January 1993	B++	1,076.30	12.09
Bell Canada 9.40s	1st mortgage bonds due February 2002	A++	930.00	10.33

issue (11 percent) is just slightly below the required rate of 11.34 percent in May 1987 for bonds of similar quality and maturity. Similar observations may be made for the other bond issues.

The Refunding Decision

From time to time a firm may decide to refund a bond issue. For example, assume you are the financial vice president for a corporation that has issued bonds at 12.5 percent only to witness a drop in interest rates to 10 percent. If you believe interest rates will not go down further and in fact believe they will go back up, you may wish to redeem the expensive 12.5 percent bonds and issue new debt at the prevailing 10 percent rate. This process is labeled a refunding operation. It is made feasible by the call provision that enables a corporation to buy back bonds at close to par rather than at high market values when interest rates are declining. Although long-term interest rates tended to move up in the 50s, 60s, 70s, and 80s, there were periods of decline in interest rates that provided good environments for refunding. The mid-1980s was one such period.

Because bond indenture agreements in Canada normally contain the "financial advantage" clause,[4] refunding of high cost debt has been more infrequent than one would expect. Dofasco's call in July 1986 of its 17 percent debentures, issued in 1982 and due in 1997, thus had particular significance in the investment community. Before the call each $1,000 worth of these bonds traded for $1,250. The day after the call announcement they were worth $1,113.00, precisely the redemption value.

A Capital Budgeting Problem

The refunding decision involves outflows in the form of financing costs related to redeeming and reissuing securities and inflows represented by savings in annual interest costs and some tax savings. In the present case assume that the corporation issued $10 million worth of

[4]This clause states that borrowers cannot use money raised more cheaply to finance the redemption of high-cost debt.

12.5 percent debt with a 25-year maturity and that the debt has been on the books for five years. The corporation now has the opportunity to buy back the old debt and effectively replace it with new debt at 10 percent interest with a 20-year life. The underwriting cost for the old issue was $125,000, and the underwriting cost for the new issue is $200,000. Other issue costs (legal, accounting, and printing) were $25,000 for the old and $30,000 for the new issue. We shall also assume that the corporation is in the 40 percent tax bracket and uses a 6 percent discount rate for refunding decisions. Since the savings from a refunding decision are certain—unlike the savings from most other capital budgeting decisions—the after-tax cost of new debt is used as the discount rate rather than the more generalized cost of capital.[5] In this case, then, the after-tax cost of new debt is 10 percent × (1 − Tax rate), or 6 percent.

Restatement of Facts

	Old Issue	*New Issue*
Size	$10,000,000	$10,000,000
Interest rate	12.5%	10%
Total life	25 years	20 years
Remaining life	20 years	20 years
Call premium	10%	—
Underwriting costs	$125,000	$200,000
Other issue costs	25,000	30,000

Tax bracket	40%
Discount rate	6%

Let's go through the capital budgeting process of defining the outflows and inflows and determining the net present value attached to the refunding decision.

[5]A minority opinion would be that there is sufficient similarity between the bond refunding decision and other capital budgeting decisions to disallow any specialized treatment. Also note that although the bondholders must still bear some risk of default, for which they are compensated, the corporation assumes no risk.

Step A—Outflow considerations

1. Payment of call premium—The first outflow is the 10 percent call premium on $10 million, or $1 million. This prepayment penalty is necessary to call in the original issue. Because it is considered a capital item, the $1 million cash expenditure will cost $1 million on an after-tax basis.

Net cost of call premium	$1,000,000

2. Underwriting cost on new issue—The second outflow is the $200,000 underwriting cost on the new issue. Any commissions or bonuses paid to an underwriter acting as agent on a best-efforts basis are tax-deductible. If the underwriter's commission arises from its acting as a principal in buying and reselling the bonds, then the underwriter's fee would be treated as a discount on issue and the tax deduction would apply in the year the bonds were redeemed. The legal, accounting, and printing costs incurred directly by the issuer in preparing the issue are tax-deductible in the year incurred. Assuming the underwriter in this case is operating on a best-efforts basis, the cash flow effect of the issue costs is:

Underwriting expense [$200,000 × (1 − t)]	$120,000
Other issue expenses [$30,000 × (1 − t)]	18,000
Total new issue expense cash flow effect	$138,000

3. Duplicate interest during overlap period—An overlap period generally occurs because the new bonds must be sold before the old ones are redeemed. We will allow one month as an estimate of the overlap period, although it could be longer. Offsetting this payment of interest on two bond issues during the overlap period is the fact that the company will be earning interest on the proceeds from the new issue until it employs them. Since interest is a tax-deductible expense the net cash flow effect of having to continue paying interest on the old issue during the overlap period is the difference between what is paid on the old issue and what is earned on the new (say 8½ percent in this case):

.125 × 1/12 × $10,000,000 × (1 − .40)	$62,500
.085 × 1/12 × $10,000,000 × (1 − .40)	42,500
	$20,000

Step B—Inflow considerations The major inflows in the refunding decision are related to the reduction of annual interest expense.

4. Cost savings in lower interest rates—The corporation will enjoy a 2.5 percent drop in interest rates, from 12.5 percent to 10 percent, on $10 million of bonds if it refunds the bond issue:

12.5% × $10,000,000	$1,250,000
10% × $10,000,000	1,000,000
Savings	$ 250,000

Since the firm is in the 40 percent tax bracket, this is equivalent to $150,000 of after-tax benefits per year for 20 years. Just take the savings and multiply by one minus the tax rate to get the after-tax benefits. Applying a 6 percent discount rate for a 20-year annuity:

$150,000 × 11.470 ($n$ = 20, i = 6%) = $1,720,500

Cost savings in lower interest rates $1,720,500

Step C—Net present value We now compare our outflows and our inflows.

Outflows		*Inflows*	
1. Net cost of call premium . . .	$1,000,000	4. Cost savings in lower interest rates	$1,720,500
2. Net cost of underwriting expense on new issue	138,000		
3. Duplicate interest during overlap	20,000		
	$1,158,000		

Present value of inflows	$1,720,500
Present value of outflows	1,158,000
Net present value	$ 562,500

The refunding decision has a positive net present value suggesting that interest rates have dropped sufficiently to favor refunding. The only question is: Will interest rates go lower—indicating an even better time for refunding? This is a consideration all firms must face, and there is no easy answer.

A number of other factors may complicate the problem. For example, the overlapping time period in the refunding procedure when both issues are outstanding and the firm is paying double interest could be longer than one month. If the bonds were issued at a discount, the difference between the redemption value and the amount the company received for the bond would be tax-deductible in the year of redemption.

In working problems the student should have minimum difficulty if he or she follows the four suggested calculations. Note, by way of review, that in each of the four calculations we had the following tax implications:

1. Payment of call premium—nontax-deductible.
2. New issue expenses—underwriting commissions are tax-deductible at either the time of issue or redemption depending on the underwriter's role. Legal, accounting, and printing costs paid directly by the issuer are tax-deductible in the year incurred.
3. Cost savings in lower interest rates—cost savings are like any form of income, and we will retain the cost savings times (1 − Tax rate).
4. Bond premiums or discounts—premiums have no tax effect. Issue discounts are tax-deductible at the time of redemption.

Advantages and Disadvantages of Debt

The financial manager must consider whether debt will contribute to or detract from the firm's operations. In certain industries, such as the airlines, very heavy debt utilization is a way of life, whereas in other industries (drugs, photographic equipment) reliance is placed on other forms of capital.

Benefits of Debt

The advantages of debt may be enumerated as:

1. Interest payments are tax-deductible. Because the corporate tax rate approaches 50 percent, the effective after-tax cost of interest is only about half the dollar amount expended.
2. The financial obligation is clearly specified and of a fixed nature (with the exception of floating rate bonds). Contrast this with selling an ownership interest in which shareholders have open-ended participation in the sharing of profits.

3. In an inflationary economy debt may be paid back with "cheaper dollars." A $1,000 bond obligation may be repaid in 10 or 20 years with dollars that have shrunk in value by 50 or 60 percent. In terms of "real dollars," or purchasing power equivalents, one might argue that the corporation should be asked to repay something in excess of $2,000. Presumably, high interest rates in inflationary periods compensate the lender for loss in purchasing power, but this is not always the case.
4. The use of debt, up to a prudent point, may lower the cost of capital to the firm. To the extent that debt does not strain the risk position of the firm, its low after-tax cost may aid in reducing the weighted overall cost of financing to the firm.

Drawbacks of Debt

Finally, we must consider the disadvantages of debt:

1. Interest and principal payment obligations are set by contract and must be met regardless of the economic position of the firm.
2. Bond indenture agreements may place burdensome restrictions on the firm such as maintenance of working capital at a given level, limits on future debt offerings, and guidelines for dividend policy. Although bondholders generally do not have the right to vote, they may take virtual control of the firm if important indenture provisions are not met.
3. Utilized beyond a given point, debt may serve as a depressant on outstanding common stock values.

Eurobond Market

A final item of interest in the bond market is the Eurobond. A Eurobond takes us out of the purely domestic framework and into foreign markets. Eurocurrencies are units of currency deposited in banks outside of the country issuing the currencies. Of such deposits, the U.S. Eurodollar is the most prevalent. A Eurobond is a bond denominated in another currency from that of the country in which the bond is issued. Eurobonds are placed by international investment dealer syndicates all over the world. An example might be a bond of a Canadian corporation, payable in U.S. dollars and sold in London,

Paris, or Frankfurt. Looking back at Table 16–1, details of Genstar's corporate debt, we see that four of the company's seven outstanding debt issues were denominated in Eurocurrencies. Three were in U.S. Eurodollars and one in Euro Swiss Francs. Disclosure requirements in the Eurobond market are less demanding than those of Canadian domestic regulatory agencies. Investors in Eurobonds are generally not able to rely on bond-rating agencies, though Moody's and Standard & Poor's have been rating selected Eurobond issues for a fee.

Intermediate Term Loans

Instead of issuing debentures, a corporation might borrow the sum needed from a financial intermediary. Banks and other commercial lenders may extend to a corporation an operating loan or a term loan. Although the differences between these types of loans are many, two stand out. First, the money on the operating line is generally advanced based on current asset security while the term loan is advanced against fixed asset security. Second, the operating loan is payable on demand while the term loan is not. The choice of lenders for term loans in Canada is wide and includes banks (both schedule A and B), trust companies, life insurance companies, credit unions and caisses populaires, specialized equipment lenders, Federal Business Development Bank (as lender of last resort), pension funds, and term lending specialists such as Commercial Capital Corporation.

The term on a term loan will generally be from 3 to 10 years although occasionally longer depending on the nature of the security and the financial strength of the borrower. The interest rate charged is often floating (for example, prime + ½ percent) although lenders will sometimes, depending on economic and market circumstances, fix the rate for the full term of the loan. Principal and interest repayments are usually made monthly or quarterly with a balloon payment of principal required at the end of the term. Figure 16–4 provides a sample of a credit offer from a term lender to a potential borrower. Take special note of the legal covenants governing the credit as extended.

Leasing as a Form of Debt

When a corporation contracts to lease an oil tanker or a computer and signs a noncancelable, long-term agreement, the transaction has all the characteristics of a debt obligation. Long-term leasing was not

Figure 16–4
Sample credit offer

Term Loan Offer
Acme Company Limited

We are pleased to make the following offer to finance:

BORROWER:	Acme Company Limited
LENDER:	XYZ Insurance Company of Canada
AMOUNT:	$3,000,000
REPAYMENT:	$25,000 per month, including principal and interest, to liquidate in 10 years. Subject to adjustment to reflect changes in Prime Lending Rate.
INTEREST:	Prime (average of 5 largest banks) + 1½%, payable monthly or fixed rate option at rates for 1-, 2-, 3- or 5-year term as set from time to time.
SECURITY:	A first fixed charge on all land, buildings, and equipment. A first floating charge on all other assets subject only to the bank charge on accounts receivable and inventory.
LEGAL COVENANTS:	1. Annual audited financial statements provided to XYZ Insurance within 90 days after fiscal year end. 2. Quarterly financial statements to be provided within 30 days of quarter end. 3. Net worth of the borrower including capital, retained earnings, and shareholders' loans is not to fall below $2,000,000 during the term of the loan. 4. Debt/equity ratio not to exceed 2:1. 5. Working capital ratio is not to be less than 1.5:1. 6. Capital expenditures not to exceed $500,000 in any fiscal year without XYZ's approval. 7. Management salaries and bonuses not to exceed $750,000 per annum without XYZ's approval. 8. An annual list of fixed assets is to be provided.

recognized as a debt obligation in the early post-World War II period, but since the mid-60s there has been a strong movement by the accounting profession to force companies to fully divulge all information about leasing obligations and to indicate the equivalent debt characteristics.

This position was made official for financial reporting purposes as a result of a Canadian Institute of Chartered Accountants (CICA) ruling in December 1978. In essence this ruling said that certain types of leases must be shown as long-term obligations on the financial statements of the firm. Prior to that lease obligations could merely be divulged in footnotes to financial statements, and large lease obligations did not have to be included in the debt structure (except for the upcoming payment). Consider the case of firm ABC, whose balance sheet is shown in Table 16–5. Prior to the CICA recommendation on leases, a footnote to the financial statements might have indicated a lease obligation of $12 million a year for the next 15 years, with a present value of $100 million. Under current practice, however, this information has been moved directly to the balance sheet, as indicated in Table 16–6.

We see that both a new asset and a new liability have been created, as indicated by the asterisks. The essence of this treatment is that a long-term, noncancelable lease is tantamount to purchasing the asset

Table 16–5

Balance Sheet
(in millions)

Current assets	$ 50	Current liabilities	$ 50
Fixed assets	150	Long-term liabilities	50
		Total liabilities	$100
		Owner's equity	100
Total assets	$200	Total liabilities and owners' equity	$200

Table 16–6

Revised Balance Sheet
(in millions)

Current assets	$ 50	Current liabilities	$ 50
Fixed assets	150	Long-term liabilities	50
*Leased property under capital lease	100	*Obligation under capital lease	100
		Total liabilities	200
		Owners' equity	100
Total assets	$300	Total liabilities and owners' equity	$300

with borrowed funds, and this should be reflected on the balance sheet. Note that between the original balance sheet (Table 16–5) and the revised balance sheet (Table 16–6) the total-debt-to-total-assets ratio has gone from 50 percent to 66.7 percent.

$$\text{Original} \quad \frac{\text{Total debt}}{\text{Total assets}} = \frac{\$100 \text{ million}}{\$200 \text{ million}} = 50\%$$

$$\text{Revised} \quad \frac{\text{Total debt}}{\text{Total assets}} = \frac{\$200 \text{ million}}{\$300 \text{ million}} = 66.7\%$$

Though this represents a substantial increase in the ratio, the impact on the firm's credit rating or stock price may be minimal. To the extent the financial markets are efficient, the information was already known by analysts who took the data from footnotes or other sources and made their own adjustments. Nevertheless, corporate financial officers fought long, hard, and unsuccessfully to keep the lease obligation off the balance sheet. They seem to be much less convinced about the efficiency of the marketplace than are financial theorists.

Capital Lease versus Operating Lease

Not all leases must be capitalized (present valued) and placed on the balance sheet. It is only under circumstances in which substantially all the benefits and risks of ownership are transferred in a lease that this treatment is necessary. Under these circumstances we have a capital (or financing) lease. Identification as a capital lease and the attendant financial treatment are required whenever any one of the four following conditions is present:

1. The arrangement transfers ownership of the property to the lessee (the leasing party) by the end of the lease term.
2. The lease contains a bargain purchase price at the end of the lease. The option price will have to be sufficiently low so that exercise of the option appears reasonably certain.
3. The lease term is equal to 75 percent or more of the estimated life of the leased property.

4. The present value of the minimum lease payments equals 90 percent or more of the fair value of the lease property at the inception of the lease.[6]

A lease that does not meet any of these four criteria is not regarded as a capital lease, but as an "operating" lease. An operating lease is usually short term and is often cancelable at the option of the lessee. Furthermore, the lessor (the owner of the asset) may provide for the maintenance and upkeep of the asset, since he is likely to get it back. An operating lease does not require the "capitalization," or presentation, of the full obligation on the balance sheet. Operating leases are used most frequently with assets such as automobiles and office equipment, while capital leases include oil drilling equipment, airplanes, rail equipment, certain forms of real estate, and other long-term assets. The greatest volume of leasing obligations is represented by capital leases.

Besides a straightforward direct lease, where a firm acquires the use of an asset offered in general to the market by a lessor, there are also sale-and-leaseback arrangements and leveraged leases. Under a sale-and-leaseback arrangement, a firm would sell an asset it already owns to another party. In turn it would then lease the asset back from that party. For example, Gulf Canada did this in 1987 with its headquarters building in Calgary. In leveraged leases three parties are involved: a lessee, a lessor, and a lender. In these instances the asset is generally financed by an equity investment by the lessor (often about 20 percent) and a loan to the lessor from a financial institution for the remainder. Leveraged leasing is common where the asset in question requires a large capital outlay.

Income Statement Effect

The capital lease calls not only for present valuing the lease obligation on the balance sheet but also for treating the arrangement for income

---

[6]The discount rate used for this test is the leasing firm's new cost of borrowing or the lessor's (the firm that owns the asset) implied rate of return under the lease. The lower of the two must be used when both are known.

statement purposes as if it were somewhat similar to a purchase-borrowing arrangement. Thus, under a capital lease the intangible asset account shown in Table 16–6 as "Leased property under capital lease" is amortized or written off over the life of the lease with an annual expense deduction. Also the liability account shown in Table 16–6 as "Obligation under capital lease" is written off through regular amortization, with an implied interest expense on the remaining balance. Thus, for financial reporting purposes the annual deductions are amortization of the asset plus implied interest expense on the remaining present value of the liability. Though the actual development of these values and accounting rules is best deferred to an accounting course, the finance student should understand the close similarity between a capital lease and borrowing to purchase an asset for financial reporting purposes.

An operating lease, on the other hand, usually calls for an annual expense deduction equal to the lease payment, with no specific amortization, as is indicated in Appendix 16B (Lease versus Purchase Decision) at the end of this chapter.

Advantages of Leasing

Why is leasing so popular? In the United States it has emerged as a $100 billion industry, with such firms as Clark Equipment, Citicorp, and U.S. Leasing International providing an enormous amount of financing. Although industry figures for the Canadian leasing market are not publicly tabulated, the Canadian market is significant but less spectacular than that of most other industrialized countries. Industry participants estimate the annual market as almost $2 billion. There are approximately 100 lessors in the Canadian equipment leasing business. Citibank Leasing Canada Ltd., probably the largest of these with 1986 sales and profits of $126 million and $13 million, respectively, was purchased by leveraged buyout specialist Onex Corporation in 1987 for $270 million. Major reasons for the popularity of leasing include the following:

1. The lessee may lack sufficient funds or the credit capability to purchase the asset from a manufacturer who is willing, however, to accept a lease agreement or to arrange a lease obligation with a third party.

2. The provisions of a lease obligation may be substantially less restrictive than those of a bond indenture.
3. There may be no down payment requirement, as would generally be the case in the purchase of an asset (leasing allows for a larger indirect loan).
4. The lessor may possess particular expertise in a given industry—allowing for expert product selection, maintenance, and eventual resale. Through this process the negative effects of obsolescence may be lessened.
5. Creditor claims on certain types of leases, such as real estate, are restricted in bankruptcy and reorganization proceedings. Leases on chattels (non-real estate items) have no such limitation.

There are also some tax factors to be considered. Where one party to a lease is in a higher tax bracket than the other party, certain tax advantages, such as an investment tax credit, may be better utilized. For example, a wealthy party may purchase an asset and take an investment tax credit then lease the asset to another party in a lower tax bracket for actual use. Also lease payments on the use of land are tax-deductible, whereas land ownership does not allow a similar deduction for depreciation. It is important to note that, to be treated as a legitimate lease contract for tax purposes, the Department of National Revenue requires that lease payments not include an excess amount implying that the lessee is purchasing the underlying asset on an installment basis. Finally, a firm may wish to engage in a sale-and-leaseback arrangement, to provide it with an infusion of capital while allowing it to continue to use the asset. Even though the dollar costs of a leasing arrangement are often higher than the dollar costs of owning an asset, the advantages cited above may outweigh the direct cost factors.

Summary

The use of debt financing by corporations has grown very rapidly since the early 1960s, and the quality of corporate debt coverage has deteriorated.

Corporate bonds may be secured by a lien on a specific asset or may carry an unsecured designation, indicating that the bondholder possesses a general claim against the corporation. A special discussion of the hierarchy of claims for firms in financial distress is presented in Appendix 16A.

Up to the early 1980s bond prices had been in a state of general decline for four decades due to rising interest rates. Nevertheless, periodic cyclical downturns in interest rates during those years have still afforded an excellent opportunity for refunding, that is, replacing high-interest-rate bonds with lower-interest-rate bonds. This was particularly true in the mid-1980s. The financial manager must consider whether the savings in interest will compensate for the additional cost of calling in the old issue and selling a new one.

Finally, the long-term, noncancelable lease should be considered as a special debt form available to the corporation. It is capitalized on the balance sheet to represent both a debt and an asset account and is amortized on a regular basis. Leasing offers a means of financing in which lessor expertise and other financial benefits can be imparted to the lessee (leasing party).

A lease versus purchase decision for an operating lease is presented in Appendix 16B.

List of Terms

par value	**call feature**
maturity date	**coupon rate**
indenture	**current yield**
secured debt	**yield to maturity**
mortgage agreement	**bond ratings**
unsecured debt	**refunding**
debenture	**capital lease**
subordinated debenture	**operating lease**
serial payments	**Eurobond**
sinking fund	**floating-rate bond**

Discussion Questions

1. Corporate debt has been expanding very dramatically since World War II. What has been the impact on interest coverage, particularly since 1972?

2. What are some of the basic features of bond agreements?
3. What is the difference between a bond agreement and a bond indenture?
4. Discuss the relationship between the coupon rate (original interest rate at time of issue) on a bond and its security provisions.
5. Take the following list of securities and arrange them in order of their priority of claims.

   Preferred stock
   Subordinated debenture
   Common stock
   Senior debentures
   Senior secured debt
   Junior secured debt

6. Which method of bond repayment reduces debt and increases the amount of common stock outstanding?
7. What is the purpose of serial repayments and sinking funds?
8. Under what circumstances would a call on a bond be exercised by a corporation? What is the purpose of a deferred call?
9. Discuss the relationship between bond prices and interest rates. What impact do changing interest rates have on the price of long-term bonds versus short-term bonds?
10. What is the difference between the following yields: coupon rate, current yield, yield to maturity?
11. How does the bond rating affect the interest rate paid by a corporation on its bonds?
12. Bonds of different risk classes will have a spread between their interest rates. Is this spread always the same? Why?
13. Explain how the bond refunding problem is similar to a capital budgeting decision.
14. What cost of capital is generally used in evaluating a bond refunding decision? Why?
15. Discuss the advantages and disadvantages of debt.

16. Explain how floating-rate bonds can save the investor from potential embarrassments in portfolio valuation.

17. What do we mean by capitalizing lease payments?

18. Explain the close parallel between a capital lease and the borrow-purchase decision from the viewpoint of both the balance sheet and the income statement.

Problems

Homework

1. The Milstead Corp. has a bond outstanding with a $90 annual interest payment, a market price of $800, and a maturity date in five years. (Assume that the par value of bonds in all the following problems is $1,000 unless otherwise specified.) Find the following:

a. The coupon rate.
b. The current rate.
c. The approximate yield to maturity.

2. The Fletcher Corporation has a bond outstanding with a coupon rate of 14 percent, a maturity of eight years, a par value of $1,000, and a market price of $1,200. Compute the yield to maturity using the approximation method.

3. The Lincoln Investment Fund buys 900 bonds of the Nichols Corporation through its broker. The bonds pay 11 percent annual interest. The yield to maturity (market rate of interest) is 14 percent. The bonds have a 25-year maturity. Assuming semiannual interest payments:

a. Compute the price of a bond (refer to semiannual interest and bond prices in Chapter 10 for review if necessary).
b. Compute the total value of the 900 bonds.

No

4. The yield to maturity for 20-year bonds is as follows for four different bond-rating categories.

A++	11.3%	A	12.0%
A+	11.6	B++	12.5

The bonds of Hamilton Corporation were rated as A+ and issued at par a few weeks ago. The bonds have just been downgraded to A. Determine the new price of the bonds, assuming a 20-year maturity and semiannual interest payments.

5. A previously issued A, 20-year industrial bond provides a return one fifth of a percent higher than the prime interest rate of 10 percent. Previously issued public utility bonds provide a yield of three eighths of a percentage point higher than previously issued industrial bonds. Finally, new issues of A public utility bonds pay one fourth of a percentage point more than previously issued public utility bonds.

   What should the interest rate be on a newly issued A public utility bond?

6. A 20-year, $1,000 par value zero-coupon bond is to be issued to yield 11 percent.

   a. What should be the initial price of the bond? (Take the present value of $1,000 for 20 years at 11 percent using Appendix B.)
   b. If immediately upon issue interest rates dropped to 9 percent, what would be the value of the zero-coupon rate bond?
   c. If immediately upon issue interest rates increased to 13 percent, what would be the value of the zero-coupon rate bond?

7. A $1,000 par value bond was issued five years ago paying 12 percent interest. The bond has 15 years remaining. Interest rates on similar debt obligations are now 10 percent in the market.

   a. What is the current price of the bond? (Use Table 16–2 to look up the answer.)
   b. Assume Mr. Sharp bought the bond three years ago when it had a price of $970. He paid 30 percent of the purchase price in cash and borrowed the rest (known as buying on margin). He used the interest payments from the bond to cover the interest costs on the loan. By what percentage did the bond price increase from the time it was purchased by Mr. Sharp to the present (value computed in part *a*)?
   c. What is Mr. Sharp's percentage gain on his cash investment?

8. The Wilshire Corp. borrowed $5 million 10 years ago. Since then inflation has averaged 5 percent per year.

a. When the firm repays the original $5 million loan this year, what will be the effective purchasing power of the $5 million?
b. In order to maintain the original $5 million purchasing power, how much should the lender be repaid?
c. If the lender knows he will only receive $5 million in payment after 10 years, how might he be compensated for the loss in purchasing power?

9. The Delta Corporation has a $20 million bond obligation outstanding that it is considering refunding. Though the bonds were initially issued at 13 percent, the interest rates on similar issues have declined to 11.5 percent. The bonds were originally for 20 years and have 16 years remaining. The new issue would be for 16 years. There is a 9 percent call premium on the old issue. The underwriting cost on the new $20 million issue is $560,000, and the underwriting cost on the old issue was $400,000 (assume the underwriters act as agents rather than principals). The company is in a 40 percent tax bracket, and it will use a 7 percent discount rate (rounded after-tax cost of debt) to analyze the refunding decision. Should the old issue be refunded with new debt?

10. The Hopkins Corporation has $60 million of bonds outstanding which were issued at a coupon rate of 14⅛ percent seven years ago. Interest rates have fallen to 13 percent. Mr. Carlson, the vice-president of finance, does not expect rates to fall any further. The bonds have 18 years left to maturity, and Mr. Carlson would like to refund the bonds with a new issue of equal amount having 18 years to maturity. The Hopkins Corporation has a tax rate of 40 percent. The underwriting cost on the old issue was 1.25 percent of the total bond value. The underwriting cost on the new issue will be 1.8 percent of the total bond value. The underwriters act as principals in the deals. The original bond indenture contained a five-year protection against a call, with a 10 percent call premium starting in the sixth year and scheduled to decline by ½ percent each year thereafter (consider the bond to be seven years old for purposes of computing the premium, with one year of reduction). Use a discount rate equal to the after-tax cost of debt rounded to the nearest whole number. Should the Hopkins Corporation refund the old issue?

11. In problem 10, what would be the after-tax cost of the call premium at the end of the 15th year (in dollar value)?

12. The Deluxe Corporation has just signed a 120-month lease on an asset with a 15-year life. The minimum lease payments are $2,000 per month ($24,000 per year) and are to be discounted back to the present at a 7 percent annual discount rate. The estimated fair value of the property is $175,000. Should the lease be recorded as a capital lease or as an operating lease?

13. The Ellis Corporation has heavy lease commitments. Prior to the 1978 CICA recommendation on leases, it merely footnoted lease obligations in the balance sheet, which appeared as follows (in millions):

Current assets	$ 50	Current liabilities	$ 10
Fixed assets	50	Long-term liabilities	30
		Total liabilities	$ 40
		Owner's equity	60
Total assets	$100	Total liabilities and owners' equity	$100

The footnotes stated that the company had $10 million in annual capital lease obligations for the next 20 years.

a. Discount these lease obligations back to the present at a 6 percent discount rate (round to nearest million dollars).
b. Construct a revised balance sheet that includes lease obligations as in Table 16–6.
c. Compute total debt to total assets on the original and revised balance sheets.
d. Compute total debt to equity on the original and revised balance sheets.
e. In an efficient capital market environment, should consequences of the CICA recommendation, as viewed in the answers to parts *c* and *d*, change stock prices and credit ratings?
f. Comment on management's perception of market efficiency (the viewpoint of the financial officer).

14. The Hegan Corporation plans to lease a $900,000 asset to the Doby Corporation. The lease will be for 10 years.

a. If the Hegan Corporation desires a 12 percent return on its investment, how much should the annual lease payments be?

b. If the Hegan Corporation is able to take a 10 percent investment tax credit and will pass the benefit along to the Doby Corporation in the form of lower lease payments (related to the Hegan Corporation's lower initial net cost), how much should the revised leased payments be? Continue to assume the Hegan Corporation desires a 12 percent return on the 10-year lease.

Selected References

Ang, James S. "The Two Faces of Bond Refunding." *Journal of Finance* 30 (June 1975), pp. 869–74.

Bogen, Jules I., ed. *Financial Handbook*. 4th ed. New York: Ronald, 1968, sec. 14.

Boot, John C. G., and George M. Frankfurter. "The Dynamics of Corporate Debt Management, Decision Rules, and Some Empirical Evidence." *Journal of Financial and Quantitive Analysis* 7 (September 1972), pp. 1957–66.

Bowlin, Oswald D. "The Refunding Decision: Another Special Case in Capital Budgeting." *Journal of Finance* 21 (March 1966), pp. 55–68.

Brennan, Michael J., and Eduardo S. Schwartz. "Bond Pricing and Market Efficiency." *Financial Analysts Journal* 38 (September–October 1982), pp. 49–56.

Brick, Ivan, and S. Abraham Ravid. "On the Relevance of Debt Maturity Structure." *Journal of Finance* 40 (December 1985), pp. 1423–37.

Collins, Robert A. "An Empirical Comparison of Bankruptcy Prediction Models." *Financial Management* 9 (Summer 1980), pp. 52–57.

Donaldson, Gordon. "New Framework for Corporate Debt Policy." *Harvard Business Review* 40 (March–April 1962), pp. 117–31.

Everett, Edward. "Subordinated Debt—Nature and Enforcement." *Business Lawyer* 20 (July 1965), pp. 953–87.

Federal Reserve Bank of Cleveland. "Direct Placement of Corporate Debt." *Economic Review*, March 1965, pp. 3–18.

Ferri, Michael G. "An Empirical Examination of the Determinants of Bond Yield Spreads." *Financial Management* 7 (August 1978), pp. 40–46.

Francis, Jack Clark. *Investment Analysis and Management.* New York: McGraw-Hill, 1972, chap. 1.

Jen, Frank C., and James E. Wert. "The Deferred Call Provision and Corporate Bond Yields." *Journal of Financial and Quantitative Analysis* 3 (June 1968), pp. 157–69.

Kolodny, Richard. "The Refunding Decision in Near Perfect Markets." *Journal of Finance* 29 (December 1974), pp. 1467–78.

Lindvall, John R. "New Issue Corporate Bonds, Seasoned Market Efficiency, and Yield Spreads." *Journal of Finance* 32 (September 1977), pp. 1057–67.

Peters, J. R. *Economics of the Canadian Corporate Bond Market.* Montreal: McGill–Queen's University Press, 1971.

Pinches, George E., and Kent A. Mingo. "The Role of Subordination and Industrial Bond Ratings." *Journal of Finance* 30 (March 1975), pp. 201–6.

Rao, Ramesh K. S. "The Impact of Yield Changes on the Systematic Risk of Bonds." *Journal of Financial and Quantitative Analysis* 17 (March 1982), pp. 115–27.

Sibley, A. M. "Some Evidence on the Cash Flow Effects of Bond Refunding." *Financial Management* 3 (Autumn 1974), pp. 50–53.

Van Horne, James C. *The Function and Analysis of Capital Market Rates.* Engelwood Cliffs, N.J.: Prentice-Hall, 1970, chaps. 4–6.

Winn, Willis J., and Arleigh Hess, Jr. "The Value of the Call Privilege." *Journal of Finance* 14 (May 1959), pp. 182–95.

Appendix 16A: Financial Alternatives for Distressed Firms

Although we have consistently considered businesses as going concerns throughout this book, we have also spoken of the risks (and securities premiums for such risks) associated with failure. For example, we stated that during uncertain economic times, a large, financially secure firm might be able to raise debt capital as much as 3 percentage points more cheaply than a medium-sized firm even if the latter is well managed. Such a differential recognizes the fact that the smaller firm may more quickly find itself in financial distress under adverse market circumstances.

A firm may be in financial distress because of *technical insolvency* or *bankruptcy.* Insolvency refers to a firm's inability to generate enough cash to pay its bills as they come due. Thus, a firm may be technically insolvent even though it has a positive net worth; there simply may not be sufficient liquid assets to meet current obligations. In other circumstances the fair market value of a firm's assets are less than its total liabilities—in other words, the firm has a negative net worth. In such a case either management or the creditors may judge that the best remedy possible is liquidation of the firm. Under the Bankruptcy Act then, either management or creditors can initiate legal action to have the firm declared a "bankrupt" and have the firm's assets liquidated. Generally, then, the term *financial failure* covers the gamut of circumstances from technical insolvency to the declaration of legal bankruptcy.

There are firms which do not fit into either of the above categories but which are still suffering from extreme financial difficulties. Perhaps they are rapidly approaching a situation in which they cannot pay their bills or where concerns over net worth deterioration may lead to bankruptcy proceedings.

Firms suffering from technical insolvency or negative net worth may participate in out-of-court settlements or in-court formal bankruptcy proceedings. Out-of-court settlements, where possible, allow the firm and its creditors to bypass certain lengthy and expensive legal proceedings. It follows, however, that if an agreement cannot be reached on a voluntary basis between a firm and its creditors, in-court procedures will be necessary.

Out-of-Court Settlement

Out-of-court settlements may take many forms. Four alternatives will be examined. The first is an *extension* in which creditors agree to allow the firm more time to meet its financial obligations. A new repayment schedule will be developed subject to the acceptance of the creditors.

A second alternative is a *composition,* under which creditors agree to accept a fractional settlement of their original claim. They may be willing to do this because they believe the firm is unable to meet its total obligations, and they wish to avoid formal bankruptcy procedures.

In the case of either a proposed extension or a composition, some creditors may not agree to go along with the arrangements. If their claims are relatively small, major creditors may allow them to be paid off immediately and in full in order to hold the agreement together. If their claims are large, no out-of-court settlement may be possible and formal bankruptcy proceedings may be necessary.

A third type of out-of-court settlement may take the form of a *creditor committee* established to run the business. Here the parties involved judge that management can no longer effectively conduct the affairs of the firm. Once the creditors' claims have been partially or fully settled, a new management team may be brought in to replace the creditor committee. Of course, the outgoing management may be willing to accept the imposition of a creditor committee only when formal bankruptcy proceedings appear likely, and they wish to avoid that stigma. There are also circumstances in which creditors are unwilling to form such a committee because they fear lawsuits from other dissatisfied creditors or from common or preferred stockholders.

A fourth type of out-of-court settlement is an *assignment,* in which liquidation of assets takes place without going through formal court action. In order to effect an assignment, creditors must agree on liquidation values and the relative priority of claims. This is not an easy task.

In actuality there may be combinations of two or more of the above described, out-of-court procedures. For example, there may be an extension as well as a composition, or a creditor committee may help to establish one or more of the alternatives.

In-Court Settlements

Proposal for an Arrangement under the Bankruptcy Act

If management believes the debtor company is worth more as a going concern than it is under liquidation, it may submit a proposal for a commercial arrangement to the court under the provisions of the Bankruptcy Act. Such a proposal may be for an extension, a composition, or both. If a restructuring of the firm's capital structure is believed necessary to rehabilitate the firm's financial health, details of that will be included as well in the proposal. As of 1986 creditors representing 75 percent of the claims[1] as well as a majority of the creditors voting must accept the proposal. If accepted by the creditors the proposal must then be ratified by the court. Ratification depends on a judgment that the plan is fair, equitable, and feasible.

An internal reorganization calls for an evaluation of current management and its operating policies. If current management is shown to be incompetent, it will probably be discharged and replaced by new management. An evaluation and possible redesign of the current capital structure is also necessary. If the firm is top-heavy with debt (as is normally the case), alternate securities such as preferred or common stock may replace part of the debt.[2] Of course, it is imperative that any restructuring be fair to all parties involved.

Therefore, under a recapitalization each of the old security holders must swap its old securities for new ones, the amount of which is determined by a current market valuation of the firm. Under what is called the *absolute priority rule*, all senior claims on asset value must be settled in full before any value can be given to a junior claimant. Thus, a bondholder must be awarded the full face value of his or her bond in a new security before preferred or common shareholders can receive any new securities. A simple example might clarify this a bit (see Table 16A–1).

Under the above example the former bondholders and preferred stockholders would receive new securities covering the full value of their former holdings, while the common stockholders would receive only the residual, or $4 million worth, of common shares. It is, in fact, quite easy to imagine a corporate reorganization where there would be no residual value left for the common stockholders (such would happen in this case if the market value of the securities at the time of reorganization were pegged at $36 million or less).

An external reorganization in which a merger partner is found for the firm may also be considered. The surviving firm must be deemed strong enough to carry out the financial and management obligations

---

[1]A study group set up by the Minister of Corporate and Consumer Affairs in 1985 has recommended a change to 66⅔ percent.

[2]Another possibility is the income bond on which interest is payable only if the firm makes money.

Table16A–1
Debt restructuring

Company A capital structure (book value) before reorganization:

Bonds	$20 million
Subordinted debentures	12 million
Preferred stock	4 million
Common stock	25 million
Total capital	$61 million

Company A capital structure after reorganization:

Bonds	$10 million
Income bonds	10 million
Common stock	20 million
Total capital	$40 million*

*$40 million would be the estimated market evaluation of these securities.

of the joint entities. Old creditors and stockholders may be asked to make concessions to ensure that a feasible arrangement is established.[3] Their motivation to do so would be that they hope to come out further ahead than if such a reorganization were not undertaken. Ideally, the firm should be merged with a strong firm in its own industry, although this is not always possible. The Canadian banking industry has found such a need to merge weaker firms with stronger firms within the industry in the mid-1980s. As a result of the concerns aroused by the failure of two Alberta-based banks, the Canadian Commercial Bank and the Northland Bank, three of the other smaller banks (Continental, Mercantile, and Bank of British Columbia) merged with stronger banks.

Liquidation

A liquidation or sell-off of assets may be recommended when an internal or external reorganization does not appear possible or when a determination is made that the assets of the firm are worth more in liquidation than through a reorganization. Priority of claims becomes

[3]That is exactly the case in the proposed takeover of Dome Petroleum by Amoco Canada, discussed further in Chapter 20. Under Amoco's proposal unsecured creditors would receive about $.35 per dollar owed them, and secured creditors would receive between $.75 and $1.00 depending on the nature of the securing assets.

extremely important in a liquidation because it is unlikely that all parties will be fully satisfied in their demands.

Secured creditors generally seize the assets upon which they have a lien. If, upon liquidation, the secured creditors realize less than their secured claims, they become normal unsecured creditors for the unsettled balance remaining.

After the claims of secured creditors are settled, the priority of claims in a bankruptcy liquidation is as follows:

1. Cost of administering the bankruptcy procedures (lawyers get in line first).
2. Wages and salaries due employees up to a maximum of $500 per worker.
3. Outstanding taxes within proscribed limits.
4. Rent in arrears within certain proscribed limits.
5. Claims for prior judgments lodged against the bankrupt.
6. Certain other claims of the Crown.
7. General or unsecured creditors are next in line. Examples of claims in this category are those held by debenture (unsecured bond) holders, trade creditors, and bankers who have made unsecured loans. There may be senior and subordinated positions within category 7, indicating that subordinated debt holders must turn over their claims to senior debt holders until complete restitution is made to the higher ranked category. Subordinated debenture holders may keep the balance if anything is left over after that payment.
8. Preferred stockholders.
9. Common stockholders.

Let us explore an example of a typical situation to determine how the above rules affect "who" receives "what" under a liquidation in bankruptcy. The sample firm, the Mitchell Corporation, has assets whose book value and liquidation value are as shown in Table 16A–2. Liabilities and stockholders' claims are also as presented in the table.

As is usually the case in bankruptcy, the liquidation value of the assets is far less than the book value ($700,000 as opposed to $1.3 million). In fact, the liquidation value of the assets will not even cover the total amount of liabilities ($700,000 as compared to $1.1 million). Since the creditor claims cannot be satisfied in full, it is an unfortunate reality that the holders of the lower-ranked (in terms of security) pre-

Table 16A–2
Financial data for the Mitchell Corporation

Assets	Book Value	Liquidation Value
Accounts receivable	$200,000	$160,000
Inventory	410,000	240,000
Machinery and equipment	240,000	100,000
Building and plant	450,000	200,000
Total assets	$1,300,000	$700,000
Liabilities and Stockholders' Claims		
Liabilities:		
Accounts payable	$ 300,000	
First lien, secured by machinery and equipment*	200,000	
Senior unsecured debt	400,000	
Subordinated debentures	200,000	
Total liabilities	1,100,000	
Stockholders' claims:		
Preferred stock	50,000	
Common stock	150,000	
Total stockholders' claims	200,000	
Total liabilities and stockholders' claims	$1,300,000	

*A lien represents a potential claim against property. The lien holder has a secured interest in the property.

ferred stock and common stock will receive nothing from the liquidation of the firm.

Before the liquidation values can be allocated, we must first consider creditor claims secured by the pledge of specific assets. Next we consider the high-priority claims. In this case there is a first lien on the machinery and equipment of $200,000. According to Table 16A–2, however, the secured creditor will only realize $100,000 on the liquidation of those assets. Therefore, the balance of their claim will be placed in the same category as those of the unsecured debt holders.

The next group of claims to be dealt with involves the high-priority liabilities listed earlier. Those will generally include, at least, the costs of administering the bankruptcy proceedings, allowable past wages due to workers, overdue taxes, and rent due. For the Mitchell Corporation those total $100,000. Since the liquidation value of assets was $700,000 and the liquidation value of the machinery and equipment providing specific security was $100,000, $500,000 is left to cover the remaining creditor demands. Table 16A–3 shows asset values available for unsatisfied secured claims and unsecured debt and the extent of the remaining claims.

In comparing the available asset values and claims in Table 16A–3, it would appear that the settlement on remaining claims should be at a 52.63 percent rate ($500,000/$950,000). The actual allocation, however, will take place as shown in Table 16A–4.

Each category receives 52.63 percent as its initial allocation. However, the subordinated debenture holders must transfer the whole of

Table 16A–3
Asset values available for unsatisfied secured claims and unsecured debt holders—and their remaining claims

Asset values:	
Asset values in liquidation	$700,000
Payment to secured creditors	−100,000
Remaining asset values	600,000
Administration, wages, taxes, rent	−100,000
Amount available to unsatisfied secured claims and unsecured debt	$500,000
Remaining claims of unsatisfied secured debt and unsecured debt:	
Secured debt (unsatisfied first lien)	$100,000
Accounts payable	250,000*
Senior unsecured debt	400,000
Subordinated debentures	200,000
	$950,000

*$50,000 of the priority claims were liabilities that arose in the course of doing business, and $50,000 were as a result of the bankruptcy proceedings themselves.

Table 16A–4
Allocations for unsatisfied secured claims and unsecured debts

(1) Category	(2) Amount of Claim	(3) Initial Allocation	(4) Amount Received
Secured debts (unsatisfied first lien)	$100,000	$ 52,630	$ 52,630
Accounts payable	250,000	131,580	131,580
Senior unsecured debt	400,000	210,530	315,790
Subordinated debentures	200,000	105,260	0
	$950,000	$500,000	$500,000

Table 16A–5
Payments and percent of claims

(1) Category	(2) Total Amount of Claim	(3) Amount Received	(4) Percent of Claim Satisfied
Secured debt (1st lien)	$200,000	$152,630	76%
Accounts payable—preferred	50,000	50,000	100
—other	250,000	131,580	53
Senior unsecured debt	400,000	315,790	79
Subordinated debentures	200,000	0	0
Preferred stock	50,000	0	0
Common stock	150,000	0	0

their $105,260 initial allocation to the senior debt holders because the latter group will realize less than full recovery of the face amount of its securities. The secured debt holders and the remaining accounts payable claims are not part of the senior subordinated arrangement and thus hold their initial positions.

Table 16A–5 summarizes the complete allocation procedure, showing the total amount of claims, the amount received, and the percent of the claim that was satisfied. The $152,630 in column (*3*) for secured debt represents the $100,000 realized from the sale of machinery and equipment and $52,630 from the allocation process summarized in Table 16A–4. After the preferred creditors the senior unsecured debt holders and the secured debt holders fared better than did the general creditors. In this example the subordinated debenture holders, preferred stock holders, and common stockholders received nothing from the bankruptcy liquidation.

List of Terms

technical insolvency
bankruptcy
extension
composition
absolute priority rule
assignment
internal reorganization
external reorganization
liquidation

Discussion Questions

16A–1. What is the difference between technical insolvency and bankruptcy?

16A–2. What are four types of out-of-court settlements? Briefly describe each.

16A–3. What is the difference between an internal reorganization and an external reorganization under formal bankruptcy procedures?

16A–4. What are the first three priority items under liquidation in bankruptcy?

Problem

16A–1. The trustee in the bankruptcy settlement for Nogo Airlines lists the following book values and liquidation values for the assets of the corporation. Liabilities and stockholders' claims are also shown below.

Assets	*Book Value*	*Liquidation Value*
Accounts receivable	$1,400,000	$1,200,000
Inventory	1,800,000	900,000
Machinery and equipment	1,100,000	600,000
Building and plant	4,200,000	2,500,000
Total assets	$8,500,000	$5,200,000

Liabilities and Stockholders' Claims

Liabilities:	
Accounts payable	$2,800,000
First lien, secured by machinery and equipment	900,000
Senior unsecured debt	2,200,000
Subordinated debenture	1,700,000
Total liabilities	7,600,000
Stockholders' claims:	
Preferred stock	250,000
Common stock	650,000
Total stockholders' claims	900,000
Total liabilities and stockholders' claims	$8,500,000

a. Compute the difference between the liquidation value of the assets and the liabilities.
b. Based on the answer to part *a*, will preferred stock or common stock participate in the distribution?
c. Given that the administrative costs of bankruptcy, workers' allowable wages, and unpaid taxes add up to $400,000, what is the total of remaining asset value available to cover secured and unsecured claims? (Wages and taxes owed totaled $50,000.)
d. After the machinery and equipment is sold to partially cover the first lien secured claim, how much will be available from the remaining asset liquidation values to cover unsatisfied secured claims and unsecured debt?
e. List the remaining asset claims of unsatisfied secured debt holders and unsecured debt holders in a manner similar to that shown at the bottom portion of Table 16A–3.
f. Compute a ratio of your answers in part *d* and part *e*. This will indicate the initial allocation ratio.
g. List the remaining claims (unsatisfied secured and unsecured) and make an initial allocation and final allocation similar to that shown in Table 16A–4. Subordinated debenture holders may keep the balance after full payment is made to senior debt holders.
h. Show the relationship of amount received to total amount of claim in a similar fashion to that of Table 16A–5. (Remember to use the sales [liquidation] value for machinery and equipment plus the allocation amount in part *g* to arrive at the total received on secured debt.)

Appendix 16B: Lease versus Purchase Decision

The classic lease versus purchase decision does not fit most capital leasing decisions anymore because of the similar financial accounting and tax treatment accorded to a capital lease and borrowing to purchase. An exception may occur when land is part of the lease arrangement. Nevertheless, the classic lease versus purchase decision is still appropriate for the operating lease.

Consider the case where a firm is considering the purchase of a $5,000 asset with a five-year life as opposed to entering into two sequential operating leases for two years and three years each. Under the operating leases the annual payments would be $1,250 on the first lease and $1,800 on the second lease. If the firm purchased the asset it would pay $1,319 annually to amortize a $5,000 loan over five years at 10 percent interest. This is based on the use of Appendix D for the present value of an annuity. Subtract the repayment of principal from the beginning balance to get the year-end balance. Note that we now know the annual amounts of interest that will be tax-deductible and thus can calculate that effect on annual cash flows.

The next task is to calculate the depreciation tax shield. In this example the asset falls into CCA Class 8 which allows a 20 percent CCA deduction. Thus, using Formula 12–1, the present value of the depreciation tax shield would be (assuming a zero salvage value):

$$\begin{aligned} \text{PV of CCA tax shield} &= \frac{Cdt}{r + d}\left[\frac{1 + .5r}{1 + r}\right] \\ &= \frac{\$5{,}000 \times .20 \times .40}{.06 + .20}\left[\frac{1 + .03}{1 + .06}\right] \\ &= \$1{,}495 \end{aligned}$$

We must now calculate the present value of the after-tax cost, or tax outflow, associated with the repayments of principal and interest and then combine that with the present value of the depreciation tax shield to find the total present value of the cost of the borrow-purchase option. (See Table 16B–1.)

Notice that both interest and CCA charges are tax-deductible expenses and thus provide a tax shield for other income. The interest tax shield can be considered on an annual cash flow basis, but the CCA tax shield, because of its unique nature, must be calculated separately.

Finally, we compare the cash outflows from leasing to the cash outflows from borrowing and purchasing. To consider the time value of money we have been discounting the annual values at an interest rate of 6 percent. This is the after-tax cost of debt to the firm, and it is computed by multiplying the interest rate of 10 percent by (1 − Tax rate). Because the costs associated with both leasing and borrowing are contractual and certain, we use the after-tax cost of debt as the discount

Table 16B–1
Net present value of borrow-purchase

Year	(1) PV of CCA Shield	(2) Payment	(3) Interest Tax Shield	(4) After-Tax Cost of (2) − (3)	(5) PV Factor of 6%	(6) Present Value
1		$1,319	($500 × .4)	$1,119	.943	$1,055
2		1,319	($418 × .4)	1,152	.890	1,025
3		1,319	($328 × .4)	1,188	.840	998
4		1,319	($229 × .4)	1,227	.792	972
5		1,319	($120 × .4)	1,271	.747	949
						4,999
	($1,495)					(1,495)
						$3,504

rate rather than the normal cost of capital. The net present value calculation for the operating lease option is shown in Table 16B–2.

Note the adjustments in Table 16B–2 for the timing of the cash flows related to the lease payments and tax shields. While the lease payments are generally made at the start of the year, the tax deductions related to them can only be claimed over the year for which the payment applies.

The borrow-purchase alternative has a lower present value of after-tax costs ($3,504 versus $4,339), which would appear to make it the more desirable alternative. However, many of the previously discussed qualitative factors that support leasing must also be considered in the decision-making process.

Table 16B–2
Net present value of operating lease outflows

Year	Payment	Tax Shield	After-Tax Cost of Leasing	Present Value Factor at 6%	Present Value
0	$1,250	$ 0	$1,250	1.000	$1,250
1	1,250	500	750	0.943	707
2	1,800	500	1,300	0.890	1,157
3	1,800	720	1,080	0.840	907
4	1,800	720	1,080	0.792	855
5	0	720	(720)	0.747	(537)
					$4,339

Problem

16B–1. The Woodland Corporation is considering whether to borrow funds and purchase an asset or lease the asset under an operating lease arrangement. If it purchases the asset the cost will be $30,000. It can borrow funds for five years at 12 percent interest. The asset will qualify for a 25 percent capital cost allowance. Assume a tax rate of 35 percent (no ITC is included in the problem).

The other alternative is to sign one lease that calls for payments of $9,500 for the first three years and a second lease that requires payments of $8,400 in Years 4 and 5. The leases would be treated as operating leases.

a. Compute the after-tax cost of the leases for the five years.

b. Compute the annual payment for the loan (round to the nearest dollar).

c. Compute the amortization schedule for the loan. (Disregard a small difference from a zero balance at the end of the loan. It is due to rounding.)

d. Determine the cash flow effect of the capital cost allowance.

e. Compute the after-tax cost of the borrow-purchase alternative.

f. Compute the present value of the after-tax cost of the two alternatives. The after-tax cost of debt should be rounded to the nearest whole number to determine the discount rate.

g. If the objective is to minimize the present value of after-tax costs, which alternative should be selected?

17 Common and Preferred Stock Financing

The ultimate ownership of the firm resides in common stock, whether it is in the form of all outstanding shares of a closely held corporation or one share of Bell Canada Enterprises. In terms of legal distinctions it is the common stockholder alone who directly controls the business. While control of the company is legally in the shareholders' hands, it is practically wielded by management on an everyday basis.[1] Of course, even though they have no power to elect board members, large creditors may also, at times, exert tremendous pressure on a firm to meet certain standards of performance.

According to a 1983 study,[2] there were about 2 million individual

[1]See Alfred D. Chandler, Jr., *The Visible Hand* (Cambridge, Mass.: Harvard University Press, 1977), for a description of the shift from owner capitalism to what he refers to as "managerial capitalism."

[2]*Canadian Shareholders: Their Profiles and Attitudes* (Study done for the Toronto Stock Exchange, 1984).

stockholders in Canada at that time. That amounts to 13 percent of the adult Canadian population as opposed to 22 percent of the U.S. population who own shares. A 1986 study[3] reports that in the three-year intervening period, the number of Canadians participating directly in the stock market had increased by 50 percent to almost 3.2 million or 18 percent of the adult population. The study also reported that 13 percent of nonshareowners intended to buy shares in the next three years. This striking increase in stock market participation among Canadians has been attributed to rising stock prices, growing investment in mutual funds (not unrelated to the first reason), and increased investment by women. Whether this spreading investment activity is a long-term trend or a temporary condition will be tested by the next sustained downturn in market prices. Currently, then, the participation by Canadians in owning common shares is increasing, but the majority of Canadians still do not buy stock in our business corporations.

Despite the fact that most adult Canadians do not own common stock directly, the increasingly large stock portfolios held by financial institutions mean that many more millions of Canadians also have a stake in the share price performance of Canadian firms. As would also be expected, management has become increasingly sensitive to these large institutional shareholders who may side with corporate raiders in voting their shares for or against merger offers or takeover attempts (these topics are covered in Chapter 20). Mutual funds, pension funds, insurance companies, and trust accounts are all examples of institutional investors. The fact that institutions accounted for 55 percent of the trading volume on the TSE in 1984 and 1985 versus 37 percent in 1980 shows both the growth and absolute size of their market impact. Although data on the amount of institutional ownership of a given firm's stock are not available, it is usually estimated that in excess of 50 percent of the stock of most of the largest, widely held Canadian corporations is owned by institutions. If that estimate is right, then institutions own over $5 billion of Bell Canada Enterprises stock, over $2.5 billion of Canadian Pacific stock, and so on.[4]

Probably because of its lack of importance in the U.S. markets,

---

[3]As yet unpublished investment survey conducted by the Toronto Stock Exchange.

[4]In terms of early 1987 prices.

preferred stock is often treated as playing a minor role in financing the corporate enterprise in Canada as well. As was discussed in Chapter 14, however, preferred stock accounted for $6 billion in new financings for Canadian corporations in 1985 as compared to $5.3 billion for common shares and $6.7 billion for bonds. Therefore, it deserves more than the passing mention it is sometimes accorded.

Preferred stock represents a hybrid security, combining some of the features of debt and common stock. Because of the fixed nature of the returns to preferred shareholders, it is probably more like debt than equity in spite of where it is placed on the balance sheet. Though the preferred stockholder does not have an ownership interest in the firm, he or she does have a priority claim to dividends superior to that of the common stockholder. On the other hand, the fact that preferred shareholders rank behind the debtholders in the event of liquidation makes the presence of preferred shares, rather than more debt, of great value to the corporate lenders.

In order to understand the rights and characteristics of the different means of financing, we shall examine the powers accorded to shareholders under each arrangement. In the case of common stock everything revolves around three key rights, namely, the residual claim to income, the voting right, and the right to purchase new shares. We shall examine each of these in detail and then consider the rights of preferred stockholders.

Common Shareholder's Claim to Income

All income that is not paid out to creditors or preferred shareholders automatically belongs to common shareholders. Thus, we say they have a residual claim to income. This is true regardless of whether these residual funds are actually paid out in dividends or retained in the corporation. Take, for example, a firm that earns $10 million before capital costs and pays $1 million in interest to bondholders and a like amount in dividends to preferred shareholders. It will then have $8 million available for common shareholders.[5] Perhaps half of that will

[5]Tax consequences related to interest are ignored for the present.

be paid out as common stock dividends. The balance will be reinvested in the business for the benefit of shareholders, with the hope of providing even greater income, dividends, and price appreciation in the future.

Realize, though, that the common shareholder does not have a legal or enforceable claim to dividends. Whereas a bondholder may force the corporation into bankruptcy for failure to make interest payments, the common shareholder must accept circumstances as they are or attempt to change management if he desires a new dividend policy.

Occasionally a company will have several classes of common stock outstanding that carry different rights and privileges. For example, Harding Carpets has Class A, Class B, Class C, and Class D common stock outstanding where the nonvoting Class A and B shares are entitled to a higher dividend than are the voting Class C and D shares. A recent innovation has come from General Motors Corporation in relation to two acquisitions. In October 1984 GM acquired Electronic Data Systems for cash and General Motors Class E common stock (total value, $2.5 billion), and in 1985 GM acquired Hughes Aircraft for cash and Class H common stock (total value, $5.8 billion). The dividends on the Class E stock are based on the income generated by EDS, and the dividends on the Class H stock are based on the earnings of Hughes Aircraft. While General Motors Class E and H shares are listed on the New York Stock Exchange, only the regular GM common shares trade on Canadian markets as yet.

The Voting Right

Because the common shareholders are the owners of the firm, they are accorded the right to vote in the election of the board of directors and on all other major issues. Common shareholders may cast their ballots as they see fit on a given issue, or they may, instead, assign the power to cast their ballots to management or to some other group interested in assembling a block of votes.[6]

As mentioned in the previous section, some corporations have dif-

[6]Referred to as *assigning a proxy.*

ferent classes of common stock with unequal voting rights.[7] For example, Canadian Tire Corporation, a retailer of a variety of automotive, sports, and household items, has both nonvoting Class A and voting common shares. The Class A shares have been issued over the years to augment the company's equity without diluting the controlling ownership. In 1983 the three children of co-founder Alfred Billes borrowed $76.6 million to buy a second 30 percent stake from the other co-founder's estate. A subsequent splitting of one common share into one voting common share and four Class A nonvoting shares allowed the Billes family heirs to maintain control over the company while at the same time paying down the debt acquired to keep control of the corporation in the family. Thus, the owners of 60 percent of the 3,450,000 voting common shares controlled the company despite the fact there were over 80 million Class A nonvoting shares as of 1987. The Class A and common shares get essentially the same treatment in terms of dividends and in terms of priority of claims in the event of liquidation. So that they have some representation in corporate policy making, the holders of the Class A shares, voting separately as a class, are entitled to select the greater of three directors or one fifth of the total number of the corporation's directors.

The Canadian Tire case has become a well-publicized example demonstrating the potential dangers of nonvoting shares. In the Canadian Tire situation there is a clause whereby Class A nonvoting shares become voting shares if a tender offer is made to purchase voting common shares and a majority of those are tendered. In December 1986 the Canadian Tire franchised dealers, who already owned 17.4 percent of the common, had made an offer to purchase 49 percent of the outstanding voting shares, and members of the Billes family had committed to tender that portion of their interests. Even though the dealers would have owned 66 percent of the voting stock if their offer succeeded, their legal advisers judged that the offer would not trigger the voting conversion for the Class A shares. This attempt to take advantage of a loophole in the wording of the clause, supposedly there to protect the rights of the Class A shareholders, incensed many among investors and investment professionals alike. As a result the Ontario Securities

[7]There are about 150 companies listed on the Toronto Stock Exchange with at least one class of stock with unusual voting rights.

Commission (OSC) held hearings into the transaction and blocked the deal from being consummated in a decision that was later upheld by the Supreme Court of Ontario.

The OSC had declared the deal was abusive because it was artificial in form, contrived only to circumvent the *coattail provision* and confound the justifiable expectations of investors.[8] If the agreement between the Billes family and the dealers had been allowed to stand, an enormous premium (over 1,000 percent over the value of the nonvoting shares) would have been paid for less than 3 percent of the outstanding shares to gain control of the corporation.[9]

While the different classes of common stock may, at times, have different voting rights, they do have a vote.[10] Bondholders and preferred stockholders, on the other hand, may vote only when a violation of their corporate agreements exists. The most common case of this is when a specified number (often two years' worth) of periodic dividends have been omitted on preferred shares. In that situation the preferred shares often acquire voting privileges, as was the case with Dome Petroleum preferreds in 1987.

Cumulative Voting

The most important voting matter is the election of the board of directors. As indicated in Chapter 1, the board has primary respon-

---

[8]This case has led to the Toronto Stock Exchange adopting new regulations for these coattail provisions relating to corporate takeovers. Of the approximately 100 provisions already in place prior to the new regulations, it was estimated that about one third were legally unenforceable.

[9]One year before there was any hint of a takeover, the voting common traded for $14⅝ while the nonvoting traded for $11⅝. The tender offer was for $160.24 per voting common share at a time when the nonvoting shares were trading for about $13.

[10]Although the creation of nonvoting shares has been a favorite manoeuvre of Canadian controlling shareholders, no company listed on the New York Stock Exchange, the world's largest and probably most regulated, is permitted to differentiate the voting rights among common shareholders. This has led to a proliferation of companies dealing in the over-the-counter market in the United States to get around this rule. The NYSE is looking into allowing such voting differentiation to combat this seeming competitive advantage of the American Stock Exchange and over-the-counter markets. Strong opposition to this proposal has come from many quarters, including Canadian institutional investors who invest a percentage of their portfolios in American stocks.

sibility for the stewardship of the corporation. If illegal or imprudent decisions are made the board members can be held legally liable to injured parties. Additionally, corporate directors serve on important subcommittees of the company and in this manner have a direct effect on corporate affairs. Examples of committees of the board include the audit committee, the long-range financial planning committee, and the compensation committee. Selection of a new chief executive officer, sometimes following a decision to prematurely remove the old one, is probably the board's single most important duty.

Election of the members of the board of directors may take place through the familiar majority voting system or by a cumulative voting method. Under majority voting any group of stockholders owning over 50 percent of the common stock may elect all of the directors. Under cumulative voting it is possible for those who hold less than a 50 percent interest to elect board members. The provision for some minority interest representation on the board is important to those who wish to reserve the right to challenge the prerogatives of the majority.

How does the cumulative voting process work? Very simply, a shareholder gets one vote for each share of stock he or she owns times one vote for each director to be elected. The shareholder may then accumulate votes in favor of a specified number of directors.

Take, as an example, a situation in which there are 10,000 shares outstanding, you own 1,001 shares, and nine directors are to be elected. Your total number of votes under a cumulative system would be:

Number of shares owned	1,001
Number of directors to be elected	9
Number of votes	9,009

Now let us consider the situation where you cast all of your ballots for only one director of your choice. With nine directors to be elected, there is no way you can be stopped from creating one of the nine highest vote getters. Since you own 1,001 shares the maximum number of shares a majority interest could control would be 8,999. This would entitle that group to 80,991 votes.

Number of shares owned (majority)	8,999
Number of directors to be elected	9
Number of votes (majority)	80,991

These 80,991 votes cannot be spread thinly enough over nine candidates to stop you from electing your one director. For example, if they are spread evenly over nine choices, each of the majority's directoral picks will receive 8,999 votes while your choice will receive 9,009 votes. Because the top nine vote getters are elected, your candidate will claim a director position.

To determine the number of shares needed to elect a given number of directors under cumulative voting, the following formula is used:

$$\text{Shares required} = \text{Number of directors desired} \times \frac{\text{Total number of shares outstanding}}{\text{Total number of directors to be elected} + 1} + 1 \qquad (17\text{–}1)$$

The formula reaffirms that in the previous instance 1,001 shares would elect one director.

$$\frac{1 \times 10{,}000}{9 + 1} + 1 = \frac{10{,}000}{10} + 1 = 1{,}001$$

If three director positions out of nine were desired, 3,001 shares would be necessary.

$$\frac{3 \times 10{,}000}{9 + 1} + 1 = \frac{30{,}000}{10} + 1 = 3{,}001$$

It thus turns out that with approximately 30 percent of the outstanding shares, a minority interest can control one third of the board. If a majority rule instead of a cumulative voting system were used, a minority interest would, of course, be able to elect no one. A group controlling 5,001 out of 10,000 outstanding shares could elect each and every director.

The following is a restatement of the proposition: If the number of minority shares outstanding under cumulative voting is known, we can determine how many directors those minority shares can elect by use of the formula:

$$\text{Number of directors that can be elected} = \frac{(\text{Shares owned} - 1) \times (\text{Total number of directors to be elected} + 1)}{(\text{Total number of shares outstanding})} \qquad (17\text{–}2)$$

Plugging 3,001 into the formula yields:

$$\frac{(3{,}001 - 1)(9 + 1)}{10{,}000} = \frac{3{,}000\ (10)}{10{,}000} = 3$$

If the formula yields an uneven result, such as 3.1 or 3.7, the fractional amount is irrelevant. This means that all results between 3 and 4 from the application of the formula indicate that three directors can be elected.

Although cumulative voting may give minority interests an opportunity to elect a representative to the board of directors, there is no requirement in Canada that directors be chosen by cumulative voting. In the United States, by way of contrast, 22 states require cumulative voting in preference to majority rule, 18 consider it preferable as part of the corporate charter, with only 10 states making no judgment on the advisability of its use.

Referring back to the voting example above, it is interesting to note that with nine directors to be elected, 1,001 shares would elect one director. If, however, the number of board members were reduced to eight, a minority group holding 1,001 shares would no longer be able to elect a board representative. That group would then need 1,112 shares to elect a director.

$$\frac{1 \times 10{,}000}{8 + 1} + 1$$

Another common method of thwarting the ambitions of the minority is to stagger the terms of directors so that only a few are elected each year. If the nine directors referred to above were elected three per year, a minority interest would then require 2,501 shares to elect a single board member. In such a case a minority holder controlling 20 percent of the shares would be denied board representation.

The Right to Purchase New Shares

In addition to a claim to residual income and the right to choose the directors, the common stockholders may also enjoy a privileged position in the offering of new securities. If the corporate charter contains a "preemptive right" provision, holders of common stock must be given the first option to purchase new shares. Even when the corporate charter does not provide a preemptive right clause, new issues of common shares are usually offered first to existing shareholders.

The preemptive right provision ensures that management cannot subvert the position of present stockholders by selling shares to outside interests without first offering them to current shareholders. If such protection were not afforded, a 20 percent stockholder might find her interest reduced to 10 percent by a major distribution of new shares to outsiders. Not only would voting rights be diluted, but proportionate claims to corporate earnings would be similarly reduced.

The Use of Rights in Financing

In Canada corporations frequently engage in rights offerings to tap this built-in market for new securities—the current shareholders. Take, for example, the mythical Walton Corporation which has 9 million shares outstanding trading at $40 per share. Walton management decides it needs to raise $30 million for new plant and equipment and, therefore, to sell 1 million new shares at $30 per share.[11] As part of the issue process the company will use a rights offering in which each old shareholder receives a first option to participate in the purchase of new shares.

Each old shareholder will receive one right for each share of stock owned and may combine a specified number of rights plus $30 cash to buy a new share of stock. Thus, the following questions must be considered:

1. How many rights should be necessary to purchase one new share of stock?
2. What is the monetary value of these rights?

Rights required Since 9 million shares are currently outstanding and 1 million new shares are to be issued, the ratio of old to new shares is

---

[11]If this were not a rights offering the discount from the current market price would be much smaller. The new shares might sell for $38 or $39.

9 to 1. On this basis the old shareholder will be able to combine nine rights plus $30 cash to purchase one new share of stock.

This means that a shareholder with 90 shares of stock would receive an equivalent number of rights that could be applied toward the purchase of 10 new shares of stock at $30 apiece. As is discussed later in this chapter, shareholders may choose to sell their rights rather than exercise them by purchasing new shares.

Monetary value of a right Anything that contributes to the privilege of purchasing a higher priced stock for $30 per share obviously has a market value. The following two-step analysis will aid in determining that value.

Nine old shares, previously worth $40 per share, bestow the capability of buying one new share for $30. This means we end up with a total market value of $390 spread over 10 shares. Therefore, upon completion of the rights offering the value of a share would theoretically equal $39.[12]

Nine old shares sold at $40 each	$360
One new share to sell at $30	30
Total value of 10 shares	$390
Average value of one share	$ 39

The rights offering thus entitles the holder to buy a stock that should carry a value of $39 for $30. With a differential between the anticipated price and the subscription price of $9 and nine rights required to participate in the purchase of one share, the value of a right becomes $1.

Average value per share	$39
Subscription price	30
Differential	$ 9
Rights required to buy one share	9
Value of a right ($9/9 shares)	$ 1

The period during which rights may be bought, sold, or exercised is usually four to six weeks after what is termed the *ex-rights* date. The

[12]A number of variables may intervene to change the value. This is a "best" approximation.

rights are issued in the same way that dividends are paid. On what is called the *record date* the company's books of record are closed, and all common shareholders listed on that date receive rights. Shares go *ex-rights* four business days prior to the record date. Investors buying the shares on or after the ex-rights date receive no rights. Between the date of the rights issue announcement and the ex-rights date, the stock is referred to as *cum-rights* or *rights-on*, bestowing on any purchaser of the stock the right to subscribe to the new issue. The following example summarizes the timing:

	Value of Stock	Value of Right
March 1–30: Stock trades cum-rights	$40	$1 (of the $40)
April 1: Stock trades ex-rights	39	1
April 5: Date of record	39	1
April 30: End of subscription period	39	—

Once the ex-right period is reached, the price of the stock will decrease by the theoretical intrinsic value of the detached right. The remaining value ($39) is the value of the share ex-rights. Though there is a time period remaining between the ex-rights date (April 1) and the end of the subscription period, the market immediately discounts the expected future dilution. Thus, the ex-rights value precisely reflects the same value as can be expected when the new, underpriced $30 stock issue is sold.

The formula for the value of the right when the stock is trading cum-rights or rights-on is:

$$R = \frac{M_o - S}{N + 1} \tag{17–3}$$

where

M_o = Market value—cum-rights, $40
S = Subscription price, $30
N = Number of rights required to purchase a new share of stock, in this case, 9

$$\frac{\$40 - \$30}{9 + 1} = \frac{\$10}{10} = \$1$$

Using Formula 17–3 we determined that the value of a right in the Walton Corporation offering was $1. An alternative formula giving precisely the same answer is:

$$R = \frac{M_e - S}{N} \tag{17–4}$$

The only new term is M_e, the market value of the stock when shares are trading ex-rights. The calculation becomes:

$$R = \frac{\$39 - \$30}{9} = \frac{\$9}{9} = \$1$$

It is important to realize that rights seldom sell at their theoretical, intrinsic value. This is because there are buying and selling costs and also because imbalances in demand and supply may develop. For example, there may be great enthusiasm for the new issue causing the market value of the right to exceed the initial theoretical value (perhaps the right will trade for $1⅜).

Effect of Rights on Shareholder's Position

At first glance a rights offering appears to bring great benefits to shareholders. But is this really the case? Does a shareholder really benefit from being able to buy a stock that is initially $40 (and later $39) for $30. Don't answer too quickly!

Think of it this way. Assume 100 people own shares of stock in a corporation and one day they decide to have the corporation sell new shares to themselves at 25 percent below current value. It cannot really make sense that they can enhance their wealth by selling their own product more cheaply to themselves. What is gained by purchasing inexpensive new shares has to be lost by diluting the value of existing outstanding shares.

Take the case of Shareholder A who owns nine shares of Walton Corporation before the rights offering and also has $30 in cash. His holdings would appear as follows:

Nine old shares at $40	$360
Cash	30
Total value	$390

If he receives and exercises nine rights to buy one new share at $30, his portfolio will contain:

Ten shares at $39 (diluted value) . . .	$390
Cash	0
Total value	$390

Clearly, he is no better off. A second alternative would be for him to sell his rights in the market and stay with his position of owning only nine shares and holding cash.

Nine shares at $39 (diluted value) . . .	$351
Proceeds from sale of rights	9
Cash	30
Total value	$390

As indicated above, whether he chooses to exercise his rights or not, the stock will still go down to a lower value (others are still diluting). Once again his overall value remains constant. The value received for the rights ($9) exactly equals the extent of dilution in the value of the original nine shares.

It would be foolish for the shareholder to throw away the rights as worthless securities. He would then suffer the pains of dilution without the offsetting gain from the sale of the rights.

Nine shares at $39 (diluted value) . . .	$351
Cash	30
Total value	$381

Empirical evidence indicates that this careless activity takes place 1 to 2 percent of the time.

Desirable Features of Rights Offerings

The student may ask, "If the shareholder is no better off in terms of total valuation, why undertake a rights offering?" There are a number of possible advantages.

As previously indicated, by giving current shareholders a first option to purchase new shares, we protect their current position in regard to voting rights and claims to earnings. Of equal importance, the use of a rights offering gives the firm a built-in market for new security issues. Because of this built-in base, distribution costs are likely to be considerably lower than under a straight public issue in which investment dealers must underwrite the full risk of distribution.[13]

Additionally, a rights offering may generate more interest in the market than would a straight public issue. There is a market not only for the stock but also for the rights. Because the subscription price is normally set 15–25 percent below current value, there is the "nonreal" appearance of a bargain, creating further interest in the offering.

The dollar value of rights traded on the exchanges is small because of the very low prices at which rights trade. Rights also have a short life—as little as several weeks—and, therefore, continuous trading in rights is not possible as it is on the common stock of the same company. During 1986 $727 million in new equity was raised on the Toronto Stock Exchange via new rights offerings, representing 6 percent of the new equity raised over that period. Over the past four years approximately 5 percent of the new equity dollars raised on the TSE was through the issuance of rights. The use of rights offerings seemed to increase as the stock market reached new highs and more common stock was sold to raise capital for corporations.

Preferred Stock Financing

Having discussed bonds (in Chapter 16) and common stock, we are now prepared to look at this intermediate or hybrid form of security known as preferred stock. You may question the validity of the term *preferred,* for preferred stock does not possess any of the most desirable characteristics of debt or common stock. In the case of debt, bondholders have a contractual claim against the corporation for the payment of interest and may force the corporation into bankruptcy if payment is not forthcoming. Common stockholders, of course, are the owners of the firm and have a residual claim to all income not paid out to others. Preferred stockholders, on the other hand, are merely entitled to receive a stipulated dividend and generally must receive the dividend prior to the payment of dividends to common stockholders. However, their right to annual dividends is not compelling to the corporation as

[13]Though investment dealers might participate in a rights offering as well, their fees are less because of the smaller risk factor.

interest on debt is, and the corporation may forgo preferred dividends when this is deemed necessary.

For example, XYZ Corporation might receive $100 per share for a new issue of preferred stock on which it specifies $12 as the annual dividend. Under normal circumstances the corporation would pay the $12 per share dividend. Let us assume it also has $1,000 bonds carrying 12.2 percent interest and shares of common stock with a market value of $50, normally paying a $3 cash dividend. The 12.2 percent interest *must* be paid on the bonds. The $12 preferred dividend has to be paid before the $3 dividend on common, but both may be waived without threat of bankruptcy. The common shareholder is the last in line to receive payment, but his potential participation in earnings is unlimited. He may not receive the $3 dividend this year but may receive much larger dividends in the future. On the other hand, the preferred shareholder's dividend will remain at $12.

Justification for Preferred Stock

Because preferred stock has few unique characteristics, why might the corporation choose to issue it, and equally important, why are investors willing to purchase the security?

One reason corporations issue preferred stock is to achieve a balance in their capital structures. It is a means of expanding the capital base of the firm without diluting the common stock ownership position or incurring contractual debt obligations. Firms that are heavy users of debt, such as public utilities and capital goods producers, may go to preferred stock to balance their sources of financing. Canadian commercial banks have become more frequent issuers of preferreds because perpetual preferred shares are counted as part of the capital in tests of the banks' capital adequacy under the Bank Act as revised in 1980.

Even in these cases there may be a drawback. While interest payments on debt are tax-deductible, preferred stock dividends are not. Thus, the interest cost on 12.2 percent debt may be only 6 to 6.5 percent on an after-tax cost basis, while the after-tax cost on 12 percent preferred stock would be the stated amount. A firm issuing the preferred stock may be willing to pay the higher after-tax cost to assure investors it has a balanced capital structure thereby lowering the costs of the other sources of funds in the capital structure.

Investor interest Primary purchasers of preferred stock are corporate investors, insurance companies, and pension funds. To the corporate investor preferred stock offers a very attractive advantage over bonds. In many cases the tax law provides that any corporation that receives either preferred or common dividends from another corporation may receive those dividends tax free. For the individual investor the preferred dividend offers the advantage of the dividend tax credit which reduces the amount of tax payable on dividend income. By contrast, the interest on bonds is usually taxable to the recipient.

Because of this tax consideration it is not surprising that corporations are able to issue preferred stock at a slightly lower pre-tax yield than debt. Figure 17–1 indicates that preferred shares have been issued during the 1980s at a substantially lower nominal yield than the much less risky Government of Canada bonds. Of course, when you adjust the yield for the tax effects (called the interest equivalent yield in the figure) it naturally turns out that the preferreds pay a premium for the extra risk involved. During the 1980s, then, new preferreds have generally paid up to 3 percentage points less than medium-term Canada bonds. When the adjustment for tax differentials is made, however, the preferreds are paying up to the equivalent of 7 percentage points more.

Figure 17–1
Yield of new issue retractable preferreds versus 5–10-year Government of Canada bonds (October 3, 1986)

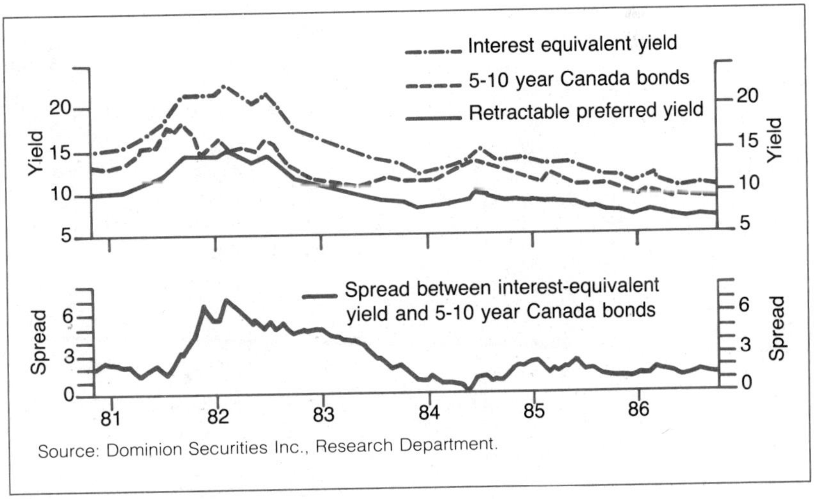

Summary of tax considerations Tax considerations work in two opposite directions. First, they make the *after-tax* cost of debt cheaper than preferred stock to the issuing corporation because interest is tax-deductible to the payer. (This is true in spite of the fact the quoted rate may be higher.) Second, tax considerations generally make the receipt of preferred dividends more valuable than corporate bond interest to the (corporate) recipient because the dividend is exempt from taxation. For the individual taxpayer the dividend tax credit reduces the amount of tax payable as compared to that payable on ordinary income. Some of the large holding companies that are such important players in Canadian capital markets quite naturally make extensive use of preferred share offerings because of the tax and capital structure effects combined. Table 17–1 summarizes the preferred share issues undertaken by one such group of companies, the Edper group, over the past few years. Some analysts have felt that such intricate use of

Table 17–1
Major Edper companies' preferred share issues (in millions)

	Financial Year		Effective Ownership
	1985	1984	
Hees	$ 386.5	$ 223.5	42% Edper
Dexleigh	97.1	22.1	33% Hees
Norcen Energy Res.	158.5	158.7	41% Hees
Brascan	497.9	433.0	23% Edper, 22% Hees
Brascade Resources	483.2	483.2	70% Brascan
Westmin Resources	110.0	110.0	62% Brascade Resources
Noranda	410.6	358.3	46% Brascade, 5% Brascan
MacMillan Bloedel	364.2	307.3	48% Noranda
Trilon	451.0	251.0	46% Brascan
Lonvest	100.0	0.0	65% Trilon
Royal Trustco	620.0	419.0	51% Trilon
Carena Bancorp	183.5	185.0	35% Edper, 35% Hees
Trizec	442.5	258.3	64% Carena
John Labatt	0.0	0.0	38% Brascan
Total	$4,305.1	$3,209.5	

Note: At least $600 million in preferred shares have been issued by the group during the 1986 financial year.
Source: *The Globe and Mail,* Toronto, December 1, 1986, pp. B1–B2.

preferred financings has allowed the Edper group to report extra large profits and minimize taxes, all while financing expansion. For example, a company with pre-tax profit of $10 million would pay about $5 million in tax. The company, it is claimed, could do much better by borrowing substantial sums to buy preferred shares. It could, for example, borrow $100 million at 10 percent. That would create an annual expense of $10 million, reducing the ordinary income to zero. Using the borrowed money to buy $100 million of preferred shares yielding about $7.5 million in dividends would increase the company's end profit by a whopping 50 percent.

Provisions Associated with Preferred Stock

A preferred stock issue contains a number of stipulations and provisions that define the stockholder's claim to income and assets.

1. Cumulative dividends—Most preferred stock issues have a cumulative claim to dividends. That is, if preferred stock dividends are not paid in any one year, they accumulate and must be paid in total before common stockholders can receive dividends. If preferred stock carries a $12 cash dividend and the company does not pay dividends for three years, preferred stockholders must receive the full $36 before common stockholders can receive anything.

The cumulative dividend feature makes a corporation very cognizant of its obligation to preferred stockholders. When a financially troubled corporation has missed a number of dividend payments under a cumulative arrangement, there may be a financial recapitalization of the corporation in which preferred stockholders receive new securities in place of the dividend arrearage. Assume the corporation has now missed five years of dividends under a $12-a-year obligation and still remains in a poor cash position. Preferred stockholders may be offered $60 or more in new common stock for forgiveness of the missed dividend payments. Preferred stockholders may be willing to cooperate in order to keep the corporation financially viable.

2. Conversion feature—Like certain forms of debt, preferred stock may be convertible into common shares. Thus, $100 in preferred stock may be convertible into *X* number of shares of common stock at the option of the holder. The topic of convertibility is discussed at length in Chapter 19, Convertibles and Warrants. In Canada it looks like a little over one quarter of preferred share issues carry a convertibility feature[14] versus about 40 percent in U.S. markets.

3. *Call feature*—Preferred stock, like debt, may be callable—that is, the corporation may retire the security prior to maturity at some small premium over par. This, of course, accrues to the advantage of the corporation and to the disadvantage of the preferred stockholder. A preferred issue carrying a call provision will be accorded a slightly higher yield than a similar issue without this feature. The same type of refunding decision applied to debt obligations in Chapter 16 could also be applied to preferred stock.

4. *Retractable feature*—A preferred share containing a provision that allows redemption of the shares at the option of the shareholder is referred to as retractable. This provision creates advantages and disadvantages for the company and shareholder in just the opposite direction as does the call provision.

5. *Participation provision*—A *small* percentage of preferred stock issues are participating; that is, they may participate over and above the quoted yield when the corporation is enjoying a particularly good year. For example, the participating feature may provide that once the common stock dividend equals the preferred stock dividend, the two classes of securities may share equally in additional payouts.

6. *Floating rate*—Beginning in the early 1980s a few preferred stock issuers made the dividend floating in nature. Typically, the dividend is changed on a quarterly basis, based on current market conditions. For example, the Royal Bank of Canada's Series E floating-rate preferred issue has dividends payable monthly at from 55 to 75 percent of the current prime bank rate depending on the price movement of

---

[14]On the TSE as of September 30, 1986, 113 out of 399 preferred share issues listed contained a convertibility feature.

the shares. Because the dividend rate only changes monthly or quarterly, there is still some small price change possibility between dividend adjustment dates. Nevertheless, it is less than the price change for regular preferred stock. A number of preferred shares currently paying a fixed return are set to revert to a floating-rate return within the next one to five years. Thus, the issuing firms have protected themselves from being locked into a fixed-rate security in perpetuity—as have the investors.

7. *Par value*—As with common shares, federally incorporated companies issue *no-par value* preferreds. However, many balance sheets still show par value preferred shares issued before the Canada Business Corporations Act was amended to disallow their issue. For example, the Royal Bank Series E preferred shares mentioned above have a par value of $100. As of the time of this writing, par value shares were still allowed for corporations incorporated under a few of the provincial corporations acts.

Comparing Features of Common and Preferred Stock and Debt

Table 17–2 compares the characteristics of common stock, preferred stock, and bonds. Consider carefully the comparative advantages and disadvantages of each.

In terms of the risk-return relationships embodied in these three classes of securities (as well as in the other investments discussed in Chapter 7), we might expect the risk-return pattern depicted in Figure 17–2. The lowest return is obtained from savings accounts, and the highest return and risk are generally associated with common stock. In between, we note that short-term instruments generally, though not always, provide lower returns than longer-term instruments. We also observe that government securities pay lower returns than issues originated by corporations because of the lower risk involved. Next on the scale after government issues is preferred stock. As previously mentioned, this hybrid form of security generally pays a lower return than

Table 17–2
Features of alternative security issues

	Common Stock	Preferred Stock	Bonds
1. Ownership and control of the firm	Belongs to common stockholders through voting rights and residual claim to income	Limited rights when dividends are missed	Limited rights under default in interest payments
2. Obligation to provide return	None	Must receive payment before common stockholder	Contractual obligation
3. Claim to assets in bankruptcy	Lowest claim of any security holder	Bondholders and creditors must be satisfied first	Highest claim
4. Cost of distribution	Highest	Moderate	Lowest
5. Risk-return trade-off	Highest risk, highest return (at least in theory)	Moderate risk, moderate return	Lowest risk, moderate return
6. Tax status of payment by corporation	Not deductible	Not deductible	Tax deductible Cost = Interest payment × (1 − Tax rate)
7. Tax status of payment to recipient	Dividend to other corporation usually tax exempt. First $1,000 of investment income to individual is tax exempt.*	Same as common stock	Interest usually fully taxable

*Applies to dividends and/or interest.

even long-term Government of Canada debt instruments because of the tax-exempt status of preferred stock dividends to corporate purchasers and because of the dividend tax credit available to individual investors. Thus, the risk-return trade-off on preferred stock does not fall on the straight line because of the enormous importance of the tax treatment.

Next, we observe increasingly high return requirements on debt, based on the presence or absence of security provisions and the priority of claims on unsecured debt. Finally, at the top of the scale is common stock. Because of its lowest priority of claim in the corporation and its volatile price movement, it has the highest demanded return.

Figure 17–2
Risk and expected return for various security classes

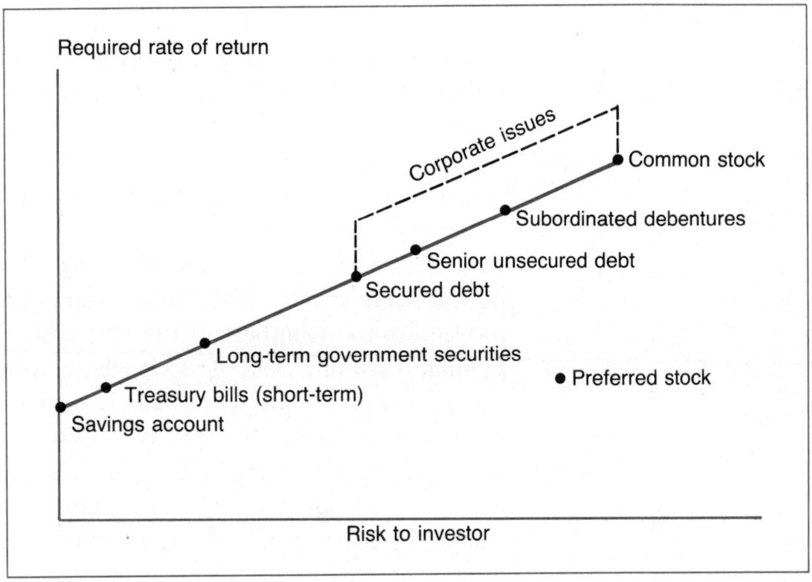

While extensive research studies have tended to validate these general patterns,[15] short-term or even intermediate-term reversals, in which investments with lower risk have outperformed investments at the higher end of the risk scale, have taken place.

Summary

Common stock is owned by over 3 million individual Canadian investors, an increase of about 50 percent in three years. In addition, institutional ownership through mutual funds, pension funds, insurance companies, trusts, and so forth is increasing every year.

Common stock ownership carries three primary rights or privileges. First, there is a residual claim to income. All funds not paid out to other classes of securities automatically belong to the common share-

[15]Roger G. Ibbotson and Rex A. Sinquefield, "Stocks, Bonds, Bills and Inflation: Year by Year Historical Returns (1926–1974)," *Journal of Business* 49, no. 1 (January 1976). Also Lawrence Fisher and James Lorie, *A Half Century of Returns on Common Stocks and Bonds* (Chicago: University of Chicago Graduate School of Business, 1977). For example, Ibbotson and Sinquefield found, over an almost 50-year period, an average return of 8.5 percent on U.S. common stocks, 3.6 percent on corporate bonds, and 3.2 percent on U.S. governments. A more recent study by Robert S. Salomon, Jr., of Salomon Bros. showed a reversal of these patterns for 1969–78.

holder; the firm may then choose to pay out these residual funds in dividends or to reinvest them for the benefit of common shareholders. Different classes of stock, such as the Harding Carpet Class A and Class B stock, may carry the right to differing dividend amounts. There can also be cases where dividends on a particular class of stock are tied to the performance of a subsidiary company.

Because common stockholders are the ultimate owners of the firm, they alone have the privilege of voting (except under default or other unusual conditions). The major voting choice for the shareholders is in electing the members of the firm's board of directors. There may be more than one class of stock whose voting rights differ. In Canada there are many examples of stock with different voting rights. The general purpose of such stock is to allow a company to raise additional equity capital without diluting the controlling ownership of a current group of shareholders. Many of the nonvoting issues contain a so-called coattail clause allowing for the participation of their holders in any premium paid by an acquirer for the voting shares. The attempted takeover of Canadian Tire by its franchised dealers has made many cognizant of the fragility of the protection provided by these clauses.

To expand the role of minority shareholders, many corporations use a system of cumulative voting in which each stockholder has voting power equal to the number of shares owned times the number of directors to be elected. By cumulating votes for a small number of selected directors, minority shareholders are sometimes able to have representation on the board.

Common shareholders may also enjoy a first option to purchase new shares. This privilege is extended through the procedure known as a rights offering. A shareholder receives one right for each share of stock owned and may combine a certain number of rights, plus cash, to purchase a new share. While the cash or subscription price is usually somewhat below the current market price, the shareholder neither gains nor loses through the process.

A hybrid, or intermediate, security, falling between debt and common stock, is preferred stock. Preferred shareholders are entitled to receive a stipulated dividend and must receive this dividend before any payment is made to common shareholders. Preferred dividends usually accumulate if they are not paid in a given year. Preferred stockholders cannot, however, initiate bankruptcy proceedings or seek legal redress if nonpayment occurs.

Finally, common stock, preferred stock, bonds, and other securities tend to receive returns over the long run in accordance with risk, with corporate issues generally paying a higher return than government securities.

List of Terms

common shareholder	**margin requirement**
cumulative voting	**preferred stock**
preemptive right	**floating-rate preferred**
rights offering	**cumulative preferred**
cum-rights	**participating preferred**
ex-rights	**convertible preferred**
majority voting	**intrinsic value**
nonvoting stock	**cumulative voting**

Discussion Questions

1. Why has corporate management become increasingly sensitive to the desires of large institutional investors?
2. What is the difference in dividend payments between Canadian Tire Class A nonvoting shares and its common shares? How do you explain the difference in their trading values?
3. Why do corporations use special categories in issuing common stock?
4. What are the possible disadvantages, from an investor's point of view, of only being able to buy nonvoting shares in a given company? What do you think of the increased tendency among Canadian companies to issue large amounts of nonvoting shares?
5. What is the purpose of cumulative voting? Are there any disadvantages to management?
6. Why has preferred stock been a much more popular source of funds for corporations in Canada than in the United States?

7. How does the preemptive right protect stockholders from dilution?
8. If common stockholders are the *owners* of the company, why do they have only the last claim on assets and only a residual claim on income?
9. Preferred stock is often referred to as a hybrid security. Why?
10. During a rights offering the underlying stock is said to sell *rights-on* and *ex-rights*. Explain the meaning of these terms and their significance to current stockholders and potential stockholders.
11. If preferred stock is riskier than bonds, why has preferred stock had lower yields than bonds in recent years?
12. A small amount of preferred stock is participating. What would your reaction be if someone said common stock is also participating?
13. What is an advantage of floating-rate preferred stock for the risk-averse investor? What is an advantage for the issuing corporation?
14. Speculate on whether it would be easier to buy control, in general, of a company listed on the TSE or one listed on the NYSE. Which situation strikes you as being better in this regard?

Problems

1. Mr. R. C. Cola owns 7,001 shares of Softdrink, Inc. There are 10 seats on the company board of directors, and the company has a total of 77,000 shares outstanding. Softdrinks, Inc., utilizes cumulative voting.

   Can Mr. Cola elect himself to the board when the vote to elect 10 directors is held next week? (Use Formula 17–2 to determine if he can elect one director.)

2. The Lindsey Corporation has been experiencing declining earnings but has just announced a 50 percent salary increase for top executives. A dissident group of stockholders wants to oust the existing board of directors. There are currently 11 directors and 60,000 shares of stock outstanding. Mr. Perk, the president of the company, has the full support of the existing board. The dissident

Homework

stockholders control proxies for 20,001 shares. Mr. Perk is worried about losing his job.

a. Under cumulative voting procedures, how many directors can the dissident stockholders elect with the proxies they now hold? How many directors could they elect under majority rule with these proxies?

b. How many shares (or proxies) are needed to elect six directors under cumulative voting?

3. Midland Petroleum is holding a stockholders' meeting next month. Ms. Ramsey is president of the company and has the support of the existing board of directors. All 11 members are up for reelection. Mr. T. B. Pickens is a dissident stockholder. He controls proxies for 40,001 shares. Ms. Ramsey and her friends on the board control 60,001 shares. Other stockholders, where loyalties are unknown, will be voting the remaining 19,998 shares. The company uses cumulative voting.

a. How many directors can Mr. Pickens be assured of electing?

b. How many directors can Ms. Ramsey and her friends be assured of electing?

c. How many directors could Mr. Pickens elect if he obtains all the proxies for the uncommitted votes? (Uneven values must be rounded down to the nearest whole number regardless of the amount.) Will he control the board?

4. In problem 3, if nine directors were to be elected and Ms. Ramsey and her friends had 60,001 shares and Mr. Pickens had 40,001 shares plus half the uncommitted votes, how many directors could Mr. Pickens elect?

5. Mr. Rogers controls proxies for 38,000 of the 70,000 outstanding shares of Ingot Industrial Company. Mr. Kermit heads a dissident group which controls the remaining 32,000 shares. Seven board members are to be elected, and cumulative voting rules apply. Mr. Rogers does not understand cumulative voting and plans to cast 100,000 of his 266,000 (38,000 × 7) votes for his brother-in-law, Mel. The remaining votes will be spread evenly over three other candidates.

a. How many directors can Mr. Kermit elect if Mr. Rogers acts as described above? Use logical analysis rather than a set formula to answer part *a*.
b. How many directors can Mr. Kermit elect if Mr. Rogers acts in an optimal manner?
c. If Mr. Rogers spreads his votes evenly over seven candidates, trying to get all his people on the board, how many directors could Mr. Kermit elect? Use logical analysis rather than a set formula to answer part *c*.

6. Madonna Fashions, Inc., has issued rights to its shareholders. The subscription price is $45, and five rights are needed along with the subscription price to buy one of the new shares. The stock is selling for $54 rights-on.

a. What would be the value of one right?
b. If the stock goes ex-rights, what would the new stock price be?

7. Skyway Airlines has announced a rights offering for its shareholders. Mr. Harold Post owns 800 shares of Skyway Airlines stock. Four rights plus $60 cash are needed to buy one of the new shares. The stock is currently selling for $72 cum-rights.

a. What is the value of a right?
b. How many of the new shares can Mr. Post buy if he exercises all his rights? How much cash would this require?
c. Mr. Post does not know if he wants to exercise his rights or sell them. What alternative would have the more positive effect on his wealth?

8. Todd Winningham IV has $4,000 to invest. He has been looking at Gallagher Tennis Clubs, Inc., common stock. Gallagher has issued a rights offering to its common stockholders. Six rights plus $38 cash will buy one new share. Gallagher's stock is selling for $50 ex-rights.

a. How many rights could Todd buy with his $4,000? Alternatively, how many shares of stock could he buy with the same $4,000 at $50 per share?
b. If Todd invests his $4,000 in Gallagher rights and the price of Gallagher stock rises to $59 per share ex-rights, what would

his total dollar profit on the rights be? (First compute profits per right.)

c. If Todd invests his $4,000 in Gallagher stock and the price of the stock rises to $59 per share ex-rights, what would his total dollar profit be?

d. What would the answer be to part *b* if the price of Gallagher's stock falls to $30 per share ex-rights instead of rising to $59?

e. What would the answer be to part *c* if the price of Gallagher's stock falls to $30 per share ex-rights?

9. Mr. and Mrs. Anderson own five shares of Magic Tricks Corporation common stock. The market value of the stock is $60. They also have $48 in cash. They have just received word of a rights offering. One new share of stock can be purchased at $48 for each five shares currently owned (based on five rights).

a. What is the value of a right?

b. What is the value of the Andersons' portfolio before the rights offering? (Portfolio in this question represents stock plus cash.)

c. If the Andersons participate in the rights offering, what will be the value of their portfolio, based on the diluted value (ex-rights) of the stock?

d. If they sell their five rights but keep their stock at its diluted value and hold onto their cash, what will be the value of their portfolio?

10. The Hamlin Corporation has some excess cash it would like to invest in marketable securities for a long-term hold. Its vice president of finance is considering three investments (Hamlin is in a 40 percent tax bracket). Which should he select, based on after-tax return: (*a*) Treasury bonds at 10.5 percent yield, (*b*) corporate bonds at 12 percent yield, or (*c*) preferred stock at 10 percent yield.

11. National Health Corporation (NHC) has a cumulative preferred stock issue outstanding which has a stated annual dividend of $9 per share. The company has been losing money and has not paid the preferred dividends for the last five years. There are 300,000 shares of preferred stock outstanding and 600,000 shares of common stock.

a. How much is the company behind in total preferred dividends?

b. If NHC earns $11 million in the coming year after taxes but before dividends, and this is all paid out to the preferred stockholders, how much will the company be in arrears (behind in payments)? Keep in mind the coming year would represent the sixth year.

c. How much would be available in common stock dividends in the coming year if $11 million is earned, as indicated in part *b*?

12. Franklin Kite Company is four years in arrears on cumulative preferred stock dividends. There are 650,000 preferred shares outstanding and the annual dividend is $7 per share. The vice president of finance sees no real hope of paying the dividends in arrears. He is devising a plan to compensate the preferred stockholders for 90 percent of the dividends in arrears.

a. How much should the compensation be?

b. Franklin will compensate the preferred stockholders in the form of bonds paying 12 percent interest in a market environment in which the going rate of interest is 14 percent. The bonds will have a 25-year maturity. Using the bond valuation table in Chapter 16 (Table 16–3), indicate the market value of a $1,000 par value bond.

c. Based on market value, how many bonds must be issued to provide the compensation determined in part *a*? (Round to the nearest whole number.)

13. The treasurer of the Newton Record Company (a corporation) currently has $100,000 invested in preferred stock yielding 9 percent. He appreciates the tax advantages of preferred stock and is considering buying $100,000 more with borrowed funds. The cost of the borrowed funds is 11 percent. He suggests this proposal to his board of directors. They are somewhat concerned by the fact that the treasurer is paying 2 percent more for funds than he is earning. The Newton Record Company is in a 40 percent tax bracket.

a. Compute the amount of the after-tax income from the additional preferred stock if it is purchased.

b. Compute the after-tax borrowing cost to purchase the additional preferred stock. That is, multiply the interest cost times $(1 - T)$.

c. Should the treasurer proceed with his proposal?

d. If interest rates and dividend yields in the market go up six months after a decision to purchase is made, what impact will this have on the outcome?

14. Walker Machine Tools has 5 million shares of common stock outstanding. The current market price of Walker common stock is $42 per share rights-on. The company's net income this year is $15 million. A rights offering has been announced in which 500,000 new shares will be sold at $36.50 per share. The subscription price plus 10 rights is needed to buy one of the new shares.

a. What are the earnings per share and price-earnings ratio before the new shares are sold via the rights offering?

b. What would the earnings per share be immediately after the rights offering? What would the price-earnings ratio be immediately after the rights offering? Assume there is no change in the market value of the stock except for the change when the stock begins trading ex-rights. (Round answers to two places after the decimal point.)

15. The Crandall Corporation currently has 100,000 shares outstanding which are selling at $50 per share. It needs to raise $900,000. Net income after taxes is $500,000. Its vice president of finance and its outside investment banker have decided on a rights offering but are not sure how much to discount the subscription price from the current market value. Discounts of 10 percent, 20 percent, and 40 percent have been suggested. Common stock is the sole means of financing for the Crandall Corporation.

a. For each discount determine the subscription price, the number of shares to be issued, and the number of rights required to purchase one share. (Round to one place after the decimal point where necessary.)

b. Determine the value of one right under each of the plans. (Round to two places after the decimal point.)

c. Compute the earnings per share before and immediately after the rights offering under a 10 percent discount from the subscription price.

d. By what percentage has the number of shares outstanding increased?

e. Stockholder X has 100 shares before the rights offering and participated by buying 20 new shares. Compute his total claim to earnings both before and after the rights offering (that is, multiply shares by the earnings per share figures computed in part *c*).

f. Should Stockholder X be satisfied with this claim over a longer period of time?

16. (*Comprehensive problem*)
Hoffman Bike Parts, Inc., is a small firm which has been very profitable over the past five years and has also exhibited a strong earnings growth trend. Mr. Hoffman owns 35 percent of the 2 million shares of common stock outstanding, but he is nevertheless worried about being taken over by a larger firm some time in the future. He has read some articles in *The Globe and Mail* about techniques used to discourage forced mergers and takeovers. Hoffman Bike Parts, Inc., currently uses majority voting for nine directors. Mr. Hoffman wonders which of the following proposals would make it easier for him to reject a takeover bid.

a. What would be the effect of cumulative voting?

b. What would be accomplished if shareholders could only vote for one third of the directors every year (staggered terms)?

c. Should Mr. Hoffman reduce or increase the number of directors? Is the answer to this question dependent on majority rule or cumulative voting?

Selected References

Bacon, P. W. "The Subscription Price in Rights Offerings." *Financial Management* 1 (September 1972), pp. 59–64.

Baumol, William J. *The Stock Market and Economic Efficiency.* New York: Fordham University Press, 1965.

Bear, Robert M., and Anthony J. Curley. "Unseasoned Financing." *Journal of Financial and Quantitative Analysis* 10 (June 1975), pp. 311–26.

Bloch, Ernest. "Pricing a Corporate Bond Issue: A Look behind the Scenes." *Essays in Money and Credit.* New York: Federal Reserve Bank of New York, 1964, pp. 72–76.

Canadian Securities Institute. *Canadian Securities Course.* Toronto, 1983, chaps. 11 and 12.

Donaldson, Gordon. "In Defense of Preferred Stock." *Harvard Business Review* 40 (July–August 1962), pp. 123–36.

Dougall, Herbert E., and Jack E. Gaumnitz. *Capital Markets and Institutions.* Englewood Cliffs, N.J.: Prentice-Hall, 1975.

Ederington, Louis H. "Uncertainty, Competition, and Costs in Corporate Bond Underwriting." *Journal of Financial Economics* 2 (March 1975), pp. 71–94.

Edmister, Robert O. "Commission Cost Structure: Shifts and Scale Economies." *Journal of Finance* 33 (May 1978), pp. 477–86.

Eibott, Peter. "Trends in the Value of Individual Stockholdings." *Journal of Business* 47 (July 1974), pp. 339–48.

Evans, G. H., Jr. "The Theoretical Value of Stock Right." *Journal of Finance* 10 (March 1955), pp. 55–61.

Fischer, Donald E., and Glenn A. Wilt, Jr. "Nonconvertible Preferred Stock as a Financing Instrument, 1950–1965." *Journal of Finance* 23 (September 1968), pp. 611–24.

Fisher, Lawrence, and James H. Lorie. *A Half Century of Returns on Common Stocks and Bonds.* Chicago: University of Chicago Graduate School of Business, 1977.

Hunter, W. T. *Canadian Financial Markets.* Peterborough: Broadview Press, 1986.

Ibbotson, Roger G., and Rex A. Sinquefield. "Stocks, Bonds, Bills, and Inflation: Year by Year Historical Returns (1926–1974)." *Journal of Business* 49 (January 1976), pp. 11–47.

Keane, S. M. "The Significance of Issue Price in Rights Issues." *Journal of Business Finance* 4 (September 1972), pp. 40–45.

Levy, Haim, and Marshall Sarnat. "Risk, Dividend Policy, and the Optimal Pricing of a Rights Offering." *Journal of Money, Credit, and Banking* 3 (November 1971), pp. 840–49.

Mikkelson, Wayne H., and M. Megan Partch. "Stock Price Effects and Costs of Secondary Distributions." *Journal of Financial Economics* 14 (June 1985), pp. 165–94.

Nelson, J. R. "Price Effects in Rights Offerings." *Journal of Finance* 20 (December 1965), pp. 647–60.

O'Neal, F. H. "Minority Owners Can Avoid Squeeze-Outs." *Harvard Business Review* 41 (March–April 1963), pp. 150–52.

Pinches, George E. "Financing with Convertible Preferred Stock, 1960–1967." *Journal of Finance* 25 (March 1970), pp. 53–63.

Soldofsky, Robert M., and Craig R. Johnson. "Rights Timing." *Financial Analysis Journal* 23 (July–August 1967), pp.101–4.

Toronto Stock Exchange. *Canadian Shareholders: Their Profiles and Attitudes*. Toronto, 1984.

18 Dividend Policy and Retained Earnings

A successful owner of a small business must continually decide what to do with the profits his firm has generated. One option is to reinvest in the business—purchasing new plant and equipment, expanding inventory, and perhaps hiring new employees. Another alternative, however, is to withdraw the funds from the business and invest them elsewhere. Prospective uses might include buying other stocks and bonds, purchasing a second business, or perhaps spending a "lost weekend" in Las Vegas.

A corporation and its shareholders must face exactly the same type of decision. Should funds associated with profits be retained in the business or paid out to shareholders in the form of dividends?

The Marginal Principle of Retained Earnings

In theory corporate directors should ask, "How can we make the best use of the funds?" The rate of return the corporation can achieve on retained earnings for the benefit of stockholders must be compared to what stockholders could earn if the funds were paid out to them in dividends. This is known as the marginal principle of retained earnings. Each potential project to be financed by internally generated funds must provide a higher rate of return than the stockholder could achieve for himself. We speak of this as the opportunity cost of using stockholder funds.

Life Cycle Growth and Dividends

One of the major influences on dividends is the corporate growth rate in sales and the subsequent return on assets. Figure 18–1 shows a corporate life cycle and the corresponding dividend policy that is most likely to be found at each stage. A small firm in the initial stages

Figure 18–1
Life cycle growth and dividend policy

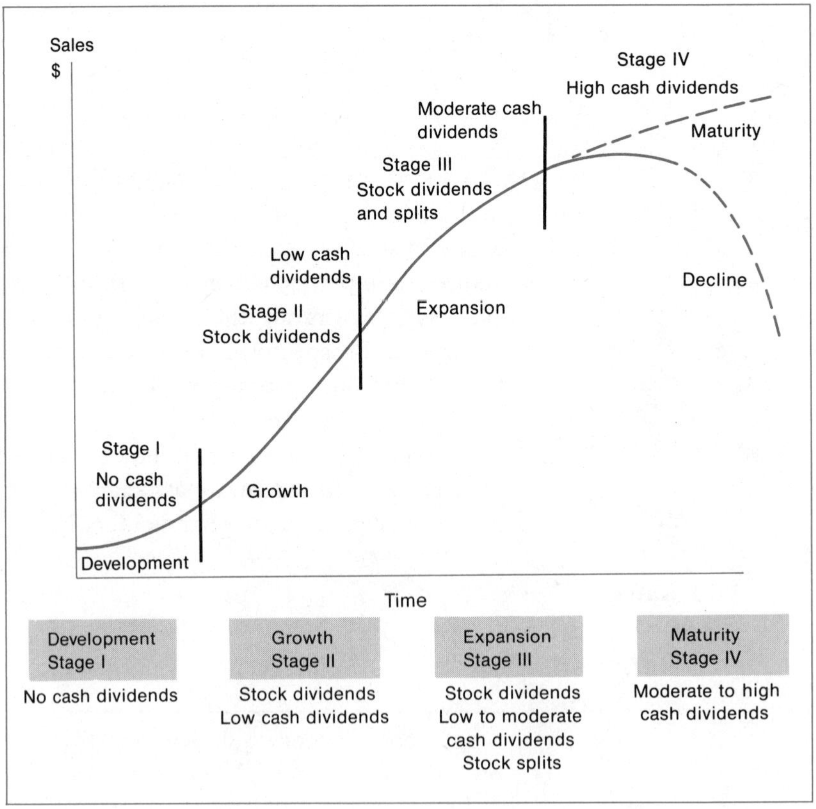

of development (Stage I) pays no dividends because it needs all of its profits (if there are any) for reinvestment in new productive assets. If the firm is successful in the marketplace, the demand for its products will create growth in sales, earnings, and assets, and the firm will move into Stage II. At this stage sales and returns on assets will be growing at an increasing rate, and earnings will still be reinvested. In the early part of Stage II stock dividends (distribution of additional shares) may be instituted, and in the latter part of Stage II *low* cash dividends may be started to inform investors that the firm is profitable but that cash is needed for internal acquisition.

After the growth period the firm enters Stage III. The expansion of sales continues, but at a decreasing rate, and returns on investment may decline as more competition enters the market and tries to take away the firm's market share. During this period the firm is more and more capable of paying cash dividends, as the asset expansion rate slows and external funds become more readily available. Stock dividends and stock splits are still common in the expansion phase, and the dividend payout ratio usually increases from a low level of 5 to 15 percent of earnings to a moderate level of 25 to 40 percent of earnings. Finally at Stage IV, maturity, the firm maintains a stable growth rate in sales similar to that of the economy as a whole, and when risk premiums are considered, its returns on assets level out to those of the industry and the economy. In unfortunate cases firms suffer declines in sales if product innovation and diversification have not taken place over the years. In Stage IV, assuming maturity rather than decline, dividends might range from 40 to 60 percent of earnings. These percentages will be different from industry to industry depending on the individual characteristics of the company, such as operating and financial leverage and the volatility of sales and earnings over the business cycle.

As the chapter continues more will be said about stock dividends, stock splits, the availability of external funds, and other variables that affect the dividend policy of the firm.

Dividends as a Passive Variable

In the preceding analysis dividends were used as a passive decision variable. They are only to be paid out if the corporation cannot make better use of the funds for the benefit of stockholders. The active decision variable is retained earnings: We decide how much to retain, and then the *residual is paid out in dividends.*

An Incomplete Theory

The only problem with the residual theory is that we have not given recognition to how shareholders feel about receiving dividends. If the shareholders' only concern is with achieving the highest return on their investment, either in the form of *corporate retained earnings remaining in the business* or *as current dividends paid out,* then there is no issue. But if shareholders have a preference for current funds, for example, over retained earnings, then our theory is incomplete. The issue is not only whether investment of retained earnings or dividends provide the highest return but also how shareholders react to the two alternatives.

While some researchers maintain that shareholders are indifferent to the division of funds between retained earnings and dividends[1] (holding investment opportunities constant), others disagree.[2] Though there is no conclusive proof one way or the other, the judgment of most researchers is that investors do have some preference between dividends and retained earnings. Certainly most financial managers believe they do.

Arguments for the Relevance of Dividends

A strong case can be made for the relevance of dividends because they *resolve uncertainty* in the minds of investors. Though earnings reinvested in the business theoretically belong to common shareholders, there is still an air of uncertainty about their eventual translation into dividends. Thus, it can be hypothesized that shareholders apply a higher discount rate (K_e) to yield a lower valuation to funds retained in the business as opposed to those that are paid out.[3]

---

[1]Merton H. Miller and Franco Modigliani, "Dividend Policy, Growth and Valuation of Shares," *Journal of Business* 34 (October 1961), pp. 411–33. Under conditions of perfect capital markets with an absence of taxes and flotation costs, it is argued that the sum of discounted value per share after dividend payments equals the total valuation before dividend payments.

[2]Myron J. Gordon, "Optimum Investment and Financing Policy," *Journal of Finance* 18 (May 1963), pp. 264–77; and John Lintner, "Dividends, Earnings, Leverage, Stock Prices, and the Supply of Capital to the Corporation," *Review of Economics and Statistics* 44 (August 1962), pp. 243–69.

[3]Ibid.

It is also argued that dividends may be viewed more favorably than retained earnings because of the *information content* they contain. In essence the corporation is telling the shareholder, "We are having a good year, and we wish to share the benefits with you." Though the corporation may be able to do just as well with the funds and perhaps provide even greater dividends in the future, some researchers find that "in an uncertain world in which verbal statements can be ignored or misinterpreted, dividend action does provide a clear-cut means of making a statement that speaks louder than a thousand words."[4]

The relevance of dividends in policy determination can also be argued from the viewpoint that the optimum dividend payout rate should be low. Because certain shareholders may be in high tax brackets, retention of funds in excess of investment needs might be recommended.

The primary contention in arguing for the relevance of dividend policy is that shareholders' needs and preferences go beyond the *marginal principle of retained earnings*. The issue is not only who can best utilize the funds (the corporation or the shareholder) but also what are the shareholders' preferences. In practice it appears that most corporations adhere to the following logic. First, a determination is made of the investment opportunities of the corporation relative to a required return (marginal analysis). This is then tempered by some subjective notion of shareholders' desires. It is not surprising that corporations with unusual growth prospects and high rates of return on internal investments generally pay a relatively low dividend (the small amount may be paid out only for its informational content).[5] For the more mature firm an analysis of both investment opportunities and stockholder preferences may indicate that a higher rate of payout is necessary. Dividend policies of selected major Canadian corporations are presented in Table 18–1. Note that in the two cases where earnings per share have been declining, continuance of historical dividend patterns has resulted in dividends exceeding after-tax earnings.

---

[4]Ezra Solomon, *The Theory of Financial Management* (New York: Columbia University Press, 1963), p. 142.

[5]Of course, such a company will be accorded a high price-earnings multiple by the very nature of its future potential. Such would make the payment of a meaningful dividend impossible. A 40 percent payout ratio for a firm with a 30 times P/E multiple translates into only a 1.2 percent dividend yield.

Table 18–1
Corporate dividend policy

	Four-Year Growth Rate in Earnings per Share (1981–1985)	Dividend Payout as Percentage of After-Tax Earnings (1981–1985)
Category 1—rapid growth:		
Magna International	36%	21%
CAE Industries	28	25
Noma Industries	41	17
Northern Telecom	30	16
Category 2—slower growth:		
Bell Canada	10	56
Alcan Aluminum	Declining	117
Stelco Inc.	Declining	104*
Bank of Nova Scotia	2	35

*Because Stelco had three years of overall losses during the 1980s while continuing to pay dividends, the dividend payout percent was averaged over the 10-year period, 1976–1985.

Dividend Stability

In considering stockholder desires in dividend policy, a primary factor is the maintenance of stability in dividend payments. Thus, corporate management must not only ask, "How many profitable investments do we have this year?" It must also ask, "What has been the pattern of dividend payments in the last few years?" Though earnings may change from year to year, the dollar amount of cash dividends tends to be much more stable, increasing in value only as new permanent levels of income are achieved while resisting any downward adjustment. Note in Figure 18–2 the smooth, generally upward sloping dividend curve and the considerably greater volatility of earnings compared to dividends for Canadian corporations since 1972.

By maintaining a record of relatively stable dividends, corporate management hopes to lower the discount rate (K_e) applied to future dividends of the firm. The operative assumption appears to be that a stockholder would much prefer to receive $1 a year for three years rather than 75 cents for the first year, $1.50 for the second year, and 75 cents for the third year—for the same $3 total. Once again we temper our policy of marginal analysis of retained earnings to include a notion of stockholder preference, with the emphasis on dividend stability.

Figure 18–2
Corporate profits and dividends

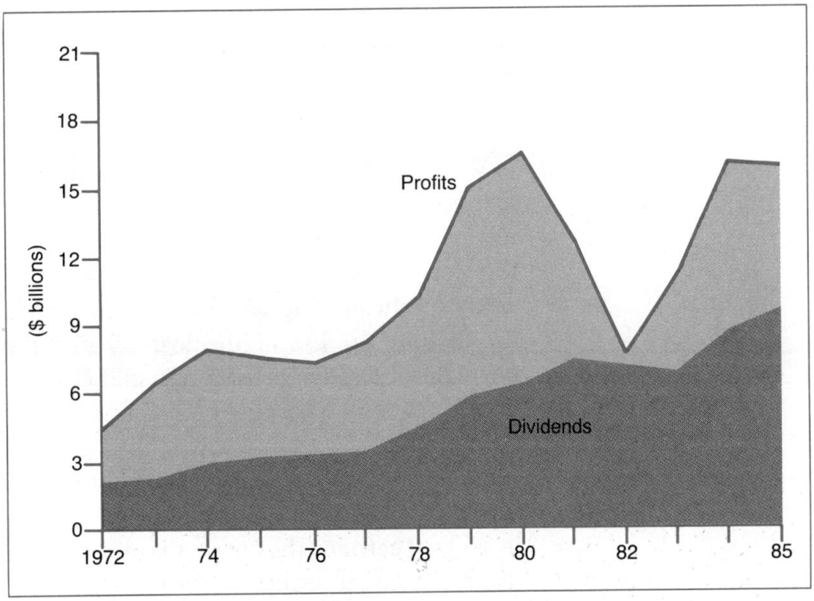

Other Factors Influencing Dividend Policy

Corporate management must also consider the legal basis of dividends, the cash flow position of the firm, and the corporation's access to capital markets. Other factors that must be considered include management's desire for control and the tax and financial position of shareholders. Each is briefly discussed.

Legal Rules

Canadian firms are not permitted to pay dividends that would impair the initial capital contributions to the firm. For this reason dividends may only be distributed from past and current earnings. To pay dividends in excess of this amount would mean that the corporation is returning to investors their original capital contributions (raiding the capital). If the ABC Company has the following statement of net worth, the maximum dividend payment possible would be $20 million.

Common stock (1 million shares)	$10,000,000
Retained earnings	20,000,000
Net worth	$30,000,000

Why all the concern about impairing permanent capital? Since the firm is going to pay dividends only to those who contributed capital in the first place, what is the problem? Clearly, there is no abuse to the stockholders, but what about the creditors? They have extended credit on the assumption that a given capital base would remain intact throughout the life of the loan. While they may not object to the payment of dividends from past and current earnings, they must have the protection of keeping contributed capital in place.[6]

Even the laws against having dividends exceed the total of past and current earnings (retained earnings) may be inadequate to protect creditors. Because retained earnings is merely an accounting concept and in no way certifies the current liquidity of the firm, a company paying dividends equal to retained earnings may, in certain cases, jeopardize the operation of the firm. Let us examine Table 18–2.

Theoretically, management could pay up to $15 million in dividends by selling off assets even though current earnings are only $1.5 million. In most cases such frivolous action would not be taken, but the mere possibility encourages creditors to closely watch the balance sheets of corporate debtors and, at times, to impose additional limits on dividend payments as a condition for the granting of credit.

Table 18–2
Dividend policy considerations

Cash	$ 1,000,000	Debt	$10,000,000
Accounts receivable	4,000,000	Common stock	10,000,000
Inventory	15,000,000	Retained earnings	15,000,000
Plant and equipment	15,000,000		$35,000,000
	$35,000,000		

Current earnings	$ 1,500,000
Potential dividends	15,000,000

[6]Of course, on liquidation of the corporation, the contributed capital to the firm may be returned to common stockholders after creditor obligations are met. Normally, stockholders who need to recoup all or part of their contributed capital sell their shares to someone else.

Company directors are also prohibited from declaring dividends when the company is insolvent or when the payment of dividends would make the company insolvent. Both legal insolvency (liabilities exceeding assets) and technical insolvency (inability to pay creditors) are included. This restriction is meant to prevent troubled firms from taking an action to the advantage of shareholders at the obvious expense of creditors.

Cash Position of the Firm

Not only do retained earnings fail to portray the liquidity position of the firm, but there are also limitations to the use of current earnings to indicate liquidity. As described in Chapter 4, Financial Forecasting, a growth firm producing the greatest gains in earnings may be in the poorest cash position. As sales and earnings expand rapidly, there is an accompanying buildup in receivables and inventory that may far outstrip cash flow generated through earnings. Note that the cash balance in Table 18–2 represents only two thirds of current earnings of $1.5 million. A firm must do a complete funds flow analysis before establishing a dividend policy.

Access to Capital Markets

The medium- to large-size firm with a good record of performance may have relatively easy access to the financial markets. A company in such a position may be willing to pay dividends now, knowing that it can sell new stocks or bonds in the future if funds are needed. Some corporations may even issue debt or stock *now* and use part of the proceeds to ensure the maintenance of current dividends. Though this policy seems at variance with the concept of a dividend as a reward, management may justify its action on the basis of maintaining stable dividends. It should be clear that in the capital-short era of the 1970s and 80s only a relatively small percentage of firms have had sufficient ease of entry to the capital markets to modify their dividend policy in this regard. Many firms may actually defer the payment of dividends because they know they will have difficulty in going to the capital markets for more funds at certain points in time as was true in the early 80s.

Desire for Control

Management must also consider the effect of the dividend policy on its collective ability to maintain control. The directors and officers of a small, closely held firm may be hesitant to pay any dividends at all for fear of diluting the cash position of the firm and forcing the owners to look to outside investors for financing. The funds may be available only through venture capital sources that wish to have a large say in corporate operations.

A larger firm with a broad base of shareholders may face a different type of threat in regard to dividend policy. Stockholders, spoiled by a past record of dividend payments, may demand the ouster of management if dividends are withheld.

Tax Position of Shareholders

The tax rates applicable to dividend income have been subject to change over the years and will likely continue to be so. However, the payment of a cash dividend is generally taxable to the recipient with some feeling the burden more heavily than others. To the wealthy lawyer or business professional, dividend income in 1986 could have attracted a net tax of up to 26 percent. The average taxpayer, on the other hand, would have paid only a low percent tax on dividend income. In the case of the corporate recipient, such as Brascan owning a controlling interest in Noranda, the dividend payment would probably have been tax-exempt. In addition, dividends to the many large institutional investors who own so much of the common equity in the market are also usually tax-exempt.

The dividend tax credit is meant to adjust for the fact that the corporation has already paid tax on the income upon which the dividend was based. In order to adjust for this double taxation, the dividend paid is grossed up to an average of the before-tax income it represents. The amount of the gross-up has been 50 percent traditionally, representing an assumption of a notional 33⅓ percent tax being paid by the corporation. If tax reform in Canada goes ahead as planned with reduced corporate rates, then we might expect the amount of the gross-up to be reduced accordingly, possibly to 33⅓ percent. The dividend tax credit is levied at 22⅔ percent of the grossed-up dividend amount while the tax payable is also computed on the grossed-up amount. Take, for example, a case where taxes must be computed on a $1,000 dividend payment to an individual whose marginal federal tax bracket is 1986's top rate of 34 percent and who lives in a province that levies provincial income tax at 50 percent of the federal amount (for all provinces except Quebec, that percentage is slightly above or below 50).

Sample calculation of tax on individual dividend receipt

Dividend received	$1,000
Gross-up	500
Taxable amount	1,500
Federal tax (at 34%)	510
Federal tax credit (22⅔% of $1,500)	340
Federal tax payable	170
Provincial tax (50% of federal)	255
Provincial tax credit (50% of federal)	170
Provincial tax payable	85
Total taxes payable	255
Net dividend ($1,000 − $255)	$ 745

The above is merely meant to show the nature of the dividend tax credit. Each taxpayer must make his or her own calculation in relation to the rules that exist for the particular year in question.

For the individual there was a plan in place as of 1986 to exempt capital gains up to $500,000 (lifetime) while amounts in excess of that would continue to be taxable at what amounts to an effective rate of one half the individual's normal tax rate. Thus, an individual in a 44 percent tax bracket would pay $220 tax on $1,000 of capital gains after the lifetime exemption was used up. However, under the planned 1988 tax reform, this $500,000 lifetime exemption is to be limited to $100,000 with the excess being taxed at two thirds rather than one half the normal tax rate.

Because of differences among investors' tax rates, certain investor preferences for dividends versus capital gains have been observed in the market. This investor behaviour is called the *clientele effect*. Investors in high marginal tax brackets usually prefer companies that reinvest most of their earnings, thus creating more growth in earnings and stock prices. The returns from such investments will be in the form of capital gains which are taxed at low rates or not at all. Companies following this dividend policy will most probably be found in the growth and expansion stages (see Figure 18–1). Investors in lower tax brackets have traditionally had a preference for dividends since the tax penalty is small at lower marginal tax rates and they will also receive regular returns on their investment. The clientele effect, then, can be used to explain the advantages of a stable dividend policy that makes investors more certain about the type and timing of their returns.

Dividend Payment Procedures

Now that we have examined the many factors that influence dividend policy, let us track the actual procedures for announcing and paying a dividend. Though dividends are quoted on an annual basis, the payments actually take place quarterly throughout the year. For example, in 1986 Imperial Oil paid $.40 per quarter in cash dividends on its Class A common shares. This meant that stockholders could expect to receive $1.60 per year in dividends. Because the stock was selling at $51 in December of 1986, we calculate the annual dividend yield to be 3.1 percent ($1.60/$51).

Three key dates are associated with the declaration of a quarterly dividend: the ex-dividend date, the dividend record date, and the dividend payment date.

On the *dividend record date* the firm examines its books to determine who is entitled to a cash dividend. In order to have your name included on the corporate books on the dividend record date, you must have bought or owned the stock before the *ex-dividend date*, which is set at the fourth business day before the dividend record date. If you bought the stock on the ex-dividend date or later your name will eventually be transferred to the corporate books, but you will have bought the stock without the right to receive the quarterly dividend. Thus, we say you have bought the stock ex-dividend.[7] In the Imperial Oil example a December 2 dividend record date resulted in an ex-dividend date of November 26 for the quarterly dividend payable January 1, 1987. Therefore, you would have had to have bought the stock before November 26 to be eligible to receive the January 1 dividend. Investors are very conscious of the date on which the stock goes ex-dividend, and the value of the stock should go down by exactly the value of the

[7] In this case the previous stockholder will receive the dividend.

dividend on the ex-dividend date (all other things being equal). Finally, in the Imperial Oil case, cheques would be sent out to the entitled stockholders on or about the *dividend payment date* of January 1.

Stock Dividend

A stock dividend represents a distribution of additional shares to common shareholders. The typical size of such a dividend is 10 percent or less of the current amount of stock outstanding. In the case of a 10 percent stock dividend, a shareholder with 100 shares would receive 10 new shares in the form of a stock dividend. Larger distributions of 20–25 percent or more are usually considered to be stock splits which are discussed later in this chapter.

Accounting Considerations for a Stock Dividend

Assume that prior to the declaration of a stock dividend the XYZ Corporation has the net worth position indicated in Table 18–3.

If a 10 percent stock dividend is declared, shares outstanding increase by 100,000 (10 percent of 1 million shares). An accounting transfer will take place between retained earnings and the two common stock accounts based on the market value of the stock dividend. If the stock is selling for $15 per share, we will assign $1 million to common stock and $500,000 to the contributed surplus account. The net worth position of XYZ after the transfer is shown in Table 18–4.

Table 18–3
XYZ Corporation's financial position before stock dividend

Capital accounts	Common stock (1 million shares issued)	$10,000,000
	Contributed surplus	5,000,000
	Retained earnings	15,000,000
	Net worth	$30,000,000

Table 18–4
XYZ Corporation's financial position after stock dividend

Capital accounts	Common stock (1.1 million shares issued)	$11,000,000
	Contributed surplus	5,500,000
	Retained earnings	13,500,000
	Net worth	$30,000,000

Value to the Investor

An appropriate question might be: Is a stock dividend of real value to the investor? Suppose your finance class collectively purchased $1,000 worth of assets and issued 10 shares of stock to each class member. Three days later it is announced that each stockholder will receive an extra share. Has anyone benefited from the stock dividend? Of course not! The asset base remains the same ($1,000), and your proportionate ownership in the business is unchanged (everyone got the same new share). You merely have more paper to tell you what you already knew.

The same logic is essentially true in the corporate setting. In the case of the XYZ Corporation, shown in Tables 18–3 and 18–4, we assumed that 1 million shares were outstanding before the stock dividend and 1.1 million shares afterward. Now let us assume the corporation had after-tax earnings of $6.6 million. Without the stock dividend, earnings per share would be $6.60, and with the dividend, $6.00.

$$\text{Earnings per share} = \frac{\text{Earnings after taxes}}{\text{Shares outstanding}}$$

Without stock dividend:

$$= \frac{\$6.6 \text{ million}}{1 \text{ million shares}} = \$6.60$$

With stock dividend:

$$= \frac{\$6.6 \text{ million}}{1.1 \text{ million shares}} = \$6.00$$

(10% decline)

Earnings per share have gone down by exactly the same percentage that shares outstanding increased. For further illustration, assuming Stockholder A had 10 shares before the stock dividend and 11 afterward, what are his total claims to earnings? As expected, they remain the same, at $66.

$$\text{Claims to earnings} = \text{Shares} \times \text{Earnings per share}$$

Without stock dividend:

$$10 \times \$6.60 = \$66$$

With stock dividend:

$$11 \times \$6.00 = \$66$$

Taking the analogy one step further, assuming the stock sold at 20 times earnings before and after the stock dividend, what is the total market value of the portfolio in each case?

$$\text{Total market value} = \text{Shares} \times \left(\begin{matrix}\text{Price/earnings} \\ \text{ratio}\end{matrix} \times \begin{matrix}\text{Earnings} \\ \text{per share}\end{matrix}\right)$$

Without stock dividend:

$$10 \times (20 \times \$6.60)$$
$$10 \times \$132 = \$1{,}320$$

With stock dividend:

$$11 \times (20 \times \$6.00)$$
$$11 \times \$120 = \$1{,}320$$

The total market value is unchanged. Note that if the stockholder sells off the 11th share to acquire cash, his or her stock portfolio will be worth $120 less than it was worth before the stock dividend.

Under the federal income tax legislation that became effective May 23, 1985, stock dividends declared and paid after that date will be treated as regular dividends. Previously, no tax was payable on stock dividends. This change in the tax law makes stock dividends less attractive to some shareholders than previously and was expected to have a negative effect on the amount of stock dividends declared in the future.

Possible Value of Stock Dividends

There are limited circumstances under which a stock dividend may be more than a financial sleight of hand. If at the time a stock dividend is declared the cash dividend per share remains constant, the stockholder will receive greater total cash dividends. Assume the annual cash dividend for the XYZ Corporation will remain $1 per share even though earnings per share decline from $6.60 to $6.00. In this instance a stockholder moving from 10 to 11 shares as the result of a stock dividend has a $1 increase in total dividends. The overall value of his portfolio may then increase in response to larger dividends.[8]

The presence of different classes of stock for which different dividend policies make sense but which have the same claim to residual income seems to present a situation where stock dividends are well suited. For example, in the Imperial Oil case considered earlier, there were both Class A and a smaller number of Class B common shares outstanding. While cash dividends were paid to the Class A shareholders, stock dividends of equal value were paid to the Class B holders. If cash had been paid to the Class A holders and no stock dividend to the Class B shareholders, one quickly sees that value would be reallocated to the Class A shareholders away from the owners of Class B stock.

Use of Stock Dividends

Stock dividends are most frequently used by growth companies as a form of "informational content" in explaining the retention of funds for reinvestment purposes. This was indicated in the discussion of the life cycle of the firm earlier in the chapter. A corporation president may state, "Instead of doing more in the way of cash dividends, we are providing a stock dividend. The funds remaining in the corporation will be used for highly profitable investment opportunities." The market reaction to such an approach may be neutral or slightly positive.

A second use of stock dividends may be to camouflage the inability of the corporation to pay cash dividends and to try to cover up the ineffectiveness of the firm's operations in generating cash flow. The president may proclaim, "Though we are unable to pay cash dividends, we wish to reward you with a 15 percent stock dividend." Well-informed investors are likely to think little of a management that uses such a strategy.

Stock Splits

A stock split is similar to a stock dividend, only more shares are distributed. For example, a two-for-one stock split would double the

[8] C. A. Barker, "Evaluation of Stock Dividends," *Harvard Business Review* 36 (July–August 1958), pp. 99–114.

number of shares outstanding. In general, distributions increasing the number of shares outstanding by more than 20–25 percent are handled as stock splits.

The accounting treatment for a stock split is somewhat different from that for a stock dividend in that there is no transfer of funds from retained earnings to the capital accounts. There is, instead, a proportionate increase in the number of shares outstanding. For example, a two-for-one stock split for the XYZ Corporation would necessitate the statement adjustments shown in Table 18–5.

In this case all adjustments are in the common stock account. Because the number of shares is doubled, the market price of the stock should drop by half. The financial literature contains much discussion about the impact of a split on overall stock value. While there might be some small positive benefit, that benefit is virtually impossible to capture after the announcement of a split has taken place.[9] Perhaps a $66 stock will only drop to $35 after a two-for-one split, but one must act very early in the process to benefit.

The primary purpose of a stock split is to lower the price of a security into a more popular trading range. A stock selling for over $50 per share may be excluded from consideration by many small investors because they generally must purchase shares in lots of 100. Splits are popular because only stronger companies that have witnessed substantial growth in market price are in a position to participate in them.

Table 18–5
XYZ Corporation before and after stock split

Before	
Common stock (1 million shares issued)	$10,000,000
Contributed surplus, common stock	5,000,000
Retained earnings	15,000,000
Total owner's equity	$30,000,000
After	
Common stock (2 million shares issued)	$10,000,000
Contributed surplus	5,000,000
Retained earnings	15,000,000
Total owner's equity	$30,000,000

[9] Keith B. Johnson, "Stock Splits and Price Changes," *Journal of Finance* 21 (December 1966), pp. 675–88.

Repurchase of Stock as an Alternative to Dividends

A firm with excess cash and inadequate investment opportunities may choose to repurchase its own shares in the market rather than pay a cash dividend. For this reason the stock repurchase decision may be thought of as an alternative to the payment of cash dividends.

We will show that the benefits of the stockholder are equal under either alternative, at least in theory. For purposes of study, assume that the Morgan Corporation's financial position may be described by the data in Table 18–6.

The firm has $2 million in excess cash, and it wishes to compare the value to stockholders of a $2 cash dividend (on the million shares outstanding) as opposed to spending the funds to repurchase shares in the market. If the cash dividend is paid, the shareholder will have $30 in stock and the $2 cash dividend. On the other hand, the $2 million may be used to repurchase shares at slightly over market value (to induce sale).[10] The overall benefit to stockholders is that earnings per share will go up as the number of shares outstanding is decreased. If the price-earnings ratio of the stock remains constant, then the price of the stock should also go up. If a purchase price of $32 is used to induce sale, then 62,500 shares will be purchased.

$$\frac{\text{Excess funds}}{\text{Purchase price per share}} = \frac{\$2{,}000{,}000}{\$32} = 62{,}500 \text{ shares}$$

Table 18–6
Financial data of Morgan Corporation

Earnings after taxes	$3,000,000
Shares	1,000,000
Earnings per share	$3
Price-earnings ratio	10
Market price per share	$30
Excess cash	$2,000,000

[10] In order to derive the desired equality between the two alternatives, the purchase price for the new shares should equal the current market price plus the proposed cash dividend under the first alternative ($30 + $2 = $32).

Total shares outstanding are reduced to 937,500 (1,000,000 − 62,500). Revised earnings per share for the Morgan Corporation become:

$$\frac{\text{Earnings after taxes}}{\text{Shares}} = \frac{\$3{,}000{,}000}{937{,}500} = \$3.20$$

Since the price-earnings ratio for the stock is 10, the market value of the stock should go to $32. Thus, we see that the consequences of the two alternatives are presumed to be the same.

(1) Funds Used for Cash Dividend		*(2)* Funds Used to Repurchase Stock	
Market value per share	$30	Market value per share	$32
Cash dividend per share	2		
	$32		

In either instance the total value is presumed to be $32. Theoretically, the stockholder would be indifferent with respect to the two alternatives. This changes somewhat, however, when taxes and transaction costs are brought into the decision-making process. Let us first look at taxes. While the cash dividend is immediately taxed in Alternative 1, the gain in Alternative 2 may be untaxed as a capital gain. Furthermore, if there is to be a capital gains tax incurred, it will be delayed until the stock is sold. From a tax viewpoint the repurchase of shares may provide maximum benefits. On the other hand one can argue that dividends put cash in the stockholders' hands without any transaction costs. If the company is buying back significant amounts of its shares, it will have to pay some premium above $30 to induce enough shareholders to sell. As well, there will be transaction costs in managing and executing the buybacks. Finally, the remaining shareholders will have to incur transaction costs if they want to realize the equivalent of the cash dividend in cash.

Other Reasons for Repurchase

In addition to using the repurchase decision as an alternative to cash dividends, corporate management may acquire its own shares in the market because it believes they are selling at bargain basement prices.

A corporation president, seeing his firm's stock price decline by 50–60 percent over a six-month period, may determine that its own stock is the best investment available to the corporation. In other words, he or she is not convinced that the current share price is a best estimate of the present value of the firm's future prospects.

By repurchasing shares the corporation is able to maintain a constant demand for its own securities and to perhaps stave off further price erosion, at least temporarily. Reacquired shares may also be useful for employee stock options or as part of a tender offer in a merger or acquisition.

Firms also often reacquire part of their shares as a protective device against being taken over by others. As the equity value of a firm decreases relative to the value of its physical assets, outsiders may attempt to gain control of the firm by using the value of the physical assets to finance the purchase of the equity. In order to reduce the availability of their companies to these highly leveraged buyouts, the managements of potential takeover targets often take on debt for the purpose of buying back some of their stock.

In 1985 28 significant stock repurchase programs were undertaken by Canadian corporations. Table 18–7 documents some of the relevant information on a few of those.

Dividend Reinvestment Plans

During the 1970s many companies started dividend reinvestment plans for their shareholders. These plans take various forms, but basically they provide the investor with an opportunity to buy additional

Table 18–7
Stock repurchases

Company	Number of Shares	Price	Repurchase P/E
Alberta Energy Corp.	6,237,500	$20.00	16.4
Norcen Energy Resources	5,000,000	15.75	8.3
Global Communications	245,600	40.00	14.2
Shaw Industries	1,400,000	11.75	18.9
Trizec Corp.	1,000,000	26.00	37.1
High Plains Oil	2,919,450	6.85	n.a.
MacLean Hunter	5,313,000	MKT	20.5
Ranger Oil	3,000,000	MKT	42.6

shares of stock with the cash dividend paid by the company. In the Imperial Oil Class A shares case discussed earlier, the shareholders can elect to reinvest their cash dividends in additional Class A shares at 5 percent less than the market price. Imperial sells authorized but unissued shares to the stockholders in this case. With this type of plan the company is the beneficiary of increased cash flow since dividends paid are returned to it for reinvestment. These types of plans have been very popular with cash-short utilities who, very often, also allow shareholders a 5 percent discount from market value at the time of the purchase. This is justified because no underwriting or distribution costs are incurred. A shareholder is often allowed to add cash payments of up to $1,000 per quarter to his or her dividend payments to buy more shares at the reduced rate.

Summary

The first consideration in the establishment of a dividend policy is the firm's ability to reinvest the funds versus that of the stockholder. To the extent the firm is able to earn a higher return, reinvestment of retained earnings may be justified. However, we must temper this "highest return theory" with a consideration of shareholder preferences and the firm's need for earnings retention and growth as presented in the life cycle growth curve.

Shareholders may be given a greater payout than the optimum determined by rational analysis in order to resolve their uncertainty about the future (that is, for informational content purposes). Conversely, stockholders may prefer a greater than normal retention in order to defer the income tax obligation associated with cash dividends. Another important consideration in establishing a dividend policy may be the shareholders' desire for steady dividend payments.

Lesser factors influencing dividend policy are legal rules relating to maximum payment, the cash position of the firm, and the firm's access to capital markets. One must also consider the desire for control by corporate management and stockholders.

An alternative (or a supplement) to cash dividends may be the use of stock dividends and stock splits. While neither of these financing devices directly changes the intrinsic value of the stockholder position, they may provide communication to shareholders and bring the stock price into a more acceptable trading range. A stock dividend may take on some actual value when total cash dividends are allowed to increase.

Nevertheless, the alert investor will watch for abuses of stock dividends—situations in which the corporation indicates that something of great value is taking place when, in fact, the new shares created merely represent the same proportionate interest for each shareholder.

The decision to repurchase shares may be thought of as an alternative to the payment of a cash dividend. Decreasing shares outstanding will cause earnings per share, and perhaps the market price, to go up. The increase in the market price may be equated to the size of the cash dividend foregone.

Many firms are now offering stockholders the option of reinvesting cash dividends in the company's common stock. Cash-short companies have been using dividend reinvestment plans in order to raise external funds. Other companies simply provide a service to shareholders by allowing them to purchase shares in the market for low transaction costs.

List of Terms

marginal principle of retained earnings
residual dividends
declaration date
ex-dividend date
dividend record date
dividend information content
dividend payout
dividend yield
life cycle curve
clientele effect
dividend payment date
stock dividends
stock split
capital gains taxes
dividend reinvestment plans
corporate stock repurchase
dividend tax credit

Discussion Questions

1. How does the marginal principle of retained earnings relate to the returns a stockholder may make in other investments?

2. Discuss the difference between a passive and an active dividend policy.

3. How does the stockholder in general feel about the relevance of dividends?

4. Explain the relationship between a company's growth possibilities and its dividend policy.

5. Discuss the major factors that may influence the firm's willingness and ability to pay dividends.

6. If you buy a stock on the ex-dividend date, will you receive the upcoming quarterly dividend?

7. Describe the importance of shareholder tax rates in setting dividend policy.

8. How is a stock split versus a stock dividend treated on the financial statements of a corporation?

9. Why might a stock dividend or a stock split be of limited value to an investor?

10. Does it make sense for a corporation to repurchase its own stock? Explain.

11. How does the life cycle curve explain the relationship between corporate growth and residual dividend theory?

12. Why might an investor prefer capital gains over dividends?

13. What advantages to the corporation and the stockholder do dividend reinvestment plans offer?

Problems

1. Sewell Enterprises earned $160 million last year and retained $100 million. What is the payout ratio?

2. In doing a five-year analysis of future dividends, the Dawson Corporation is considering the following two plans. The values represent dividends per share.

Year	Plan A	Plan B
1	$1.50	$ .50
2	1.50	2.00
3	1.50	.20
4	1.60	4.00
5	1.60	1.70

a. How much in total dividends per share will be paid under each plan over the five years?

b. Mr. Bright, the vice president of finance, suggests that stockholders often prefer a stable dividend policy to a highly variable one. He will assume that stockholders apply a lower discount rate to dividends that are stable. The discount rate to be used for Plan A is 10 percent; the discount rate for Plan B is 12 percent. Which plan will provide the higher present value for the future dividends? (Round to two places to the right of the decimal point.)

3. The following companies have different financial statistics. What dividend policies would you recommend for them? Explain your reasons.

	Turtle Co.	Hare Corp.
Growth rate in sales and earnings	5%	20%
Cash as a percentage of total assets.	15	2

4. The Ontario Freight Company's common stock is selling for $40 the day before the stock goes ex-dividend. The annual dividend yield is 6.7 percent, and dividends are distributed quarterly. Based solely on the impact of the cash dividend, by how much should the stock go down on the ex-dividend date? What will the new price of the stock be?

5. Below are the earnings per share and the dividends per share of three companies.

XYZ Co.		ABC Co.		Widget Co.	
EPS	DPS	EPS	DPS	EPS	DPS
$2.00	$1.00	$2.00	$1.00	$2.00	$1.00
2.10	1.05	2.10	1.00	2.10	.75
2.40	1.20	2.40	1.00	2.40	1.00
2.80	1.40	2.80	1.00	2.80	1.50
3.00	1.50	3.00	1.20	3.00	1.00

a. What are the payout ratios for each company on an annual basis?
b. Can you explain some of the reasons for such differences in payout patterns?
c. Which company would you prefer to own as a stockholder? Why? What other kinds of information would you want before you invested your money?

6. The King Petroleum Company has the following capital section on its balance sheet. Its stock is currently selling for $7 per share.

Common stock (100,000 shares)	$100,000
Contributed surplus	150,000
Retained earnings	250,000
	$500,000

The firm intends to declare a 10 percent stock dividend and then pay a 25¢ cash dividend (which also causes a reduction of retained earnings).

Show the capital section of the balance sheet after the first transaction and then after the second transaction.

7. Phillips Rock and Mud is trying to determine the maximum amount of cash dividends it can pay this year. Assume its balance sheet is as follows:

Assets

Cash	$ 312,500
Accounts receivable	800,000
Fixed assets	987,500
Total assets	$2,100,000

Liabilities and Owners' Equity

Accounts payable	$ 445,000
Long-term payable	280,000
Common stock (250,000 shares)	500,000
Retained earnings	875,000
Total liabilities and owners' equity	$2,100,000

a. From a legal perspective, what is the maximum amount of dividends per share the firm could pay? Is this realistic?
b. In terms of cash availability, what is the maximum amount of dividends per share the firm could pay?

c. Assume the firm earned a 16 percent return on owners' equity last year. If the board wishes to pay out 60 percent of earnings in the form of dividends, how much will dividends per share be?

8. The Adams Corporation has earnings of $750,000, with 300,000 shares outstanding. Its P/E ratio is eight. The firm is holding $400,000 of funds to invest or pay out in dividends. If the funds are retained, the after-tax return on investment will be 15 percent, and this will add to present earnings. The 15 percent is the normal return anticipated for the corporation, and the P/E ratio would remain unchanged. If the funds are paid out in the form of dividends, the P/E ratio will increase by 10 percent because the stockholders are in a very low tax bracket and have a preference for dividends over retained earnings. Which plan will maximize the market value of the stock?

9. Wilson Pharmaceuticals' stock has done very well in the market during the last three years. It has risen from $45 to $70 per share. The firm's current statement of owners' equity is as follows:

Common stock (4 million shares issued, 12 million shares authorized)	$ 40,000,000
Contributed surplus	15,000,000
Retained earnings	45,000,000
Net worth	$100,000,000

a. What changes would occur in the statement of owners' equity after a two-for-one stock split?

b. What would the statement of owners' equity look like after a three-for-one stock split?

c. Assume Wilson earned $14 million. What would be its earnings per share before and after the two-for-one stock split? The three-for-one stock split?

d. What would be the price per share after the two-for-one stock split? The three-for-one stock split? (Assume the price-earnings ratio stays the same.)

e. Should a stock split change the price-earnings ratio for Wilson?

10. Slick Products sells marked playing cards to blackjack dealers. It has not paid a dividend in many years but is currently contemplating some kind of dividend. The capital accounts for the firm are as follows:

Common stock (150,000 shares)	$150,000
Contributed surplus	150,000
Retained earnings	400,000
Net worth	$700,000

The company's stock is selling for $6 per share, and it earned $0.60 per share this year, indicating a P/E ratio of 10.

a. What adjustments would have to be made to the capital accounts for a 10 percent stock dividend?

b. What adjustments would be made to EPS and the stock price? (Assume the P/E ratio remains constant.)

c. How many shares would an investor end up with if he or she originally had 100 shares?

d. What is the investor's total investment worth before and after the stock dividend if the P/E ratio remains constant? (There may be a small difference due to rounding.)

e. Has Slick Products pulled a magic trick, or has it given the investor something of value? Explain.

11. The purpose of this problem is to compare the after-tax income on a $20,000 investment for the following two investors and two possible investments. Mr. Trucks's marginal tax rate is 30 percent. This is his only investment. Mrs. Carr's marginal tax rate is 50 percent. This is her only investment. Investment A provides $2,500 in dividends and no capital gains. Investment B provides no dividends but $2,500 of capital gains.

a. Calculate the after-tax return for Mr. Trucks in Investment A and Investment B.

b. Calculate the after-tax return for Mrs. Carr in Investment A and Investment B.

c. Indicate the difference in after-tax income between the two investors in Investment A.

d. Indicate the difference in after-tax income between the two investors in Investment B.

e. In the answers to parts *c* and *d*, why is there a smaller difference between the answers for one investment than for the other?

12. The Belton Corporation has $5 in earnings after taxes and 1 million shares outstanding. The stock trades at a P/E of 10. The firm has $4 million in excess cash.

a. Compute the current price of the stock.
b. If the $4 million is used to pay dividends, how much will dividends per share be?
c. If the $4 million is used to repurchase shares in the market at a price of $54 per share, how many shares will be required? (Round to the nearest share.)
d. What will the new earnings per share be? (Round to the nearest cent.)
e. If the P/E ratio remains constant, what will the price of the securities be? By how much, in terms of dollars, did the repurchase increase the stock price?

Assume Stockholder X has owned 100 shares of Belton stock for a number of years. He is in a 45 percent tax bracket.

f. How much is his after-tax dollar return on his 100 shares with the cash dividend?
g. How much is his after-tax return on his 100 shares with the $4 gain from the corporate stock repurchase if he sells his stock? (There, of course, would be no cash dividend.)

13. The Hastings Sugar Corporation has the following pattern of net income each year and associated capital expenditures projects. The firm can earn a higher return on the projects than the shareholders could earn if the funds were paid out as dividends.

Year	*Net Income*	*Profitable Capital Expenditure*
1	$10 million	$ 7 million
2	15 million	11 million
3	9 million	6 million
4	12 million	7 million
5	14 million	8 million

The Hastings Corporation has 2 million shares outstanding. (The following questions are separate from each other.)

a. If the marginal principle of retained earnings is applied, how much in total cash dividends will be paid over the five years?
b. If the firm simply uses a payout ratio of 40 percent of net income, how much in total cash dividends will be paid?
c. If the firm pays a 10 percent stock dividend in Years 2 through 5 and also pays a cash dividend of $2.40 per share for each of the five years, how much in total cash dividends will be paid?
d. Assume the payout ratio in each year is to be 30 percent of net income, and the firm will pay a 20 percent stock dividend in Years 2 through 5. How much will dividends per share for each year be?

Selected References

Barker, C. A. "Evaluation of Stock Dividends." *Harvard Business Review* 36 (July–August 1958), pp. 99–114.

Bierman, Harold, Jr., and Richard West. "The Acquisition of Common Stock by the Corporate Issuer." *Journal of Finance* 21 (December 1966), pp. 687–96.

Black, Fischer, and Myron Scholes. "The Effects of Dividend Yield and Dividend Policy on Common Stock Prices and Returns." *Journal of Financial Economics* 1 (May 1974), pp. 1–22.

Brigham, Eugene F., and Myron J. Gordon. "Leverage, Dividend Policy, and the Cost of Capital." *Journal of Finance* 23 (March 1968), pp. 85–104.

Dielmen, T.; R. Wright; and T. Nantell. "Price Effects of Stock Repurchasing: A Random Coefficient Regression Approach." *Journal of Financial and Quantitative Analysis* 15 (March 1980), pp. 175–89.

Elton, Edwin J., and Martin J. Gruber. "The Cost of Retained Earnings—Implications of Share Repurchase." *Industrial Management Review* 9 (Spring 1968), pp. 87–104.

Fama, Eugene F. "The Empirical Relationships between the Dividend and Investment Decisions of Firms." *American Economic Review* 64 (June 1974), pp. 304–18.

Friend, Irwin, and Marshall Puckett. "Dividends and Stock Prices." *American Economic Review* 54 (September 1964), pp. 656–82.

Gordon, Myron J. "Optimum Investment and Financing Policy." *Journal of Finance* 18 (May 1963), pp. 264–72.

Grinblatt, Mark S.; Ronald W. Masulis; and Sheridan Titman. "The Valuation Effects of Stock Splits and Stock Dividends." *Journal of Financial Economics* 13 (December 1984), pp. 461–90.

Johnson, Keith B. "Stock Splits and Price Changes." *Journal of Finance* 21 (December 1966), pp. 675–86.

Kalay, Avner. "Stockholder-Bondholder Conflict and Dividend Constraints." *Journal of Financial Economics* 59 (July 1982), pp. 211–33.

______. "The Ex-dividend Day Behavior of Stock Prices: A Reexamination of the Clientele Effect." *Journal of Finance* 37 (September 1982), pp. 1059–70.

Lintner, John. "Distribution of Income of Corporations among Dividends, Retained Earnings, and Taxes." *American Economic Review* 46 (May 1956), pp. 97–113.

______. "Dividends, Earnings, Leverage, Stock Prices, and the Supply of Capital to Corporations." *Review of Economics and Statistics* 44 (August 1962), pp. 243–69.

Miller, Merton H., and Franco Modigliani. "Dividend Policy, Growth, and the Valuation of Shares." *Journal of Business* 34 (October 1961), pp. 411–33.

Pettit, R. Richardson. "Dividend Announcements, Security Performance, and Capital Market Efficiency." *Journal of Finance* 27 (December 1972), pp. 993–1007.

Solomon, Ezra. *The Theory of Financial Management*. New York: Columbia University Press, 1963.

Terborgh, George. "Inflation and Profits." *Financial Analysis Journal* 30 (May–June 1974), pp. 19–23.

Van Horne, James C., and John G. McDonald. "Dividend Policy and New Equity Financing." *Journal of Finance* 26 (May 1971), pp. 507–19.

Walter, James E. "Dividend Policies and Common Stock Prices." *Journal of Finance* 11 (March 1956), pp. 29–41.

19 Convertibles and Warrants

There are as many types of securities as there are innovative corporate treasurers or forward-looking portfolio managers. In the inflation-disinflation, volatile-interest-rate period of the 1970s and 1980s, investors have looked to security features providing special downside protection as well as capital appreciation potential. Many of these securities were originally an outgrowth of the wheeler-dealer, fast-buck period of the late 1960s. The particular emphasis in this chapter is on convertible securities and warrants.

Convertible Securities

A convertible security is a bond or share of preferred stock that can be converted, at the option of the holder, into common stock. Thus, the owner has a fixed-income security that can be transferred to a common stock interest if and when the affairs of the firm indicate such a conversion is desirable. For purposes of discussion we will refer to convertible bonds (debentures), although the same principles apply to convertible preferred stock.

When a convertible debenture is initially issued, a conversion ratio to common stock is specified. The ratio indicates the number of shares of common stock to which the debenture may be converted. Assume that in 1983 the Williams Company issued $10 million of 25-year, 6 percent convertible debentures, with each $1,000 bond convertible into 20 shares of common stock. The conversion ratio of 20 may also be expressed in terms of a conversion price. To arrive at the conversion price we divide the face value of the bond by the conversion ratio of 20. In the case of the Williams Company the conversion price is $50.

Value of the Convertible Bond

As a first consideration in evaluating a convertible bond, we must examine the value of the conversion privilege. In the above case we might assume the common stock is selling at $45 per share, so that the total conversion value is $900 ($45 × 20). Nevertheless, the bond may sell for par or face value ($1,000) in anticipation of future developments in the common stock and because interest payments are being received on the bonds. With the bond selling for $1,000 and a $900 conversion value, there is a $100 conversion premium, representing the dollar difference between market value and conversion value. The conversion premium generally will be influenced by the expectations of future performance of the common stock. If investors are optimistic about the prospects of the common stock, the premium may be large.

If the price of the common stock really takes off and goes to $60 per share, the conversion privilege becomes quite valuable. The bonds, which are convertible into 20 shares, will go up to at least $1,200 and perhaps more. Note that you do not have to convert to common immediately but may enjoy the movement of the convertible in concert with the common.

What happens if the common stock goes in the opposite direction? Assume that instead of going from $45 to $60 the common stock simply drops from $45 to $25—what will happen to the value of the convertible debenture? We know the value of a convertible bond will go down in response to the drop in the common stock, but will it fall all the way down to \$500 (20 × \$25 per share)? The answer is clearly no because the debenture still has value as an interest-bearing security. If the going market rate of interest in straight debt issues of similar maturity (25 years) and quality is 8 percent, we would say the debenture has a pure bond value of \$785.46.[1] Thus, a convertible bond has a floor value[2] but no upside limitation. The price pattern for the convertible bond is depicted in Figure 19–1.

We see the effect on the convertible bond price as the common stock price, shown along the horizontal axis, is assumed to change. Note that the floor value for the convertible is well above the conversion

Figure 19–1
Price movement pattern for a convertible bond

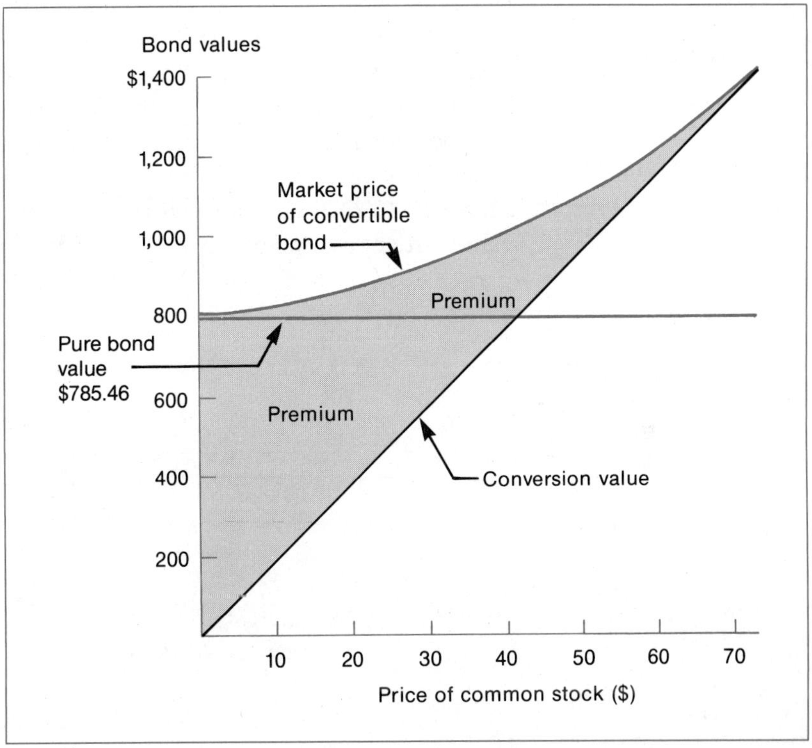

[1]Based on discounting procedures covered in Chapter 10, Valuation and Rates of Return.

[2]The floor value can change if interest rates in the market change. For ease of presentation we shall assume they are constant for now.

value when the common stock price is very low. As the common stock price moves to higher levels, the convertible bond moves in concert with the conversion value. Representative information on outstanding convertible bonds is presented in Table 19–1.

Looking at the BCE Development Corp. bond in Table 19–1 allows an illustration of what is meant by floor value. Following a severe downturn in Western Canadian real estate markets in the early 1980s, the common stock had fallen to $3.20 per share. That leaves us with a conversion value of only $492.10 (each bond was convertible into about 154 common shares). Because the convertible bond has maintained its 10¾ percent coupon payment, however, the bond price failed to decline past its floor value of $900.00. At this price the rather high-risk bond yields 12.24 percent to maturity.

In the MacLean Hunter and Molsons situations the bonds are trading well above the face value of $1,000 because the conversion privilege has become very valuable. In those cases, with yields to maturity of 2.33 percent and 5.37 percent, respectively, the interest payments have little effect on establishing the market value. The Bank of Montreal Mortgage Corp. bonds are selling at a premium over their conversion value but are at a point where a positive change in the common stock

Table 19–1
Pricing patterns for convertible bonds outstanding (October 1986)

Issuc, Coupon, Maturity, and Rating	*(1) Conversion Value*	*(2) Asking Price of Bond*	*(3) Call Price (percent of par)*	*(4) Yield to Maturity on Bond*	*(5) Market Rate for Bond of Similar Maturity and Quality*
Bank of Montreal Mortgage Corp. 11.75, 1994, A++	$ 981.10	$1,100.00	106.70%	9.18%	9.5%
Dickenson Mines 8.50, 1995	1,266.20	1,300.00	—	4.42	N/A
Irwin Toy 14.50, 1992, B	682.90	1,100.00	108.70	12.06	N/A
MacLean Hunter 8.25, 2004, B++	1,839.70	1,850.00	106.41	2.33	12.5
Royal Bank 11.25, 1991, A++	1,074.80	1,100.00	106.00	8.80	9.5
Molsons 8.50, 2000, A	1,259.00	1,310.00	106.13	5.33	12.3
BCE Development Corp 10.75, 2001, C	492.10	900.00	107.75	12.24	N/A

price would probably affect the market value of the bonds. A decline in stock price would probably not have much effect on the bond price since the yield would support it at the floor value.

Is This Fool's Gold?

At times some among us seem to believe that the creation of convertible securities has repealed the principle of an inherent trade-off between risk and return—that in order to get superior returns we must take larger than normal risks. With convertible bonds we appear to limit our risk while maximizing our return potential.

A close examination shows we have merely created a more complicated combination of risks and potential returns. For example, once convertible debentures begin going up in value, say to $1,100 or $1,200, the downside protection becomes pretty meaningless. In the case of the Williams Company in our earlier example, the floor is at $785.46. If an investor were to buy the convertible bond at $1,200, he would be exposed to $414.54 in potential losses (hardly adequate protection for a true risk averter). Also if interest rates in the market rise, the floor price, or pure bond value, could fall, creating more downside risk.

A second drawback with convertible bonds is that the purchaser is invariably asked to accept below-market rates of interest on the debt instrument. The interest rate on convertibles is generally one third below that for instruments in a similar risk class at time of issue. In the sophisticated environment of the bond and stock markets, one seldom gets an additional benefit without having to suffer a corresponding disadvantage.

The student will also recall that the purchaser of a convertible bond pays a premium over the conversion value. For example, if a $1,000 bond were convertible into 20 shares of common at $45 per share, a $100 conversion premium might be involved initially. If the same $1,000 were invested directly in common stock at $45 per share, 22.2 shares could be purchased. If the shares go up in value we have 2.2 more shares on which to garner a profit.

Last, convertibles may suffer from the attachment of a call provision giving the corporation the option of redeeming the bonds at a specified price above par ($1,000) in the future. In a subsequent section we will see how the corporation can use this device to force the conversion of the bonds.

None of these negatives is meant to detract from the fact that convertibles carry some inherently attractive features if they are purchased with investor objectives in mind. If the investor wants downside protection he or she should search out convertible bonds trading below par, perhaps within 10–15 percent of the floor value. Though a fairly large move in the stock may be necessary to generate upside profit, the investor has the desired protection and some hope for capital appreciation.

Advantages and Disadvantages to the Corporation

Having established the fundamental characteristics of the convertible security from the investor viewpoint, let us now turn the coin over and examine the factors a corporate financial officer must consider in weighing the advisability of a convertible offer for the firm.

Not only has it been established that the interest rate paid on convertible issues is lower than that paid on a straight debt instrument, but the convertible feature may be the only device for allowing smaller corporations access to the bond market. In this day of debt-ridden corporate balance sheets, investor acceptance of new debt may be contingent upon a special sweetener such as the ability to convert to common.

Convertible debentures are also attractive to a corporation that believes its stock is currently undervalued. You will recall that in the case of the Williams Company, $1,000 bonds were convertible into 20 shares of common stock at a conversion price of $50. Since the common stock had a current price of $45 and new shares of stock might be sold at only $44,[3] the corporation effectively received $6 over current market price, assuming future conversion. However, conversion will probably only occur if the stock price rises past $50. One can, then, plausibly argue that if the firm had delayed the issuance of common stock or convertibles for a year or two, the stock might have gone up from $45 to $60 and new common stock might have been sold at this lofty price.

---

[3]There is always a bit of underpricing to ensure the success of a new offering.

To translate this to overall numbers for the firm, if a corporation needs $10 million in funds and offers straight stock now at a net price of $44, it must issue 227,272 shares ($10 million/$44 per share). With convertibles the number of shares potentially issued is only 200,000 shares ($10 million/$50). Finally, if no stock or convertible bonds are issued now and the stock goes up to a level at which new shares can be offered at a net price of $60, only 166,667 will be required ($10 million/$60).

According to *Value Line Convertibles,* the typical convertible bond issued in 1985 in U.S. markets had a 20 percent conversion premium at issue. Although comprehensive data is not compiled on Canadian convertible securities, that level of premium seems close to the norm. For example, when the MacLean Hunter convertible debenture was issued in 1984, its equivalent share price was $8.69 as against the conversion price of $10.125 per share. This indicates a 16.5 percent premium. The conversion premium on the Royal Bank bonds was 13.2 percent on issue, while that on the BCE Development bonds was more like 23 percent. Small companies with less than a top-grade credit rating are obvious users of the convertible bond vehicle, although top-grade borrowers sometimes use them as well as is demonstrated by the presence of Bank of Montreal Mortgage Corporation and the Royal Bank in Table 19–1.

A matter of concern to the corporation is the accounting treatment accorded to convertibles. In the funny-money days of the conglomerate merger movement of the 1960s, corporate management often chose convertible securities over common stock because the convertibles had a nondilutive effect on earnings per share. As is indicated in a later section on reporting earnings for convertibles, the rules were changed in 1970, and this is no longer the case.

Important to the success of a convertible issue is the presumed ability of the corporation to force the security holder to convert the present instrument to common stock. We will examine this process.

Forcing Conversion

How does a corporation, desirous of shifting outstanding debt to common stock, force conversion? The principal device is the call provision, as discussed in Chapter 16, Long-Term Debt and Lease Financing. We know that when the value of the common stock goes up, the convertible security will move in a similar fashion. Table 19–1 indicates that convertible debentures may go up substantially in value. Some particularly successful convertibles have actually doubled in price. For this reason the holder of a convertible bond has no immediate incentive to convert to common unless the company calls the bond.

As an example of forcing a call we will use the MacLean Hunter convertible bond from Table 19–1. At the time of issue the corporation established a future privilege for calling in the bond at 6.41 percent above par value—thus, the $1,000 debenture was redeemable at $1,064.10. Most bonds have a 5 to 10 percent call premium often declining as the bond gets closer to maturity. The MacLean Hunter bond has risen in value to $1,850 per $1,000 bond. The conversion value is almost exactly the same as the price. An owner of this bond is entitled to 9.876 common shares per bond. If MacLean Hunter wishes to force conversion it merely announces it will call the issue at $1,064.10. Bondholders have the choice between converting to 9.876 shares of stock worth $1,839.70 or accepting the call price of $1,064.10. All rational bondholders will take the shares because of their higher value. The term *forced conversion* derives from the fact that in such a situation, the bondholder has no choice but to convert.

Conversion may also be encouraged through a step-up in the conversion price over time. When the BCE Development bond was issued, for example, the contract specified the following conversion provisions.

	Conversion Price	*Conversion Ratio*
First seven years	$ 6.50	153.8 shares
Next three years	11.58	86.4 shares
Next two years	14.58	68.6 shares

At the end of each time period there is a strong inducement to convert rather than accept an adjustment to a higher conversion price and a lower conversion ratio. Of course, the effectiveness of this step-up provision in forcing conversion is dependent on postive share price performance. In the BCE Development case, unless the share price recovers markedly, the conversion privilege has no attraction at even the current $6.50 conversion price.

Accounting Considerations with Convertibles

Prior to 1970 the full impact of the conversion privilege as it applied to convertible securities, warrants (long-term options to buy stock), and other dilutive securities was not adequately reflected in reported earnings per share. Since all of these securities may generate additional common stock in the future, the potential effect of dilution should be considered. Let us examine the unadjusted (for conversion) financial statements of the XYZ Corporation in Table 19–2.

An analyst would hardly be satisfied in accepting the unadjusted earnings per share figure of $1 for the XYZ Corporation. In computing earnings per share we have not accounted for the 400,000 additional shares of common stock that could be created by converting the bonds.

How then do we make this full disclosure? According to the Canadian Institute of Chartered Accountants recommendations issued in January 1970, we need to compute earnings per share as if the common shares related to conversions had actually been issued at the beginning of the accounting period.

$$\text{Fully diluted earnings per share} = \frac{\text{Adjusted after-tax earnings}}{\text{Fully diluted shares}} \qquad (19\text{–}1)$$

Table 19–2
XYZ Corporation

1. *Capital section of balance sheet:*	
Common stock (1 million shares)	$10,000,000
4.5% convertible debentures (10,000 debentures of $1,000 convertible into 40 shares per bond, or a total of 400,000 shares)	10,000,000
Retained earnings	20,000,000
Net worth	$40,000,000
2. *Condensed income statement:*	
Earnings before interest and taxes	$ 2,450,000
Interest (4.5% of $10 million)	450,000
Earnings before taxes	2,000,000
Taxes (50%)	1,000,000
Earnings after taxes	$ 1,000,000

3. *Earnings per share:*

$$\frac{\text{Earnings after taxes}}{\text{Shares of common outstanding}} = \frac{\$1{,}000{,}000}{1{,}000{,}000} = \$1$$

Earnings must be redefined to add to the numerator of the EPS ratio the costs related to the convertible securities. Thus, the adjustment would include adding dividends paid on convertible preferred shares, interest (after-tax) on convertible debt, and imputed interest (after-tax) on the cash that would have been received had warrants, rights, and options been exercised. The denominator in the ratio includes common shares outstanding, the common share equivalent of all convertible preferred shares and bonds, the common shares that would be issued if all outstanding rights to purchase common shares were exercised, and the common shares that would be issued if all outstanding warrants and other options were exercised. Conversions that result in a higher earnings per share or lower loss per share (that is, antidilutive) are ignored as are conversion privileges that do not become effective within 10 years.

We get new earnings per share for the XYZ Corporation by assuming that 400,000 new shares would have been created from potential conversion while, at the same time, allowing for the reduction in interest payments that would have taken place as a result of the conversion of the debt to common stock. Since before-tax interest payments on the convertibles are $450,000 annually for the XYZ Corporation, the after-tax cost is about $225,000. The assumption is that had conversion taken place at the beginning of the year, this after-tax interest cost would have been saved, augmenting the reported income by $225,000. Thus, fully diluted earnings per share for XYZ Corporation become $.88.

$$\text{Fully diluted earnings per share} = \frac{\text{Adjusted earnings after tax}}{\text{Fully diluted shares}}$$

$$= \frac{\overset{\text{Reported earnings}}{\$1{,}000{,}000} + \overset{\text{Interest savings}}{\$225{,}000}}{1{,}000{,}000 + 400{,}000} = \frac{\$1{,}225{,}000}{1{,}400{,}000} = \$0.88/\text{share}$$

The result of calculating the fully diluted earnings per share amount is a reduction of 12 percent from the basic earnings per share. The new figure is the one that would be used by a sophisticated investor in analyzing the value of a common share of XYZ Corporation.

Some Final Comments on Convertible Securities

While convertible debentures in the U.S. market are of such importance they encourage much investor activity and research,[4] in Canada they account for a small percentage of capital market activity. For instance, a review of the industrial bond price listings compiled by the Financial Post Information Service[5] reveals that only 31 of 811 industrial bond issues listed as outstanding were convertibles. Such stalwart investment favorites as Bell Canada have no outstanding convertible debenture issues.[6] Bell Canada, however, did have two separate convertible preferred share issues outstanding as of late 1986.

Table 19–3 demonstrates some information on a sample of convertible preferred shares outstanding in late 1986. In the Bell Canada Enterprises preferred share example, we see that the share is basically trading on the basis of the price of the common stock. There is a very slight discount because the common dividend yield is higher than the preferred dividend yield when the preferred stock price is in the $37 range. The preferred shares of Bow Valley and Dofasco are trading pretty much on the basis of current yield because the conversion premium has become so large. The Bank of Montreal preferred and the MacMillan Bloedel preferred are trading at a slight premium over the

Table 19–3
Convertible preferred shares

Issue, Conversion	*Market Value*	*Conversion Value*	*Conversion Premium*	*Preferred Yield*	*Common Yield*
Bell Canada Enterprises $2.05, 1992	$37.13	$37.25	0%	5.5%	6.3%
Bow Valley $2.05, 1995	19.63	12.79	53	10.4	1.8
Bank of Montreal $2.85, 1991	36.63	32.38	13	7.8	6.1
Dofasco $2.60 Ser 1, 1995	34.25	22.63	51	7.6	4.1
MacMillan Bloedel $2.08, 1991	26.75	23.74	13	7.8	2.7

[4]For example, in August 1986 Goldman-Sachs, a New York investment firm, issued a comprehensive, 64-page research report on convertible debentures in U.S. markets.

[5]Financial Post Information Service, *Canadian Bond Prices (1985)*, Toronto: MacLean Hunter, 1986.

[6]Bell had 26 separate bond issues outstanding at the end of 1985.

conversion value while still generating a current return higher than that on the common shares. In the MacMillan Bloedel case there was a straight preferred share yielding 8.58 percent. This infers that investors were willing to forgo .78 percent per year in current income in order to have the opportunity to benefit from future common share price appreciation.

Financing through Warrants

A warrant is an option to buy a stated number of shares of stock at a specified price over a given period of time. Abitibi-Price warrants, for example, entitle the holder to buy one share of common stock for $30 any time up until June 15, 1990. If the value of Abitibi-Price common stock were to go up to $40 or $50, the warrants would take on substantial value. On the other hand, if the share price stays far below $30 as June 15, 1990, approaches, the warrants will become almost worthless.

Traditionally, warrants were issued as a sweetener in a bond offering, making the issue of the debt feasible when it might not otherwise be so. More recently warrants have been issued in conjunction with preferred share issues, common share issues, and even as a stand-alone fund-raising issue. When warrants are attached to another security issue, like a bond, the combination of bond and attached warrants is called a unit. Warrants are usually detachable from the other security in the unit and generally trade on the Toronto Stock Exchange or the Montreal Exchange. After warrants are exercised the other security to which they were attached remains in existence.

The value of a warrant is dependent on the eventual market price movement of the underlying common stock above a certain stated value. If no chance is perceived of the stock price rising above the option price before the exercise date, the warrant will be worthless. This makes warrants highly speculative investments. If a $30 common stock were to move to $35 overnight, the effect on a low-priced warrant might be dramatic.

In the U.S. experience, United Airlines warrants moved from 4½ to 126 between 1962 and 1966. The potential for downward movement was demonstrated in the case of LTV warrants, which plummeted in value from 83 to 2¼ in the 1968–70 bear market. The decline in value of ATCO Ltd. warrants on the Toronto Stock Exchange from $1.75 in early 1984 to $.21 in 1986 represented a substantial percentage decline in value over a relatively short period and thus illustrates well the degree of risk entailed in investing in warrants.

Valuation of Warrants

Because the value of a warrant is tied closely to the price of the underlying common stock, a formula for the minimum value (often referred to as intrinsic value) of a warrant can be developed:

$$\text{Minimum value of a warrant} = \left[\text{Market value of common stock} - \text{Option price of warrant}\right] \times \text{Number of shares each warrant entitles holder to purchase} \qquad (19\text{–}3)$$

Using the data from Table 19–4 we see that CB Pak common stock was trading for $19.88 in November 1986. Each warrant carried with

Table 19–4
Relationships determining warrant prices (November 1986)

(1) Firm	(2) Warrant Price	(3) Stock Price	(4) Exercise Price	(5) Number of Shares	(6) Intrinsic Value	(7) Speculative Premium	(8) Due Date
Abitibi-Price	$ 4.90	$24.75	$30.00	1	$– 5.25	$10.15	6/15/90
Asamera Inc..	1.40	11.50	15.25	1	– 3.75	5.15	10/15/89
Canada Northwest Energy	1.10	14.25	20.00	1	– 5.75	6.85	6/18/93
CB Pak	6.50	19.88	14.50	1	5.38	1.12	12/15/87
CIBC (B).	2.90	19.38	22.00	1	– 2.62	5.52	9/30/88
Nova Alberta	17.63	5.88	0.00	3	17.64	0	7/31/96
Trans Canada Pipeline	2.21	16.50	19.25	1	– 2.75	4.96	7/13/89

it the right to purchase one share of CB Pak common stock at \$14.50 per share until late 1987. From Formula 19–3 the minimum, or intrinsic, value is derived as \$5.38 or (\$19.88 − \$14.50) × 1. Since the life of the warrant is only 13 more months, its speculative premium is \$1.12. Investors are willing to pay this premium because a small percentage gain in the stock price may generate large percentage increases in the warrant price. Formula 19–4 demonstrates the calculation of the speculative premium.

$$\text{Speculative premium of a warrant} = \text{Warrant price} - \text{Intrinsic value} \qquad (19\text{–}4)$$

In the Abitibi-Price situation one sees that the speculative premium is substantial reflecting in part the fact there are almost four years until the end of the exercise period. In that case the \$10.15 speculative premium is:

$$\$10.15 = \$4.90 - (\$-5.25)$$

Thus, even though the Abitibi-Price stock was trading substantially below the option price on the warrant, the warrant had a substantial value in the marketplace. Investors were willing to purchase the warrant in the hope the common stock price would rise sufficiently within the next four years to make the option provision valuable. Although the "speculative premium" in the Abitibi-Price case seems high at \$10.15 on a \$24.75 common share, it should be remembered that the normal expectation of investors on the stock might be it would appreciate by 12 percent or so per year. If that were the case, the current price would have built into it an expectation of a price of \$37 or so for the common stock 43½ months hence, when the warrant's option expires.

The typical relationship between the warrant price and the intrinsic value of a warrant is depicted in Figure 19–2. In the case depicted, the warrant entitles the holder to purchase one new common share for \$20. At common stock prices less than \$20 the intrinsic value of the warrant is negative, but investors are still willing to assign some value to it in the marketplace. As the market value of the stock increases markedly above \$20, we see that the difference between the market price of the warrant and its intrinsic value diminishes. Two reasons may be offered for this declining premium.

Figure 19–2
Market price relationships for a warrant

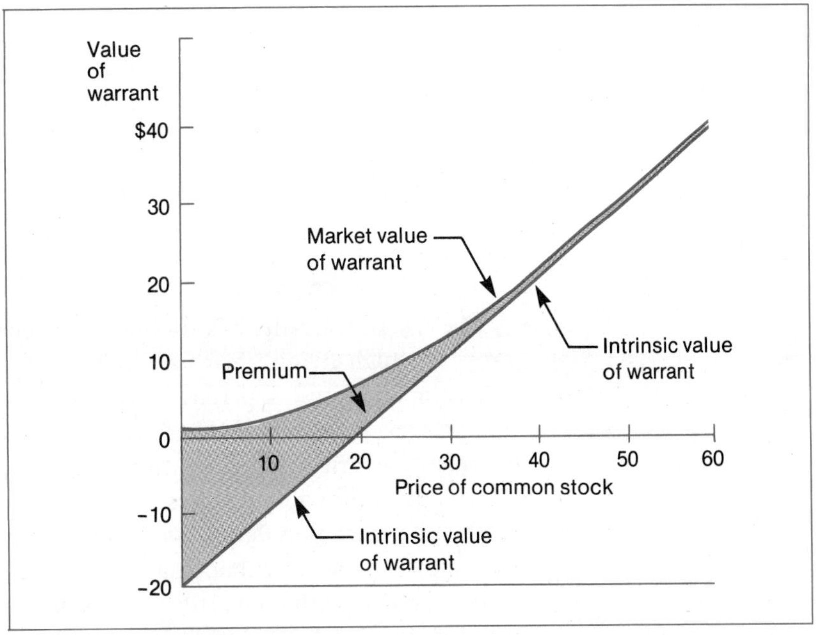

First, the speculator loses the ability to use leverage to generate high returns as the price of the stock goes up. When the price of the stock is relatively low, say $25, and the warrant is in the $5 range, a 10-point (or 50 percent) movement in stock price could mean a 200 percent gain in the value of the warrants. Table 19–5 describes this leveraging effect.

Use of Warrants in Corporate Finance

Let us consider for a moment the suitability of warrants for corporate financing purposes. As previously discussed, warrants may allow for the issuance of debt under difficult circumstances. While a straight debt issue may not be acceptable or may be accepted only at very high interest rates, the same security may be well received because of the inclusion of detachable warrants. Warrants may also be included as an add-on in a merger or acquisition agreement. For example, a firm might offer $20 million cash plus 10,000 warrants in exchange for all of the outstanding shares of the acquisition target.

Table 19–5
Leverage in valuing warrants

Low Stock Price	*High Stock Price*
Stock price, \$25; warrant price, \$5 + 10-point movement in stock price New warrant price, \$15 (10-point gain)	Stock price, \$50; warrant price, \$30 + 10-point movement in stock price New warrant price, \$40 (10-point gain)
Percentage gain in warrant $= \frac{\$10}{\$5} \times 100 = 200\%$	Percentage gain in warrant $= \frac{\$10}{\$30} \times 100 = 33\%$

The use of warrants has traditionally been associated with such aggressive "high flying" firms as real estate investment trusts, airlines, and conglomerates. A perusal of the daily stock quotations in the mid-80s, however, reveals that warrants have become a very popular investment security issued by firms ranging from chartered banks to speculative mining companies.

Despite their popularity, warrants may not be as desirable as convertible securities as a financing device for creating new common stock. A corporation with convertible debentures outstanding may force the conversion of debt to common stock through a call while no similar device is available to the firm with warrants. The only possible inducement for causing an early exercise of the warrant might be a step-up in option price—whereby the warrant holder may pay a progressively higher option price if he or she does not exercise by a given date.

The capital structure of the firm after the exercise of a warrant is somewhat different from that created after the conversion of a debenture. In the case of a warrant the original debt outstanding remains in existence after the detachable warrant is exercised, whereas the conversion of a debenture extinguishes the former debt obligation.[7]

Accounting Considerations with Warrants

As with convertible securities, the potential dilutive effect of warrants must be considered. All warrants are included in computing both

[7] It should be pointed out that a number of other financing devices can blur this distinction. See Jerry Miller, "Accounting for Warrants and Convertible Bonds," *Management Accounting*, January 1973, pp. 26–28.

basic and fully diluted earnings per share.[8] The accountant must compute the number of new shares that could be created by the exercise of all warrants, with the provision that the total can be reduced by the assumed use of the cash proceeds to purchase a partially offsetting amount of shares at the market price. Assume warrants to purchase 10,000 shares at $20 are outstanding and the current price of the stock is $50. We show the following:

1. New shares created	10,000
2. Reduction of shares from cash proceeds (computed below)	4,000
Cash proceeds—10,000 shares @ $20 = $200,000	
Current price of stock—$50	
Assumed reduction in shares outstanding from cash proceeds—$200,000/$50 = 4,000	
3. Assumed net increase in shares from exercise of warrants (10,000 − 4,000)	6,000

In computing earnings per share we will add 6,000 shares to the denominator, with no adjustment to the numerator. This, of course, will lead to some dilution in earnings per share. Its importance must be interpreted by the company management and by investors alike.

Summary

A number of security devices related to the debt and common stock of the firm became popular in the 1960s and in subsequent decades. Each security offers downside protection or upside potential, or a combination of these features.

A convertible security is a bond or share of preferred stock that can be converted into common stock at the option of the holder. Thus, the holder has a fixed-income security that will not go below a minimum amount because of the interest or dividend payment feature, and at the same time he or she has a security that is potentially convertible to common stock. If the common stock goes up in value, the convertible security will appreciate as well. From a corporate viewpoint the firm may force conversion to common stock through a call feature and thus

[8]Under most circumstances, if the market price is below the option price, dilution need not be considered.

achieve a balanced capital structure. Interest rates on convertibles are usually lower than those on straight debt issues. The same is true for dividends on convertible preferred shares.

A warrant is an option to buy a stated number of shares of stock at a specified price over a given time period. The warrant has a large potential for appreciation if the stock goes up in value. Traditionally, warrants have been used primarily as sweeteners for debt instruments or as add-ons in merger tender offers. Their use as investment vehicles in recent years has become quite extensive. When warrants are exercised, the basic debt instrument to which they may have been attached is not eliminated, as is the case for a convertible debenture. The potential dilutive effect of warrants and convertible securities is an important consideration in computing earnings per share.

List of Terms

convertible security
conversion ratio
conversion price
conversion value
conversion premium
pure bond value
floor price
forced conversion
step-up in conversion
basic earnings per share
warrant
fully diluted earnings per share
financial sweetener
minimum warrant value
speculative warrant premium
leverage
intrinsic value

Discussion Questions

1. How can a company force conversion of a convertible bond?
2. What are the basic advantages to the corporation of issuing convertible securities?
3. Explain the difference between basic earnings per share and fully diluted earnings per share.

4. Why, in the case of a convertible preferred share, are investors willing to pay a premium over the theoretical value (straight preferred value or conversion value)?

5. Why is it said that convertible securities have a floor price?

6. Find the prices of the following two convertible preferred shares in a newspaper: Rogers Cablesystem Series VIII and Noranda Pref. C.

a. Explain what factors cause their prices to be different from their par values of $25.
b. What will happen to the straight preferred value if long-term interest rates decline?

7. What is meant by a step-up in the conversion price?

8. What adjustments to earnings after taxes are necessary in order to compute earnings per share when convertible preferred shares are outstanding? When warrants are outstanding?

9. Explain how convertible bonds and warrants are similar and different.

10. Explain why warrants generally are issued (why are they used in corporate finance?).

11. What are the reasons that warrants sell above their intrinsic values?

Problems

1. National Motors, Inc., has warrants outstanding that allow the holder to purchase 1.5 shares per warrant at $28 per share (option price). Thus, each individual share can be purchased at $28 under the warrant. The common stock is currently selling for $35. The warrant is selling for $14.

a. What is the intrinsic (minimum) value of this warrant?
b. What is the speculative premium on this warrant?
c. What should happen to the speculative premium as the expiration date approaches?

2. H & B Brewing Company has a convertible bond trading at 85. (Bond quotes represent percentage of par value. Thus 70 represents $700, 80 represents $800, and so on.) It matures in 10 years and carries a coupon rate of 4½ percent. The conversion price is $20, and the common stock is currently selling for $10 per share on the TSE.

   a. Compute the conversion premium.
   b. At what price does the common stock need to sell for the conversion value to be equal to the current bond price?

3. The Big Bear Manufacturing Company has a convertible bond outstanding trading in the marketplace at $850. The par value is $1,000, the coupon rate is 8 percent, and the bond matures in 20 years. The conversion price is $50, and the company's common stock is selling for $35 per share. Interest is paid semiannually.

   a. What is the conversion value?
   b. If similar bonds which are not convertible are currently yielding 12 percent, what is the pure bond value of this convertible bond? (Use semiannual analysis as described in Chapter 10.)

4. Western Olive Company of Alberta has a convertible bond outstanding with a coupon rate of 9 percent and a maturity date of 15 years. It is rated AAA, and competitive, nonconvertible bonds of the same risk class carry a 10 percent return. The conversion ratio is 25. Currently, the common stock is selling for $30 per share on the Toronto Stock Exchange.

   a. What is the conversion price?
   b. What is the conversion value?
   c. Compute the pure bond value. (Use semiannual analysis.)
   d. Draw a graph that includes the floor price and the conversion value but not the convertible bond price.
   e. Which will influence the bond price more—the pure bond value or the conversion value?

5. Alice Overland Truck Company has convertible bonds outstanding that are callable at $1,080. The bonds are convertible into 22 shares of common stock. The stock is currently selling for $58.75 per share.

a. If the firm announces it is going to call the bonds at $1,080, what action are bondholders likely to take, and why?
b. Assume that instead of the call feature the firm has the right to drop the conversion ratio from 22 down to 20 after 5 years and down to 18 after 10 years. If the bonds have been outstanding for 4 years and 11 months, what will the price of the bonds be if the stock price is $60? Assume the bonds carry no conversion premium.
c. Further assume you anticipate in two months that the common stock price will be up to $63. Considering the conversion feature, should you convert now or continue to hold the bond for at least two more months?

6. Assume you can buy a warrant for $6 that gives you the option to buy one share of common stock at $15 per share. The stock is currently selling at $18 per share.

a. What is the intrinsic value of the warrant?
b. What is the speculative premium on the warrant?
c. If the stock rises to $27 per share and the warrant sells at its theoretical value without a premium, what will be the percentage increase in the stock price and the warrant price if you bought the stock and the warrant at the prices stated above, $6 and $18? Explain this relationship.

7. The Big D Investment Company bought 100 Newsome Corporation warrants one year ago and would like to exercise them today. The warrants were purchased at $30 each, and they expire when trading ends today (assume there is no speculative premium left). Newsome common stock is selling today for $60 per share. The option price is $36, and each warrant entitles the holder to purchase two shares of stock, each at the option price.

a. If the warrants are exercised today, what would Big D's total profit or loss be?
b. What is Big D's percentage rate of return?

8. Assume in Problem 7 that Newsome common stock was selling for $50 per share when Big D Investment Company bought the warrants.

a. What was the intrinsic value of a warrant at that time?
b. What was the speculative premium per warrant when the warrants were purchased? The purchase price, as indicated above, was $30.
c. What would Big D's total dollar profit or loss have been had they invested the $3,000 directly in Newsome Corporation's common stock one year ago at $50 per share? Recall the current value is $60 per share.
d. What would the percentage rate of return be on this common stock investment? Compare this to the rate of return on the warrant computed in Problem 7*b*.

9. Mr. Hymen Flyer has $1,000 to invest in the market. He is considering the purchase of 50 shares of Volatile Corporation at $20 per share. His broker suggests he may wish to consider purchasing warrants instead. The warrants are selling for $5, and each warrant allows him to purchase one share of Volatile common stock at $18 per share.

a. How many warrants can Mr. Flyer purchase for the same $1,000?
b. If the price of this stock goes to $30, what would be his total dollar and percentage return on the stock?
c. At the time the stock goes to $30, the speculative premium on the warrant goes to 0 (though the intrinsic value of the warrant goes up). What would be Mr. Flyer's total dollar and percentage return on the warrant?
d. Assuming the speculative premium remains $3.50 over the intrinsic value, how far would the price of the stock have to fall before the warrant has no value?

10. The Bedrock Tombstone Company has net income of $350,000 in the current fiscal year. There are 100,000 shares of common stock outstanding along with convertible bonds that have a total face value of $800,000. The $800,000 is represented by 800 different $1,000 bonds. Each $1,000 bond pays 5 percent interest and was issued when the average A+ bond yield was 9 percent. The conversion ratio is 20. The tax rate is 46 percent. Calculate Bedrock's earnings per share.

11. Using the information from Problem 10, assume the average A+ bond yield was 7 percent instead of 9 percent at the time the convertible bonds were issued. All other facts are the same.

a. What are the unadjusted earnings per share for Bedrock?
b. Indicate the value for fully diluted earnings per share for Bedrock.

12. Anderson Electronics has 2 million shares of stock outstanding. It also has two convertible bond issues with terms as follows:
10 percent convertible (1999, $15,000,000)
8 percent convertible (2008, $20,000,000).
The issue with the 10 percent coupon rate was first sold when average A+ bonds were yielding 14 percent and is convertible into 400,000 shares. The issue with the 8 percent coupon rate was first sold when A+ bonds were yielding 13 percent and is convertible into 500,000 shares. Earnings after taxes are $6 million, and the tax rate is 50 percent.

a. Compute both unadjusted and fully diluted earnings per share for Anderson Electronics.
b. Now assume Anderson Electronics has warrants outstanding which allow the holder to buy 100,000 shares of stock at $30 per share. The stock is currently selling for $50 per share. Compute fully diluted earnings per share, considering the possible impact of both the warrants and convertibles.
c. Assume that in addition to the convertible bonds and the warrants, Anderson Electronics has 100,000 shares of convertible preferred stock paying $1.875 in dividends annually. Recompute fully diluted earnings per share.

13. The Loud Communications Company has $1 million in 10 percent convertible bonds outstanding. Each bond has a $1,000 par value. The conversion ratio is 50, the stock price is $24, and the bond matures in 10 years. The bonds are currently selling at a conversion premium of $100 over their conversion value.

a. If the price of Loud Communications common stock rises to $33 this date next year, what would your rate of return be if you bought a convertible bond today and sold it in one year? Assume that on this date next year the conversion premium has shrunk from $100 to $20.
b. Assume the yield on similar nonconvertible bonds has fallen to 8 percent at the time of sale. What would the pure bond value be then? (Use semiannual analysis.) Would the pure bond value have a significant effect on valuation then?

14. Lomas Exploration Ltd. has 1,000 convertible bonds ($1,000 par value) outstanding, each of which may be converted to 40 shares. The $1 million worth of bonds has 25 years to maturity. The current price of the stock is $32 per share. The firm's net income in the most recent fiscal year was $270,000. The bonds pay 12 percent interest and were issued when the average A+ bond rate was 13.2 percent. The corporation has 160,000 shares of common stock outstanding. Current market rates on long-term bonds of equal quality are 14 percent. A 50 percent tax rate is applicable.

a. Compute fully diluted earnings per share.

b. Assume the bonds currently sell at a 5 percent conversion premium over straight conversion value (based on a stock price of $32). However, as the price of the stock increases from $32 to $45 due to new events, there will be an increase in the bond price, but the conversion premium will be zero. Under these circumstances, determine the rate of return on a convertible bond investment that is part of this price change, based on the appreciation in value.

c. Now assume the stock price fell to $19 per share because a competitor introduced a new product. Would the straight conversion value be greater than the pure bond value, based on the interest rates stated above? (See Table 16–3 in Chapter 16 to get the bond value without having to go through the actual computation.)

d. Referring to part *c*, if the convertible traded at a 20 percent premium over the straight conversion value, would the convertible be priced above the pure bond value?

e. If long-term interest rates in the market go down to 10 percent while the stock price is $29, with a 6 percent conversion premium, what would the difference be between the market price of the convertible bond and the pure bond value? Assume 25 years to maturity and once again use Table 16–3 for part of your answer.

f. If Lomas were able to retire the convertibles and to replace them with 40,000 shares of common stock selling at $32 per share and paying a 5.5 percent dividend yield (dividend to price ratio), would the after-tax cash outflow related to the convertible be greater or less than the cash outflow related to the stock?

15. (*Comprehensive problem*)
AC&C (Alberta Cable and Communications) has $10 million of convertible bonds outstanding with a coupon rate of 9 percent, while interest rates are currently 7 percent for bonds of equal risk. The bonds were originally sold when the average A+ bond rate was 8 percent, and they have 20 years left to maturity. The bond may be called at a 10 percent premium as well as converted into 20 shares of common stock. The tax rate for the company is 50 percent.

AC&C common stock is currently selling for $60 per share, and it pays a dividend of $5 per share. The expected income for the company is $16.15 million on the 2 million shares of common stock currently outstanding.

Make a thorough analysis of this bond and determine whether AC&C should call the bond at the 10 percent call premium. In your analysis, consider the following:

a. The impact of the call on unadjusted and fully diluted earnings per share and the common stock price (assume the call forces conversion).
b. The consequences of your decision on future financing flexibility.
c. The net change in cash outflows to the company.
d. If the bond is called, will the stockholders take the call price or the 20 shares of common stock?
e. Assuming the bondholders could have converted the bonds into common stock whenever they desired, would you as a bondholder have waited for the company to call your bond and thereby force a decision on your part? Explain.

Selected References

Alexander, Gordon J., and Roger O. Stover. "Pricing in the New Issue Convertible Debt Market." *Financial Management* 6 (Fall 1977), pp. 35–39.

Bacon, Peter W., and Edward L. Winn, Jr. "The Impact of Forced Conversion on Stock Prices." *Journal of Finance* 24 (December 1969), pp. 871–74.

Baumol, William J.; Burton G. Malkiel; and Richard E. Quandt. "The Valuation of Convertible Securities." *Quarterly Journal of Economics* 80 (February 1966), pp. 48–59.

Black, Fischer, and Myron Scholes. "The Pricing of Options and Corporate Liabilities." *Journal of Political Economy* 81 (May-June 1973), pp. 637–54.

________. "The Valuation of Option Contracts and a Test of Market Efficiency." *Journal of Finance* 27 (May 1972), pp. 399–417.

Brealey, Richard A. *Security Prices in a Competitive Market*. Cambridge, Mass.: MIT Press, 1971, chaps. 16 and 17.

Brennan, M. J., and E. S. Schwartz. "Convertible Bonds: Valuation and Optimal Strategies for Call and Conversion." *Journal of Finance* 32 (December 1977), pp. 1699–1715.

Brigham, Eugene F. "An Analysis of Convertible Debentures: Theory and Some Empirical Evidence." *Journal of Finance* 21 (March 1966), pp. 35–54.

Chen, A. H. Y. "A Model of Warrant Pricing in a Dynamic Market." *Journal of Finance* 25 (December 1970), pp. 1041–59.

Dawson, Steve. "A Somber Fifteenth Euro-Convertible Bond Reunion." *Journal of Portfolio Management*, Winter 1985, pp. 85–87.

Frank, Werner G., and Jerry J. Weygandt. "Convertible Debt and Earnings per Share: Pragmatism vs. Good Theory." *Accounting Review* 45 (April 1970), pp. 280–89.

Hayes, Samuel L., III, and Henry B. Reiling. "Sophisticated Financing Tool: The Warrant." *Harvard Business Review* 47 (January-February 1969), pp. 137–50.

Lewellen, Wilbur G., and George A. Racette. "Convertible Debt Financing." *Journal of Financial and Quantitative Analysis* 7 (December 1973), pp. 777–92.

Marr, Wayne M., and G. Rodney Thompson. "The Pricing of New Convertible Bond Issues." *Financial Management* 13 (Summer 1984), pp. 38–40.

Mikkelson, Wayne H. "Convertible Calls and Stock Price Declines." *Financial Analysts Journal*, January-February 1985, pp. 63–69.

Miller, Jerry. "Accounting for Warrants and Convertible Bonds." *Management Accounting*, January 1973, pp. 26–28.

Pinches, George E. "Financing with Convertible Preferred Stocks, 1960–1967." *Journal of Finance* 25 (March 1970), pp. 53–64.

Rush, David F., and Ronald W. Melicher. "An Empirical Examination of Factors which Influence Warrant Prices." *Journal of Finance* 29 (December 1974), pp. 1449–66.

Samuelson, Paul A. "Rational Theory of Warrant Pricing." *Industrial Management Review* 6 (Spring 1965), pp. 13–31.

Schwartz, Eduardo S. "The Valuation of Warrants: Implementing a New Approach." *Journal of Financial Economics* 4 (January 1977), pp. 79–94.

Shelton, John P. "The Relation of the Price of a Warrant to the Price of Its Associated Stock." *Financial Analysts Journal* 23 (May-June and July-August 1967), pp. 143–51 and 88–99.

Sinkey, Joseph F., and James A. Miles. "The Use of Warrants in the Bail Out of First Pennsylvania Bank: An Application of Option Pricing." *Financial Management* 27 (Autumn 1982), pp. 27–32.

Soldofsky, Robert M. "Yield-Risk Performance of Convertible Securities." *Financial Analysts Journal* 39 (March-April 1971), pp. 61–65.

PART

SIX

Expanding the Perspective of Corporate Finance

Introduction

The final two topics, mergers and international finance, have become particularly important in the Canadian financial environment of the 1980s. This has occurred in large part as a result of decisions by corporate managements to have their firms grow and diversify away from traditional product lines and across international borders.

Managers have long viewed mergers as offering the potential for risk reduction by combining diversified business operations under common control. However, the achievement of such risk reduction can be an elusive process, as overly optimistic planners often find obstacles in their way. The successful merger must be based on realistic expectations and a careful consideration of post-merger performance. We shall evaluate both of these factors in Chapter 20.

As we enter the late 1980s mergers are occurring at a record pace in Canada. In fact, some critics have argued that buying and selling existing companies is all our entrepreneurial class knows how to do anymore.

Although tying simple typologies to anything as complex and differentiated as the Canadian industrial sector is a dangerous pastime, we might roughly classify merger activity in the past 10 years into two categories. In the late 1970s and early 1980s much of the activity was a result of decisions by large foreign-based firms to liquify their investments in Canada. Oftentimes the Canadian subsidiary no longer fit into the companies' new global strategies aimed at either rationalizing production worldwide or concentrating on a few core businesses. In other words, the thrust was not Canada as an attractive place to invest but the opposite. In the mid-1980s mergers are much more proactive as companies are often buying operating assets and market position at less than replacement cost. As to motive in this latter period, some mergers were clearly aimed at diversifying risk, while others were undertaken to reinforce the firm's ability to compete in its basic industry. Gulf Canada's $3.3 billion purchase of Hiram Walker Resources was an attempt to diversify its dependence on the oil and gas sector as a result of falling oil prices. On the other hand, Amoco Canada's proposed $5.1 billion purchase of Dome Petroleum is intended to augment Amoco's ability to be a major player in Canada's oil and gas industry.

In the merger chapter we examine the significant financial and management variables that influence the merger decision, including the price paid, the accounting implications, the stock market effect, and the motivations of the participating parties. Because merger-related decision making involves the valuation of a firm as a whole, the chapter provides an important umbrella for tying together topics discussed throughout the text.

The importance of the firm doing business globally is considered in Chapter 21. In an ever-shrinking world the financial manager must be prepared to make decisions that have worldwide effects. Because of Canada's enormous economic dependence on international trade, this issue is of great importance.

In prior chapters basic business decisions were considered primarily in terms of the direct "dollar" impact on profitability. As the business firm moves into foreign markets and deals in deutsche marks, Swiss francs, and Japanese yen, the foreign exchange implications of decisions must also be considered. For example, a firm may suddenly have to make a future payment in a currency that is rapidly appreciating in value. How is this circumstance to be handled? It is imperative that the financial manager understand his or her options in the international arena.

Although foreign investments may carry unusual political and economic risks, they also allow for expanded market potential. Local customs and requirements in regard to taxation and payment of dividends must be caefully examined.

Finally, international financing arrangements, such as the Eurodollar market and Eurobond market, which were touched on in Part Three of the book, are now given expanded coverage.

20 External Growth through Mergers

> If ever anyone creates a dance for the Canadian business community, it ought to be called the takeover tango. In the past year or so, the nation's corporate captains have shown a remarkable ability to quickstep into each other's boardrooms and waltz through some complex acquisitions and mergers.[1]

The concepts involved in financial planning, risk–return analysis, valuation, capital budgeting, and portfolio management are fundamental to any consideration of the decision-making process related to mergers and acquisitions. Thus, besides addressing a very important topic in managerial finance, Chapter 20 integrates much of the material discussed throughout the text.

[1]David Hatter, "Tripping the Light Fantastic with the Takeover Tango," *The Financial Post 500*, Summer 1986.

The Canadian Merger Environment

The 1,198 acquisitions reported in 1986 represented the greatest merger activity in Canadian history.[2] The fact that 647 of those were made by foreign entities, 437 U.S.-based, demonstrates Canada's large dependence on foreign capital, especially from U.S. multinationals.

In deals where the transaction value was over $500,000, a total of $19.3 billion was spent on acquiring 238 companies.[3] Table 20–1 summarizes some of the data on these larger mergers. The price-earnings ratios and premiums over market paid on the resource sector transactions were substantially higher than on the others, indicating that the acquirers were more optimistic about the future of this sector than was the market as a whole.

During the late 1970s and early 1980s the divestiture thrust of many large foreign-based companies led to a number of leveraged buyouts of Canadian operations that no longer had any place in the global strategy of their multinational parent companies. The implementation, in 1980, of the National Energy Policy, whose provisions favored Canadian-owned energy companies, also led to the sale of Canadian oil and gas operations by foreign companies. For example, the $4.1 billion

Table 20–1 Mergers by industry, 1986

	All Sectors	*Resource Sector*	*Manufacturing Sector*	*Service Sector*
Total value*	$19,300	$6,600	$6,900	$5,700
Number of transactions	238	50	83	107
Average value*	$81	$132	$83	$54
Average P/E	19 times	27 times	13 times	18 times
Average premium	20.6%	33.7%	14.2%	14.0%

*In millions.

Source: Harris-Bentley Limited, *Mergers and Acquisitions in Canada,* 1987.

[2]See Harris-Bentley Limited, *Mergers and Acquisitions in Canada,* 1987.

[3]One Canadian company, Olympia & York, was involved in transactions totaling almost $13 billion in 1985 and 1986.

purchase of Hudson's Bay Oil and Gas from U.S.-based Conoco by Dome Petroleum was a key ingredient in one of the most interesting and nearly disastrous sagas in Canadian corporate history. In fact, Dome spent nearly $10 billion (in 1986 inflation-adjusted dollars) on seven oil company acquisitions, while PetroCanada, created as a federal crown corporation in 1976, bought five oil companies for $6.5 billion.[4]

The major theme of the latest merger movement is that it is cheaper to acquire other companies than it is to expand through new product development or the purchase of new plant and equipment. Amoco Canada's offer of $5.1 billion for Dome Petroleum is clearly based on the premise that duplicating Dome's holdings of oil and gas reserves through drilling projects, or some other means, would be more expensive. Table 20–2 documents a number of the larger mergers that occurred in the two-year period ending in May 1987.

Table 20–2 Some large mergers involving Canadian companies, 1985–1987

Company Acquired	*Purchaser*	*Price (in thousands)*	*Percent Control Purchased*
Union Enterprises	Unicorp	$ 215,000	51%
Gulf Canada	Olympia & York	2,800,000	60
Abitibi-Price	Gulf Canada	1,200,000	89
Canada Trustco	Genstar	841,000	94
Kidd Creek Mines	Falconbridge	615,000	100
Dome Petroleum*	Amoco Canada	5,100,000	100
Hiram Walker-Gooderham & Worts	Allied-Lyons†	2,600,000	100
Hiram Walker Resources	Gulf Canada	3,300,000	70
Home Oil	Interprovincial Pipeline	1,100,000	100
Allied Stores‡	Campeau Corp.	4,900,000	100
Burlington Industries*‡	Domtex	1,800,000	100
Genstar	Imasco	2,500,000	100
Canadian Pacific Air	Pacific Western	300,000	100

*Not yet complete as of May 11, 1987.
†Great Britain-based company.
‡U.S.-based company.

[4] Jean Murphy, "Counting the Cost of the Decade's Mergers," *The Financial Post 500*, Summer 1987, pp. 61–64.

The Domino Effect of Merger Activity

An attempt by one company to buy control of another often leads to a whole series of mergers. Two of the most common reasons for this are so that: (1) the target company can avoid being taken over or (2) the acquirer can pay for what it has bought. Because so many of Canada's industrial corporations are subsidiaries of foreign multinationals, the chain of merger activity often begins with a transaction in another country.

In relation to the above, an important development in the U.S. economy has been the unfriendly buyout, in which a major acquiring company identifies a target company and attempts to acquire it without management permission. This activity spread from the oil industry with unfriendly takeover attempts by T. Boone Pickens on Gulf Oil, Phillips Petroleum, and Union Oil of California (Unocal).

The interwoven nature of Canadian and U.S. merger activity is demonstrated by the Gulf situation. To fend off Pickens, Gulf's management arranged to have the company bought by a *white knight,*[5] Chevron (formerly Standard Oil of California), for a record $13.3 billion (U.S.). In order to reduce the financial strain imposed by the large purchase price, Chevron had Gulf sell its shares of Gulf Canada for $2.8 billion (Canadian) to the Reichmann brothers' Olympia & York Corporation. However, the chain of interrelated mergers did not stop there. In order to raise the financing for the deal, Olympia & York sold to Gulf Canada its stake in Abitibi-Price, one of Canada's largest forest products companies, for $1.2 billion. Then, to raise the capital for the Abitibi-Price acquisition, Gulf Canada, in turn, sold a portion of its assets to Petro-Canada for $890 million, to Ultramar for $120 million, and to Norcen Energy for $300 million.

The ensuing decline in the price of oil then led the Reichmanns, through Gulf Canada, to make a successful unsolicited takeover bid for Hiram Walker Resources in an attempt to diversify away from an overdependence on oil and gas. The price tag on that takeover was $3.3 billion. After being taken over by Gulf, Walker then sold off its ownership of Home Oil to Interprovincial Pipeline for $1.1 billion.

---

[5]The intrigue surrounding merger manoeuverings has resulted in a colorful set of descriptive terms, some of which will be highlighted throughout this discussion.

This one chain of interrelated events not only demonstrates the linked nature of the U.S. and Canadian merger markets but also the intricacies of the financial arrangements that underlay the financing of many of the large merger transactions.

Although hostile takeovers in Canada are much less prevalent than in the United States because of the scarcity of widely held companies, they still occur. The takeover of Hiram Walker by Gulf Canada and that of Union Enterprises by Unicorp are two notable recent examples. In the latter situation the target gas utility company spent $125 million to buy a meat packing company, Burns Foods. By swallowing a so-called *poison pill* a takeover target contrives to have more debt and/or less liquid assets to become less attractive to the would-be acquirer. In the Hiram Walker situation, the acquisition target made a deal to sell its *crown jewel,* its distilling operations, to Allied-Lyons of Britain for $2.6 billion.[6] In neither case did the *shark repellent* strategy adopted fend off the would-be acquirer although it did increase the overall costs of the transaction and make the final prize less valuable to the buyer.

Foreign Acquisitions

A relatively recent phenomenon has been the increased tendency of firms from Canada and other countries to purchase major U.S. firms. Data show that non-U.S. purchasers accounted for 13 percent of the dollar value of all merger deals in the U.S. market in 1985—double the 1984 volume.

In 1986 Robert Campeau of Toronto executed a successful $4.9 billion bid to take over Allied Stores of New York. His success against Allied's chosen white knight, Edward DiBartolo, was due to the financial support of his U.S. investment advisors and also their ingenuity in assembling the required block of shares. Campeau's stated objective was to diversify his company's dependence on the Canadian real estate market. Purchases of retail chains have been popular in recent years because of the so-called *hidden assets* on the balance sheet in terms of real estate worth far more than its stated value on the books.

---

[6]Part of Allied-Lyons' reason for making the bid for Walker was to make itself too expensive to be taken over by Elders IXL Ltd., a brewing company based in Australia. The much smaller Elders had bid $3.3 billion, which it intended to borrow, for Allied.

As this is written, another Canadian firm, Domtex, has offered $2 billion for Burlington Industries of North Carolina. Domtex's intent is to strengthen its capability to compete effectively in the North American textile industry in anticipation of a free trade agreement between Canada and the United States. Burlington, although much larger than Domtex, seemed available as a takeover target because of disenchantment with its management by the investment community. Among Burlington's responses has been a threat to invoke a *Pac-Man defence* whereby it would attempt to buy control of Domtex before Domtex gained control of it. Just as in the electronic video game, the winner is the company that swallows the other first.

Government Regulation of Takeovers

Who knows what company will be a takeover target by the time you read this chapter. The absolute size of the recent merger deals listed in Table 20–2 and the corporate concentration they imply has caused some to be concerned. Unlike in the United States, where fears of undue corporate concentration have been entrenched in antitrust laws since the beginning of the 20th century, Canadians have generally been unconcerned about high concentration levels of corporate power.[7] However, on June 19, 1986, the Competition Act came into force replacing the toothless Combines Investigation Act.[8] The new act makes a merger or acquisition illegal if it "lessens competition substantially in a given market." Importantly, charges under the new act are civil rather than criminal which increases the chances of a conviction if, in fact, competition will be seriously impaired by a merger. The Bureau of Competition Policy, which reviews the merger in relation to the act, can prohibit an acquisition, order sale of certain assets as part of its approval, or even unwind a completed deal. Although there is no doubt the new act will make private firms more reluctant to propose merger deals because of the possibility of public disclosure of details, it remains to be seen if it has any effect on the mega-transactions involving public entities.

[7]See, for example, Minister of Supply and Services Canada, *Report of the Royal Commission on Corporate Concentration*, 1978.

[8]Under the Combines Investigation Act there had never been a single successful prosecution of a merger in a contested case in 75 years.

If Canadians have been generally unconcerned about corporate concentration, the same cannot be said about foreign ownership. Canadian nationalists made this a major political issue during the 1960s, which led to the establishment of the Foreign Investment Review Agency (FIRA) under the Foreign Investment Review Act by the early 1970s. Under the watchful eye of FIRA virtually no large takeovers of Canadian firms by foreigners occurred. However, FIRA was replaced by Investment Canada in 1984 in an attempt to make Canada a more hospitable place for foreign capital. In late 1986 and early 1987 a number of Canadian companies, including Carling O'Keefe, Husky Oil, and British Columbia Forest Products, were taken over by foreign companies.

Investment Canada requires there be some evidence that the takeover of a Canadian company by a foreign entity will result in a net gain for Canada as a whole. In the Amoco Canada proposal to take over Dome Petroleum, Amoco's Chicago-based parent company stated publicly it would refrain from repatriating any dividends to the United States for five years. That commitment was an attempt to calm Canadian fears about oil industry profits flowing south of the 49th parallel rather than being reinvested in Canadian industry. However, the fact that the proposed takeover is so large in a politically sensitive industry may still test the resolve of the present Canadian government to encourage foreign investment.

In the rest of this chapter we shall examine in more general terms the motives for business combinations; the establishment of negotiated terms of exchange, with the associated accounting implications; and the stock market effect of mergers (including unfriendly takeovers). In the final section of the chapter we examine the holding company device.

Motives for Business Combinations

In Canada there is no specific definition of what constitutes a merger. In contrast, the term *merger* in the United States denotes the acquisition of one company by another followed by the liquidation of the acquired company into the acquiring company. Such rarely happens in Canada. Instead, the acquirer usually buys a majority, sometimes all of the voting shares of the selling company, but both remain after the acquisition as separate legal entities. This normal situation in Canada is commonly referred to by both the merger and acquisition labels.

The term *amalgamation* does, however, have a precise legal definition in Canada. An amalgamation is a statutory combination under one of the provincial corporations or companies acts, the Canada Corporations Act, or the Canada Business Corporations Act. In this chapter we will use the term *merger* to connote any transaction by which two or more companies are combined, either under a statutory amalgamation or just in terms of ownership.

Financial Motives

The motives for mergers are both financial and nonfinancial in nature. We examine the financial motives first. As discussed in Chapter 13, a merger allows the acquiring firm to enjoy a potentially desirable *portfolio effect* by achieving risk reduction while perhaps maintaining the firm's rate of return. If two firms that benefit from opposite phases of the business cycle combine, their variability in performance may be reduced. Risk-averse investors may then discount the future performance of the merged firm at a lower rate and thus assign it a higher valuation than was assigned to the separate firms. The same point can be made in regard to multinational mergers. Through merger a firm with holdings in diverse economic and political climates can enjoy some reduction in the risks that derive from foreign exchange translation, government politics, military takeovers, and localized recessions.

While the portfolio diversification effect of a merger is intellectually appealing—with each firm becoming a mini-internal capital market unto itself—the practicalities of the situation can become quite complicated. One of the major forces of merger activity in the mid- to late 1960s was the desire for diversification. A lesson we have learned from the frenzied takeover strategies of many U.S.-based conglomerates of that time is that too much diversification can strain the managerial capabilities of a firm, even one with excellent management talent. One form of evidence of the lack of success of some mergers is the fact that many of the acquisitions we see involve the sale of a previously acquired subsidiary by one company to another. For example, after undertaking a diversification strategy for decades, Canadian Pacific initiated a divestiture program which moved it out of the airline and mining industries in a very short time span. Divestiture programs are usually undertaken either to reduce the debt incurred under the old acquisition strategies or to redeploy assets consistent with new corporate strategies.

A second financial motive is the *improved financing posture* a merger can create as a result of expansion in size. Larger firms may enjoy greater access to financial markets and thus be in a better position to raise debt and equity capital. Such firms may also be able to attract larger and more prestigious investment bankers to handle future financing.

Greater financing capability may also be inherent in the merger itself. This is likely to be the case if the acquired firm has a strong cash position or a low debt-equity ratio that can be used to expand borrowing by the acquiring company.

One of the popular acquisition devices in the 1980s has been the leveraged buyout. As discussed in Chapter 15, the leveraged buyout results when either existing management or an outsider makes an offer to "go private" by retiring all the shares of the company. The buying group borrows the necessary money, using the assets of the acquired firm as collateral. The buying group then repurchases all the shares and expects to retire the debt over time with the cash flow from operations or the sale of corporate assets.

A final financial motive is the *tax loss carry-forward* that might be available in a merger if one of the firms has previously sustained a tax loss. An operating loss may be carried forward up to seven years.[9] In any event, a tax loss carry-forward must be used up as quickly as possible when there are offsetting profits. In situations like the Dome merger mentioned earlier in the chapter, where the potential acquiree has incurred substantial losses in recent years, the tax loss carry-forward may provide significant value to an acquiring company.

As an example of tax loss benefits, assume Firm A acquires Firm B, which has a $220,000 tax loss carry-forwrd. We look at Firm A's financial position before and after the merger. Based on the carry-forward, the company is able to reduce its total taxes from $120,000 to $32,000, and thus it could pay $88,000 for the carry-forward alone

---

[9]Revenue Canada might challenge the use of tax loss carry-forwards in the case of a merger whose only purpose was to gain the tax shields associated with the carry-forwards. The expectation is that the acquirer will run and operate the company after purchase, not just liquidate it.

(this is on a nondiscounted basis). The tax shield value of a carry-forward is equal to the loss involved times the tax rate ($220,000 × 40 percent = $88,000).

	1988	*1989*	*1990*	*Total Values*
Firm A (without merger):				
Before-tax income	$100,000	$100,000	$100,000	$300,000
Taxes (40%)	40,000	40,000	40,000	120,000
Income available to stockholders	$ 60,000	$ 60,000	$ 60,000	$180,000
Firm A (with merger and associated tax benefits):				
Before-tax income	$100,000	$100,000	$100,000	$300,000
Tax loss carry-forward	100,000	100,000	20,000	220,000
Net taxable income	0	0	80,000	80,000
Taxes (40%)	0	0	32,000	32,000
Income available to stockholders	$100,000	$100,000	$ 68,000	$268,000

As would be expected, income available to stockholders has gone up by a like amount ($268,000 − $180,000 = $88,000). Of course, Firm B's anticipated operating gains and losses for future years must also be taken into consideration in arriving at a purchase price.

Nonfinancial Motives

The nonfinancial motives for mergers and consolidations include the desire to expand management and marketing capabilities as well as the acquisition of new products. Companies in traditional lines of business may attempt to expand into more dynamic industries in order to upgrade their image. Bell Canada is an example of a company that is expanding away from its regulated telephone core business, while acquisitions by large real estate companies like Olympia & York and Campeau are aimed at redeploying some assets in more exciting areas.

While mergers may be directed toward either horizontal integration (that is, the acquisition of competitors) or vertical integration (the acquisition of buyers or sellers of goods and services to the company), the new competition laws should preclude the substantial elimination of competition. For this reason mergers may become directed more toward companies in allied but not directly related fields. The pure conglomerate merger of firms in totally unrelated firms is still undertaken but after more careful deliberation than in the past.

Perhaps the greatest management motive for a merger is the possible synergistic effect. Synergy is said to take place when the whole is greater than the sum of the parts. This "2 + 2 = 5" effect may be the result of eliminating overlapping functions in production and marketing as well as meshing together various engineering and administrative capabilities. In terms of planning related to mergers, there is often a tendency to overestimate the possible synergistic benefits that might accrue.[10]

Motives of Selling Stockholders

Most of our discussion has revolved around the motives of the acquiring firm that initiates a merger. Likewise, the selling stockholders may be motivated by a desire to receive the acquiring company's stock—which may have greater acceptability or activity in the marketplace than the stock they hold. Also when cash is offered instead of stock, this gives the selling stockholders an opportunity to diversify their holdings into many new investments. As will be discussed later in the chapter, the selling stockholders generally receive an attractive price for their stock that may well exceed its current market or book value. An exchange offer may represent an opportunity to get a value approaching the replacement costs for their assets in an inflationary environment.

In addition, officers of the selling company may receive attractive postmerger management contracts as well as directorships in the acquiring firm. In some circumstances they may be allowed to operate the company as a highly autonomous subsidiary after the merger (though this is probably the exception).[11]

---

[10]T. Hogarty, "The Profitability of Corporate Mergers," *Journal of Business* 43 (July 1970), pp. 317–27.

[11]This is most likely to happen when the acquiring firm is in a different business and therefore not likely to try and integrate the acquired company into the operating system of its new parent.

A final motive of the selling stockholders may simply be the bias against smaller businesses that has developed in this country and around the world. Real clout in the financial markets may dictate being part of a larger organization. These motives should not be taken as evidence that all or even most officers or directors of smaller firms wish to sell out—a matter we shall examine further when we discuss negotiated offers versus takeover attempts.

Terms of Exchange

In determining the price that will be paid for a potential acquisition, a number of factors are considered, including earnings, dividends, and growth potential. We shall divide our analysis between cash purchases and stock-for-stock exchanges in which the acquiring company trades stock rather than paying cash for the acquired firm.

Cash Purchases

The cash purchase of another company can be viewed within the context of a capital budgeting decision. Instead of purchasing new plant or machinery, the purchaser has opted to acquire a *going concern*. For example, assume that the Invest Corporation is analyzing the acquisition of the Sell Corporation for $1 million. The Sell Corporation has expected cash flow (after-tax earnings plus depreciation) of $100,000 per year for the next 5 years and $150,000 per year for the 6th through the 20th year. Furthermore, the synergistic benefits of the merger (in this case, combining production facilities) will deduct $10,000 per year from operating costs. Finally, the Sell Corporation has a $50,000 tax loss carry-forward that can be used immediately by the Invest Corporation. Assuming a 40 percent tax rate, the $50,000 loss carry-forward will generate $20,000 extra in after-tax profits immediately. The Invest Corporation has a 10 percent cost of capital, and this is assumed to remain stable with the merger. Our analysis would be as follows:

Cash outflow:	
Purchase price	$1,000,000
Less tax shield benefit from tax loss carry-forward ($50,000 × 40%)	20,000
Net cash outflow	$ 980,000

Cash inflows:		
Years 1–5: $100,000	Cash inflow	
10,000	Synergistic benefit	
$110,000	Total cash inflow	
Present value of $110,000 × 3.791		$ 417,010
Years 6–20: $150,000	Cash inflow	
10,000	Synergistic benefit	
$160,000	Total cash inflow	
Present value of 160,000 × 4.723		755,680
Total present value of inflows		$1,172,690

The present value factor for the first five years (3.791) is based on $n = 5, i = 10$ percent, and can be found in Appendix D. For the 6th through the 20th year, we take the present value factor in Appendix D for $n = 20, i = 10$ percent, and subtract from this the present value factor for $n = 5, i = 10$ percent. This allows us to isolate the 6th through the 20th year with a factor of 4.723 (8.514 − 3.791).

The net present value of the investment is:

Total present value of inflows	$1,172,690
Net cash outflow	980,000
Net present value	$ 192,690

The acquisition appears to represent a desirable alternative for the expenditure of cash with a positive net present value of $192,690. As previously indicated, in the market environment of the late 1970s and 1980s many firms could be purchased at a value below the replacement costs of their assets and thus represented a potentially desirable capital investment.

Stock-for-Stock Exchange

On a stock-for-stock exchange we use a somewhat different analytical approach, emphasizing the earnings per share impact of exchanging securities (and ultimately the market valuation of those earnings). The analysis is primarily from the viewpoint of the acquiring firm. The shareholders of the acquired firm are concerned mainly about the initial price they are paid for their shares and about the outlook for the acquiring firm.

Assume Expand Corporation is considering the acquisition of Small Corporation. Significant financial information on the firms before the merger is provided in Table 20–3.

We begin our analysis with the assumption that one share of Expand Corporation ($30) will be traded for one share of Small Corporation ($30). (In actuality, Small Corporation will probably demand more than $30 per share because the acquired firm usually gets some premium over the current market value. We will later consider the impact of paying such a premium.)

If 50,000 new shares of Expand Corporation are traded in exchange for all the old shares of Small Corporation, Expand Corporation will then have 250,000 shares outstanding. At the same time, its claim to earnings will go to $700,000 when the two firms are combined. Postmerger earnings per share will be $2.80 for the Expand Corporation, as indicated in Table 20–4.

A number of observations are worthy of note. First, the earnings per share of Expand Corporation have increased as a result of the merger, rising from $2.50 to $2.80. This has occurred because Expand Corporation's P/E ratio was higher than that of Small Corporation at the time of the merger (12 versus 7.5). *Whenever a firm acquires another*

Table 20–3
Financial data on potential merging firms

	Small Corporation	*Expand Corporation*
Total earnings	$200,000	$500,000
Number of shares of stock outstanding	50,000	200,000
Earnings per share	$4.00	$2.50
Price–earnings ratio (P/E)	7.5 ×	12 ×
Market price per share	$30.00	$30.00

Table 20–4
Postmerger earnings per share

Total earnings: Small ($200,000) + Expand ($500,000)	$700,000
Shares outstanding in surviving corporation: Old (200,000) + New (50,000)	250,000

$$\text{New earnings per share for Expand Corporation} = \frac{\$700{,}000}{250{,}000} = \$2.80$$

entity whose P/E ratio is lower than its own, there is an immediate increase in earnings per share. The P/E ratio comparison is an important variable we shall follow closely in our subsequent discussion.

As previously indicated, it is unlikely Small Corporation will give up its shares at the current market value of $30 per share. We shall now assume that Expand Corporation is willing to pay 33 percent over market value. This would imply that the shareholders of Small Corporation would receive $40 worth of stock for each share of stock outstanding. Since Expand shares are trading at $30 per share, it must offer 1⅓ shares of Expand Corporation for each share of Small Corporation. This means Expand Corporation will have to issue 66,667 new shares (50,000 old shares of Small Corporation × 1⅓). Postmerger earnings per share for Expand Corporation are now shown in Table 20–5 to be $2.62.

Even though Expand Corporation has paid the shareholders of Small Corporation a 33 percent premium over market value, it has still been able to increase its earnings per share from $2.50 premerger (Table 20–4) to $2.62 postmerger (Table 20–5). Why? Once again its P/E ratio was higher than that paid to Small Corporation in the exchange transaction. Expand Corporation enjoys a P/E of 12 times earnings, while Small Corporation was purchased at a 33 percent premium over its current P/E of 7.5, or at 10 times earnings. As previously stated, whenever a firm purchases another company at a lower P/E ratio than its own, there is an immediate increase in earnings per share.

One might also wish to determine whether the stockholders of Small Corporation have benefited from the latest suggested merger transaction. In terms of market values they have come out ahead, whereas in terms of earnings per share they have lost out. Both results are indicated in Table 20–6.

Previous research has indicated that stockholders of the *acquired* company are more concerned with the market value exchanged than

Table 20–5
Adjusted postmerger earnings per share

Total earnings: Small ($200,000) + Expand ($500,000)	$700,000
Shares outstanding in surviving corporation:	
Old (200,000) + New (66,667)	266,667

$$\text{New earnings per share for Expand Corporation} = \frac{\$700{,}00}{266{,}667} = \$2.62$$

Table 20–6
Postmerger analysis of the acquired firm

A. *Trade in market value*
One share of Small Corporation ($30) traded for 1⅓ shares of Expand Corporation ($40 total value)
Gain: $10

B. *Trade in earnings per share*
One share of Small Corporation previously represented $4.00 in earnings per share (Table 20–3): 1⅓ shares of Expand Corporation represent $3.48 in earnings per share (the $2.62 postmerger value in Table 20–5 times 1.33)
Dilution in earnings per share: $0.52

with the earnings, dividends, or book value exchanged.[12] Thus, the $10 increase in market value will probably compensate for the decrease in the claims to earnings per share.[13] The stockholders can always sell out after the merger and take a $10 capital gain. At times, however, stockholders may be concerned about trading or maintaining parity in dividends per share. The acquiring company may offer fixed-income securities as well as common stock to maintain parity.

Long-Term Considerations

In Table 20–5 we showed the earnings per share for Expand Corporation to be $2.62 as a result of the merger—a 12-cent gain over the premerger figure of $2.50. Although Expand Corporation is enjoying an *immediate* appreciation in earnings per share, we must still consider the long-run impact of the merger and its influence on our ultimate objective of market value maximization.

Consider this: The reason Expand Corporation was able to enjoy an immediate appreciation in earnings per share as a result of the merger was that it had a higher P/E ratio than Small Corporation. The reason for Expand's higher P/E ratio may be that it had superior growth

[12]Frank K. Reilly, "What Determines the Ratio of Exchange in Corporate Mergers?" *Financial Analysts Journal* 18 (November–December 1962), pp. 47–50. Also Lynn E. Dellenbarger, "A Study of Relative Stock Equity Values in Fifty Mergers of Listed Industrial Corporations, 1950–57," *Journal of Finance* 18 (September 1963), p. 565.

[13]Earnings-per-share parity would indicate an exchange ratio of 1.6 Expand Corporation shares for each Small Corporation share ($4.00/2.50 = 1.6). The $4.00 represents Small Corporation's premerger EPS, while the $2.50 is Expand Corporation's premerger EPS.

prospects, less risk, a better product in the marketplace, more rigorous accounting procedures, or a number of other factors.

We shall assume for now the differential in the P/E ratios can be explained in large measure by differing growth prospects. Perhaps Expand Corporation, without the merger, could be expected to grow at 10 percent per year, while Small Corporation would only grow by 6 percent. Since Expand Corporation is initially contributing $50,000 to earnings and Small Corporation $20,000, the postmerger weighting on earnings is five sevenths and two sevenths, respectively. Without considering any postmerger operating benefits (synergy), the new weighted growth rate for Expand Corporation after the merger would be:

$$\frac{5}{7}(10\%) + \frac{2}{7}(6\%) = 7.14\% + 1.71\% = 8.85\%$$

The net effect is that Expand Corporation will suffer a decline of 1.15 percent in its growth rate at the same time it enjoys a 12-cent immediate increase in earnings per share ($2.50 to $2.62). We look at the combined effect of these two variables in Table 20–7 as we extend the time horizon to 10 years.

Table 20–7
Anticipated earnings per share for Expand Corporation with and without the merger, over 10 years

	Without Merger			With Merger (Small Corporation)		
Year	Beginning Earnings per Share	Growth Rate	Anticipated Earnings per Share	Beginning Earnings per Share	Growth Rate	Anticipated Earnings per Share
1	$2.50	10%	$2.75	$2.62	8.85%	$2.85
2	2.75		3.03	2.85		3.10
3	3.30		3.33	3.10		3.37
4	3.33		3.66	3.37		3.66
5	3.66		4.03	3.66		3.98
6	4.03		4.43	3.98		4.33
7	4.43		4.87	4.33		4.71
8	4.87		5.36	4.71		5.13
9	5.36		5.90	5.13		5.58
10	5.90		6.49	5.58		6.07

Although earnings per share will be 12 cents higher immediately as a result of the merger, the slower postmerger growth rate of 8.85 percent indicates that after four years there is an indifference point between earnings with and without the merger (at $3.66). After 10 years *not merging* would actually provide 42 cents more in earnings per share ($6.49 versus $6.07). The long-term dilutive effect on earnings is the result of the differential growth rates and the absence of synergy. If the merger produced synergy by increasing the operating effectiveness of the combined firms by 15 percent, the immediate effect would be to increase earnings per share to $3.01 ($2.62 × 1.15) and 10th-year earnings to $6.98 ($6.07 × 1.15). Nevertheless, as has been pointed out, synergistic benefits may be difficult to achieve.

Buying a Company at a Higher P/E Ratio

As an alternative strategy, assume Expand Corporation is considering the acquisition of Growth Corporation. Although Growth Corporation is currently the same in size as Small Corporation, it enjoys a relatively high P/E ratio (14×) and a strong anticipated growth in earnings per share (18 percent). Financial information for Growth Corporation is presented in Table 20–8 along with data for Expand Corporation.

In order to effect a merger, we shall assume Expand Corporation will pay the shareholders of Growth Corporation a 40 percent premium over market value. With each share of Growth Corporation currently selling at $56 per share, this would indicate a price of $78.40 per share ($56 × 1.4). To purchase 50,000 shares of Growth Corporation, the total value exchanged would be $3,920,000.

Table 20–8
Financial data for potential merging firms

	Growth Corporation	*Expand Corporation*
Total earnings	$200,000	$500,000
Number of shares of stock outstanding	50,000	200,000
Earnings per share	$4.00	$2.50
Price–earnings ratio (P/E)	14 ×	12 ×
Market price per share	$56.00	$30.00
Growth rate in earnings per share	18%	10%

$78.40	Price per share
× 50,000	Shares
$3,920,000	Total price

Since $30 shares of Expand Corporation are to be traded in the merger, 130,667 shares must be given to the shareholders of Growth Corporation.

$$\frac{\text{Purchase price}}{\text{Value of Expand}} = \frac{\$3{,}920{,}000}{\$30} = 130{,}667 \text{ shares}$$

Postmerger earnings per share are $2.12, as indicated in Table 20–9.

The earnings per share of Expand Corporation have been diluted from $2.50 to $2.12 as a result of the merger. Once again, the reason can be found in the relative P/E ratios. Growth Corporation is being purchased at a 40 percent premium over its current P/E ratio of 14, or at 19.6 times earnings. Since Expand Corporation's P/E ratio is only 12, dilution has set in. Nevertheless, a strong inducement factor for Expand Corporation is the high rate of increase in earnings per share of 18 percent for the Growth Corporation. On a weighted basis, this will increase the postmerger earnings per share growth rate of Expand Corporation to 12.28 percent.

$$\frac{5}{7}(10\%) + \frac{2}{7}(18\%) = 7.14\% + 5.14\% = 12.28\%$$

Rounding to 12.3 percent, the anticipated stream of future earnings for Expand Corporation with and without the Growth Corporation merger is indicated in Table 20–10.

In spite of the initial dilution in earnings per share, Expand Corporation will eventually benefit from the merger with 10th-year earnings per share at a level 30 cents higher than without merger. If the

Table 20–9
Postmerger earnings per share

Total earnings: Growth ($200,000) + Expand ($500,000).	$700,000
Shares outstanding in surviving corporation:	
Old (200,000) + New (130,667)	330,667

$$\text{New earnings per share for Expand Corporation} = \frac{\$700{,}000}{330{,}667} = \$2.12$$

Table 20–10
Anticipated earnings for Expand Corporation with and without a merger with Growth Corporation, over 10 years

	Without Merger			With Merger (Growth Corporation)		
Year	Beginning Earnings per Share	Growth Rate	Anticipated Earnings per Share	Beginning Earnings per Share	Growth Rate	Anticipated Earnings per Share
1	$2.50	10%	$2.75	$2.12	12.3%	$2.38
2	2.75		3.03	2.38		2.67
3	3.03		3.33	2.67		3.00
4	3.33		3.66	3.00		3.37
5	3.66		4.03	3.37		3.79
6	4.03		4.43	3.79		4.26
7	4.43		4.87	4.26		4.79
8	4.87		5.36	4.79		5.38
9	5.36		5.90	5.38		6.04
10	5.90		6.49	6.04		6.79

analysis is extended to 15 years, the difference between the two alternatives becomes approximately $1.70. Although it may take a dilutive, high-growth acquisition longer to show positive benefits, the eventual gains may be substantial. Of course, the presence of synergy would shorten the break-even period and expand the long-term positive benefits.

A comparison of the two merger plans with a nonmerger strategy for Expand Corporation is presented in Figure 20–1.

The earnings-per-share impact of a merger is influenced by the exchange ratio (relative price-earnings ratios as reflected in the terms), the relative growth rates of the firms, and the relative sizes of the firms. In regard to the last variable, if Growth Corporation had the same earnings as Expand Corporation, there would be a tremendous dilution in earnings per share down to $1.90, followed by an annual increase in earnings per share of 14 percent. Earnings per share would grow to over $7 after 10 years.

Market Value Maximization

The basic merger plans diagrammed in Figure 20–1 indicate the possibilities in buying a slow-growth firm at a relatively low P/E ratio and a high-growth firm at a relatively high P/E ratio. There is no right or wrong decision as such. The ultimate answer lies in the concept of market value maximization. We must try to assess how shareholders (present and potential) will view the merger. Thus, we must consider not only the immediate impact on earnings per share but also the effect on the surviving firm's postmerger P/E ratio. While the merger with Small Corporation will increase Expand Corporation's earnings per share from \$2.50 to \$2.62, will there be a decrease in Expand Cor-

Figure 20–1
Impact of alternative plans on Expand Corporation

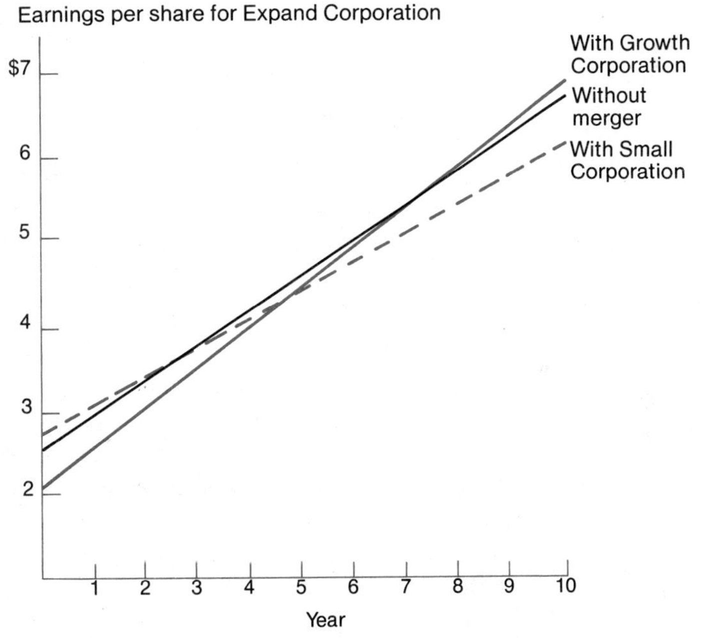

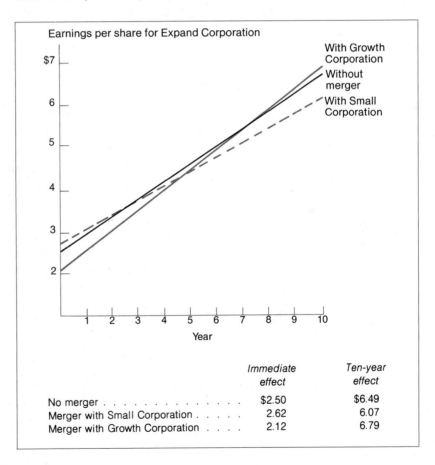

	Immediate effect	Ten-year effect
No merger	\$2.50	\$6.49
Merger with Small Corporation	2.62	6.07
Merger with Growth Corporation	2.12	6.79

poration's postmerger P/E ratio because of the decrease in the corporate growth rate from 10 percent to 8.85 percent? Similarly, will the dilution in earnings per share from $2.50 to $2.12 as a result of the Growth Corporation acquisition be more than offset by an imposing increase in the corporate growth rate from 10 percent to 12.3 percent and a possible increase in the P/E ratio? In Table 20–11 we look at possible postmerger P/E ratios and stock prices for Expand Corporation, assuming a merger with Growth Corporation.

Undoubtedly, a corporate treasurer would like to study all these possibilities in the context of a premerger price of $30 per share. Based on similar experiences of other companies in the industry or on past corporate history, relative probabilities of outcomes may be assigned and the expected value determined. (See Problem 9 at the end of the chapter.)

Portfolio Effect

Inherent in all our discussion is the importance of the merger's portfolio effect on the risk-return posture of the firm. The reduction or increase in risk may influence the P/E ratio as much as the change in the growth rate. To the extent we are diminishing the overall risk of the firm in a merger, the P/E ratio may increase even if the potential earnings growth is unchanged. Business risk reduction may be achieved through acquiring another firm that is influenced by a set of factors in the business cycle opposite from those that influence our own firm, while financial risk reduction may be achieved by restructuring our postmerger financial arrangements to include less debt.

Table 20–11
Postmerger valuation based on increased level of P/E ratio (current level of 12)*

	Potential Increase in P/E Ratio (percent)				
	1%	*10%*	*20%*	*30%*	*40%*
New P/E ratio	12.1 ×	13.2 ×	14.4 ×	15.6 ×	16.8 ×
Postmerger earnings	$2.12	$2.12	$2.12	$2.12	$2.12
Postmerger market value	$25.65	$27.98	$30.53	$33.07	$35.62

*Additional analysis could also be done based on a declining P/E ratio.

Perhaps Expand Corporation is diversifying from a heavy manufacturing industry into the real estate/housing industry. While heavy manufacturing industries move with the business cycle, the real estate/housing industry tends to be countercyclical. Even though the expected value of earnings per share may remain relatively constant as a result of the merger, the standard deviation of possible outcomes may decline as a result of risk reduction through diversification, as is indicated in Figure 20–2.

We see that the expected value of the earnings per share has remained constant in this instance but that the standard deviation has gone down. Because there is less risk in the corporation, the investor may be willing to assign a higher valuation, thus increasing the price-earnings ratio.

Like synergy, however, countercyclical effects are hard to capture as the relationships of different businesses to the general business cycle vary somewhat over time. In addition, some have argued persuasively that it is more efficient for the shareholder to diversify his or her portfolio than it is for an individual firm to do so. The final irony is that because diversified companies are so difficult to classify as to business prospects, and so forth, they often command a lower P/E than the average of those that would have been assigned to the individual parts. This is one of the reasons diversified companies, like Canadian Pacific at present, periodically decide to go through massive divestments to concentrate on fewer businesses.

Figure 20–2
Risk reduction portfolio benefits

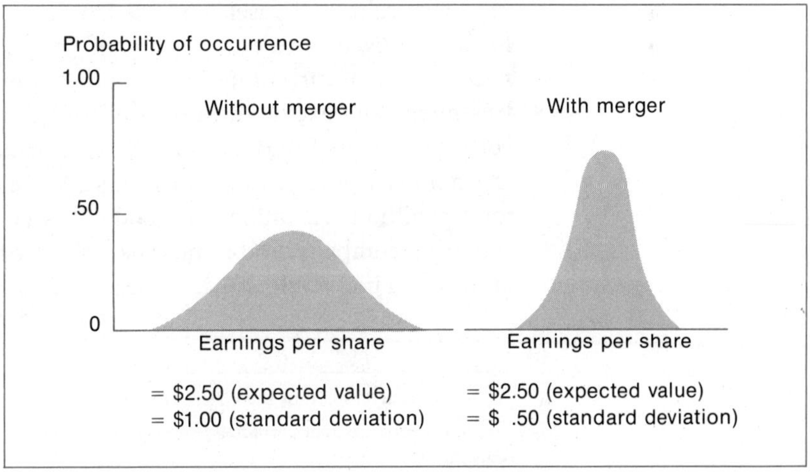

Accounting Considerations in Mergers and Acquisitions

Over the past 20 years the role of financial accounting has probably had no greater significance than in the area of mergers and acquisitions. When a price substantially above book value is paid for a potential acquisition, goodwill may be created on the books of the acquiring firm, and the writing off of this goodwill over time can have a negative impact on earnings per share. Most firms would like to avoid the creation of goodwill if at all possible. Let's see what the issues and the options are.

A merger can be treated on the books of the acquiring firm as either a *pooling of interests* or a *purchase of assets.* Business combinations in which the ownership interests of two or more companies are joined through an exchange of shares and in which none of the parties involved can be identified as an acquirer can be considered pooling of interests. The financial statements of the firms are combined, subject to some minor adjustments, and no goodwill is created.[14] Pooling of interest accounting treatment is rare since the adoption of the foregoing definition by the accounting profession in the early 1970s. Its widespread use up until that time, however, does make an understanding of the pooling of interest method useful.

Goodwill may be created when the second type of merger recording—a purchase of assets—is used. Because of the criteria described for a pooling of interests, a purchase of assets treatment is generally necessary in all current mergers. Under a purchase of assets accounting treatment, any excess of purchase price over book value must be recorded as goodwill and written off over a maximum period of 40 years.[15] If a company purchases a firm with a $4 million book value (net worth) for $6 million, $2 million of goodwill is created on the books of the acquiring company, and it must be written off over a period of 40 years or less.[16] This would cause at least a $50,000-per-year reduction in

[14]See Section 1580.10 of the *CICA Handbook.*

[15]An exception is that certain assets may be revalued upward at the time of merger, thus reducing the magnitude of the goodwill created.

[16]Because of the premiums often paid to induce a possible acquisition, payments well in excess of book value are not unusual.

reported earnings ($2 million/40 years).[17] Goodwill is classified as an *eligible capital expenditure* under the Income Tax Act. As such, one half can be amortized for tax purposes at a rate of 10 percent on a declining balance basis (similar to the CCA treatment discussed in Chapter 12).

The main reason we look at the pooling of interests versus the purchase of assets accounting treatment is to recognize the potentially beneficial effect, historically but not currently, to a corporation of exchanging common stock rather than nonequity compensation (cash, bonds, preferred stock, and so on) and thus perhaps qualifying as a pooling of interests. Although merely issuing common stock no longer qualifies for a pooling treatment, a share exchange more readily qualifies a merger for a tax-free exchange under Sections 85(1) or 87(4) of the Income Tax Act. Under a tax-free exchange the stockholders of the acquired firm may defer any capital gains taxes until the newly acquired shares have actually been sold. Thus, there would be no immediate tax for trading a share of stock in Growth Corporation that was purchased 10 years ago at $5 for $78.40 in Expand Corporation stock. If and when the Expand Corporation stock is sold, the tax will be recognized. If the tender offer were $78.40 in cash, there would be an immediate tax obligation.

In analyzing accounting and tax considerations, we see that up until the early 1970s, the acquiring corporation had some inducement to offer common stock to qualify as a pooling of interests when the exchange offer exceeded book value. We also see that the stockholders of the acquired firm still have some incentive to receive common stock when the exchange offer exceeds their initial cost basis in order to avoid immediate taxes. During the 1960s and part of the 1970s, common stock, often supplemented by convertible securities and warrants, was a frequently used mode of exchange.[18] In the merger movement of the late 1970s and in the 1980s, cash offers have come into vogue.

Why? First of all, stockholders of the acquired firms have become somewhat disenchanted with the performance of the acquiring companies' stock and, at times, the stock market in general. For this reason

[17]According to the *CICA Handbook*, Section 1580.58, goodwill should be amortized using the straight-line method over its estimated life but not to exceed 40 years. The auditors will often recommend a shorter amortization period.

[18]The popularity of the last two items was reduced somewhat in January 1970 by the introduction of tough new accounting standards for the dilutive effects of convertibles and warrants, as described in Chapter 19.

they have been willing to take cash, pay a tax, and invest in a new, diversified set of investments. Acquiring corporations have gone along with the cash tender offer pattern in order to satisfy the demands of selling stockholders.

Also by using cash instead of stock, a corporation may diminish the perceived dilutive effect of a merger. If Small Corporation or Growth Corporation had been acquired for straight cash by Expand Corporation, no new shares would have been issued, and earnings per share would have gone up proportionately by the amount of new after-tax earnings. This latter argument tends to be weakened by recognition of the fact that cash tendered in a merger has a substantial capital cost associated with it and, furthermore, that new shares of stock may later have to be authorized and sold to finance the cash drain.

Negotiated versus Tendered Offers

Traditionally, mergers have been negotiated in a friendly atmosphere between officers and directors of the participating corporations. Product lines, quality of assets, and future growth prospects are discussed, and eventually an exchange ratio is hammered out and presented to the investment community and the financial press.

If the potential buyer cannot come to agreement on merger terms with the potential seller's management, there are still two alternatives open to it. First, it can ask the seller's stockholders for the right to vote their shares at the company's next annual meeting. This gives rise to what is known as a *proxy fight* as management and the potential buyers vie for the right to vote a majority of the stockholders' shares. This right to vote the shares of another stockholder is called a *proxy.*

Rather than engage in a lengthy and expensive proxy fight, the potential seller can elect to make a *tender offer* through a stock exchange directly to the target company's stockholders. If the tender offer is lucrative enough to attract over 50 percent of the voting stock, the buyer will gain control and be able to conclude the merger.

As previously mentioned, the U.S.-based merger wave of the late 1970s and the 1980s has helped to create a wholly new atmosphere. The takeover *tender offer,* in which a company attempts to acquire a target firm against its will, has come into vogue. Early in the chapter we reviewed some of the antitakeover manoeuvres initiated by takeover targets who have attempted to avoid being acquired. In the notable recent examples, like the Union Enterprises or the Hiram Walker Resources cases, the defensive tactics have merely served to increase the cost of the takeovers without preventing them.

Though a tender offer may please the company's shareholders, its management faces the dangers of seeing the company going down the wrong path in a merger and perhaps of their being personally ousted. In order to avoid an unfriendly takeover, management may turn to a white knight for salvation, buy in portions of their own shares to restrict the amount of stock available for a takeover, take a poison pill, stagger the elections for corporate directors,[19] change the corporate by-laws regarding shareholder approval procedures in takeover situations, and so on.

One of the key rules for avoiding being targeted as a takeover candidate is to never get caught with too large a cash position. A firm with large cash balances serves as an ideal target for a *leveraged* takeover. The acquiring company is able to negotiate a bank loan based on the target company's assets and to then go into the marketplace to make a cash tender offer. Firms with strong asset or market positions and low earnings are also prime takeover targets. This is certainly the situation in the takeover battle currently raging between Domtex, the Canadian textile company, and Burlington Industries, the largest textile company in the United States.

While a takeover bid may not appeal to management, it is often very enticing to shareholders. Herein lies the basic problem. The bidding may get so high that shareholders demand action. The desire of management to maintain the status quo can come into conflict with the objective of shareholder wealth maximization. For example, Hiram Walker's management feared, in the Gulf offer to take over their company, that the Reichmanns would sell off assets as they did in the Gulf takeover and therefore dramatically alter Hiram Walker as an operating entity. How do we consider that against the fact the shareholders were being offered a 15 percent premium over the previous value of their holdings?[20] The issue is even more interesting if we consider that ex-

[19]This makes it more difficult for an outside group to gain control of the board even after it has bought a majority of the outstanding shares.

[20]The offer was eventually increased so that it represented a 36 percent premium. It is common for bidding companies to start much lower than their eventual final offer as happened in this case.

cellent decisions made by the management team may have actually been responsible for the attractiveness of the company as a takeover target as was clearly the case when Campeau Corporation took over Allied Stores.[21]

The proliferation of nonvoting shares in Canada may complicate a given takeover situation. In many cases clauses in the corporation's by-laws attempt to include the nonvoting equity holders in the premium stock pricing generated by a takeover bid. This is generally done by stipulating that a tender offer aimed at securing voting control must include an offer to purchase the nonvoting shares as well as the voting. As we saw in Chapter 17 in the Canadian Tire case, however, these clauses are sometimes open to varying interpretation. In the situations where there are no provisions for inclusion of the nonvoting shareholders in a control takeover bid, the nonvoting shareholder loses the opportunity to make substantial gains in the event the firm is taken over.

Premium Offers and Stock Price Movements

Although premiums of 15–20 percent over market value in a merger or acquisition were considered normal historically, some very high premiums have been paid in the 1980s. For example, Dome Petroleum's purchase of Hudson's Bay Oil and Gas involved a premium of approximately 75 percent over market. In the more recent takeover of Hiram Walker by Gulf Canada the premium was 36 percent.

The high premiums of the late 1970s and the 1980s may be related to market values for securities in general. To the extent replacement value exceeds market value, a high premium over market value may be justified. In addition, the motivation of the acquiring company in making the purchase was sometimes not to turn around a poor performer but to take advantage of the superior market or product position of the acquired company.

Researchers into takeover activity in the U.S. markets, where data are plentiful, have found that acquirees have superior price performance

[21]For more information, see H. Allan Conway, *Allied Stores Corporation (B)*, #9–381–087 (Boston: Harvard Business School Case Clearing House, 1980).

on a risk-adjusted basis.[22] It is not surprising that a company which is offered a large premium over its current market value has a major upside movement. The only problem for the investor is that much of this activity may take place before the public announcement of the merger offer. If a firm is selling at $25 per share when informal negotiations begin, it may be $34 by the time an announced offer of $40 is made. Still, there are good profits to be made by investing at $34 if the merger goes through.

The risk with this strategy or of any merger-related investment strategy is that the merger may be called off. In that case the merger candidate's stock, which shot up from $25 to $34, may fall back to $25, and the "Johnny-come-lately" investor would lose $9 per share.

All this information on price movement patterns has significance to corporate financial managers, who must understand and react to the motivations of investors. For example, once individuals and institutions have bought at a premium price anticipating the takeover, they will do everything possible to see that the merger goes through. This, at a minimum, will include voting all their shares in favor of a merger. On a more active basis, it may encompass a strategy of influencing other large shareholders, and it could ultimately include an attempt to discredit the management of a target company in the eyes of shareholders.

Mergers and the Market for Corporate Control

The high level of activity in corporate mergers is sometimes justified by the proposition that a competitive market for corporate control is an effective brake on any tendency for agent managers to diverge from striving to maximize shareholder wealth. However, to the extent that activity in this so-called market for corporate control creates financial value for shareholders, results of some studies suggest all of the excess value is transferred to the selling shareholders.

Although the evidence seems to support the general conclusion that the shareholders of acquired companies realize substantial excess re-

[22]Gershon Mandelker, "Risk and Return: The Case of Merging Firms," *Journal of Financial Economics* 1 (December 1974), pp. 303–35. Mandelker found the merger effect beginning to influence the acquiree's stock seven months before consummation of the merger, with the measure of excessive returns becoming positive at that point.

turns when a merger occurs, the results of many U.S.-based studies suggest that the shareholders of bidder firms realize negligible excess returns on takeovers. Because the bidding firms in the U.S. situation are generally much larger than the acquired firms and because the bidding firms' corporate strategies are often based on active acquisition programs,[23] however, those research results are at least partially muddied by measurement problems.

A recent study of Canadian merger activity between 1964 and 1983 came to what may be a significantly different conclusion in regard to the sharing of abnormal returns between buyer and seller.[24] As Figure 20–3 shows, the data from that study showed that, consistent with

Figure 20–3
Abnormal returns relative to merger announcements

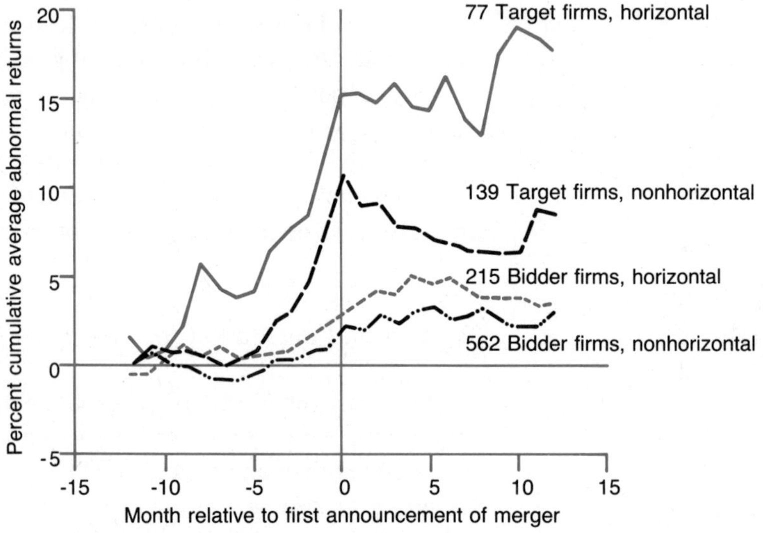

Monthly cumulative average abnormal returns relative to the merger announcement; four-digit SIC horizontal versus non-horizontal mergers, 1964–83.

Source: B. Espen Eckbo, "Mergers and the Market for Corporate Control: The Canadian Evidence," *Canadian Journal of Economics* 19, no. 2 (May 1986), p. 248.

---

[23]In effect, the expectation of its making attractive acquisitions may be already discounted in the company's normal share price.

[24]B. Espen Eckbo, "Mergers and the Market for Corporate Control: The Canadian Evidence," *Canadian Journal of Economics* 19, no. 2 (May 1986), pp. 236–60.

U.S.-based studies, target firms received higher abnormal returns, on average than did the bidder firms. Unlike the U.S. studies, however, the bidder firms did, in fact, receive significant abnormal returns on average. In addition, Figure 20–3 indicates there were generally higher abnormal returns in cases where the mergers were related, especially for the acquirees.

Thus, the evidence to this point seems to infer there may be some overall benefit to merger activity. In many cases, if value is actually created, it can be attributed to a new management team changing the status quo. This may be particularly appropriate in a company where the previous management had become too wedded to investing in the traditional industry regardless of whether the cost of capital was higher than the potential returns. Whether the buyer gets some of the value created by the merger is still a question requiring further research.

Holding Companies

Although the holding company in the United States as a corporate entity has been declining in prominence since the early 20th century, it is still a very important part of the ownership and control structure of the Canadian economy. A holding company is one that has control over one or more other firms. In order to establish voting control, the holding company may own less than a majority interest but is able to determine policy as a result of widely spread minority interests among the other shareholders. Brascan, controlling shareholder of Labatt's Breweries, Royal Trustco, London Life Insurance, Royal-LePage Real Estate, Great Lakes Holdings, Noranda Mines, and Westmin Resources, among other important financial and industrial entities, is one example of the many important holding companies in the Canadian economy. Another is Canadian Pacific, whose holdings included, as of early 1987, Canadian International Paper, PanCanadian Petroleum, AMCA International, Algoma Steel, Maple Leaf Mills, Great Lakes Forest Products, Marathon Realty, and Fording Coal.

The primary advantage of the holding company is that it affords unusual opportunities for leverage. Assume Giant Holding Corporation has the investment interests in Companies A, B, and C shown in Table 20–12. All numbers are assumed to represent millions of dollars. Also assume Giant Holding Corporation has effective voting control of the

Table 20–12
Assets, liabilities, and owners' equity of Giant Holding Corporation and related companies (in millions)

GIANT HOLDING CORPORATION

Assets		Liabilities and Owners' Equity	
Common shareholdings:			
Company A	$10	Long-term debt	$15
Company B	15	Preferred stock	10
Company C	20	Common stock equity	20
	$45		$45

COMPANY A

Assets		Liabilities and Owners' Equity	
Current assets	$ 50	Current liabilities	$ 20
Plant and equipment	50	Long-term debt	30
	$100	Common stock equity	50
			$100

COMPANY B

Assets		Liabilities and Owners' Equity	
Current assets	$ 60	Current liabilities	$ 10
Plant and equipment	60	Long-term debt	70
	$120	Common stock equity	40
			$120

COMPANY C

Assets		Liabilities and Owners' Equity	
Current assets	$ 80	Current liabilities	$ 20
Plant and equipment	120	Long-term debt	100
	$200	Common stock equity	80
			$200

three companies because of the widely dispersed interests of these companies' other owners. It owns 20 percent of the equity of Company A, as indicated by Giant Holding Corporation's balance sheet holding of $10 million in Company A (an asset) and Company A's common stock equity account of $50 million. In the case of Company B the ratio is 37.5 percent ($15 million/$40 million), while for Company C it is 25 percent ($20 million/$80 million). Through these interlocking positions, Giant Holding Corporation controls $420 million in assets (the combined assets of the three companies). Note that it is doing this with only $20 million of common stock equity in its own firm. Its equity-to-"assets controlled" ratio is 4.8 percent ($20 million/$420 million). If we really want to get creative, we can assume another holding company has control of Giant Holding Corporation with only a small investment in it, thus creating additional levels of ownership.

The holding company device also benefits from the isolation of the "legal" risks of the firms. Theoretically, if Company C loses money, this will not *legally* affect the other firms because Company C is a separate legal entity with separate shareholders.

The fact that dividends paid from one Canadian corporation to another are free of tax makes the holding company form of organization much more common in Canada than in the United States, where those dividends would be partially taxable. In Canada holding companies have often placed their investments in subsidiary companies in preferred rather than common shares as the dividends paid on preferred tend to be higher than those on common stock.

Drawbacks

The drawbacks are those inherent in any pyramiding arrangement. Although Companies A, B, and C are separate legal entities and one cannot force the bankruptcy of another, as has been implied there can be an indirect chain effect that is disastrous. For example, if Company A has a bad year, it may be unable to pay dividends to the holding company, which, in turn, may be unable to pay interest on the $15 million it has in long-term debt. The more complicated the arrangement, the more vulnerable the operation is to reversals.

The complicated administrative policies and procedures of a holding company are also worthy of note. With multiple managements, boards of directors, dividend policies, and reporting systems, the expenses are high and the opportunities for problems substantial.

Summary

Corporations may seek external growth through mergers in order to achieve risk reduction, to improve access to the financial markets through increased size, or to obtain tax loss carry-forward benefits. A merger may also expand the marketing and management capabilities of the firm and allow for new-product development. While some mergers promise synergistic benefits (the 2 + 2 = 5 effect), this can be an elusive feature, with initial expectations exceeding the subsequent realities.

The cash purchase of another corporation takes on many of the characteristics of a classical capital budgeting decision. In a stock-for-stock exchange, there is often a trade-off between immediate gain or dilution in earnings per share and future growth. If a firm buys another firm with a P/E ratio lower than its own, there is an immediate increase in earnings per share, but the long-term earnings growth prospects must also be considered. The ultimate objective of a merger, as is true of any financial situation, is shareholder wealth maximization, and the immediate and delayed effects of the merger must be evaluated in this context.

The accounting considerations in a merger are also important. Where the purchase price exceeds the book value of the acquired firm (after postmerger asset value adjustments), goodwill may be created which must be written off directly against future earnings per share. In order to avoid goodwill creation, many earlier mergers were treated as poolings of interests rather than purchases of assets. Virtually all current mergers, however, must be accounted for as purchases of assets with the attendant possibility of creating goodwill.

During the 1980s the unsolicited tender offer for a target company gained in popularity. Offers were made at values well in excess of the current market price, and management of the target company became trapped in the dilemma of maintaining its current position versus agreeing to the wishes of the acquiring company and even the target company's own shareholders.

The interlocking nature of takeover activities is striking. This arises from takeovers in foreign markets affecting the parent of a multinational subsidiary, from activities undertaken by a target firm to avoid being taken over, and from after-purchase spin-offs to generate cash to pay the cost of the acquisition.

Finally, the holding company is viewed as a means of accumulating large asset control with a minimum equity investment through leveraging the investment. The holding company is an important participant in the Canadian industrial and financial infrastructure. Surprisingly, there has been little research into the administrative problems inherent in this important form of organization.

List of Terms

merger
amalgamation
portfolio effect
market value maximization
tax loss carry-forward
synergy
terms of exchange
Competition Act
market for corporate control
tender offer
goodwill
purchase of assets
pooling of interests
merger premium
leveraged buyout
holding company
Investment Canada
Foreign Investment Review Agency

Discussion Questions

1. Briefly discuss three significant features of the merger movement of the late 1970s and the 1980s.
2. Is risk reduction in the firm's portfolio of undertakings likely to be best achieved through horizontal integration, vertical integration, or conglomerate-type acquisitions?
3. If a firm wishes to achieve immediate appreciation in earnings per share as a result of a merger, how can this be best accomplished in terms of exchange variables? What is a possible drawback to this approach in terms of long-range considerations?
4. What is the essential difference between a pooling of interests and a purchase of assets accounting treatment of a merger? What is the effect of including goodwill?
5. If the Amoco Canada and Dome Petroleum merger is completed, suggest three forms of synergy that might take place.
6. Generally a stockholder of the selling corporation will demand a higher price if cash consideration is tendered. Explain why this might be the case.

7. Explain how the weak stock market of the late 1970s served as an impetus to the merger wave of the late 1970s and 1980s.

8. It is possible for the postmerger P/E ratio to move in a direction opposite to that of the immediate postmerger earnings per share. Explain why this could happen.

9. Explain why unusually high premiums have sometimes been paid in the latest merger movement.

10. Suggest some ways in which firms have tried to avoid being a takeover target.

11. Why do management and stockholders often have divergent viewpoints about the desirability of a takeover?

12. How can the ordinary investor benefit from a possible merger? What is the danger in investing in a proposed merger target? Explain.

13. Compare the use of leverage in a holding company to the concept of operating and financial leverage explained in Chapter 5. Does a holding company have any tax complications related to dividends?

14. Why has the United States been traditionally concerned about corporate concentration arising from merger activity while Canada's concern has been much more with foreign ownership?

Problems

1. Assume the Arrow Corporation is considering the acquisition of Failure Unlimited. The latter has a $400,000 tax loss carry-forward. The projected earnings for Arrow Corporation are as follows:

	1988	*1989*	*1990*	*Total Value*
Before-tax income	$160,000	$200,000	$320,000	$680,000
Taxes (45%)	72,000	90,000	144,000	306,000
Income available to stockholders	$ 88,000	$110,000	$176,000	$374,000

a. How much will the total taxes of Arrow Corporation be reduced as a result of the tax loss carry-forward?

b. How much will the total income available to stockholders be for the three years if the acquisition takes place?

2. The McCoy Corporation desires to expand. It is considering a cash purchase of Hatfield Enterprises for $2.6 million. Hatfield has a $500,000 tax loss carry-forward that could be used immediately by the McCoy Corporation, which is paying taxes at the rate of 40 percent. Best estimates predict that Hatfield will provide $380,000 per year in cash flow (after-tax income plus depreciation) for the next 20 years. If the McCoy Corporation has a cost of capital of 14 percent, should the merger be undertaken?

3. Kemp's Supply Sidemolding is considering a cash acquisition of Roth Homebuilding for $2.2 million. Kemp's hopes that Roth will provide the following pattern of cash inflows and synergistic benefits for the next 20 years. There is no tax loss carry-forward.

	Years		
	1–5	*6–15*	*16–20*
Cash inflow (after tax)	$220,000	$240,000	$280,000
Synergistic benefits (after tax)	20,000	22,000	40,000

The cost of capital for the acquiring firm is 12 percent. Should the merger be undertaken? (If you have any difficulty with delayed time value of money problems, consult Chapter 9.)

4. Ann Newberg helped start the Lovely Fragrance Company in 1951. At the time she purchased 100,000 shares of stock at $.10 per share. In 1988 she has the opportunity to sell her interest in the company to Holly Cosmetics for $50 cash per share. At valuation day, her shares were worth $10 each. She has not used any of her lifetime capital gains tax exemption to this point.

a. If she sells out her interest, what will be the value for before-tax profit, capital gains taxes (rough estimate), and after-tax profit?

b. Assume instead of cash she accepts stock valued at $50 per share. She holds the stock for five years and then sells it for

$87.50 (the stock pays no cash dividends). What will be the value for before-tax profit, capital gains taxes, and after-tax profit?

c. Using a 10 percent discount rate, compare the after-tax profit figure in part *b* to part *a*.

5. A merger between Pica Corporation and Elite Corporation is under consideration. The financial information for these firms is as follows:

	Elite Corporation	*Pica Corporation*
Total earnings	$300,000	$600,000
Number of shares of stock outstanding	100,000	300,000
Earnings per share	$3	$2
Price-earnings ratio	8 ×	12 ×
Market price per share	$24	$24

a. On a share-for-share exchange basis, what will the postmerger earnings per share be?

b. If Pica Corporation pays a 25 percent premium over the market value of Elite Corporation, how many shares will be issued?

c. With the 25 percent premium, what will the postmerger earnings per share be? (Round to the nearest cent.)

d. With a 50 percent premium, how many shares will be issued and what will be the postmerger earnings per share?

e. With a 75 percent premium, how many shares will be issued and what will be the postmerger earnings per share?

f. Explain what has happened in parts *a, c, d,* and *e* in terms of relative P/E ratios and the earnings per share impact of the acquisition.

6. In the case of the Pica and Elite merger described in Problem 5, assume a 100 percent premium will be paid, but there is a 20 percent synergistic benefit to total earnings from the merger. Will the postmerger earnings go up or down based on your calculations?

7. Median Corporation is considering a share-for-share exchange with Passive Corporation. The financial information for these firms is as follows:

	Passive Corporation	Median Corporation
Total earnings	$10,000,000	$15,000,000
Number of shares of stock outstanding	4,000,000	10,000,000
Earnings per share	$2.50	$1.50
Price-earnings ratio	4 ×	10 ×
Market price per share	$10.00	$15.00

Median Corporation had agreed to pay Passive Corporation a 20 percent premium over market value. Without the merger, Median Corporation will grow at a 12 percent rate for the next 10 years. Passive Corporation is expected to grow by 2 percent per year.

a. Compute the postmerger earnings per share. (Round to the nearest cent.)

b. Compute the anticipated postmerger growth rate for the combined firms for the next 10 years. Weight the combined growth rate on the basis of relative earnings contributed to the merged firm.

c. Project earnings per share annually for the next 10 years for Median Corporation based on no merger and based on a merger with Passive Corporation.

8. As a second alternative, Median Corporation (in Problem 7) is also considering a merger with Dynamo Corporation. The financial information for these firms is as follows:

	Dynamo Corporation	Median Corporation
Total earnings	$5,000,000	$15,000,000
Number of shares of stock outstanding	2,500,000	10,000,000
Earnings per share	$2.00	$1.50
Price-earnings ratio	12×	10×
Market price per share	$24.00	$15.00

Median Corporation has agreed to pay Dynamo Corporation a 50 percent premium over market value. As previously stated, without the merger Median would grow at a 12 percent rate for the next

10 years. Dynamo Corporation is expected to grow at a 24 percent rate for the next 10 years.

a. Compute the postmerger earnings per share. (Round to the nearest cent.)
b. Compute the anticipated postmerger growth rate for the combined firms for the next 10 years.
c. Project earnings per share annually for the next 10 years for Median Corporation based on no merger (already computed) and based on a merger with Dynamo Corporation.

9. Based on the answers developed to Problems 7 and 8:

a. Briefly describe the characteristics of the Median Corporation merger with Passive Corporation in terms of initial dilution, break-even point, and impact after 10 years. Do the same for the Median Corporation–Dynamo Corporation merger. (No graphs are necessary.)
b. In the case of the merger between Median Corporation and Dynamo Corporation, assume the following possible immediate postmerger P/E ratios with the associated probabilities. Compute an expected value for the price of Median Corporation stock after the merger.

P/E	*Probability*
10	.20
12	.40
14	.30
16	.10

c. In regard to the Median Corporation–Dynamo Corporation merger, if the firms had wished to trade strictly on the basis of earnings per share, what would the exchange ratio be?
d. In regard to the Median Corporation–Dynamo Corporation merger, if 12 percent initial synergy were involved, what would the merger's break-even time period be? (That is, after how many years would earnings per share with and without merger be approximately equal?)

10. Assume the Shelton Corporation is considering the acquisition of Cook Inc. The expected earnings per share for the Shelton Corporation will be $3.00 with or without the merger. However, the standard deviation of the earnings will go from \$1.89 to \$1.20 with the merger because the two firms' results are negatively correlated.

a. Compute the coefficient of variation for the Shelton Corporation before and after the merger.
b. Discuss the possible impact on Shelton's postmerger P/E ratio, assuming investors are risk averse.

11. General Meters is considering two mergers. The first is with Firm A in its own volatile industry, the auto speedometer industry, whereas the second is a merger with Firm B in an industry that moves in the opposite direction (and will tend to level out performance due to negative correlation).

a. Compute the mean, standard deviation, and coefficient of variation for both investments (consult Chapter 13 to review statistical concepts if necessary).

General Meters Merger with Firm A		*General Meters Merger with Firm B*	
Possible Earnings (\$ millions)	*Probability*	*Possible Earnings (\$ millions)*	*Probability*
\$40	.30	\$10	.25
50	.40	50	.50
60	.30	90	.25

b. Assuming investors are risk averse, which alternative can be expected to bring the higher valuation?

12. The Heisman Corporation is considering the acquisition of the O'Brien Corporation. The book value of the O'Brien Corporation is \$30 million, and the Heisman Corporation is willing to pay \$80 million in cash and preferred stock. No upward adjustment of assets is anticipated. The Heisman Corporation has 2 million shares outstanding. A purchase of assets financial recording will be used, with a 40-year write-off of goodwill.

a. How much will the annual amortization be?
b. How much will the annual amortization be on a per share basis?
c. Is any tax benefit involved?
d. Explain how the recording of goodwill could have been avoided.

13. Maxima Corporation, a holding company, has investments in three other firms.

ALPHA CORPORATION

Assets		Liabilities and Owners' Equity	
Current assets	$ 80	Current liabilities	$ 40
Plant and equipment	120	Long-term debt	40
		Common stock equity	120
	$200		$200

BETA CORPORATION

Assets		Liabilities and Owners' Equity	
Current assets	$100	Current liabilities	$ 30
Plant and equipment	200	Long-term debt	70
		Common stock equity	200
	$300		$300

DELTA CORPORATION

Assets		Liabilities and Owners' Equity	
Current assets	$150	Current liabilities	$ 90
Plant and equipment	150	Long-term debt	110
		Common stock equity	100
	$300		$300

Maxima Corporation has voting control of the three other corporations, with the following investment interests in each: 25 percent of the equity in Alpha, 20 percent of the equity in Beta, and 10 percent of the equity in Delta. Maxima Corporation's long-term debt is equal to 30 percent of its assets; its preferred stock is equal to 20 percent; and its common stock is equal to 50 percent.

a. Fill in the table below for Maxima Corporation.

Assets		Liabilities and Owners' Equity	
Common stockholdings			
Alpha Corporation	______	Long-term debt	______
Beta Corporation	______	Preferred stock	______
Delta Corporation	______	Common stock equity	______
Total	______	Total	______

b. Compute the percentage of Maxima Corporation's equity to the total holding company assets in the three corporations.

Selected References

Appleyard, A. R., and G. K. Yarrow. "The Relationship between Take-Over Activity and Share Valuation." *Journal of Finance* 30 (December 1975), pp. 1239–49.

Asquith, P. "Merger Bids, Uncertainty, and Stockholder Returns." *Journal of Financial Economics* 11 (April 1983), pp. 51–83.

Austin, Douglas V. "The Financial Management of Tender Offer Take-Overs." *Financial Management* 3 (Spring 1974), pp. 37–43.

Belkaoui, Ahmed. "Financial Ratios as Predictors of Canadian Take-overs." *Journal of Business Finance and Accounting* 5 (1978), pp. 83–107.

Block, Stanley B. "The Effects of Mergers and Acquisitions on the Market Value of Common Stock." *Southern Journal of Business* 4 (October 1969), pp. 189–95.

Bradley, James W., and Donald H. Korn. "Acquisition and Merger Trends Affecting the Portfolio Manager." *Financial Analysts Journal* 33 (November–December 1977), pp. 65–70.

Clark, John T. *Business Merger and Acquisition Strategies*. Englewood Cliffs, N.J.: Prentice-Hall, 1985.

Conn, Robert L., and James F. Nielsen. "An Empirical Test of the Larson-Gonedes Exchange Ratio Determination Model." *Journal of Finance* 32 (June 1977), pp. 749–59.

Cummin, Robert I. "Unfriendly Corporate Takeovers—Old Style." *Financial Analysts Journal* 85 (June–August 1982).

Dellenbarger, Lynn E. "A Study of Relative Common Stock Equity Values in Fifty Mergers of Listed Industrial Corporations, 1950–57." *Journal of Finance* 18 (September 1963), p. 565.

Dodd, Peter, and Richard Ruback. "Tender Offers and Stockholder Returns." *Journal of Financial Economics* 5 (December 1977), pp. 351–73.

Eckbo, B. Espen. "Mergers and the Market for Corporate Control: The Canadian Evidence." *Canadian Journal of Economics* 19, no. 2 (May 1986), pp. 236–60.

Falk, Haim, and L. Gordon. "Business Combination Decisions: A U.S./Canada Study." *Decision Sciences*, 1979, pp. 604–17.

Hogarty, T. "The Profitability of Corporate Mergers." *Journal of Business* 43 (July 1970), pp. 317–27.

Jensen, M. C., and R. S. Ruback. "The Market for Corporate Control: The Scientific Evidence." *Journal of Financial Economics* 11 (April 1983), pp. 5–50.

Larson, Kermit D., and Nicholas J. Gonedes. "Business Combinations: An Exchange Ratio Determination Model." *Accounting Review* 44 (October 1969), pp. 720–28.

Levinson, Harry. "A Psychologist Diagnoses Merger Failures." *Harvard Business Review,* March–April 1970.

Lewellen, Wilber G. "A Pure Financial Rationale for Conglomerate Merger." *Journal of Finance* 26 (May 1971), pp. 521–37.

MacBeth, Michael. "Survival Mergers: How Four Firms Did It." *Canadian Business* 55, no. 8 (August 1982), pp. 72–80.

Mandelker, Gershon. "Risk and Return: The Case of Merging Firms." *Journal of Financial Economics* 1 (December 1974), pp. 303–35.

McKenzie, G. G. "Myths and Realities of Corporate Takeovers." *Canadian Business Review,* Spring 1987, pp. 26–28.

Melicher, Ronald W., and David F. Rush. "Evidence on the Acquisition Related Performance of Conglomerate Firms." *Journal of Finance* 29 (March 1974), pp. 141–49.

Mergers & Acquisitions in Canada, 1987. Toronto: Harris-Bentley Limited, 1987.

Merjos, Anna. "Costly Propositions—Some Big Mergers Have Lately Fallen through." *Barron's,* May 14, 1979, pp. 9–13.

Modigliani, Franco, and Richard A. Cohn. "Inflation, Rational Valuation, and the Market." *Financial Analysts Journal* 35 (March–April 1979), pp. 24–44.

Morin, Desmond B., and Warren Chippendale, eds. *Acquisitions and Mergers in Canada*. 2nd ed. Toronto: Metheun, 1977.

Murphy, Jean. "Counting the Cost of the Decade's Mergers." *The Financial Post 500,* Summer 1987, pp. 61–64.

Oppenheimer, Henry, and Stanley Block. "An Examination of the Characteristics Associated with Merger Activity during the 1975–78 Period." Financial Management Association Meetings, 1980.

Parker, John R. E., and George C. Baxter. *Corporate Combinations and Intercorporate Investments*. Toronto: Canadian Institute of Chartered Accountants, 1980.

Reilly, Frank K. "What Determines the Ratio of Exchange in Corporate Mergers?" *Financial Analysts Journal* 18 (November–December 1962), pp. 47–50.

Salter, Malcolm S. and Wolf A. Weinhold. *Diversification via Acquisition: Creating Value*. New York: Free Press, 1979.

Scott, James H., Jr. "On the Theory of Conglomerate Mergers." *Journal of Finance* 32 (September 1977), pp. 1235–49.

Shrieves, Ronald E., and Mary M. Pashley. "Evidence of the Association between Mergers and Capital Structure." *Financial Management* 13 (Autumn 1984), pp. 39–48.

Stanbury, William T., and G. B. Reschenthaler. "Reforming Canadian Competition Policy: Once More unto the Breach." *The Canadian Business Law Journal* 5 (September 1981), pp. 381–437.

Stevens, Donald L. "Financial Characteristics of Merged Firms: A Multivariate Analysis." *Journal of Financial and Quantitative Analysis* 8 (March 1973), pp. 149–58.

21 International Financial Management

Introduction

During the post-World War II era advances in communications and transportation systems brought people everywhere closer together. Think of the rise in production in the Far East of products aimed for sale primarily in North America and Europe. Prior to the 1960s such production in low-wage countries for consumption in more affluent countries would not have been possible. In this shrinking world it has become easier to interact with others through trade, regardless of geographic origin, location, or nationality. The political systems that emerged from World War II also contributed to the establishment of trade relations between nations. Under the Marshall Plan the United States helped the war-torn nations of Western Europe rebuild their economies. Western Europe, Canada, and Japan experienced sustained growth, much of it related to the economy of the industrial colossus to Canada's south—the United States. As the economies of Western nations grew in this manner, their trade relations also strengthened. Concurrently, European nations formed the European Common Market in an effort to promote better trade relations among themselves. Technology and capital also started to flow among these nations. During the 1950s and 1960s the United States became the dominant partner in the world economy. The U.S. dollar received worldwide acceptance, and the members of the international trading community started using it as reserve currency. With the rise of the industrial might of Japan, Korea, and other countries, this hegemony of the United States in world commerce has lessened. In fact, the enormous trade deficits and external debt being incurred by the United States in recent years is a source of great uncertainty in world markets.

Today the world economy is more integrated than ever, and nations are dependent on one another for many valuable and scarce resources. Just as Canada is dependent on Japan for a large portion of the automobiles used here, Japan is dependent on Canada for the coal it uses to make the steel that is incorporated in those cars. Even the major Eastern Block country, the USSR, has been dependent on Canada and the United States for agricultural commodities and high-technology goods for many years. This growing interdependence necessitates the development of sound international business relations, which, in turn, will enhance the prospects for future international cooperation and understanding. It is virtually impossible for any country to isolate itself from the impact of international developments in an integrated world economy.

The significance of international business operations becomes more apparent if we look at the importance of foreign sales relative to the size of the Canadian economy. In 1985, for example, Canada exported $136 billion worth of goods and services out of a total production of $462 billion. That means some 32 percent of Canada's production went into international trade. In addition, since $94 billion of those exports went to the United States, we depend on that economy to absorb over 20 percent of Canada's total production of goods and services. Thus, to a greater extent than any other industrialized economy except West Germany, Canada is truly "open" to the forces of world trade. In comparison, the United States, a major player in international trade by any measure, exports slightly less than 10 percent of its domestic production.

In such a trade-oriented economy it is natural that many of our industrial firms would be heavily involved in international operations. For example, Abitibi-Price, the large forest products company, made 62 percent of total sales outside of Canada in 1985, while for Northern Telecom, the telecommunications equipment manufacturer, foreign sales accounted for 72 percent of its $5.8 billion total. All of the country's major commercial banks also derive a significant percentage of their earnings from foreign operations. At the end of 1985 Canada's largest bank, the Royal Bank, had $33.5 billion in assets outside of Canada. That represented 38 percent of the bank's total assets. The Bank of Nova Scotia had an even larger 52 percent of its $59 billion in assets tied up in international operations.

Just as foreign operations affect the performance of Canadian business firms, developments in international financial markets also affect our lifestyles. If you have been vacationing in Acapulco every winter, you might have been pleasantly surprised in 1987 that it didn't cost you as much as it had in 1986. The primary reason was the precipitous drop in the value of the Mexican peso against the Canadian dollar. For a similar reason, Banff National Park is attracting more and more Japanese tourists, probably partially because of the declining value of the Canadian dollar against the Japanese yen, especially in 1986. On the other side of the ledger, if you went out in 1987 to buy a Japanese automobile, you would have noticed a tremendous price increase versus what it would have cost only two years earlier. Thus, the fluctuations in currency values affect many of us in one way or another as about 30 percent of our purchases are for products and services from other countries.

This chapter deals with the international dimensions of corporate finance. We believe this chapter provides a basis for understanding the complexities of international financial decisions. Such an understanding is important whether you work for a multinational manufacturing firm, a large commercial bank, a major brokerage firm, or any firm involved in international transactions or are just involved in managing your own personal financial affairs.

International business operations, by their very nature, are often complex, risky, and require special understanding. Many major Canadian banks have had to learn the lessons of international finance through painful experience. In the worldwide recession of 1981–83, many less developed, Third World countries found difficulty in repaying their bank debt obligations due to declining exports. In order to prevent the default of these countries on mammoth amounts of debt owed to the commercial banking system, the ingenuity of world financial institutions was, and continues to be, severely tested.

In the following section of this chapter a description of the international business firm and its environment is presented. Then foreign exchange rates and the variables influencing foreign currency values are explained, and strategies for dealing with foreign exchange risk are examined. The foreign investment decision is then illustrated through an example, and finally, international financing sources are discussed.

The Multinational Corporation: Nature and Environment

The focus of international financial management has been the multinational corporation (MNC). One might ask: Just what is a multinational corporation? Some definitions of a multinational corporation require that a minimum percentage (often 30 percent or more) of a firm's business activities be carried on outside its national borders. For purposes of our discussion, however, a firm doing business across its national borders will be considered a multinational enterprise. Such multinational corporations can take several forms. Four are briefly examined.

Exporter An MNC could produce a product domestically and export some of that production to one or more foreign markets. This is generally considered the least risky method of going international—reaping the benefits of foreign demand without committing any long-term investment to a foreign country.

Licensing agreement A firm with exporting operations may get into trouble when a foreign government imposes or substantially raises an import tariff to a level at which the exporter cannot compete effectively with the local domestic manufacturers. The foreign government may even ban all imports into the country at times. When this happens, the exporting firm may grant a license to an independent local producer to use the firm's technology in return for a license fee or a royalty. In essence, then, the MNC will be exporting technology rather than the product to that foreign country. Another advantage of licensing over straight export might arise when some adaptation of the product for local preference is desirable.

Joint venture As an alternative to licensing, the MNC may establish a joint venture with a local foreign manufacturer. The legal, political, and economic environments around the globe are more conducive to the joint venture arrangement than any of the other modes of operations. Historical evidence also suggests that a joint venture with a local entrepreneur exposes the firm to the least amount of political risk. Consequently, this position is preferred by most business firms and by foreign governments as well.

Fully owned foreign subsidiary Although the joint venture form is desirable for many reasons, it may be hard to find a willing and cooperative local entrepreneur with sufficient capital to participate. Under these conditions the MNC may have to set up foreign operations alone. For political reasons, however, a wholly owned foreign subsidiary is becoming more of a rarity in the mid-80s. During the remainder of this chapter we will use the term *foreign affiliate* to refer to either a joint venture or a fully owned subsidiary.

As the firm crosses its national borders, it usually faces an environment that is riskier and more complex than its domestic surroundings. Sometimes the social and political environment can be hostile. In spite of these difficult challenges, foreign affiliates often are more profitable than domestic businesses. A purely domestic firm faces several basic risks, such as the risk related to maintaining sales and market share, the financial risk of too much leverage, the risk of a poor equity market, and so on. In addition to these types of risks, the foreign affiliate is exposed to foreign exchange risk and political risk. While the foreign affiliate experiences a larger amount of risk than a domestic firm, it actually lowers the portfolio risk of its parent corporation by stabilizing the combined operating cash flows for the MNC. This risk reduction occurs because foreign and domestic economies are less than perfectly correlated.

Foreign business operations are more complex because the host country's economy may be different from the domestic economy. The rate of inflation in many foreign countries is likely to be higher than that in Canada even though our inflation performance over the past 20 years has been less than satisfactory. The rules of taxation are usually different. The structure and operation of financial markets and institutions also vary from country to country, as do financial policies and practices.

The presence of a foreign affiliate should benefit the host country's economy. In fact, foreign affiliates have been a decisive factor in shaping the pattern of trade, investment, and the flow of technology between and among nations. They can have a significant positive impact on a host country's economic growth, employment, trade, and balance of payments. This positive contribution, however, is occasionally overshadowed by allegations of wrongdoing. For example, some host countries have charged that foreign affiliates subverted their governments and caused instability in their currencies' exchange rates. The less developed countries (LDCs) have, at times, alleged that foreign businesses exploit their labor with low wages. The multinational companies are also under constant criticism in their home countries where labor unions charge the MNCs with exporting jobs, capital, and technology to foreign nations while avoiding their fair share of taxes.

In spite of all these criticisms, the multinational companies have managed to survive and prosper. The MNC is well positioned to take advantage of imperfections in global markets. Furthermore, since current global resource distribution favors the MNC's survival and growth, it may be concluded that the multinational corporation is here to stay.

Foreign Exchange Rates

Suppose you are planning to spend a semester in Paris studying French culture and you have been granted a $1,000 scholarship to support you while you are there. To put your plan into operation you will need French currency (that is, French francs—FF) so you can pay for your expenses during your stay in France. How many French francs you can obtain for $1,000 will depend on the exchange rate at the particular time you offer your Canadian dollars for sale in exchange for French francs. The relationship between the values of two currencies is known as the exchange rate. The exchange rate between Canadian dollars and French francs can be stated as dollars per francs or francs per dollar. For example, the quotation of $0.22 per franc is the same as FF 4.54 per dollar. At this exchange rate you can purchase 4,540 French francs with $1,000. *The Globe and Mail* publishes exchange rates for the major foreign currencies at the end of each week. Table 21–1 illustrates the currencies of a number of countries and their exchange rates relative to the Canadian dollar. This table lists the number of units (or fractions thereof) of a foreign currency that one could purchase with one Canadian dollar (foreign currency units/$).

As you can readily notice from this table, the exchange rates change over time. By comparing exchange rates in September 1985 with those of February 1987, you will observe that one dollar would buy less of most foreign currencies as time went on. In other words, the value of the Canadian dollar, its exchange rate, had fallen against most of these currencies between 1985 and 1987. For example, one dollar would have bought 6.5 French francs in September 1985 but only 4.54 French francs in February 1987. In other words, the purchasing power of the

Table 21–1
Selected currencies and exchange rates—number of foreign currency units you can purchase with one Canadian dollar

		Exchange Rate (per $1)	
Country	*Currency Unit*	*September 9, 1985*	*February 13, 1987*
Austria	Schilling	15.0277	9.5929
Brazil	Cruzado	5.2544	13.3635
China	Renminbi	2.1561	2.7725
Denmark	Kronë	7.7475	5.1471
France	Franc	6.5008	4.5413
Germany (West)	Deutsche mark	2.1390	1.3628
India	Rupee	8.9137	9.7132
Italy	Lira	1417.0000	969.8300
Japan	Yen	177.2300	114.4700
Mexico	Peso	254.5167	753.0726
Netherlands	Guilder	2.3956	1.5385
Portugal	Escudo	127.0258	106.0708
South Africa	Rand	1.8839	1.5615
Spain	Peseta	125.5293	96.3128
Sweden	Krona	6.2673	4.8585
Switzerland	Franc	1.7655	1.1534
United Kingdom	Pound	0.5506	0.4899
United States	Dollar	0.7300	0.7449

dollar against the franc plummeted over 30 percent in only 1½ years. By taking the reciprocal of these two values, we could also say the French franc was worth .1538 (1/6.5008) dollars in September 1985 and .2202 (1/4.5413) dollars in February 1987. Thus, had you received your $1,000 scholarship a few semesters earlier, it would have bought you FF 6,500 and a much higher standard of living during your stay in Paris.

Over a longer time period the dollar was extremely weak against many foreign currencies during most of the 1970s and early 1980s. Then in the mid-1980s, up to the 1985 data in the table, the dollar improved substantially against major currencies. During 1986 the dollar's value, in general, fell once again. The magnitude of the fall was largely a result of a determined effort by the United States federal government to force major trading countries such as Germany and Japan to realign their currencies at a higher value vis à vis the U.S. dollar. Thus, over the period covered by Table 21–1 the Canadian dollar actually appreciated against the U.S. dollar even as it fell 36 percent against the deutsche mark and 35 percent against the Japanese yen. No doubt, foreign exchange relationships will continue to be volatile as the U.S. administration uses exchange rate adjustments as an attempted solution to its massive trade deficit and Canada's economic performance continues to be heavily dependent on trade with the United States.

Factors Influencing Exchange Rates

The present international monetary system consists of a mixture of "freely" floating exchange rates and fixed rates. The currencies of Canada's major trading partners are traded in free markets. In such a market the exchange rate between two currencies is determined by the supply of and the demand for those currencies. This activity, however, is subject to intervention by many countries' central banks. Factors that tend to increase the supply or decrease the demand schedule for a given currency will bring down the value of that currency in foreign exchange markets. Similarly, the factors that tend to decrease the supply or increase the demand for a currency will raise the value of that currency. Since fluctuations in currency values result in foreign exchange risk, the financial executive must understand the factors causing these changes in currency values. Although the value of a currency is determined by the aggregate supply and demand for that currency, this alone does not help our financial manager understand or predict the changes in exchange rates. Fundamental factors such as inflation, interest rates, foreign trade balances, and government policies are quite important in explaining both the short-term and long-term fluctuations of a currency value.

Inflation A parity between the purchasing powers of two currencies establishes the rate of exchange between the two currencies. Suppose apples are the commodity of value in Canada and in Germany and that it takes $1.00 to buy one dozen apples in Toronto and 2.50 deutsche marks to buy the same apples in Frankfurt, Germany. Then the rate of exchange between the Canadian dollar and the deutsche mark is DM 2.50/$1.00 or $0.40/DM. If the price of apples doubles in Toronto while the prices in Frankfurt remain the same, the purchasing power of a dollar in Toronto will drop 50 percent. Consequently, you will be able to exchange $1.00 for only DM 1.25 in foreign currency markets (or now receive $.80, or double the previous rate, per DM). This means that currency exchange rates tend to vary inversely with their respective purchasing powers in order to provide the same or similar purchasing power in each country. This is called the *purchasing power parity theory.* When the inflation rate between two countries is different, the exchange rate adjusts to correspond to the relative purchasing powers of the countries.

Interest rates Another economic variable that has a significant influence on the exchange rate is the interest rate. As a student of finance you readily recognize that investment capital flows in the direction of higher yield for a given level of risk. This flow of short-term capital between money markets occurs because investors seek equilibrium through arbitrage buying and selling. If investors can earn 10 percent interest per year in Canada and 16 percent per year in Britain, they will prefer to invest in Britain, provided the inflation rate and perceived risk are the same in both countries. As investors sell Canadian dollars to buy British pounds, the value of the pound will appreciate relative to the dollar. At the same time, the increased demand for British securities will also tend to reduce the interest rate differential between the United Kingdom and Canada. Thus, interest rates and exchange rates adjust until the foreign exchange market and the money market reach equilibrium. This interplay between interest rate differentials and exchange rates is called the *interest rate parity theory.*

Balance of payments The term *balance of payments* refers to a system of government accounts that catalogs the flow of economic transactions between the residents of a given country and the residents of all other countries (the balance of payments statement for Canada is prepared by Statistics Canada). It resembles the Cash Flow statement presented in Chapter 2 and keeps track of the country's exports and imports as well as the flow of capital and gifts. When a country sells (exports) more goods and services to foreign countries than it purchases (imports) from abroad, it will have a surplus in its balance of trade. Japan, for example, through its aggressive competition in world markets, exports far more goods than it imports and has been enjoying large trade surpluses for many years. Since the foreigners who buy Japanese goods are expected to pay their bills in yen, the demand for the yen and, consequently, its value increase in foreign currency markets. On the other hand, continuous deficits in the balance of payments are expected to depress the value of a currency because such deficits would increase the supply of that currency relative to the demand.

Government policies A national government may, through its central bank, intervene in the foreign exchange market, buying and selling currencies as it sees fit to support the value of its currency relative to others. Sometimes a given country may deliberately pursue a policy of maintaining an undervalued currency in order to promote cheap exports. In communist countries the currency values are set by government decree. Even in some free market countries, the central banks fix the exchange rates, subject to periodic review and adjustment. At times some nations affect the foreign exchange rate indirectly by restricting the flow of funds into and out of the country. Monetary and fiscal policies also affect the currency value in foreign exchange markets. For example, expansionary monetary policy and excessive government spending are primary causes of inflation, and continual use of such policies eventually reduces the value of the country's currency. In the Canadian example, a rapid expansion of the money supply in the late 1970s and increasingly large government deficits have had much to do with the decline in our foreign exchange rate (for example, from US $1.05 in 1976 to US $.74 in 1987).

Other factors Other factors may also affect the demand for a country's currency and, therefore, its exchange rate. In this section we will highlight some of the commonly observed other factors. A pronounced and extended stock market rally in a country attracts investment capital from other countries, thus creating a huge demand by foreigners for that country's currency. This increased demand will tend to increase the value of that currency. Similarly, a significant drop in demand for a country's principal exports worldwide is expected to result in a corresponding decline in the value of its currency. The South African rand and British pound are two examples from recent history. A precipitous drop in gold prices in the South African situation and an apparent oil glut in the British situation are cited as the reasons for the depreciation of these two currencies during the 1980–85 period. Political turmoil within a country has often been responsible for driving capital out of a country into more stable countries. A mass exodus of capital, due to the fear of political risk, undermines the value of a country's currency in the foreign exchange market. If widespread labor strikes appear to weaken the nation's economy, they also will have a depressing influence on its currency value.

Although a wide variety of factors that can influence exchange rates have been discussed, a few words of caution are in order. All of these variables will not necessarily influence all currencies to the same degree. Some factors may have an overriding influence on one currency's value, while their influence on another currency may be negligible at that point in time. In other words, exchange rates are partial measures of our confidence in the future performance of a particular economy. An event that may utterly destroy our confidence in one economy's future may not do so in another.

Spot Rates and Forward Rates

When you look into a major financial newspaper you will discover that two exchange rates exist simultaneously for most major currencies—the spot rate and the forward rate. The spot rate for a currency is the exchange rate at which the currency is traded for immediate delivery. For example, you might walk into the local branch of the Toronto Dominion Bank and ask for French francs. The banker will indicate the rate at which the franc is selling, say FF 4.5/$. If you are satisfied with the rate, you buy 4,500 francs with $1,000 and walk out the door. This is a *spot market* transaction at the retail level.

The trading of currencies for future delivery is called a forward market transaction. To illustrate, suppose Imperial Oil expects to receive FF 60 million from a French customer 90 days from now. Given the recent volatility in foreign exchange markets, it is not certain, however, what these francs will be worth in dollars 90 days from today. In order to eliminate this uncertainty the treasurer at Imperial contacts a bank and offers to sell FF 60 million for Canadian dollars 90 days from now. In their negotiation the two parties may agree on an exchange rate of FF 5/$. Since the exchange rate is established for future delivery, it is a *forward rate*. After 90 days Imperial Oil delivers FF 60 million to the bank and receives $12 million. The difference between spot and forward exchange rates, expressed in dollars per unit of foreign currency, may be seen in the following values quoted on February 13, 1987.

Rates	Deutsche Mark (DM) ($/DM)	British Pound (£) ($/£)
Spot	$0.7338	$2.0412
30-day forward	0.7357	2.0358
90-day forward	0.7420	2.0255
180-day forward	0.7464	2.0135

The forward exchange rate of a currency is generally slightly different from the spot rate prevailing at that time. Since the forward rate deals with a future time, the expectations regarding the future value of that currency are reflected in the forward rate. Forward rates may be greater than the current spot rate (trade at a premium) or less than the current spot rate (trade at a discount). On February 13, 1987, forward rates on the deutsche mark were at a premium in relation to the spot rate, while the forward rates for the British pound were at a discount from the spot rate. This means that, on that day, the participants in the foreign exchange market expected the deutsche mark to appreciate relative to the Canadian dollar in the near-term future, while they expected the British pound to depreciate against the dollar. It is very common to express the discount or premium as an annualized percentage deviation from the spot rate. The percentage discount or premium is computed with the following formula:

$$\text{Forward premium (or discount)} = \frac{\text{Forward rate} - \text{Spot rate}}{\text{Spot rate}} \times \frac{12}{\text{Length of forward contract (in months)}} \times 100\% \qquad (21\text{–}1)$$

For example, on February 13, 1987, the 90-day forward contract in deutsche marks was selling at a 4.47 percent premium:

$$\frac{0.7420 - 0.7338}{0.7338} \times \frac{12}{3} \times 100\% = 4.47\%$$

while the 90-day forward contract in pounds was trading at a 3.08 percent discount:

$$\frac{2.0255 - 2.0412}{2.0412} \times \frac{12}{3} \times 100\% = -3.08\%$$

Normally, the forward premium or discount is between 0.5 percent and 10 percent.

The spot and forward transactions take place in what is called the over-the-counter market. Foreign currency dealers (usually large commercial banks or investment dealers) and their customers (importers, exporters, investors, multinational firms, and so forth) negotiate the exchange rate, the length of the forward contract, and the commission in a mutually agreeable fashion. Although the length of a typical forward contract may generally vary between one month and six months, contracts for longer maturities are not uncommon. The dealers, however, may require higher returns for longer contracts.

Cross rates If we have currency quotations in Canadian dollars only, we will have to make some further calculations if we are interested in the cross rates for currencies other than the dollar. For example, on February 13, 1987, the deutsche mark was selling for $0.7338 and the British pound was selling for $2.0412. The cross rate between the mark and the pound was then 2.7818 DM/£ (pound). In determining this value, we know one dollar will buy 1.3628 marks (1/0.7338) and a pound is equal to 2.0412 dollars. Thus, 1.3628 deutsche marks per *dollar* times 2.0412 *dollars* per pound equals 2.7818 deutsche marks per pound.

Managing Foreign Exchange Risk

When the parties associated with a commercial transaction are located in the same country, the transaction is denominated in a single currency. International transactions inevitably involve more than one currency (because the parties are domiciled residents of different countries). Since most foreign currency values fluctuate from time to time, the monetary value of an international transaction measured in either the seller's currency or the buyer's currency is likely to change when payment is delayed. As a result, the seller may receive less revenue than expected or the buyer may have to pay more than the expected amount for the merchandise. Thus the term *foreign exchange risk* refers to the possibility of a drop in revenue or an increase in cost in an international transaction due to a change in foreign exchange rates. Importers, exporters, investors, and multinational firms are all exposed to this foreign exchange risk.

The international monetary system has undergone a significant change over the last 15 years. The free trading, Western nations basically went from a fixed exchange rate system to a "freely" floating rate system. For the most part the new system proved its agility and resilience during the most turbulent years of oil price hikes and hyperinflation of the last decade. The free market exchange rates responded and adjusted well to these adverse conditions. Consequently, the exchange rates fluctuated over a much wider range than before. The increased volatility of exchange markets forced many multinational firms, importers, and exporters to pay more attention to the function of foreign exchange risk management.

The foreign exchange risk of a multinational company is divided into three types of exposure. They are: accounting, or translation, exposure; transaction exposure; and economic exposure. An MNC's foreign assets and liabilities, which are denominated in foreign currency units, are exposed to losses and gains due to changing exchange rates. This is called accounting, or translation, exposure. The amount of loss or gain resulting from this form of exposure, and the treatment of it in the parent company's books, depends on the accounting rules established by the parent company's government. In Canada the rules are spelled out in the CICA Accounting Recommendations, Section 1650. Under the accounting recommendations set forward in June 1983 all foreign currency denominated assets and liabilities are converted at the rate of exchange in effect on the date of balance sheet preparation. All translation gains or losses are incorporated in the parent's consolidated income statement for that period. Thus, the impact of the accounting exposure resulting from the translation of a foreign subsidiary's balance sheet on reported earnings of multinational firms is substantial.

The foreign exchange gains and losses resulting from international transactions, which are known as transaction gains and losses, are reflected in the income statement for the current period. As a consequence of these transactional gains and losses, the volatility of reported earnings per share increases. Three different strategies can be used to minimize this transaction exposure.

1. Hedging in the forward exchange market.
2. Hedging in the money market.
3. Hedging in the currency futures market.

Forward exchange market hedge To see how the transaction exposure can be covered in forward markets, suppose British Telephone purchases a large telephone switching station from Northern Telecom of Canada for £1.267 million on February 13, 1987, and NorTel is promised the payment in British pounds in 90 days. Since NorTel is now exposed to exchange risk by agreeing to receive the payment in British pounds in the future, it is up to Northern Telecom to find a way to reduce this exposure, if it so desires. One simple method is to hedge the exposure in the forward exchange market. To establish the forward cover, NorTel would sell a forward contract, on February 13, to deliver the £1.267 million 90 days from then in exchange for $2.5663 million. On May 14, 1987, Northern Tel receives payment from British Telephone and delivers the £1.267 million to the bank that signed the contract. In return, the bank delivers $2.5663 million to Northern Tel. Thus, through this international transaction, Northern Telecom receives the same dollar amount it expected three months ago regardless of what happened to the value of the British pound in the interim. In contrast, if the sale had been invoiced in Canadian dollars, British Telephone, not Northern Tel, would have been exposed to the exchange risk.

Money market hedge A second way to eliminate transaction exposure in this example is to borrow money in British pounds and convert them to Canadian dollars immediately. When the accounts receivable from the sale is collected three months later, the loan is cleared with the proceeds. This strategy consists of the following steps: On February 13, 1987,

1. Borrow £1,230,000 (£ 1,267,000/1.03 = £ 1,230,000) at the rate of 12 percent per year for three months. You borrow less than the full amount of £ 1,267,000 in recognition of the fact that interest must be paid on the loan. Twelve percent interest for 90 days translates into 3 percent. Thus £ 1,267,000 is divided by 1.03 to arrive at the size of the loan prior to the interest payment.
2. Convert the British pounds into Canadian dollars in the spot market.

Then on May 14, 1987 (90 days later),

3. Receive the payment £ 1,267,000 from British Telephone.
4. Clear the loan with the proceeds from that payment.

The money market hedge basically calls for matching the exposed asset (accounts receivable) with a liability (loan payable) in the same currency. Some firms prefer this money market hedge because of the earlier availability of funds this method provides.

Currency futures market hedge Transaction exposure associated with a foreign currency can also be covered in the currency futures market. The International Monetary Market (IMM) of the Chicago Mercantile Exchange began trading in futures contracts in foreign currencies on May 16, 1972. Trading in currency futures contracts also made a debut on the London International Financial Futures Exchange (LIFFE) in September 1982. Other markets have also developed around the world. Just as futures contracts are traded in corn, wheat, hogs, and beans, foreign currency futures contracts are traded in these markets. Although the futures market and forward market are similar in concept, they differ in their operations. To illustrate the hedging process in the currency futures market, suppose that in June the Bank of Montreal considers lending 500,000 deutsche marks to a German subsidiary of a Canadian parent company for six months. It purchases the deutsche marks in the spot market, delivers them to the borrower, and simultaneously hedges its transaction exposure by selling December contracts in deutsche marks for the same amount. In December when the loan is cleared, the bank sells the deutsche marks in the spot market and buys back the December deutsche mark contracts. The transactions are illustrated as follows for the spot and futures market:

Date	*Spot Market*	*Futures Market*
June 1	Buys DM 500,000 at $0.7420/ DM = $371,000	Sells DM 500,000 for December delivery at $0.7380/DM = $369,000
December 1	Sells DM 500,000 at $0.7340/ DM = $367,000 Loss = $4,000	Buys DM 500,000 at $.07340/ DM = $367,000 Gain = $2,000

While the loan was outstanding the deutsche mark dropped its value in relation to the Canadian dollar. Had the bank remained unhedged, it would have lost $4,000. By hedging in the futures market the bank reduced the loss to $2,000. A $2,000 gain in the futures market was used to cancel out half of the $4,000 loss in the spot market.

Hedging is not the only means companies have for protecting themselves against foreign exchange risk. Over the years multinational companies have developed elaborate foreign asset management programs that involve such strategies as switching cash and other current assets into strong currencies while piling up debt and other liabilities in depreciating currencies. Companies also encourage the quick collection of bills in weak currencies by offering sizable discounts while extending liberal credit in strong currencies.

Foreign Investment Decisions

At the end of 1982 1,146 Canadian firms had direct investments in 3,240 foreign concerns. The fact that 6 percent of these Canadian enterprises accounted for 78 percent of the value of these investments

Figure 21–1
Risk reduction from international diversification

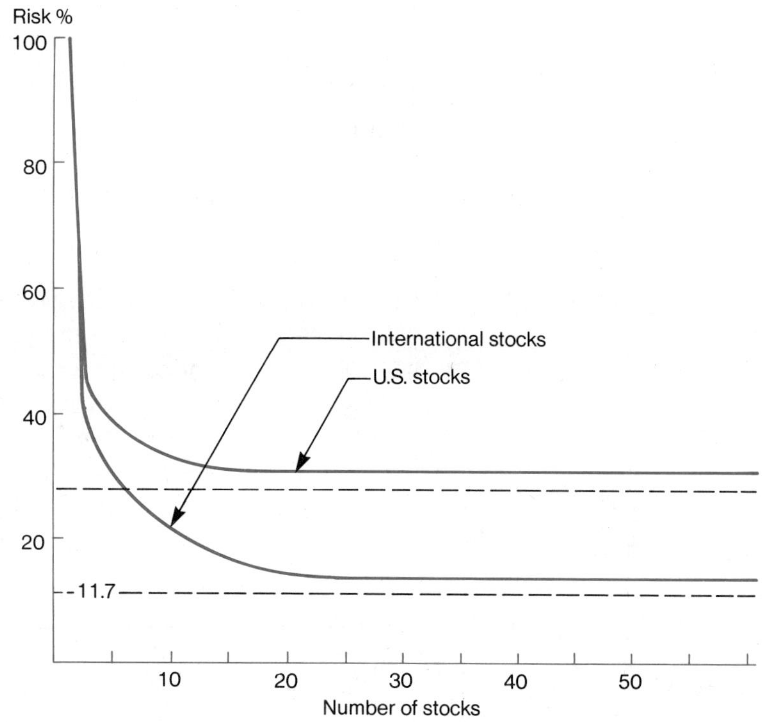

Source: Bruno H. Solnik, "Why Not Diversify Internationally Rather Than Domestically?" *Financial Analysts Journal* 30 (July–August, 1974), p. 51.

paring single-country versus multicountry investment portfolios, implies that further reduction in investment risk can be achieved by diversifying across national boundaries. International stocks, in Figure 21–2, show a consistently lower percentage of risk compared to any given number of U.S. stocks in a portfolio. Some argue, however, that institutional and political constraints, language barriers, and lack of adequate information on foreign investments prevent investors from diversifying across nations. Multinational firms, on the other hand, through their unique position around the world, can derive the benefits of international diversification.[1] This is due, at least partially, to their

[1] This point is sometimes debated by those who suggest that multinationals are subject to the financial market conditions existing in their own home country.

ability to operate as an efficient internal capital market bypassing many of the frictions that exist among and within nation-based capital, managerial, and technology markets.[2]

While the U.S.-based firms took the lead in establishing overseas subsidiaries during the 1950s and 1960s, the European and Japanese firms started this activity in the 1970s. Because of this slowdown in U.S. expansion abroad, the flow of foreign direct investment into Canada has proceeded at a much slower rate since the mid-1970s. This slower relative growth is due, in part, to a number of takeovers by Canadians of foreign-owned energy companies as the result of the provisions of the National Energy Policy, announced in 1980.

Even though the rate of growth since 1977 has slowed to about 5.5 percent annually, foreign investments in Canada were $84 billion at the end of 1985. Much of this investment is a legacy of the establishment of American branch plants in Canada following the Second World War. As Figure 21–3 documents, the United States's dominant share

Figure 21–3
Foreign direct investment in Canada by geographic source

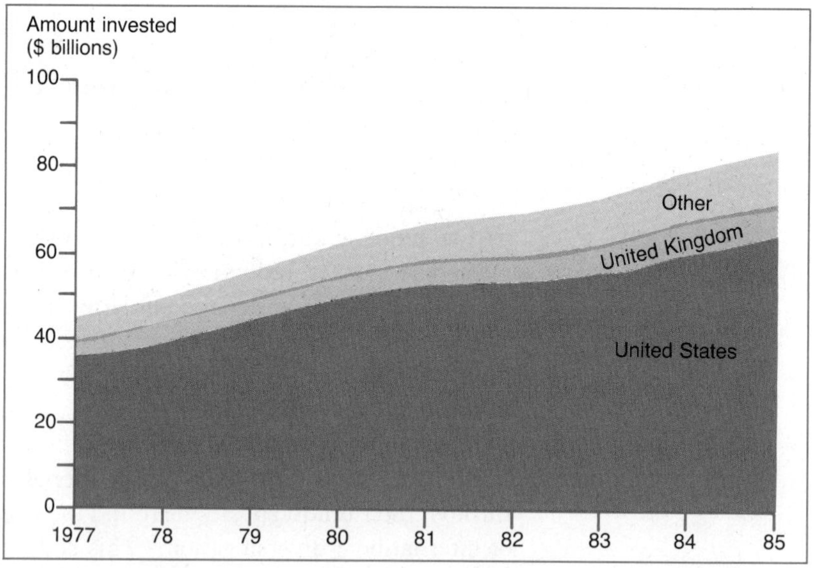

[2] See Alan M. Rugman, "Internalization Theory and Corporate International Finance," *California Management Review* 22, no. 2 (1980), pp. 73–79, for further information on this important point.

of foreign direct investment in Canada dropped about four percentage points to 76 percent of the total between 1977 and 1985. Over that time Asia's share rose two percentage points to 3 percent of total direct investment, largely as a result of increased Japanese activity. Given the large capital surpluses Japan is generating as a result of its positive international balance of trade, that trend should continue and possibly accelerate.

A particularly thorny issue in the history of Canadian development has been the extent of foreign control of industrial enterprise in our economy. In the 1960s it was estimated that as much as two thirds of the manufacturing capacity and 80 percent of the petroleum and gas industry were controlled by foreign-based firms (especially American multinationals). By 1980 the degree of foreign ownership of the productive capacity had declined but still stood at 51 percent in manufacturing (the United States controlled 40 percent), 50 percent in petroleum and natural gas (U.S.-based, 38 percent), and 49 percent in mining and smelting (29 percent U.S. controlled). This foreign domination of ownership of important sectors of the Canadian economy has been blamed for many ills, not the least of which is the failure of our firms to invest heavily in new product research and development.

Analysis of Political Risk

Decisions by business firms to make direct investments in foreign countries are taken with a relatively long time horizon in view. This is natural because of the time period necessary to recover the initial investment on large capital projects. The government may change hands several times during the foreign firm's tenure in that country. In the case of many countries, there is the concern that when a new government takes over, it may not be as friendly or as cooperative as the previous administration. An unfriendly government can interfere with the foreign affiliates in many ways. It may impose foreign exchange restrictions, or the foreign ownership share may be limited to a set percentage of the total. Repatriation (transfer) of a subsidiary's profit to the parent company may be blocked, at least temporarily. In the most extreme cases of interference the government may even expropriate (take over) the foreign subsidiary's assets. The multinational company may experience a sizable loss of income and/or property as a result of this political interference. Many well-known U.S. firms like Anaconda, ITT, and Occidental Petroleum have lost hundreds of millions of dollars in politically unstable countries. It has been reported that in the late 1970s and early 1980s, more than 60 percent of U.S. companies doing business abroad suffered some form of politically inflicted damage.[3] The experience of Canadian international enterprise is littered with far fewer examples of foreign government expropriation, probably due to the fact that the amount Canadian firms have invested directly in Third World countries has been insignificant. Nonetheless, analysis of foreign political risk deserves much attention in multinational firms who are considering investing outside of the major industrial nations.

The best approach to protection against political risk is for the firm to conduct a thorough investigation of the country's political stability long before it makes any investment in that country. To this end companies have been using different methods for assessing political risk. Some firms hire consultants to provide them with a report of political risk analysis. Others form their own advisory committees (little state departments) consisting of top-level managers from headquarters and foreign subsidiaries. After ascertaining the country's political risk level, the multinational firm can use one of the following strategies to guard against such risk:

1. One strategy is to establish a joint venture with a local entrepreneur. By bringing a local partner into the deal, the MNC not only limits its financial exposure but also minimizes antiforeign feelings. It may also enhance its chances of commercial success by including a partner who knows the culture intimately.
2. Another risk management tactic is to enter into a joint venture, preferably with firms from other countries. For example, Chevron may pursue its oil production operation in Zaire in association with Royal Dutch Petroleum and Nigerian National Petroleum as partners. The foreign government will be more hesitant to antagonize a number of partner firms of many nationalities at the same time.
3. When the perceived political risk level is high, insurance against such risks can be obtained in advance. Export Development Cor-

[3] Ronald Alsop, "Foreign Ventures," *The Wall Street Journal,* March 30, 1981, p. 1.

poration (EDC), a federal government agency, sells insurance policies to qualified firms. This agency can insure against losses due to expropriation, war or revolution, or any resulting impossibility of repatriating revenues or capital. Many firms have made use of this service over the years. Private insurance companies such as Lloyds of London, American International Group Inc., CIGNA, and others issue similar policies to cover political risk. Political-risk umbrella policies do not come cheaply. Coverage for projects in "fairly safe" countries can cost anywhere from 0.3 percent to 12 percent of the insured values per year. Needless to say, they are more expensive or unavailable in troubled countries. EDC's rates are lower than those of private insurers, and its policies extend for 20 years, compared to three years or less for private insurance policies.

Cash Flow Analysis and the Foreign Investment Decision

Direct foreign investments are often relatively large in size. As we mentioned previously, these investments are exposed to some extraordinary risks such as foreign exchange fluctuations and political interference, which are nonexistent for domestic investments. Therefore, the final decision is often made at the board of directors level after considering the financial feasibility and the strategic importance of the proposed investment. Financial feasibility analysis for foreign investments is basically conducted in the same manner as it is for domestic capital budgets. Certain important differences exist, however, in the treatment of foreign tax credits, foreign exchange risk, and remittance of cash flows. To see how these are handled in foreign investment analysis, let us consider a hypothetical illustration.

Q Systems Inc., a Quebec-based manufacturer of word processing equipment, is considering the establishment of a manufacturing plant in Salaysia, a country in Southeast Asia. The Salaysian plant will be a wholly owned subsidiary of Q Systems, and its estimated cost is 90 million ringgits (2 ringgits = $1). Based on the exchange rate between ringgits and dollars, the cost in dollars is $45 million. In addition to selling in the local Salaysian market, the proposed subsidiary is expected to export its word processors to the neighboring markets in Singapore, Hong Kong, and Thailand. Expected revenues and operating costs are as shown in Table 21–2. The country's investment climate, which reflects the foreign exchange and political risks, is rated BBB (considered fairly safe) by a leading Asian business journal. After considering the investment climate and the nature of the industry, Q Systems has set a target rate of return of 20 percent for this foreign investment. Salaysia has a 25 percent corporate income tax rate and has waived the withholding tax on dividends repatriated (forwarded) to the parent company. A dividend payment ratio of 100 percent is intended for the foreign subsidiary. Q Systems' marginal tax rate is 46 percent.

It was agreed by Q Systems and the Salaysian government that the subsidiary will be sold to a Salaysian entrepreneur after six years for an estimated 30 million ringgits. The plant will be depreciated over a

Table 21–2
Cash flow analysis of a foreign investment

	Projected Cash Flows (millions ringgits unless otherwise stated)						
	Year 1	*Year 2*	*Year 3*	*Year 4*	*Year 5*	*Year 6*	
Revenues	45.00	50.00	55.00	60.00	65.00	70.00	
− Operating expenses	28.00	30.00	30.00	32.00	35.00	35.00	
− Depreciation	10.00	10.00	10.00	10.00	10.00	10.00	
Earnings before Salaysian taxes	7.00	10.00	15.00	18.00	20.00	25.00	
− Salaysian income tax (25%)	1.75	2.50	3.75	4.50	5.00	6.25	
Earnings after foreign income taxes	5.25	7.50	11.25	13.50	15.00	18.75	
= Dividends repatriated	5.25	7.50	11.25	13.50	15.00	18.75	
Gross Canadian taxes (46% of foreign earnings before taxes)	3.22	4.60	6.90	8.28	9.20	11.50	
− Foreign tax credit	1.75	2.50	3.75	4.50	5.00	6.25	
Net Canadian taxes payable	1.47	2.10	3.15	3.78	4.20	5.25	
After-tax dividend received by Q Systems	3.78	5.40	8.10	9.72	10.80	13.50	
Exchange rate (ringgits/$)	2.00	2.04	2.08	2.12	2.16	2.21	
After-tax dividend (Can. $)	1.89	2.65	3.89	4.58	5.00	6.11	
IF_{pv} (at 20%)	0.833	0.694	0.579	0.482	0.402	0.335	
PV of dividends ($)	1.57 +	1.84 +	2.25 +	2.21 +	2.01 +	2.05	= $11.93

period of six years using the straight-line method. The cash flows generated through depreciation cannot be remitted to the parent company until the subsidiary is sold to the local private entrepreneur six years from now. The Salaysian government requires the subsidiary to invest the depreciation-generated cash flows in local government bonds yielding an after-tax rate of 15 percent. The depreciation cash flows thus compounded and accumulated can be returned to Q Systems when the project is terminated.

Although the value of ringgits in the foreign exchange market has remained fairly stable for the past three years, the projected budget deficits and trade deficits of Salaysia, according to a consultant hired by Q Systems, is likely to result in a gradual devaluation of ringgits against the Canadian dollar at the rate of 2 percent per year for the next six years.

Note the analysis in Table 21–2 is primarily done in terms of ringgits. Expenses (operating, depreciation, and Salaysian income taxes) are subtracted from revenues to arrive at earnings after foreign income taxes. These earnings are then repatriated (forwarded) to Q Systems in the form of dividends. Dividends repatriated thus begin at 5.25 ringgits (in millions) in Year 1 and increase to 18.75 ringgits in Year 6. The next item, gross Canadian taxes, refers to the unadjusted Canadian tax obligation. Dividends received from a foreign subsidiary, unlike those received from a Canadian subsidiary, are fully taxable. In the case of Q Systems this rate is equal to 46 percent of foreign earnings before taxes (earnings before Salaysian taxes).[4] For example, gross Canadian taxes in the first year are equal to:

Earnings before Salaysian taxes	7.00
46% of foreign pre-tax earnings	46%
Gross Canadian taxes	3.22

From gross Canadian taxes, Q Systems may take a foreign tax credit equal to the amount of Salaysian income tax paid. Gross Canadian taxes minus this foreign tax credit are equal to net Canadian taxes payable. Finally, after-tax dividends received by Q Systems are equal to dividends repatriated minus Canadian taxes payable. In the first year, the values are:

[4]If foreign earnings had not been repatriated, there is a possibility that this tax obligation would not be due.

Dividends repatriated	5.25
Less: Net Canadian taxes payable	1.47
After-tax dividends received by Q	3.78

The figures for after-tax dividends received by Q Systems are all stated in ringgits (the analysis up to this point has been in ringgits). These ringgits will now be converted into dollars. The initial exchange rate is two ringgits per dollar, and this will go up by 2 percent per year.[5] For the first year, 3.78 million ringgits will be translated into $1.89 million. After-tax dividends in Canadian dollars grow from $1.89 million in Year 1 to $6.11 million in Year 6. The last two rows of Table 21–2 show the present value of these dividends at a 20 percent discount rate. The *total* present value of estimated after-tax dividends to be received by Q Systems adds up to $11.93 million. Of course, we do know that repatriated dividends will be just one part of the cash flow. The second part consists of depreciation-generated cash flow accumulated and reinvested in Salaysian government bonds at 15 percent per year. The compound value of reinvested depreciation cash flows (10 million ringgits per year) is:

10 million ringgits × 8.754 = 87.54* million ringgits after six years

*Compound sum at 15 percent for six years (see Appendix C at end of book).

These 87.54 million ringgits must next be translated into dollars and then discounted back to the present. Since the exchange rate is forecast at 2.21 ringgits per dollar in the sixth year (fourth line from the bottom in Table 21–2), the dollar equivalent of 87.54 million ringgits becomes:

87.54 million ringgits ÷ 2.21 = $39.61 million

The $39.61 million can now be discounted back to the present by using the present value factor for six years at 20 percent (see Appendix B).

$39.61	million
0.335	IF_{pv}
$13.27	million

[5]The 2 percent appreciation means the dollar is equal to an increasing amount of ringgits each year. The dollar is appreciating relative to ringgits, and ringgits are depreciating relative to the dollar. Since Q Systems' earnings are in ringgits, they are being converted at a less desirable rate each year. Q Systems may eventually decide to hedge its foreign exchange risk exposure.

The final benefit to be received is the 30 million ringgits when the plant is sold six years from now. We first convert this to dollars and then take the present value.

$$30 \text{ million ringgits} \div 2.21 = \$13.57 \text{ million}$$

The present value of $13.57 million after six years at 20 percent is:

$$\begin{array}{ll} \$13.57 & \text{million} \\ \underline{0.335} & IF_{pv} \\ \$\ 4.55 & \text{million} \end{array}$$

The present value of all cash inflows in dollars is equal to:

Present value of dividends	$11.93 million
Present value of repatriated depreciation	13.27
Present value of plant sale	4.55
Total value of inflows	$29.75 million

The cost of the project was initially specified as 90 million ringgits, or $45 million. Thus, we see the total present value of inflows in dollars is less than the cost, and the project has a negative net present value.

Total present value of inflows	$ 29.75 million
Cost	45.00
Net present value	$−15.25 million

The project is not acceptable on the basis of net present value criteria. However, before such a recommendation is made to the board of directors, the financial analyst must reconsider the project and assess its strategic importance for the firm. One must debate whether the specific foreign project is consistent with the firm's overall long-term goals. If the firm wants to use this foreign project as a base for its future marketing of small computers in this part of the world, then the negative net present value should not be the decisive factor in making the decision. As a next step, you need to consider any special circumstances of a nonroutine nature that may have led the firm to consider this foreign investment. For example, if Q Systems' North American domestic market share is eroding, a new market penetration like the one under consideration may be part of a much larger decision that is crucial for the firm's future.[6]

Financing International Business Operations

When the parties to an international transaction are well known to each other and the countries involved are politically stable, sales are generally made on credit, as is customary in domestic business operations. If the foreign importer is relatively new and/or the political environment is volatile, the possibility of nonpayment by the importer is worrisome for the exporter. In order to reduce the risk of nonpayment, an exporter will generally request that the importer furnish a letter of credit. The importer's bank normally issues the letter of credit in which the bank promises to subsequently pay out the money for the merchandise. For example, assume Canadian Western Farms (CWF) is negotiating with a South Korean trading company to export soybean meal. The two parties reach agreement on price, method of shipment, timing of shipment, destination point, and so forth. Once the basic terms of sale have been agreed to, the South Korean trading company (importer) applies for a letter of credit from its commercial bank in Seoul. The Korean bank, if it so desires, issues such a letter of credit, which specifies in detail all the steps that must be completed by the Canadian exporter before payment is made. If CWF complies with all specifications in the letter of credit and submits to the Korean bank the proper documentation to prove it has done so, the Korean bank guarantees the payment on the due date. On that date the Canadian firm is paid by the Korean bank, not by the buyer of the goods. Therefore, all the credit risk to the exporter is absorbed by the importer's bank, which is in a good position to evaluate the creditworthiness of the importing firm.

---

[6]The impact of the 20 percent discount rate should also be considered. At discount rates commonly applied to conventional domestic investments, often closer to 10 percent, the project would be accepted on a net present value basis.

The exporter who requires cash payment or a letter of credit from foreign buyers of marginal credit standing is likely to lose orders to competitors. Instead of risking the loss of business, Canadian firms can find an alternative way to reduce the risk of nonpayment by foreign customers. This alternative method consists of obtaining export credit insurance. The insurance policy provides assurance to the exporter that should the foreign customer default on payment, the insurance company will pay for the shipment. The Export Development Corporation, an agency of the Canadian federal government, provides this kind of insurance to exporting firms.

Funding of Transactions

Assistance in the funding of foreign transactions may take many forms.

Export Development Corporation (EDC) This agency of the federal government facilitates the financing of Canadian exports through its miscellaneous programs. In its credit insurance EDC protects the exporter by insuring 90 percent of the value of export sales. The EDC also guarantees loans made by financial institutions to foreign purchasers of Canadian products. EDC can also make capital projects possible by financing them in instances where there is no commercial credit available. In these cases the Canadian supplier receives payment from the proceeds of the loan to the foreign buyer. Such capital goods might include communications equipment, heavy machinery—especially for use in energy-related projects, radar systems, and the like.

Loans from the parent company or a sister affiliate An apparent source of funds for a foreign affiliate is its parent company or its sister affiliates. In addition to contributing equity capital the parent company often provides loans of varying maturities to its foreign affiliate. Although the simplest arrangement is a direct loan from the parent to the foreign subsidiary, such a loan is rarely extended because of foreign exchange risk, political risk, and tax treatment. Instead, the loans are often channeled through an intermediary to a foreign affiliate. *Parallel loans* and *fronting loans* are two examples of such indirect loan arrangements between a parent company and its foreign affiliate. A typical parallel loan arrangement is depicted in Figure 21–4.

Figure 21–4
A parallel loan arrangement

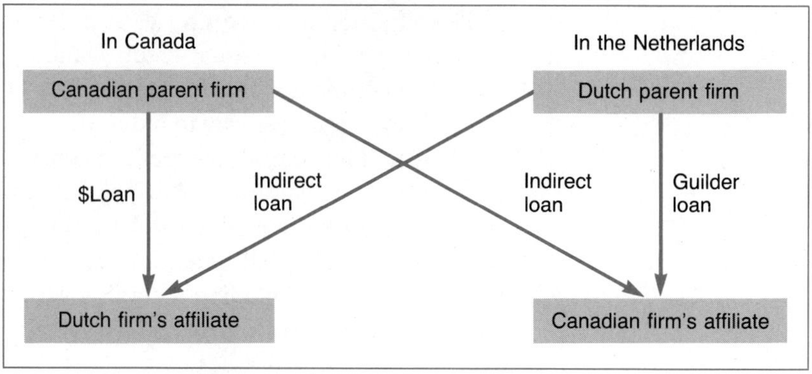

In this illustration a Canadian firm wanting to lend funds to its Dutch affiliate locates a Dutch parent firm that wants to transfer funds to its Canadian affiliate. Avoiding the exchange markets entirely, the Canadian parent lends dollars to the Dutch affiliate in Canada, while the Dutch parent lends guilders to the Canadian affiliate in the Netherlands. At maturity the two loans would each be repaid to the original lender. Notice that neither loan carries any foreign exchange risk in this arrangement. In essence, both parent firms are providing indirect loans to their affiliates.

A fronting loan is simply a parent's loan to its foreign subsidiary channeled through a financial intermediary, usually a large international bank. A schematic of a fronting loan is shown in Figure 21–5.

In the example the Canadian parent company deposits funds in an Amsterdam bank, and that bank, in turn, lends the same amount to its affiliate in the Netherlands. In this manner the bank fronts for the parent by extending a risk-free (fully collateralized) loan to the foreign affiliate. In the event of political turmoil, the foreign government is more likely to allow the Canadian subsidiary to repay the loan to a large international bank than to allow the same affiliate to repay the loan to its parent company. Thus, the parent company reduces its political risk substantially by using a fronting loan instead of transferring funds directly to its foreign affiliate.

Even though the parent company would prefer that its foreign subsidiary maintain its own financial arrangements, many banks are apprehensive about lending to a foreign affiliate without a parent guarantee. In fact, a large portion of bank lending to foreign affiliates is based on

Figure 21–5
A fronting loan arrangement

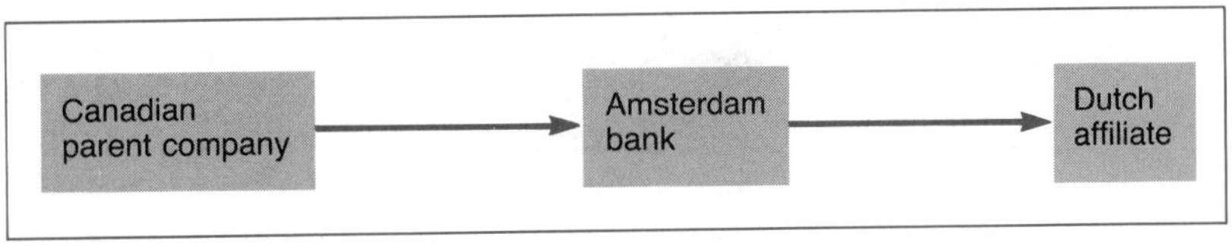

some sort of a guarantee by the parent firm. Usually because of its multinational reputation, the parent company has a better credit rating than its foreign affiliates. The lender advances funds on the basis of the parent's creditworthiness even though the affiliate is expected to pay back the loan. The terms of a parent guarantee may vary greatly, depending upon the closeness of the parent-affiliate ties, the parent-lender relations, and the home country's legal jurisdiction.

Eurocurrency loans The Eurocurrency market is an important source of short-term loans for many multinational firms and their foreign affiliates. A Eurocurrency is a unit of currency held on deposit in a bank outside of the country issuing the currency.

For example, the predominant Eurocurrency, Eurodollars, are generally U.S. dollars deposited in European banks. A substantial portion of these deposits is held by European branches of U.S. commercial banks. About 85–90 percent of these deposits are in the form of straight term deposits with the banks for a specific maturity and at a fixed interest rate. The remaining 10–15 percent of these deposits represent negotiable certificates of deposit with maturities varying from one week to five years or longer. However, maturities of three months, six months, and one year are most common in this market.

Since the early 1960s the Eurodollar market alone has become nearly a trillion-dollar market and has established itself as a significant part of world credit markets. The participants in these markets are diverse in character and are geographically widespread. Hundreds of corporations and banks, mostly from the United States, Canada, Western Europe, and Japan, are regular borrowers and depositors in this market.

The Eurocurrency market became an increasingly important source of short-term financing for the multinational company during the early 1980s. The lower costs and greater credit availability of the Eurocurrency market continue to attract borrowers. The lower borrowing costs in the Eurocurrency market are often attributed to the smaller overhead costs for lending banks and the absence of a compensating balance requirement. The lending rate for borrowers in the Eurocurrency market is based on the London Interbank Offered Rate (LIBOR), which is the interest rate for large deposits. Interest rates on loans are calculated by adding premiums to this basic rate. The size of this premium varies from 0.25 percent to 0.50 percent, depending on the customer, length of the loan period, size of the loan, and so on. Although the rates in the Eurocurrency market tend to be cheaper than domestic rates in either Canada or the United States, the LIBOR rate does tend to be more volatile than the banks' prime rates because of the volatility of supply and demand in the Eurocurrency market.

Lending in the Eurocurrency market is almost exclusively done by commercial banks. Large Eurocurrency loans are often syndicated by a group of participating banks. The loan agreement is put together by a lead bank known as the manager, which is usually one of the largest U.S. or European banks. The manager charges the borrower a once-and-for-all fee or commission of 0.25 percent to 1 percent of the loan value. A portion of this fee is kept by the lead bank, and the remainder is shared by all the participating banks. The aim of forming a syndicate, of course, is to diversify the risk, which would be too large for any single bank to handle by itself. Multicurrency loans and revolving credit arrangements can also be negotiated in the Eurocurrency market to suit borrowers' needs.

Eurobond market When long-term funds are needed, borrowing in the Eurobond market is a viable alternative for leading multinational corporations. The annual turnover of $2.5 trillion of Eurobonds per year indicates the size of this market. These Eurobond issues are sold simultaneously in several different national capital markets but are denominated in a currency different from that of the nation in which the bonds are issued. The most widely used currency in the Eurobond market is the U.S. dollar with almost 67 percent of all the issues denominated in that currency. The next currency in importance is the deutsche mark. Eurobond issues are underwritten by an international syndicate of banks and securities firms. Eurobonds of longer than seven years in maturity generally have a sinking fund provision.

Disclosure requirements in the Eurobond market are much less stringent than those required by the securities commissions in Canada and the United States. Furthermore, the registration costs in the Eurobond market are generally lower than those charged in Canada and the United

States. In addition, the Eurobond market offers tax flexibility for borrowers and investors alike. Since most Eurobonds are issued by a fully owned offshore finance subsidiary located in a tax-haven country such as Luxembourg, there are no withholding taxes on interest paid. Wealthy investors often buy Eurobonds through Swiss bank accounts so their interest income can be kept anonymous. All these advantages of Eurobonds enable the borrowers to raise funds at a lower cost. Nevertheless, a caveat may be in order with respect to the effective cost of borrowing in the Eurobond market. When a multinational firm borrows by floating a foreign currency denominated debt issue on a long-term basis, it creates transaction exposure, a kind of foreign exchange risk. If the foreign currency appreciates in value during the bond's life (think of what happened to the deutsche mark compared to the Canadian and American dollars in 1986), the cost of servicing the debt could be prohibitively high. Many Canadian multinational firms borrowed at an approximate 7 percent coupon interest by selling Eurobonds denominated in deutsche marks and Swiss francs in the late 1960s and early 1970s. Nevertheless, these firms experienced an average debt service cost of approximately 13 percent, which is almost twice as much as the coupon rate. This increased cost occurred because the Canadian dollar fell with respect to these currencies. Therefore, currency selection for denominating Eurobond issues must be made with extreme care and foresight. To lessen the impact of foreign exchange risk, some recently issued Eurobond issues were denominated in multicurrency units.

One sector of the Eurobond market, that for banks' perpetual floating rate notes (worth over $23 billion Canadian), has been an important source of long-term capital for the major commercial banks of Canada and other industrialized nations. Because of payment defaults by Third World nations on their huge debts owed to the international commercial banking industry, however, this source of funds (or *perps* as they are called) for the Canadian banks will probably not be available in the future.

International equity markets The entire amount of equity capital comes from the parent company for a wholly owned foreign subsidiary, but a majority of foreign affiliates are not owned completely by their parent corporations. In fact, in countries like India and Malaysia, majority ownership of a foreign affiliate must be held by the local citizens. In some other countries the parent corporations are allowed to own their affiliates completely in the initial stages, but they are required to relinquish partial ownership to local citizens after five or seven years. In order to avoid nationalistic reactions to wholly owned foreign subsidiaries, multinational firms such as Unilever Ltd., Schlumberger, General Motors, Ford Motor Company, and IBM sell shares to worldwide stockholders. It is also believed that widespread foreign ownership of the firm's common stock encourages the loyalty of foreign stockholders and employees toward the firm. Thus, selling common stock to residents of foreign countries is not only an important financing strategy, but it is also a risk-minimizing strategy for many multinational corporations.

As you learned in Chapter 14, a well-functioning secondary market is essential to entice investors into owning shares. To attract investors from all over the world, reputable multinational firms list their shares on major stock exchanges around the world. For instance, about 40 Canadian companies are listed on the New York Stock Exchange while a few more are listed on the American Stock Exchange. Even more foreign firms would sell stock issues in the United States and list on NYSE and AMEX were it not for the tough and costly disclosure rules in effect in that country and enforced by the Securities and Exchange Commission. Many foreign corporations such as Hoechst, Honda, Hitachi, Sony, Magnet Metals Ltd., DeBeers, and the like accommodate American investors by issuing American Depository Receipts (ADRs). All the American-owned shares of a foreign company are placed in trust in a New York bank. The bank, in turn, will issue its depository receipts to the American stockholders and will maintain a stockholder ledger on these receipts, thus enabling the holders of ADRs to sell or otherwise transfer them as easily as they transfer any American company shares. Most ADRs trade in the over-the-counter market, although a few are listed on the New York Stock Exchange. ADR prices tend to move parallel with the prices of the underlying securities in their home markets.

Looking elsewhere around the world, approximately 70 U.S. firms have listed their shares on the Toronto Stock Exchange and some 50 on the Montreal Exchange. Similarly, more than 100 U.S. firms have listed their shares on the London Stock Exchange. Approximately 160 foreign issues are listed on the Bourse de Paris, including 37 U.S. stocks. In addition, a number of foreign securities are traded on the

French hors côté (OTC) market. Fully half the stocks listed on the Amsterdam stock exchange are foreign. A handful of Canadian firms have recently been listed on the Tokyo Stock Exchange.

To obtain exposure in an international financial community, listing securities on world stock exchanges is a step in the right direction for a multinational firm. This international exposure also brings an additional responsibility for the MNC to understand the preferences and needs of heterogeneous groups of investors of various nationalities. The MNC may have to print and circulate its annual financial statements in many languages. Some foreign investors are more risk averse than their counterparts in North America, preferring dividend income over less certain capital gains.

Common stock ownership among individuals in countries like Japan and Norway is insignificant, with financial institutions holding substantial amounts of common stock issues. For example, only 5–10 percent of Japanese households own stock, while more than 70 percent have deposit accounts with commercial banks. Institutional practices around the globe also vary significantly when it comes to issuing new securities. Unlike the current Canadian situation (which will change in the near future), European commercial banks play a dominant role in the securities business. They underwrite stock issues, manage portfolios, vote the stock they hold in trust accounts, and hold directorships on company boards. In Germany the banks also run an over-the-counter market in many stocks.

The International Finance Corporation Whenever a multinational company has difficulty raising equity capital due to lack of adequate private risk capital in a foreign country, the firm may explore the possibility of selling partial ownership to the International Finance Corporation (IFC), a unit of the World Bank Group. The International Finance Corporation was established in 1956 and is owned by 119 member countries of the World Bank. Its objective is to further economic development by promoting private enterprises in these countries. The profitability of a project and its potential benefit to the host country's economy are the two criteria the IFC uses to decide whether to assist a venture. The IFC participates in private enterprise through buying equity shares of a business or providing long-term loans, or a combination of the two, for up to 25 percent of the total capital. The IFC expects the other partners to assume managerial responsibility, and it does not exercise its voting rights as a stockholder. The IFC helps finance new ventures as well as the expansion of existing ones in a variety of industries. Once the venture is well established, the IFC sells its investment position to private investors in order to free up its capital.

Some Unsettled Issues in International Finance

As firms become multinational in scope, the nature of their financial decisions also becomes more complex. A multinational firm has access to more sources of funds than a purely domestic corporation. Interest rates and market conditions vary between the alternate sources of funds, and corporate financial practices may differ significantly between countries. For example, the debt ratios in many foreign countries are higher than those used by Canadian firms—which are, in turn, higher than those used by American firms. A foreign affiliate of a Canadian or an American firm faces a dilemma in its financing decision: Should it follow the parent firm's norm or that of the host country? Who must decide this? Will it be decided at the corporate headquarters in Toronto or by the foreign affiliate? This matter of control over financial decisions has important strategic overtones for the multinational firm.

Dividend policy is another area of debate. Should the parent company dictate the dividends the foreign affiliate must distribute or should it be left completely to the discretion of the foreign affiliate? Foreign government regulations also often influence this decision. Questions like these do not have clear-cut answers. The complex environment in which the MNCs operate does not permit simple, clear-cut solutions. Obviously, each situation has to be evaluated individually, and specific guidelines for decision making must be established. Such coordination, it is to be hoped, will result in cohesive policies in the areas of working capital management, capital structure optimization, and dividend payouts throughout the MNC network.

Summary

When a domestic business firm crosses its national borders to do business in other countries, it enters a riskier and more complex environment. A multinational firm is exposed to foreign exchange risk and political risk in addition to the usual business and financial risks. In general, international business operations have been more profitable than domestic operations, and this higher profitability is one factor that motivates business firms to go overseas. International operations account for a significant proportion of the earnings for many North American firms. Multinational firms have played a major role in promoting economic development and international trade for several decades. Canada had more often been the site of rather than the source of such multinational investments, especially prior to 1977. Now, however, Canadian firms are investing significant sums in other countries, most notably in the United States.

International business transactions are denominated in foreign currencies. The rate at which one currency unit is converted into another is called the exchange rate. In today's global monetary system the exchange rates of major currencies are fluctuating rather freely. These freely floating exchange rates expose multinational business firms to foreign exchange risk. To deal with this foreign currency exposure effectively, the financial executive of an MNC must understand foreign exchange rates and how they are determined. Foreign exchange rates are influenced by differences in inflation rates among countries, by differences in interest rates, by governmental policies, and by the expectations of the participants in the foreign exchange markets. The international financial manager can reduce the firm's foreign currency exposure by hedging in the forward exchange market, in the money markets, and in the currency futures market.

Multinational companies have made billions of dollars worth of direct investments in foreign countries over the years. Lower production costs overseas, tax deferral provisions, less foreign competition, and benefits of international diversification are some of the motivational factors behind the flow of direct investment between nations. Foreign direct investments are usually quite large in size, and many of them are exposed to enormous political risk. Although discounted cash flow analysis is applied to screen the projects in the initial stages, strategic considerations and political risk are often the overriding factors in reaching the final decision. One of the most important differences between domestic and international investments is that the information on foreign investments is generally less complete and often less accurate. Therefore, analyzing a foreign investment proposal is more difficult than analyzing a domestic investment project.

Financing international trade and investment is another important area of international finance one must understand in order to raise funds at the lowest cost possible. The multinational firm has access to both the domestic and foreign capital markets. The Export Development Corporation aids in financing Canadian exports to foreign countries. Borrowing in the Eurobond market may appear less expensive at times, but the effect of foreign exchange risk on debt-servicing cost must be weighed carefully before borrowing in these markets. Floating common stock in foreign capital markets is another viable financing alternative for many multinational companies. The International Finance Corporation, a subsidiary of the World Bank, also provides debt capital and equity capital to qualified firms. These alternative sources of financing may differ significantly with respect to cost, terms, and conditions. Therefore, the financial executive must carefully locate and use the proper means to finance international business operations.

List of Terms

multinational corporation
balance of payments
expropriation
currency futures
transaction exposure
translation exposure
earnings repatriation
parallel loan
fronting loan
Eurocurrency
Eurobond
Export Development Corporation (EDC)
purchasing power parity theory
interest rate parity theory
foreign exchange rate
foreign exchange risk
letter of credit
London Interbank Offered Rate (LIBOR)
American Depository Receipts (ADRs)

Discussion Questions

1. What risks does a foreign affiliate of a multinational firm face in today's business world?

2. What are some allegations made against foreign affiliates of multinational firms and against the multinational firms themselves?

3. List the factors that affect the value of a currency in foreign exchange markets.

4. Explain how exports and imports tend to influence the value of a currency.

5. Differentiate between the spot exchange rate and the forward exchange rate.

6. What is meant by translation exposure in terms of foreign exchange risk?

7. What factors influence a Canadian business firm to look to expand in international markets?

8. What procedure(s) would you recommend for a multinational company in studying exposure to political risk? What actual strategies can be used to guard against such risk?

9. What factors beyond the normal domestic analysis go into a financial feasibility study for a multinational firm?

10. What is a letter of credit?

11. Explain the functions of the following agencies: Export Development Corporation (EDC); International Finance Corporation (IFC).

12. What are the differences between a parallel loan and a fronting loan?

13. What is LIBOR? How does it compare to the Canadian banks' domestic prime rates?

14. What is the danger or concern in floating a Eurobond issue?

15. What are ADRs?

16. Comment on any dilemmas that multinational firms and their foreign affiliates may face in regard to debt ratio limits and dividend payouts.

Problems

1. Using the foreign exchange rates for February 13, 1987, in Table 21–1, determine the number of Canadian dollars required to buy the following amounts of foreign currencies.

   a. 10,000 guilders.
   b. 2,000 deutsche marks.
   c. 100,000 yen.
   d. 5,000 Swiss francs.
   e. 20,000 kronas.

2. Obtain a recent Monday edition of *The Globe and Mail—Report on Business* and recalculate the currency exchanges of Problem 1. How do these figures compare to those obtained in the above problem? Has the dollar strengthened or weakened against these currencies?

3. *The Globe and Mail* reported the following spot and forward rates for the Swiss franc ($/SF) as of February 13, 1987:

Spot	$0.8670
30-day forward	0.8698
90-day forward	0.8758
180-day forward	0.8846

   a. Was the Swiss franc selling at a discount or premium in the forward market on February 13, 1987?
   b. What was the 30-day forward premium (or discount)?
   c. What was the 90-day forward premium (or discount)?
   d. Suppose you executed a 90-day forward contract to exchange 100,000 Swiss francs into Canadian dollars. How many dollars would you get 90 days hence?
   e. Assume a Swiss bank entered into a 180-day forward contract with TD Bank to buy $100,000. How many francs will the Swiss bank deliver in six months to get the Canadian dollars?

4. Suppose a Danish kronë is selling for $0.1943 and an Irish punt is selling for $0.9430. What is the exchange rate (cross rate) of the Danish kronë to the Irish punt? That is, how many Danish kronës are equal to an Irish punt?

5. Suppose a Netherland guilder is selling for \$0.6500 and a Maltan pound is selling for \$2.8369. What is the exchange rate (cross rate) of the Netherland guilder to the Maltan pound? That is, how many Netherland guilders are equal to a Maltan pound?

6. From the base price level of 100 in 1968, German and U.S. price levels in 1985 stood at 160 and 213, respectively. If the 1968 US\$/DM exchange rate was U.S. \$0.30/DM, what should the exchange rate have been in 1985?

7. In Problem 6, if the United States had somehow managed no inflation since 1968, what should the exchange rate have been in 1985, using the purchasing power parity theory?

8. An investor in Canada bought a one-year Australian security valued at 108,696 Australian dollars. The Canadian dollar equivalent was \$100,000. The Australian security earned 12 percent during the year, but the Australian dollar depreciated five cents against the Canadian dollar during the time period. After transferring the funds back to Canada, what was the investor's return on his \$100,000? Determine the total ending value of the Australian investment in Australian dollars and then translate this value to Canadian dollars. Then compute the return on the \$100,000 investment.

9. You are the vice president of finance for Exploratory Resources, headquartered in Calgary. In January 19XX your firm's American subsidiary obtained a six-month loan of 1 million American dollars from a bank in Calgary to finance the acquisition of an oil producing property in Oaklahoma. The loan will also be repaid in American dollars. At the time of the loan the spot exchange rate was U.S. \$0.7366/Canadian dollar and the U.S. currency was selling at a discount in the forward market. The June 19XX futures contract (face value = \$100,000 per contract) was quoted at U.S. \$0.7426.

   a. Explain how the Calgary bank could lose on this transaction.
   b. How much is the bank expected to lose due to foreign exchange risk?
   c. If there is a \$100 total brokerage commission per contract, would you still recommend the bank hedge in the currency futures market?

10. The Livingston Corporation has a wholly owned foreign subsidiary in Jamaica. The subsidiary earns $5 million per year before taxes in Jamaica. The foreign income tax rate is 20 percent. Livingston's subsidiary repatriates the entire after-tax profit in the form of dividends to the Livingston Corporation. The Canadian corporate tax rate is 46 percent of foreign earnings before taxes. Disregard any problems associated with exchange rates.

a. Complete the table below.

Before-tax earnings	______
Foreign income tax @ 20%	______
Earnings after foreign income taxes	______
Gross Canadian taxes	______
Foreign tax credit	______
Net Canadian taxes payable	______
After-tax cash flow	______

b. Now assume there is a 10 percent withholding tax on dividends in Jamaica. Recompute the answer to part *a* by completing the following table.

Before-tax earnings	______
Foreign income tax @ 20%	______
Earnings after foreign income taxes	______
Gross dividends distributed	______
Withholding tax	______
Net dividends repatriated	______
Gross Canadian taxes	______
Foreign tax credit	______
Net Canadian taxes payable	______
After-tax cash flow	______

11. The Office Automation Corporation is considering a foreign investment. The initial cash outlay will be $8 million. The current foreign exchange rate is 2 francs = $1. Thus, the investment in foreign currency will be 16 million francs. The assets have a useful life of five years and no expected salvage value. The firm uses a straight-line method of depreciation. Sales are expected to be 20 million francs and operating cash expenses 10 million francs every year for five years. The foreign income tax rate is 25 percent. The foreign subsidiary will repatriate all after-tax profits to Office Automation in the form of dividends. Furthermore, the depreciation cash flows (equal to each year's depreciation) will be repatriated during the same year they accrue to the foreign subsidiary. The applicable cost of capital that reflects the riskiness of the cash flows is 16 percent. The Canadian tax rate is 46 percent.

a. Should the Office Automation Corporation undertake the investment if the foreign exchange rate is expected to remain constant during the five-year period?

b. Should the Office Automation undertake the investment if the foreign exchange rate is expected to be as follows:

Year 0	\$1 = 2.0 francs
Year 1	\$1 = 2.2 francs
Year 2	\$1 = 2.4 francs
Year 3	\$1 = 2.7 francs
Year 4	\$1 = 2.9 francs
Year 5	\$1 = 3.2 francs

Selected References

Aggarwal, Raj. "International Differences in Capital Structure Norms." *Management International Review* 21, no. 1 (1981), pp. 75–88.

Alsop, Ronald. "Foreign Ventures." *The Wall Street Journal,* March 30, 1981, p. 1.

Dufey, Gunter, and Ian Giddy. *The International Money Market.* Englewood Cliffs, N.J.: Prentice-Hall, 1978.

Eiteman, David, and Arthur Stonehill. *Multinational Business Finance.* 3rd ed. Reading, Mass.: Addison-Wesley Publishing, 1982.

Errunza, Viharg. "Determinants of Financial Structure in the Central American Common Market." *Financial Management* 8 (Autumn 1979), pp. 72–77.

Folks, William R., Jr. "Decision Analysis for Exchange Risk Management." *Financial Management* 1 (Winter 1972), pp. 101–12.

"Foreign Manufacturing Investments in the United States." The Conference Board, March 1981, p. 1.

Gentry, James A; D. R. Mehta; S. K. Bhattacharya; R. Cobbaut; and J. Scaringella. "An International Study of Management Perceptions of the Working Capital Process." *Journal of International Business Studies* 10 (Spring–Summer 1979), pp. 28–38.

"The Hundred Largest U.S. Multinationals." *Forbes*, July 5, 1982, pp. 126–28.

Kolhagen, Steven W. "The Performance of Foreign Exchange Markets: 1971–1974." *Journal of International Business Studies* 6 (Fall 1975), pp. 33–39.

Lessard, Donald R. "World, National, and Industrial Factors in Equity Returns." *Journal of Finance* 29 (May 1974), pp. 379–91.

McGuinness, Norman W., and H. A. Conway. "World Product Mandates: The Need for Directed Search Strategies." In *Managing the Multinational Subsidiary*, ed. Hamid Etemad and Louise Dulude. New York: St. Martin Press, 1986.

Murray, D. "The Tax Sensitivity of U.S. Direct Investment in Canadian Manufacturing." *Journal of International Money and Finance* 34, no. 3 (1981).

Naidu, G. N. "How to Reduce Transaction Exposure in International Lending." *The Journal of Commercial Bank Lending* 63 (June 1981), pp. 39–46.

———, and Tai Shin. "Effectiveness of Currency Futures Market in Hedging Foreign Exchange Risk." *Management International Review* 21, no. 4 (1981), pp. 5–16.

Remmers, L.; A. Stonehill; R. Wright; and T. Beekhuisen. "Industry and Size as Debt Ratio Determinants in Manufacturing Internationally." *Financial Management* 3 (Summer 1974), pp. 24–32.

Ricks, David A., and R. A. Ajami. "Motives of Non-American Firms in Investing in the United States." *Journal of International Business Studies* 12 (Winter 1981), pp. 25–34.

Rogalski, Richard, and Joseph Vinso. "Price Level Variations as Predictors of Flexible Exchange Rates." *Journal of International Business Studies* 8 (Summer–Spring 1977), pp. 71–81.

Rugman, Alan M. "Internalization Theory and Corporate International Finance." *California Management Review* 22, no. 2 (1980), pp. 73–79.

———. *Multinationals in Canada: Theory, Performance and Economic Impact*. Boston: Martinus Nijhoff, 1980.

Rummel, R. J., and David A. Heenan. "How Multinationals Analyze Political Risk." *Harvard Business Review* 56 (January–February 1978), pp. 67–76.

Shapiro, Alan C. *Multinational Financial Management*. Boston: Allyn & Bacon, 1982.

Solnik, Bruno H. "Why Not Diversify Internationally Rather than Domestically?" *Financial Analysts Journal* 30 (July–August 1974), pp. 48–54.

Stanley, Marjorie T. "Capital Structure and Cost of Capital for the Multinational Firm." *Journal of International Business Studies* 12 (Spring–Summer 1981), pp. 103–20.

Tang, Roger Y. W. *Multinational Transfer Pricing: Canadian and British Perspectives*. Toronto: Butterworths, 1981.

Weston, J. Fred, and Bart W. Sorge. *Guide to International Financial Management*. New York: McGraw-Hill, 1977.

Appendices

Appendix A Compound sum of $1, IF_s $S = P(1+i)^n$

Period	Percent										
	1%	2%	3%	4%	5%	6%	7%	8%	9%	10%	11%
1	1.010	1.020	1.030	1.040	1.050	1.060	1.070	1.080	1.090	1.100	1.110
2	1.020	1.040	1.061	1.082	1.103	1.124	1.145	1.166	1.188	1.210	1.232
3	1.030	1.061	1.093	1.125	1.158	1.191	1.225	1.260	1.295	1.331	1.368
4	1.041	1.082	1.126	1.170	1.216	1.262	1.311	1.360	1.412	1.464	1.518
5	1.051	1.104	1.159	1.217	1.276	1.338	1.403	1.469	1.539	1.611	1.685
6	1.062	1.126	1.194	1.265	1.340	1.419	1.501	1.587	1.677	1.772	1.870
7	1.072	1.149	1.230	1.316	1.407	1.504	1.606	1.714	1.828	1.949	2.076
8	1.083	1.172	1.267	1.369	1.477	1.594	1.718	1.851	1.993	2.144	2.305
9	1.094	1.195	1.305	1.423	1.551	1.689	1.838	1.999	2.172	2.358	2.558
10	1.105	1.219	1.344	1.480	1.629	1.791	1.967	2.159	2.367	2.594	2.839
11	1.116	1.243	1.384	1.539	1.710	1.898	2.105	2.332	2.580	2.853	3.152
12	1.127	1.268	1.426	1.601	1.796	2.012	2.252	2.518	2.813	3.138	3.498
13	1.138	1.294	1.469	1.665	1.886	2.133	2.410	2.720	3.066	3.452	3.883
14	1.149	1.319	1.513	1.732	1.980	2.261	2.579	2.937	3.342	3.797	4.310
15	1.161	1.346	1.558	1.801	2.079	2.397	2.759	3.172	3.642	4.177	4.785
16	1.173	1.373	1.605	1.873	2.183	2.540	2.952	3.426	3.970	4.595	5.311
17	1.184	1.400	1.653	1.948	2.292	2.693	3.159	3.700	4.328	5.054	5.895
18	1.196	1.428	1.702	2.206	2.407	2.854	3.380	3.996	4.717	5.560	6.544
19	1.208	1.457	1.754	2.107	2.527	3.026	3.617	4.316	5.142	6.116	7.263
20	1.220	1.486	1.806	2.191	2.653	3.207	3.870	4.661	5.604	6.727	8.062
25	1.282	1.641	2.094	2.666	3.386	4.292	5.427	6.848	8.623	10.835	13.585
30	1.348	1.811	2.427	3.243	4.322	5.743	7.612	10.063	13.268	17.449	22.892
40	1.489	2.208	3.262	4.801	7.040	10.286	14.974	21.725	31.409	45.259	65.001
50	1.645	2.692	4.384	7.107	11.467	18.420	29.457	46.902	74.358	117.39	184.57

Appendix A (*concluded*) Compound sum of $1

	Percent										
Period	12%	13%	14%	15%	16%	17%	18%	19%	20%	25%	30%
1	1.120	1.130	1.140	1.150	1.160	1.170	1.180	1.190	1.200	1.250	1.300
2	1.254	1.277	1.300	1.323	1.346	1.369	1.392	1.416	1.440	1.563	1.690
3	1.405	1.443	1.482	1.521	1.561	1.602	1.643	1.685	1.728	1.953	2.197
4	1.574	1.630	1.689	1.749	1.811	1.874	1.939	2.005	2.074	2.441	2.856
5	1.762	1.842	1.925	2.011	2.100	2.192	2.288	2.386	2.488	3.052	3.713
6	1.974	2.082	2.195	2.313	2.436	2.565	2.700	2.840	2.986	3.815	4.827
7	2.211	2.353	2.502	2.660	2.826	3.001	3.185	3.379	3.583	4.768	6.276
8	2.476	2.658	2.853	3.059	3.278	3.511	3.759	4.021	4.300	5.960	8.157
9	2.773	3.004	3.252	3.518	3.803	4.108	4.435	4.785	5.160	7.451	10.604
10	3.106	3.395	3.707	4.046	4.411	4.807	5.234	5.696	6.192	9.313	13.786
11	3.479	3.836	4.226	4.652	5.117	5.624	6.176	6.777	7.430	11.642	17.922
12	3.896	4.335	4.818	5.350	5.936	6.580	7.288	8.064	8.916	14.552	23.298
13	4.363	4.898	5.492	6.153	6.886	7.699	8.599	9.596	10.699	18.190	30.288
14	4.887	5.535	6.261	7.076	7.988	9.007	10.147	11.420	12.839	22.737	39.374
15	5.474	6.254	7.138	8.137	9.266	10.539	11.974	13.590	15.407	28.422	51.186
16	6.130	7.067	8.137	9.358	10.748	12.330	14.129	16.172	18.488	35.527	66.542
17	6.866	7.986	9.276	10.761	12.468	14.426	16.672	19.244	22.186	44.409	86.504
18	7.690	9.024	10.575	12.375	14.463	16.879	19.673	22.091	26.623	55.511	112.46
19	8.613	10.197	12.056	14.232	16.777	19.748	23.214	27.252	31.948	69.389	146.19
20	9.646	11.523	13.743	16.367	19.461	23.106	27.393	32.429	38.338	86.736	190.05
25	17.000	21.231	26.462	32.919	40.874	50.658	62.669	77.388	95.396	264.70	705.64
30	29.960	39.116	50.950	66.212	85.850	111.07	143.37	184.68	237.38	807.79	2,620.0
40	93.051	132.78	188.88	267.86	378.72	533.87	750.38	1,051.7	1,469.8	7,523.2	36,119.
50	289.00	450.74	700.23	1,083.7	1,670.7	2,566.2	3,927.4	5,988.9	9,100.4	70,065.	497,929.

Source: Maurice Joy, *Introduction to Financial Management* (Homewood, Ill.: Richard D. Irwin, 1977).

Appendix B Present value of $1, IF_{pv} $P = S\left[\frac{1}{(1+i)^n}\right]$

Period	1%	2%	3%	4%	5%	6%	7%	8%	9%	10%	11%	12%
1	0.990	0.980	0.971	0.962	0.952	0.943	0.935	0.926	0.917	0.909	0.901	0.893
2	0.980	0.961	0.943	0.925	0.907	0.890	0.873	0.857	0.842	0.826	0.812	0.797
3	0.971	0.942	0.915	0.889	0.864	0.840	0.816	0.794	0.772	0.751	0.731	0.712
4	0.961	0.924	0.885	0.855	0.823	0.792	0.763	0.735	0.708	0.683	0.659	0.636
5	0.951	0.906	0.863	0.822	0.784	0.747	0.713	0.681	0.650	0.621	0.593	0.567
6	0.942	0.888	0.837	0.790	0.746	0.705	0.666	0.630	0.596	0.564	0.535	0.507
7	0.933	0.871	0.813	0.760	0.711	0.665	0.623	0.583	0.547	0.513	0.482	0.452
8	0.923	0.853	0.789	0.731	0.677	0.627	0.582	0.540	0.502	0.467	0.434	0.404
9	0.914	0.837	0.766	0.703	0.645	0.592	0.544	0.500	0.460	0.424	0.391	0.361
10	0.905	0.820	0.744	0.676	0.614	0.558	0.508	0.463	0.422	0.386	0.352	0.322
11	0.896	0.804	0.722	0.650	0.585	0.527	0.475	0.429	0.388	0.350	0.317	0.287
12	0.887	0.788	0.701	0.625	0.557	0.497	0.444	0.397	0.356	0.319	0.286	0.257
13	0.879	0.773	0.681	0.601	0.530	0.469	0.415	0.368	0.326	0.290	0.258	0.229
14	0.870	0.758	0.661	0.577	0.505	0.442	0.388	0.340	0.299	0.263	0.232	0.205
15	0.861	0.743	0.642	0.555	0.481	0.417	0.362	0.315	0.275	0.239	0.209	0.183
16	0.853	0.728	0.623	0.534	0.458	0.394	0.339	0.292	0.252	0.218	0.188	0.163
17	0.844	0.714	0.605	0.513	0.436	0.371	0.317	0.270	0.231	0.198	0.170	0.146
18	0.836	0.700	0.587	0.494	0.416	0.350	0.296	0.250	0.212	0.180	0.153	0.130
19	0.828	0.686	0.570	0.475	0.396	0.331	0.277	0.232	0.194	0.164	0.138	0.116
20	0.820	0.673	0.554	0.456	0.377	0.312	0.258	0.215	0.178	0.149	0.124	0.104
25	0.780	0.610	0.478	0.375	0.295	0.233	0.184	0.146	0.116	0.092	0.074	0.059
30	0.742	0.552	0.412	0.308	0.231	0.174	0.131	0.099	0.075	0.057	0.044	0.033
40	0.672	0.453	0.307	0.208	0.142	0.097	0.067	0.046	0.032	0.022	0.015	0.011
50	0.608	0.372	0.228	0.141	0.087	0.054	0.034	0.021	0.013	0.009	0.005	0.003

Appendix B (*concluded*) Present value of $1

Period	*13%*	*14%*	*15%*	*16%*	*17%*	*18%*	*19%*	*20%*	*25%*	*30%*	*35%*	*40%*	*50%*
1	0.885	0.877	0.870	0.862	0.855	0.847	0.840	0.833	0.800	0.769	0.741	0.714	0.667
2	0.783	0.769	0.756	0.743	0.731	0.718	0.706	0.694	0.640	0.592	0.549	0.510	0.444
3	0.693	0.675	0.658	0.641	0.624	0.609	0.593	0.579	0.512	0.455	0.406	0.364	0.296
4	0.613	0.592	0.572	0.552	0.534	0.515	0.499	0.482	0.410	0.350	0.301	0.260	0.198
5	0.543	0.519	0.497	0.476	0.456	0.437	0.419	0.402	0.320	0.269	0.223	0.186	0.132
6	0.480	0.456	0.432	0.410	0.390	0.370	0.352	0.335	0.262	0.207	0.165	0.133	0.088
7	0.425	0.400	0.376	0.354	0.333	0.314	0.296	0.279	0.210	0.159	0.122	0.095	0.059
8	0.376	0.351	0.327	0.305	0.285	0.266	0.249	0.233	0.168	0.123	0.091	0.068	0.039
9	0.333	0.300	0.284	0.263	0.243	0.225	0.209	0.194	0.134	0.094	0.067	0.048	0.026
10	0.295	0.270	0.247	0.227	0.208	0.191	0.176	0.162	0.107	0.073	0.050	0.035	0.017
11	0.261	0.237	0.215	0.195	0.178	0.162	0.148	0.135	0.086	0.056	0.037	0.025	0.012
12	0.231	0.208	0.187	0.168	0.152	0.137	0.124	0.112	0.069	0.043	0.027	0.018	0.008
13	0.204	0.182	0.163	0.145	0.130	0.116	0.104	0.093	0.055	0.033	0.020	0.013	0.005
14	0.181	0.160	0.141	0.125	0.111	0.099	0.088	0.078	0.044	0.025	0.015	0.009	0.003
15	0.160	0.140	0.123	0.108	0.095	0.084	0.074	0.065	0.035	0.020	0.011	0.006	0.002
16	0.141	0.123	0.107	0.093	0.081	0.071	0.062	0.054	0.028	0.015	0.008	0.005	0.002
17	0.125	0.108	0.093	0.080	0.069	0.060	0.052	0.045	0.023	0.012	0.006	0.003	0.001
18	0.111	0.095	0.081	0.069	0.059	0.051	0.044	0.038	0.018	0.009	0.005	0.002	0.001
19	0.098	0.083	0.070	0.060	0.051	0.043	0.037	0.031	0.014	0.007	0.003	0.002	0
20	0.087	0.073	0.061	0.051	0.043	0.037	0.031	0.026	0.012	0.005	0.002	0.001	0
25	0.047	0.038	0.030	0.024	0.020	0.016	0.013	0.010	0.004	0.001	0.001	0	0
30	0.026	0.020	0.015	0.012	0.009	0.007	0.005	0.004	0.001	0	0	0	0
40	0.008	0.005	0.004	0.003	0.002	0.001	0.001	0.001	0	0	0	0	0
50	0.002	0.001	0.001	0.001	0	0	0	0	0	0	0	0	0

Source: Maurice Joy, *Introduction to Financial Management* (Homewood, Ill.: Richard D. Irwin, 1977).

Appendix C Compound sum of an annuity of $1, IF_{sa} $S = R\left[\frac{(1+i)^n - 1}{i}\right]$

Period	1%	2%	3%	4%	5%	6%	7%	8%	9%	10%	11%
1	1.000	1.000	1.000	1.000	1.000	1.000	1.000	1.000	1.000	1.000	1.000
2	2.010	2.020	2.030	2.040	2.050	2.060	2.070	2.080	2.090	2.100	2.110
3	3.030	3.060	3.091	3.122	3.153	3.184	3.215	3.246	3.278	3.310	3.342
4	4.060	4.122	4.184	4.246	4.310	4.375	4.440	4.506	4.573	4.641	4.710
5	5.101	5.204	5.309	5.416	5.526	5.637	5.751	5.867	5.985	6.105	6.228
6	6.152	6.308	6.468	6.633	6.802	6.975	7.153	7.336	7.523	7.716	7.913
7	7.214	7.434	7.662	7.898	8.142	8.394	8.654	8.923	9.200	9.487	9.783
8	8.286	8.583	8.892	9.214	9.549	9.897	10.260	10.637	11.028	11.436	11.859
9	9.369	9.755	10.159	10.583	11.027	11.491	11.978	12.488	13.021	13.579	14.164
10	10.462	10.950	11.464	12.006	12.578	13.181	13.816	14.487	15.193	15.937	16.722
11	11.567	12.169	12.808	13.486	14.207	14.972	15.784	16.645	17.560	18.531	19.561
12	12.683	13.412	14.192	15.026	15.917	16.870	17.888	18.977	20.141	21.384	22.713
13	13.809	14.680	15.618	16.627	17.713	18.882	20.141	21.495	22.953	24.523	26.212
14	14.947	15.974	17.086	18.292	19.599	21.015	22.550	24.215	26.019	27.975	30.095
15	16.097	17.293	18.599	20.024	21.579	23.276	25.129	27.152	29.361	31.772	34.405
16	17.258	18.639	20.157	21.825	23.657	25.673	27.888	30.324	33.003	35.950	39.190
17	18.430	20.012	21.762	23.698	25.840	20.213	30.840	33.750	36.974	40.545	44.501
18	19.615	21.412	23.414	25.645	28.132	30.906	33.999	37.450	41.301	45.599	50.396
19	20.811	22.841	25.117	27.671	30.539	33.760	37.379	41.446	46.018	51.159	56.939
20	22.019	24.297	26.870	29.778	33.066	36.786	40.995	45.762	51.160	57.275	64.203
25	28.243	32.030	36.459	41.646	47.727	54.865	63.249	73.106	84.701	98.347	114.41
30	34.785	40.588	47.575	56.085	66.439	79.058	94.461	113.28	136.31	164.49	199.02
40	48.886	60.402	75.401	95.026	120.80	154.76	199.64	259.06	337.89	442.59	581.83
50	64.463	84.579	112.80	152.67	209.35	290.34	406.53	573.77	815.08	1,163.9	1,668.8

Appendix C (*concluded*) Compound sum of an annuity of $1

	Percent										
Period	*12%*	*13%*	*14%*	*15%*	*16%*	*17%*	*18%*	*19%*	*20%*	*25%*	*30%*
1	1.000	1.000	1.000	1.000	1.000	1.000	1.000	1.000	1.000	1.000	1.000
2	2.120	2.130	2.140	2.150	2.160	2.170	2.180	2.190	2.200	2.250	2.300
3	3.374	3.407	3.440	3.473	3.506	3.539	3.572	3.606	3.640	3.813	3.990
4	4.779	4.850	4.921	4.993	5.066	5.141	5.215	5.291	5.368	5.766	6.187
5	6.353	6.480	6.610	6.742	6.877	7.014	7.154	7.297	7.442	8.207	9.043
6	8.115	8.323	8.536	8.754	8.977	9.207	9.442	0.683	9.930	11.259	12.756
7	10.089	10.405	10.730	11.067	11.414	11.772	12.142	12.523	12.916	15.073	17.583
8	12.300	12.757	13.233	13.727	14.240	14.773	15.327	15.902	16.499	19.842	23.858
9	14.776	15.416	16.085	16.786	17.519	18.285	19.086	19.923	20.799	25.802	32.015
10	17.549	18.420	19.337	20.304	21.321	22.393	23.521	24.701	25.959	33.253	42.619
11	20.655	21.814	23.045	24.349	25.733	27.200	28.755	30.404	32.150	42.566	56.405
12	24.133	25.650	27.271	29.002	30.850	32.824	34.931	37.180	39.581	54.208	74.327
13	28.029	29.985	32.089	34.352	36.786	39.404	42.219	45.244	48.497	68.760	97.625
14	32.393	34.883	37.581	40.505	43.672	47.103	50.818	54.841	59.196	86.949	127.91
15	37.280	40.417	43.842	47.580	51.660	56.110	60.965	66.261	72.035	109.69	167.29
16	42.753	46.672	50.980	55.717	60.925	66.649	72.939	79.850	87.442	138.11	218.47
17	48.884	53.739	59.118	65.075	71.673	78.979	87.068	96.022	105.93	173.64	285.01
18	55.750	61.725	68.394	75.836	84.141	93.406	103.74	115.27	128.12	218.05	371.52
19	63.440	70.749	78.969	88.212	98.603	110.29	123.41	138.17	154.74	273.56	483.97
20	72.052	80.947	91.025	102.44	115.38	130.03	146.63	165.42	186.69	342.95	630.17
25	133.33	155.62	181.87	212.79	249.21	292.11	342.60	402.04	471.98	1,054.8	2,348.80
30	241.33	293.20	356.79	434.75	530.31	647.44	790.95	966.7	1,181.9	3,227.2	8,730.0
40	767.09	1,013.7	1,342.0	1,779.1	2,360.8	3,134.5	4,163.21	5,529.8	7,343.9	30,089.	120,393.
50	2,400.0	3,459.5	4,994.5	7,217.7	10,436.	15,090.	21,813.	31,515.	45,497.	280,256.	165,976.

Source: Maurice Joy, *Introduction to Financial Management* (Homewood, Ill.: Richard D. Irwin, 1977).

Appendix D Present value of an annuity of $1, IF_{pva} $A = R\left[\frac{1 - \frac{1}{(1+i)^n}}{i}\right]$

Period	1%	2%	3%	4%	5%	6%	7%	8%	9%	10%	11%	12%
	Percent											
1	0.990	0.980	0.971	0.962	0.952	0.943	0.935	0.926	0.917	0.909	0.901	0.893
2	1.970	1.942	1.913	1.886	1.859	1.833	1.808	1.783	1.759	1.736	1.713	1.690
3	2.941	2.884	2.829	2.775	2.723	2.673	2.624	2.577	2.531	2.487	2.444	2.402
4	3.902	3.808	3.717	3.630	3.546	3.465	3.387	3.312	3.240	3.170	3.102	3.037
5	4.853	4.713	4.580	4.452	4.329	4.212	4.100	3.993	3.890	3.791	3.696	3.605
6	5.795	5.601	5.417	5.242	5.076	4.917	4.767	4.623	4.486	4.355	4.231	4.111
7	6.728	6.472	6.230	6.002	5.786	5.582	5.389	5.206	5.033	4.868	4.712	4.564
8	7.652	7.325	7.020	6.733	6.463	6.210	5.971	5.747	5.535	5.335	5.146	4.968
9	8.566	8.162	7.786	7.435	7.108	6.802	6.515	6.247	5.995	5.759	5.537	5.328
10	9.471	8.983	8.530	8.111	7.722	7.360	7.024	6.710	6.418	6.145	5.889	5.650
11	10.368	9.787	9.253	8.760	8.306	7.887	7.499	7.139	6.805	6.495	6.207	5.938
12	11.255	10.575	9.954	9.385	8.863	8.384	7.943	7.536	7.161	6.814	6.492	6.194
13	12.134	11.348	10.635	9.986	9.394	8.853	8.358	7.904	7.487	7.103	6.750	6.424
14	13.004	12.106	11.296	10.563	9.899	9.295	8.745	8.244	7.786	7.367	6.982	6.628
15	13.865	12.849	11.939	11.118	10.380	9.712	9.108	8.559	8.061	7.606	7.191	6.811
16	14.718	13.578	12.561	11.652	10.838	10.106	9.447	8.851	8.313	7.824	7.379	6.974
17	15.562	14.292	13.166	12.166	11.274	10.477	9.763	9.122	8.544	8.022	7.549	7.102
18	16.398	14.992	13.754	12.659	11.690	10.828	10.059	9.372	8.756	8.201	7.702	7.250
19	17.226	15.678	14.324	13.134	12.085	11.158	10.336	9.604	8.950	8.365	7.839	7.366
20	18.046	16.351	14.877	13.590	12.462	11.470	10.594	9.818	9.129	8.514	7.963	7.469
25	22.023	19.523	17.413	15.622	14.094	12.783	11.654	10.675	9.823	9.077	8.422	7.843
30	25.808	22.396	19.600	17.292	15.372	13.765	12.409	11.258	10.274	9.427	8.694	8.055
40	32.835	27.355	23.115	19.793	17.159	15.046	13.332	11.925	10.757	9.779	8.951	8.244
50	39.196	31.424	25.730	21.482	18.256	15.762	13.801	12.233	10.962	9.915	9.042	8.304

Appendix D (*concluded*) Present value of an annuity of $1

Period	13%	14%	15%	16%	17%	18%	19%	20%	25%	30%	35%	40%	50%
1	0.885	0.877	0.870	0.862	0.855	0.847	0.840	0.833	0.800	0.769	0.741	0.714	0.667
2	1.668	1.647	1.626	1.605	1.585	1.566	1.547	1.528	1.440	1.361	1.289	1.224	1.111
3	2.361	2.322	2.283	2.246	2.210	2.174	2.140	2.106	1.952	1.816	1.696	1.589	1.407
4	2.974	2.914	2.855	2.798	2.743	2.690	2.639	2.589	2.362	2.166	1.997	1.849	1.605
5	3.517	3.433	3.352	3.274	3.199	3.127	3.058	2.991	2.689	2.436	2.220	2.035	1.737
6	3.998	3.889	3.784	3.685	3.589	3.498	3.410	3.326	2.951	2.643	2.385	2.168	1.824
7	4.423	4.288	4.160	4.039	3.922	3.812	3.706	3.605	3.161	2.802	2.508	2.263	1.883
8	4.799	4.639	4.487	4.344	4.207	4.078	3.954	3.837	3.329	2.925	2.598	2.331	1.922
9	5.132	4.946	4.772	4.607	4.451	4.303	4.163	4.031	3.463	3.019	2.665	2.379	1.948
10	5.426	5.216	5.019	4.833	4.659	4.494	4.339	4.192	3.571	3.092	2.715	2.414	1.965
11	5.687	5.453	5.234	5.029	4.836	4.656	4.486	4.327	3.656	3.147	2.752	2.438	1.977
12	5.918	5.660	5.421	5.197	4.988	4.793	4.611	4.439	3.725	3.190	2.779	2.456	1.985
13	6.122	5.842	5.583	5.342	5.118	4.910	4.715	4.533	3.780	3.223	2.799	2.469	1.990
14	6.302	6.002	5.724	5.468	5.229	5.008	4.802	4.611	3.824	3.249	2.814	2.478	1.993
15	6.462	6.142	5.847	5.575	5.324	5.092	4.876	4.675	3.859	3.268	2.825	2.484	1.995
16	6.604	6.265	5.954	5.668	5.405	5.162	4.938	4.730	3.887	3.283	2.834	2.489	1.997
17	6.729	6.373	6.047	5.749	5.475	5.222	4.988	4.775	3.910	3.295	2.840	2.492	1.998
18	6.840	6.467	6.128	5.818	5.534	5.273	5.033	4.812	3.928	3.304	2.844	2.494	1.999
19	6.938	6.550	6.198	5.877	5.584	5.316	5.070	4.843	3.942	3.311	2.848	2.496	1.999
20	7.025	6.623	6.259	5.929	5.628	5.353	5.101	4.870	3.954	3.316	2.850	2.497	1.999
25	7.330	6.873	6.464	6.097	5.766	5.467	5.195	4.948	3.985	3.329	2.856	2.499	2.000
30	7.496	7.003	6.566	6.177	5.829	5.517	5.235	4.979	3.995	3.332	2.857	2.500	2.000
40	7.634	7.105	6.642	6.233	5.871	5.548	5.258	4.997	3.999	3.333	2.857	2.500	2.000
50	7.675	7.133	6.661	6.246	5.880	5.554	5.262	4.999	4.000	3.333	2.857	2.500	2.000

Source: Maurice Joy, *Introduction to Financial Management* (Homewood, Ill.: Richard D. Irwin, 1977).

N	N^2	$\sqrt{N}$	$\sqrt{10N}$	N	N^2	$\sqrt{N}$	$\sqrt{10N}$
				50	2 500	7.071 068	22.36068
1	1	1.000 000	3.162 278	51	2 601	7.141 428	22.58318
2	4	1.414 214	4.472 136	52	2 704	7.211 103	22.80351
3	9	1.732 051	5.477 226	53	2 809	7.280 110	23.02173
4	16	2.000 000	6.324 555	54	2 916	7.348 469	23.23790
5	25	2.236 068	7.071 068	55	3 025	7.416 198	23.45208
6	36	2.449 490	7.745 967	56	3 136	7.483 315	23.66432
7	49	2.645 751	8.366 600	57	3 249	7.549 834	23.87467
8	64	2.828 427	8.944 272	58	3 364	7.615 773	24.08319
9	81	3.000 000	9.486 833	59	3 481	7.681 146	24.28992
10	100	3.162 278	10.00000	60	3 600	7.745 967	24.49490
11	121	3.316 625	10.48809	61	3 721	7.810 250	24.69818
12	144	3.464 102	10.95445	62	3 844	7.874 008	24.89980
13	169	3.605 551	11.40175	63	3 969	7.937 254	25.09980
14	196	3.741 657	11.83216	64	4 096	8.000 000	25.29822
15	225	3.872 983	12.24745	65	4 225	8.062 258	25.49510
16	256	4.000 000	12.64911	66	4 356	8.124 038	25.69047
17	289	4.123 106	13.03840	67	4 489	8.185 353	25.88436
18	324	4.242 641	13.41641	68	4 624	8.246 211	26.07681
19	361	4.358 899	13.78405	69	4 761	8.306 824	26.26785
20	400	4.472 136	14.14214	70	4 900	8.366 600	26.45751
21	441	4.582 576	14.49138	71	5 041	8.426 150	26.64583
22	484	4.690 416	14.83240	72	5 184	8.485 281	26.83282
23	529	4.795 832	15.16575	73	5 329	8.544 004	27.01851
24	576	4.898 979	15.49193	74	5 476	8.602 325	27.20294
25	625	5.000 000	15.81139	75	5 625	8.660 254	27.38613
26	676	5.099 020	16.12452	76	5 776	8.717 798	27.56810
27	729	5.196 152	16.43168	77	5 929	8.774 964	27.74887
28	784	5.291 503	16.73320	78	6 084	8.831 761	27.92848
29	841	5.385 165	17.02939	79	6 241	8.888 194	28.10694
30	900	5.477 226	17.32051	80	6 400	8.944 272	28.28427
31	961	5.567 764	17.60682	81	6 561	9.000 000	28.46050
32	1 024	5.656 854	17.88854	82	6 724	9.055 385	28.63564
33	1 089	5.744 563	18.16590	83	6 889	9.110 434	28.80972
34	1 156	5.830 952	18.43909	84	7 056	9.165 151	28.98275
35	1 225	5.916 080	18.70829	85	7 225	9.219 544	29.15476
36	1 296	6.000 000	18.97367	86	7 396	9.273 618	29.32576
37	1 369	6.082 763	19.23538	87	7 569	9.327 379	29.49576
38	1 444	6.164 414	19.49359	88	7 744	9.380 832	29.66479
39	1 521	6.244 998	19.74842	89	7 921	9.433 981	29.83287
40	1 600	6.324 555	20.00000	90	8 100	9.486 833	30.00000
41	1 681	6.403 124	20.24846	91	8 281	9.539 392	30.16621
42	1 764	6.480 741	20.49390	92	8 464	9.591 663	30.33150
43	1 849	6.557 439	20.73644	93	8 649	9.643 651	30.49590
44	1 936	6.633 250	20.97618	94	8 836	9.695 360	30.65942
45	2 025	6.708 204	21.21320	95	9 025	9.746 794	30.82207
46	2 116	6.782 330	21.44761	96	9 216	9.797 959	30.98387
47	2 209	6.855 655	21.67948	97	9 409	9.848 858	31.14482
48	2 304	6.928 203	21.90890	98	9 604	9.899 495	31.30495
49	2 401	7.000 000	22.13594	99	9 801	9.949 874	31.46427
50	2 500	7.071 068	22.36068	100	10 000	10.00000	31.62278

Appendix E (*continued*) Tables of squares and square roots

N	N^2	$\sqrt{N}$	$\sqrt{10N}$	N	N^2	$\sqrt{N}$	$\sqrt{10N}$
100	10 000	10.00000	31.62278	150	22 500	12.24745	38.72983
101	10 201	10.04988	31.78050	151	22 801	12.28821	38.85872
102	10 404	10.09950	31.93744	152	23 104	12.32883	39.98718
103	10 609	10.14889	32.09361	153	23 409	12.36932	39.11521
104	10 816	10.19804	32.24903	154	23 716	12.40967	39.24283
105	11 025	10.24695	32.40370	155	24 025	12.44990	39.37004
106	11 236	10.29563	32.55764	156	24 336	12.45000	39.49684
107	11 449	10.34408	32.71085	157	24 649	12.52996	39.62323
108	11 664	10.39230	32.86335	158	24 964	12.56981	39.74921
109	11 881	10.44031	33.01515	159	25 281	12.60952	39.87480
110	12 100	10.48809	33.16625	160	25 600	12.64911	40.00000
111	12 321	10.53565	33.31666	161	25 921	12.68858	40.12481
112	12 544	10.58301	33.46640	162	26 244	12.72792	40.24922
113	12 769	10.63015	33.61547	163	26 569	12.76715	40.37326
114	12 996	10.67708	33.76389	164	26 896	12.80625	40.49691
115	13 225	10.72381	33.91165	165	27 225	12.84523	40.62019
116	13 456	10.77033	34.05877	166	27 556	12.88410	40.74310
117	13 689	10.81665	34.20526	167	27 889	12.92285	40.86563
118	13 924	10.86278	34.35113	168	28 224	12.96148	40.98780
119	14 161	10.90871	34.49638	169	28 561	13.00000	41.10961
120	14 400	10.95445	34.64102	170	28 900	13.03840	41.23106
121	14 641	11.00000	34.78505	171	29 241	13.07670	41.35215
122	14 884	11.04536	34.92850	172	29 584	13.11488	41.47288
123	15 129	11.09054	35.07136	173	29 929	13.15295	41.59327
124	15 376	11.13553	35.21363	174	30 276	13.19091	41.71331
125	15 625	11.18034	35.35534	175	30 625	13.22876	41.83300
126	15 876	11.22497	35.49648	176	30 976	13.26650	41.95235
127	16 129	11.26943	35.63706	177	31 329	13.30413	42.07137
128	16 384	11.31371	35.77709	178	31 684	13.34166	42.19005
129	16 641	11.35782	35.91657	179	32 041	13.37909	42.30839
130	16 900	11.40175	36.05551	180	32 400	13.41641	42.42641
131	17 161	11.44552	36.19392	181	32 761	13.45362	42.54409
132	17 424	11.48913	36.33180	182	33 124	13.49074	42.66146
133	17 689	11.53256	36.46917	183	33 489	13.52775	42.77850
134	17 956	11.57584	36.60601	184	33 856	13.56466	42.89522
135	18 225	11.61895	36.74235	185	34 225	13.60147	43.01163
136	18 496	11.66190	36.87818	186	34 596	13.63818	43.12772
137	18 769	11.70470	37.01351	187	34 969	13.67479	43.24350
138	19 044	11.74734	37.14835	188	35 344	13.71131	43.35897
139	19 321	11.78983	37.28270	189	35 721	13.74773	43.47413
140	19 600	11.83216	37.41657	190	36 100	13.78405	43.58899
141	19 881	11.87434	37.54997	191	36 481	13.82027	43.70355
142	20 164	11.91638	37.68289	192	36 864	13.85641	43.81780
143	20 449	11.95826	37.81534	193	37 249	13.89244	43.93177
144	20 736	12.00000	37.94733	194	37 636	13.92839	44.04543
145	21 025	12.04159	38.07887	195	38 025	13.96424	44.15880
146	21 316	12.08305	38.20995	196	38 416	14.00000	44.27189
147	21 609	12.12436	38.34058	197	38 809	14.03567	44.38468
148	21 904	12.16553	38.47077	198	39 204	14.07125	44.49719
149	22 201	12.20656	38.60052	199	39 601	14.10674	44.60942
150	22 500	12.24745	38.72983	200	40 000	14.14214	44.72136

N	N^2	$\sqrt{N}$	$\sqrt{10N}$	N	N^2	$\sqrt{N}$	$\sqrt{10N}$
200	40 000	14.14214	44.72136	250	62 500	15.81139	50.00000
201	40 401	14.17745	44.83302	251	63 001	15.84298	50.09990
202	40 804	14.21267	44.94441	252	63 504	15.87451	50.19960
203	41 209	14.24781	45.05552	253	64 009	15.90597	50.29911
204	41 616	14.28296	45.16636	254	64 516	15.93738	50.39841
205	42 025	14.31782	45.27693	255	65 025	15.96872	50.49752
206	42 436	14.35270	45.38722	256	65 536	16.00000	50.59644
207	42 849	14.38749	45.49725	257	66 049	16.03122	50.69517
208	43 264	14.42221	45.60702	258	66 564	16.06238	50.79370
209	43 681	14.45683	45.71652	259	67 081	16.09348	50.89204
210	44 100	14.49138	45.82576	260	67 600	16.12452	50.99020
211	44 521	14.52584	45.93474	261	68 121	16.15549	51.08816
212	44 944	14.56022	46.04346	262	68 644	16.18641	51.18594
213	45 369	14.59452	46.15192	263	69 169	16.21727	51.28353
214	45 796	14.62874	46.26013	264	69 696	16.24808	51.38093
215	46 225	14.66288	46.36809	265	70 225	16.27882	51.47815
216	46 656	14.69694	46.47580	266	70 756	16.30951	51.57519
217	47 089	14.73092	46.58326	267	71 289	16.34013	51.67204
218	47 524	14.76482	46.69047	268	71 824	16.37071	51.76872
219	47 961	14.79865	46.79744	269	72 361	16.40122	51.86521
220	48 400	14.83240	46.90415	270	72 900	16.43168	51.96152
221	48 841	14.86607	47.01064	271	73 441	16.46208	52.05766
222	49 284	14.89966	47.11688	272	73 984	16.49242	52.15362
223	49 729	14.93318	47.22288	273	74 529	16.52271	52.24940
224	50 176	14.96663	47.32864	274	75 076	16.55295	52.34501
225	50 625	15.00000	47.43416	275	75 625	16.58312	52.44044
226	51 076	15.03330	47.53946	276	76 176	16.61325	52.53570
227	51 529	15.06652	47.64452	277	76 729	16.64332	52.63079
228	51 984	15.09967	47.74935	278	77 284	16.67333	52.72571
229	52 441	15.13275	47.85394	279	77 841	16.70329	52.82045
230	52 900	15.16575	47.95832	280	78 400	16.73320	52.91503
231	53 361	15.19868	48.06246	281	78 961	16.76305	53.00943
232	53 824	15.23155	48.16638	282	79 524	16.79286	53.10367
233	54 289	15.26434	48.27007	283	80 089	16.82260	53.19774
234	54 756	15.29706	48.37355	284	80 656	16.85230	53.29165
235	55 225	15.32971	48.47680	285	81 225	16.88194	53.38539
236	55 696	15.36229	48.57983	286	81 796	16.91153	53.47897
237	56 169	15.39480	48.68265	287	82 369	16.94107	53.57238
238	56 644	15.42725	48.78524	288	82 944	16.97056	53.66563
239	57 121	15.45962	48.88763	289	83 521	17.00000	53.75872
240	57 600	15.49193	48.98979	290	84 100	17.02939	53.85165
241	58 081	15.52417	49.09175	291	84 681	17.05872	53.94442
242	58 564	15.55635	49.19350	292	85 264	17.08801	54.03702
243	59 049	15.58846	49.29503	293	85 849	17.11724	54.12947
244	59 536	15.62050	49.39636	294	86 436	17.14643	54.22177
245	60 025	15.65248	49.49747	295	87 025	17.17556	54.31390
246	60 516	15.68439	49.59839	296	87 616	17.20465	54.40588
247	61 009	15.71623	49.69909	297	88 209	17.23369	54.49771
248	61 504	15.74802	49.79960	298	88 804	17.26268	54.58938
249	62 001	15.77973	49.89990	299	89 401	17.29162	54.68089
250	62 500	15.81139	50.00000	300	90 000	17.32051	54.77226

N	N^2	$\sqrt{N}$	$\sqrt{10N}$	N	N^2	$\sqrt{N}$	$\sqrt{10N}$
300	90 000	17.32051	54.77226	350	122 500	18.70829	59.16080
301	90 601	17.34935	54.86347	351	123 201	18.73499	59.24525
302	91 204	17.37815	54.95453	352	123 904	18.76166	59.32959
303	91 809	17.40690	55.04544	353	124 609	18.78829	59.41380
304	92 416	17.43560	55.13620	354	125 316	18.81489	59.49790
305	93 025	17.46425	55.22681	355	126 025	18.84144	59.58188
306	93 636	17.49288	55.31727	356	126 736	18.86796	59.66574
307	94 249	17.52142	55.40758	357	127 449	18.89444	59.74948
308	94 864	17.54993	55.49775	358	128 164	18.92089	59.83310
309	95 481	17.57840	55.58777	359	128 881	18.94730	59.91661
310	96 100	17.60682	55.67764	360	129 600	18.97367	60.00000
311	96 721	17.63519	55.76737	361	130 321	19.00000	60.08328
312	97 344	17.66352	55.85696	362	131 044	19.02630	60.16644
313	97 969	17.69181	55.94640	363	131 769	19.05256	60.24948
314	98 596	17.72005	56.03670	364	132 496	19.07878	60.33241
315	99 225	17.74824	56.12486	365	133 225	19.10497	60.41523
316	99 856	17.77639	56.21388	366	133 956	19.13113	60.49793
317	100 489	17.80449	56.30275	367	134 689	19.15724	60.58052
318	101 124	17.83255	56.39149	368	135 424	19.18333	60.66300
319	101 761	17.86057	56.48008	369	136 161	19.20937	60.74537
320	102 400	17.88854	56.56854	370	136 900	19.23538	60.82763
321	103 041	17.91647	56.65686	371	137 641	19.26136	60.90977
322	103 684	17.94436	56.74504	372	138 384	19.28730	60.99180
323	104 329	17.97220	56.83309	373	139 129	19.31321	61.07373
324	104 976	18.00000	56.92100	374	139 876	19.33908	61.15554
325	105 625	18.02776	57.00877	375	140 625	19.36492	61.23724
326	106 276	18.05547	57.09641	376	141 376	19.39072	61.31884
327	106 929	18.08314	57.18391	377	142 129	19.41649	61.40033
328	107 584	18.11077	57.27128	378	142 884	19.44222	61.48170
329	108 241	18.13836	57.35852	379	143 641	19.46792	61.56298
330	108 900	18.16590	57.44563	380	144 000	19.49359	61.64414
331	109 561	18.19341	57.53260	381	145 161	19.51922	61.72520
332	110 224	18.22087	57.61944	382	145 924	19.54483	61.80615
333	110 889	18.24829	57.70615	383	146 689	19.57039	61.88699
334	111 556	18.27567	57.79273	384	147 456	19.59592	61.96773
335	112 225	18.30301	57. 87918	385	148 225	19.62142	62.04837
336	112 896	18.33030	57.96551	386	148 996	19.64688	62.12890
337	113 569	18.35756	58.05170	387	149 769	19.67232	62.20932
338	114 224	18.38478	57.13777	388	150 544	19.69772	62.28965
339	114 921	18.41195	58.22371	389	151 321	19.72308	62.36986
340	115 600	18.43909	58.30952	390	152 100	19.74842	62.44998
341	116 281	18.46619	58.39521	391	152 881	19.77372	62.52999
342	116 694	18.49324	58.48077	392	153 664	19.79899	62.60990
343	117 649	18.52026	58.56620	393	154 449	19.82423	62.68971
344	118 336	18.54724	58.65151	394	155 236	19.84943	62.76942
345	119 025	18.57418	58.73670	395	156 025	19.87461	62.84903
346	119 716	18.60108	58.82176	396	156 816	19.89975	62.92853
347	120 409	18.62794	58.90671	397	157 609	19.92486	63.00794
348	121 104	18.65476	58.99152	398	158 404	19.94994	63.08724
349	121 801	18.68154	59.07622	399	159 201	19.97498	63.16645
350	122 500	18.70829	59.16080	400	160 000	20.00000	63.24555

Appendix E (*continued*) Tables of squares and square roots

N	N^2	$\sqrt{N}$	$\sqrt{10N}$	N	N^2	$\sqrt{N}$	$\sqrt{10N}$
400	160 000	20.00000	63.24555	450	202 500	21.21320	67.08204
401	160 801	20.02498	63.32456	451	203 401	21.23676	67.15653
402	161 604	20.04994	63.40347	452	204 304	21.26029	67.23095
403	162 409	20.07486	63.48228	453	205 209	21.28380	67.30527
404	163 216	20.09975	63.56099	454	206 116	21.30728	67.37952
405	164 025	20.12461	63.63961	455	207 025	21.33073	67.45369
406	164 836	20.14944	63.71813	456	207 936	21.35416	67.52777
407	165 649	20.17424	63.79655	457	208 849	21.37756	67.60178
408	166 464	20.19901	63.87488	458	209 764	21.40093	67.67570
409	167 281	20.22375	63.95311	459	210 681	21.42429	67.74954
410	168 100	20.24846	64.03124	460	211 600	21.44761	67.82330
411	168 921	20.27313	64.10928	461	212 521	21.47091	67.89698
412	169 744	20.29778	64.18723	462	213 444	21.49419	67.97058
413	170 569	20.32240	64.26508	463	214 369	21.51743	68.04410
414	171 396	20.34699	64.34283	464	215 296	21.54066	68.11755
415	172 225	20.37155	64.42049	465	216 225	21.56386	68.19091
416	173 056	20.39608	64.49806	466	217 156	21.58703	68.26419
417	173 889	20.42058	64.57554	467	218 089	21.61018	68.33740
418	174 724	20.44505	64.65292	468	219 024	21.63331	68.41053
419	175 561	20.46949	64.73021	469	219 961	21.65641	68.48357
420	176 400	20.49390	64.80741	470	220 900	21.67948	68.55655
421	177 241	20.51828	64.88451	471	221 841	21.70253	68.62944
422	178 084	20.54264	64.96153	472	222 784	21.72556	68.70226
423	178 929	20.56696	65.03845	473	223 729	21.74856	68.77500
424	179 776	20.59126	65.11528	474	224 676	21.77154	68.84706
425	180 625	20.61553	65.19202	475	225 625	21.79449	68.92024
426	181 476	20.63977	65.26808	476	226 576	21.81742	68.99275
427	182 329	20.66398	65.34524	477	227 529	21.84033	69.06519
428	183 184	20.68816	65.42171	478	228 484	21.86321	69.13754
429	184 041	20.71232	65.49809	479	229 441	21.88607	69.20983
430	184 900	20.73644	65.57439	480	230 400	21.90800	69.28203
431	185 761	20.76054	65.65059	481	231 361	21.93171	69.35416
432	186 624	20.78461	65.72671	482	232 324	21.95450	69.42622
433	187 489	20.80865	65.80274	483	233 280	21.97726	69.50820
434	188 356	20.83267	65.87868	484	234 256	22.00000	69.57011
435	189 225	20.85665	65.95453	485	235 225	22.02272	69.64194
436	190 096	20.88061	66.03030	486	236 196	22.04541	69.71370
437	190 969	20.90454	66.10598	487	237 169	22.06808	69.78530
438	191 844	20.92845	66.18157	488	238 144	22.09072	69.85700
439	192 721	20.95233	66.25708	489	239 121	22.11334	69.92853
440	193 600	20.97618	66.33250	490	240 100	22.13594	70.00000
441	194 481	21.00000	66.40783	491	241 081	22.15852	70.07139
442	195 364	21.02380	66.48308	492	242 064	22.18107	70.14271
443	196 249	21.04757	66.55825	493	243 049	22.20360	70.21396
444	197 136	21.07131	66.63332	494	244 036	22.22611	70.28513
445	198 025	21.09502	66.70832	495	245 025	22.24860	70.35624
446	198 916	21.11871	66.78323	496	246 016	22.27106	70.42727
447	199 809	21.14237	66.85806	497	247 009	22.29350	70.49823
448	200 704	21.16601	66.93280	498	248 004	22.31519	70.56912
449	201 601	21.18962	67.00746	499	249 001	22.33831	70.63993
450	202 500	21.21320	67.08204	500	250 000	22.36068	70.71068

N	N^2	$\sqrt{N}$	$\sqrt{10N}$	N	N^2	$\sqrt{N}$	$\sqrt{10N}$
500	250 000	22.36068	70.71068	550	302 500	23.45208	74.16198
501	251 001	22.38303	70.78135	551	303 601	23.47339	74.22937
502	252 004	22.40536	70.85196	552	304 704	23.49468	74.29670
503	253 009	22.42766	70.92249	553	305 809	23.51595	74.36397
504	254 016	22.44994	70.99296	554	306 916	23.53720	74.43118
505	255 025	22.47221	71.06335	555	308 025	23.55844	74.49832
506	256 036	22.49444	71.13368	556	309 136	23.57965	74.56541
507	257 049	22.51666	71.20393	557	310 249	23.60085	74.63243
508	258 064	22.53886	71.27412	558	311 364	23.62202	74.69940
509	259 081	22.56103	71.34424	559	312 481	23.64318	74.76630
510	260 100	22.58318	71.41428	560	313 600	23.66432	74.83315
511	261 121	22.60531	71.48426	561	314 721	23.68544	74.89993
512	262 144	22.62742	71.55418	562	315 844	23.70654	74.96666
513	263 169	22.64950	71.62402	563	316 969	23.72762	75.03333
514	264 196	22.67157	71.69379	564	318 096	23.74686	75.09993
515	265 225	22.69361	71.76350	565	319 225	23.76973	75.16648
516	266 256	22.71563	71.83314	566	320 356	23.79075	75.23297
517	267 289	22.73763	71.90271	567	321 489	23.81176	75.29940
518	268 324	22.75961	71.97222	568	322 624	23.83275	75.36577
519	269 361	22.78157	72.04165	569	323 761	23.85372	75.43209
520	270 400	22.80351	72.11103	570	324 900	23.87467	75.49834
521	271 441	22.82542	72.18033	571	326 041	23.89561	75.56454
522	272 484	22.84732	72.24957	572	327 184	23.91652	75.63068
523	273 529	22.86919	72.31874	573	328 329	23.93742	75.69676
524	274 576	22.89105	72.38784	574	329 476	23.95830	75.76279
525	275 625	22.91288	72.45688	575	330 625	23.97916	75.82875
526	276 676	22.93469	72.52586	576	331 776	24.00000	75.89466
527	277 729	22.95648	72.59477	577	332 929	24.02082	75.96052
528	278 784	22.97825	72.66361	578	334 084	24.04163	76.02631
529	279 841	23.00000	72.73239	579	335 241	24.06242	76.09205
530	280 900	23.02173	72.80110	580	336 400	24.08319	76.15773
531	281 961	23.04344	72.86975	581	337 561	24.10394	76.22336
532	283 024	23.06513	72.93833	582	338 724	24.12468	76.28892
533	284 089	23.08679	73.00685	583	339 889	24.14539	76.35444
534	285 156	23.10844	73.07530	584	341 056	24.16609	76.41989
535	286 225	23.13007	73.14369	585	342 225	24.18677	76.48529
536	287 296	23.15167	73.21202	586	343 396	24.20744	76.55064
537	288 369	23.17326	73.28028	587	344 569	24.22808	76.61593
538	289 444	23.19483	73.34848	588	345 744	24.24871	76.68116
539	290 521	23.21637	73.41662	589	346 921	24.26932	76.74634
540	291 600	23.23790	73.48469	590	348 100	24.28992	76.81146
541	292 681	23.25941	73.55270	591	349 281	24.31049	76.87652
542	293 764	23.28089	73.62056	592	350 464	24.33105	76.94154
543	294 849	23.30236	73.68853	593	351 649	24.35159	77.00649
544	295 936	23.32381	73.75636	594	352 836	24.37212	77.07140
545	297 025	23.34524	73.82412	595	354 025	24.39262	77.13624
546	298 116	23.36664	73.89181	596	355 216	24.41311	77.20104
547	299 209	23.38803	73.95945	597	356 409	24.43358	77.26578
548	300 304	23.40940	74.02702	598	357 604	24.45404	77.33046
549	301 401	23.43075	74.09453	599	358 801	24.47448	77.39509
550	302 500	23.45208	74.16198	600	360 000	24.49490	77.45967

N	N^2	$\sqrt{N}$	$\sqrt{10N}$	N	N^2	$\sqrt{N}$	$\sqrt{10N}$
600	360 000	24.49490	77.45967	650	422 500	25.49510	80.62258
601	361 201	24.51530	77.52419	651	423 801	25.51470	80.68457
602	362 404	24.53569	77.58868	652	425 409	25.53240	80.80130
603	363 609	24.55606	77.65307	653	426 409	25.55386	80.80842
604	364 816	24.57641	77.71744	654	427 716	25.57342	80.87027
605	366 025	24.59675	77.78175	655	429 025	25.59297	80.93207
606	367 736	24.61707	77.84600	656	430 336	25.61250	80.99383
607	368 449	24.63737	77.91020	657	431 649	25.63201	81.05554
608	369 664	24.65766	77.97435	658	432 964	25.65151	81.11720
609	370 881	24.67793	78.03845	659	434 281	25.67100	81.17881
610	372 100	24.69818	78.10250	660	435 600	25.69047	81.24038
611	373 321	24.71841	78.16649	661	436 921	25.70992	81.30191
612	374 544	24.73863	78.23043	662	438 244	25.72936	81.36338
613	375 769	24.75884	78.29432	663	439 569	25.74879	81.42481
614	376 996	24.77902	78.35815	664	440 896	25.76820	81.48620
615	378 225	24.79919	78.42194	665	442 225	25.78759	81.54753
616	379 456	24.81935	78.48567	666	443 556	25.80698	81.60882
617	380 689	24.83948	78.54935	667	444 889	25.82634	81.67007
618	381 924	24.85961	78.61298	668	446 224	25.84570	81.73127
619	383 161	24.87971	78.67655	669	447 561	25.86503	81.79242
620	384 400	24.89980	78.74008	670	448 900	25.88436	81.85353
621	385 641	24.91987	78.80355	671	450 241	25.90367	81.91459
622	386 884	24.93993	78.86698	672	451 584	25.92296	81.97561
623	388 129	24.95997	78.93035	673	452 929	25.94224	82.03658
624	389 376	24.97999	78.99367	674	454 276	25.96151	82.09750
625	390 625	25.00000	79.05694	675	455 625	25.98076	82.15838
626	391 876	25.01999	79.12016	676	456 976	26.00000	82.21922
627	393 129	25.03997	79.18333	677	458 329	26.01922	82.28001
628	394 384	25.05993	79.24645	678	459 684	26.03843	82.34076
629	395 641	25.07987	79.30952	679	461 041	26.05763	82.40146
630	396 900	25.09980	79.37254	680	462 400	26.07681	82.46211
631	398 161	25.11971	79.43551	681	463 761	26.09598	82.52272
632	399 424	25.13961	79.49843	682	465 124	26.11513	82.58329
633	400 689	25.15949	79.56130	683	466 489	26.13427	82.64381
634	401 956	25.17936	79.62412	684	467 856	26.15339	82.70429
635	403 225	25.19921	79.68689	685	469 225	26.17250	82.76473
636	404 496	25.21904	79.74961	686	470 596	26.19160	82.82512
637	405 769	25.23886	79.81228	687	471 969	26.21068	82.88546
638	407 044	25.25866	79.87490	688	473 344	26.22975	82.94577
639	408 321	25.27845	79.93748	689	474 721	26.24881	83.00602
640	409 600	25.29822	80.00000	690	476 100	26.26785	83.06624
641	410 881	25.31798	80.06248	691	477 481	26.28688	83.12641
642	412 164	25.33772	80.12490	692	478 864	26.30589	83.18654
643	413 449	25.35744	80.18728	693	480 249	26.32489	83.24662
644	414 736	25.37716	80.24961	694	481 636	26.34388	83.30666
645	416 025	25.39685	80.31189	695	483 025	26.36285	83.36666
646	417 316	25.41653	80.37413	696	484 416	26.38181	83.42661
647	418 609	25.43619	80.43631	697	485 809	26.40076	83.48653
648	419 904	25.45584	80.49845	698	487 204	26.41969	83.54639
649	421 201	25.47548	80.56054	699	488 601	26.43861	83.60622
650	422 500	25.49510	80.62258	700	490 000	26.45751	83.66600

N	N^2	$\sqrt{N}$	$\sqrt{10N}$	N	N^2	$\sqrt{N}$	$\sqrt{10N}$
700	490 000	26.45751	83.66600	750	562 500	27.38613	86.60254
701	491 401	26.47640	83.72574	751	564 001	27.40438	86.66026
702	492 804	26.49528	83.78544	752	565 504	27.42262	86.71793
703	494 209	26.51415	83.84510	753	567 009	27.44085	86.77557
704	495 616	26.53300	83.90471	754	568 516	27.45906	86.83317
705	497 025	26.55184	83.96428	755	570 025	27.47726	86.89074
706	498 436	26.57066	84.02381	756	571 536	27.49545	86.94826
707	499 849	26.58947	84.08329	757	573 049	27.51363	87.00575
708	501 264	26.60827	84.14274	758	574 564	27.53180	87.06320
709	502 681	26.62705	84.20214	759	576 081	27.54995	87.12061
710	504 100	26.64583	84.26150	760	577 600	27.56810	87.17798
711	505 521	26.66458	84.32082	761	579 121	27.58623	87.23531
712	506 944	26.68333	84.38009	762	580 644	27.60435	87.29261
713	508 369	26.70206	84.43933	763	582 169	27.62245	87.34987
714	509 796	26.72078	84.49852	764	583 696	27.64055	87.40709
715	511 225	26.73948	84.55767	765	585 225	27.65863	87.46428
716	512 656	26.75818	84.61578	766	586 756	27.67671	87.52143
717	514 089	26.77686	84.67585	767	588 289	27.69476	87.57854
718	515 524	26.79552	84.73488	768	589 824	27.71281	87.63561
719	516 961	26.81418	84.79387	769	591 361	27.73085	87.69265
720	518 400	26.83282	84.85281	770	592 900	27.74887	87.74964
721	519 841	26.85144	84.91172	771	594 441	27.76689	87.80661
722	521 284	26.87006	84.97058	772	595 984	27.78489	87.86353
723	522 729	26.88866	85.02941	773	597 529	27.80288	87.92042
724	524 176	26.90725	85.08819	774	599 076	27.82086	87.97727
725	525 625	26.92582	85.14693	775	600 625	27.83882	88.03408
726	527 076	26.94439	85.20563	776	602 176	27.85678	88.09086
727	528 529	26.96294	85.26429	777	603 729	27.87472	88.14760
728	529 984	26.98148	85.32294	778	605 284	27.89265	88.20431
729	531 411	27.00000	85.38150	779	606 841	27.91057	88.26098
730	532 900	27.01851	85.44004	780	608 400	27.92848	88.31761
731	534 361	27.03701	85.49854	781	609 961	27.94638	88.37420
732	535 824	27.05550	85.55700	782	611 524	27.96426	88.43076
733	537 289	27.07397	85.61542	783	613 089	27.98214	88.48729
734	538 756	27.09243	85.67380	784	614 656	28.00000	88.54377
735	540 225	27.11088	85.73214	785	616 225	28.01785	88.60023
736	541 696	27.12932	85.79044	786	617 796	28.03569	88.65664
737	543 169	27.14774	85.84870	787	619 369	28.05352	88.71302
738	544 644	27.16616	85.90693	788	620 944	28.07134	88.76936
739	546 121	27.18455	85.96511	789	622 521	28.08914	88.82567
740	547 600	27.20294	86.02325	790	624 100	28.10694	88.88194
741	549 081	27.22132	86.08136	791	625 681	28.12472	88.93818
742	550 564	27.23968	86.13942	792	627 264	28.14249	88.99438
743	552 049	27.25803	86.20745	793	628 849	28.16026	89.05055
744	553 536	27.27636	86.25543	794	630 436	28.17801	89.10668
745	555 025	27.29469	86.31338	795	632 025	28.19574	89.16277
746	556 516	27.31300	86.37129	796	633 616	28.21347	89.21883
747	558 009	27.33130	86.42916	797	635 209	28.23119	89.27486
748	559 504	27.34959	86.48609	798	636 804	28.24889	89.33085
749	561 001	27.36786	86.54479	799	638 401	28.26659	89.38680
750	562 500	27.38613	86.60254	800	640 000	28.28427	89.44272

N	N^2	$\sqrt{N}$	$\sqrt{10N}$	N	N^2	$\sqrt{N}$	$\sqrt{10N}$
800	640 000	28.28427	89.44272	850	722 500	29.15476	92.19544
801	641 601	28.30194	89.49860	851	724 201	29.17190	92.24966
802	643 204	28.31960	89.55445	852	725 904	29.18904	92.30385
803	644 809	28.33725	89.61027	853	727 609	29.20616	92.35800
804	646 416	28.35489	89.66605	854	729 316	29.22328	92.41212
805	648 025	28.37252	89.72179	855	731 025	29.24038	92.46621
806	649 636	28.39014	89.77750	856	732 736	29.25748	92.52027
807	651 249	28.40775	89.83318	857	734 449	29.27456	92.57429
808	652 864	28.42534	89.88882	858	736 164	29.29164	92.62829
809	654 481	28.44293	89.94443	859	737 881	29.30870	92.68225
810	656 100	28.46050	90.00000	860	739 600	29.32576	92.73618
811	657 721	28.47806	90.05554	861	741 321	29.34280	92.79009
812	659 344	28.49561	90.11104	862	743 044	29.35984	92.84396
813	660 969	28.51315	90.16651	863	744 769	29.37686	92.89779
814	662 596	28.53069	90.22195	864	746 496	29.39388	92.95160
815	664 225	28.54820	90.27735	865	748 225	29.41088	93.00538
816	665 856	28.56571	90.33272	866	749 956	29.42788	93.05912
817	667 489	28.58321	90.38805	867	751 689	29.44486	93.11283
818	669 124	28.60070	90.44335	868	753 424	29.46184	93.16652
819	670 761	28.61818	90.49862	869	755 161	29.47881	93.22017
820	672 400	28.63564	90.55385	870	756 900	29.49576	93.27379
821	674 041	28.65310	90.60905	871	758 641	29.51271	93.32738
822	675 684	28.67054	90.66422	872	760 384	29.52965	93.38094
823	677 329	28.68798	90.71935	873	762 129	29.54657	93.43447
824	678 976	28.70540	90.77445	874	763 876	29.56349	93.48797
825	680 625	28.72281	90.82951	875	765 625	29.58040	93.54143
826	682 276	28.74022	90.88454	876	767 376	29.59730	93.59487
827	683 929	28.75761	90.93954	877	769 129	29.61419	93.64828
828	685 584	28.77499	90.99451	878	770 884	29.63106	93.70165
829	687 241	28.79236	91.04944	879	772 641	29.64793	93.75500
830	688 900	28.80972	91.10434	880	774 400	29.66479	93.80832
831	690 561	28.82707	91.15920	881	776 161	29.68164	93.86160
832	692 224	28.84441	91.21403	882	777 924	29.69848	93.91486
833	693 889	28.86174	91.26883	883	779 689	29.71532	93.96808
834	695 556	28.87906	91.32360	884	781 456	29.73214	94.02027
835	697 225	28.89637	91.37833	885	783 225	29.74895	94.07444
836	698 896	28.91366	91.43304	886	784 996	29.76575	94.12757
837	700 569	28.93095	91.48770	887	786 769	29.78255	94.10868
838	702 244	28.94823	91.54234	888	788 544	29.79933	94.23375
839	703 921	28.96550	91.59694	889	790 321	29.81610	94.28680
840	705 600	28.98275	91.65151	890	792 100	29.83287	94.33981
841	707 281	29.00000	91.70605	891	793 881	29.84962	94.39280
842	708 964	29.01724	91.76056	892	795 664	29.86637	94.44575
843	710 649	29.03446	91.81503	893	797 449	29.88311	94.49868
844	712 336	29.05168	91.86947	894	799 236	29.89983	94.55157
845	714 025	29.06888	91.92388	895	801 025	29.91655	94.60444
846	715 716	29.08608	91.97826	896	802 816	29.93326	94.65728
847	717 409	29.10326	92.03260	897	804 609	29.94996	94.71008
848	719 104	29.12044	92.08692	898	806 404	29.96665	94.76286
849	720 801	29.13760	92.14120	899	808 201	29.98333	94.81561
850	722 500	29.15476	92.19544	900	810 000	30.00000	94.86833

N	N^2	$\sqrt{N}$	$\sqrt{10N}$	N	N^2	$\sqrt{N}$	$\sqrt{10N}$
900	810 000	30.00000	94.86833	950	902 500	30.82207	97.46794
901	811 801	30.01666	94.92102	951	904 401	30.83829	97.51923
902	813 604	30.03331	94.97368	952	906 304	30.85450	97.57049
903	815 409	30.04996	95.02631	953	908 209	30.87070	97.62172
904	817 216	30.06659	95.07891	954	910.116	30.88689	97.67292
905	819 025	30.08322	95.13149	955	912 025	30.90307	97.72410
906	820 836	30.09938	95.18403	956	913 936	30.91925	97.77525
907	822 649	30.11644	95.23655	957	915 849	30.93542	97.82638
908	824 464	30.13304	95.28903	958	917 764	30.95158	97.87747
909	826 281	30.14963	95.34149	959	919 681	30.96773	97.92855
910	828 100	30.16621	95.39392	960	921 600	30.98387	97.97959
911	829 921	30.18278	95.44632	961	923 521	31.00000	98.03061
912	831 744	30.19934	95.49869	962	925 444	31.01612	98.08160
913	833 569	30.21589	95.55103	963	927 369	31.03224	98.13256
914	835 396	30.23243	95.60335	964	929 296	31.04835	98.18350
915	837 225	30.24897	95.65563	965	931 225	31.06445	98.23441
916	839 056	30.26549	95.70789	966	933 156	31.08054	98.28530
917	840 889	30.28201	95.76012	967	935 089	31.09662	98.33616
918	842 724	30.29851	95.81232	968	937 024	31.11270	98.38699
919	844 561	30.31501	95.86449	969	938 961	31.12876	98.43780
920	846 400	30.33150	95.91663	970	940 900	31.14482	98.48858
921	848 241	30.34798	95.96874	971	942 841	31.16087	98.53933
922	850 084	30.36445	96.02083	972	944 784	31.17691	98.59006
923	851 929	30.38092	96.07289	973	946 729	31.19295	98.64076
924	853 776	30.39735	96.12492	974	948 676	31.20897	98.69144
925	855 625	30.41381	96.17692	975	950 625	31.22499	98.74209
926	857 476	30.43025	96.22889	976	952 576	31.24100	98.79271
927	859 329	30.44667	96.28084	977	954 529	31.25700	98.84331
928	861 184	30.46309	96.33276	978	956 484	31.27299	98.89388
929	863 041	30.47950	96.38465	979	958 441	31.28898	98.94443
930	864 900	30.49590	96.43651	980	960 400	31.30495	98.99495
931	866 761	30.51229	96.48834	981	962 361	31.32092	99.04544
932	868 624	30.52868	96.54015	982	964 324	31.33688	99.09591
933	870 489	30.54505	96.59193	983	966 144	31.34021	99.10321
934	872 356	30.56141	96.64368	984	968 256	31.36877	99.19677
935	874 225	30.57777	96.69540	985	970 225	31.38471	99.24717
936	876 096	30.59412	96.74709	986	972 196	31.40064	99.29753
937	877 969	30.61046	96.79876	987	974 169	31.41656	99.34787
938	879 844	30.62679	96.85040	988	976 144	31.43247	99.39819
939	881 721	30.64311	96.90201	989	978 121	31.44837	99.44848
940	883 600	30.65942	96.95360	990	980 100	31.46427	99.49874
941	885 481	30.67572	97.00515	991	982 081	31.48015	99.54898
942	887 364	30.69202	97.05668	992	984 064	31.49603	99.54920
943	889 249	30.70831	97.10819	993	986 049	31.51190	99.64939
944	891 136	30.72458	97.15966	994	988 036	31.52777	99.69955
945	893 025	30.74085	97.21111	995	990 025	31.54362	99.74969
946	894 916	30.75711	97.26253	996	992 016	31.55947	99.79980
947	896 809	30.77337	97.31393	997	994 009	31.57531	99.84989
948	898 704	30.78961	97.36529	998	996 004	31.59114	99.89995
949	900 601	30.80584	97.41663	999	998 001	31.60696	99.94999
950	902 500	30.82207	97.46794	1000	1 000 000	31.62278	100.00000

Glossary

A

aging of accounts receivable Analyzing accounts by the amount of time they have been on the books.

amalgamation A statutory combination of two or more firms under one of the provincial corporations or companies acts, the Canada Corporations Act, or the Canada Business Corporations Act.

American Depository Receipts (ADR) These receipts represent the ownership interest in a foreign company's common stock. The shares of the foreign company are put in trust in a New York bank. The bank, in turn, issues its depository receipts to the American shareholders of the foreign firm. Many ADRs are listed on the NYSE, and many more are traded in the over-the-counter market.

annuity A series of consecutive payments or receipts of equal amount.

asset-based public offerings Public offerings backed by receivables as collateral. Essentially, a firm factors (sells) its receivables in the securities markets.

asset utilization ratios A group of ratios that measures the speed at which the firm is turning over or utilizing its assets. We measure inventory turnover, fixed asset turnover, total asset turnover, and the average time it takes to collect accounts receivable.

assignment The liquidation of assets without going through formal court procedures. In order to affect an assignment creditors must agree on liquidation values and the relative priority of claims.

average collection period The average amount of time accounts receivable have been on the books. It may be computed by dividing accounts receivable by average daily credit sales.

B

balance of payments The term refers to a system of government accounts that catalogs the flow of economic transactions between countries.

balance sheet A financial statement that indicates what assets the firm owns and how those assets are financed in the form of liabilities or ownership interest.

bank rate The rate of interest the Bank of Canada charges on loans to the chartered banks. A monetary tool for management of the money supply.

bankers' acceptance Short-term securities that frequently arise from foreign trade. The acceptance is a draft drawn on a bank for approval for future payment and is subsequently presented to the payer.

bankruptcy The market value of a firm's assets are less than its liabilities, and the firm has a negative net worth. The term is also used to describe in-court procedures associated with the reorganization or liquidation of a firm.

bear market A falling or lethargic stock market. The opposite of a bull market.

beta A measure of the volatility of returns on an individual stock relative to the market. Stocks with a beta of 1.0 are said to have risk equal to that of the market (equal volatility). Stocks with betas greater than 1.0 have more risk than the market, while those with betas of less than 1.0 have less risk than the market.

blanket inventory liens A secured borrowing arrangement in which the lender has a general claim against the inventory of the borrower.

bond ratings Bonds are rated according to risk by the Canadian Bond Rating Service (CBRS) and by the Dominion Bond Rating Service (DBRS). A bond rated A++ by CBRS has the lowest risk while a bond with a C rating has the highest risk. The rate of interest a corporation must pay to issue debt securities is heavily influenced by its bond rating.

book value (See net worth.)

break-even analysis A numerical and graphical technique used to determine at what point the firm will break even (revenue = cost). To compute the break-even point, we divide fixed costs by price minus variable cost per unit.

brokers Members of organized stock exchanges who have the ability to buy and sell securities on the floor of their respective exchanges. Brokers act as agents between buyers and sellers.

bull market A rising stock market. There are many complicated interpretations of this term, usually centering on the length of time the market should be rising in order to meet the criteria for classification as a bull market. For our purposes a bull market exists when stock prices are strong and rising and investors are optimistic about future market performance.

Bureau of Competition Policy Federal agency set up to review mergers in relation to the Competition Act to determine if they lessen competition substantially in given markets.

C

call premium The premium paid by a corporation to call in a bond or preferred stock issue before the maturity date.

call provision Used for bonds and some preferred stock. A call provision allows the corporation to retire securities before maturity by forcing their holders to sell securities back to it at a set price.

capital Sources of long-term financing available to the business firm.

capital asset pricing model A model that relates the risk-return tradeoffs of individual assets to market returns. A security is presumed to receive a risk-free rate of return plus a premium for risk.

capital cost allowance (CCA) Declining balance method of accelerated depreciation the Income Tax Act allows as a tax-deductible expense.

capital gains taxes Taxes on gains from holding assets. The individual may exclude 50 percent (scheduled to be reduced to 33⅓ percent) of the gain from taxation and currently may shelter, over his or her lifetime, $100,000 of capital gains from any tax.

capital lease A long-term, noncancelable lease that has many of the characteristics of debt. Under generally accepted accounting practices, the lease obligation must be shown directly on the balance sheet.

capital markets Competitive markets for equity securities or debt securities with maturities of more than one year. The best examples of capital market securities are common stock, bonds, and preferred stock.

capital rationing Occurs when a corporation has more dollars of capital budgeting projects with positive net present values than it has money to invest in them. Therefore, some projects that should be accepted are excluded because financial capital is rationed.

carrying costs The cost to hold an asset, usually inventory. For inventory, carrying costs include such items as interest, warehousing costs, insurance, and material-handling expenses.

cash budget A series of monthly or quarterly budgets that indicate cash receipts, cash payments, and the borrowing requirements for meeting financial requirements. It is constructed from the pro forma income statement and other supportive schedules.

cash flow A value equal to income after taxes plus noncash expenses. In capital budgeting decisions, the usual noncash expense is depreciation.

cash flow statement Reports the cash flow effects of all changes between a beginning and ending balance sheet for a period of time. It is often referred to as a statement of changes in financial position.

certificates of deposit A certificate offered by banks, trust companies, and other financial institutions for the deposit of funds at a given interest rate over a specified time period.

clientele effect The effect of investor preferences for dividends or capital gains. Investors tend to purchase securities that meet their needs.

coefficient of correlation The degree of associated movement between two or more variables. Variables that move in the same direction are said to be positively correlated, while negatively correlated variables move in opposite directions.

coefficient of variation A measure of risk determination computed by dividing the standard deviation for a series of numbers by the expected value. Generally, the larger the coefficient of variation, the greater the risk.

combined leverage The total or combined impact of operating and financial leverage.

commercial paper An unsecured promissory note that large corporations issue to investors. The minimum amount is usually $25,000.

common equity The common stock or ownership capital of the firm. Common equity may be supplied through retained earnings or the sale of new common stock.

common shareholder Holders of common stock are the owners of the company. Common shareholders elect the members of the board of directors, who in turn help select the top management.

compensating balances A bank requirement that business customers maintain a minimum average balance. The required amount is usually computed as a percentage of customer loans outstanding or as a percentage of the future loans to which the bank has committed itself.

composition An out-of-court settlement in which creditors agree to accept a fractional settlement on their original claim.

compound sum The future value of a single amount or an annuity when compounded at a given interest rate for a specified time period.

conglomerate A corporation made up of many diverse, often unrelated divisions. This form of organization is thought to reduce risk but may create problems of coordination.

constant dollar accounting One of two methods of inflation-adjusted accounting that have been recommended by the Canadian Institute of Chartered Accountants for use by larger firms. Financial statements are adjusted to reflect changing price levels using a general price index like the consumer price index. If the firm elects to follow the recommendation, this is shown as supplemental information in the firm's annual report.

consumer price index An economic indicator published monthly by Statistics Canada. It measures the rate of inflation for consumer goods.

contribution margin The contribution to fixed costs from each unit of sales. The margin may be computed as price minus variable cost per unit.

conversion premium The market price of a convertible bond or preferred stock minus the security's conversion value.

conversion price The conversion ratio divided into the par value. The price of the common stock at which the security is convertible. An investor would usually not convert the security into common stock unless the market price were greater than the conversion price.

conversion ratio The number of shares of common stock an investor will receive if he exchanges a convertible bond or convertible preferred stock for common stock.

conversion value The conversion ratio multiplied by the market price per share of common stock.

convertible security A security that may be traded in to the company for a different form or type of security. Convertible securities are usually bonds or preferred stock that may be exchanged for common stock.

corporate stock repurchase A corporation may repurchase its shares in the market as an alternative to paying a cash dividend. Earnings per share usually go up, and if the price-earnings ratio remains the same, the shareholder will receive the same dollar benefit as through a cash dividend. Furthermore, the increase in stock price is a capital gain, whereas the cash dividend would be taxed as ordinary income. A corporation may also justify the repurchase of its stock because it is at a very low price or to maintain constant demand for the shares. Reacquired shares may be used for employee options or as part of a tender offer in a merger or acquisition. Firms may also reacquire part of their shares as a protective device against being taken over as a merger candidate.

corporation A form of ownership in which a separate, legal entity is created. A corporation may sue or be sued, engage in contracts, and acquire property. It has a continual life and is not dependent on any one shareholder for maintaining its legal existence. A corporation is owned by shareholders who enjoy the privilege of limited liability. There is, however, the potential for double taxation in the corporate form of organization: the first time at the corporate level in the form of profits and again at the shareholder level in the form of dividends.

cost-benefit analysis A study of the incremental costs and benefits that can be derived from a given course of action.

cost of capital The cost of alternative sources of financing to the firm. (See, also, weighted average cost of capital.)

cost of goods sold The cost specifically associated with units sold during the time period under study.

coupon rate The actual interest rate on the bond, usually payable in semiannual installments. The coupon rate normally stays constant during the life of the bond and indicates what the bondholder's annual dollar income will be.

credit terms The repayment provisions that are part of a credit arrangement. An example would be a 2/10, net 30 arrangement in which the customer may deduct 2 percent from the invoice price if payment takes place in the first 10 days. Otherwise the full amount is due.

cum rights The situation in which the purchase of a share of common stock includes a right attached to the stock.

cumulative preferred stock If dividends from one period are not paid to the preferred shareholders, they are said to be in arrears and are then added to the next period's dividends. When dividends on preferred stock are in arrears, no dividends can legally be paid to the common shareholders. The cumulative dividend feature is very beneficial to preferred shareholders since it assures them they will receive all dividends due before common shareholders can get any dividends.

cumulative voting Allows shareholders more than one vote per share. They are allowed to multiply their total shares by the number of directors being elected to determine their total number of votes. This system enables minority shareholders to elect directors even though they do not have 51 percent of the vote.

currency futures contract A futures contract that may be used for hedging or speculation in foreign exchange.

current cost accounting The second method of inflation-adjusted accounting recommended by the CICA for use by larger companies. Financial statements are adjusted to reflect changing price levels using specific price indices related to the specific types of goods being adjusted. If the firm elects to follow the recommendation, this is shown as supplemental information in the firm's annual report.

current yield The yearly dollar interest payment divided by the current market price.

D

dealers Participants in the market who transact security trades over-the-counter from their own inventory of stocks and bonds. They are often referred to as market makers since they stand ready to buy and sell their securities at quoted prices.

debenture A long-term unsecured corporate bond. Debentures are usually issued by large, prestigious firms having excellent credit ratings in the financial community.

debt utilization ratios A group of ratios that indicates to what extent debt is being used and the prudence with which it is being managed. Calculations include debt to total assets, times interest earned, and fixed charge coverage.

decision tree A tabular or graphical analysis that lays out the sequence of decisions that are to be made and highlights the differences between choices. The presentation resembles branches on a tree.

declaration date The day on which the board of directors officially states that a dividend will be paid.

deferred annuity An annuity that will not begin until some time period in the future.

degree of combined leverage A measure of the total combined effect of operating and financial leverage on earnings per share. The percentage change in earnings per share is divided by the percentage change in sales at a given level of operation. Other algebraic statements are also used, such as Formula 5–7 and footnote 5 in Chapter 5.

degree of financial leverage A measure of the impact of debt on the earnings capability of the firm. The percentage change in earnings per share is divided by the percentage change in earnings before interest and taxes at a given level of operation. Other algebraic statements are also used, such as Formula 5–5.

degree of operating leverage A measure of the impact of fixed costs on the operating earnings of the firm. The percentage change in operating income is divided by the percentage change in volume at a given level of operation. Other algebraic statements are also used, such as Formula 5–3 and footnote 3 in Chapter 5.

dilution of earnings This occurs when additional shares of stock are sold without creating an immediate increase in income. The result is a decline in earnings per share until earnings can be generated from the funds raised.

discount rate The interest rate at which future sums or annuities are discounted back to the present.

discounted loan A loan in which the calculated interest payment is subtracted or discounted in advance. Because this lowers the amount of available funds, the effective interest rate is increased.

disinflation A leveling off or slowing down of price increases.

dividend information content This theory of dividends assumes that dividends provide information about the financial health and economic expectations of the company. If this is true, corporations must actively manage their dividends to provide the market with information.

dividend payment date The day on which a shareholder of record will receive his or her dividend.

dividend payout The percentage of after-tax earnings paid out as dividends. It can be computed by dividing dividends per share by earnings per share.

dividend record date Shareholders owning the stock on the holder-of-record date are entitled to receive a dividend. In order to be listed as an owner on the corporate books, the investor must have bought the stock before it went ex-dividend.

dividend reinvestment plans Plans that provide the investor with an opportunity to buy additional shares of stock with the cash dividends paid by the company.

dividend tax credit Tax credit accorded to individuals receiving corporate dividends. Its purpose is to compensate for the fact that corporate earnings are taxed in the hands of the corporation and possibly again in the hands of the shareholder.

dividend valuation model A model for determining the value of a share of stock by taking the present value of an expected stream of future dividends.

dividend yield Dividends per share divided by market price per share. Dividend yield indicates the percentage return a shareholder will receive on dividends alone.

dual trading Exists when one security, such as Alcan common stock, is traded on more than one stock exchange. This practice is quite common for larger TSE-listed companies which are often also listed on the Montreal Exchange.

Dun & Bradstreet A credit-rating agency that publishes information on hundreds of thousands of business establishments through its *Reference Book*.

Du Pont System of Ratio Analysis An analysis of profitability that breaks down return on assets between the profit margin and asset turnover. The second, or modified, version shows how return on assets is translated into return on equity through the amount of debt the firm has. Actually, return on assets is divided by (1 − debt/assets) to arrive at return on equity.

E

earnings per share The earnings available to common shareholders divided by the number of common stock shares outstanding.

economic indicators Hundreds of indicators exist. Each is a specialized series of data. The data are analyzed for their relationship to economic activity, and the indicator is classified as either a lagging indicator, a leading indicator, or a coincident economic indicator.

economic ordering quantity (EOQ) The most efficient ordering quantity for the firm. The EOQ will allow the firm to minimize the total ordering and carrying costs associated with inventory.

efficient frontier A line drawn through the optimum point selections in a risk-return trade-off diagram. Each point represents the best possible trade-off between risk and return (the highest return at a given risk level or the lowest risk at a given return level).

efficient market hypothesis Hypothesis which suggests that markets adjust very quickly to new information and that it is very difficult for investors to select portfolios of securities that outperform the market. The efficient market hypothesis may be stated in many different forms as indicated in Chapter 14.

electronic funds transfer A system in which funds are moved between computer terminals without the use of written checks.

Eurobonds Bonds payable or denominated in the borrower's currency but sold outside the country of the borrower, usually by an international syndicate.

Eurocurrency A unit of currency held on deposit in a bank outside of the country issuing the currency.

Eurodollar loan A loan from a foreign bank denominated in dollars.

ex-dividend date Four business days before the holder-of-record date. On the ex-dividend date the purchase of the stock no longer carries with it the right to receive the dividend previously declared.

expectations theory of interest rates This theory explains the shape of the term structure relative to expectations for future short-term interest rates. It is thought that long-term rates are an average of the expected short-term rates. Therefore, an upward-sloping yield curve would indicate that short-term rates will rise.

expected value A representative value from a probability distribution arrived at by multiplying each outcome by the associated probability and summing up the values.

Export Development Corporation (EDC) Agency of the federal government whose role is to facilitate the financing of Canadian exports through credit insurance, loan guarantees, special loans, and so forth.

expropriation The action of a country in taking away or modifying the property rights of a corporation or individual.

ex-rights The situation in which the purchase of common stock during a rights offering no longer includes rights to purchase additional shares of common stock.

extension An out-of-court settlement in which creditors agree to allow the firm more time to meet its financial obligations. A new repayment schedule will be developed, subject to the acceptance of creditors.

external corporate funds Corporate financing raised through sources outside of the firm. Bonds, common stock, and preferred stock fall in this category.

F

factoring receivables Selling accounts receivable to a finance company.

federal budget deficit Government expenditures are greater than government tax revenues, and the government must borrow to balance revenues and expenditures. These deficits act as an economic stimulus.

federal budget surplus Government tax receipts are greater than government expenditures. A rarity during the last 20 years. These surpluses have a dampening effect on the economy.

field warehousing An inventory financing arrangement in which collateralized inventory is stored on the premises of the borrower but is controlled by an independent warehousing company.

FIFO A system of writing off inventory into cost of goods sold in which the items purchased first are written off first. Referred to as first-in, first-out.

financial capital Common stock, preferred stock, bonds, and retained earnings. Financial capital appears on the corporate balance sheet under long-term liabilities and equity.

financial disclosure Presentation of financial information to the investment community.

financial futures market A market that allows for the trading of financial instruments related to a future point in time. A purchase or sale takes place in the present, with a reversal necessitated in the future to close out the position. If a purchase (sale) takes place initially, then a sale (purchase) will be necessary in the future.

financial intermediary A financial institution such as a bank or a life insurance company that directs other people's money into such investments as government and corporate securities.

financial lease A long-term noncancelable lease. The financial lease has all the characteristics of long-term debt except that the lease payments are a combination of interest expense and amortization of the cost of the asset.

financial leverage A measure of the amount of debt used in the capital structure of the firm.

financial sweetener Usually refers to equity options, such as warrants or conversion privileges, attached to a debt security. The sweetener lowers the nominal interest cost to the corporation.

fiscal policy The tax policies of the federal government and the spending associated with its tax revenues.

fixed costs Costs that remain relatively constant regardless of the volume of operations. Examples are rent, depreciation, property taxes, and executive salaries.

float The difference between the corporation's recorded cash balance on its books and the amount credited to the corporation by the bank.

floating rate bond The interest payment on the bond changes with market conditions rather than the price of the bond.

floating rate preferred stock The quarterly dividend on the preferred stock changes with market conditions. The market price is considerably less volatile than it is with regular preferred stock.

floor price Usually equal to the pure bond or preferred share value. A convertible bond will not sell at less than its pure bond value even when its conversion value is below the pure bond value.

flotation cost The distribution cost of selling securities to the public. The cost includes the underwriter's spread and any associated fees.

forced conversion Occurs when a company calls a convertible security that has a conversion value greater than the call price. Investors will take the higher of the two values and convert the security to common stock rather than take a lower cash call price.

foreign exchange rate The relationship between the value of two or more currencies. For example, the exchange rate between Canadian dollars and French francs is stated as dollars per franc or francs per dollar.

foreign exchange risk A form of risk that refers to the possibility of experiencing a drop in revenue or an increase in cost in an international transaction due to a change in foreign exchange rates. Importers, exporters, investors, and multinational firms alike are exposed to this risk.

four pillars of finance Traditional separation of financial institution roles in Canada among chartered banks, trusts, insurance companies, and securities dealers.

fourth market A market of stocks and bonds in which there is direct dealing between financial institutions, such as investment dealers, insurance companies, pension funds, and mutual funds.

fronting loan A parent company's loan to a foreign subsidiary is channeled through a financial intermediary, usually a large international bank. The bank fronts for the parent in extending the loan to the foreign affiliate.

fully diluted earnings per share Equals adjusted earnings after tax divided by the fully diluted number of shares. Earnings are redefined to add to the numerator the costs related to convertible securities. The denominator includes common shares outstanding, the common share equivalent of all convertible shares and bonds, and common shares that could be issued as a result of outstanding rights, warrants, and other options.

futures contract A contract to buy or sell a commodity at some specified price in the future.

G

going private The process by which all publicly owned shares of common stock are repurchased or retired, thereby eliminating listing fees, annual reports, and other expenses involved with publicly owned companies.

golden parachute Highly attractive termination payments made to current management in the event of a takeover of the company.

goodwill An intangible asset that reflects value above that recognized in the tangible assets of the firm. It arises when one firm acquires another for an amount greater than the acquired firm's book value.

H

hedging To engage in a transaction that partially or fully reduces a prior risk exposure by taking a position that is the opposite of your initial position. As an example, you buy some copper now but also engage in a contract to sell copper in the future at a set price.

historical cost accounting The traditional method of accounting in which financial statements are developed based on original cost minus depreciation.

holding company A company that has voting control of one or more other companies. It often has less than a 50 percent interest in each of these other companies.

hurdle rate The minimum acceptable rate of return in a capital budgeting decision.

I

income statement A financial statement that measures the profitability of the firm over a period of time. All expenses are subtracted from sales to arrive at net income.

indenture A legal contract between the borrower and the lender that covers every detail regarding a bond issue.

indexing An adjustment for inflation. Indexing may be used to revalue assets on the balance sheet and to automatically adjust wages, tax deductions, interest payments, and a wide variety of other categories to account for inflation.

inflation The phenomenon of price increase with the passage of time.

inflation premium A premium to compensate the investor for the eroding effect of inflation on the value of the dollar. In the 1980s the inflation premium has been about 4 percent. In the late 1970s it was in excess of 10 percent.

installment loan A borrowing arrangement in which a series of equal payments are used to pay off the loan.

interest factor (*IF*) The tabular value to insert into the various formulas. It is based on the number of periods (n) and the interest rate (i).

interest rate parity theory A theory based on the interplay between interest rate differentials and exchange rates. If one country has a higher interest rate than another country after adjustments for inflation, interest rates and foreign exchange rates will adjust until the foreign exchange rates and money market rates reach equilibrium (are properly balanced between the two countries).

internal corporate funds Funds generated through the operations of the firm. The principal sources are retained earnings and cash flow added back from depreciation and other noncash expenses.

internal rate of return (IRR) A discounted cash flow method for evaluating capital budgeting projects. The IRR is a discount rate which makes the present value of the cash inflows equal to the present value of the cash outflows.

International diversification Achieving diversification through many different foreign investments that are influenced by a variety of factors.

International Finance Corporation (IFC) An affiliate of the World Bank established with the sole purpose of providing partial seed capital for private ventures around the world. Whenever a multinational company has difficulty raising equity capital due to lack of adequate private risk capital, the firm may explore the possibility of selling equity or debt (totaling up to 25 percent) to the International Finance Corporation.

inventory profits Profits generated as a result of an inflationary economy in which old inventory is sold at large profits because of increasing prices. This is particularly prevalent under FIFO accounting.

inverted yield curve A downward-sloping yield curve. Short-term rates are higher than long-term rates.

Investment Canada Agency set up by the federal government to review proposed foreign direct investments in Canada.

investment tax credit (ITC) Direct dollar giveback to a firm for investing in certain assets sometimes for use in specific geographic areas or in specific businesses. These incentives range from 7 percent of the value of the investment to 50 percent.

investment underwriter A financial organization that specializes in selling primary offerings of securities. Investment underwriters can also perform other financial functions such as advising clients, negotiating mergers and takeovers, and selling secondary offerings.

L

leading indicators Selected statistics that, on average, indicate changes in the business cycle ahead of the economy as a whole. These relate to capital investment, business starts and failures, employment, profits, stock prices, inventory adjustment, housing starts, and the prices of some commodities.

lease A contractual arrangement between the owner of equipment (lessor) and the user of equipment (lessee) which calls for the lessee to pay the lessor an established lease payment. There are two kinds of leases, financial leases and operating leases.

letter of credit A credit letter normally issued by the importer's bank in which the bank promises to pay out the money for the merchandise when delivered.

level production Equal monthly production used to smooth out production schedules and employ manpower and equipment more efficiently and at a lower cost.

leverage The use of fixed-charge items with the intent of magnifying the potential returns to the firm.

leveraged buyout Existing management or an outsider makes an offer to "go private" by retiring all the shares of the company. The buying group borrows the necessary money, using the assets of the acquired firm as collateral. The buying group then repurchases all the shares and expects to retire the debt over time with the cash flow from operations or the sale of corporate assets.

LIBOR (See London Interbank Offered Rate.)

life cycle curve A curve illustrating the growth phases of a firm. The dividend policy most likely to be employed during each phase is often illustrated.

LIFO A system of writing off inventory into cost of goods sold in which the items purchased last are written off first. Referred to as last-in, first-out. Rarely used in Canada because of tax treatment.

limited partnership A special form of partnership to limit liability for most of the partners. Under this arrangement, one or more partners are designated as general partners and have unlimited liability for the debts of the firm, while the other partners are designated as limited partners and are only liable for their initial contribution.

liquidation A procedure that may be carried out under the formal bankruptcy laws when an internal or external reorganization does not appear to be feasible and it appears the assets are worth more in liquidation than through a reorganization. Priority of claims becomes extremely important in a liquidation because it is unlikely that all parties will be fully satisfied in their demands.

liquidity The relative convertibility of short-term assets to cash. Thus, marketable securities are highly liquid assets, while inventory may not be.

liquidity ratios A group of ratios that allows one to measure the firm's ability to pay off short-term obligations as they come due. Primary attention is directed to the current ratio and the quick ratio.

listing requirements Financial standards corporations must meet before their common stock can be traded on a stock exchange. Listing requirements are not standard but are set by each exchange.

lockbox system A procedure used to expedite cash inflows to a business. Customers are requested to forward their checks to a post-office box in their geographic region, and a local bank picks up the checks and processes them for rapid collection. Funds are then wired to the corporate home office for immediate use.

London Interbank Offered Rate (LIBOR) An interbank rate applicable for large deposits in the London market. It is a benchmark rate just like the prime interest rate in Canada. Interest rates on Eurodollar loans are determined by adding premiums to this basic rate. Most often LIBOR is lower than the Canadian prime rate.

M

majority voting All directors must be elected by a vote of more than 50 percent. Minority shareholders are unable to achieve any representation on the board of directors.

managing underwriter An investment dealer who is responsible for the pricing, prospectus development, and legal work involved in the sale of a new issue of securities.

margin The amount paid by a client who uses credit to buy a security, the balance being loaned by the broker. The margin requirement is 50 percent or greater depending on the exchange and the price level of the stock being bought on margin.

marginal cost of capital The cost of the last dollar of funds raised. It is assumed each dollar is financed in proportion to the firm's optimum capital structure.

marginal principle of retained earnings The corporation must be able to earn a higher return on its retained earnings than a shareholder would receive after paying taxes on the distributed dividends.

market efficiency Markets are considered to be efficient when (1) prices adjust rapidly to new information; (2) there is a continuous market in which each successive trade is made at a price close to the previous price (the faster the price responds to new information and the smaller the differences in price changes, the more efficient the market); and (3) the market can absorb large dollar amounts of securities without destabilizing the prices.

market maker (See dealers.)

market risk premium A premium over and above the risk-free rate. It is represented by the difference between the market return (K_m) and the risk-free rate (R_f), and it may be multiplied by the beta coefficient to determine additional risk-adjusted return on a security.

market stabilization Intervention in the secondary markets by an investment dealer to stabilize the price of a new security offering during the offering period. The purpose of market stabilization is to provide an orderly market for the distribution of the new issue.

market value maximization The concept of maximizing the wealth of shareholders. This calls for a recognition not only of earnings per share but also how they will be valued in the marketplace.

maturity date The date on which the bond is retired and the principal (par value) is repaid to the lender.

merger The combination of two or more companies.

merger premium The part of a buyout or exchange offer which represents a value over and above the market value of the acquired firm.

minimum warrant value The market value of the common stock minus the option price of the warrant multiplied by the number of shares of the common stock that each warrant entitles the holder to purchase.

monetary policy Management by the Bank of Canada of the money supply and the resultant interest rates.

money market The part of the capital market in which short-term financial obligations are bought and sold. The securities comprising this market include federal government Treasury bills and other of its securities maturing within three years, commercial paper, bankers' acceptances, and trust company guaranteed investment certificates.

mortgage agreement A loan which requires real property (plant and equipment) as collateral.

multinational corporation (MNC) A firm doing business across its national borders is considered a multinational enterprise. Some definitions require a minimum percentage (often 30 percent or more) of a firm's business activities to be carried on outside its national borders.

mutually exclusive The selection of one choice precludes the selection of any competitive choice. For example, several machines can do an identical job in capital budgeting. If one machine is selected, the other machines will not be used.

N

net present value (NPV) The NPV equals the present value of the cash inflows minus the present value of the cash outflows with the cost of capital used as a discount rate. This method is used to evaluate capital budgeting projects. If the NPV is positive, a project should be accepted.

net present value profile A graphical presentation of the potential net present values of a project at different discount rates. It is very helpful in comparing the characteristics of two or more investments.

net trade credit A measure of the relationship between the firm's accounts receivable and accounts payable. If accounts receivable exceed accounts payable, the firm is a net provider of trade credit; otherwise, it is a net user.

net worth, or book value Owners' equity minus preferred stock ownership. Basically, net worth is the common shareholders' interest as represented by amounts raised through the sale of common stock, and retained earnings. If you take all the assets of the firm and subtract its liabilities and preferred stock, you arrive at net worth.

nominal GNP GNP (gross national product) in current dollars without any adjustments for inflation.

nominal yield A return equal to the coupon rate.

nonfinancial corporation A firm not in the banking or financial services industry. The term would primarily apply to manufacturing, mining, wholesaling, and retail firms.

nonlinear break-even analysis Break-even analysis based on the assumption that cost and revenue relationships to quantity may vary at different levels of operation. Most of our analysis is based on *linear* break-even analysis.

normal yield curve An upward-sloping yield curve. Long-term interest rates are higher than short-term rates.

O

open-market operations The purchase and sale of government securities in the open market by the Bank of Canada for its own account. This is the most common method for managing the money supply and works by increasing or decreasing the cash reserves in the banking system.

operating lease A short-term, nonbinding obligation that is easily cancelable.

operating leverage A reflection of the extent to which fixed assets and fixed costs are utilized in the business firm.

optimum capital structure A capital structure that has the best possible mix of debt, preferred stock, and common equity. The optimum mix should provide the lowest possible cost of capital to the firm.

over-the-counter markets Markets for securities (both bonds and stock) in which market makers, or dealers, transact purchases and sales of securities by trading from their own inventories of securities.

owners' equity The total ownership position of preferred and common shareholders.

P

par value Sometimes referred to as the face value or the principal value of the bond. Most bond issues have a par value of $1,000 per bond. Older issues of common and preferred stock may also have an assigned par value.

parallel loan A Canadian firm that wishes to lend funds to a foreign affiliate (such as a Dutch affiliate) locates a foreign parent firm (such as a Dutch parent firm) that wishes to loan money to a Canadian affiliate. Avoiding the foreign exchange markets entirely, the Canadian parent lends dollars to the Dutch affiliate in Canada, while the Dutch parent lends guilders to the Canadian affiliate in the Netherlands. At maturity the two loans would each be repaid to the original lender. Notice that neither loan carries any foreign exchange risk in this arrangement.

participating preferred stock A small number of preferred stock issues are participating with regard to corporate earnings. For such issues, once the common stock dividend equals the preferred stock dividend, the two classes of securities may share equally (or in some ratio) in additional dividend payments.

partnership A form of ownership in which two or more partners are involved. Like the sole proprietorship, a partnership arrangement carries unlimited liability for the owners.

payback A value that indicates the time period required to recoup an initial investment. The payback does not include the time-value-of-money concept.

percent-of-sales method A method of determining future financial needs that is an alternative to the development of pro forma financial statements. We first determine the percentage relationship of various asset and liability accounts to sales, and then we show how that relationship changes as our volume of sales changes.

permanent current assets Current assets that will not be reduced or converted to cash within the normal operating cycle of the firm. Though from a strict accounting standpoint the assets should be removed from the current assets category, they generally are not.

perpetuity An investment without a maturity date.

planning horizon The length of time it takes to conceive, develop, and complete a project and to recover the cost of the project on a discounted cash flow basis.

pledging receivables Using accounts receivable as collateral for a loan. The firm usually may borrow 60 to 80 percent of the value of acceptable collateral.

point-of-sales terminals Computer terminals in retail stores that either allow digital input or use optical scanners. The terminals may be used for inventory control or other purposes.

pooling of interests A method of financial recording for mergers in which the financial statements of the firms are combined, subject to minor adjustments, and goodwill is *not* created. The use of this method is rarely allowed anymore.

portfolio effect The impact of a given investment on the overall risk-return composition of the firm. A firm must consider not only the individual investment characteristics of a project but also how the project relates to the entire portfolio of undertakings.

preemptive right The right of current common shareholders to maintain their ownership percentage on new issues of common stock.

preferred stock A hybrid security combining some of the characteristics of common stock and debt. The dividends paid are not tax-deductible expenses for the corporation, as is true of the interest paid on debt.

present value The current or discounted value of a future sum or annuity. The value is discounted back at a given interest rate for a specified time period.

price-earnings ratio The multiplier applied to earnings per share to determine current value. The P/E ratio is influenced by the earnings and sales growth of the firm, the risk or volatility of its performance, the debt-equity structure, and other factors.

prime rate The rate the bank charges its most creditworthy customers.

private placement The sale of securities directly to a financial institution by a corporation. This eliminates the middleman and reduces the cost of issue to the corporation.

profitability ratios A group of ratios that indicates the return on sales, total assets, and invested capital. Specifically, we compute the profit margin (net income to sales), return on assets, and return on equity.

pro forma balance sheet A projection of future asset, liability, and shareholders' equity levels. Notes payable or cash is used as a plug or balancing figure for the statement.

pro forma financial statements A series of projected financial statements. Of major importance are the pro forma income statement, the pro forma balance sheet, and the cash budget.

pro forma income statement A projection of anticipated sales, expenses, and income.

prospectus Legal document, prepared in conformity with the requirements of the appropriate provincial securities commission, describing securities offered for sale to the public.

proxy Written authorization given by a shareholder to someone else to represent him or her and vote his or her shares at a shareholders' meeting.

public placement The sale of securities to the public through the investment underwriter process.

public warehousing An inventory financing arrangement in which inventory, used as collateral, is stored with and controlled by an independent warehousing company.

purchase of assets A method of financial recording for mergers in which the difference between the purchase price and the adjusted book value is recognized as goodwill and amortized over a maximum time period of 40 years.

purchasing power parity theory A theory based on the interplay between inflation and exchange rates. A parity between the purchasing powers of two countries establishes the rate of exchange between the two currencies. Currency exchange rates, therefore, tend to vary inversely with their respective purchasing powers in order to provide the same or similar purchasing power.

pure bond value The value of the convertible bond if its present value is computed at a discount rate equal to interest rates on straight bonds of equal risk, without conversion privileges.

R

real capital Long-term productive assets (plant and equipment).

real GNP GNP (gross national product) in current dollars adjusted for inflation.

real rate of return The rate of return an investor demands for giving up the current use of his or her funds on an inflation-adjusted basis. It is payment for forgoing current consumption. Historically, the real rate of return demanded by investors has been of the magnitude of 2 to 3 percent. However, throughout the 1980s the real rate of return has been much higher; that is, 5 to 7 percent.

refunding The process of retiring an old bond issue before maturity and replacing it with a new issue. Refunding will occur when interest rates have fallen and new bonds may be sold at lower interest rates.

reinvestment assumption An assumption must be made concerning the rate of return that can be earned on the cash flows generated by capital budgeting projects. The NPV method assumes the rate of reinvestment to be the cost of capital, while the IRR method assumes the rate to be the actual internal rate of return.

repatriation of earnings Returning earnings to the multinational parent company in the form of dividends.

replacement cost The cost of replacing the existing asset base at current prices as opposed to original cost.

replacement cost accounting Financial statements based on the present cost of replacing assets.

required rate of return That rate of return investors demand from an investment to compensate them for the amount of risk involved.

reserve requirements The amount of funds commercial banks must hold in reserve for each dollar of deposits. Reserve requirements are set by the Bank of Canada and are different for savings and checking accounts. Low reserve requirements are stimulating; high reserve requirements are restrictive.

residual dividends This theory of dividend payout states that a corporation will retain as much earnings as it may profitably invest. If any income is left after investments, it will pay dividends. This theory assumes that dividends are a passive decision variable.

restructuring Redeploying the asset and liability structure of the firm. This can be accomplished through repurchasing shares with cash or borrowed funds, acquiring other firms, or selling off unprofitable or unwanted divisions.

rights offering A sale of new common stock by issuing rights to existing shareholders. Usually one right will be issued for every share held. A certain number of rights may be used to buy shares of common stock from the company at a set price that is lower than the market price.

rights-on (See cum rights.)

risk A measure of uncertainty about the outcome from a given event. The greater the variability of possible outcomes, on both the high side and the low side, the greater the risk.

risk-adjusted discount rate A discount rate used in the capital budgeting process that has been adjusted upward or downward from the basic cost of capital to reflect the risk dimension of a given project.

risk averse An aversion or dislike for risk. In order to induce most people to take larger risks, there must be increased potential for return.

risk-free rate of interest Rate of return on an asset that carries no risk. The return on Government of Canada short-term Treasury bills is often used as an approximation of this rate although some studies have concluded that a rate related to longer-term government bonds would be better.

risk premium A premium associated with the special risks of an investment. Of primary concern are two types of risk, business risk and financial risk. Business risk relates to the inability of the firm to maintain its competitive position and sustain stability and growth in earnings. Financial risk relates to the inability of the firm to meet its debt obligations as they come due. The risk premium will also differ (be greater or less) for different types of investments (bonds, stocks, and so forth).

S

secondary offering The sale of a large block of stock in a publicly traded company, usually by estates, foundations, or large individual shareholders.

secondary trading The buying and selling of publicly owned securities in secondary markets such as the Toronto Stock Exchange and the over-the-counter markets.

secured debt A general category of debt which indicates the loan was obtained by pledging assets as collateral. Secured debt has many forms and usually offers some protective features to a given class of bondholders.

security market line A line or equation that depicts the risk-related return of a security based on a risk-free rate plus a market premium related to the beta coefficient of the security.

self-liquidating assets Assets that are converted to cash within the normal operating cycle of the firm. An example is the purchase and sell-off of seasonal inventory.

semiannual compounding A compounding period of every six months. For example, a five-year investment in which interest is compounded semiannually would indicate an n value equal to 10 and an i value at one half the annual rate.

semivariable costs Costs that are partially fixed but still change somewhat as volume changes. Examples are utilities and repairs and maintenance.

serial bond A bond issued by one company or government unit with a series of different maturity dates and interest rates that correspond to rates on competitive bonds with the same maturity and risk.

shareholder wealth maximization Maximizing the wealth of the firm's shareholders through achieving the highest possible value for the firm in the marketplace. It is the overriding objective of the firm and should influence all decisions.

simulation A method of dealing with uncertainty in which future outcomes are anticipated. The model may use random variables for inputs. By programming the computer to randomly select inputs from probability distributions, the outcomes generated by a simulation are distributed about a mean, and instead of generating one return or net present value, a range of outcomes with attendant standard deviations is provided.

sinking fund A method for retiring bonds in an orderly process over the life of a bond. Each year or semiannually a corporation sets aside a sum of money equal to a certain percentage of the total issue. These funds are then used by a trustee to purchase the bonds in the open market and retire them. This method will prevent the corporation from being forced to refund or raise a large amount of capital at maturity to retire the total bond issue.

sole proprietorship A form or organization that represents single-person ownership and offers the advantages of simplicity of decision making and low organizational and operating costs.

speculative warrant premium The market price of the warrant minus the warrant's intrinsic value.

spontaneous sources of funds Funds arising through the normal course of business such as accounts payable generated from the purchase of goods for resale.

standard deviation A measure of the spread or dispersion of a series of numbers around the expected value. The standard deviation tells us how well the expected value represents a series of values.

step-up in conversion A feature that is sometimes written into the contract which allows the conversion ratio to decline in steps over time. This feature encourages early conversion when the conversion value is greater than the call price.

stock dividend A dividend paid in stock rather than cash. A book transfer equal to the market value of the stock dividend is made from retained earnings to the capital stock and paid-in capital accounts. The stock dividend may be symbolic of corporate growth, but it does not increase the total value of the shareholders' wealth.

stock split A division of shares by a ratio set by the board of directors—two for one, three for one, three for two, and so on. Stock splits usually indicate the company's stock has risen in price to a level the directors feel limits the trading appeal of the stock. Any par value is divided by the ratio set, and new shares are issued to the current shareholders of record to increase their shares to the stated level. For example, a two-for-one split would increase your holdings from one share to two shares.

straight-line depreciation A method of depreciation which takes the depreciable cost of an asset and divides it by the asset's useful life to determine the annual depreciation expense. Straight-line depreciation creates uniform depreciation expenses for each of the years in which an asset is depreciated.

subordinated debenture An unsecured bond in which payment to the holder will take place only after designated senior debenture holders are satisfied.

synergy The recognition that the whole may be equal to more than the sum of the parts. The "2 + 2 = 5" effect.

T

tax loss carry-forward A loss that can be carried forward for a number of years to offset future taxable income and perhaps be utilized by another firm in a merger or an acquisition.

technical insolvency A firm cannot pay its bills as they come due.

temporary current assets Current assets that will be reduced or converted to cash within the normal operating cycle of the firm.

tender offer takeover An unfriendly acquisition which is not initially negotiated with the management of the target firm. A tender offer is usually made directly to the shareholders of the target firm.

term loan An intermediate-length loan in which credit is generally extended from 1 to 10 years. The loan is usually repaid in monthly or quarterly installments over its life.

term structure of interest rates The relationship between interest rates and maturities for securities of equal risk. Usually government securities are used for the term structure.

terms of exchange The buyout ratio or terms of trade in a merger or an acquisition.

third market An over-the-counter market in listed securities. This market was created by traders attempting to buy and sell listed securities at lower commissions than could be obtained on the exchanges.

tight money A term to indicate time periods in which financing may be difficult to find and interest rates may be quite high by normal standards.

Toronto Stock Exchange (TSE) The largest organized security exchange in Canada.

trade credit Credit provided by sellers or suppliers in the normal course of business.

transaction exposure Foreign exchange gains and losses resulting from *actual* international transactions. These may be hedged through the foreign exchange market, the money market, or the currency futures market.

translation exposure The foreign-located assets and liabilities of a multinational corporation which are denominated in foreign currency units and are exposed to losses and gains due to changing exchange rates. This is called accounting, or translation, exposure.

Treasury bills Short-term obligations of the federal government with maturities of up to one year.

treasury shares Corporate stock that has been reacquired by the corporation.

trend analysis An analysis of performance made over a number of years in order to ascertain significant patterns.

trust receipt An instrument acknowledging that the borrower holds the inventory and proceeds for sale in trust for the lender.

TSE 300 Index Value-weighted index made up of 300 stocks that trade on the Toronto Stock Exchange.

U

undepreciated capital cost (UCC) The amount within a given CCA class (or pool) of assets available for tax-deductible depreciation. The maximum amount of CCA that can be expensed in a given year in relation to a particular CCA class is the UCC multiplied by the applicable CCA rate. Special adjustments have to be made for in-year purchases and sales of assets in the class.

underwriting The process of selling securities and, at the same time, assuring the seller a specified price. Underwriting is done by investment dealers and represents a form of risk taking.

underwriting spread The difference between the price a selling corporation receives for an issue of securities and the price at which the issue is sold to the public. The spread is the fee investment dealers and others receive for selling securities.

underwriting syndicate A group of investment dealers formed to share the risk of a security offering and also to facilitate the distribution of the securities.

unsecured debt A loan which requires no assets as collateral but allows the bondholder a general claim against the corporation rather than a lien against specific assets.

V

variable costs Costs that move directly with a change in volume. Examples are raw materials, factory labor, and sales commissions.

W

warrant An option to buy securities at a set price for a given period of time. Warrants commonly have a life of one to five years.

warrant intrinsic value (See minimum warrant value.)

weighted average cost of capital The computed cost of capital determined by multiplying the cost of each item in the optimal capital structure by its weighted representation in the overall capital structure and summing up the results.

white knight A firm management calls upon to help it avoid an unwanted takeover offer. It is an invited suitor.

working capital management The financing and management of the current assets of the firm. The financial manager determines the mix between temporary and permanent current assets and the nature of the financing arrangement.

Y

yield The interest rate that equates a future value or an annuity to a given present value.

yield curve A curve that shows interest rates at a specific point in time for all securities having equal risk but different maturity dates. Usually government securities are used to construct such curves. The yield curve is often also referred to as the term structure of interest rates.

yield to maturity The required rate of return on a bond issue. It is the discount rate used in present valuing future interest payments and the principal payment at maturity. It is used interchangeably with market rate of interest.

Z

zero-coupon rate bond A bond sold at a deep discount from face value. The return to the investor is the difference between the investor's cost and the face value received at the end of the life of the bond.

Index

A